Organizations: Systems, Control and Adaptation

The Wiley Series in

MANAGEMENT AND ADMINISTRATION

ELWOOD S. BUFFA, *Advisory Editor*
University of California, Los Angeles

MANAGEMENT SYSTEMS
Peter P. Schoderbek

OPERATIONS MANAGEMENT: PROBLEMS AND MODELS, SECOND EDITION
Elwood S. Buffa

PROBABILITY FOR MANAGEMENT DECISIONS
William R. King

PRINCIPLES OF MANAGEMENT: A MODERN APPROACH, THIRD EDITION
Henry H. Albers

MODERN PRODUCTION MANAGEMENT, THIRD EDITION
Elwood S. Buffa

CASES IN OPERATIONS MANAGEMENT: A SYSTEMS APPROACH
James L. McKenney and Richard S. Rosenbloom

ORGANIZATIONS: STRUCTURE AND BEHAVIOR, VOLUME I, SECOND EDITION
Joseph A. Litterer

ORGANIZATIONS: SYSTEMS, CONTROL AND ADAPTATION, VOLUME II
Joseph A. Litterer

MANAGEMENT AND ORGANIZATIONAL BEHAVIOR: A MULTIDIMENSIONAL APPROACH
Billy J. Hodge and Herbert J. Johnson

MATHEMATICAL PROGRAMMING: AN INTRODUCTION TO THE DESIGN AND APPLICATION OF OPTIMAL DECISION MACHINES
Claude McMillan

DECISION MAKING THROUGH OPERATIONS RESEARCH
Robert J. Thierauf and Richard A. Grosse

QUALITY CONTROL FOR MANAGERS & ENGINEERS
Elwood G. Kirkpatrick

PRODUCTION SYSTEMS: PLANNING, ANALYSIS AND CONTROL
James L. Riggs

ORGANIZATIONS:

Systems, Control and Adaptation

VOLUME II

Second Edition

JOSEPH A. LITTERER

Graduate School of Business Administration

University of Illinois

JOHN WILEY & SONS, INC.

NEW YORK · LONDON · SYDNEY · TORONTO

10 9 8 7 6 5 4 3 2 1

Library of Congress Catalogue Card Number: 77-88314

SBN 471 54111 7 (cloth) SBN 471 54112 5 (paper)

Printed in the United States of America

Preface

THERE ARE A NUMBER OF PURPOSES FOR WHICH AN ANTHOLOGY OF WRITINGS on organizations might be prepared. One would be to present the latest work in the field. Another would be to bring together the important work in a particular approach to organizations, such as theories of decision making in organizations. A third would be to assemble those writings that treat the basic issues, developments, and topics in the field. These different purposes would have distinctly different implications for a new edition of the anthology. With the first approach, each new edition would likely be a new collection. With the last approach, new editions would include only very important new work, with many of the selections likely to remain in one edition after another. The impetus for new editions then would only come, in part, from new developments in the field.

The purpose of this book can be stated quite simply: to bring together the most important writings on organizations. Doing this is a bit more difficult. There is the problem of scope—what are we defining as the area of organizations? There is a problem of depth—how intensively are various aspects to be covered? Then, of course, the nastiest of all problems, what are the most important writings within those boundaries?

Several ideas have led us to believe that the answers to these problems used in the first edition should be modified. The scope of the subject should be expanded to include (as separate topics) control and systems, which had been lumped with other topics in the first edition. A number of topics should be examined more intensively: work flows, conditional aspects for combinations of various organization elements, and impact of environment on organizational matters, to name the more important. Finally, this dynamic field has produced a number of important developments in theory and empirical research in recent years, providing us with more of a selection. All of these factors combine to make a new edition necessary.

This expansion in boundaries and the newer work that has come out have greatly magnified the difficulty noted in the first edition, namely, the amount of material that ought to be included is so large that it far exceeds the capacity of a single (or several) volumes. To permit the selection to do any reasonable justice to the field, it was decided to bring out the second edition in two volumes. This decision raised the problem of how to divide the selections between the two volumes so that the volumes would be as self-contained as possible, yet would permit the items in each to be relatively easy to integrate.

The scheme adopted is provided by Boulding, who has observed that we can differentiate among systems on the basis of levels of abstraction.[1] At the most elementary level are structures or frameworks. They identify parts and the relationship among them in a static fashion. Here we study anatomy, classification schemes for plants, rocks, or insects; or positions, departments, and hierarchical levels into which they are placed. At the second level, the parts move and do something in a fixed and predetermined way. This is identified as the level of clockworks. Here we are concerned with completeness and fit and, in the most elementary fashion, with functions and purposes. For our purposes, we call this the level of the simple steady state. It is here that we study mechanics or kinematics, friction, work flow, or conflict. We apply this study to automatic washing machines or production control systems.

At the next level, things become more complex. Now we are interested not only in the intended purpose but whether it is actually being achieved. For example, an automatic washer, once started, will go through all cycles, whether the clothes in the machine are dirty or not or, for that matter, even if there are no clothes in the washer. At this new level, performance is compared with a standard or goal and, when deviating, is adjusted. Here our concern is not that tools be used as desired, but with organisms that have the capacity to control their own operations to achieve an end. Control is studied not as compliance but as cybernetics. This control involves not only the performance of the total organism but also the adjustment the parts make to one another. We are therefore concerned with the interdependency of the parts in a way only hinted at on the previous levels.

At the fourth level, we are concerned with the interrelationship between the organism and others in its environment. The third level is that of closed systems, the fourth of open systems. Added to the question of how to adjust performance to meet objectives is the far more complex issue of how to change objectives to meet new requirements of the environment. Boulding identifies several additional levels, but they are less well understood and have not yet been reached by organizations in their developments.

Volume I deals with the first two levels as they pertain to organizations: Structure and the Simple Steady State. Volume II will deal with the third and fourth levels of abstraction and will deal with Systems, Cybernetics, and Open and Closed Systems.

Most of the selections retained from the first edition (twelve have been deleted) appear in Volume I. Some, notably those dealing with organizational adaptation, have been moved to the second volume. Both volumes have been organized to reflect the levels-of-abstraction concept, but both the subject and the readings make it impossible to follow it exactly.

I am grateful for the kind cooperation of the authors and publishers of the material reproduced.

Joseph A. Litterer

Friendship Long Island, Maine, 1969

[1] Kenneth E. Boulding, "General System Theory—The Skeleton of a Science," *Management Science*, April 1956, pp. 197–208.

Contents

Introduction

In fairness I must warn the reader that this is going to be a difficult volume. It will be difficult because of the great diversity you will find in the selections included. This does not merely mean the differences in the skills of various writers to make their prose clear and interesting; it also means the diversity that comes from the range of disciplines they are writing for, the different levels of abstraction they use, and the adequateness of the concepts available for them to use in expressing their ideas. However, an additional difficulty in reading the volume is caused by the fact that the aspects of organizations we are now covering are very complex and difficult to deal with in verbal communication. This has stimulated efforts to handle this material more precisely and easily with mathematics. Unfortunately, there are many things we want to express about organizations for which mathematics is even less useable than verbal languages. We use English for this volume, then, because it is the most general language available for the topic.

General Systems and Organizations

Systems as a concept was mentioned frequently in Volume I and will be even more prevalent in this volume. It would be well to make some distinctions about this topic before going further. Systems or, as it is frequently called, General Systems, is a new and emerging discipline and, as its title suggests, is a general discipline. Usually, scientific disciplines concern themselves with a particular sector of the empirical world.[1] Hence the disciplines of physiology, chemistry, and psychology all tackle different but definable types of phenomena and, through research, develop theories that explain to some degree of satisfaction what is going on in that sector. However, a discipline like mathematics is concerned with developing knowledge that does not of necessity have any connection with the empirical world. While particular mathematical knowledge may be abstracted from a particular aspect of the empirical world, its validity does not rest on its usefulness in that sector but on other tests that are internal to mathematics itself. Hence, if it is valid mathematically, it may well be useful in many other sectors of science than the one in which it originated. While mathematics is not part of any other field, it may be used in any field. That is, it does not give us any content, but it does help us understand the relationships among the content of any field. It gives us a language of science.

General Systems theories are not as abstract or as general as those of mathematics; however, they are considerably more so than the specific formulations of specialized disciplines. As a recognized differentiated area, it is very new and, therefore, its boundaries are only poorly defined, its concepts relatively few and underdeveloped, and it as yet has few scientists who identify themselves fully with the field. Hence, work in the area is done "part time" as scientists in different disciplines develop General Systems theories to cope with immediate problems in their specialities, much as a physicist may develop some new mathematics to cope with a particular problem he is facing. Furthermore, the work is not carried on in

[1] For further discussion of the ideas in this section, the reader is referred to Kenneth E. Boulding, "General Systems—The Skeleton of Science," *Management Science*, Vol. 2, No. 2, April 1956, pp. 197–208.

any systematic fashion nor is there any real integration and ordering of what is known. In spite of these limitations and difficulties, the field is there, growing, and already immensely useful to us.

If mathematics can be said to provide a language of science, then General Systems may be viewed as providing a skeleton of science. It is concerned with those generalities of theory that occur in more than one specialized discipline and, in fact, may not be able fully to be developed within the confines of one discipline. Once such a concept is developed and its generality beyond the field in which it was first developed is established, it is no longer necessary for those in other specialities to discover it for themselves. Hence, although homeostasis may have been first discovered in the speciality of physiology, once we recognize that it is a general theory applicable at least to all living organisms, we can now go back to look for the specific forms it will take in other fields such as psychology, sociology, organizations, and zoology. We have a structure, a framework, that permits us to identify some of the general characteristics of a theory in any one of a number of specialized fields. Once known, we can ask what specific form or content these elements take or have in a particular discipline. Thus it is not sufficient to say that a particular discipline has a property like homeostasis because it has General Systems properties. It is necessary to investigate the particulars by which this occurs in that field.

Part One of this volume covers material on General Systems for exactly these reasons. Our intent is to examine this general discipline because it will throw considerable light on the general outline of theories that will explain organizations, not because the study of General Systems is the study of organizations.

The Content of Volume II

In this book we have been following one of the ideas presented by General Systems Theory: that there are different levels of theory.[2] We could use this formulation to differentiate among specialized disciplines if we could show that each tended to have its most natural "level." Or one could say that General Systems Theory is really an array of theories, each of which can be differentiated into levels on some continuum of complexity. It is this route that we have chosen for this book. The specific theories about organizations have been differentiated according to the complexity of the level of General Systems Theory they most closely resemble.[3] The first volume dealt with those organization theories and data that belonged to the first two levels—those of Frameworks and those of Clockworks of the Simple Steady State. This volume takes up the next two levels. The third is that of control where the essential ingredient of feedback is introduced, and the fourth is that of open systems. Here, differentiation of the organism from its environment and properties of self-maintenance become central to our concern. Our theories and knowledge about organizations at this level are fragmentary, but those we have are also complex.

We begin with a section on General Systems. This part could be placed at the beginning of Volume I to provide a general framework or at the end of this volume to suggest an overall way to tie together the many things covered. It is placed here because it is felt that this material will be most needed at this point in the progression of the ideas we are covering. The complexity of the relationships covered in the first two levels of systems concepts is not so great that the knowledge of organizations we have is not capable of adequately handling the topic. However, the specific organization theories available for the areas we are about to enter are still in an early state of development and are often more useful when put into some perspective. The perspective provided by General Systems Theory for much of what is currently going on in the field of organizations is directed to finding out how organizations carry out control, make the adjustments to survive, and bring about integration of several different purposes and, at the same time, facilitate their very uniqueness —topics so complex and involved that, without simplification by some more general theories, they become fragmentated into a vast set of unconnected bits. In this respect, General Systems Theory aids the study of organizations in much the same way that calculus and Newtonian physics aid the study of astronomy. They give us a way of approaching the spe-

[2] Boulding, *op. cit.*

[3] See Volume I for a discussion of the levels of General System Theory.

cific knowledge we have of stars so that we can better understand and explain how they move and how they fit into solar systems. Calculus and physics are not astronomy; yet, without them, astronomy would amount to little more than a vast collection of poorly ordered data. We use General Systems Theory, then, to orient our thinking and to give us some of the conceptual tools to order and to understand the information we have about organizations.

In Part Two, we take up some aspects of organizations, not previously covered, that are aspects of systems in general, but appropriate for consideration at the level of the steady state. In Volume I, we discussed the interdependency among elements in a system, but largely in the context of cause-effect chains and the interrelations between these chains. Although accurate, this is likely to leave the reader with a very underdeveloped picture of the richness and the complexity of the way elements fit together. Here, we are concerned with not only how activities fit together to make a product but how the technical system within which the activities are embedded are supported and facilitated by a managerial system; how the personality of the individual fits with this technical-managerial system; how each adjusts to the totality they constitute; how this totality fits with goals of the organization, and so on. Earlier, we considered organizations as instruments for satisfying many goals. We now look at the capabilities that organizations have of satisfying different classes of goals; the problems that can arise from divergence of individual and organization goals; the disruptive forces that can emerge from this; and the processes by which organizations counter this to keep themselves intact.

With these steady state properties of organizations examined, we take a big step in Part Three and consider the organization as an open system. Our examination up to now has been as if the organization were isolated from the environment with no inputs of information or energy. Convenient for analysis, it is, nonetheless, a completely unrealistic picture. Organizations exist in a world of other organizations and of individuals who expect things from it and must be drawn upon for inputs. As some of the General Systems theorists have suggested, life itself can be seen as coming from the existence of open systems, the need to differentiate an identity, and to sustain it. We are here concerned with the following questions: how can we identify organizations in a social milieu, what do they do, why are they tolerated, how do they get an identity, and how do they maintain it? In what ways and on what points does the environment influence the internal character of the organization and in what ways and for what purposes do organizations influence their environment?

Viewing organizations as open systems leaves the organization open to many disturbances, demands, and difficulties, previously assumed away. It brings to the fore a most crucial question: how are the various elements of the organization controlled and coordinated to produce the means of satisfying the needs and goals of the many who have claim on the organization? This is the topic of Part Four, namely, control over organization elements and activities to insure that they achieve desired outcome in an internal phenomenon, that is, they are self-regulating. Although this is a simple statement at first glance, it is indeed one of the most distinguishing characteristics of an organization or of a living thing. This gives us a convenient handle to distinguish organizations from nonorganizations as, for example, when we view a unit embedded in an organization or raise the question of whether it is an organization itself or a nonseparable part of the larger one. It is often very hard to tell except by asking the question "Does it have fully developed internal control processes or does it have some of its behaviors controlled externally?" Some departments in organizations pass this test; many do not.

Control is very largely a process involving information. Much of our attention in this part, then, is on information and the ways in which it moves or does not move through organizations.

Through the first four parts of the book, we have been treating organizations very tenderly, either protecting them from any outside disturbances or considering only those organizational responses to disturbances that involve adjustments of existing elements within ranges that do not entail basic modifications in them. In the last section, however, we consider what happens when the organization has to engage in substantial modification of one or more elements to be able to cope with new conditions or goals.

We have often observed that organizations are instruments for achieving goals or objectives. At the same time, we have given no attention to the issue of where or how goals are developed. A typical answer to this is that the goals of an organization are those given to it by the sources of authority that brought it into existence, for example, the government or the owners, or that the goals of the organization are those of the people at the top of the organization, such as the president or the general. This is a simple but, as this part shows, not a very adequate or satisfactory explanation. Many parties, not often thought to be legitimately concerned with organization goals, can be contributing to them in ways and through processes quite different from those we might initially expect.

Much of this volume has been concerned with how organizations adjust and adapt where two unstated conditions prevail: (1) the change to which the organization must respond does not endanger the immediate existence of the organization, and (2) the organization has an adequate time span in which to respond to the new situation. When these conditions do not exist, the organization is faced with a crisis, and we find that often it operates in ways quite different than when faced with noncrisis situations.

Finally, one of the characteristics that organizations share with living things is that they grow. Growth leads to additions of functions, capacities, members, and relationships. Acquiring and adjusting to these is a complex and difficult experience.

The contents of Volume II cover the most complex and difficult aspects of organizations —those that arise from the fact that an organization is an open system and, therefore, does take on properties of goal seeking, adaptation, and growth. Such lifelike processes have been difficult to study in many fields, and they are difficult to study in the area of organizations; yet they represent the most important and intellectually stimulating subjects. Because they are, however, we can all too easily leap to an easy or oversimplified solution or explanation. As several writers in Part One have observed, the first obligation of the philosopher is to warn his audience about himself. Even before this, it would seem that the philosopher must warn himself about himself. For that reason, the reader of this book should make a special note of the way our perceptions of phenomena are molded and limited by our intellectual heritage. We should also observe those readers of our scientific concepts and how they have left us with blind spots, particularly in those areas important to understanding organizations. These authors are often as much concerned with helping us understand how to orient ourselves toward the topic as they are in having us understand the topic. Perhaps the most useful thought to keep in mind as we move into the next section on general systems and, from it, to the following sections on organization, viewed as systems, is what sort of glasses should be used to view organizations and what should be looked for with these glasses.

Organizations: Systems, Control and Adaptation

PART ONE

General Systems

PART ONE

THE PERIOD beginning in the latter half of the 1700's has often been called the age of science. It is frequently pointed out that George Washington would have been more at home in the world of Julius Caesar eighteen hundred years before he was born than he would be today, two hundred years after he was in his prime. This great change is largely the direct or indirect result of research adding to our fund of knowledge. At one time, science was the concern of the occasional person who had the talent, time and the interest to search for new knowledge. Today, science employs a large number of people, who must depend on training as well as talent, who work full time in research as a profession rather than as a hobby, and who, in their work, use large amounts of physical and human resources.

While the overall impact and output of science has been great, progress has not been uniform for all sciences. In the physical sciences, work has been rapid, voluminous, and reasonably integrated. The biological sciences have exhibited fewer of these characteristics and the social sciences fewer yet. Part of these differences can perhaps be ascribed to the seniority of the sciences. Many of the physical sciences have systematic bodies of literature that go back for several centuries. Many of the social sciences, such as psychology and sociology, have literatures that go back only a little past the turn of the century. It is doubtful, however, if seniority is the only or, for that matter, the most important reason for the differences.

One difficulty faced by men in any area of science is to determine what can be studied, what questions should be asked. This often requires a scaling down of ambitions. Science does not just explore questions even though some may be very interesting and of "fundamental" importance. For example, it is not useful for a person to say, "I am interested in falling bodies. To study this, I am going to determine what characteristics of apples make them want to fall from branches to the ground and what characteristics the stars or the moon do not possess which keeps them from wanting to fall to the earth." An interesting question, but one which in the past has gotten men involved with determining the intrinsic characteristics of apples or stars. The physical sciences "took off" when investigators realized that the search for properties, while interesting, was essentially an intellectual "dry well." Newton may have started with an apple falling from a tree, but what he gave us was a way of determining the movement of an object; a way of describing behavior.

Biologists may observe that living things die and then ask "what is life." To search for the essential property that gives life has proven to be a frustrating task. Social scientists may observe that some men are important in the social world because they are leaders and therefore ask, "What are the traits which leaders possess that differentiate them from others such as followers?" Much study of this question yielded no answer. If such questions are answerable, it is not going to be by any direct assault on the problem. Recognizing that the physical sciences had faced the same difficulty, researchers in other fields decided to learn from their experience and, thereby, innocently stumbled into new problems which would lead to frustrations.

To switch from a study of properties to the study of behavior and relationships may be a useful reorientation for all science. But it has become quite apparent that the strategy for doing this in the physical sciences is not applicable in the social sciences and perhaps not in many areas of the biological sciences. In the physical sciences, great progress has been made by breaking large problems into smaller ones, to break wholes into parts, and parts into more basic elements until, finally, manageable components are derived. They are manageable because they are fewer in number and there are fewer relationships between them and, therefore, they are conceptually easier to handle. But the process has also identified specific things for which data are desired and, while the task of measuring may be difficult, it is usually possible to specify what must be done to measure. This permits the other aspect of the strategy to be followed—increased precision of measurement so that meaningful statements can be made.

Unfortunately, this approach is not useable in sciences concerned with life or lifelike phenomena. Getting at parts or elements while life exists may be impossible and, without life, the parts may not exist. But we are getting a little ahead of our story. The point we are concerned with is that any science is aided and limited by the tools and concepts it possesses. If we think that the way of all science is to break wholes into parts, then in some areas we shall not only get confusing and frustrating results, but we shall also be unaware of the real source of our problem. Better analysis or more precise measurement is not going to be a solution. Scientists in a number of fields have concerned themselves with this problem. The first part of this book contains articles in which these men examine the basic frameworks of the various sciences and work toward a framework called General Systems which will include all science and be of particular use to the biological and social sciences.

One intention of these writers is to distinguish between the general properties of science and the particular forms or uses taken in the physical sciences. Models and theories play a central role in all science (Von Bertalanffy, Rapoport, Hall, and Fagan). They also show that there are quite different sources of models and uses to which they can be put (Deutsch, Hall, and Fagan), and that the general mode of analysis in the biological and social sciences is different from that of the physical sciences. A fundamental difference arises because the physical sciences can use closed or deterministic systems in their analysis. Other fields of science cannot. A basically different type of theoretical construction is required. The biological and social scientist must deal with the wholeness of the unit under study. Yet the wholes with which they are dealing are so complex that, unless simplified in some way, they are impossible to study. The attempt to find some way of simplifying this problem provides the motivation for the development of General Systems Theory.

As it became apparent to investigators in a number of disciplines that the problems they had were not unique to their discipline, they also came to suspect that the solution to the problems probably could not be found within the discipline itself. What was needed was some metadiscipline which could include and therefore be useful in analyzing the problems in any scientific discipline. Mathematics is one of the most important of the general disciplines. General Systems emerges as another tool for coping with problems in many disciplines.

Some Characteristics that Define General Systems

The various authors in this section identify some of the properties by which General Systems can be recognized. Among them are the following:

1. *Interrelatedness of Objects, Attributes, and Events.* Perhaps the most frequently cited characteristic of a system is that it is comprised of a number of interrelated elements. These elements may be objects or things such as people or gears and opinions or chemicals. They may also be attribute of these things, such as the weight of a part, the tension on a spring, the acidity of a chemical, or the personality of an individual. Or they can be events that occur, such as a threatening speech by a national leader, a reduction in communications between nations, an increase of feelings of being threatened within nations and, ultimately, war. By saying these are interrelated we mean that the characteristic of any element, object, attribute, or event is dependent on the other attributes or events or objects that exist. Furthermore, that a change in any one means some adjustment or change in the others. This comes about because there is some transfer of energy, information, or both. Elements, in effect, feed upon each other and so could not even exist alone.

2. *Wholism.* This is often and briefly stated in the observation that the whole is greater than the sum of its parts. For example, several thousand bricks may be a pile or they may also be a wall around the garden or of a building. Here again we enter one of the difficult areas of general systems. Is a set of bricks just a wall, or is it a part of a building, is the building part of a city, is the city part of a nation? Any element contributes to a system, but all too typically that system is part of another system, and the question then is, "What is the system under study?" This depends to a considerable degree upon the interests of the observer or person who is concerned with defining a system. We seem to have the essential ingredients for a system whenever we can find the complete cycle of events. By this we mean that most systems have a time dimension during which events occur in some order. Typically, there is a time when the order is repeated and a new cycle begins. A minimum requirement for a system seems to be a complete cycle of events, although obviously it may contain several sets of cycles. Hence a production worker may have six operations that he repeats every three minutes for a complete cycle. His production cycle then would be the six. However, if we are interested in his work-rest cycle, we may recognize that every two hours he receives a ten-minute break; therefore, he begins by performing his work cycle, repeats this sixty times, then pauses for a ten-minute period and, finally, is working again for a still different cycle. This, however, is part of a larger cycle that includes arriving at work, working for two hours, a ten-minute break, working for an hour and fifty minutes, having a half-hour lunch, working again throughout the afternoon, going home, sleeping, and coming back to work again the next day. Each of these satisfy the necessary minimal conditions for a system in that they have a cycle. The definition of system, therefore, is somewhat arbitrary.

3. *Goal Seeking.* It has often been observed that large complex systems appear to have considerable stability. For example, there are some corporations that have repeatedly paid quarterly dividends to their stockholders for periods of thirty, forty, or even more years. Such regularity should not suggest, however, that the other elements in the system are equally stable. They may in truth vary greatly. The stability is a characteristic of the whole, not of the parts. Looked at more generally, business firms, typically, tend to break even or perhaps make a profit. This is not to say that every year they make a profit. There may be other years in which they break even and other years in which they make a very handsome return. In fact, even during a good year, there may be months or quarters in which the firm is actually losing money. Nonetheless, performance is such that the firm *tends toward* a position of breaking even or making a profit. That is, an equilibrium position, a position to a system tends to return after it has been disturbed. This return is usually a result of compensating actions on part of the system. Hence it can appear that the system is attempting or seeking to return to this point or, as it is sometimes expressed, the organization or system is seeking this goal. Complex systems may have more than one point of equilibrium. Often, as performance approaches one equilibrium point, the system is pulled out of equilibrium on another. Hence a complex system

may appear to have multiple goals, not all of them, however, obtainable simultaneously.

4. *Regulation*. The fact that individual elements or their properties can be changed to bring overall performance toward some equilibrium point or goal clearly suggests that such systems are regulated or, more accurately, they are self-regulating. The authors included in this part identify at least three different types of regulation.

(a) ADJUSTMENT. The first of the two types of regulation are identified by Von Bertalanffy as primary regulations. In a broad sense, this is where a whole is reestablished from parts. For example, if we had a collection of marbles in a round goblet and were able to remove one of the marbles from the lower portion of the pile, all the others would shift down until they again came to rest in the bottom of the goblet.

(b) CONTROL. This is described by Von Bertalanffy as secondary regulation, where there are fixed arrangements for control, usually and typically by feedback.

(c) LEARNING. The third type of regulation is described by Stagner and Rapoport and, essentially, involves those situations in which the system, after having been disturbed several times and having exercised some control to again reach equilibrium, changes its internal characteristics so that it can anticipate similar disturbances in the future and, thereby, will now act differently toward them. Hence a university administration, which finds that for several spring semesters in a row it has to contend with student panty raids, "learns" that it had better have the Dean of Students and his assistants maintain close contact with the student body in the spring and also not permit any of the university police force to take vacations at that time. It may go one step further and organize a spring festival to drain off excess student energies.

5. *Inputs and Outputs*. Almost by definition, systems, if they are open systems, receive things from the environment. In a broad sense, these are usually categorized as energy and information. But systems also deliver something to their environment which, in turn, is the input of some other system or systems. Hence, all systems are dependent on receiving inputs produced by other systems and produce something needed by other systems.

6. *Transformation*. What systems deliver to the environment is not the same, or at least in the same form, as was received by the system. Some transformation has occurred in the cycle of events used to define the system.

7. *Hierarchy*. It has been earlier suggested that one system may contain within it several other systems. This nesting of systems within systems is referred to as hierarchy (Simon). The fact that complex systems can be "decomposed" into smaller and, usually, less complex systems offers one of the main avenues of analysis suggested for General Systems Theory.

8. *Entropy*. A characteristic of closed systems is that they run down. That is, the energy differentials between the different elements of the system disappear and they all reach a common level. This phenomenon of running down is called increasing entropy. Maximum entropy, then, would occur when all elements of a system are at the same level of energy. In living systems this is the condition of death. Almost every one of our writers discusses entropy in one form or another. Several indicate that negative entropy and information appear to be the same sort of thing. Hence, increasing information is the same as decreasing entropy. We can also view negative entropy as organization. That is, the more differentiated elements are, the more systematically they are arranged, the greater is the negative entropy. Open systems, while they have a tendency toward "running down," may not, for they receive inputs of energy and information from their environment and, thus, can continually increase their negative entropy.

9. *Differentiation*. Open systems typically tend to become more complex. More specialized units appear to take care of different problems that the system faces. Some cope with different sectors of the environment, others perform tasks and still others control sequences of tasks so that goals may be attained.

10. *Equifinality*. In closed systems, if an initial state can be defined, the final state can be

unequivocally determined. In open systems, however, this is not the case. An initial state can have several possible final states. Furthermore, the same final state may be arrived at from several initial starting places.

These, then, are the most predominant characteristics that the writers covered, in part, and used to identify general systems. In many instances, several writers fully discuss the same topic and while there is some overlap, each usually makes his own addition to our knowledge. Much work still has to be done in the area of General Systems. Even in this meager beginning, however, we have the ingredients to permit us to begin at a more meaningful analysis of organizations, as we shall see in the following four parts.

General System Theory—A Critical Review

LUDWIG VON BERTALANFFY

It is more than 15 years since the writer has first presented, to a larger public, the proposal of a General System Theory (Bertalanffy 1947, 1950, 1956). Since then, this conception has been widely discussed and was applied in numerous fields of science. When an early reviewer (Egler, 1953) found himself "hushed into awed silence" by the idea of a General System Theory, now in spite of obvious limitations, different approaches and legitimate criticism, few would deny the legitimacy and fertility of the interdisciplinary systems approach.

Even more: The systems concept has not remained in the theoretical sphere, but became central in certain fields of applied science. When first proposed, it appeared to be a particularly abstract and daring, theoretical idea. Nowadays "systems engineering," "research," "analysis" and similar titles have become job denominations. Major industrial enterprises and government agencies have departments, committees or at least specialists to the purpose; and many universities offer curricula and courses for training.

Thus the present writer was vindicated when he was among the first to predict that the concept of "system" is to become a fulcrum in modern scientific thought. In the words of a practitioner of the science,

> In the last two decades we have witnessed the emergence of the "system" as a key concept in scientific research. Systems, of course, have been studied for centuries, but something new has been added. . . . The tendency to study systems as an entity rather than as a conglomeration of parts is consistent with the tendency in contemporary science no longer to isolate phenomena in narrowly confined contexts, but rather to open interactions for examination and to examine larger and larger slices of nature. Under the banner of *systems research* (and its many synonyms) we have also witnessed a convergence of many more specialized contemporary scientific developments. . . . These research pursuits and many others are being interwoven into a cooperative research effort involving an ever-widening spectrum of scientific and engineering disciplines. We are participating in what is probably the most comprehensive effort to attain a synthesis of scientific knowledge yet made (Ackoff, 1959).

This, however, does not preclude but rather implies that obstacles and difficulties are by no means overcome as is only to be expected in a major scientific reorientation. A reassessment of General Systems Theory, its foundations, achievements, criticisms and prospects therefore appears in place. The present study aims at this purpose.

According to the Preface to the VIth volume of *General Systems* by Meyer (1961), the greatest number of the enquiries made asks for "new statements describing the method and significance of the idea." Another central theme is "the organismic viewpoint." As one of the original proponents of the *Society for General Systems Research* and founders of the organismic viewpoint in biology (cf. Bertalanffy, 1962) the author feels obliged to answer this challenge as well as readily admitted limitations of his knowledge and techniques permit.

1. The Rise of Interdisciplinary Theories

The motives leading to the postulate of a general theory of systems can be summarized under a few headings.

1. Up to recent times the field of science as a nomothetic endeavor, i.e., trying to establish

From *General Systems: the Yearbook of the Society for General Systems Research*, Vol. VII, 1962, pp. 1–20. Reprinted by permission of the Society for General Systems Research.

an explanatory and predictive system of laws, was practically identical with theoretical physics. Few attempts at a system of laws in non-physical fields gained general recognition; the biologist would first think of genetics. However, in recent times the biological, behavioral and social sciences have come into their own, and so the problem became urgent whether an expansion of conceptual schemes is possible to deal with fields and problems where application of physics is not sufficient or feasible.

2. In the biological, behavioral and sociological fields, there exist predominant problems which were neglected in classical science or rather which did not enter into its considerations. If we look at a living organism, we observe an amazing order, organization, maintenance in continuous change, regulation and apparent teleology. Similarly, in human behavior goal-seeking and purposiveness cannot be overlooked, even if we accept a strictly behavioristic standpoint. However, concepts like organization, directiveness, teleology, etc., just do not appear in the classic system of science. As a matter of fact, in the so-called mechanistic world view based upon classical physics, they were considered as illusory or metaphysical. This means, to the biologist for example, that just the specific problems of living nature appeared to lie beyond the legitimate field of science.

3. This in turn was closely connected with the structure of classical science. The latter was essentially concerned with two-variable problems, linear causal trains, one cause and one effect, or with few variables at the most. The classical example is mechanics. It gives perfect solutions for the attraction between two celestial bodies, a sun and a planet, and hence permits to exactly predict future constellations and even the existence of still undetected planets. However, already the three-body problem of mechanics is unsolvable in principle and can only be approached by approximations. A similar situation exists in the more modern field of atomic physics (Zacharias 1957). Here also two-body problems such as that of one proton and electron are solvable, but trouble arises with the many-body problem. One-way causality, the relation between "cause" and "effect" or of a pair or few variables cover a wide field. Nevertheless, many problems particularly in biology and the behavioral and social sciences, essentially are multivariable problems for which new conceptual tools are needed. Warren Weaver (1948), cofounder of information theory, had expressed this in an often-quoted statement. Classical science, he stated, was concerned either with linear causal trains, that is, two-variable problems; or else with unorganized complexity. The latter can be handled with statistical methods and ultimately stems from the second principle of thermodynamics. However, in modern physics and biology, problems of organized complexity, that is, interaction of a large but not infinite number of variables, are popping up everywhere and demand new conceptual tools.

4. What has been said are not metaphysical or philosophic contentions. We are not erecting a barrier between inorganic and living nature which obviously would be inappropriate in view of intermediates such as viruses, nucleoproteins and self-duplicating units in general which in some way bridge the gap. Nor do we protest that biology is in principle "irreducible to physics" which also would be out of place in view of the tremendous advances of physical and chemical explanation of life processes. Similarly, no barrier between biology and the behavioral and social sciences is intended. This, however, does not obviate the fact that in the fields mentioned we do not have appropriate conceptual tools serving for explanation and prediction as we have in physics and its various fields of application.

5. It therefore appears that an expansion of science is required to deal with those aspects which are left out in physics and happen to concern just the specific characteristics of biological, behavioral, and social phenomena. This amounts to new conceptual models to be introduced. Every science is a model in the broad sense of the word, that is a conceptual structure intended to reflect certain aspects of reality. One such model is the system of physics—and it is an incredibly successful one. However, physics is but *one* model dealing with certain aspects of reality. It needs not to have monopoly, nor is it *the* reality as merchanistic methodology and metaphysics presupposed. It apparently does not cover all aspects and represents, as many specific problems in biology and behavioral science show, a

limited aspect. Perhaps it is possible to introduce other models dealing with aspects outside of physics.

These considerations are of a rather abstract nature. So perhaps some personal interest may be introduced by telling how the present author was led into this sort of problem.

When, some 40 years ago, I started my life as a scientist, biology was involved in the mechanism-vitalism controversy. The mechanistic procedure essentially was to resolve the living organism into parts and partial processes: the organism was an aggregate of cells, the cell one of colloids and organic molecules, behavior a sum of unconditional and conditioned reflexed, and so forth. The problems of organization of these parts in the service of maintenance of the organism, of regulation after disturbances and the like were either bypassed or, according to the theory known as vitalism, explainable only by the action of soul-like factors, little hobgoblins as it were, hovering in the cell or the organism—which obviously was nothing less than a declaration of bankruptcy of science. In this situation, I was led to advocate the so-called organismic viewpoint. In one brief sentence, it means that organisms are organized things and, as biologists, we have to find out about it. I tried to implement this organismic program in various studies on metabolism, growth, and biophysics of the organism. One way in this respect was the so-called theory of open systems and steady states which essentially is an expansion of conventional physical chemistry, kinetics and thermodynamics. It appeared, however, that I could not stop on the way once taken and so I was led to a still further generalization which I called "General System Theory." The idea goes back for some considerable time—I presented it first in 1937 in Charles Morris' philosophy seminar at the University of Chicago. However, at this time theory was in bad reputation in biology, and I was afraid of what Gauss, the mathematician, called the "clamor or the Boeotians." So I left my drafts in the drawer, and it was only after the war that my first publications in this respect appeared.

Then, however, something interesting and surprising happened. It turned out that a change in intellectual climate had taken place, making model building and abstract generalizations fashionable. Even more: quite a number of scientists had followed similar lines of thought. So General System Theory, after all, was not isolated or a personal idiosyncrasy as I have believed, but rather was one within a group of parallel developments.

Naturally, the maxims enumerated above can be formulated in different ways and using somewhat different terms. In principle, however, they express the viewpoint of the more advanced thinkers of our time and the common ground of system theorists. The reader may, for example, compare the presentation given by Rapoport and Horvath (1959) which is an excellent and independent statement and therefore shows even better the general agreement.

There is quite a number of novel developments intended to meet the goals indicated above. We may enumerate them in a brief survey:

1. Cybernetics, based upon the principle of feedback or circular causal trains providing mechanisms for goal-seeking and self-controlling behavior.
2. Information theory, introducing the concept of information as a quantity measurable by an expression isomorphic to negative entropy in physics, and developing the principles of its transmission.
3. Game theory, analyzing in a novel mathematical framework, rational competition between two or more antagonists for maximum gain and minimum loss.
4. Decision theory, similarly analyzing rational choices, within human organizations, based upon examination of a given situation and its possible outcomes.
5. Topology or relational mathematics, including non-metrical fields such as network and graph theory.
6. Factor analysis, i.e., isolation by way of mathematical analysis, of factors in multivariable phenomena in psychology and other fields.
7. General system theory in the narrower sense (G.S.T.), trying to derive from a general definition of "system" as complex of interacting components, concepts characteristic of organized wholes such as interaction, sum, mechanization, centralization, competition, finality, etc., and to apply them to concrete phenomena.

While systems theory in the broad sense has the character of a basic science, it has its correlate in applied science, sometimes subsumed under the general name of Systems Science. This development is closely connected with modern automation. Broadly speaking, the following fields can be distinguished (Ackoff, 1960; Hall, 1962):

Systems Engineering, i.e., scientific planning, design, evaluation, and construction of man-machine systems;

Operations research, i.e., scientific control of existing systems of men, machines, materials, money, etc.

Human Engineering, i.e., scientific adaptation of systems and especially machines in order to obtain maximum efficiency with minimum cost in money and other expenses.

A very simple example for the necessity of study of "man-machine systems" is air travel. Anybody crossing continents by jet with incredible speed and having to spend endless hours waiting, queuing, being herded in airports can easily realize that the physical techniques in air travel are at their best, while "organizational" techniques still are on a most primitive level.

Although there is considerable overlapping, different conceptual tools are predominant in the individual fields. In systems engineering, cybernetics and information theory, also general system theory *s.s.*, are used. Operations research uses tools such as linear programming and game theory. Human engineering, concerned with the abilities, physiological limitations and variabilities of human beings, includes biomechanics, engineering psychology, human factors, etc., among its tools.

The present survey is not concerned with applied systems science; the reader is referred to Hall's book as an excellent textbook of systems engineering (1962). However it is well to keep in mind that the systems approach as a novel concept in science has a close parallel in technology. The systems viewpoint in recent science stands in a similar relation to the so-called "mechanistic" viewpoint, as stands systems engineering to physical technology.

All these theories have certain features in common. *Firstly*, they agree in the emphasis that something should be done about the problems characteristic of the behavioral and biological sciences, but not dealt with in conventional physical theory. *Secondly*, these theories introduce concepts and models in comparison to physics: for example, a generalized system concept, the concept of information compared to energy in physics. *Thirdly*, these theories are particularly concerned with multivariable problems, as mentioned before. *Fourthly*, these models are interdisciplinary and transcend the conventional fields of science. If, for example, you scan the *Yearbooks* of the *Society for General Systems Research*, you notice the breadth of application: Considerations similar or even identical in structure are applied to phenomena of different kinds and levels, from networks of chemical reactions in a cell to populations of animals, from electrical engineering to the social sciences. Similarly, the basic concepts of cybernetics stem from certain special fields in modern technology. However, starting with the simplest case of a thermostat which by way of feedback maintains a certain temperature and advancing to servomechanisms and automation in modern technology, it turns out that similar schemes are applicable to many biological phenomena of regulation or behavior. Even more, in many instances there is a formal correspondence or isomorphism of general principles or even of special laws. Similar mathematical formulations may apply to quite different phenomena. This entails that general theories of systems, among other things, are labor-saving devices: A set of principles may be transferred from one field to another, without the need to duplicate the effort as has often happened in science of the past. *Fifthly* and perhaps most important: Concepts like wholeness, organization, teleology and directiveness appeared in mechanistic science to be unscientific or metaphysical. Today they are taken seriously and as amenable to scientific analysis. We have conceptual and in some cases even material models which can represent those basic characteristics of life and behavioral phenomena.

An important consideration is that the various approaches enumerated are not, and should not be considered to be monopolistic. One of the important aspects of the modern changes in scientific thought is that there is no unique and all-embracing "world system." All scientific constructs are models representing certain aspects or perspectives of reality. This even applies to theoretical physics: far from being a metaphysical presentation of ultimate reality (as the materialism of the past proclaimed and modern positivism still implies) it is but one of these models and, as recent developments show, neither exhaustive nor unique. The various "systems theories" also are models that mirror different aspects. They are not mutually exclusive and often combined in application. For example, certain phenomena may be amenable to scientific exploration by way of cybernetics, others by way of general system theory *s.s.;* or even in the same phenomenon, certain aspects may be describable in the one or the other way. Cybernetics combine the information and feedback models, models of the nervous system net and information theory, etc. This, of course, does not preclude but rather implies the hope for further synthesis in which the various approaches of the present toward a theory of "wholeness" and "organization" may be integrated and unified. Actually, such further syntheses, e.g., between irreversible thermodynamics and information theory, are slowly developing.

The differences of these theories are in the particular model conceptions and mathematical methods applied. We therefore come to the question in what ways the program of systems research can be implemented.

2. Methods of General Systems Research

Ashby (1958a) has admirably outlined two possible ways or general methods in systems study:

> Two main lines are readily distinguished. One, already well developed in the hands of von Bertalanffy and his co-workers, takes the world as we find it, examines the various systems that occur in it—zoological, physiological, and so on—and then draws up statements about the regularities that have been observed to hold. This method is essentially empirical. The second method is to start at the other end. Instead of studying first one system, then a second, then a third, and so on, it goes to the other extreme, considers the set of all conceivable systems and then reduces the set to a more reasonable size. This is the method I have recently followed.

It will easily be seen that all systems studies follow one or the other of these methods or a combination of both. Each of these approaches has its advantages as well as shortcomings.

1. The first method is empirico-intuitive; it has the advantage that it remains rather close to reality and can easily be illustrated and even verified by examples taken from the individual fields of science. On the other hand, the approach lacks mathematical elegance and deductive strength and, to the mathematically minded, will appear naïve and unsystematic.

Nevertheless, the merits of this empirico-intuitive procedure should not be minimized.

The present writer has stated a number of "system principles," partly in the context of biological theory and without explicit reference to G.S.T. (Bertalanffy, 1960a, pp. 37–54), partly in what emphatically was entitled an "Outline" of this theory (1950). This was meant in the literal sense: It was intended to call attention to the desirability of such field, and the presentation was in the way of a sketch or blueprint, illustrating the approach by simple examples.

However, it turned out that this intuitive survey appears to be remarkably complete. The main principles offered such as wholeness, sum, centralization, differentiation, leading part, closed and open system, finality, equifinality, growth in time, relative growth, competition, have been used in manifold ways (e.g., general definition of system: Hall and Fagen, 1956; types of growth: Keiter, 1951–52; systems engineering: Hall, 1962; social work: Hearn, 1958). Excepting minor variations in terminology intended for clarification or due to the subject matter, no principles of similar significance were added—even though this would be highly desirable. It is perhaps even more significant that this also applies to considerations which do not refer to the present writer's work and hence cannot be said to be unduly influenced by it. Perusal of studies such as those by Beer (1961) and Kremyanski (1960) on principles, Bradley and Calvin (1956) on the network of chemical reactions, Haire (1959) on growth or organizations, etc., will easily show that they are also using the "Bertalanffy principles."

2. The way of deductive systems theory was followed by Ashby (1958b). A more informal presentation which summarizes Ashby's reasoning (1962) leads itself particularly well to analysis.

Ashby asks about the "fundamental concept

of machine" and answers the question by stating "that its internal state, and the state of its surroundings, defines uniquely the next state it will go to." If the variables are continuous, this definition corresponds to the description of a dynamic system by a set of ordinary differential equations with time as the independent variable. However, such representation by differential equations is too restricted for a theory to include biological systems and calculating machines where discontinuities are ubiquitous. Therefore the modern definition is the "machine with input": It is defined by a set S of internal states, a set I of input and mapping f of the product set $I \times S$ into S. "Organization," then, is defined by specifying the machine's states S and its conditions I. If S is a product set ($S = \pi_i T_i$), with i as the parts and T is specified by the mapping f." A "self-organizing" system, according to Ashby, can have two meanings, namely: (1) The system starts with its parts separate, and these parts then change toward forming connections (example: cells to the embryo, first having little or no effect on one another, join by formation of dendrites and synapses to form the highly interdependent nervous system). This first meaning is "changing from unorganized to organized." (2) The second meaning is "changing from a bad organization to a good one" (examples: a child whose brain organization makes it fire-seeking at first, while a new brain organization makes him fire-avoiding; an automatic pilot and plane coupled first by deleterious positive feedback and then improved). "There the organization is bad. The system would be 'self-organizing' if a change were automatically made" (changing positive into negative feedback). But "*no machine can be self-organizing in this sense*" (author's underscores). For adaptation (e.g., of the homeostat or in a self-programming computer) means that we start with a set S of states, and that f changes into g, so that organization is a variable, e.g., a function of time $\alpha(t)$ which has first the value f and later the value g. However, this change "cannot be ascribed to any cause in the set S; *so it must come from some outside agent, acting on the system S as input*" (our underscores). In other terms, to be "self-organizing" the machine S must be coupled to another machine.

This concise statement permits observation of the limitations of this approach. We completely agree that description by differential equations is not only a clumsy but, in principle, inadequate way to deal with many problems of organization. The author was well aware of this emphasizing that a system of simultaneous differential equations is by no means the most general formulation and is chosen only for illustrative purposes (Bertalanffy, 1949).

However, in overcoming this limitation, Ashby introduced another one. His "modern definition" of system as a "machine with input" as reproduced above, supplants the general system model by another rather special one: the cybernetic model, i.e., a system open to information but closed with respect to entropy transfer. This becomes apparent when the definition is applied to "self-organizing systems." Characteristically, the most important kind of these has no place in Ashby's model, namely, systems organizing themselves by way of progressive differentiation, evolving from states of lower to states of higher complexity. This is, of course, the most obvious form of "self-organization," apparent in ontogenesis, probable in phylogenesis, and certainly also valid in many social organizations. We have here not a question of "good" (i.e., useful, adaptive) or "bad" organization which, as Ashby correctly emphasizes, is relative on circumstances; increase in differentiation and complexity—whether useful or not—is a criterion that is objective and at least on principle amenable to measurement (e.g., in terms of decreasing entropy, of information). Ashby's contention that "no machine can be self-organizing," more explicitly, that the "change cannot be ascribed to any cause in the set S" but "must come from some outside agent, an input" amounts to exclusion of self-differentiating systems. The reason that such systems are not permitted as "Ashby machines" is patent. Self-differentiating systems that evolve toward higher complexity (decreasing entropy) are, for thermodynamic reasons, possible only as open systems, i.e., systems importing matter containing free energy to an amount overcompensating the increase in entropy due to irreversible processes within the system ("import of negative entropy"). However, we cannot say that "this change comes from some outside agent, an input"; the differentiation within a developing embryo and organism is due to its internal laws of organization, and the input (e.g., oxygen supply which may vary quantitatively, or nutrition which can vary qualitatively within a broad spectrum) makes it only possible energetically.

The above is further illustrated by additional examples given by Ashby. Suppose a digital computer is carrying through multiplications at random; then the machine will "evolve" toward showing even numbers (because products even x even as well as even x odd give numbers even), and eventually only zeroes will be "surviving." In still another version Ashby quotes Shannon's Tenth Theorem, stating that if a correction channel has capacity H, equivocation of the amount H can be removed, but no more. Both examples illustrate the working of closed systems: The "evolution" of the computer is one toward disappearance of differentiation and establishment of maximum homogeneity (analog to the Second Principle in closed systems); Shannon's Theorem similarly concerns closed systems where no negative entropy is fed in. Compared to the information content (organization) of a living system, the imported matter (nutrition, etc.) carries not information but "noise." Nevertheless, its negative entropy is used to maintain or even to increase the information content of the system. This is a state of affairs apparently not provided for in Shannon's Tenth Theorem, and understandably so as he is not treating information transfer in open systems with transformation of matter.

In both respects, the living organism (and other behavioral and social systems) is not an Ashby machine because it evolves toward increasing differentiation and inhomogeneity, and can correct "noise" to a higher degree than an inanimate communication channel. Both, however, are consequences of the organism's character as an open system.

Incidentally, it is for similar reasons that we cannot replace the concept of "system" by the generalized "machine" concept of Ashby. Even though the latter is more liberal compared to the classic one (machines defined as systems with fixed arrangement of parts and processes), the objections against a "machine theory" of life (Bertalanffy, 1960a, p. 16–20 and elsewhere) remain valid.

These remarks are not intended as adverse criticism of Ashby's or the deductive approach in general; they only emphasize that there is no royal road to General Systems Theory. As every other scientific field, it will have to develop by an interplay of empirical, intuitive and deductive procedures. If the intuitive approach leaves much to be desired in logical rigor and completeness, the deductive approach faces the difficulty of whether the fundamental terms are correctly chosen. This is not a particular fault of the theory or of the workers concerned but a rather common phenomenon in the history of science; one may, for example, remember the long debate as to what magnitude—force or energy—is to be considered as constant in physical transformations until the issue was decided in favor of $mv^2/2$.

In the present writer's mind, G.S.T. was conceived as a working hypothesis; being a practicing scientist, he seems the main function of theoretical models in the explanation, prediction and control of hitherto unexplored phenomena. Others may, with equal right, emphasize the importance of axiomatic approach and quote to this effect examples like the theory of probability, non-Euclidean geometries, more recently information and game theory, which were first developed as deductive mathematical fields, and later applied in physics or other sciences. There should be no quarrel about this point. The danger, in both approaches, is to consider too early the theoretical model as being closed and definitive—a danger particularly important in a field like general systems which is still groping to find its correct foundations.

3. Homeostasis and Open Systems

Among the models mentioned, cybernetics in its application as homeostasis, and G.S.T. in its application to open systems lend themselves most readily for interpretation of many empirical phenomena. The relation of both theories is not always well understood, and hence a brief discussion is in place.

The simplest feedback scheme can be represented as follows (Fig. 1). Modern servomechanisms and automation, as well as many phenomena in the organism, are based upon feedback arrangements far more complicated than

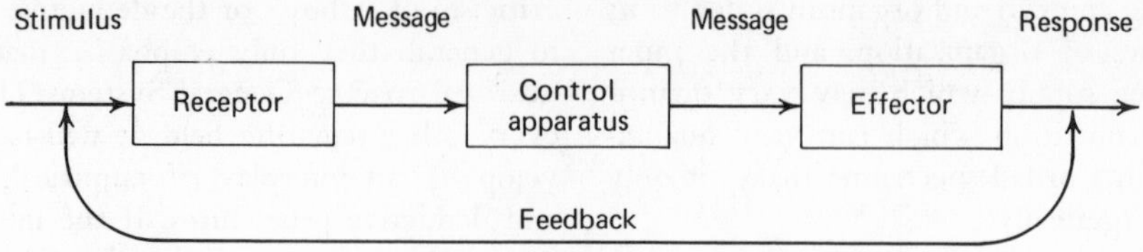

Fig. 1. Simple feedback model.

the simple scheme (Fig. 1) but the latter is the elementary prototype.

In application to the living organism, the feedback scheme is represented by the concept of homoeostasis.

Homeostasis, according to Cannon, is the ensemble of organic regulations which act to maintain the steady state of the organism and are effectuated by regulating mechanisms in such a way that they do not occur necessarily in the same, and often in opposite, direction to what a corresponding external change would cause according to physical laws. The simplest example is homeothermy. According to Van't Hoff's rule in physical chemistry, a decrease in temperature leads to slowing down of the rate of chemical reactions, as it does in ordinary physico-chemical systems and also in poikilothermic animals. In warm-blooded animals, however, it leads to the opposite effect, namely, to an increase of metabolic rate, with the result that the temperature of the body is maintained constant at approximately 37°C. This is effectuated by a feedback mechanism. Cooling stimulates thermogenic centers in the brain thalamus which "turn on" heat-producing mechanisms in the body. A similar feedback pattern is found in a great variety of physiological regulations. Regulation of posture and the control of actions in animals and man toward a goal are similarly controlled by feedback mechanisms.

In contradistinction to cybernetics concerned with feedback arrangements, G.T.S. is interested in dynamic interaction within multivariable systems. The case particularly important for the living organism is that of open systems. It amounts to saying that there is a system into which matter is introduced from outside. Within the system, the material undergoes reactions which partly may yield components of a higher complexity. This is what we call anabolism. On the other hand, the material is catabolized and the end products of catabolism eventually leave the system. A simple model of an open system is indicated in Fig. 2.

A few main characteristics of open as compared to closed systems are in the fact that, appropriate system conditions presupposed, an open system will attain a steady state in which its composition remains constant, but in contrast to conventional equilibria, this constancy is maintained in a continuous exchange and flow of component material. The steady state of open systems is characterized by the principle of equifinality; that is, in contrast to equilibrium states in closed systems which are determined by initial conditions, the open system may attain a time-independent state independent of initial conditions and determined only by the system parameters. Furthermore, open systems show thermodynamic characteristics which are apparently paradoxical and contradictory to the second principle. According to the latter, the general course of physical events (in closed systems) is toward increasing en-

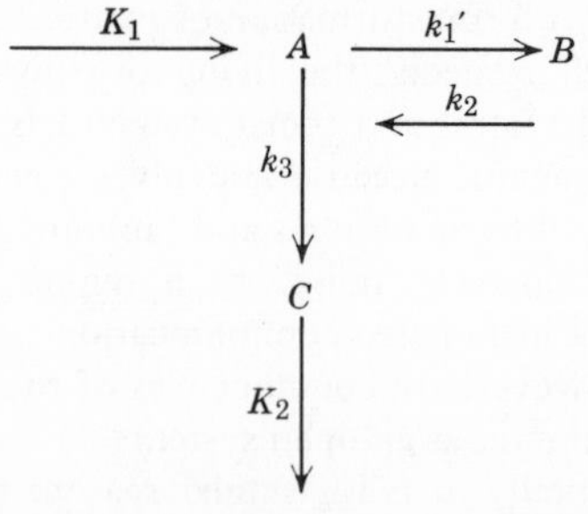

Fig. 2. Model of a simple open system. The component A *is introduced into the system and transformed, in a reversible reaction, into* B; *it is catabolized in an irreversible reaction, into* C *which eventually is excreted.* K_1, K_2 *are constants of import and export, respectively;* k_1, k_2, k_3 *are reaction constants. The model approximately corresponds, for example, to protein turnover in an animal organism.* A *representing amino acids,* B *proteins, and* C *products of excretion.*

tropy, leveling down of differences and states of maximum disorder. In open systems, however, with transfer of matter import of "negative entropy" is possible. Hence, such systems can maintain themselves at a high level, and even evolve toward an increase of order and complexity—as is indeed one of the most important characteristics of life processes (cf. Bertalanffy, 1956).

The open-system model also has a wide application. According to its character, it is particularly applicable to phenomena showing nonstructural, dynamic interaction of processes, such as those of metabolism, growth, metabolic aspects of excitation, etc.

Speaking more generally, living systems can be defined as hierarchically organized open systems, maintaining themselves, or developing toward a steady state. Disease is the life process regulating toward normalcy after disturbance, owing to the equifinality of biological systems and with the assistance of the physician. In this way, the *vis medicatrix naturae* of old is divested of its metaphysical paraphernalia; it is not a vitalistic agent but an expression of the dynamics of living systems, maintaining and reestablishing, so far as possible, the steady state.

In this way, the theory of open systems accounts for basic characteristics of the living organism which have baffled physicists, biologists, and philosophers, and appeared to be violations of the laws of physics, explainable only by vitalistic factors beyond the competence of science and scientific explanation.

Thus "feedback" and "open systems" are two models for biological and possibly behavioral phenomena. It should be made clear that the term "homeostasis" can be used in two ways. It is either taken in the original sense as proferred by Cannon and illustrated by examples like maintenance of body temperature and other physiological variables by feedback mechanisms—or else the term is often used as a synonym for organic regulation and adaptation in general. This is a question of semantics. However, it is a wise rule in the natural sciences to use terms in the sense originally attached to them by their authors. So I propose to use the word homeostasis in its narrower but well-defined sense, and this has important consequences, as it reveals certain limitations which are often forgotten.

As was already emphasized, regulations of the homeostasis or feedback type are abundant in the mature higher organism. However, it is clear from the scheme (Fig. 1) or any other flow diagram that feedback represents a machine-like arrangement, that is, an order of processes based upon fixed arrangements and representing linear, though circular, causal trains. The primary phenomena of organic regulation, e.g., the regulations in early embryonic development, in regeneration, etc. appear to be of a different nature. It seems that the primary regulations in the organism result from dynamic interaction within a unitary open system that reestablishes its steady state. Superimposed upon this by way of progressive mechanization are secondary regulatory mechanisms governed by fixed structures especially of the feedback type.

Although the homeostasis model transcends directiveness in self-regulating circular processes, it still adheres to the machine theory of the organism. This also applies to a second aspect. An essential component of the mechanistic view is a utilitarian conception which is deeply connected with the economic outlook of the 19th and early 20th centuries. This is well-known, for example, in the history of Darwinism: Struggle for existence and survival of the fittest are a biological version of the economic model of free competition. This utilitarian or economic viewpoint also prevails in the concept of homeostasis: The organism is essentially envisaged as an aggregate mechanism for maintenance of minimum costs. However, there seem to be plenty of non-utilitarian structures and functions in the living world.

The concept of homeostasis also retains a third aspect of the mechanistic view. The organism is essentially considered to be a reactive system. Outside stimuli are answered by proper responses in such a way as to maintain the system. The feedback model (Fig. 1) is essentially the classical stimulus-response scheme, only the feedback loop being added. However, an overwhelming amount of facts shows that primary organic behavior as, for example, the first movements of the fetus, are not reflex responses to external stimuli, but rather spontaneous mass activities of the whole embryo or larger areas. Reflex reactions answering external stimuli and following a structured path appear to be superimposed upon primitive automatisms, ontogenetically and phylogenetically, as secondary regulatory mechanisms. These considerations win particular importance in the theory of behavior, as we shall see later on.

In this sense, it appears that in development and evolution dynamic interaction (open system) precedes mechanization (structured arrangements particularly of a feedback nature). In a similar way, G.S.T. can logically be considered the more general theory; it includes systems with feedback constraints as a special case, but this assertion would not be true vice versa. It need not be emphasized that this statement is a program for future systematization and integration of G.S.T. rather than a theory presently achieved.

4. Criticism of General System Theory

A discussion of G.S.T. must take account of the objections raised, both to clarify misunderstanding and to utilize criticism for improvement (cf. also Bertalanffy *et al.*, 1951).

A "devastating" criticism of "General Behavior Systems Theory" by Buck (1956) would hardly deserve discussion were it not for the fact that it appeared in the widely read *Minnesota Studies in the Philosophy of Science*, a leading publication of modern positivism. In passing, it should be noted that the lack of interest in, or even hostility of logical positivists against, G.S.T. is a rather remarkable phenomenon. One would expect that a group whose program is "Unified Science" should be concerned with a novel approach to this problem, however immature it may still be. The opposite is the case; no contribution or even pertinent criticism came forward from these quarters. The reason is not difficult to see. Abandoning the debatable but challenging position of Logical Positivism and replacing it by a rather tame "Empirical Realism" (Feigl, 1956), modern positivists have come back to what is generally agreed among modern scientists, avoiding commitments which trespass and would imply an adventure of thought. It needs to be said that modern positivism has been a singularly sterile movement. It is paradoxical that the declared "philosophers of science" have neither contributed any empirical research nor new idea to modern science—while professional or half-time philosophers who were justly censored for their "mysticism," "metaphysics," or "vitalism," indubitably did. Eddington and Jeans in physics. Driesch in biology, Spengler in history are but a few examples.

Buck's critique is not directed against the present author but against J. G. Miller and his Chicago group (Miller *et al.*, 1953). Its essence is in the "So what?" argument: Supposing we find an analogy or formal identity in two "systems," it means nothing. Compare, for example, a chessboard and a mixed dinner party; a general statement expressing the alternation of black and white squares on the one hand, and of men and women on the other can be made. "If one is tempted to say 'All right, so they're structurally analogous, so what?' my answer is 'So, nothing.' " In the same vein, Buck pokes fun at some of Miller's more hazardous comparisons, such as of the behavior of slime molds and Londoners during the *blitz*. He asks, "What are we to conclude from all this? That Londoners are a form of slime mold? That myxamoebae are a sort of city dweller?" Or "if no conclusion, why bother with the analogy at all?"

As proof of the emptiness of analogies Buck offers the example of a scientist, A, who finds a formula for the rate of formation of frost in a refrigerator; of another, B, formulating the rate of carbon deposit in an automobile motor; and a "general systems theorist," C, who notices that both formulas are the same. The similarity of mathematical expressions and models is, according to Buck, "sheer coincidence"—it does not prove that a refrigerator is an automobile or vice versa, but only that both are "systems" of some sort. This, however, is a meaningless statement; for

> One is unable to think of anything, or of any combination of things, which could not be regarded as a system. And, of course, a concept that applies to everything is logically empty.

Regardless of the question whether Miller's is a particularly felicitous presentation, Buck has simply missed the issue of a general theory of systems. Its aim is not more or less hazy analogies; it is to establish principles applicable to entities not covered in conventional science. Buck's criticism is, in principle, the same as if one would criticize Newton's law because it draws a loose "analogy" between apples, planets, ebb and tide and many other entities; or if one would declare the theory of probability meaningless because it is concerned with the "analogy" of games of dice, mortality statistics, molecules in a gas, the distribution of hereditary characteristics, and a host of other phenomena.

The basic role of "analogy"—or rather of isomorphisms and models is science—has been lucidly discussed by Ashby (1958b; cf. also Bertalanffy 1960a, p. 200, on degrees of explanation; Oppenheimer, 1956 on the scientific use of analogy; Ackoff, 1959 on analogues and analogies). Hence a few remarks in answer to Buck will suffice.

The "So what?" question mistakes a method which is fundamental in science although—like every method—it can be misused. Even Buck's first example is not a meaningless pseudoproblem; in the "analogy" of chessboard and dinner party topology may find a common structural principle that is well worth stating. Generally speaking, the use of "analogy" (isomorphism, logical homology)—or; what amounts to nearly the same, the use of conceptual and material models—is not a half-poetical play but a potent tool in science. Where would physics be without the analogy or model of "wave," applicable to such dissimilar phenomena as water waves, sound waves, light and electromagnetic waves, "waves" (in a rather Pickwickian sense) in atomic physics? "Analogies" may pose fundamental problems, as for example, the analogy (logically not dissimilar from that of chessboard and dinner party) of Newton's and Coulomb's law which raises the question (one of the most basic for "Unified Science") of a general field theory unifying mechanics and electrodynamics. It is commonplace in cybernetics that systems which are different materially; e.g., a mechanical and an electrical system, may be formally identical; far from considering this as a meaningless So what? the researcher has to work out the common structure (flow diagram), and this may be of incomparable value for practical technology.

A similar lack of understanding is manifest in the criticism of the system concept. By the same token ("One is unable to think of anything" which would not show the properties in question) mechanics would have to be refused as "logically empty" because every material body shows mass, acceleration, energy, etc. In the following paragraphs of his paper, Buck has some glimpse of this truism, but he soon comes back to ridiculing Miller's use of "analogies."

Although Buck justly criticizes certain unfortunate formulations, his misunderstanding of the basic problems involved makes one wonder how his essay found its way into a treatise on "Philosophy of Science."

At an incomparably higher level stands the criticism by the Soviet authors, Lektorsky and Sadovsky (1960). The writers give a sympathetic and fair presentation of Bertalanffy's G.S.T. sketching diligently its gradual evolution from "organismic biology" and the theory of open systems. In view of the above criticism by Buck the following quotation (l.c., p. 173f.) is of interest:

> Bertalanffy emphasizes the idea that a general system theory is not an investigation of hazy and superficial analogies. . . . Analogies as such have little value, since differences can always be found among phenomena as well as similarities. Bertalanffy declares that the kind of isomorphism with which general system theory is concerned is a consequence of the fact that in some respects corresponding abstractions and conceptual models can be applied to different phenomena.

"We can only welcome (the) goal (of G.S.T.)," write Lektorsky and Sadovsky, "i.e., the attempt to give a general definition of the concept of 'organized system,' to classify logically various types of systems and to work out mathematical models for describing them . . . Bertalanffy's theory of organization and of organized complexes is a special scientific discipline. At the same time it certainly fulfills a definite methodological function" (i.e., avoiding duplication of effort in various disciplines by a single formal apparatus). "Its mathematical apparatus can be utilized for analyzing a comparatively large class of systemed objects of interest to biologists, chemists, biochemists, biophysicists, psychologists and others."

The criticism of the Russian authors is directed against imperfections of G.S.T. which, unfortunately, cannot be denied: "Bertalanffy's definition is rather a description (not pretending to precision) of the class of events which we may call systems than a strictly logical definition." "The description contains no trace of logical elegance." "Elementary methods of analysis and synthesis are insufficient for the analysis of systems." Fairly enough the authors concede that "The flaws we have noted speak only for the fact that general system theory, like any scientific theory, should develop further and in the process of development should strive for more adequate reflection of the objects of investigation."

The "main flaws of the theory," according to Lektorsky and Sadovsky, are in the lack of "methodology" (i.e., presumably of rules to establish and to apply system principles) and in considering G.S.T. "a philosophy of modern science." With respect to the first item, the present study is devoted to just this problem. The second point is a misunderstanding. G.S.T. in its present form is one—and still very imperfect—model among others. Were it completely developed, it would indeed incorporate the "organismic" world view of our time, with its emphasis on problems of wholeness, organization, directiveness, etc., in a similar way as when previous philosophies have presented a mathematical world view (philosophies *more geometrico*), a physicalistic one (the mechanistic philosophy based upon classical physics), etc., corresponding to scientific development. Even then, this "organismic" picture would not claim to be a "Nothing-but" philosophy: It would remain conscious that it only presents certain aspects of reality (richer and more comprehensive than previous ones, as corresponds to the advance of science), but never exhaustive, exclusive or final.

According to the authors, Marxist-Leninist philosophy "formulates a series of most important methodological principles of analysis of complex systems"; Soviet scientists "attempt to give a general definition of the notion of systems and to obtain a classification." Difficulties in international communication make it unfortunately impossible to the present writer to evaluate these claims.

Another criticism backed by the same *Weltanschauung* is that of Kamarýt (1961). The main arguments are:

1. Underestimation of the structural and morphologic aspects of organization of the theory of open systems (and implicitly in G.S.T.). The theory of open system does not "solve" the problem of life, its origin and evolution which is successfully attacked in modern biochemistry, submicroscopic morphology, physiological genetics, etc. The reply to this is that the functional and processual aspect has been emphasized in the theory, particularly in contradistinction to structural, homeostatic mechanisms. But neither the importance of the latter is denied, nor of course the specificity of the material basis of life. "Morphology and physiology are different and complementary ways of studying the same integrated object." (Bertalanffy, 1960a, p. 139) If one wishes, this may be called a "dialectic unity of structure and function" (Kamraýt).

2. Neglect of "qualitative specifity" of biological open system and of the specific "chemodynamics" of the first. The reply is: Thermodynamic considerations (of machines, chemical reactions, organisms, etc.) permit balance statements regarding the system as a whole, without entering into, or even knowing partial reactions, components, organization, etc., in detail. Hence part of the "theory of open systems" is concerned with such over-all balances of the system as a whole. If, however, the theory is applied to individual processes such as formation of proteins, behavior of tracers in the organism, ionic steady states, etc., the "specifity" of the respective components enters as a matter of course.

5. Advances of General System Theory

The decisive question is that of the explanatory and predictive value of the "new theories" attacking the host of problems around wholeness, teleology, etc. Of course, the change in intellectual climate which allows to see new problems which were overlooked perviously, or to see problems in a new light, is in a way more important than any single and special application. The "Copernican Revolution" was more than the possibility somewhat better to calculate the movement of the planets; general relativity more than an explanation of a very small number of recalcitrant phenomena in physics; Darwinism more than a hypothetical answer to zoological problems; it was the changes in the general frame of reference that mattered (cf. Rapoport, 1959). Nevertheless, the justification of such change ultimately is in specific achievements which would not have obtained without the new theory.

There is no question that new horizons have

been opened up but the relations to empirical facts often remain tenuous. Thus, information theory has been hailed as a "major breakthrough" but outside the original technological field contributions have remained relatively scarce. In psychology, they are so far limited to rather trivial applications such as rote learning, etc. (Rapoport, 1956, Attneave, 1959). When, in biology, DNA is spoken of as "coded information" and of "breaking the code" when the structure of nucleic acids is elucidated, this is more a *façon de parler* than added insight into the control of protein synthesis. "Information theory, although useful for computer design and network analysis, has so far not found a significant place in biology" (Bell, 1962). Game theory, too, is a novel mathematical development which was considered to be comparable in scope to Newtonian mechanics and the introduction of calculus; again, "the applications are meager and faltering" (Rapoport, 1959; the reader is urgently referred to Rapoport's discussions on information and game theory which admirably analyze the problems here mentioned). The same is seen in decision theory from which considerable gain in applied systems science was expected; but as regards the much-advertised military and business games, "there has been no controlled evaluation of their performance in training, personnel selection, and demostration" (Ackoff, 1959).

A danger in recent developments should not remain unmentioned. Science of the past (and partly still the present) was dominated by one-sided empiricism. Only collection of data and experiments were considered as being "scientific" in biology (and psychology); "theory" was equated with "speculation" or "philosophy," forgetting that a mere accumulation of data, although steadily piling up, does not make a "science." Lack of recognition and support for development of the necessary theoretical framework and unfavorable influence on experimental research itself (which largely became an at-random, hit-or-miss endeavor) was the consequence (cf. Weiss, 1962). This has, in certain fields, changed to the contrary in recent years. Enthusiasm for the new mathematical and logical tools available has led to feverish "model building" as a purpose in itself and often without regard to empirical fact. However, conceptual experimentation at random has no greater chances of success than at-random experimentation with biological, psychological, or clinical material. In the words of Ackoff (1959), there is the fundamental misconception in game (and other) theory to mistake for a "problem" what actually is only a mathematical "exercise." One would do well to remember the old Kantian maxim that experience without theory is blind, but theory without experience a mere intellectual play.

The case is somewhat different with cybernetics. The model here applied is not new; although the enormous development in the field dates from the introduction of the name, Cybernetics (Wiener, 1948), application of the feedback principle to physiological processes goes back to R. Wagner's work nearly 40 years ago (cf. Kment, 1959). The feedback and homeostasis model has since been applied to innumerable biological phenomena and—somewhat less persuasively—in psychology and the social sciences. The reason for the latter fact is, in Rapoport's words (1956) that

> usually, there is a well-marked negative correlation between the scope and the soundness of the writings. . . . The sound work is confined either to engineering or to rather trivial applications; ambitious formulations remain vague.

This, of course, is an ever-present danger in all approaches to general systems theory: doubtless, there is a new compass of thought but it is difficult to steer between the scylla of the trivial and the charybdis of mistaking neologisms for explanation.

The following survey is limited to "classical" general system theory—"classical" not in the sense that it claims any priority or excellence, but that the models used remain in the framework of "classical" mathematics in contradistinction to the "new" mathematics in game, network, information theory, etc. This does not imply that the theory is merely application of conventional mathematics. On the contrary, the system concept poses problems which are partly far from being answered. In the past, system problems have led to important mathematical developments such as Volterra's theory of integro-differential equations, of systems with "memory" whose behavior depends not only on actual conditions but also on previous history. Presently important problems are waiting for further developments, e.g., a general theory of non-linear differential equations, of steady states and rhythmic phenomena, a generalized principle of least action, the thermodynamic definition of steady states, etc.

It is, of course, irrelevant whether or not research was explicitly labeled as "general system theory." No complete or exhaustive review is intended. The aim of this unpretentious survey will be fulfilled if it can serve as a sort of guide to research done in the field, and to areas that are promising for future work.

Open Systems. The theory of open systems is an important generalization of physical theory, kinetics and thermodynamics. It has led to new principles and insight, such as the principle of equifinality, the generalization of the second thermodynamic principle, the possible increase of order in open systems, the occurrence of periodic phenomena of overshoot and false start, etc. The possibility of measuring organization in terms of entropy ("chain entropy" of high molecular compounds showing a certain order of component molecules Schulz, 1951) deserves further attention.

The extensive work done cannot be reviewed here. Principles and comprehensive bibliographies may be found in Bertalanffy, 1953, 1960b; Bray and White, 1957, etc. It should be briefly mentioned, however, that apart from theoretical developments, the field has two major applications, i.e., in industrial chemistry and in biophysics.

The applications of "open systems" in biochemistry, biophysics, physiology, etc., are too numerous to permit more than brief mentioning in the present study. The impact of the theory follows from the fact that the living organism, the cell as well as other biological entities essentially are steady states (or evolving toward such states). This implies the fundamental nature of the theory in the biological realm, and a basic reorientation in many of its specialties. Among others, the theory was developed and applied in such fields as, e.g., the network of reactions in photosynthesis (Bradley and Calvin, 1956), calculation of turnover rates in isotope experiments, energy requirements for the maintenance of body proteins, transport processes, maintenance of ion concentrations in the blood (Dost, 1953) radiation biology, excitation and propagation of nerve impulses, and others. The organism is in a steady state not only with respect to its chemical components, but also to its cells; hence the numerous modern investigations on cell turnover and renewal have also to be included here. Beside the work already cited, results and impending problems in biophysics and related fields may be found in Netter (1959).

There are certainly relations between irreversible thermodynamics of open systems, cybernetics, and information theory, but they are still unexplored. First approaches to these problems are those by Foster, Rapoport and Trucco (1957) and by Tribus (1961). Another interesting approach to metabolizing systems was made by Rosen (1960) who instead of conventional reaction equations, applied "relational theory" using mapping by way of block diagrams.

Beyond the individual organism, systems principles are also used in population dynamics and ecologic theory (review: J. R. Bray, 1958). Dynamic ecology, i.e., the succession and climax of plant populations, is a much-cultivated field which, however, shows a tendency to slide into verbalism and terminological debate. The systems approach seems to offer a new viewpoint. Whittacker (1953) has described the sequence of plant communities toward a climax formation in terms of open systems and equifinality. According to this author, the fact that similar climax formations may develop from different initial vegetations is a striking example of equifinality, and one where the degree of independence of starting conditions and of the course development has taken appears even greater than in the individual organism. A quantitative analysis on the basis of open systems in terms of production of biomass, with climax as steady state attained, was given by Patten (1959).

The open-system concept has also found application in the earth sciences, geomorphology (Chorley, in press) and meteorology (Thompson, 1961) drawing a detailed comparison of modern meteorological concepts and Bertalanffy's organismic concept in biology. It may be remembered that already Prigogine in his classic (1947) mentioned meteorology as one possible field of application of open systems.

Growth-in-Time. The simplest forms of growth which, for this reason, are particularly apt to show the isomorphism of law in different fields, are the exponential and the logistic.

Examples are, among many others, the increase of knowledge of number of animal species (Gessner, 1951), publications on drosophila (Hersh, 1942), of manufacturing companies (Haire, 1959). Boulding (1956) and Keiter (1951–52) have emphasized a general theory of growth.

The theory of animal growth after Bertalanffy (and others)—which, in virtue of using overall physiological parameters ("anabolism," "catabolism") may be subsumed under the heading of G.S.T. as well as under that of biophysics—has been surveyed in its various applications (Bertalanffy, 1960b).

Relative Growth. A principle which is also of great simplicity and generality concerns the relative growth of components within a system. The simple relationship of allometric increase applies to many growth phenomena in biology (morphology, biochemistry, physiology, evolution).

A similar relationship obtains in social phenomena. Social differentiation and division of labor in primitive societies as well as the process of urbanization (i.e., growth of cities in comparison to rural population) follow the allometric equation. Application of the latter offers a quantitative measure of social organization and development, apt to replace the usual, intuitive judgments (Narroll and Bertalanffy, 1956). The same principle apparently applies to the growth of staff compared to total number of employees in manufacturing companies (Haire, 1959).

Competition and Related Phenomena. The work in population dynamics by Volterra, Lotka, Gause and others belongs to the classics of G.S.T., having first shown that it is possible to develop conceptual models for phenomena such as the "struggle for existence" that can be submitted to empirical test. Population dynamics and related population genetics have since become important fields in biological research.

It is important to note that investigation of this kind belongs not only to basic but also to applied biology. This is true of fishery biology where theoretical models are used to establish optimum conditions for the exploitation of the sea (survey of the more important models: Watt, 1958). The most elaborate dynamic model is by Beverton and Holt (1957; short survey: Holt, w.y.) developed for fish populations exploited in commercial fishery but certainly of wider application. This model takes into account recruitment (i.e., entering of individuals into the population), growth (assumed to follow the growth equations after Bertalanffy), capture (by exploitation), and natural mortality. The practical value of this model is illustrated by the fact that it has been adopted for routine purposes by the Food and Agriculture Organization of the United Nations, the British Ministry of Agriculture and Fisheries and other official agencies.

Richardson's studies on armaments races (cf. Rapoport, 1957, 1960), notwithstanding their shortcomings, dramatically show the possible impact of the systems concept upon the most vital concerns of our time. If rational and scientific considerations matter at all, this is one way to refute such catch words as *Si vis pacem para bellum.*

The expressions used in population dynamics and the biological "struggle for existence," in econometrics, in the study of armament races (and others) all belong to the same family of equations (the system discussed in Bertalanffy, 1950). A systematic comparison and study of these parallelisms would be highly interesting and rewarding (cf. also Rapoport, 1957, p. 88). One may, for example, suspect that the laws governing business cycles and those of population fluctuations according to Volterra stem from similar conditions of competition and interaction in the system.

In a non-mathematical way, Boulding (1953) has discussed what he calls the "Iron Laws" of social organizations: the Malthusian law, the law of optimum size of organizations, existence of cycles, the law of oligopoly, etc.

Systems Engineering. The theoretical interest of systems engineering and operations research is in the fact that entities whose components are most heterogeneous—men, machines, buildings, monetary and other values, inflow of raw material, outflow of products and many other items—can successfully be submitted to systems analysis.

As already mentioned, systems engineering employs the methodology of cybernetics, information theory, network analysis, flow and block diagrams, etc. Considerations of G.S.T. also enter (Hall, 1962). The first approaches are concerned with structured, machine-like aspects (yes-or-no decisions in the case of information theory); one would suspect that

G.S.T. aspects will win increased importance with dynamic aspects, flexible organizations, etc.

Personality Theory. Although there is an enormous amount of theorizing on neural and psychological function in the cybernetic line based upon the brain-computer comparison, few attempts have been made to apply G.S.T. in the narrower sense to the theory of human behavior (e.g., Krech, 1956; Menninger, 1957). For the present purposes, the latter may be nearly equated with personality theory.

We have to realize at the start that personality theory is at present a battlefield of contrasting and controversial theories. Hall and Lindzey (1957, p. 71) have justly stated: "All theories of behavior are pretty poor theories and all of them leave much to be desired in the way of scientific proof"—this being said in a textbook of nearly 600 pages on "Theories of Personality."

We can therefore not well expect that G.S.T. can present solutions where personality theorists from Freud and Jung to a host of modern writers were unable to do so. The theory will have shown its value if it opens new perspectives and viewpoints capable to experimental and practical application. This appears to be the case. There is quite a group of psychologists who are committed to an organismic theory of personality, Goldstein and Maslow being well-known representatives. Biological considerations may therefore be expected to advance the matter.

There is, of course, the fundamental question whether, first, G.S.T. is not essentially a physicalistic simile, inapplicable to psychic phenomena; and secondly whether such model has explanatory value when the pertinent variables cannot be defined quantitatively as is in general the case with psychological phenomena.

(1) The answer to the first question appears to be that the systems concept is abstract and general enough to permit application to entities of whatever denomination. The notions of "equilibrium," "homeostasis," "feedback," "stress," etc., are no less of technologic or physiological origin but more or less successfully applied to psychological phenomena. System theorists agree that the concept of "system" is not limited to material entities but can be applied to any "whole" consisting of interacting "components" (cf. the definition of "system" given by Bertalanffy, 1950, with Ackoff, 1690, p. 1; Ashby, 1962, p. 260 f.). Systems engineering is an example where components are partly not physical and metric.

(2) If quantitation is impossible, and even if the components of a system are ill-defined, it can at least be expected that certain principles will qualitatively apply to the whole *qua* system. At least "explanation on principle" (see below) may be possible.

Bearing in mind these limitations, on concept which may prove to be of a key nature is the organismic notion of the organism as a spontaneously active system. In the present author's words,

> Even under constant external conditions and in the absence of external stimuli the organism is not a passive but a basically active system. This applies in particular to the function of the nervous system and to behavior. It appears that internal activity rather than reaction to stimuli is fundamental. This can be shown with respect both to evolution in lower animals and to development, for example, in the first movements of embryos and fetuses (Bertalanffy, 1960a).

This agrees with what von Holst has called the "new conception" of the nervous system, based upon the fact that primitive locomotor activities are caused by central automatisms that do not need external stimuli. Therefore, such movements persist, for example, even after the connection of motoric to sensory nerves had been severed. Hence the reflex in the classic sense is not the basic unit of behavior but rather a regulatory mechanism superimposed upon primitive, automatic activities. A similar concept is basic in the theory on instinct. According to Lorenz, innate releasing mechanisms (I.R.M.) play a dominant role, which sometimes go off without an external stimulus (invacuo or running idle reactions): A bird which has no material to build a nest may perform the movements of nest building in the air. These considerations are in the framework of what Hebb called the "conceptual C.N.S. of 1930–1950." The more recent insight into activating systems of the brain emphasizes differently, and with a wealth of experimental evidence, the same basic concept of the autonomous activity of the C.N.S.

The significance of these concepts becomes

apparent when we consider that they are in fundamental contrast to the conventional stimulus-response scheme which assumes that the organism is an essentially reactive system answering, like an automaton, to external stimuli. The dominance of the S-R scheme in contemporary psychology needs no emphasis, and is obviously connected with the *zeitgeist* of a highly mechanized society. This principle is basic in psychological theories which in all other respects are opposite, for example, in behavioristic psychology as well as in psychoanalysis. According to Freud it is the supreme tendency of the organism to get rid of tensions and drives and come to rest in a state of equilibrium governed by the "principle of stability" which Freud borrowed from the German philosopher, Fechner. Neurotic and psychotic behavior, then, is a more or less effective or abortive defense mechanism tending to restore some sort of equilibrium (according to D. Rappaport's analysis (1960) of the structure of psychoanalytic theory: "economic" and "adaptive points of view").

Charlotte Buhler (1959), the well-known child psychologist, has aptly epitomized the theoretical situation:

> In the fundamental psychoanalytic model, there is only one basic tendency, that is toward *need gratification* or *tension reduction*. . . . Present-day biologic theories emphasize the "spontaneity" of the organism's activity which is due to its built-in energy. The organism's autonomous functioning, its "drive to perform certain movements" is emphasized by Bertalanffy. . . . These concepts represent *a complete revision of the original homeostasis principle* which emphasized exclusively the tendency toward equilibrum. It is the original homeostasis principle with which psychoanalysis identified its theory of discharge of tensions as the only primary tendency (Underscores partly ours).

In brief, we may define our viewpoint as "Beyond the Homeostasis Principle":

1. The S-R scheme misses the realms of play, exploratory activities, creativity, self-realization, etc.
2. The economic scheme misses just specific, human achievements—the most of what loosely is termed "human culture".
3. The equilibrium principle misses the fact that psychological and behavioral activities are more than relaxation of tensions; far from establishing an optimal state, the latter may entail psychosis-like disturbances as, e.g., in sensory-deprivation experiments.

It appears that the S-R and psychoanalytic model is a highly unrealistic picture of human nature and, in its consequences, a rather dangerous one. Just what we consider to be specific human achievements can hardly be brought under the utilitarian, homeostasis, and stimulus-response scheme. One may call mountain climbing, composing of sonatas or lyrical poems "psychological homeostasis"—as has been done—but at the risk that this physiologically well-defined concept loses all meaning. Furthermore, if the principle of homeostatic maintenance is taken as a golden rule of behavior, the so-called well-adjusted individual will be the ultimate goal, that is a well-oiled robot maintaining itself in optimal biological, psychological and, social homeostasis. This is a *Brave New World*—not, for some at least, the ideal state of humanity. Furthermore, that precarious mental equilibrium must not be disturbed. Hence in what somewhat ironically is called progressive education, the anxiety not to overload the child, not to impose constraints and to minimize all directing influences—with the result of a previously unheard-of crop of illiterates and juvenile delinquents.

In contrast to conventional theory, it can safely be maintained that not only stresses and tensions but equally complete release from stimuli and the consequent mental void may be neurosogenic or even psychosogenic. Experimentally this is verified by the experiments with sensory deprivation when subjects, insulated from all incoming stimuli, after a few hours develop a so-called model psychosis with hallucinations, unbearable anxiety, etc. Clinically it amounts to the same when insulation leads to prisoners' psychosis and to exacerbation of mental disease by isolation of patients in the ward. In contrast, maximal stress need not necessarily produce mental disturbance. If conventional theory were correct, Europe during and after the war, with extreme physiological as well as psychological stresses, should have been a gigantic lunatic asylum. As a matter of fact, there was statistically no increase either in neurotic or psychotic disturbances, apart from easily explained acute disturbances such as combat neurosis.

We so arrive at the conception that a great deal of biological and human behavior is beyond the principles of utility, homeostasis and stimulus-response, and that it is just this which is characteristic of human and cultural activities. Such new look opens new perspectives not only in theory, but in practical implications with respect to mental hygiene, education, and society in general.

What has been said can also be couched in philosophical terms. If existentialists speak of the emptiness and meaninglessness of life, if they see in it a source not only of anxiety but of actual mental illness, it is essentially the same viewpoint: that behavior is not merely a matter of satisfaction of biological drives and of maintenance in psychological and social equilibrium but that something more is involved. If life becomes unbearably empty in an industrialized society, what can a person do but develop a neurosis? The principle which may loosely be called spontaneous activity of the psychophysical organism, is a more realistic formulation of what the existentialists want to say in their often obscure language. And if personality theorists like Maslow or Gardner Murphy speak of self-realization as human goal, it is again a somewhat pompous expression of the same.

Theoretical History. We eventually come to those highest and ill-defined entities that are called human cultures and civilizations. It is the field often called "philosophy of history." We may perhaps better speak of "theoretical history," admittedly in its very first beginnings. This name expresses the goal to form a connecting link between "science" and the "humanities"; more in particular, between the "social sciences" and "history."

It is understood, of course, that the techniques in sociology and history are entirely different (polls, statistical analysis against archival studies, internal evidence of historic relics, etc.). However, the object of study is essentially the same. Sociology is essentially concerned with a temporal cross-section as human societies *are;* history with the "longitudinal" study how societies *become* and develop. The object and techniques of study certainly justify practical differentiation; it is less clear, however, that they justify fundamentally different philosophies.

The last statement already implies the question of constructs in history, as they were presented, in grand form, from Vico to Hegel, Marx, Spengler, and Toynbee. Professional historians regard them at best as poetry, at worst as fantasies pressing, with paranoic obsession, the facts of history into a theoretical bed of Procrustes. It seems history can learn from the system theorists, not ultimate solutions but a sounder methodological outlook. Problems hitherto considered to be philosophical or metaphysical can well be defined in their scientific meaning, with some interesting outlook at recent developments (e.g., game theory) thrown into the bargain.

Empirical criticism is outside the scope of the present study. For example, Geyl (1958) and many others have analyzed obvious misrepresentations of historical events in Toynbee's work, and even the non-specialist reader can easily draw a list of fallacies especially in the later, Holy-Ghost inspired volumes of Toynbee's *magnum opus*. The problem, however, is larger than errors in fact or interpretation or even the question of the merits of Marx's, Spengler's or Toynbee's theories; it is whether, in principle, models and laws are admissible in history.

A widely held contention says that they are not. This is the concept of "nomothetic" method in science and "idiographic" method in history. While science to a greater or less extent can establish "laws" for natural events, history, concerned with human events of enormous complexity in causes and outcome and possibly determined by free decisions of individuals, can only describe, more or less satisfactorily, what has happened in the past.

Here the methodologist has his first comment. In the attitude just outlined, academic history condemns constructs of history as "intuitive," "contrary to fact," "arbitrary," etc. And, no doubt, the criticism is pungent enough vis-à-vis Spengler or Toynbee. It is, however, somewhat less convincing if we look at the work of conventional historiography. For example, the Dutch historian, Peter Geyl, who made a strong argument against Toynbee from such methodological considerations, also wrote a brilliant book about Napoleon (1949), amounting to the result that there are a dozen or so different interpretations—we may safely say, *models*—of Napoleon's character and career within academic history, all based upon "fact" (the Napoleonic period happens to be one of the best documented) and all flatly contradicting each other. Roughly speaking, they range from Napoleon as the brutal tyrant and egotistic enemy of human freedom to Napoleon the wise planner of a unified Europe; and if one is a Napoleonic student (as the present writer happens to be in a small way), one can easily produce some original documents refuting misconceptions occurring even in generally accepted, standard histories. You cannot have it both ways. If even a figure like Napoleon, not very remote in time and with the best of historical documentation, can be interpreted contrarily, you cannot well blame the "philosophers of history" for their intuitive procedure, subjective bias, etc., when they deal with the enormous phenomenon of universal history. What you have in both cases is a conceptual model which always will represent certain aspects only, and for this reason will be one-sided or even lopsided. Hence the construction of conceptual models in history is not only permissible but, as a matter of fact, is at the basis of any historical interpretation as distinguished from mere enumeration of data, i.e., chronicle or annals.

If this is granted, the antithesis between idiographic and nomothetic procedure reduces to what psychologists are wont to call the "molecular" and "molar" approach. One can analyze events within a complex whole—individual chemical reactions in an organism, perceptions in the psyche, for example; or one can look for over-all laws covering the whole such as growth and development in the first or personality in the second instance. In terms of history, this means detailed study of individuals, treaties, works of art, singular causes and effects, etc., or else over-all phenomena with the hope of detecting grand laws. There are, of course, all transitions between the first and second considerations; the extremes may be illustrated by Carlyle and his hero worship at one pole and Tolstoy (a far greater "theoretical historian" than commonly admitted) at the other.

The question of a "theoretical history" therefore is essentially that of "molar" models in the field; and this is what the great constructs of history amount to when divested of their philosophical embroidery.

The evaluation of such models must follow the general rules for verification or falsification. First, there is the consideration of empirical bases. In this particular instance it amounts to the question whether or not a limited number of civilizations—some twenty at the best—provide a sufficient and representative sample to establish justified generalizations. This question and that of the value of proposed models will be answered by the general criterion: whether or not the model has explanatory and predictive value, i.e., throws new light upon known facts and correctly foretells facts of the past or future not previously known.

Although elementary, these considerations nevertheless are apt to remove much misunderstanding and philosophical fog which has clouded the issue.

1. As had been emphasized, the evaluation of models should be simply pragmatic in terms of their explanatory and predictive merits (or lack thereof); *a priori* considerations as to their desirability or moral consequences do not enter.

Here we encounter a somewhat unique situation. There is little objection against so-called "synchronic" laws, i.e., supposed regularities governing societies at a certain point in time; as a matter of fact, beside empirical study this is the aim of sociology. Also certain "diachronic" laws, i.e., regularities of development in time, are undisputed such as, e.g., Grimm's law stating rules for the changes of consonants in the evolution of Indo-Germanic languages. It is commonplace that there is a sort of "life cycle"—stages of primitivity, maturity, baroque dissolution of form and eventual decay for which no particular external causes can be indicated—in individual fields of culture, such as Greek sculpture, Renaissance painting or German music. Indeed, this even has its counterpart in certain phenomena of biological evolution showing, as in ammonites or dinosaurs, a first explosive phase of formation of new types, followed by a phase of speciation and eventually of decadence.

Violent criticism comes in when this model is applied to civilization as a whole. It is a legitimate question—Why often rather unrealistic models in the social sciences remain matters of academic discussion, while models of history encounter passionate resistance? Granting all factual criticism raised against Spengler or Toynbee, it seems rather obvious that emotional factors are involved. The highway of science is strewn with corpses of deceased theories which just decay or are preserved as mummies in the museum of history of science. In contrast, historical constructs and especially theories of historical cycles appear to touch a raw nerve, and so opposition is much more than usual criticism of a scientific theory.

2. This emotional involvement is connected with the question of "Historical Inevitability" and a supposed degradation of human "freedom." Before turning to it, discussion of mathematical and non-mathematical models is in place.

Advantages and shortcomings of mathematical models in the social sciences are well known (Arrow, 1956; Rapoport, 1957). Every mathematical model is an oversimplification, and it remains questionable whether it strips actual events to the bones or cuts away vital parts of their anatomy. On the other hand, so far as it goes, it permits necessary deduction with often unexpected results which would not be obtained by ordinary "common sense."

In particular, Rashevsky has shown in several studies how mathematical models of historical processes can be constructed (Rashevsky, 1951, 1952).

On the other hand, the value of purely qualitative models should not be underestimated. For example, the concept of "ecologic equilibrium" was developed long before Volterra and others introduced mathematical models; the theory of selection belongs to the stock-in-trade of biology, but the mathematical theory of the "struggle for existence" is comparatively recent, and far from being verified under wildlife conditions.

In complex phenomena, "explanation on principle" (Hayek, 1955) by qualitative models is preferable to no explanation at all. This is by no means limited to the social sciences and history; it applies alike to fields like meteorology or evolution.

3. "Historical inevitability"—subject of a well-known study by Sir Isaiah Berlin (1954) —dreaded as a consequence of "theoretical history," supposedly contradicting our direct experience of having free choices and eliminating all moral judgment and values—is a phantasmogoria based upon a world view which does not exist any more. As, in fact, Berlin emphasizes, it is founded upon the concept of the Laplacean spirit who is able completely to predict the future from the past by means of deterministic laws. This has no resemblance with the modern concept of "laws of nature." All "laws of nature" have a statistical character. They do not predict an inexorably determined future but probabilities which, depending on the nature of events and on the laws available, may approach certainty or else remain far below it. It is nonsensical to ask or fear more "inevitability" in historical theory than is found in sciences with relatively high sophistication like meteorology or economics.

Paradoxically, while the cause of free will rests with the testimony of intuition or rather immediate experience and can never be proved objectively ("Was it Napoleon's free will that led him to the Russian Campaign?"), determinism (in the statistical sense) can be proved, at least in small-scale models. Certainly business depends on personal "initiative," the individual "decision" and "responsibility" of the entrepreneur; the manager's choice whether or not to expand business by employing new appointees, is "free" in precisely the sense as Napoleon's choice whether or not to accept battle at Austerlitz. However, when the growth curve of industrial companies is analyzed, it is found that "arbitrary" deviations are followed by speedy return to the normal curve, as if invisible forces were active. Haire (1959, p. 283) states that "the return to the pattern predicted by earlier growth suggests the operation of *inexorable forces* operating on the social organism" (or underscores).

It is characteristic that one of Berlin's points is "the fallacy of historical determinism (appearing) from its utter inconsistency with the common sense and everyday life of looking at human affairs." This characteristic argument is of the same nature as the advice not to adopt the Copernican system because everybody can see that the sun moves from morning to evening.

4. Recent developments in mathematics even allow to submit "free will"—apparently the philosophical problem most recalcitrant against scientific analysis—to mathematical examination.

In the light of modern systems theory, the alternative between molar and molecular, nomothetic and idiographic approach can be given a precise meaning. For mass behavior, system laws would apply which, if they can be mathematized, would take the form of differential equations of the sort of those used by Richardson (cf. Rapoport, 1957) mentioned above. Free choice of the individual would be described by formulations of the nature of game and decision theory.

Axiomatically, game and decision theory are concerned with "rational" choice. This means a choice which "maximizes the individual's utility or satisfaction," that "the individual is free to choose among several possible courses of action and decides among them at the basis of their consequences," that he "selects, being informed of all conceivable consequences of his actions, what stands highest on his list," he "prefers more of a commodity to less, other things being equal," etc. (Arrow, 1956). Instead of economical gain, any higher value may be inserted without changing the mathematical formalism.

The above definition of "rational choice" includes everything that can be meant by "free will." If we do not wish to equate "free will" with complete arbitrariness, lack of any value judgment and therefore completely inconsequential actions (like the philosopher's favorite example: It is my free will whether or not to wiggle my left little finger) it is a fair definition of those actions with which the moralist, priest or historian is concerned: free decision between alternatives based upon insight into the situation and its consequences and guided by values.

The difficulty to apply the theory even to simple, actual situations is of course enormous; so is the difficulty in establishing over-all laws. However, without explicit formulation, both approaches can be evaluated in principle—leading to an unexpected paradox.

The "principle of rationality" fits—not the majority of human actions but rather the "unreasoning" behavior of animals. Animals and organisms in general do function in a "ratiomorphic" way, maximizing such values as maintenance, satisfaction, survival, etc.; they select, in general, what is biologically good for them, and prefer more of a commodity (e.g., food) to less.

Human behavior, on the other hand, falls far short of the principle of rationality. It is not even necessary to quote Freud to show how small is the compass of rational behavior in man. Women in a supermarket, in general, do not maximize utility but are susceptible to the tricks of the advertiser and packer; they do not make a rational choice surveying all possibilities and consequences; and do not even prefer more of the commodity packed in an inconspicuous way to less when packed in a big red box with attractive design. In our society, it is the job of an influential specialty—advertisers, motivation researchers, etc.—to *make* choices irrational which essentially is done by coupling biological factors—conditioned reflex, unconscious drives—with symbolic values (cf. Bertalanffy, 1956).

And there is no refuge by saying that this irrationality of human behavior concerns only trivial actions of daily life; the same principle applies to "historical" decisions. That wise old mind, Oxenstierna, Sweden's Chancellor during the Thirty Years' War, has perfectly expressed this by saying: *Nescis, mi fili, quantilla ratione mundus regatur*—you don't know, my dear boy, with what little reason the world is governed. Reading newspapers or listening to the radio readily shows that this applies perhaps even more to the 20th than the 17th century.

Methodologically, this leads to a remarkable conclusion. If one of the two models is to be applied, and if the "actuality principle" basic in historical fields like geology and evolution is adopted (i.e., the hypothesis that no other principles of explanation should be used than can be observed as operative in the present)—then it is the statistical or mass model which is backed by empirical evidence. The business of the motivation and opinion researcher, statistical psychologist, etc., is based upon the premise that statistical laws obtain in human behavior; and that, for this reason a small but well-chosen sample allows for extrapolation to the total population under consideration. The generally good working of a Gallup poll and prediction verifies the premise—with some incidental failure like the well-known example of the Truman election thrown in, as is to be expected with statistical predictions. The opposite contention—that history is governed by "free will" in the philosophical sense (i.e., rational decision for the better, the higher moral value or even enlightened self-interest) is hardly supported by fact. That here and then the statistical law is broken by "rugged individualists" is in its character. Nor does the role played in history by "great men" contradict the systems concept in history; they can be conceived as acting like "leading parts," "triggers" or "catalyzers" in the historical process—a phenomenon well accounted for in the general theory of systems (Bertalanffy, 1950).

5. A further question is the "organismic analogy" unanimously condemned by historians. They combat untiringly the "metaphysical," "poetical," "mythical" and thoroughly unscientific nature of Spengler's assertion that civilizations are a sort of "organisms," being born, developing according to their internal laws and eventually dying. Toynbee (e.g., 1961) takes great pains to emphasize that he did not fall into Spengler's trap—even though it is somewhat difficult to see that his civilizations, connected by the biological relations of "affiliation" and "apparentation," even (according to the latest version of his system) with a rather strict time span of development, are not conceived organismically.

Nobody should know better than the biologist that civilizations are no "organism." It is trivial to the extreme that a biological organism, a material entity and unity in space and time, is something different from a social group consisting of distinct individuals, and even more from a civilization consisting of generations of human beings, of material products, institutions, ideas, values, and what not. It implies a serious underestimate of Vico's, Spengler's (or any normal individual's) intelligence to suppose that they did not realize the obvious.

Nevertheless, it is interesting to note that, in contrast to the historians' scruples, sociologists do not abhor the "organismic analogy" but rather take it for granted. For example, in the words of Rapoport and Horvath (1959):

> There is some sense in considering a real organization as an organism, that is, there is reason to believe that this comparison need not be a sterile metaphorical analogy, such as was common in scholastic speculation about the body politic. Quasi-biological functions are demonstrable in organizations. They maintain themselves; they sometimes reproduce or metastasize; they respond to stresses; they age, and they die. Organizations have discernible anatomies and those at least which transform material inputs (like industries) have physiologies.

Or Sir Geoffrey Vickers (1957):

> Institutions grow, repair themselves, reproduce themselves, decay, dissolve. In their external relations they show many characteristics of organic life. Some think that in their internal relations also human institutions are destined to become increasingly organic, that human cooperation will approach ever more closely to the integration of cells in a body. I find this prospect unconvincing (and) unpleasant. (N.B. so does the present author.)

And Haire (1959, p. 272):

> The biological model for social organizations—and here, particularly for industrial organizations—means taking as a model the living organism and the processes and principles that regulate its growth and development. It means looking for lawful processes in organizational growth.

The fact that simple growth laws apply to social entities such as manufacturing companies, to urbanization, division of labor, etc., proves that in these respects the "organismic analogy" is correct. In spite of the historians' protests, the application of theoretical models, in particular, the model of dynamic, open and adaptive systems (McClelland, 1958) to the historical process certainly makes sense. This does not imply "biologism," i.e., reduction of social to biological concepts, but indicates system principles applying in both fields.

6. Taking all objections for granted—poor method, errors in fact, the enormous complexity of the historical process—we have nevertheless reluctantly to admit that the cyclic models of history pass the most important test of scientific theory. The predictions made by Spengler in the *Decline of the West*, by Toynbee when forecasting a time of trouble and contending states, by Ortega Y Gasset in the *Uprise of the Masses*—we may as well add *Brave New World* and *1984*—have been verified to a disquieting extent and considerably better than any respectable models of the social scientists.

Does this imply "historic inevitability" and inexorable dissolution? Again, the simple answer was missed by moralizing and philosophizing historians. By extrapolation from the life cycles of previous civilizations nobody could have predicted the Industrial Revolution, the Population Explosion, the development of atomic energy, the emergence of underdeveloped nations, and the expansion of Western civilization over the whole globe. Does this refute the alleged model and "law" of history? No—it only says that this model—as every one in science—mirrors only certain aspects or facets of reality. Every model becomes dangerous only when it commits the "Nothing-but" fallacy which mars not only theoretical history, but the models of the mechanistic world picture, of psychoanalysis and many others as well.

We have hoped to show in this survey General System Theory has contributed toward the expansion of scientific theory; has led to new insights and principles; and has opened up new problems that are "researchable," i.e., are amenable to further study, experimental or mathematical. The limitations of the theory and its applications in their present status are obvious; but the principles appear to be essentially sound as shown by their application in different fields.

REFERENCES

Ackoff, R. L. Games, decisions, and organizations. *General Systems* IV, 145–150, 1959.

———. Systems, organizations, and interdisciplinary research. *General Systems* V, 1–8, 1960.

Arrow, K. J. Mathematical models in the social sciences. *General Systems* I, 29–47, 1956.

Ashby, W. R. General systems theory as a new discipline. *General Systems* III, 1–6, 1958a.

———. *An Introduction to Cybernetics*. 3rd impr., Wiley, New York, 1958b.

———. Principles of the self-organizing system. In: H. von Foerster, G. W. Zopf, Jr. (eds.), *Principles of Self-organization*. Pergamon Press, New York, 1962, pp. 255–278.

Attneave, F. *Application of Information Theory to Psychology. Holt,* New York, 1959.

Beer, St. Below the twilight arch. A mythology of systems. *General Systems* V, 9–20, 1960.

Bell, E. Oogenesis. C. P. Raven (review). *Science* 135, 1056, 1962.

von Bertalanffy, L. Vom Sinn und der Einheit der Wissenschaften. *Der Student*. Wien, 2, No. 7/8, 1947.

———. Zu einer allgemeinen systemlehre. *Biologia Generalis* 19, 114–129, 1949.

———. An outline of general system theory. *Brit. J. Philos. Sci.* 1, 134–165, 1950.

———. *Biophysik des fliessgleichgewichts*. (Transl. by W. Westphal). Vieweg, Braunschweig, 1953.

———. General system theory. *General Systems* I, 1–10, 1956.

———. A biologist looks at human nature. *Scientific Monthly* 82, 33–41, 1956.

———. *Problems of Life. An evaluation of Modern Biological and Scientific Thought*. (1952). Torchbook edition, Harper, New York, 1960a.

———. Principles and theory of growth. In: W. W. Nowinski (ed.), *Fundamental Aspects of Normal and Malignant Growth*. Elsevier, Amsterdam, 1960b, pp. 137–259.

———. *Modern Theories of Development. An Introduction to Theoretical Biology*. (1933). Torchbook edition, Harper, New York, 1962.

von Bertalanffy, L., Hempel, C. G., Bass, R. E., and Jonas, H. General system theory: A new approach to unity of science. *Human Biol.* 23, 302–361, 1951.

Beverton, R. J. H., and Holt, S. J. On the dynamics of exploited fish populations. *Fishery Investigation,* Ser. II, vol. XIX. Her Majesty's Stationery Office, London, 1957.

Boulding, K. E. *The Organizational Revolution*. Harper, New York, 1953.

———. Toward a general theory of growth. *General Systems* I, 66–75, 1956.

Bradley, D. F., and Calvin, M. Behavior: Imbalance in a network of chemical transformation. *General Systems* I, 56–65, 1956.

Bray, J. R. Notes toward an ecology theory. *Ecology* 9, 770–776, 1958.

Bray, H. G., and White, K. *Kinetics and Thermodynamics in Biochemistry*. Academic Press, New York, 1957.

Buck, R. C. On the logic of general behavior systems theory. In: H. Feigel and M. Scriven (eds.), *Minnesota Studies in the Philosophy of Science*, vol. I, Univer. of Minnesota Press, Minneapolis, 1956, pp. 223–238.

Buhler, Ch., Theoretical observations about life's basic tendencies. *Amer. J. Psychother.* 13, 501–581, 1959.

Chorley, R. J. Geomorphology and general systems theory. In press.

Dost, R. H. *Der Blutspiegel*. Kinetik der Konzentrationsabläufe in der Körperflussigkeit. Thieme, Leipzig, 1953.

Egler, F. E. Bertalanffian organismicism. *Ecology* 34, 443–446, 1953.

Feigl, H. Some major issues and developments in the philosophy of science of logical empiricism. In: H. Feigl and M. Scriven (eds.), *Minnesota Studies in the Philosophy of*

Science, vol. I, Univer. of Minnesota Press, Minneapolis, 1956, pp. 3–37.

Foster, C. Rapoport, A., and Trucco, E. Some unsolved problems in the theory of non-isolated systems. *General Systems* II, 9–29, 1957.

Gessner, F. Wieviel Tiere bevölkern die Erde? *Orion*, 33–35, 1952.

Geyl, P., *Napoleon for and Against*. Cape, London, 1949 (1957).

———. *Debates with Historians.* Meridian Books, New York, 1958.

Haire, M. Biological models and empirical histories of the growth of organizations. In: M. Haire (ed.), *Modern Organization Theory*. Wiley, New York, 1959, pp. 272–306.

Hall, A. D. *A Methodology for Systems Engineering*. Nostrand, Princeton, 1962.

Hall, A. D., and Fagen, R. E. Definition of system. *General Systems* I, 18–28, 1956.

Hall, C. S., and Lindzey, G. *Theories of Personality*. Wiley, New York, 1957.

Hayek, F. A. Degrees of explanation. *Brit J. Philos. Sci.*, 6, 209–225, 1955.

Hearn, G. *Theory Building in Social Work*. Univer. of Toronto Press, Toronto, 1958.

Hersh, A. H. Drosophila and the course of research. *Ohio J. of Science* 42, 198–200, 1942.

Holt, S. J. The application of comparative population studies to fisheries biology—an exploration. In: E. D. Le Cren and M. W. Holdgate (eds.), *The Exploitation of Natural Animal Populations*. Blackwell, Oxford, without year.

Kamaryt, J. Die Bedeutung der Theorie des offenen Systems in der gegenwaertigen Biologie. *Deutsche Z fuer Philosophie* 9, 2040–2059, 1961.

Keiter, F., Wachstum und Reifen im Jugendalter. *Koelner Z. fuer Soziologie* 4, 165–174, 1951–52.

Kment, H. The problem of biological regulation and its evolution in medical view. *General Systems* IV, 75–82, 1959.

Kremyanskiy, V. I. Certain peculiarities of organisms as a "system" from the point of view of physics, cybernetics, and biology. *General Systems* V, 221–230, 1960.

Lektorsky, V. A., and Sadovsky, V. N. On principles of system research (related to L. Bertalanffy's general system theory). *General Systems* V, 171–179, 1960.

McClelland, Ch. A. Systems and history in international relations. Some perspectives for empirical research and theory. *General Systems* III, 221–247, 1958.

Meyer, R. L. Preface. *General Systems* VI, III–IV, 1961.

Miller, J. G., et al. Symposium. Profits and problems of homeostatic models in the behavioral sciences. *Chicago Behavioral Sciences Publications No. 1*, 1953.

Naroll, R. S., and von Bertalanffy, L. The principle of allometry in biology and the social sciences. *General Systems* I, 76–89, 1956.

Netter, H. *Theoretische Biochemie*. Springer, Berlin, 1959.

Oppenheimer, R. Analogy in science. *Amer. Psychol.* 11, 127–135, 1956.

Patten, B. C. An introduction to the cybernetics of the ecosystem: The trophic-dynamic aspect. *Ecology* 40, 221–231, 1959.

Prigogine, I. *Etude thermodynamique des phénomènes irréversibles*. Dunod, Paris, 1947.

Rapoport, A. The promise and pitfalls of information theory. *Behav. Sci.* 1, 303–315, 1956.

———. Lewis F. Richardson's mathematical theory of war. *General Systems* II, 55–91, 1957.

———. Critiques of game theory. *Behav. Sci.* 4, 49–66, 1959.

———. *Fights, Games, and Debates*. Univer. of Mich. Press, Ann Arbor, 1960.

Rapoport, A., and Horvath, W. J. Thoughts on organization theory and a review of two conferences. *General Systems* IV, 87–93, 1959.

Rappaport, D. The structure of psycho-analytic theory. *Psychol. Issues* 2, Monogr. 6, pp. 39–64, 1960.

Rashevsky, N. The effect of environmental factors on the rates of cultural development. *Bull. Math. Biophysics*, 14, 193–201, 1952.

Rosen, R. A relational theory of biological systems. *General Systems* V, 29–55, 1960.

Schulz, G. V. Energetische und statistische Voraussetzungen fuer die Synthese der Makromolekuele im Organismus. *Z Electrochem. u. angew. phys. Chemie* 55, 569–574, 1951.

Thompson, J. W. The organismic conception in meteorology. *General Systems* VI, 45–49, 1961.

Toynbee, A. J. *A Study of History. Vol. XII Reconsiderations*. Oxford Univer. Press, New York, 1961.

Tribus, M. Information theory of the basis for thermostatics and thermodynamics. *General Systems* VI, 127–138, 1967.

Vickers, G. Control, stability and choice. *General Systems* II, 1–8, 1957.

Watt, K. E. F. The choice and solution of mathematical models for predicting and maximizing the yield of a fishery. *General Systems* III, 101–121, 1958.

Weaver, W. Science and complexity. *American Scientist* 36, 536–644, 1948.

Whittaker, R. H. A consideration of climax theory: The climax as a population and pattern. *Ecol. Monographs* 23, 41–78, 1953.

Weiss, P. Experience and experiment in biology. *Science* 136, 468–471, 1962.

Wiener, N. *Cybernetics*. Wiley, New York, 1948.

Zacharias, J. R. Structure of physical science. *Science* 125, 427–428, 1957.

Definition of System[1]

A. D. HALL AND R. E. HAGEN

1. Introduction

The plan of the present paper is to discuss properties of systems more or less abstractly; that is to define *system* and to describe the properties that are common to many systems and which serve to characterize them.

2. Definition of "System"

Unfortunately, the word "system" has many colloquial meanings, some of which have no place in a scientific discussion. In order to exclude such meanings, and at the same time provide a starting point for exposition we state the following definition:

> *A system is a set of objects together with relationships between the objects and between their attributes.*

Our definition does imply of course that a system has properties, functions or purposes distinct from its constituent objects, relationships and attributes.

The "definition" above is certainly terse and vague enough to merit further comments, the first of which should, in all fairness, be a note of caution. The "definition" is in no sense intended or pretended to be a definition in the mathematical or philosophical sense. Definitions of the mathematical or philosophical type are precise and self contained, and settle completely and unambiguously the question of the meaning of a given term. The definition given above certainly does not meet these requirements; indeed, one would be hard-pressed to supply definition of system that does. This difficulty arises from the concept we are trying to define; it simply is not amenable to complete and sharp description.

In order to reduce the vagueness inherent in our definition, we now elaborate on the terms *objects*, *relationships*, and *attributes*.

2.2 *Objects*. Objects are simply the parts of components of a system, and these parts are unlimited in variety. Most systems in which we will be interested consist of physical parts: atoms, stars, switches, masses, springs, wires, bones, neurons, genes, muscles, gases, etc. We also admit as objects abstract objects such as mathematical variables, equations, rules and laws, processes, etc.

2.2 *Attributes*. Attributes are properties of objects. For example, in the preceding cases, the objects listed have, among others, the following attributes:

atoms—the number of planetary electrons, the energy states of the atoms, the number of atomic particles in the nucleus, the atomic weight.
stars—temperature, distances from other stars, relative velocity.
switches—speed of operation, state.
masses—displacement, moments of inertia, momentum, velocity, kinetic energy, mass.
springs—spring tension, displacement.
wires—tensile strength, electrical resistance, diameter, length.

2.3 *Relationships*. The relationships to which we refer are those that "tie the system together." It is, in fact, these relationships that make the notion of "system" useful.

For any given set of objects it is impossible to say that no inter-relationships exist since, for example, one could always consider as relationships the distances between pairs of the objects. It would take us too far afield to try to

---

From *General Systems: the Yearbook of the Society for General Systems Research*, Vol. I, 1956, pp. 18–28. Reprinted by permission of the Society for General Systems Research.

[1] Revised version of introductory chapter of *Systems Engineering*, text for a course at Bell Telephone Laboratories, New York. Reprinted with permission of Bell Telephone Laboratories.

be precise and exclude certain "trivial" relationships or to introduce a philosophical notion such as causality as a criterion. Instead we will take the attitude that the relationships to be considered in the context of a given set of objects depend on the problem at hand, important or interesting relationships being included, trivial or unessential relationships excluded. The decision as to which relationships are important and which trivial is up to the person dealing with the problem; i.e. the question of triviality turns out to be relative to one's interest. To make the idea explicit, let us consider a few simple examples.

3. Examples of Physical Systems

First, suppose the parts are a spring, a mass, and a solid ceiling. Without the obvious connections, these components are unrelated (except for some logical relationships that might be thought of, such as being in the same room, etc.). But hang the spring from the ceiling and attach the mass to it and the relationships (of physical connectedness) thus introduced give rise to a more interesting system. In particular, new relationships are introduced between certain attributes of the parts as well. The length of the spring, the distance of the mass from the ceiling, the spring tension and the size of the mass are all related. The system so determined is *static;* that is, the attributes do not change with time. Given an initial displacement from its rest position however, the mass will have a certain velocity depending on the size of the mass and the spring tension; its position changes with time, and in this case the system is *dynamic*.

A more complex example is given by a high-fidelity sound system. The parts of this system are more numerous, but for simplicity we could consider only the turntable and arm of the record player, the amplifier, the speaker and the cabinet. Again, without connections, these parts in themselves would not behave as a sound reproducing system. With connections, in this case electrical coupling of input to output, these parts and their attributes are related in that the performance in each stage is dependent on performance in the other stages; mechanical vibrations in the speaker are related to currents and voltages in the amplifier, etc.

4. Examples of Abstract or Conceptual Systems

An example of a nonphysical nature is given by a set of real variables. The most obvious property of a real variable is its numerical size; in other words in this example *object* and *attribute* are closely related (in fact, in any example an object is ultimately specified by its attributes. Familiar relationships between variables take the form of equations. For concreteness, consider two variables x_1 and x_2 satisfying the two linear equations.

$$\begin{aligned} a_1x_1 + a_2x_2 &= c_1 \\ b_1x_1 + b_2x_2 &= c_2 \end{aligned} \qquad (1)$$

The equations provide constraints on the variables; together the two equations constitute a system of linear equations; the parts of the system are the variables x_1 and x_2, the relationships being determined by the constants and the simultaneous restrictions on the given quantities. The system of equations (1) might be termed *static*, by way of analogy with the static spring and mass system. The analogy is determined by the fact that the numbers which satisfy the equations are fixed, just as the length of the spring is fixed in the mechanical analogue.

On the other hand, introduction of a time parameter t gives rise, for example, to equations of the form

$$\begin{aligned} \frac{dx}{dt} &= a_1x_1 + a_2x_2 \\ \frac{dx}{dt} &= b_1x_1 + b_2x_2 \end{aligned} \qquad (2)$$

The system (2) might, by further analogy with the spring and mass example, be termed *dynamic*. Here the solutions are functions of time just as the length of the spring in the dynamic system is a function of time.

The terms "static" and "dynamic" are always in reference to the system of which the equations are an abstract model. Abstract mathematical and/or logical relationships are themselves always timeless.

5. Abstract Systems as Models

The two examples of the preceding section provide more than incidental illustrations of the idea of system; they suggest one of the most fruitful ways of analyzing physical systems, a way that will be immediately recognized as a fundamental method of science: the method of abstraction.

A return to the simple example of the coupled mass and spring provides a direct illustration of the idea. In the static case, the attributes of interest are the spring constant K, displacement x, and weight W. These are related (within elastic limits by Hooke's law) by the linear equation

$$Kx = W \tag{3}$$

which is of the form (1) for one variable. This further suggests the intimate relationship between an abstract system such as (1) and its *physical realization.* To study the physical system, we substitute for it an abstract system with analogous relationships and the problem becomes a mathematical one. In the dynamic case as well, it is not hard to show that the same sort of analogy obtains, the system being replaced in this case by a differential equation instead of a linear algebraic equation.

This practice is certainly a familiar one to physicists, chemists and engineers; usually it is spoken of as the creation of a mathematical *model.* The extent to which a model agrees with the actual behavior of a system is a measure of the applicability of the particular model to the situation in question. On the other hand, the ease with which a given system can be represented accurately by a mathematical model is a measure of the ease of analyzing the given system.

In order to be completely amenable to mathematical analysis, a system must possess rather special properties. First, the relationships must be known explicitly; secondly, the attributes of importance must be quantifiable and not so numerous as to defy listing, and finally the mode of behavior (as would be given by a physical law such as Hooke's law), under the given set of relationships must be known. Unfortunately, it is a rare system indeed that has all these properties; more exactly, systems possess these qualities in degrees, the more interesting systems such as living organisms exhibiting less of a conformance than simpler systems such as mechanical systems of which the spring and mass is a special case.

6. Definition of Environment

At this point it seems worthwhile to introduce the notion of *environment* of systems. Environment for our purposes can best be defined in a manner quite similar to that used to define system, as follows:

> *For a given system, the environment is the set of all objects a change in whose attributes affect the system and also those objects whose attributes are changed by the behavior of the system.*

The statement above invites the natural question of when an object belongs to a system and when it belongs to the environment; for if an object reacts with a system in the way described above should it not be considered a part of the system? The answer is by no means definite. In a sense, a system together with its environment makes up the universe of all things of interest in a given context. Subdivision of this universe into two sets, system and environment, can be done in many ways which are in fact quite arbitrary. Ultimately it depends on the intentions of the one who is studying the particular universe as to which of the possible configurations of objects is to be taken as the system. A few examples may serve to illustrate this idea.

7. Systems and Their Environments

First, let us return to one of our original examples, the high fidelity sound system. Suppose the whole system is situated in a living room, and that a record is being played over the system. The environment of the system could consist of the record being played, the room in which it is situated, and the listener. It is easily seen that each of these objects bears some relationship to the behavior of the system; the record determines the succession of electrical impulses and mechanical vibrations in the various stages of the system. The output of the system, in turn, affects the pattern of sound waves in the room as well as the mental state of the listener (which for a high-fi "bug" might range from sheer ecstasy to nervous apprehension depending on the excellence of the output). Any or all of these environmental objects could be considered to be part of the system instead of the environment. For certain purposes this might be an artificial designation. Each time a different record is played, one would be considering a different system in this case, whereas actually the system of interest to a sound engineer would not include any specific record, and so would not change in nature from record to record. On the other hand, if one is interested in a system to reproduce one specific announcement, it would make more sense to consider the record as part of the system.

The example above is cited only to make clear what is meant by system and environment and why the dichotomy of sets of related objects into system and environment depends essentially on the point of view at hand. However, the general problem of specifying the environment of a given system is far from trivial. To specify completely an environment one needs to know all the factors that affect or are affected by a system; this problem is in general as difficult as the complete specification of the system itself. As in any scientific activity, one includes in the universe of system and environment all those objects which feels are the most important, describes the inter-relationships as thoroughly as possible and pays closest attention to those attributes of most interest, neglecting those attributes which do not play essential roles. One "gets away" with this method of idealization rather well in physics and chemistry; mass-less strings, friction-less air, perfect gases, etc. are commonplace assumptions and simplify greatly the description and analysis of mechanical and thermodynamical universes. Biologists, sociologists, economists, psychologists, and other scientists interested in animate systems and their behavior are not so fortunate. In these fields it is no mean task to pick out the essential variables from the nonessential; that is, specification of the universe and subsequent dichotomization into system and environment is in itself, apart from analysis of the inter-relationships, a problem of fundamental complexity.

8. Subsystems

It is clear from the definition of system and environment that any given system can be further subdivided into subsystems. Objects belonging to one subsystem may well be considered as part of the environment of another subsystem. Consideration of a subsystem, of course, entails a new set of relationships in general. The behavior of the subsystem might not be completely analogous with that of the original system. Some authors [1] refer to the property *hierarchical order* of systems; this is simply the idea expressed above regarding the partition of systems into subsystems. Alternatively, we may say that the elements of a system may themselves be systems of lower order.

In passing it may be worthwhile to note that this idea of examining subsystems and their behavior has a rather widespread significance in mathematics, particularly in set theory and modern algebra. Just to mention an example, the study of groups (collections of mathematical objects having certain algebraic properties) includes considerations of the properties of subgroups; moreover, subgroups do not necessarily "behave" (behavior here is in the algebraic sense) the same as their parent groups in all respects.

Returning to our example of the high-fidelity system, we see that the idea of division into subsystem is clearly illustrated. The amplifier itself is a system of considerable complexity; the pick-up arm and speaker, themselves systems of a different character can be quite naturally considered as parts of the environment of amplifier. In turn, the amplifier could be further divided into its stages, and each circuit considered as a separate subsystem.

9. Macroscopic vs. Microscopic Views of Systematic Behavior

One technique for studying systems which are exceedingly complex is to consider in detail the behavior of certain of its subsystems. Another method is to neglect the minute structure and observe only the macroscopic behavior of the system as a whole. Both the methods above are common and familiar in many fields, and are of fundamental importance. Before discussing these ideas further, we cite a familiar example.

The difference between these two approaches can be seen by considering the roles of the physiologist and psychologist in the study of the human system. The physiologist is interested in the internal properties and characteristics of the body; he isolates and studies separately the functions of the various internal organs in relationships to bodily activity. When studying the heart, for example, the blood stream, lungs, kidneys, etc. might well be considered as parts of the environment. On the other hand, the psychologist, while not completely neglecting visceral conditions, is primarily concerned with patterns of behavior of the system under various external conditions. It may well be that the psychologist could theoretically improve his knowledge by a complete physiological approach. From the practical standpoint this may be virtually impossible. The variables and their relationships are still beyond description and comprehension; the psychologist is left with the realization that his investigation of behavior is more fruitful from a macroscopic point of view.

10. Some Macroscopic Properties of Systems

So far we have been talking in detail about systems as though by implication there were in the background some sort of unified theory of systems. Actually, there is as yet no such theory, although attempts have been made at one. It is always a good idea when considering such general theories to be sure the types of system under discussion are clearly understood and, where generalizations to systems of other types are claimed, to see if all the analogies and correspondences used are valid.

Nevertheless, there are some properties that belong to certain classes of systems, and are worth mentioning briefly. Also, there are some valid and useful analogies concerning the behavior and properties of certain types of systems that often aid in analysis, at least conceptually, of particular systems. As a notable example, the concept of entropy, useful in thermodynamic systems, has an interesting and valuable analogue in the concept of entropy as defined for message sources in information theory. Other familiar examples are found in the close analogies between electrical, mechanical and acoustical systems, a simple instance being an R-L-C circuit and its mechanical analogue, the coupled mass, spring and resistive dashpot.

Properties that are frequently mentioned by various authors [1, 2] in discussing systems are:

Wholeness and Independence. In our definition of system we noted that all systems have relationships between objects and between their attributes. If every part of the system is so related to every other part that a change in a particular part causes a change in all the other parts and in the total system, the system is said to behave as a *whole* or *coherently*. At the other extreme is a set of parts that are completely unrelated: that is, a change in each part depends only on that part alone. The variation in the set is the physical sum of the variations of the parts. Such behavior is called *independence* or *physical summativity*.

Wholeness or coherence and independence or summativity are evidently not two properties, but extremes of the same property. We may speak of 100% wholeness being at the same end of a scale with 0% independence, but such use of these terms would be merely a matter of verbal convenience. While wholeness and independence may be matters of degree, no sensible method of measuring them yet exists. Nevertheless, the property provides a useful qualitative notion. In fact, since all systems have some degree of wholeness, this property is used by some writers to define "system."

Since all systems have wholeness in some degree, we have no difficulty illustrating the property. Near the 100% end of the scale we have such systems as passive electrical networks and their mechanical analogues. At the other end of the scale we have difficulty finding examples. In fact, most of the literature uses the term "heap" or "complex" to describe a set of parts which are mutually independent and the term "system" is used only when some degree of wholeness exists. We prefer to call sets of parts with complete independence "degenerate systems" because, as we noted before, it is impossible to deny systematic relationships in a heap of sand or odds and ends, or for mechanical forces acting according to the parallelogram of forces.

Progressive Segregation. The concepts of wholeness and summativity can be used to define another qualitative property often observed in physical systems. Most nonabstract systems change with time. If these changes lead to a gradual transition from wholeness to summativity, the system is said to undergo *progressive segregation.* We can illustrate this very simply with equations (2) by letting the "mutual" or "transfer" terms a_2 and b_1 become functions of time. If these terms decrease to zero as a limit we will have two independent systems represented by the equations, or we can say that the larger system, consisting of two simultaneous equations, becomes a "degenerate system."

We can distinguish two kinds of progressive segregation. The first, and simplest kind, illustrated above, corresponds to decay. It is as though, through much handling, the parts of a jigsaw puzzle become so rounded that a given piece no longer fits the other pieces better than another. Or suppose an open-wire carrier telephone system were suddenly deprived of maintenance. Vacuum tubes would wear out, poles would rot, and so on, and eventually there would be a group of parts that no longer behaved as a system.

The second kind of progressive segregation corresponds to growth. The system changes in the direction of increasing division into subsystems and sub-subsystems or differentiation of functions. This kind of segregation seems to appear in systems involving some creative process or in evolutionary and developmental processes. An example is embryonic development, in which the germ passes from wholeness to a state where it behaves like a sum of regions which develop independently into specialized organs. Another example, often observed in the creation and development of a new communication system, occurs when an idea appears, or a need is defined, and the original conception of a system segregates through planning effort into subsystems whose design and development eventually proceed almost independently.

Progressive Systematization. This is simply the opposite of progressive segregation, a process in which there is change toward wholeness. It may consist of strengthening of preexisting relations among the parts, the development of relations among parts previously unrelated, the gradual addition of parts and relations to a system, or some combination of these changes. As an example, consider the development of the long distance telephone network. First, local telephone exchanges sprang up about the country. Then exchanges were joined with trunk lines. As transmission techniques improved, more exchanges were added at greater distances. Later, toll dialing was added, placing the network at the command of operators and eventually at the command of customers. The record has been one of increasing unification of the whole system.

It is possible for progressive segregation and systematization to occur in the same system. These two processes can occur simultaneouly and go on indefinitely so that the system can exist in some kind of steady state as with the processes of anabolism and catabolism in the human body. These processes can also occur sequentially. Consider the early history of America during which groups of people colonized various parts of the country. These groups became more and more independent of their parent countries. Gradually, the new country became more coherent as more interchanges occurred between the groups, a new government was formed, etc.

Centralization. A *centralized* system is one in which one element or subsystem plays a major or dominant role in the operation of the system. We may call this the *leading part* or say that the system is *centered* around this part. A small change in the leading part will then be reflected throughout the system, causing considerable change. It is like a trigger with a small change being amplified in the total system. An example from politics might be a totalitarian regime, decisions of an autocrat affecting behavior of the entire system.

Either progressive segregation of progressive systematization may be accompanied by *progressive centralization;* as the system evolves one part emerges as a central and controlling agency. In the case of embryonic development previously noted, segregation does not proceed to the limit for several reasons, the most important perhaps is that the brain emerges as the controlling and unifying part.

11. Natural and Man-Made Systems

To enhance the meaning of "system" we distinguish natural systems and man-made systems. Engineers are directly interested in man-made systems; however in the environment of these man-made systems are natural systems which also require investigation since their properties interact with the system under study. Furthermore, there are certain properties that both types of systems have in common; man-made systems are often copies of natural systems or at least are constructed to perform analogous functions.

11.1 *Natural Systems.* The description of these is the task of the astronomer, physicist, chemist, biologist, physiologist, etc., and again the amount one can say about a given natural system depends on the number of essential variables involved.

Open and Closed Systems. Most organic systems are *open,* meaning they exchange materials, energies, or information with their environments. A system is *closed* if there is no import or export of energies in any of its forms such as information, heat, physical materials, etc., and therefore no change of components, an example being a chemical reaction taking place in a sealed insulated container. An open system becomes closed if ingress or egress of energies is cut off.

Whether a given system is open or closed depends on how much of the universe is included in the system and how much in the environment. By adjoining to the system that part of the environment with which an exchange takes place, the system becomes closed. For instance, in thermodynamics, the second law is universally applicable to closed systems; it seems to be violated for organic processes. For the organic system and its environment, however, the second law still holds.[3]

ADAPTIVE SYSTEMS. Many natural systems, especially living ones, show a quality usually called *adaptation.* That is, they possess the ability to react to their environments in a way that is favorable, in some sense, to the continued operation of the system. It is as though systems of this type have some prearranged "end" and the behavior of the system is such that it is led to this end despite unfavorable environmental conditions. The "end" might be mere survival; evolutionary theory is based heavily on the notion of adaptation to environment.

There are many examples of adaptive behavior in the body. Many of these are mechanisms that tend to keep within certain physiological limits various bodily conditions such as body temperature, physical balance, etc. Mechanisms of this sort are sometimes called "homeostatic mechanisms." One example is the inborn reaction to cold by shivering, tending to resist a drop in body temperature by a compensating movement producing warmth. Closely related to the concept of adaptation, learning and evolution is the notion of *stability.*

STABLE SYSTEMS. A system is stable with respect to certain of its variables if these variables tend to remain within defined limits. The man-made thermostat is an example of a device to insure stability in the temperature of a heating system; the notion of stability is familiar also in mechanics and especially in the communications field. Note that a system may be stable in some respects and unstable in others. An adaptive system maintains stability for all those variables which must, for favorable operation, remain with limits. In physiology, "motor co-ordination" is intimately connected with stability; clumsiness, tremor, and ataxia are examples of deficient or impaired motor co-ordination and instability.

SYSTEMS WITH FEEDBACK. Certain systems have the property that a portion of their outputs or behavior is fed back to the input to affect succeeding outputs. Such systems are familiar enough to the communications engineer; servomechanisms in general are man-made systems utilizing the principle of feedback. Systems with feedback occur quite frequently in nature as well; posture control in the human body is an example. It is a well known fact that the nature, polarity, and degree of feedback in a system have a decisive effect on the stability or instability of the system.

11.2 *Man-Made Systems.* Man-made systems exhibit many of the properties possessed by natural systems; simple notions such as wholeness, segregation and summativity have meaning for both types of system. On the other hand, it has not been until recently that man-made machines have shown what might be termed adaptive behavior even on a modest scale. Other kinds of man-made systems, such as language and systems of social organization, have always shown adaptive behavior.

Adaptation for man-made systems is not strictly analogous to that for natural systems;

in fact, what might be considered mystical behavior on the part of a natural system is perfectly explainable for the man-made system. Any seemingly purposeful or intelligent behavior on the part of a machine has been built into it by its designer. Also, adaptive behavior on the part of a machine is not to ensure the survival of the machine necessarily, but instead to insure a specified performance in some respect.

There are, in addition to the differences above, some additional considerations in connection with man-made systems that seem to have less bearing on natural systems.

COMPATIBILITY (OR HARMONY). Often the problem arises of constructing a system to match a given environment, or what amounts to virtually the same thing, of adding new parts to already existing systems, or of connecting two systems to operate a tandem. There is no guarantee that a system constructed for a given purpose will function properly if its environment is changed (not all fountain pens write under water). Similarly, two systems independently might be quite satisfactory in certain respects, but in tandem could have completely different and not necessarily favorable characteristics.

Systems might be compatible in some respects and incompatible in others; it depends on the purpose for which the systems are introduced as well as the environmental factors. Also, systems may be compared as to the degree of compatibility with a given system. In terms of the high fidelity system, we might consider as an example the problem of matching a speaker to the rest of the outfit. Different speakers would function with varying degrees of success; some of the environmental factors might be the size of the room, the amount of money available to spend on the speaker, etc., A speaker with perfectly matched impedance and excellent mechanical construction might produce beautiful results in the given setting, but if it cost a few thousand dollars it could easily be called incompatible with respect to at least one environmental factor.

OPTIMIZATION. Compatibility considerations lead naturally to the problem of optimization. As the term implies, it means adapting the system to its environment to secure the best possible performance in some respect. Optimum performance in one respect does not necessarily mean optimum performance is another; again it is a question of intent on the part of the system planner. Often, the factor of interest in an optimization problem is economic: how much bandwidth to allocate to a telephone channel, how many interoffice trunks to provide, etc. Note that the optimum bandwidth for transmitting all the subtle voice characteristics is not the same as the optimum from an economic standpoint.

11.3 *Systems with Randomness.* In either natural or man-made systems it is sometimes necessary to take into account random behavior. What randomness means and when to introduce it in analysis of a system are questions that can be hotly debated by philosophers. In practice it is usually introduced as a factor when the variables that may affect a given attribute are so great in number or so inaccessible that there is no choice but to consider behavior as subject to chance. One example is the noise in a vacuum tube due to random emission of electrons from the cathode.

Random variables enter in at both the microscopic and macroscopic levels. Statistical mechanics and modern physics are both dependent on assumptions of microscopic randomness. Economic conditions, numbers of potential customers, etc. are macroscopic factors also subject to chance fluctuation.

The operation of some systems with randomness can best be described in terms of stochastic processes (also called random processes or time series). Familiar examples in the field of communications are random message sources and disturbing noise in information theory, and the theory of waiting lines in telephone traffic.

12. Isomorphism

As has been suggested before, there are instances in many sciences where the techniques and general structure bears an intimate resemblance to similar techniques and structures in other fields. A one-to-one correspondence between objects which preserves the relationships between the objects is called an *isomorphism.* For instance in the electrical-mechanical duality, an R-L-C circuit is isomorphic to its mechanical dual since each circuit element has its corresponding mechanical interpretation and the relationships are formally the same.

Isomorphisms of this type are rather numerous; in fact, their prevalence has led to several attempts at unifying various fields of science using the idea of "system" as a fundamental concept, but these attempts are as yet incomplete. There are, however, several disciplines with more modest aims that have achieved notable success. To quote a well-known mathematician,

> As for practical usefulness, it should be borne in mind that for a mathematical theory to be applicable it is by no means necessary that it be able to provide accurate models of observed phenomena. Very often in applications the constructive role of mathematical theories is less important than the economy of thought and experimentation resulting from the ease with which qualitatively reasonable working hypotheses can be eliminated by mathematical arguments. For example, in geology we are confronted with random processes which have been going on for millions of years, some of them covering the surface of the earth. We observe that certain species go through a period of prosperity and steady increase, only to die out suddenly and without apparent reason. Is it really necessary to assume cataclysms working one-sidely against certain species, or to find other explanations? The Volterra-Lotka theory of struggle for existence teaches us that even under constant conditions situations are bound to arise which would appear to the naive observer exactly like many of the cataclysms of geology. Similarly, although it is impossible to give an accurate mathematical theory of evolution, even the simplest mathematical model of a stochastic process, together with observations of age, geographical distribution, and sizes of various genera and species, makes it possible to deduce valuable information concerning the influence on evolution of various factors such as selection, mutation and the like. In this way undecisive qualitative arguments are supplemented by a more convincing quantitative analysis.

In addition to the Volterra-Lotka theory mentioned in the quotation above, there are other theories of the same nature unifying several subdomains of science. Mathematical biology, for instance, has had considerable success in this direction. There have been attempts at proposing a mathematical theory of history, cybernetics is widely quoted (and seldom understood) as unifying the communication field with the study of the behavior of living organisms, demography is a study of the growth and spread of populations, etc., but these attempts, while offering hope that certain areas will be unified eventually, are yet incomplete.

That there are isomorphisms, either total or partial, is neither accidental nor mystical. It just amounts to the fact that many systems are structurally similar when considered in the abstract. For example telephone calls, radioactive disintegrations and impacts of particles, all considered as random events in time have the same abstract nature and can be studied by exactly the same mathematical model. It is not surprising then that properties shown by systems of gases with diffusion are useful in analyzing waiting lines of telephone calls and vice versa.

13. The State-Determined System

As an example of the notion of isomorphism, to illustrate some of the macroscopic properties discussed, and to enhance further in a more concrete way the meaning of "system," we will examine the so-called state-determined system. Known to mathematicians as the time-invariant system, it has simple properties and widespread interpretations.

13.1 *Definition of State-Determined System.* Suppose that a system is completely specified by n variables $x_1, x_2, \ldots x_n$. Then the state of the system is uniquely describable by a set of n numbers. To borrow terminology from physics, the set of all points in n-dimensions describing possible states of a system is called *phase space*.

To describe the behavior of a system of this type, it is sufficient to specify the possible paths in phase space or in other words the succession of states through which the system passes. For simplicity let us assume that two variables determine the system. Then phase space is the ordinary Euclidean plane, and possible paths are curves in the plane.

If a system has the property that, given an initial state, the path is uniquely determined re-

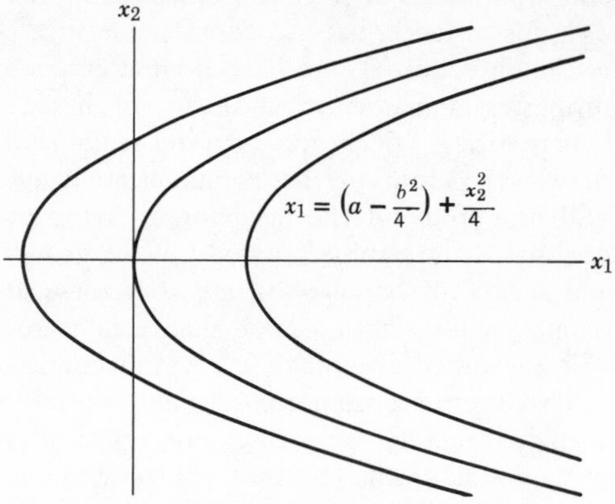

Fig. 1(a)

gardless of how the system arrived at the initial state, the system is called state-determined.

Such systems have the following important mathematical property which we shall state but not prove:

For a system to be state-determined it is necessary and sufficient that its variables satisfy a system of equations of the form

$$\frac{dx_1}{dt} = f_1(x_1, \ldots, x_n)$$
$$\vdots \qquad (4)$$
$$\frac{dx_n}{dt} = f_n(x_1, \ldots, x_n)$$

where the functions $f_1, \ldots, f_n$ are single-valued functions of their arguments. For instance, the system described in (2) is by this theorem state-determined.

The absence of t in equations (4) is what Margenau [5] regards as the essence of causality. The same set is used by Ashby [6] to define "absolute" systems, and by von Bertalanffy [1] to demonstrate the possibility of a "General Systems Theory." When the constants of the set become functions of time, as in progressive segregation or systematization, the definition is no longer satisfied.

As examples, first of a system which is state-determined and then of one which is not to illustrate the theorem above, consider the following system with lines of behavior given by the equations

$$x_1 = a + bt + t^2 \qquad (5)$$
$$x_2 = b + 2t.$$

This system is state-determined. For if the curves so defined are plotted in the (x_1, x_2) plane it is easily seen that they are all parabolas with vertices on the x_1 axis and opening to the right; thus they do not intersect and exactly one of the parabolas passes through each point of the plane (see Figure 1*a*).

Also, the curves determined by (5) satisfy the differential equations

$$\frac{dx_1}{dt} = x_2 \qquad (6)$$
$$\frac{dx_2}{dt} = 2$$

which are of the form (4) with $f_1(x_1, x_2) = x_2$ and $f_1(x_1, x_2) = 2$: a verification of the theorem.

On the other hand, a system with lines of behavior given by

$$x_1 = a + bt + t^2 \qquad (7)$$
$$x_2 = b + t$$

is not state-determined. The curves in this case are again parabolas, but this time the vertices do not all lie on the x_1 axis, so that a given parabola will intersect other parabolas of the family (see Figure 1*b*). By differentiating (7) and substituting in (7) it can be seen that curves so defined satisfy the differential equations

$$\frac{dx_1}{dt} = x_2 + t \qquad (8)$$
$$\frac{dx_2}{dt} = 1$$

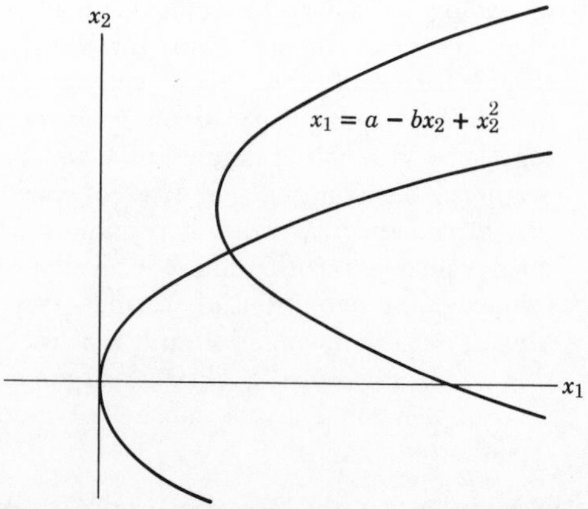

Fig. 1(b)

which is not of the form (4) since $\frac{dx_1}{dt}$ depends not only on x_2 but on t as well.

Systems of equations of the form (4) arise in many fields. The most familiar are in mechanics, circuit theory, etc. That they should frequently occur is borne out by the underlying structure; whenever a system is *state-determined* (that is, from a given state the future progress, or line of behavior, is completely determined), it can be described by equations of this type.

13.2 *Properties of State-Determined Systems.* We can use the system (4) to illustrate some of the concepts we have spoken of previously.

In case $f_1, \ldots, f_n$ are all zero, the system is static. That is the variables to do change with time. If this is not the case, the system is dynamic; at least one of the variables does change with time. The degree of "wholeness" of the system is determined by the nature of the functions $f_1, \ldots, f_n$. If each of these functions depends strongly on each of the variables, the system shows a high degree of wholeness; a change in any variable then affects appreciable changes in all the rest. On the other hand if each of the functions depends on only one of the variables, the system does not have strong connections. In particular, if the equations degenerate to the form

$$\frac{dx_1}{dt} = f_1(x_1)$$
$$\frac{dx_n}{dt} = f_n(x_n), \qquad (9)$$

the parts function independently, a change in any variable depending only on the condition of that variable.

On the other hand, the pair of equations below illustrate the type of relationships that might characterize a system with wholeness.

$$\frac{dx_1}{dt} = x_1 x_2$$
$$\frac{dx_2}{dt} = x_1^2 + x_2^2 \qquad (10)$$

In (10) each variable affects the other in a completely symmetric manner.

Finally, a centralized system might have the form

$$\frac{dx_1}{dt} = x_1$$
$$\frac{dx_2}{dt} = x_1^3 + x_2, x_1 > x_2 > 1 \qquad (11)$$

the part represented by x_1 playing the central role in determining changes in the system.

One simple form in which equations of the type (4) frequently appear is

$$\frac{dx}{dt} = ax;\ x(0) = x_0 \qquad (12)$$

This applies, for instance, whenever the rate of change of the number of elements in a system is proportional to the number already there; for example to unlimited growth of populations when a is positive, or to the decay of radium when a is negative. The solution (line of behavior) is of course the exponential

$$x = x_0 e^{at} \qquad (13)$$

A second simple example of this type is

$$\frac{dx}{dt} = 2x + bx^2\ x(0) = x_0 \qquad (14)$$
$$b < 0$$

the solution of which has the form

$$x = \frac{ax_0}{(a + bx_0)e^{-at} - bx_0} \qquad (15)$$

The curve described in (15) in contrast to that in)13) approaches the limiting value $-\frac{a}{b}$ as t gets large. This curve is usually called a logistic curve, and arises in applications concerned with growth processes occurring in situations where the growth is limited by factors analogous to saturation. Specific instances in which growth processes are described fairly well by a logistic curve include the growth of human populations in a limited living space (from demography), the growth of a railway or communications network in a given area, and the law of autocatalytic reaction (from physical chemistry) describing how a compound formed in a closed reaction vessel catalyzes its own formation until all the molecules are transformed.

The examples above are given because the solutions are simple and have many familiar interpretations. The general case, in which there are n variables and hence n equations is more complicated; examples with more than one variable would require more mathematical notation than it seems worthwhile to include, and so will not be considered.

Finally, the notion of stability can be illustrated for state-determined systems by considering the lines of behavior in phase space. Consider again, for simplicity, the two-variable case where lines of behavior are a family of curves in the plane. For a given region in the plane, a line of behavior from a point in the region is stable if it never leaves the region. This corresponds with our earlier definition of stability; that is, if the line of behavior is confined to a certain prescribed region when starting from a point in the region, it follows that the variables involved are constrained to operate within given limits. As a simple example suppose a vehicle is operating on a fuel supply, and that the velocity of the vehicle depends on the rate of flow of fuel which is in turn controlled by a governor sensitive to velocity. The governor, for instance, might be arranged to allow an increasing rate of flow until a critical velocity is attained and then cut down the rate of flow until the velocity drops below another critical level, and then increase the flow again, etc. Plotting a typical line of behavior (rate of flow against velocity), one sees that a closed loop (of a shape depending on the details of the system) is obtained. The system is stable because both rate of fuel flow and velocity are constrained to vary within prescribed limits.

14. Summary and Additional Remarks

The preceding sections discuss the notion of system and introduce some related ideas frequently encountered in the literature pertaining to systems in general. We admit that the ideas so introduced and the examples illustrating them are for the most part simple and familiar ones, and that the level of sophistication involved is considerably below that required for solution of actual technical problem.

The role of the scientist or engineer is complex and important. His work involves among other things analyses of systems, synthesis of systems, and evaluation of systems operations.

To analyze systems, a scientist must be aware of models available as aids to analysis as well as their limitations. Knowledge of when to use a mathematical model, and which model to use is vital; appreciation of the inter-play between a theoretical and an empirical approach to systems analysis is equally essential. There are models other than mathematical ones; at time a physical model, whether a scale model of the actual system or an analogy to it is far more effective and accurate for analysis of a given system than is an abstract model which fits poorly and is overly complex. On the other hand, as mentioned in the section on isomorphism, there are occasions when a mathematical model, even though simple and relatively inaccurate, can introduce surprising clarifications and simplifications. The section on state-determined systems was included to emphasize this idea; to be state-determined a system must have very special properties, and it would be naive to suspect that complex systems of interest are so simple. Yet, with the proper amount of care and understanding, one can use the framework of state-determined systems with good results in surprisingly diverse situations. Appreciation of similarities or isomorphisms often leads to discovering new and unsuspected connections and unifications.

Synthesis of systems is much more difficult. Here since and engineering begin to take on aspects of art. A systems designer or planner not only must construct systems that work harmoniously individually and in tandem, he must also know a lot about the environment that the system is intended to match. Consideration of environmental factors requires foresight and experience; no one can ever foresee all the variables of importance and a choice of which to include is often a difficult one to make.

Finally, in evaluating system performance, the scientist is confronted with a problem somewhat different in nature from analysis or synthesis of systems. Often one is concerned with the evaluation of large scale operations which must be studied without interrupting the process; a good example is a traffic study in an operating telephone central office. Deciding what the level of performance is requires certain criteria where often no quantitative criteria exist. For instance, in evaluating a traffic system, one must decide what effect delays have on the quality of service. If the traffic service is providing dial tone, an average delay of a few minutes is probably unacceptable, whereas a similar average delay for overseas service is commonplace. It is often necessary to adopt arbitrary levels of performance as standard; again this requires a combination of sound judgment and a knowledge of environment.

In summary, a scientist in his analysis, evaluation and synthesis of systems is not concerned primarily with the pieces of hardware that make up a system, but with the concept of system as a whole; its internal relations, and its behavior in the given environment. In this paper we have given explicitly a few of the notions concerning system and environment that enter implicitly or tacitly into any piece of scientific work.

REFERENCES

1. L. von Bertalanffy, "An Outline of General Systems Theory, "The British Journal of the Philosophy of Science, Vol. I, No. 2, 1950.
2. L. S. Stebbing, "A Modern Introduction to Logic," T. Y. Crowell Co., N. Y., 1930.
3. L. von Bertalanffy, "The Theory of Open Systems in Physics and Biology," *Science*, January, 1950, Vol. III.
4. W. Feller, "On the Theory of Stochastic Processes with Particular Reference to Applications." Proc. Berkeley *Symp. on Math. Stat. and Probability*, Univ. of Cal. Press, 1949.
5. H. Margenau, "The Nature of Physical Reality," McGraw Hill, New York, 1950.
6. W. R. Ashby, "Design for a Brain," Chapman and Hall, London, 1952.

Toward a General Theory for the Behavioral Sciences

JAMES G. MILLER

General Behavior Systems Theory

Of the various possible integrations of the relevant data, we have found most profit in what we call *general behavior system stheory*. Systems are bounded regions in space-time, involving energy interchange among their parts, which are assoicated in functional relationships, and with their environments. General systems theory is a series of related definitions, assumptions, and postulates about all levels of systems from atomic particles through atoms, molecules, crystals, viruses, cells, organs, individuals, small groups, societies, planets, solar systems, and galaxies. General behavior systems theory is a subcategory of such theory, dealing with living systems, extending roughly from viruses through societies. Perhaps the most significant fact about living things is that they are open systems, with important inputs and outputs. Laws which apply to them differ from those applying to relatively closed systems.

All behavior can be conceived of as energy exchange within an open system or from one such system to another. Any exchange of energy across a boundary results in some alteration or distortion of the energy form. Those specific functions of systems which we can stipulate and whose magnitude we can measure in a relative scale, we will call "variables" if they are within the system and "parameters" if they are in its environment. Each system except the largest of all—the universe—has its environment. The system and its environment together constitute a suprasystem. Each system except the smallest has subsystems, which are any components of an organism that can affect a variable.

Inputs and outputs may be either coded or uncoded. Coding is a linkage within subsystems whereby process A_1 is coupled with process A_2 so that either will elicit the other in the future. Coding involves conditioning, learning, or pairing of two processes in a system and the memory or retention of this union over a period of time. Any action is uncoded unless—like speech or gesture—it has some added significance as a result of such a bond. It then conveys information.

All living systems tend to maintain steady states of many variables, by negative feedback mechanisms which distribute information to subsystems to keep them in orderly balance. Not only are subsystems ordinarily kept in equilibrium, but systems are also usually in balance with their environments, which have outputs into systems and inputs from them. This prevents variations in the environment from destroying systems, either by collapse or by explosion. There is a range of stability for any parameter or variable in any system. It is that range within which the rate of correction is minimal or zero and beyond which correction does occur. Inputs (or loads), either coded or uncoded, which, by lack or excess, force the variables beyond the range of stability constitute stresses and produce strains within the system. These strains may or may not be capable of being reduced, depending upon the equilibratory resources of the system.

The above general statement can be translated into terminology of several behavioral sciences. In individual psychology, for instance, the system has generally been known as the organism; the input, as the stimulus; and the output, as the response. Uncoded inputs, we have recognized, can result in strains or disequilibria within the organism which are known as primary or somagenic drives. Coded inputs result in secondary, learned, acquired, or psychogenic drives. Reduction of strains is called drive satisfaction. When inputs or loads create strains great enough to call into play complex subsystems to restore equilibrium, we

---

From *American Psychologist*, Vol. 10, 1955, pp. 513–531. Reprinted by permission of the author and the publisher, the American Psychological Association.

sometimes refer to such processes as "defense mechanisms." When these mechanisms fail, severe disruption of the steady state of the organism, known as mental or physical illness, or ultimately death, occurs. The total of the strains within the individual resulting from his genetic input and variations in the input from his environment is often referred to as his values. The relative urgency of reducing these individual strains determines his hierarchy of values.

Specific Aspects of the Theory

System. Our definition of "system" is very general, and at first sight might appear to apply to almost everything in the world. And, of course, the function of general theory is to be inclusive. However, it may be helpful to indicate what is not a system. The dark-colored half of the Pied Piper was not a system. The opposing lines of two football teams in scrimmage, independent of their backs, would not ordinarily be considered together as a system. If the Headless Horseman of Washington Irving had not been fictional, he could not have held his head in his arm and yet behave like an intact system. All the blondes in the United States are themselves not a system unless they are organized by some sort of communication, like the Red-headed League of A. Conan Doyle. In simple, naive, common-sense terms, then, a real system is all of a thing. Even though it is possible to construct a conceptual system which includes grandpa's mustache, Chinese hokku poetry, and the Brooklyn Bridge, this would not correspond to a real system of general systems theory, because these things are not surrounded by a single boundary, are not continuous in space-time, and do not have recognizable functional interrelationships.

Some may wonder whether "system" is identical with "Gestalt." Are there laws of the whole which do not apply to specific parts? We hold that both the parts, or subsystems, and the whole behave according to similar laws. However, the fact that subsystems are equilibrated together by systemwide organizing processes (even though these mechanisms can be explained by the behavior of component parts) means that there are characteristics of the whole which do not apply to any part. This is true of systems at every level.

Boundary. Boundaries of systems are not always clear-cut and round like the rind of a watermelon. Sometimes they have intricate geometrical design, more like the surface of a branching coral, but even more complex than that. A naval task force maneuvering blind at sea can be a system, even though its boundary is complicated and in continual flux. It is a system organized by communications which require at least a small filament of contiguous space-time of ether, to transmit radio, radar, or other signals. When a typhoon hits the *Caine* and her sister destroyers, wiping out radio and radar contact, then the flotilla is no longer a system, because usual functional interrelationships are impossible. Communications make feasible complex organizations of systems, like the American Psychological Association or the United Nations. A given individual or behaving subsystem can, of course, be part of several systems at the same time, equilibrating at least partially with all of them. To deal with this fact the concept of "role" has been developed in social psychology.

Subsystems. How could one disprove our contention that every system except the smallest has subsystems? The answer is that if one found a homogeneous distribution of energy in any system, so that no boundary between its subsystems was discoverable, then that system would have no subsystems. How does one locate a boundary, i.e., a region where energy or information exchange is significantly less than inside or outside the system? One decides upon the order of magnitude of difference in rate of exchange of information or energy which one will accept as indication of a boundary. Let us call this amount d. This differs according to the level of system with which one intends to deal. Then, having decided on this, one can empirically locate the boundary as that region where there is d less interchange of energy and information than either outside or inside. In general, d is progressively less from larger systems to smaller so that ordinarily it is great for societies, less for individuals, and much less for cells.

We know a good deal about the input-output relations of the peripheral sensory and motor subsystems, but it is extremely difficult with present methods to determine these relations for processes in the human central subsystems. Electronic technicians know that if there is only one subsystem between two test electrodes which contact the input and the output respectively, 100 per cent of the variance will be in that subsystem; if, however, there are two subsystems, and there is no way to put a test electrode between those systems, all the variance may be in Subsystem A; all of it may be in Subsystem B; or the variance may be accounted for by an infinite set of possible combinations of the relationships between the two. Extremely complex mathematics is required to study the input-output alterations of multiple systems whose components cannot be isolated. For this reason precise study of central subsystems of the individual—often said to be the main variables of his "personality"—presents a difficult or impossible scientific problem by present methods.

Coding. In living organisms the important process of coding, which makes it possible for energy exchange also to be information exchange, is accomplished by at least three means, which are perhaps basically the same, but which for convenience can be classified as (*a*) instinct; (*b*) imprinting; and (*c*) conditioning or learning. The first is irreversible; the second may be; and the last is reversible. Instinct is a "wiring in" of the relationship before birth, either in the endocrine or in the nervous system. Imprinting is "wired in" before birth or hatching and stamped in by "social releasers" during early hours after birth or hatching. Conditioning or learning is usually acquired after birth, and it may be lost.

As the link between energy theory and information theory, the process of coding is of prime importance. While both the biological and the social sciences share a dual concern with energy transfer and information transfer, the predominant emphasis of the biological sciences is energy transfer, whereas that of the social sciences is information transfer. The social sciences deal chiefly with verbal or symbolic behavior. Information theory abets the union of the natural and the social sciences, but is probably more likely to be useful to the latter. General behavior systems theory incorporates most aspects of modern information theory, but it is more encompassing, for it deals with the transmission of both information and energy, and with the relationships between information and energy transfer.

Ancient philosophers, including Aristotle and Plato, were concerned with the metaphysical question of the relation of form to matter. Plato thought matter to be the feminine aspect of the universe, a "receptacle" capable of accepting any form. To him form was the masculine aspect of life, which, when united with matter, produced the real or concrete object. So reproduction could be explained, being a special case of the more general notion that any object—as we would say, any "system"—was the union of form and matter. The form could be in the head of the sculptor and he could put it into the rough matter of Carrara marble in order to fashion a bust. This form could also have been wrought in brass, iron, or other substances. Conversely, some other form, like a table or chair, could have been imposed on the marble. Together, form and matter were thought to define the object.

These conceptualizations were sheerly metaphysical until recent years, when certain empirical and quantitative discoveries have made possible a more precise linkage between these notions, bringing them closer to science.

First came the work in the late nineteenth century, which developed the second law of thermodynamics, the law of entropy. Energy (E) and entropy (S) were seen to have a specific relationship. Then in the early twentieth century, Einstein produced his theory of relativity which included the basic equation:

$$E = mc^2,$$

energy equals mass times the square of the speed of light.

Within the last ten years, Wiener and Shannon have written equations which connect the notion of entropy with the notion of information. The basic equation is:

$$S = -H.$$

That is, entropy equals the negative of information (H).

What does this all mean? It has many implications, but a simple illustration might be as follows:

If an electric impulse of random character, like a lightning stroke, were to be sent over a wire and fed into a speaker, you would hear noise. A similar current passing into a television set would show "snow" on the screen. So the ultimate result of entropy, randomly distributed energy, produces noise when conveyed over a communication system to a speaker. On the other hand if a modulated current, including only selected frequencies, is conveyed over such a circuit, you will hear a tone; on a television screen you will see organized form. That is, as energy distribution becomes less random, "noise" (which in information theory is the negative of information) tends to disappear, and information tends to increase.

Anyone who has listened on a many-party, old-fashioned country telephone line knows that the higher the noise level the less the information that can get across. As noise is decreased in communication systems, more and more of the message can be conveyed.

Let us now observe the following combination of the above equations:

$$E = mc^2$$
$$|$$
$$S = -H.$$

This demonstrates that there is a highly complex, but nevertheless understood, and to a degree quantifiable relationship between mass (matter or energy) and information. It is not pure coincidence that the word "form" appears as a syllable in the word "information." We find, therefore, that dimensions of energy transmission and information transmission, in some ways like the matter and form of the ancient Greeks, are in recent years for the first time quantitatively relatable.

This suggests a basic role for information theory in general science. Information, which can be measured quantitatively in bits or similar units, can convey qualitative or formal structural aspects of any system. It can describe the nonrandom relationships in which energy is organized. Information and energy coexist as companionate aspects of every system. Perhaps this fact may lead to better understanding of the special case of the system known as the brain and the messages or information conveyed or stored in it.

As mentioned before, we are attempting to employ only dimensions and units related to the centimeter–gram–second system in quantifying all aspects of behavior, coded and uncoded. Perhaps it would be better to coin a word to represent our precise meaning and say that we employ "*u*-units." Under this term we include: First, measures that can actually be made in centimeters, grams, and seconds, like the size of a system, its weight, or the length of its existence. In addition, we include complex dimensions of the natural sciences, whose relationships to centimeters, grams, and seconds have been demonstrated, like the temperature dimensions scaled in degrees above absolute zero. Furthermore, because we believe that equations can be written which indicate the systematic relationships between units of information and the units of energy measured by the CGS system, we include units of information like bits in our *u*-units.

We recognize the arbitrary nature of all coding. Almost any configuration of energy can in some language or other represent or symbolize almost anything else. However, once these code linkages are developed as traces in the brain or in the programming of an electronic computer, they are then processed according to principles of energy transformation which can ultimately be measured in the derivatives of CGS units of the natural sciences. It is of these various sorts of units we speak when we employ the phrase *u*-units.

We envisage a far-off scientific Utopia in which we can reduce to comparable dimensions the Oedipus complex, repression, submissiveness, physiological traces, acculturation, the pH of blood, and every other factor related to behavior. At present the social sciences wrestle with a congeries of completely unconnected terms and dimensions. It is true that factor analysis has made efforts to improve this situation. Factor analysis attempts to plot the domain of a number of dimensions whose relationships previously were unknown. When this is done you still may not know the relationships between one domain and another, but you could presumably pyramid a whole series of factor analyses until ultimately a common dimensionality of behavior emerged, relating all the terminologies of the behavioral sciences. However, it may be more rapid and effective simply to translate these terms into the dimensions of the natural sciences. This may be true, first, because scientists have had a good deal of experience with these particular modes of measurement. Second, because use of such dimensions permits quantitative comparisons between the actions of nonliving systems and the behavior of living ones. And third, because no one is particularly ego involved with these dimensions. This is not true of most terminological systems and scaling techniques in the social sciences that often are emotionally toned for representatives of various schools or viewpoints.

Even though many of the problems of such a translation to CGS units have not yet been worked through, a few examples can be given of how some behavioral traits can be measured in such units. A phlegmatic person can of course be recognized by his usual rate of motion in space; so can a hyperkinetic or manic patient. The trait of "initative" may be viewed as originating motion in space, and "passivity" as waiting to be moved. When one individual directs more initiative toward a second person than the latter does toward the former, the first is "dominant" and the second "submissive."

These and many other behavioral traits, however, are frequently evidenced in words and gestures. On first thought, such symbolic behavior might seem unamenable to description in *u*-units. What sorts of equilibrations in what subsystems can explain the intricate, subtle intonations, speech, and acts of a civilized man?

Let us assume that memories of past experiences are stored in the brain as traces, whose nature we do not exactly understand but which we may call "information analogs." These analogs are combined in the nervous system, perhaps in much the same way as electronic computers handle information. When this process is complete, a specific behavioral output is elicited, but this is a resultant act of a more complex process than a simple reduction of strain in a subsystem. Of course the molecular activities which transfer information analogs in the brain at cellular and subcellular levels follow the natural laws of systems just as do electronic calculating machines. Therefore decision-making and other "higher mental processes" ultimately are explainable in terms of general behavior systems theory.

Equifinality. The concept of *equifinality* advanced by Bertalanffy (3) explains purposive behavior in animals and men more effectively than vitalistic assumptions, and also more consistently with our general theoretical framework. Teleological notions of goal striving are not necessary if we accept this principle. It operates only in open systems which circumvent the effects of the second thermodynamics law of entropy, since materials necessary to create and maintain a certain organization may be selected from the input and surplus products or wastes be rejected in the output. For example consider a chemical system made up of two solutions, silver nitrate and hydrochloric acid, which when combined precipitate silver chloride. If an indefinitely large input of both substances is available and output is possible for this system, then the rate of precipitation will become constant at a specific equilibrium level. Moreover, this rate will not depend on the amounts of silver nitrate and hydrochloric acid present at the beginning of the experiment. There could be either a dram or 100 gallons of each. Rather, it depends on the solubility characteristics of the components (H^+, Cl^-, Ag^+, and NO_3^-). This reaction, then, looks as if it always strives teleologically toward the same goal—that is a specific rate of precipitation—no matter whether the system at first was poor or rich in silver nitrate or hydrochloric acid. Actually, however, it is clear that this "equifinal" result is determined by the nature of the constituents of the system.

We contend that this is true of all behaving systems. Whether an infant be three months premature and weigh two pounds or be born of a diabetic mother and so weigh fifteen pounds, he will ordinarily be of normal weight a few months later. The small one will grow more rapidly than an average baby and the big one less rapidly. This may appear like vitalistic teleology, but it can be explained simply by stating that the constituents of human subsystems determine what their equilibrium levels shall be. Many of these together, in turn, fix the size of the child.

So the "goals" which "impel" the rat to run the maze, the woman to marry, and the candidate to file for public office, can be interpreted as internal strains which elicit efforts to achieve inputs of energy and information that will reduce the strains toward an equilibrium point. And no matter whether he is nurtured at court to become Pharaoh or cast away in the bulrushes, a man will search until he finds an environment with inputs capable of diminishing the particular drives within him—strains established by his genetic inputs as modified by later inputs of energy and information, by learning or acculturation.

Formal Identities

Implied throughout the above discussion is the principle that similar aspects of systems follow similar laws. Examples are propositions, to be considered in detail later, such as the statement that the growth of all systems in time is comparable within certain ranges. Or that transmissions across all boundaries involve step functions. Or that spatial spread of state throughout all systems follows comparable laws. Our attempt is to see how much of all behavior we can explain by a series of such formal identities, recognizing of course the differences or disanalogies which exist between one behaving system and another.

We must remain continuously alert to the danger of neglecting these differences, a danger which arises from the fact that a chief goal of any general theory is to recognize, describe, and measure pervasive similarities, formal identities, or analogies.

The analogy has often suffered vilification from scientists and philosophers. Still, if it is carefully employed, it is scientifically useful. Perhaps the phrase "formal identity" is more acceptable, but that term is essentially equivalent to some senses of "analogy." As clear a definition of "analogy" as any is that of John Stuart Mill, who used it as an adjective in the phrase "analogical reasoning," whose sense he formulated as follows: "Two things resemble each other in one or more respects: a certain proposition is true of the one, therefore it is true of the other. . . . Every resemblance which can be shown to exist affords ground for expecting an indefinite number of other resemblances" (7). Currently there are several ways the term "analogy" is used. One is as a statement of the subjective experience of an observer that two or more phenomena appear similar to him or arouse in him similar feelings. This is a statement about his private experience and as such it is irrelevant for operational science. To some persons it is a purely literary term like "metaphor" or "simile," which is frequently modified by the slighting adverb "mere" and which is of artistic value to the writers of poetry and prose, but not to scientists. Another usage is a logical one, referring to a form of inference whereby it is argued that, if two or more things are similar in some respects, they will probably be similar in others, though not necessarily all others. It is apparent that there is no general agreement about the word among different disciplines. "Analogy," for example, means one thing specific to logicians and something quite different but equally specific to biologists.

Any general scientific use of the word should indicate that analogies or formal identities are the bases of all inductions which underlie scientific laws. The perception of similarity among phenomena must precede their classification. Then one can generalize, predicting that if some members of a class of phenomena are observed to operate in a certain way, so will the other members of that population, even though they have not been observed. So recognition of analogy or formal identity underlies all generalization and all science.

In modern electromechanical analog computers one can find a good example of the scientific use of quantitative analogies or formal identities. An analog computer (cf. 2) employs differing amounts of some physical quantity to match similarly differing amounts of some measurement. For example, in the differential analyzer designed by Vannevar Bush and finished at the Massachusetts Institute of Technology in 1942, a small wheel presses on a large disc, which is supported on a vertical axle running through a block. This block can be moved back and forth in a horizontal direction by turning a long screw. In the operation of the analog computer, one turn of the screw represents a certain amount of one variable in a differential equation. One turn of the vertical axle represents a certain amount of another variable. And the resultant turn of the small wheel riding on the disc represents, turn by turn, a third unknown variable in the equation. For example, if the screw represents the speed at which a train travels and the disc measures the time, then the small wheel might measure the distance traveled. Such a mechanism can successfully solve differential equations, even though the motions of the various parts have only analogous relationships to the variables involved. Indeed, this analogous operation represents one of the most successful—if not the most successful—way now known to solve many differential equations. Such an analog is similar to a physical model, and operations carried out on such a model can accurately quantify aspects of some comparable phenomenon of the real world.

Throughout this article the word "system" used without modifiers refers to "real" systems which exist in the veridical world of space-time coordinates. They should therefore be distinguished from formal or "conceptual" systems, which are mathematical or logical in character. The latter can, but do not always, describe such real systems. A formal identity between two conceptual systems is an "isomorphy." A formal identity between two real systems is a "homology"—a common biological concept. (A special case of homology is a formal identity between an inanimate and an animate system, like Lillie's iron wire homology of neural conduction, or Ashby's Homeostat [1].) And finally the term "model" may well be reserved for a formal identity between a conceptual system and a real system, although it is sometimes used also for homologies like Lillie's.

Generalization, or the use of analogy in the social sciences, has often bogged down in semantic difficulties. This has led to unnecessary disagreements between generalists and those concerned primarily with the special case. For example, Freud was impressed with the similarities between a number of related types of experiences which he included under his conception "sexuality." He recognized the similarity between physiological sexual gratification on the one hand, sensual satisfaction from art, music and other sensory experiences, and feelings of love and affection. In stressing these similarities in order to make a generalization, he at times neglected the differences between them, although he undoubtedly recognized them and would have acknowledged them immediately if they had been pointed out. There are theorists like Freud, concerned with making broad generalizations among dissimilar phenomena, in every discipline.

On the other hand, in every field we find persons who are concerned with a specific case, whether it be a clinical study of a specific individual or a complete analysis of all the characteristics of the culture of a single tribe on a Pacific island. They tend to emphasize the differences between the phenomenon they study and other phenomena. However, if similarities between their special case and other such cases were called to their attention, they would be willing to recognize them.

In mathematics the relation between similarity and disparity, between formal identity and individual difference, between analogy and disanalogy, can be easily made clear. The similarity is described by a general function, like $ax + by = cz$. The differences are indicated by constants written into the same equation or mathematical sentence, like $3x + 7y = 6.4z$, which is different from $7x + 8.5y = 17z$.

In prose, which is the usual language of the social sciences, conveyance of such ideas is more difficult. It is ordinarily inconvenient—though possible—to construct a sentence which has as its combined subject both a similarity and a difference, both preceding the main verb. Not accustomed to such cumbersome linguistic usage, we commonly make a straight assertion of either the similarity or the difference, which results in a false bifurcation we do not intend, and we neglect the opposite consideration which we would readily admit to be true. We often proceed to the logical and emotional fallacy of committing ourselves to the importance of one and neglecting the other, and so arise many of the schoolistic battles in the social sciences.

Between any two phenomena there is an analogy and between any two phenomena there is also a disanalogy. We hope to develop a theory in which both are recognized, the analogies by general functions and the disanalogies by constants.

Table 1 illustrates the general paradigm of how we intend to proceed. The first vertical column under "Propositions" represents one formal identity, the growth function, which within certain ranges is an exponential curve. This may be observed at all levels of behaving systems—cell, organ, individual, group, and society—and perhaps in some aspects of nonliving systems like electronic circuits. The next column represents the formal identity of boundary functions, which, as will be explained later, appear to be step functions. The third column represents a diffusion proposition concerning spread of states in space. So we might go on for many propositions which are true of all systems.

On the other hand, the constants differ for

each level. Growth for the cell is most conveniently measured in micra; for the organ in millimeters; for the individual in centimeters; for the group in meters; and for the society in kilometers. Similar spatial constants would at each level apply to diffusion rates, etc.

Table 1. General Paradigm of Behavior Theory Propositions

SYSTEM LEVEL	UNIT	PROPOSITIONS		
		GROWTH FUNCTION	BOUNDARY FUNCTION	DIFFUSION FUNCTION
Cell	μ			
Organ	mm			
Individual	cm			
Group	m			
Society	Km			
Electronic circuit	From μ to Km			

There are also other constants for different types of systems according to the materials of which they are constituted, their densities, and many other factors. There is, then, a systematic "horizontal" relationship among constants of the systems described in Table 1 which represents the disanalogy between levels, just as there is a systematic "vertical" relationship within columns, representing the analogies. The ultimate problem of predicting behavior is to learn what are the quantitative characteristics of the general laws on the one hand and the individual differences on the other, using both in a specific prediction. Such is the basic strategy of the program for empirical testing of general behavior systems theory.

This is a specific method. It does not deal in vague, poetic, or metaphorical similarities between systems which are not operationally demonstrable, like "growth" in size and "growth" in tactfulness. Nor does it simply identify comparable processes in different systems, as for example storage of information in electronic memories; traces in the nervous system; secretarial minutes of committees; and libraries of a nation. But this method does make predictions of behavior by transferring a set of assumptions, definitions, and theorems from one class of behaving systems to another, at the same time making allowance for the distinctive specific characteristics of the systems being considered. This does not differ from the classical method of the natural sciences, from the method of Newton and many others. Newton made a real contribution in developing his laws so that they explained at once the fall of an apple from a tree, the flowing of the tides, and the revolution of the earth, even though these are vastly dissimilar phenomena. Yet such generalization can be effective only when these analogies or formal identities are recognized, even though no proper scientist may blind himself to the fact that there are also always disanalogies.

A Critique of Analogy

What have been the common sources of dissatisfaction with analogy in science?

We have already referred to a frequent basis for such discontent—the confusion of poetical or metaphorical analogy with comparisons which are useful scientifically. Suppose that one says "He has a heart of gold." Suppose one adds that "Gold is heavy." Syllogistic logic then concludes "Therefore his heart is heavy." But this makes no operational sense. Science cannot be made from logical operations upon metaphors.

Another cause for dissatisfaction with analogy, already mentioned, is the tendency of those who generalize through analogies to neglect the obvious disanalogies. An example of this is Spiru C. Haret's book *Mécanique Sociale* (5), which appeared in 1910 and in which the author based a theory of sociology on the attraction of people to each other precisely according to the inverse square law of gravitation. It is possible that unself-critical recognition of similarities is appropriate in the initial stages of scholarly enquiry, but no scientific task can be completed until the degree of comparability is precisely determined, as well as the degree and forms of the dissimilarities. It is an interesting idea, relevant to some aspects of general behavior systems theory, that the development of societies historically has been in some ways similar to biological evolution. But a vast amount of effort has been wasted in the last seventy-five years by theorists who have compared the two without being precisely clear about the facts of both biological evolution and social process, and also without being accurate concerning the details of how they are similar and how they differ.

Much of the criticism of analogy in behavioral science has been directed particularly at formal models like the ones we expect to incorporate into general behavior systems theory. One such argument is that models simply describe what was already known and do not reveal anything new. Certainly this is not true of all models, as for instance those concerning the learning process, which have led to the discovery of many new facts. This criticism is apt only when applied to poor models. It has been clearly shown that models are useful in natural science if they are properly employed. There is no a priori reason why this should not also be true in the behavioral sciences.

One often hears the comment that formal models are useful only to a limited degree in the social sciences because many of the data of those areas are not quantifiable. It may appear that such behavioral phenomena as foreign relations and politics or cultural customs and content of language are difficult to measure. But important aspects of such behavior can at least be rank ordered. If cardinal numbers cannot be used, ordinal numbers can, and this has been the first entrance into measurement of other young, complex sciences.

There is truth in the critique that the value of formal models is sometimes sharply restricted because inappropriate parameters are chosen, and consequently the relevant variables in the situation being analyzed are not made apparent. This may happen if model builders are not intimately acquainted with social or behavioral phenomena. This criticism applies to poor models and not to all models. If appropriate parameters are chosen, the model can be progressively modified to approximate more and more closely to the real system. If model builders are sufficiently informed about the phenomena that they select the proper dimensions, they can throw much light on the nature of the process they are studying.

It is sometimes said that, because of the many variables, it is more difficult to use formal models in the behavioral than in other sciences. But models have been used to study complex, multivariant problems in the physical and biological sciences. Continually techniques are being developed to deal with such problems, including the giant electronic computers which can handle a previously unthinkable order of magnitude of variables. Precise application of a model, also, may reveal certain variables to be irrelevant which we otherwise might have considered. This can simplify the problem.

Another criticism is that models are always in error, never being precisely correct. It is hard to say how correct a model must be to be scientifically useful. The answer is that there is probably no correct model, but the goal is to find one which will explain the largest number of known facts. As further empirical data are collected and more thinking goes on, models usually are rejected and more satisfactory ones substituted. The purpose of the scientific process is to improve the goodness of fit of the model to the empirical data, that is, its predictive power. Ordinarily this is a long process of making successively better approximations. Actually models can describe complex phenomena like the social structure of a community more economically, precisely, and fully than most verbal descriptions. In addition they can suggest new variables or relationships to investigate. From models explicit predictions can be made, whereas in the past social scientists have typically made very loose predictions if they have made them at all. Furthermore, it is possible to calculate the error of the outcome of a prediction, which has not been a common social science method.

Another criticism often made of the use of models is that if you find several sorts of behavior which can be described by the same model, you have shown nothing necessarily valuable. It may be simple coincidence if you discover that the rate at which a snowball forms on rolling down hill, the rate at which a new political party picks up members, and the rate at which an audience enters a theater are similar quantitative functions. So what? The answer to this is of basic significance for general behavior systems theory. If the comparable functions are for processes which by other criteria have similar status in different systems, and if the general or "vertical" functions (cf. Table 1) in specific systems have "horizontal" constants identical to or of known relationship to constants determined for other general functions for that system, the observations have importance and are much more than coincidence.

It is sometimes said that in the social sciences, with the exception of economics and psychology, no formal models have been developed which can be helpfully applied to social phenomena. This is not a criticism of models, as has been implied. When relevant basic assumptions are made and proper variables are selected, there is no reason why all social phenomena cannot be profitably analyzed by formal models.

Some have found fault in formal models because assumptions must be made before a model can be built. Merely adding assumptions, they contend, does not advance behavioral science. One can reply that this does not differ from the scientific method of the physical sciences. Assumptions are tested by each step of application of any model. As experiment after experiment is performed which checks the model, assumptions get more and more support, or else the assumptions or other aspects of the model are altered to include new parameters or variables, in order to predict the phenomena more accurately. This is more productive than a traditional procedure in social science, which has been to build assumption upon assumption in a complex theoretical structure, without being certain that they refer to important facts and without constantly testing them.

It is said that formal models in the behavioral sciences suffer by being caricatures of human beings, seeming to have nothing about them like the warm reality of human life. So models of the learning process seem to have little in common with the way children pick up facts in school. The only reply to this is that you cannot judge a model in terms of such appearances, but rather by its effectiveness in explaining and predicting. To the physicist, the granitic Rock of Gibraltar, for instance, is just a mass of seething subatomic particles.

To some thoughtful persons it appears that indicating similarities between either formal models or real systems on the one hand, and man's behavior on the other, can never fathom the complexities and richness of human experience. Others recognize that we ordinarily lose ability to observe objectively as the subject matter becomes more and more like ourselves. Freud realized the scientific need to allow for this effect, which in the psychoanalytic relationship he labeled "countertransference." Few antivivisectionists strive to prevent cruelty to bread molds and amebae, but many are concerned for the welfare of cats and dogs. An earthquake on a Mediterranean isle will disturb us more than the disappearance of a moon of Jupiter, even though the latter phenomenon is much vaster. The question is whether our ego involvement with ourselves, other humans, and organisms like us does not prevent us from recognizing otherwise obvious similarities between us and other behaving or acting systems in the universe.

One final criticism can be made of naive formal models which do not distinguish between energy transmission and information transmission or uncoded and coded behavior. This is a critique of poor models and not of all models. It is usually unproductive to compare a physical model not involving information transfer—like the oscillations of a pendulum—with a behavioral phenomenon which involves information transfer and highly symbolic components—like the swings of business cycles. Formal identities between various sorts of systems are valuable only if they make this distinction. Persons eager to advance rapidly our understanding of behavior at times manifest their impatience by hurriedly taking a model from physics or biology and applying it to human behavior. This commonly leads to unjustifiable oversimplification, particularly because information transfer is a much more significant aspect of group and social behavior than it is of physical action or biological function.

Electronic Models

Since we are concerned with quantitative formal identities among various kinds of systems, it is natural that we should be interested not only in formal models of behavior but also in homologies with electronic systems. It may someday be possible to develop a comparative psychology or sociology dealing not with animals but with electronic models. These are in some ways less adequate than animals, in that they do not have some characteristics of life inherent in protoplasm. But they are better in other ways. Greater precision is possible in quantifying their actions. Also one can manipulate their parts and alter any of their circuits quantitatively by electronic "surgery," without danger of destroying them.

The modern giant electronic computers are open systems with significantly large magnitudes of inputs and outputs. Consequently, their action is in many interesting ways like living behavior. Figure 1 depicts the chief subsystems typical of such a computer. It has two sorts of input: input of energy (the line voltage which operates the machine) and input of information (a teletype tape which conveys the coded problem into the decoding subsystem of the machine). Coded data and instructions are decoded and fed electronically through the control to the memory. The control then, as directed, takes the appropriate information electronically out of the memory and puts it into an electronic calculator which manipulates voltages or other analogs of numbers, adding or subtracting (or carrying out more complex mathematical operations, all of which are derivatives of addition or subtraction). The subtotals, and finally the totals, are returned to the memory, the ultimate answers then being coded in the encoder subsystem for information output on a teletype tape or by a typewriter.

Some of these electronic devices contain internal monitoring or checking circuits, not unlike human proprioceptor or pain pathways, which transmit a "squeal signal" whenever anything goes wrong in any of the subsystems. In fact, some electronic systems can perform automatic repairing functions, replacing units or rectifying circuits when the "squeal" indicates they are worn out or operating improperly.

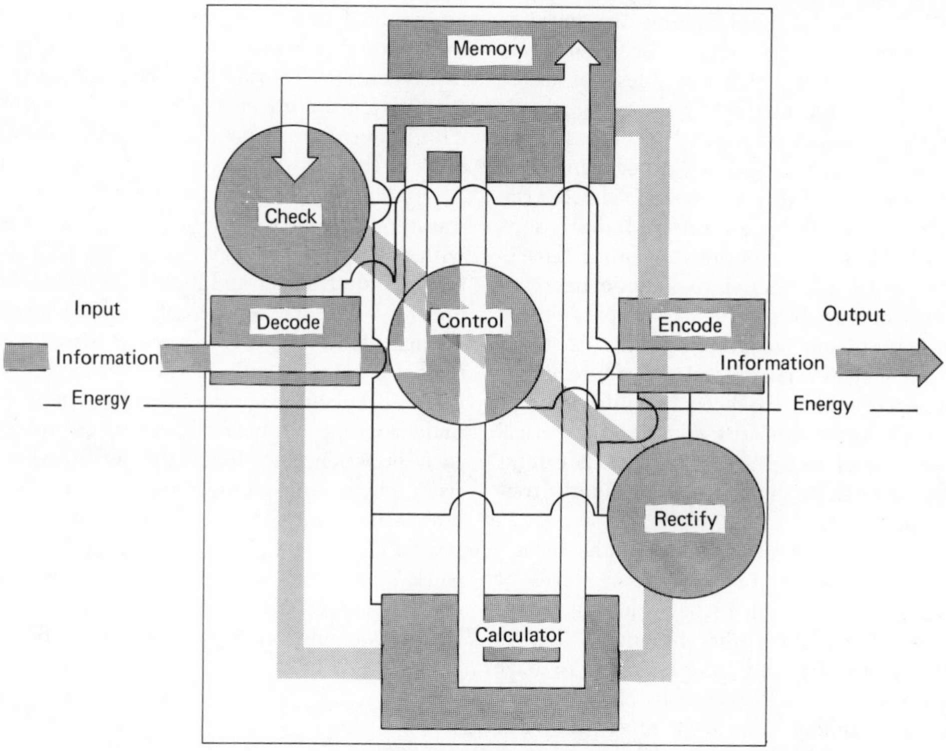

Fig. 1. Diagram of a typical electronic computer.

In individual animals and human beings these same processes occur. There is sensory input at the boundary of the system as well as energy input, like intake of food, sunlight, water, and so forth. You also find the decoder (whatever the subsystem be that interprets speech and gesture); the memory; the internal communication system; the internal motor system; the association areas; the executive, decision-maker, or "calculator" which determines the outcome; and the output, either coded or uncoded. There are also pain or proprioception "checking" circuits, and repair or rectification mechanisms. At the level of the small group, you again find these functions—the secretary's written minutes representing one sort of memory; the chairman representing the control; and so on. Similarly in a society there are intelligence services providing information from outside; import agencies bringing in material supplies; an executive in control; an army and diplomats to provide output; and internal communication and transport services. A first step in comparing these various sorts of systems is to recognize their comparable functions. But to obtain greatest profit from the comparison, we must press further and state propositions about them which are quantifiable and testable.

Propositions

Several dozen specific theorems or propositions, each empirically testable at the levels of cell, organ, individual, small group and society—often for both energy and information exchange—have been derived by us or related by us to our general theoretical framework. In some cases it is clear that electronic systems can be built to which they would also apply. The testing of these propositions would involve empirical research to discover exactly under what conditions and within what ranges they do or do not apply, and what are the related variables which, when altered, change the character of the general function. Only a few of these propositions can be mentioned here.

Proposition 1. The rate of growth of a system in a medium which has an essentially unrestricted amount of energy available for input is—within certain ranges—exponential. How this proposition can be tested at various levels is suggested in Table 2. The formal identities mentioned in this table are assumed to exist because of a general characteristic of all behaving systems or perhaps of all systems. An exponential growth curve appears in any expansion process in a system in which further subsystems are constantly being produced which are capable of expanding themselves or dividing into or producing other subsystems. If the newly produced subsystems could not also expand or reproduce, the total function would more likely be linear than exponential. Information transfer will probably increase exponentially in growing systems for one (or combination) of several reasons: either (*a*) there are more units, multiplying exponentially, to transmit information; or (*b*) there are more combinations of interaction possible; or (*c*) if information transmission facilitates drive reduction or equilibration among the subsystems, there is exponentially more of this sort of interaction to occur. Of course a whole program of research is required to discover which, if any, of these alternatives is correct.

There are probably several shapes of exponential growth curves, differing in different classes of systems. It is also apparent that the constants involved in growth functions will differ from level to level of systems. (Cells, as we have said, grow in micra and societies in kilometers.) The growing period of cells is measured in hours and of societies in decades. Furthermore, there are species differences: hamsters grow faster than dogs. All these other considerations must be weighed in making a prediction about growth of a system.

The original proposition states that an essentially unrestricted input of energy is required if the growth curve is to be exponential. This is a limiting condition which must be stated, because of course malnourished ova, children, or societies do not grow at the same rate as those with plenty of food. Furthermore, there appear in most living systems to be mechanisms that slow growth after a period, so that this proposition obviously applies only within certain ranges. The nature of these limiting mechanisms is an intriguing question for study.

We have discussed this first proposition at a length which we cannot devote to the others. It is apparent that, while there is a rationale behind the proposition, it might be disproved at any or all levels. If it is valid, it can be valid for various reasons. The explanations may even be different at various levels, or for energy and information transmissions. But we believe it most likely that an unavoidable characteristic of all systems in space-time accounts for the formal identity we have pointed out. Only an extensive set of integrated empirical studies can reveal the facts about even this single proposition.

Table 2. Proposition 1: The Growth Proposition

SYSTEM	ENERGY TRANSFER	INFORMATION TRANSFER
Cell	Measure the rate of growth of a yeast cell or ameba under the microscope.	None thought of.
Organ	Measure by repeated X ray the rate of growth of a bone or other organ in the embryo.	Measure by electrodes implanted in the brain of an embryo the rate of increase of impulse transmission with maturation.
Individual	Measure the volumes of embryos of different ages and plot the volumes against the ages.	A broad extension of the above to the whole nervous system, together with measurement of the rate of increase of hormonal secretion will indicate the general magnitude of increase of total information transmission in the individual.
Group	Measure the rate at which a crowd gathers around the goal posts to tear them down after a big football game (or around the President when he appears unexpectedly on a county courthouse lawn; or around a sudden street fist fight).	Measure in words per minute the rate at which a group of eight strangers in a European railway train compartment begin to interact.
Society	Collect or analyze population growth figures to test the validity of Malthus' law.	This is extremely difficult to measure because the experimental method cannot be used, and societies do not develop *de novo*, but from fragments of former civilizations. The historical method is difficult to use here because of the great differences of communication methods in different eras. Perhaps the rate of increase of message transmission across a boundary, after the end of a civil war or of the partition of a country, could be measured.

Let us turn, more briefly, to other propositions, any one of which raises similar complex issues and implies a major research program for its confirmation or disproof.

Proposition 2. Greater energy is required for a transmission across a boundary than for a transmission in the suprasystem immediately outside a boundary or in the system immediately inside it. Step-functions, whose importance for behavior is outlined by Ashby (1), are characteristic of transmission across boundaries. Neurophysiological and psychophysical threshold phenomena commonly appear to be functions of this type. At the level of the cell, more pressure is necessary to rupture the membrane than to move mechanically in the tissue fluids outside or the cytoplasm inside. More pressure is necessary to rupture a spleen or liver than to move through the space outside the capsule of such an organ, or inside it. As we have noted there is much work concerning thresholds for the individual. Special output of effort is necessary to join a group like a fraternity or country club, as well as to pass through customs and immigration across a border into the society of a new country. This extra physical effort or symbolic activity at boundaries can easily be measured to test this proposition.

Proposition 3. Spread of energy or information throughout systems is quantitatively comparable. After a transmission crosses a boundary into a system, it ordinarily diffuses. Rapoport (10) has written moderately complex probability equations describing the spread of excitation in a "random net," originally conceived as a net of interconnected neurons. Later the same type of equation was found applicable to the spread of epidemics, and the spread of information or rumors in a group or

Proposition 4. There is always a constant systematic distortion—or better alteration—between input of energy or information into a system and output from that system. Manuals issued by the manufacturers indicate the input-output "distortion characteristics" of vacuum tubes. The distortion can be determined for any electronic system, like an amplifier. A comparable alteration occurs when glucose enters a cell and lactic acid comes out. Sound frequencies pass through the cochlea of the ear and come out in volleys on the eighth nerve. A Rorschach card is an identical stimulus for many patients, but the characteristic distortions of each one result in different responses from each patient. Communication between one person and another inevitably results in distortion because these individuals are not coded identically, and for other reasons. This is often illustrated in the old parlor game when one person whispers a story to his neighbor on his right, and he to his neighbor on the right, and so on around a circle. When it gets back to the originator it is nearly always greatly altered. Likewise distortion may occur in the passage of information from one group to another, say when a report of the Bureau of Labor Statistics is interpreted first by the CIO and then by the NAM. Distortion also appears in the crossing of such massive barriers between cultures as the Iron Curtain.

Such alterations may be explained by another, interrelated proposition:

Proposition 5. The distortion of a system is the sum of the effects of processes which subtract from the input to reduce strains in subsystems or add to the output to reduce such strains. Though ultimately all our propositions should presumably interdigitate to form the organized conceptual structure of general behavior systems theory, at present their precise interrelationships usually are not clear. Propositions 4 and 5 are exceptions, however, for the latter suggests a measurable explanation for the process mentioned in the former. Such alteration or distortion can be explained by the fact that every system takes out of its input essentials for the maintenance of its own equilibrium, rejecting all substances that do not contribute to that steady state. This alters the output. Particular systems distort some categories of input more than they do others, because of their specific equilibratory needs. In human beings we find certain alterations in sense organs; others in perceptual areas; others in association areas; others in motor areas; and so on. The difference between the energy input which we call a stimulus and the output which we term a response is the sum of all of these changes.

Proposition 6. When variables in a system return to equilibrium after stress, the rate of *return and the strength of the restorative forces are stronger than a linear function of the amount of displacement from the equilibrium point.* To test this statement one could set up a number of experimental conditions in which the equilibrium range of a variable in a behaving system could be determined. Stimuli could then be applied to this system to disturb it a specified amount away from this point of equilibrium. The rate at which it returned to equilibrium and the strength of the forces restoring it could be measured and compared with similar measurements when there were greater or lesser degrees of disturbance from equilibrium. The characteristics of the curves for different sorts of behaving systems could then be compared quantitatively.

For example, the rate of motion and the amount of energy expended by an ameba moving out of cold or hot fluids into fluids of comfortable temperature might be measured. Or similar studies might be made of amebas moving out of acid or alkaline fluids to those of optimal pH.

At the level of the human individual, the rate of return to a position of balance and the amount of energy expended in return to it, after various amounts of displacement, could be measured. Similarly, the "fire-power" of the defense employed by a player in a simplified chess game to re-establish the equilibrium of his pieces after it had been disturbed by losses of various categories of men could be measured. This would permit quantification of forces restoring equilibrium in a problem-solving situation.

At the level of social phenomena, the strength of various degrees of disturbing influences on group activity could be calculated and measures made of the rate of return to equilibrium and strength of restorative forces employed by the group to establish balance. In various experimental balloting situations in small groups, votes could be used as quantitative indices of the strength of these equilibrating forces.

Disanalogies among various species of systems as to methods of returning to equilibrium depend upon the subsystems or mechanisms of defense available to them for maintaining their study states. Amebae can swim out of an overly acid medium, but sessile forms cannot. The prisoner sings for the wings of a bird, who would be able to fly the coop he is locked in. A man recognizes the threat in an approaching tornado and takes cover, but a child may not have learned about such storms and so may be killed. However, the existence of such disanalogies does not make the general proposition less applicable.

Proposition 7. Living systems respond to continuously increasing stress first by a lag in response, then by an overcompensatory response, and finally by catastrophic collapse of the system. Selye (11) investigated the effects of varying degrees of many physiological stresses on the organism. He has employed such stresses as extreme variation in temperature and intravenous injections of glucose and typhoid toxoid into animals. The charts of his data, of which Figure 2 is representative, show for each stress an initial dip in the curve in the direction of the final collapse, which is the alarm reaction. It is followed by a rise of the curve above the level normally maintained by the organism, which constitutes a sort of overcompensation or overdefensiveness. As the stress is increased, more and more defenses are called into play until finally no additional ones are available and the system collapses suddenly into death.

We have collected data which suggest that coded or symbolic stresses like those in battle may well elicit response curves similar to those of Selye. While extreme stress always worsens performance, moderate stress can improve it above ordinary levels. One of the tests which shows such improvement is the crossing out of C's randomly distributed in a field of O's. However, the same stress increases microtrembling of the fingers, the same fingers used in crossing out C's. It is thus clear that while finger muscle performance worsens, compensatory defense mechanisms come into play so that the total operation of crossing out C's improves. This is an illustration of how certain subsystems may develop strain under stress but the whole system compensates for it.

All this conforms with Ashby's (1) notion of a multistable or ultrastable system. An analogy to such a system is an Army cot made up of a number of wire links. Pressure on the central link will at first be compensated for by the central link alone; but as pressure increases the ring of immediately contiguous links will be called into play; then the next ring; and so on. In the end the cot can support 1,000 pounds on wires, none of which alone could carry 80 pounds without breaking.

Proposition 8. Systems which survive employ the least expensive defenses against stress first and increasingly more expensive ones later. In individual psychology we speak of the physiological or somatic drives, the needs for water, air, vitamins, proteins, and the like, and the psychogenic drives which are concerned essentially with the social environment, coded inputs. Either lack or excess of rate of input of either of these two sorts constitutes a stress, and the system must respond readily to defend itself against such stress if it is to maintain equilibrium. The equilibrium is not static, as

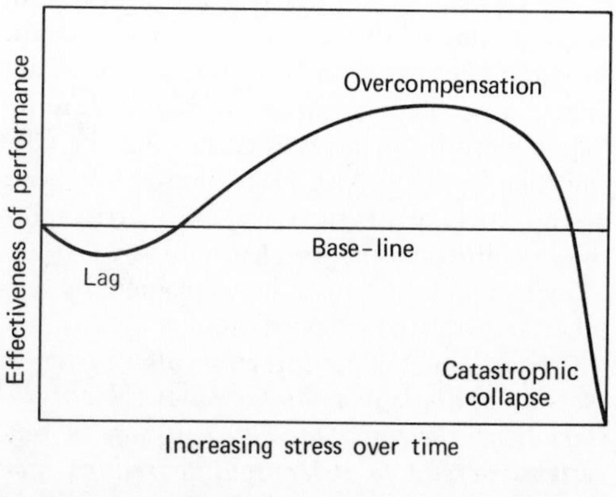

Fig. 2. Representative curve of effectiveness of performance as stress is increased over a period of time.

when a ball rolled up an incline returns to its original position in a trough at the bottom, but is rather the dynamic interaction of forces in flux to maintain a steady state in a rapidly changing environment, like a salmon struggling up the Columbia River to spawn.

If a continuously increasing amount of acid is injected into a dog's veins, a number of mechanisms will be brought into play to defend or protect the steady pH of the blood from this stress. The first which appears to reach its maximal effectiveness will probably be overbreathing, which produces generalized alkalosis to compensate for the acidosis. Excretion of a more acid urine than usual and the "chloride shift" from blood plasma to red cells are other mechanisms which can aid in counteracting the stress, and which probably will achieve their maximal effects later than overbreathing does. It is possible that those organisms which can survive longest under such stress are those which first mobilize the protective mechanisms that employ the most easily replaceable inputs (e.g., oxygen), and only under more extreme conditions use the mechanisms involving inputs not so easily replaceable from their environment. At any rate, this hypothesis can be experimentally tested.

A person's defense mechanisms to protect against coded, psychodynamic stresses are comparable to the physiological mechanisms, and may ordinarily be mobilized in order of their expensiveness. For example, if a man is unable to solve a problem or achieve a goal, he may lower his level of aspiration and say, "Well, I'll try something simpler." This is relatively inexpensive. The next thing he may do is rationalize his behavior, saying, "I could have done it if I had had more time." This is a little more expensive since it places him in a tactically difficult position. Someone might say, "All right, take all the time you need," and he would then be shown to be unable to do it. Repression, a yet more expensive defense, might be his next way of handling the stress if he is forced to continue working toward his goal. His "attention might turn to other things," but that would leave the unresolved strain within him, which some have said can cause psychosomatic symptoms—a serious consequence. Finally, to avoid the frustration of the unsolved problem constantly obtruding on him, he may deny the reality of his total input and a psychotic state may result which can cut him off from close human contact and in other ways be extremely expensive to him.

Proposition 9. Systems which survive perform at an optimum efficiency for maximum power output, which is always less than maximum efficiency. This is a principle suggested by Odum and Pinkerton (8). They apply it to living and nonliving systems at several levels—weights on a pulley (Atwood's machine); water wheels which run grindstones; electric batteries which charge other batteries; metabolism; animal food capture; photosynthesis; a plant community; and a civilization. This principle applies to all systems the notion of efficiency from physics or economics, and the concepts of survival from evolutionary theory. It questions the traditional view that the most efficient system survives and suggests that this is true only if, on occasion, it can also put out maximum power. It also broadens natural selection theory to apply to all systems under stress in a changing suprasystem, from cells, organs, and individuals through groups like clubs and corporations to societies which, like Rome, can fall. Unless in a battle an animal can, by an "emergency reaction" like that described by Cannon, transfer blood flow temporarily from the gut to the extremities, he will fight less well and blood in a cut will clot less effectively. This is directly related to survival. Also, if the cooks in an army under attack, as in the Battle of the Bulge, are not permitted to leave their stoves and pick up guns to aid in a maximum effort, the army may not survive. Throughout all these examples runs a single principle.

Proposition 10. When a system's negative feedback discontinues, its steady state vanishes, and at the same time its boundary disappears and the system terminates. At this moment it becomes part of a larger system which is its environment, and at the same time divides into several subsystems. This hypothesis mentions two independent variables which can be measured separately. One is the degree of negative feedback or the steadiness of the equilibrium in the system; the other is the permeability of the boundary. If too much water enters a red cell, it will swell up and eventually rupture. It can be demonstrated physiologically that the osmotic equilibrium within the cells disappears at about the same time that the cell membrane ruptures. Separate molecules of the cells then become small systems in the much larger system of the circulating blood. A similar sequence occurs in physiological death. It may also occur in the breakdown of psychological defense mechanisms. Certainly a comparable process is seen when a committee dealing with a practical problem cannot agree. It finally dissolves, the members dispersing while the next larger organizational unit, which set up the committee, takes over the responsibility for settling the issue.

Proposition 11. The dimensionality of the output of a system is always less than the dimensionality of the input. This principle is derived by Platt (9) from electronic amplifier theory. Amplifiers are systems which increase the volume of a specific output, but along with amplification there is always selection or discrimination. For example, a high fidelity phonograph amplifies only certain vibrations of the needle in the groove. It does not amplify the motion of the pick-up arm, the light in the room, the temperature of the room, the pressure of the air, the line voltage input, or many other variables in the input to the amplifier from its environment. Consequently the dimensionality of its output involves fewer variables than its input. This is true of sense organs. It is also probably true of any individual, group, or society which makes decisions among options and follows one rather than another, for selection and amplification always go hand in hand.

Proposition 12. Decentralization of the maintenance of variables in equilibrium is always more expensive of energy than centralization, although it can increase utility (i.e., the rate of strain reduction). This is an example of the group of propositions that combines economic concepts with other behavioral notions.

Proposition 13. As decentralization increases, subsystems increasingly act without the benefit of information existing elsewhere in the system.

Proposition 14. The more subsystems there are in efficient systems, the more variables they can maintain in equilibrium, but there are also proportionately more subsystems whose destruction will result in collapse of the system.

Proposition 15. The equilibratory range of a system for a specific variable increases proportionately to the amount of storage of the input in the case of a lack strain along that variable, or spillage of the input in the case of an excess strain.

Proposition 16. When reduction of several strains is not possible simultaneously, the order in which they are reduced in systems which survive is from strongest to weakest, if the effort required for their reduction is identical.

Proposition 17. There is a range of optimal rates for development of coding. If it develops too rapidly, the system cannot properly equilibrate to the probable variations in input; if it develops too slowly the system cannot profit adequately from past inputs. In other words, since the environment varies somewhat, two events may not always be associated tomorrow as they were yesterday. One-trial learning would lead to the rigid and maladaptive expectation that they would be. On the other hand a system that never learns from past experience cannot adapt so well as one that does. The optimum learning rate for adaptive systems that survive is somewhere between these two.

Proposition 18. Up to a maximum, the more energy in a system devoted to information processing (as opposed to metabolic and motor activity), the more likely the system is to survive. In general evolution appears to have resulted in the more complex species having more and more of their total cells devoted to information collection and processing, e.g., larger and larger nervous systems. No one has yet demonstrated a species which failed to survive because too much of its total mass was neural tissue.

Proposition 19. When one living species (the predator) feeds on another (the prey) in a given suprasystem and both species continue to survive, an oscillation of numbers of predators and prey occurs around an equilibrium point. This is the cat-and-rat farm situation, or the ecological problem of foxes and rabbits. As the foxes increase in number they eat more rabbits. As the rabbits decrease in number, there is less food for the foxes and so fewer of them survive. Then rabbits rapidly become more numerous. When cells or organs or individuals of other species compete for food, or oxygen, related phenomena are observed, of which this is a special case.

These, then, are a few illustrative propositions. Some may be correct; others may be wholly wrong; still others may require modification. To test all of them at all levels would be a vast empirical program. We intend to embark on it piecemeal, realizing that the waters are murky and full of shoals, and that our vision is limited. We shall try it, though, because of the alluring distant shore of an integrated behavior theory.

The Role of Subjectivity

All of this discussion has dealt with publicly observable evidence. Some readers will have wondered about the place of subjective experience in all this. This traditional enigma is too important to avoid entirely—we cannot in day-to-day life deny our subjectivity. Since operational science yields no relevant facts, we can only state a belief about this issue—a belief that the most satisfactory solution seems to be Whitehead's. He contended (12) that there is a subjective pole to all phenomena occurring in each subsystem and system. In complex living systems we recognize this as experience. Its character in simple systems is unimaginable to us—less comprehensible than the "blooming, buzzing confusion" of James. In order to have experience continuous over a period of time, all the equilibratory mechanisms which add up to what we call the behavior of the individual, the group, or the society are essential. The concept of responsibility in the law—for example, in the law of torts which concerns damage of one's boundary or limitation of one's input or output, or the law of contracts and civil rights which guarantees coded inputs and outputs—depends on the morality that we may not destroy the equilibrium of other systems which we suspect are experiencing as we do. Social systems remain organized because they are capable of handling larger numbers of stresses and maintaining the experience of all their members more adequately than any individual can. It may be that ultimately, through having explained behavior scientifically, we can understand the proccesses which enable each of us to maintain his experiencing subjectivity. And, by application of our findings to living and nonliving systems at various levels, we may be able to improve the external human and nonhuman conditions which provide satisfaction in experience. This ultimately is what makes the behavioral sciences important.

This article is an affirmative statement of a general position. Very many aspects of so vast a problem obviously cannot be considered in such short space, so in many ways it is incomplete. An effort is made to embrace core subject matter from several biological and social sciences, including such notions as natural selection, efficiency, homeostasis, and other powerful concepts which appear to have cross-disciplinary implications. Obviously no approach to a general theory of behavior at present could encompass even a small percentage of the phenomena which must be considered. The negative criticisms of this view could consume as much if not more space than this positive presentation. As we have observed earlier, models and theories are never perfect but simply approach the limit of correct explanation, and another theory that explains more than this will probably appear soon and should properly supplement this one. At the moment we have only a sketchy map which perhaps shows the route to a first approximation of a general behavior theory. Only a program of empirical testing such as we are now undertaking can demonstrate how much value, if any, it may have.

REFERENCES

1. Ashby, W. R. *Design for a brain.* New York: Wiley, 1952.
2. Berkeley, E. C. *Giant brains, or machines that think.* New York: Wiley, 1949.
3. Bertalanffy, L. v. The theory of open systems in physics and biology. *Science,* 1950, **111,** 23–28.
4. Congressional Record, 79th Congress, Second Session, 9–10.
5. Haret, S. C. *Mécanique sociale.* Paris: Gauthier-Villars, 1910.
6. House of Representatives, 2514, 82nd Congress, Second Session, 9–10.
7. Mill, J. S. *A system of logic.* New York: Harper, 1874, 393–4.
8. Odum, H. T., & Pinkerton, R. C. Time's speed regulator. *Amer. Scientist,* 1955, **43,** 331–343.
9. Platt, John R. Personal communication, 1955.
10. Rapoport, A. Some mathematical models of the spread of information through a population. Chicago: Behavioral Sciences Publication, No. 1, 1953, 19–23.
11. Selye, H. *The physiology and pathology of exposure to stress; A treatise based on the concepts of the general-adaptation syndrome and the diseases of adaptation.* Montreal: Acta, 1950.
12. Whitehead, A. N. *Adventures of ideas.* New York: Macmillan, 1933.

Stability and Adaptation

ROSS ASHBY

Stability

4/1. The words "stability," "steady state," and "equilibrium" are used by a variety of authors with a variety of meanings, though there is always the same underlying theme. As we shall be much concerned with stability and its properties, an exact definition must be provided.

The subject may be opened by a presentation of the three standard elementary examples. A cube resting with one face on a horizontal surface typifies "stable" equilibrium; a sphere resting on a horizontal surface typifies "neutral" equilibrium; and a cone balanced on its point typifies "unstable" equilibrium. With neutral and unstable equilibria we shall have little concern, but the concept of "stable equilibrium" will be used repeatedly.

These three dynamic systems are restricted in their behaviour by the fact that each system contains a fixed quantity of energy, so that any subsequent movement must conform to this invariance. We, however, shall be considering systems which are abundantly supplied with free energy so that no such limitation is imposed. Here are two examples.

The first is the Watt's governor. A steam-engine rotates a pair of weights which, as they are rotated faster, separate more widely by centrifugal action; their separation controls mechanically the position of the throttle; and the position of the throttle controls the flow of steam to the engine. The connexions are arranged so that an increase in the speed of the engine causes a decrease in the flow of steam. The result is that if any transient disturbance slows or accelerates the engine, the governor brings the speed back to the usual value. By this return the system demonstrates its stability.

Chapters 4 and 5 from *Design for a Brain*. New York: Wiley, 1960, pp. 44–70. Reprinted by permission of the publisher.

The second example is the thermostat, of which many types exist. All, however, work on the same principle: a chilling of the main object causes a change which in its turn causes the heating to become more intense or more effective; and vice versa. The result is that if any transient disturbance cools or overheats the main object, the thermostat brings its temperature back to the usual value. By this return the system demonstrates its stability.

4/2. An important feature of stability is that it does not refer to a material body or "machine" but only to some aspect of it. This statement may be proved most simply by an example showing that a single material body can be in two different equilibrial conditions at the same time. Consider a square card balanced exactly on one edge; to displacements at right angles to this edge the card is unstable; to displacements exactly parallel to this edge it is, theoretically at least, stable.

The example supports the thesis that we do not, in general, study physical bodies but only entities carefully abstracted from them. The matter will become clearer when we define stability in terms of the results of primary operations. This may be done as follows.

4/3. Consider a corrugated surface, laid horizontally, with a ball rolling from a ridge down towards a trough. A photograph taken in the middle of its roll would look like Figure 1. We might think of the ball as being unstable because it has rolled away from the

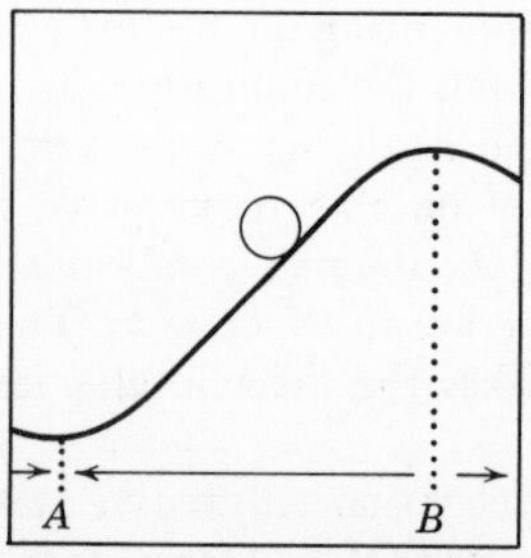

Fig. 1

ridge, until we realise that we can also think of it as stable because it is rolling towards the trough. The duality shows we are approaching the concept in the wrong way. The situation can be made clearer if we remove the ball and consider only the surface. The top of the ridge, as it would affect the roll of a ball, is now recognised as a position of unstable equilibrium, and the bottom of the trough as a position of stability. We now see that, if friction is sufficiently marked for us to be able to neglect momentum, the system composed of the single variable "distance of the ball laterally" is state-determined, and has a definite, permanent field, which is sketched in Figure 1.

From *B* the lines of behaviour diverge, but to *A* they converge. We conclude tentatively that the concept of "stability" belongs not to a material body but to a field. It is shown by a field if the lines of behaviour converge. (An exact definition is given in S. 4/8.)

4/4. The points *A* and *B* are such that the ball, if released on either of them, and mathematically perfect, will stay there. Given a field, a state of equilibrium is one from which the representative point does not move. When the primary operation is applied, the transition from that state can be described as "to itself".

(Notice that this definition, while saying what happens *at* the equilibrial state, does not restrict how the lines of behaviour may run around it. They may converge in to it, or diverge from it, or behave in other ways.)

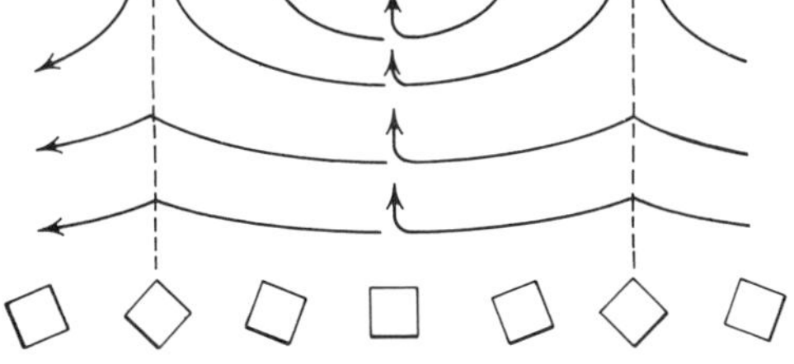

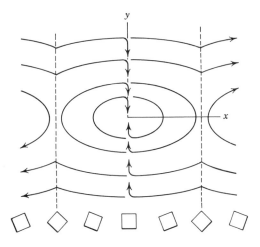

Fig. 2. Field of the two-variable system described in the text. Below is shown the cube as it would appear in elevation when its main face, shown by a heavier line, is tilted through the angle x.

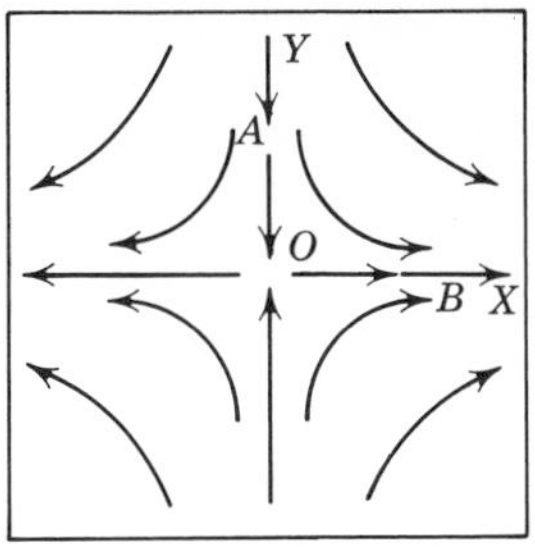

Fig. 3

Although the variables do not change value when the system is at a state of equilibrium, this invariance does not imply that the "machine" is inactive. Thus, a motionless Watt's governor is compatible with the engine working at a non-zero rate.

4/5. To illustrate that the concept of stability belongs to a field, let us examine the fields of the previous examples.

The cube resting on one face yields a state-determined system which has two variables:

(x) the angle at which the face makes with the horizontal, and
(y) the rate at which this angle changes.

(This system allows for the momentum of the cube.) If the cube does not bounce when the face meets the table, the field is similar to that sketched in Figure 2. The stability of the cube when resting on a face corresponds in the field to the convergence of the lines of behaviour to the centre.

The square card balanced on its edge can be represented approximately by two variables which measure displacements at right angles (x) and parallel (y) to the lower edge. The field will resemble that sketched in Figure 3. Displacement from the origin *O* to *A* is followed by a return of the representative point to *O*, and this return corresponds to the stability. Displacement from *O* to *B* is followed by a departure from the region under consideration, and this departure corresponds to the instability. The uncertainty of the movements near *O* corresponds to the uncertainty in the behaviour of the card when released from the vertical position.

The Watt's governor has a more complicated field, but an approximation may be obtained without difficulty. The system may be specified to an approximation sufficient for our purpose by three variables:

(x) the speed of the engine and governor (r.p.m.),
(y) the distance between the weights, or the position of the throttle, and
(z) the velocity of flow of the steam.

(y represents either of two quantities because they are rigidly connected). If, now, a disturbance suddenly accelerates the engine, increasing x, the increase in x will increase y; this increase in y will be followed by a decrease of z, and then by a decrease of x. As the changes occur not in jumps but continuously, the line of behaviour must resemble that sketched in Figure 4. The other lines of the field could be added by considering what would happen after other disturbances (lines starting from points other than A). Although having different initial states, all the lines would converge towards O.

4/6. In some of our examples, for instance that of the cube, the lines of behaviour terminate in point at which all movement ceases. In other examples the movement does not wholly cease; many a thermostat settles down, when close to its resting state, to a regular small oscillation. We shall seldom be interested in the details of what happens at the exact centre.

4/7. More important is the underlying theme that in all cases the stable system is characterised by the fact that after a displacement we can assign some *bound* to the subsequent movement of the representative point, whereas in the unstable system such limitation is either impossible or depends on facts outside the subject of discussion. Thus, if a thermostat is set at 37° C. and displaced to 40°, we can predict that in the future it will not go outside specified limits, which might be, in one apparatus, 36° and 40°. On the other hand, if the thermostat has been assembled with a component reversed so that it is unstable (S. 4/14) and if it is displaced to 40°, then we can give no limits to its subsequent temperatures; unless we introduce such new topics as the melting-point of its solder.

4/8. These considerations bring us to the definitions. Given the field of a state-determined system and a region in the field, the region is stable if the lines of behaviour from all points in the region stay within the region.

Thus, in Figure 1 make a mark on either side of A to define a region. All representative points within are led to A, and none can leave the region; so the region is stable. On the other hand, no such region can be marked around B (unless restricted to the single point of B itself).

The definition makes clear that change of either the field or the region may change the result of the test. We cannot, in general, say of a given system that it is stable (or unstable) unconditionally. The field of Figure 2 showed this, and so does that of Figure 3. (In the latter the regions restricted to any part of the y-axis with the origin are stable; all others are unstable.)

The examples above have been selected to test the definition severely. Often the fields are simpler. In the field of the cube, for instance, it is possible to draw many boundaries, all oval, such that the regions inside them are stable. The field of the Watt's governor is also of this type.

A *field* will be said to be stable if the whole region it fills is stable; the *system* that provided the field can then be called stable.

4/9. Sometimes the conditions are even simpler. The system may have only one state of equilibrium and the lines of behaviour may all either converge in to it or all diverge from it. In such a case the indication of which way the lines go may be given sufficiently by the sim-

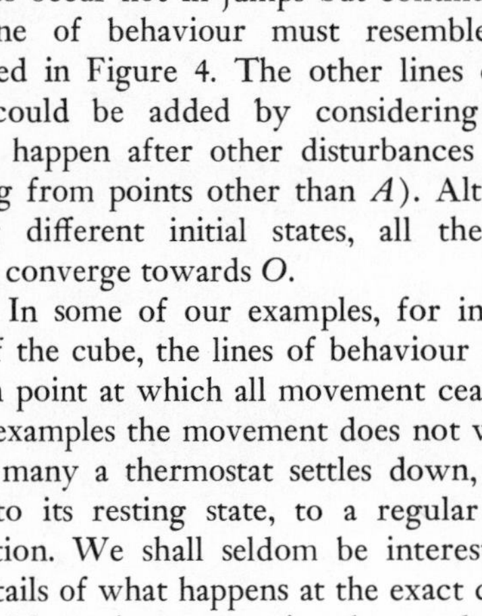

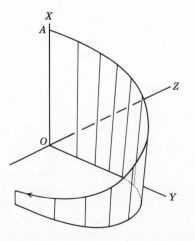

Fig. 4. One line of behaviour in the field of the Watt's governor. For clarity, the resting state of the system has been used as origin. The system has been displaced to A *and then released.*

ple, unqualified, statement that "it is stable" (or not). A system can be described adequately by such an unqualified statement (without reference to the region) only when its field, i.e. its behaviour, is suitably simple.

4/10. If a line of behaviour is re-entrant to itself, the system undergoes a recurrent cycle. If the cycle is wholly contained in a given region, and the lines of behaviour lead *into* the cycle, the cycle is stable.

Such a cycle is commonly shown by thermostats which, after correcting any gross displacement, settle down to a steady oscillation. In such a case the field will show, not convergence to a point but convergence to a cycle, such as is shown exaggerated in Figure 5.

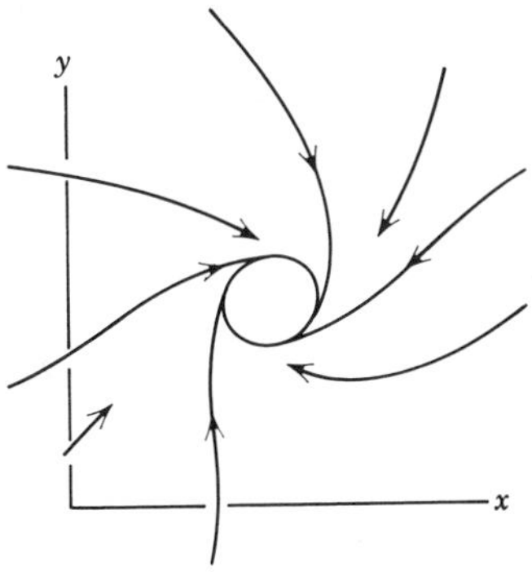

Fig. 5

4/11. This definition of stability conforms to the requirement of S. 2/10; for the observed behaviour of the system determines the field, and the field determines the stability.

The Diagram of Immediate Effects

4/12. The description given in S. 4/1 of the working of the Watt's governor showed that it is arranged in a functional circuit: the chain of cause and effect is re-entrant. Thus if we represent "*A* has a direct effect on *B*" or "*A* directly disturbs *B*" by the symbol $A \rightarrow B$, then the construction of the Watt's governor may be represented by the diagram:

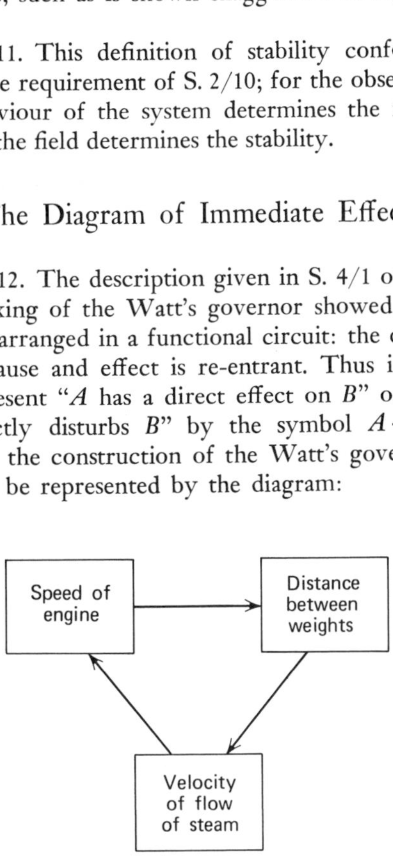

(The number of variables named here is partly optional.)

I now want to make clear that this type of diagram, if accurately defined, can be derived *wholly from the results of primary operations.* No metaphysical or borrowed knowledge is necessary for its construction. To show how this is done, take an actual Watt's governor as example.

Each pair of variables is taken in turn. Suppose the relation between "speed of engine" and "distance between weights" is first investigated. The experimenter would fix the variable "velocity of flow of steam" and all other extraneous variables that might interfere to confuse the direct relation between speed of engine and distance between weights. Then he would try various speeds of the engine, and would observe how these changes affected the behaviour of "distance between the weights." He would find that changes in the speed of the engine were regularly followed by changes in the distance between the weights. Thus the transition of the variable "distance between weights" (one distance changing to another) *is* affected by the value of the speed of the engine. He need know nothing of the nature of the ultimate physical linkages, but he would observe the fact. Then, still keeping "velocity of flow of steam" constant, he would try various distances between the weights, and would observe the effect of such changes on the speed of the engine; he would find them to be without effect. He would thus have established that there is an arrow from left to right but not from right to left in

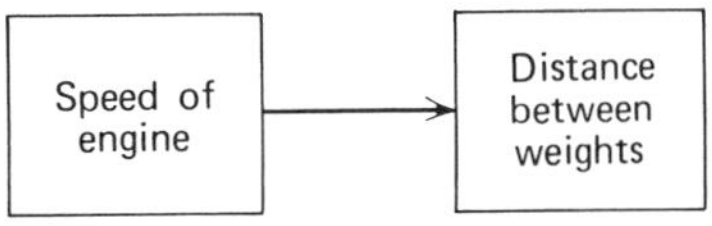

This procedure could then be applied to the two variables "distance between weights" and "velocity of flow of steam", while the other variable "speed of engine" was kept constant.

And finally the relations between the third pair could be established.

The method is clearly general. To find the immediate effects in a system with variables A, B, C, D . . . take one pair, A and B say; hold all other variables C, D . . . constant; note B's behaviour when A starts at A_1; and also its behaviour when A starts at A_2. If these behaviours of B are the same, then there is no immediate effect from A to B. But if the B's behaviours are unequal, and regularly depend on what value A starts from, then there *is* an immediate effect, which we may symbolise by $A \rightarrow B$.

By interchanging A and B in the process we can then test for $B \rightarrow A$. And by using other pairs in turn we can determine all the immediate effects. The process consists purely of primary operations, and therefore uses no borrowed knowledge. We shall frequently use this diagram of immediate effects.

4/13. It should be noticed that this arrow, though it sometimes corresponds to an actual material channel (a rod, a wire, a nerve fibre, etc.), has fundamentally nothing to do with material connexions but is *a representation of a relation between the behaviours at A and B*. Strictly speaking, it refers to A and B only, and not to anything between them.

That it is the functional, behaviourial, relation between A and B that is decisive (in deciding whether we may hypothesise a channel of communication between them) was shown clearly on that day in 1888 when Heinrich Hertz gave his famous demonstration. He had two pieces of apparatus (A and B, say) that manifestly were not connected in any material way; yet whenever at any arbitrarily selected moment he closed a switch in A a spark jumped in B, i.e., B's behaviour depended at any moment on the position of A's switch. Here was a flat contradiction: materially the two systems were *not* connected, yet functionally their behaviours *were* connected. All scientists accepted that the *behavioural* evidence was final—that some linkage was demonstrated.

Feedback

4/14. A gas thermostat also shows a functional circuit or feedback; for it is controlled by a capsule which by its swelling moves a lever which controls the flow of gas to the heating flame, so the diagram of immediate effects would be:

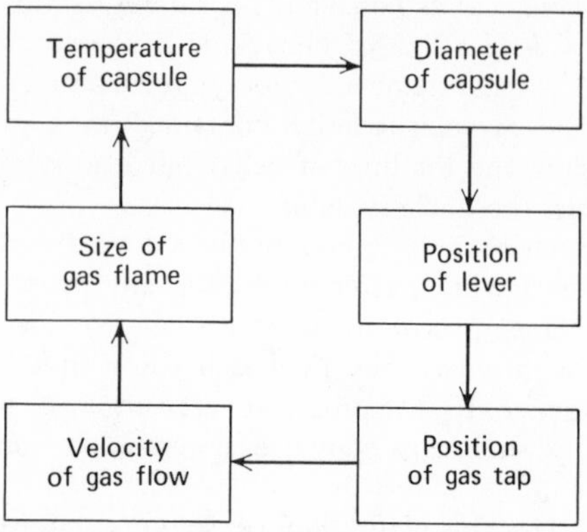

The reader should verify that each arrow represents a physical action which can be demonstrated if all variables other than the pair are kept constant.

Another example is provided by "reaction" in a radio receiver. We can represent the action by two variables linked in two ways:

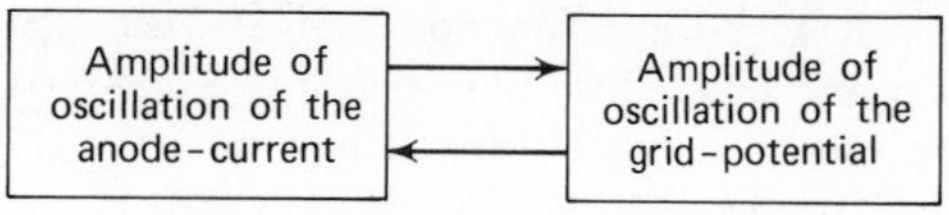

The lower arrow represents the grid-potential's effect within the valve on the anode-current. The upper arrow represents some arrangement of the circuit by which fluctuation in the anode current affects the grid-potential. The effect represented by the lower arrow is determined by the valve-designer, that of the upper by the circuit-designer.

Such systems whose variables affect one another in one or more circuits possess what the radio-engineer calls "feedback"; they are also sometimes described as "servo-mechanisms." They are at least as old as the Watt's governor and may be older. But only during the last decade has it been realised that the possession of feedback gives a machine potentialities that are not available to a machine lacking it. The development occurred mainly during the last war, stimulated by the demand for automatic methods of control of searchlight, anti-aircraft guns, rockets, and torpedoes, and facilitated by the great advances that had occurred in electronics. As a result, a host of new machines appeared which acted with powers of self-adjustment and correction never before achieved. Some of their main properties will be described in S. 4/16.

The nature, degree, and polarity of the feedback usually have a decisive effect on the stability or instability of the system. In the Watt's governor or in the thermostat, for instance, the connexion of a part in reversed position, reversing the polarity of action of one component on the next, may, and probably will, turn the system from stable to unstable. In the reaction circuit of the radio set, the stability or instability is determined by the quantitative relation between the two effects.

Instability in such systems is shown by the development of a "runaway." The least disturbance is magnified by its passage round the circuit so that it is incessantly built up into a larger and larger deviation from the central state. The phenomenon is identical with that referred to as a "vicious circle."

4/15. The examples shown have only a simple circuit. But more complex systems may have many interlacing circuits. If, for instance, four variables all act on each other, the diagram of immediate effects would be that shown in Figure 6 (*A*). It is easy to verify that such a system contains twenty interlaced circuits, two of which are shown at *B* and *C*.

The further development of the theory of systems with feedback cannot be made without mathematics. But here it is sufficient to note two facts: a system which possesses feedback is usually actively stable or actively unstable; and whether it is stable or unstable depends on the quantitative details of the particular arrangement.

Goal-Seeking

4/16. Every stable system has the property that if displaced from a state of equilibrium and released, the subsequent movement is so matched to the initial displacement that the system is brought back to the state of equilibrium. *A variety of disturbances will therefore evoke a variety of matched reactions.* Reference to a simple field such as that of Figure 2 will establish the point.

This pairing of the line of return to the initial displacement has sometimes been regarded as "intelligent" and peculiar to living things. But a simple refutation is given by the ordinary pendulum: if we displace it to the right, it develops a force which tends to move it to the left; and if we displace it to the left, it develops a force which tends to move it to the right. Noticing that the pendulum reacted with forces which though varied in direction always pointed towards the centre, the mediaeval scientist would have said "the pendulum seeks the centre." By this phrase he would have recognised that the behaviour of a stable system may be described as "goal-seeking." Without introducing any metaphysical implications we may recognise that this type of behaviour does occur in the stable dynamic systems. Thus Figure 7 shows how, as the control setting of a thermostat was altered, the temperature of the apparatus always followed it, the set temperature being treated as if it were a goal.

Such a movement occurs here in only one dimension (temperature), but other goal-seeking devices may use more. The radar-controlled searchlight, for example, uses the reflected impulses to alter its direction of aim so as to minimise the angle between its direction of aim and the bearing of the source of the reflected impulses. So if the aircraft swerves, the searchlight will follow it actively, just as the temperature followed the setting. Such a system is goal-seeking in two dimensions.

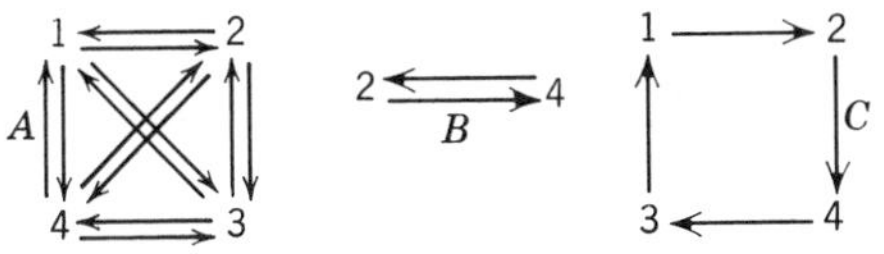

Fig. 6

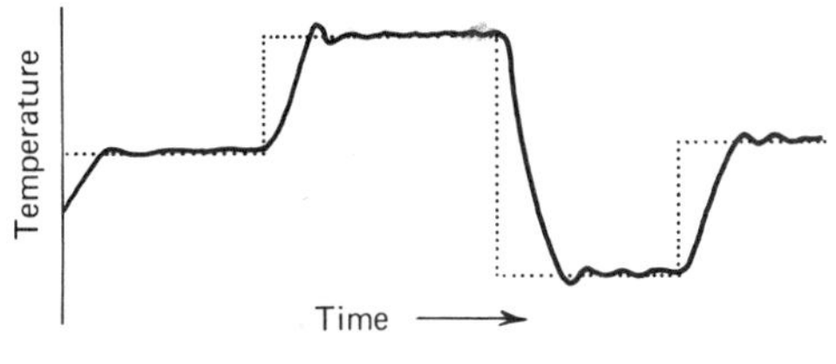

Fig. 7. Tracing of the temperature (solid line), of a thermostatically controlled bath, and of the control setting (broken line).

The examples show the common feature that each is "error-controlled": each is partly controlled by the deviation of the system's state from the state of equilibrium (which, in these examples, can be moved by an outside operation). The thermostat is affected by the difference between the actual and the set temperatures. The searchlight is affected by the difference between the two directions. Thus, *machines with feedback are not subject to the oft-repeated dictum that machines must act blindly and cannot correct their errors.* Such a statement is true of machines without feedback, but not of machines in general.

Once it is appreciated that feedback can be used to correct any deviation we like, it is easy to understand that there is no limit to the complexity of goal-seeking behaviour which may occur in machines quite devoid of any "vital" factor. Thus, an automatic anti-aircraft gun may be controlled by the radar-pulses reflected back both from the target aeroplane and from its own bursting shells, in such a way that it tends to minimise the distance between shell-burst and plane. Such a system, wholly automatic, cannot be distinguished by its behaviour from a humanly operated gun: both will fire at the target, following it through all manœuvres, continually using the errors to improve the next shot. It will be seen, therefore, that a system with feedback may be both wholly automatic and yet actively and complexly goal-seeking. There is no incompatibility.

4/17. It will have been noticed that stability, as defined, in no way implies fixity or rigidity. It is true that the stable system usually has a state of equilibrium at which it shows no change; but the lack of change is deceptive if it suggests rigidity: if displaced from the state of equilibrium it will show active, perhaps extensive and complex, movements. The stable system is restricted only in that it does not show the unrestricted divergencies of instability.

Stability and the Whole

4/18. An important feature of a system's stability (or instability) is that *it is a property of the whole system and can be assigned to no part of it.* The statement may be illustrated by a consideration of the first diagram of S. 4/14 as it is related to the practical construction of the thermostat. In order to ensure the stability of the final assembly, the designer must consider:

1. The effect of the temperature on the diameter of the capsule, i.e. whether a rise in temperature makes the capsule expand or shrink.
2. Which way an expansion of the capsule moves the lever.
3. Which way a movement of the lever moves the gas-tap.
4. Whether a given movement of the gas-tap makes the velocity of gas-flow increase or decrease.
5. Whether an increase of gas-flow makes the size of the gas-flame increase or decrease.
6. How an increase in size of the gas-flame will affect the temperature of the capsule.

Some of the answers are obvious, but they must none the less be included. When the six answers are known, the designer can ensure stability only by arranging the components [chiefly by manipulating (2), (3), and (5) so that as a whole they form an appropriate combination. Thus five of the effects may be decided, yet the stability will still depend on how the sixth is related to them. *The stability belongs only to the combination; it cannot be related to the parts considered separately.*

In order to emphasise that the stability of a system is independent of any conditions which may hold over the parts which compose the whole, some further examples will be given.

1. Two systems may be joined so that they act and interact on one another to form a single system: to know that the two systems when separate were both stable is to know nothing about the stability of the system formed by their junction: it may be stable or unstable.

2. Two systems, both unstable, may join to form a whole which is stable.

3. Two systems may form a stable whole if joined in one way, and may form an unstable whole if joined in another way.

4. In a stable system the effect of fixing a variable may be to render the remainder unstable.

Such examples could be multiplied almost indefinitely. They illustrate the rule that the stability (or instability) of a dynamic system depends on the parts and their interrelations as a whole.

4/19. The fact that the stability of a system is a property of the system as a whole is related to the fact that *the presence of stability always implies some co-ordination of the actions between the parts.* In the thermostat the necessity for co-ordination is clear, for if the components were assembled at random there would be only an even chance that the assembly would be stable. But as the system and the feedbacks become more complex, so does the achievement of stability become more difficult and the likelihood of instability greater. Radio engineers know only too well how readily complex systems with feedback become unstable, and how difficult is the discovery of just that combination of parts and linkages which will give stability. As the number of variables increases so usually do the effects of variable on variable have to be coordinated with more and more care if stability is to be achieved.

Adaptation as Stability

5/1. The concept of "adaptation" has so far been used without definition; this vagueness must be corrected. Not only must the definition be precise, but it must, by S. 2/10,[1] be given in terms that can be reduced wholly to primary operations.

5/2. The suggestion that an animal's behaviour is "adaptive" if the animal "responds correctly to a stimulus" may be rejected at once. First, it presupposes an action by an experimenter and therefore cannot be applied when the free-living organism and its environment affect each other reciprocally. Secondly, the definition provides no meaning for "correctly" unless it means "conforming to what the experimenter thinks the animal ought to do." Such a definition is useless.

Homeostasis

5/3. I propose the definition that *a form of behaviour is* adaptive *if it maintains the essential variables* (S. 3/14) [2] *within physiological limits.* The full justification of such a definition would involve its comparison with all the known facts—an impossibly large task. Nevertheless it is fundamental in this subject and I must discuss it sufficiently to show how fundamental it is and how wide is its applicability.

First I shall outline the facts underlying Cannon's concept of "homeostasis." They are not directly relevant to the problem of learning, for the mechanisms are inborn; but the mechanisms are so clear and well known that they provide an ideal basic illustration. They show that:

1. Each mechanism is "adapted" to its end.
2. Its end is the maintenance of the values of some essential variables within physiological limits.
3. Almost all the behaviour of an animal's vegetative system is due to such mechanisms.

5/4. As first example may be quoted the mechanisms which tend to maintain within limits to concentration of glucose in the blood. The concentration should not fall below about 0·06 per cent or the tissues will be starved of their chief source of energy; and the concentration should not rise above about 0.18 per cent or other undesirable effects will occur. If the blood-glucose falls below about 0·07 per cent the adrenal glands secret adrenaline which makes the liver turn its stores of glycogen into glucose; this passes into the blood and the fall is opposed. In addition, a falling blood-glucose stimulates the appetite so that food is taken, and this, after digestion, provides glucose. On the other hand, if it rises excessively, the secretion of insulin by the pancreas is increased, causing the liver to remove glucose from the blood. The muscles and skin also remove it; and the kidneys help by excreting glucose into the urine if the concentration in the blood exceeds 0·18 per cent. Here then are five activities all of which have the same final effect. Each one acts so as to *restrict* the fluctuations which might otherwise occur. Each may justly be described as "adaptive," for it acts to preserve the animal's life.

The temperature of the interior of the warm-blooded animal's body may be disturbed by exertion, or illness, or by exposure to the weather. If the body temperature becomes raised, the skin flushes and more heat passes from the body to the surrounding air; sweat-

[1] *Design for a Brain*, pp. 19–20.
[2] *Design for a Brain*, pp. 41–42.

ing commences, and the evaporation of the water removes heat from the body; and the metabolism of the body is slowed, so that less heat is generated within it. If the body is chilled, these changes are reversed. Shivering may start, and the extra muscular activity provides heat which warms the body. Adrenaline is secreted, raising the muscular tone and the metabolic rate, which again supplies increased heat to the body. The hairs or feathers are moved by small muscles in the skin so that they stand more erect, enclosing more air in the interstices and thus conserving the body's heat. In extreme cold the human being, when almost unconscious, reflexly takes a posture of extreme flexion with the arms pressed firmly against the chest and the legs fully drawn up against the abdomen. The posture is clearly one which exposes to the air a minimum of surface. In all these ways, the body acts so as to maintain its temperature within limits.

The amount of carbon dioxide in the blood is important in its effect on the blood's alkalinity. If the amount rises, the rate and depth of respiration are increased, and carbon dioxide is exhaled at an increased rate. If the amount falls, the reaction is reversed. By this means the alkalinity of the blood is kept within limits.

The retina works best at a certain intensity of illumination. In bright light the nervous system contracts the pupil, and in dim relaxes it. Thus the amount of light entering the eye is maintained within limits.

If the eye is persistently exposed to bright light, as happens when one goes to the tropics, the pigment-cells in the retina grow forward day by day until they absorb a large portion of the incident light before it reaches the sensitive cells. In this way the illumination on the sensitive cells is kept within limits.

If exposed to sunshine, the pigment-bearing cells in the skin increase in number, extent, and pigment-content. By this change the degree of illumination of the deeper layers of the skin is kept within limits.

When dry food is chewed, a copious supply of saliva is poured into the mouth. Saliva lubricates the food and converts it from a harsh and abrasive texture to one which can be chewed without injury. The secretion therefore keeps the frictional stresses below the destructive level.

The volume of the circulating blood may be disturbed by haemorrhage. Immediately after a severe haemorrhage a number of changes occur: the capillaries in limbs and muscles undergo constriction, driving the blood for these vessels to the more essential internal organs; thirst becomes extreme, impelling the subject to obtain extra supplies of fluid; fluid from the tissues passes into the blood-stream and augments its volume; and clotting at the wound helps to stem the haemorrhage. A haemorrhage has a second effect in that, by reducing the number of red corpuscles, it reduces the amount of oxygen which can be carried to the tissues; the reduction, however, itself stimulates the bone-marrow to an increased production of red corpuscles. All these actions tend to keep the variables "volume of circulating blood" and "oxygen supplied to the tissues" within normal limits.

Every fast-moving animal is liable to injury by collision with hard objects. Animals, however, are provided with reflexes that tend to minimise the chance of collision and of mechanical injury. A mechanical stress causes injury—laceration, dislocation, or fracture—only if the stress exceeds some definite value, depending on the stressed tissue—skin, ligament, or bone. So these reflexes act to keep the mechanical stresses within physiological limits.

Many more examples could be given, but all can be included within the same formula. Some external disturbance tends to drive an essential variable outside its normal limits; but the commencing change itself activates a mechanism that *opposes* the external disturbance. By this mechanism the essential variable is maintained within limits much narrower than would occur if the external disturbance were unopposed. The narrowing is the objective manifestation of the mechanism's adaptation.

5/5. The mechanisms of the previous section act mostly within the body, but it should be noted that some of them have acted partly through the environment. Thus, if the body-temperature is raised, the nervous system lessens the generation of heat within the body and the body-temperature falls, but only because the body is continuously losing heat to its surroundings. Flushing of the skin cools the body only if the surrounding air is cool; and sweating lowers the body-temperature only if the surrounding air is unsaturated. Increasing respiration lowers the carbon dioxide content of the blood, but only if the atmosphere contains less than 5 per cent. In each case the chain of cause and effect passes partly through the environment. The mechanisms that work wholly within the body and those that make extensive use of the environment are thus only the extremes of a continuous series. Thus, a thirsty animal seeks water: if it is a fish it does no more than swallow, while if it is an antelope in the veldt it has to go through an elaborate process of search, of travel, and of finding a suitable way down to the river or pond. The homeostatic mechanisms thus extend from those that work wholly within the animal to those that involve its widest-ranging activities; *the principles are uniform throughout.*

Generalized Homeostasis

5/6. Just the same criterion for "adaptation" may be used in judging the behaviour of the free-living animal in its learned reactions. Take the type-problem of the kitten and the fire. When the kitten first approaches an open fire, it may paw at the fire as if at a mouse, or it may crouch down and start to "stalk" the fire, or it may attempt to sniff at the fire, or it may walk unconcernedly on to it. Every one of these actions is liable to lead to the animal's being burned. Equally the kitten, if it is cold, may sit far from the fire and thus stay cold. The kitten's behaviour cannot be called adapted, for the temperature of its skin is not kept within normal limits. The animal, in other words, is not acting homeostatically for skin temperature. Contrast this behaviour with that of the experienced cat: on a cold day it approaches the fire to a distance adjusted so that the skin temperature is neither too hot nor too cold. If the fire burns fiercer, the cat will move away until the skin is again warmed to a moderate degree. If the fire burns low the cat will move nearer. If a red-hot coal drops from the fire the cat takes such action as will keep the skin temperature within normal limits. Without making any enquiry at this stage into what has happened to the kitten's brain, we can at least say that whereas at first the kitten's behaviour was not homeostatic for skin temperature, it has now become so. Such behaviour is "adapted": it preserves the life of the animal by keeping the essential variables within limits.

The same thesis can be applied to a great deal, if not all, of the normal human adult's behaviour. In order to demonstrate the wide application of this thesis, and in order to show that even Man's civilised life is not exceptional, some of the surroundings which he has provided for himself will be examined for their known physical and physiological effects. It will be shown that each item acts so as to narrow the range of variation of his essential variables.

The first requirement of a civilised man is a house; and its first effect is to keep the air in which he lives at a more equable temperature. The roof keeps his skin at a more constant dryness. The windows, if open in summer and closed in winter, assist in the maintenance of an even temperature, and so do fires and stoves. The glass in the windows keeps the illumination of the rooms nearer the optimum, and artificial lighting has the same effect. The chimneys keep the amount of irritating smoke in the rooms near the optimum, which is zero.

Many of the other conveniences of civilisation could, with little difficulty, be shown to be similarly variation-limiting. An attempt to demonstrate them all would be interminable. But to confirm the argument we will examine a motor-car, part by part, in order to show its homeostatic relation to man.

Travel in a vehicle, as contrasted with travel on foot, keeps several essential variables within narrower limits. The fatigue induced by walking for a long distance implies that some variables, as yet not clearly known, have exceeded limits not transgressed when the subject is carried in a vehicle. The reserves of food in the body will be less depleted, the skin on the soles of the feet will be less chafed, the muscles will have endured less strain, in winter the body will have been less chilled, and in summer it will have been less heated, than would have happened had the subject travelled on foot.

When examined in more detail, many ways are found in which it serves us by maintaining our essential variables within narrower limits. The roof maintains our skin at a constant dryness. The windows protect us from a cold wind, and if open in summer, help to cool us. The carpet on the floor acts similarly in winter, helping to prevent the temperature of the feet from falling below its optimal value. The jolts of the road cause, on the skin and bone of the human frame, stresses which are much lessened by the presence of springs. Similar in action are the shock-absorbers and tyres. A collision would cause an extreme deceleration which leads to very high values for the stress on the skin and bone of the passengers. By the brakes these very high values may be avoided, and in this way the brakes keep the variables "stress on bone" within narrower limits. Good headlights keep the luminosity of the road within limits narrower than would occur in their absence.

The thesis that "adaptation" means the maintenance of essential variables within physiological limits is thus seen to hold not only over the simpler activities of primitive animals but over the more complex activities of the "higher" organisms.

5/7. Before proceeding further, it must be noted that the word "adaptation" is commonly used in two senses which refer to different processes.

The distinction may best be illustrated by the inborn homeostatic mechanisms: the reaction to cold by shivering, for instance. Such a mechanism may undergo two types of "adaptation." The first occurred long ago and was the change from a species too primitive to show such a reaction to a species which, by natural selection, had developed the reaction as a characteristic inborn feature. The second type of "adaptation" occurs when a member of the species, born with the mechanism, is subjected to cold and changes from not-shivering to shivering. The first change involved the development of the mechanism itself; the second change occurs when the mechanism is stimulated into showing its properties.

In the learning process, the first stage occurs when the animal "learns": when it changes from an animal not having an adapted mechanism to one which has such a mechanism. The second stage occurs when the developed mechanism changes from inactivity to activity. In this chapter we are concerned with the characteristics of the developed mechanism. The processes which led to its development are discussed in Chapter 9.[3]

5/8. We can now recognise that "*adaptive*" *behaviour is equivalent to the behaviour of a stable system, the region of the stability being the region of the phase-space in which all the essential variables lie within their normal limits.*

[3] *Design for a Brain.*

The view is not new (though it can now be stated with more precision):

> Every phase of activity in a living being must be not only a necessary sequence of some antecedent change in its environment, but must be so adapted to this change as to tend to its neutralisation, and so to the survival of the organism. . . . It must also apply to *all* the relations of living beings. It must therefore be the guiding principle, not only in physiology . . . but also in the other branches of biology which treat of the relations of the living animal to its environment and of the factors determining its survival in the struggle for existence.
>
> (Starling.)

> In an open system, such as our bodies represent, compounded of unstable material and subjected continuously to disturbing conditions, constancy is in itself evidence that agencies are acting or ready to act, to maintain this constancy.
>
> (Cannon.)

> Every material system can exist as an entity only so long as its internal forces, attraction, cohesion, etc., balance the external forces acting upon it. This is true for an ordinary stone just as much as for the most complex substances; and its truth should be recognised also for the animal organism. Being a definite circumscribed material system, it can only continue to exist so long as it is in continuous equilibrium with the forces external to it: so soon as this equilibrium is seriously disturbed the organism will cease to exist as the entity it was.
>
> (Pavlov.)

McDougall never used the concept of "stability" explicitly, but when describing the type of behaviour which he considered to be most characteristic of the living organism, he wrote:

> Take a billiard ball from the pocket and place it upon the table. It remains at rest, and would continue to remain so for an indefinitely long time, if no forces were applied to it. Push it in any direction, and its movement in that direction persists until its momentum is exhausted, or until it is deflected by the resistance of the cushion and follows a new path mechanically determined. . . . Now contrast with this an instance of behaviour. Take a timid animal

Table 1. All forms of Animal Behavior, Classified by Holmes

Behaviour	Non-adaptive			Useless tropistic reaction.
				Misdirected instinct.
				Abnormal sex behaviour.
				Pathological behaviour.
				Useless social activity.
				Superfluous random movements.
	Adaptive	Self-maintaining	Sustentative	Capture, devouring of food.
				Activities preparatory, as making snares, stalking.
				Collection of food, digging.
				Migration.
				Caring for food, storing, burying, hiding.
				Preparing of food.
			Protective	Against enemies—fight, flight.
				Against inanimate forces.
				Reactions to heat, gravity, chemicals.
				Against inanimate objects.
			Ameliorative	Rest, sleep, play, basking.
		Race-maintaining	(With these we are not concerned.)	

such as a guinea-pig from its hole or nest, and put it upon the grass plot. Instead of remaining at rest, it runs back to its hole; push it in any other direction, and, as soon as you withdraw your hand, it turns back towards its hole; place any obstacle in its way, and it seeks to circumvent or surmount it, restlessly persisting until it achieves its end or until its energy is exhausted.

He could hardly have chosen an example showing more clearly the features of stability.

Survival

5/9. Are there aspects of "adaptation" not included within the definition of "stability?" Is "survival" to be the sole criterion of adaptation? Is it to be maintained that the Roman soldier who killed Archimedes in Syracuse was better "adapted" in his behaviour than Archimedes?

The question is not easily answered. It is similar to that of S. 3/4 [4] where it was asked whether all the qualities of the living organism could be represented by number; and the answer must be similar. It is assumed that we are dealing primarily with the simpler rather than with the more complex creatures, though the examples of S. 5/6 have shown that some at least of man's activities may be judged properly by this criterion.

In order to survey rapidly the types of behaviour of the more primitive animals, we may examine the classification of Holmes, who intended his list to be exhaustive but constructed it with no reference to the concept of stability. The reader will be able to judge how far our formulation S. 5/8) is consistent with his scheme, which is given in Table 1.

For the primitive organism, and excluding behaviour related to racial survival, there seems to be little doubt that the "adaptiveness" of behaviour is properly measured by its tendency to promote the organism's survival.

5/10. A most impressive characteristic of living organisms is their mobility, their tendency to change. McDougall expressed this characteristic well in the example, of S. 5/8. Yet our formulation transfers the centre of interest to the state of equilibrium, to the fact that the essential variables of the adapted organism change *less* than they would if it were

[4] *Design for a Brain*, p. 32.

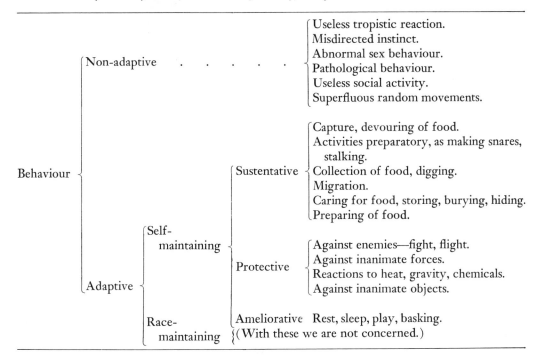

unadapted. Which is important: constancy or change?

The two aspects are not incompatible, for *the constancy of some variables may involve the vigorous activity of others.* A good thermostat reacts vigorously to a small change of temperature, and the vigorous activity of some of its variables keeps the other within narrow limits. The point of view taken here is that the constancy of the essential variables is fundamentally important, and that the activity of the other variables is important only in so far as it contributes to this end.

Stability and Co-ordination

5/11. So far the discussion has traced the relation between the concepts of "adaptation" and of "stability." It will now be proposed that "motor co-ordination" also has an essential connexion with stability.

"Motor-co-ordination" is a concept well understood in physiology, where it refers to the ability of the organism to combine the activities of several muscles so that the resulting movement follows accurately its appropriate path. Contrasted to it are the concepts of clumsiness, tremor, ataxia, athetosis. It is suggested that the presence or absence of co-ordination may be decided, in accordance with our methods, by observing whether the movement does, or does not, deviate outside given limits.

The formulation seems to be adequate provided that we measure the limb's deviations from some line which is given arbitrarily, usually by a knowledge of the line followed by the normal limb. A first example is given by Figure 8, which shows the line traced by the point of an expert fencer's foil during a lunge. An inco-ordination would be shown by a divergence from the intended line.

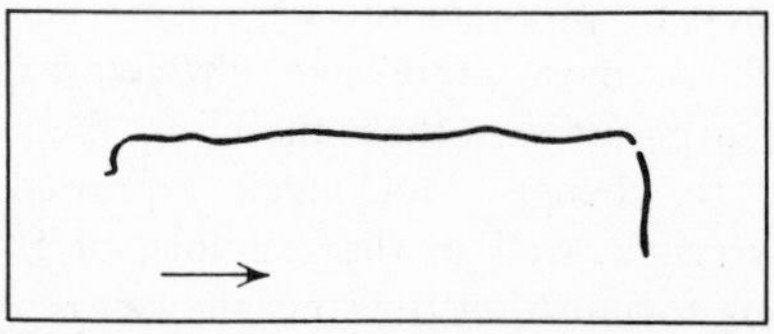

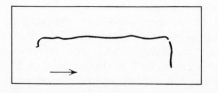

Fig. 8

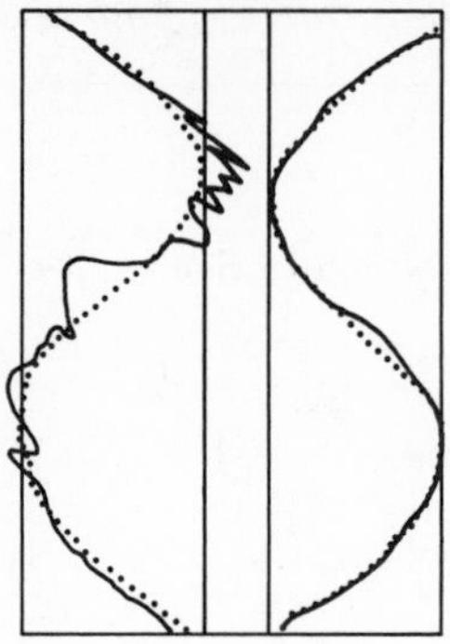

Fig. 9. Record of the attempts of a patient to follow the dotted lines with the left and right hands. (By the courtesy of Dr. W. T. Grant of Los Angeles.)

A second example is given by the record of Figure 9. The subject, a patient with a tumour in the left cerebellum, was asked to follow the dotted lines with a pen. The left- and right-hand curves were drawn with the respective hands. The tracing shows clearly that the co-ordination is poorer in the left hand. What criterion reveals the fact? The essential distinction is that the deviations of the lines from the dots are larger on the left than on the right.

The degree of motor co-ordination achieved may therefore be measured by the smallness of the deviations from some standard line. Later it will be suggested that there are mechanisms which act to maintain variables within narrow limits. If the identification of this section is accepted, such mechanisms could be regarded as appropriate for the co-ordination of motor activity.

5/12. So far we have noticed in stable systems only their property of keeping variables within limits. But such systems have other properties of which we shall notice two. They are also shown by animals, and are then sometimes considered to provide evidence that the organism has some power of "intelligence" not shared by non-living systems. In these two instances the assumption is unnecessary.

The first property is shown by a stable system when the lines of behaviour do not return directly, by a straight line, to the state of equilibrium (*e.g.* Figure 4). When this occurs, variables may be observed to move away from their values in the state of equilibrium, only to return to them later. Thus, suppose in Figure 10 that the field is stable and that at the equilibrial state R x and y have the values X and Y. For clarity, only one line of behaviour is drawn. Let the system be displaced to A and is subsequent behaviour observed. At first, while the representative point moves towards B, y hardly alters; but x, which started at X', moves to X and goes past it to X''. Then x remains almost constant and y changes until the representative point reaches C. Then y stops changing, and x changes towards, and reaches, its resting value X. The system has now reached a state of equilibrium and no further changes occur. This account is just a transcription into words of what the field defines graphically.

Now the shape and features of any field depend ultimately on the real physical and chemical construction of the "machine" from which the variables are abstracted. The fact that the line of behaviour does not run straight from A to R must be due to some feature in the "machine" such that if the machine is to get from state A to state R, states B and C must be passed through of necessity. Thus, if the machine contained moving parts, their shapes might prohibit the direct route from A to R; or if the system were chemical the prohibition might be thermodynamic. But in either case, if the observer watched the machine work, and thought it alive, he might say: "How clever! x couldn't get from A to R directly because this bar was in the way; so x went to B, which made y carry x from B to C; and once at C, x could get straight back to R. I believe x shows foresight."

Both points of view are reasonable. A stable

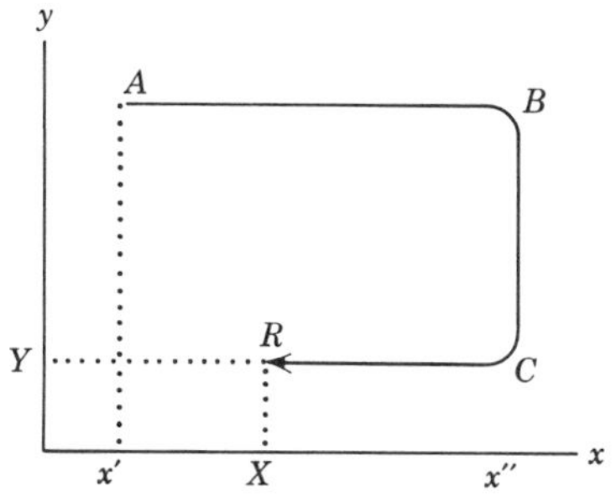

Fig. 10

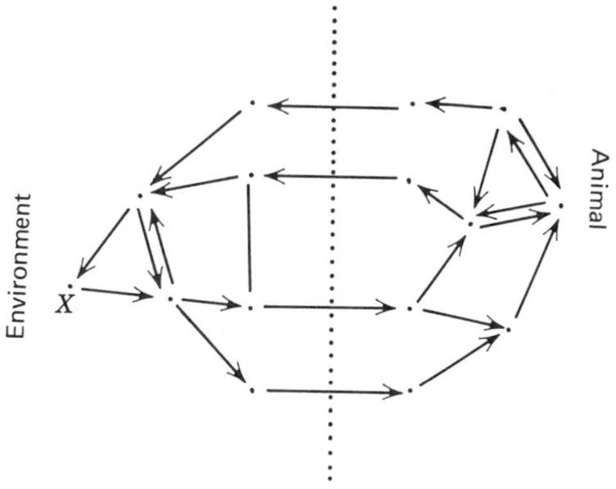

Fig. 11

system may be regarded both as blindly obeying the laws of its nature, and also as showing skill in getting back to its state of equilibrium in spite of obstacles.[5]

5/13. The second property is shown when an organism reacts to a variable with which it is not directly in contact. Suppose, for instance, that the diagram of immediate effects (S. 4/12) is that of Figure 11; the variables have been divided by the dotted line into "animal" on the right and "environment" on the left, and the animal is not in direct contact with the variable marked X. The system is assumed to be stable, i.e. to have arrived at the "adapted" condition. (S. 5/7). If disturbed, its changes will show co-ordination of part with part (S. 5/12), and this co-ordination will hold over the whole system (S. 4/18). It follows that the behaviour of the "animal"-part will be co-ordinated with the behaviour of X although the "animal" has no immediate contact with it.

[5] I would like to acknowledge that much of what I am describing was arrived at independently by G. Sommerhoff. I met his *Analytical Biology* only when the first edition of *Design for a Brain* was in proof, and I could do no more than add his title to my list of references. Since then it has become apparent that our work was developing in parallel, for there is a deep similarity of outlook and method in the two books. The superficial reader might notice some differences and think we are opposed, but I am sure the distinctions are only on minor matters of definition or emphasis. The reader who wishes to explore these topics further should consult his book as a valuable independent contribution.

In the higher organisms, and especially in Man, the power to react correctly to something not immediately visible or tangible has been called "imagination", or "abstract thinking", or several other names whose precise meaning need not be discussed at the moment. Here we should notice that the co-ordination of the behaviour of one part with that of another part not in direct contact with it is simply an elementary property of the stable system.

5/14. Let us now re-state our problem in the new vocabulary. If, for brevity, we omit minor qualifications, we can state it thus: A determinate "machine" changes from a form that produces chaotic, unadapted behaviour to a form in which the parts are so co-ordinated that the whole is stable, acting to maintain its essential variables within certain limits—how can this happen? For example, what sort of a thermostat could, if assembled at random, re-arrange its own parts to get itself stable for temperature?

It will be noticed that the new statement involves the concept of a machine changing its internal organization. So far, nothing has been said of this important concept; so it will be treated in the next chapter.

Homeostasis as a Unifying Concept in Personality Theory

ROSS STAGNER

The task of personality theory is to achieve generalizations having maximum applicability with maximum predictive value. Such generalizations may relate to personality as a feature of all human organisms, or to personality as the unique totality of a single individual. The most fruitful generalizations would seem to be those which are useful in both of these areas.

It is proposed here that the principle of homeostasis—the law that organisms seek to maintain constancy of inner tissue conditions—can be expanded into a major generalization in the field of personality theory. This principle can be shown to have value in illuminating personality considered both as a universal and as a unique phenomenon.

While the concept of homeostasis in itself needs no restatement here, the particular sequence of ideas to be developed calls for a beginning at the basic physiological level. Treating this very briefly, we shall then discuss in more detail some broader implications of the concept.

Homeostasis was first identified as a major biological concept in connection with the maintenance of essential tissue equilibria, such as the oxygen, temperature, glucose and other inner constants (31, 8). These inner constancies correspond to the basic biological needs upon which behavioristic theorists develop their conception of personality dynamics.

According to this view, any disturbance of essential constancy leads to tension, restless activity, contacting the needed substance, and restoration of equilibrium. As metabolism consumes glucose, for example, the hunger tension arises. Seeking-behavior results in the location and ingestion of food; the return to equilibrium is accompanied by quiescence.

It is, however, obvious that the organism does not simply continue to restore those biological equilibria which are essential to the existence of our protoplasm. While critics of homeostatic theory have suggested that this view offers only a static explanation of behavior, a recurrent restoration of a preexisting state, such interpretations are unfair to the theory. When a given tissue constancy is first disturbed, the organism mobilizes energy for action which ceases when the equilibrium is restored. *Recurrence* of this same disturbance is another matter. (1) The organism perceives minimal physiological changes as *cues* and *anticipates* the disturbance. Forestalling action therefore becomes possible. (We eat before we experience intense hunger pangs.) We suggest that energy mobilization for forestalling tactics must be explained in terms of a *cortical tension* which reflects the visceral-proprioceptive pattern of the original biological disequilibration. (2) The organism perceives environmental objects as potential sources of equilibrium-restoration and behaves differently toward them (hoarding food, building houses or nests, etc.). Thus, repeated disequilibration results in continuous modification of the organism and its perception of the external world. *Dynamic homeostasis* involves the maintenance of tissue constancies by establishing a constant physical environment—by reducing the variability and disturbing effects of external stimulation. Thus the organism does not simply restore the prior equilibrium. A new, more complex and more comprehensive equilibrium is established.

But it is not only the changes in physical situations which disturb tissue constancies. Persons become increasingly important to us from birth onward. To the infant the presence of mother is a *sign* of tissue constancy and physical-milieu constancy. The absence of mother becomes a sign of disequilibrium and threat. Thus, the mother's appearance, voice, etc., can become valued as a means to biological equilibrium. In the same way other changes in the social environment may come to function as signals for biological disturbance, and set off anxiety tensions, energy mobilization,

From *Psychological Review,* Vol. 58, 1951, pp. 5–17. Reprinted by permission of the author and the publisher.

and vigorous action toward the restoration of social-milieu constancy (12). The organism may then take anticipatory measures to prevent change in the *social* environment on subsequent occasions.

This sequence of events leads to the view of personality sketched in Figure 1, where it is suggested that the individual, dynamically striving to preserve his inner tissue constancies, moves successively to build a constant physical environment (second level), and a constant social environment (third level). These may be thought of as envelopes protecting the biological constancies. It is assumed that, in the typical sequence, demand for physical constancy emerges first and demand for social constancy second, the latter being based in considerable part upon the need for physical uniformity. This leads to the prediction that threats to the organism's physical environment will generally produce more vigorous energy-mobilizations than threats to the social constancies; and that actual biological disequilibrium will dominate over either of the others. For the most part this prediction is verified: under the pressure of physical hazard, social amenities disappear (13); and under extreme hunger or pain, the physical environment is likely to be disregarded. We shall consider later the case in which this prediction is not verified.

Homeostasis and Perceptual Constancy

Before elaborating further on the motivational aspects of homeostatic theory, it is desirable that we introduce a new thread into the pattern. An important part of stage two (the establishment of a constant physical milieu) is perceptual in character. The so-called "perceptual constancies" (size constancy, color constancy, etc.) must be introduced here if we are to get a clear picture of the extensive role played by the homeostatic principle in personality organization.

Every undergraduate student of psychology learns that objects tend to be visually perceived as having a constant size, shape and color under varying illuminations and at varying distances. It is noted that these external conditions make it physically impossible to have a constant retinal image; perceptual constancies are therefore central in basis. The teacher does not always point out to the undergraduate that such constancies have survival value; but it is fairly obvious that man could not have survived under primitive conditions if he failed to identify the small image of a saber-tooth tiger before it reached the size associated with immediate physical danger.

When observed from this point of view, the perceptual constancies appear to be another facet of homeostasis. The organism needs a constant external environment if it is to maintain constant tissue states. In attempting to reduce the variability of external stimuli (threats to equilibrium or sources of needed substances), the organism must deal with objects. But objects, as stimuli affecting the distance receptors, are protean in size, shape and color. Under such conditions adjustment is most difficult. The organism therefore *learns* to perceive identical objects as possessing these constant attributes.

The excellent treatment by Hebb (18) of the problem of perception has made it unnecessary to defend this suggestion. As Hebb has noted, the Gestalt emphasis on native factors in object perception should be restricted to the perception of *unity;* that is, the awareness of form and closure. The evidence he cites bears rather convincingly on the notion that *identity* must be a product of learning; indeed, it would seem that more than normal faith in mysterious organismic powers would be required to explain size-constancy on a nativistic basis.[1]

Hebb has placed rather less emphasis than seems justified upon the fact that perception is itself a purposive, need-directed process dominated by organismic homeostasis. It is interesting in this connection to consider the work of Adelbert Ames, Jr. (3), and the variety of research activities stimulated thereby (9, 17, *et al.*). It appears from these findings that even so simple a perception as that of two lines of light in a dark room is modified by the set or purpose of the observer, and that the perceived characteristics (size, shape and distance) of objects inhere in their relations to the purpose

[1] There is even reason, according to Raney and Carmichael (29, p. 16), to believe that both sensitivity and response are determined initially by inner, metabolic factors; and that outside stimuli acquire "meaning" in their function of interrupting or facilitating such endogenous behavior.

of the perceiver. Since—as the first section of this paper indicated—purposive activities can be subsumed under the homeostatic category, this line of reasoning confirms the view that the perceptual constancies are also to be considered as homeostatic manifestations.

Helson (19) has argued persuasively, and the data of other researchers agree, that the frame of reference of the individual tends toward a constant organization about a point determined by the geometric mean of his experiences with the class of stimuli presented. This suggests that the organism builds not merely a constancy for characteristics of individual objects, but also constancy for classes of objects. Thus Hastorf (17) notes that subjects make a projected rectangle of light larger when operating under the task-set of representing an envelope than when representing a calling card.

This is possibly the explanation for the finding of Bruner and Goodman (7) that poor children make a circle representing a 25-cent piece larger than it is made by well-to-do children. It may be that the "physically real" value (purchasing power) was greater for the poorer children; thus constancy would favor the larger size.

Physical perception of objects, and of classes of objects, as possessing constant characteristics, will aid survival. It becomes possible to contact needed substances and avoid noxious stimuli, to deal adaptively with physical reality; whereas reactions based directly upon the protean, ever-changing peripheral receptor process would induce only behavioral confusion.[2] We must maintain external as well as internal constancy.

Constancies in Social Perception

Perceptual constancies may very well contribute in a major way to the establishment of the uniform social milieu which has been suggested as the third level of homeostatic adjustment. Successful adaptation of the child to demands of his parents is unquestionably facilitated if he behaves on a "constancy hypothesis" with respect to them. Where reality constantly frustrates this tendency (very inconsistent real behavior by a parent), maladjustment seems invariably to result.

In later social development the same pattern appears. Our perception of individual personalities follows the constancy principle. If I observe Mr. Smith behaving in a weak, futile, ineffectual manner today, I shall be predisposed to perceive those same characteristics in his actions tomorrow (the so-called "halo" effect). This phenomenon is likewise adaptive and homeostatic in character. The person, in his efforts to achieve tissue constancy, must operate on some hypothesis as regards external reality. Since the constancy hypothesis proves useful in dealing with inanimate objects, it tends to be transferred to dealing with people. Further, infantile experiences usually reinforce the constancy hypothesis. Mother has a dependable relationship with food, comfort and security. Strangers are often associated with disturbance of equilibrium, thwarting of needs, pain, discomfort and insecurity. Thus the perception of specific individuals, and of classes of people, may become organized as constants and this may aid in adjustment. Unfortunately, or fortunately, as one chooses to view the phenomenon, humans do not in reality manifest such constancy as does an inanimate object. The perception of personality-constancy is thus projective and inaccurate in many instances, but is adhered to nevertheless.

Once a delineated percept for a given individual or group is established, it tends to persist. We overlook in our friends behavior that we bitterly criticize elsewhere. Undesirable characteristics simply are not perceived. Conversely, disliked individuals are seen as having "bad" traits even when no objective basis for this perception can be identified.[3]

Leeper (24) demonstrated the establishment of a constant percept for an ambiguous figure. By showing a picture which allowed only one

[2] We are intrigued, in this connection, with the work reported by Eysenck (11) and others on dark-vision of anxiety neurotics. It appears that such patients show a far greater loss of visual efficiency under dark adaptation than normals or hysterics. Could this be due, in anxiety cases, to the presence of a deep insecurity about these perceptual constancies? Does it mean that children who, for any reason, fail to stabilize firmly these percepts—under widely varying physical conditions—are prone to develop anxiety neurosis?

[3] A methodical analysis of perceptual constancies in the social field will be found in the recent monograph by Gustav Ichheiser (20). While we are in disagreement with minor parts in this treatment, it is generally supplementary to the basic thesis presented here.

alternative (from the ambiguous drawing) to be seen, he was able to fix the perception so that it was virtually impossible for subjects to get the other object. Edwards (10) verified the existence of a selective tendency based on established perceptions, tending to maintain constancy. He presented a speech containing an identical number of pro-New Deal and anti-New Deal statements to his subjects. Republicans remembered mostly anti-New Deal items (and distorted some favorable remarks into hostile comments); Democrats remembered pro-New Deal facts and ignored the others. Thus a percept of an idea or social object, once established, obeys the constancy principle.

The effect of reality (experience followed by action directed toward the object) no doubt is in the direction of modifying constancies established on an unrealistic basis. This process, in the field of physical reality, probably proceeds promptly and reliably. In social perceptions it is slower and less dependable. As the various studies of stereotypes of social groups indicate, such pictures develop without much basis in reality. Even when world events clearly have a bearing on the qualitative nature of this stereotype, it is modified but slowly (35). Thus we may generalize that a fundamental tendency of personality seemed to be one of perceiving constancy in individuals (or groups of individuals), and to behave toward them in terms of these perceived constancies.[4]

There is reason to believe (28, p. 107) that the preservation of a constant external environment is an aid to the development of a well-integrated ego. While we need not accept the analytic metaphor that "objects are internalized," we are on safe ground in stating that habits will function smoothly, and perceptual expectancies will be adequately related to objective reality, if this physical constancy is maintained.

The constancy of the social milieu is also important. The child establishes certain expectancies with regard to his parents—their personalities and behavior. He attains security as their actions fit into these expectancies. Furthermore, he imitates them, and develops certain expectancies for his own behavior patterned on theirs (the Freudian ego-ideal). Now, as Jacobson (21) and Plant (28) have noted, the effect of disappointment as regards their characteristics can be quite destructive of ego-integration, especially about the Oedipus age. It is worthy of note that both of these authors equate disappointment to disillusion. In our scheme this is equivalent to the disturbance of a perceptual constancy in the social field.

Need and Preference

Let us now turn to a criticism of homeostatic theory which is of considerable importance. This approach may be represented by P. T. Young (37), who has pointed out cogently that rats and humans may be motivated to more vigorous action by preference than by homeostatic need. The answer to this criticism can best be given in terms of perceptual phenomena.

We have already emphasized that the organism responds selectively to external stimuli when motivated by homeostatic tensions. Thus, certain perceived qualities of objects come to function as *cues* directing behavior toward these objects. It seems likely (1) that some such cues are innately given, in the sense that selective threshold differences are built into our nervous system. For example, mother's milk must be acceptable to the infant if the latter is to survive. We may therefore hypothesize that mammalian strains not provided with differential sensitivity to warm, sweet liquids were eliminated early in biological history. It is true, of course, that there are other substances which offer these cues (*cf.* Young's rats who chose saccharine solutions) but which are not homeostatic in character.

A realistic approach to behavior theory requires a consideration of the fact that modern conditions face the organism with new objects of indeterminate homeostatic significance. Man (presumably by Darwinian selection processes) is so biologically constituted that he has sensory mechanisms capable of reporting on most of the noxious stimuli having any considerable probability of occurrence in primitive life. Furthermore, these sensory selectivi-

[4] See Murphy (27, pp. 331–339) for a treatment of these phenomena in a rather different theoretical context.

ties are triggered to visceral tensions in such a way that violent activity is released by the perception of this cue (physical pain, for example).

Man has not, however, evolved sensory mechanisms for the detection of X-rays, gamma rays, and other noxious stimuli present in modern life. This does not constitute a criticism of homeostatic theory, but only a recognition of the fact that some new sources of tissue disequilibrium have been invented. Organic disturbances must set off behavioral activity by way of afferent fibers. When the sensory mechanism is inadequate to detect a harmful stimulus, no homeostatic protective action is possible.

Similarly, modern living presents us with many stimulus objects *perceived as identical* with those having homeostatic value. If these are preferred, though useless, it may mean an "error" on the part of the integrating mechanism; it does not invalidate the theory.

A further point merits consideration, namely the fact (2) that learning to identify objects as equilibrium-restoring is never mathematically perfect. The organism operates on a probability basis. In the language of hypothesis-learning, we may say something like this: "In the past, most warm, sweet liquids have served as tension-reducers. The probabities are high that this warm, sweet liquid is also need-satisfying in character." The phenomena of stimulus equivalence and positive transfer suggest that, within certain limits of discrimination threshold, objects presenting similar cues will be perceived as identical. Thus rats and men may *prefer* substances which are not homeostatic in function, but are incorrectly identified as such.

Preference for foods may be changed either by satiating with the preferred food or by creating a need for the nonpreferred substance (37). However, in the latter case it is necessary to break up the physically perceivable situation so that the preferred food does not affect the distance receptors simultaneously with the non-preferred. Otherwise the constancy based on former needs and tensions appears capable of blocking the establishment of a new habit adequate to the new need.

This seems to have considerable bearing on the success of reform or therapy. If the delinquent (or neurotic) is simply replaced in the environment which led him to develop maladjustive patterns of perceiving and acting, these are likely to be reinstated and to continue to dominate the motor system.

Young's own experiments (38) show conclusively that preferences can be built upon a homeostatic need. It thus appears far more defensible to hold that homeostasis is the primary motivational principle involved, and that preference (palatability, affectivity) is simply a derivative based upon (1) inherent sensitivity thresholds of homeostatic significance, or (2) non-discriminable differences from signs of homeostatic goal-objects.

At this point it will be well also to deal briefly with two less fundamental criticisms of homeostatic motivation theory. One of these calls attention to the fairly obvious fact that, in the short run at least, people often indulge in behavior which is disequilibrating; the other, that behavior directed to the maintenance of a constant state sometimes takes such a form as to prevent the achievement of that state. Neither of these objections seems to carry much weight.

The relationship between short-run disequilibrium and long-run equilibrium has been dealt with rather adequately by Freeman (14), following the excellent analysis by Freud (16). That men do in fact go on fasts, climb mountains, hunt dangerous animals and in other ways disturb constant states is a truism. That such behavior violates the principle of homeostasis is not a truism.

The organism is constantly faced with the necessity for maintaining a variety of constant states and hence with the task of determining priorities. It seems safe to assume that within the biological needs, the relative survival significance of a given demand is keyed to dominance of the motor system: that is, that the hierarchy of physiological drives is a function of the threat to survival implied by a given deprivation. As we move from this level to the maintenance of a constant physical and a constant social environment, we encounter more difficulty in ascertaining the principles upon which dominance is based. It should be clear, nonetheless, that the organism in some way evolves standards of value, in terms of which choice is made as to the particular constancy which gets priority. Probably the history of the individual is decisive in this respect.

The facts indicate that the epithet "coward" may be more disturbing to equilibrium than the physical danger of facing a wild animal. Or, the humiliation of losing valued social status may be more upsetting than the physiological disequilibrium induced by mountain climbing. In terms of the view presented here, such choices will be functions of the perception of these alternatives, and this in turn will depend upon the number and kind of reinforcements related to such percepts. In one boy's family, physical prowess is constantly praised and rewarded; in another, it is ignored or depreciated. There is a significant relationship here to Freud's reality-principle; a short-run or minor disequilibrium may be accepted in order to achieve a long-run or major equilibrium. A fruitful approach to this problem is that of Mowrer (26), which utilizes the observation that some people orient their behavior to the rewards or punishments physically present or near in *time,* neglecting those to follow in the future. In the context of the present paper, the phenomenon is one of *perceiving as larger* that which is closer in time.

The second objection refers to those acts which ostensibly aim at restoring equilibrium but in fact prevent it. Thus we have the instance of the insecure, affection-starved woman who, in demanding love from people, so frightens them that she becomes even more insecure. When phrased thus, the problem promptly vanishes. No proponent of homeostatic theory has ever claimed that the organism did not make errors. Probably a young lion, trying to catch game, often is overeager and loses his dinner; this may be considered unfortunate—for him—but does not deny the applicability of homeostasis to his behavior.

This difference, of course, needs to be noted; the lion learns to correct his seeking behavior, or else he dies. The neurotic does not, without guidance, learn to identify and eliminate his errors; on the contrary, he is most likely to establish an artificial constancy, perhaps on a fantasy level, in which his acts are not errors. That such inherently unstable equilibria lead to a piling up of residual tension and so eventually to breakdown has been aptly stated by Freeman (14), as in a different context by all the psychoanalysts. Sex conflicts lead to neuroses, whereas conflicts about food do not, because an unstable equilibrium with regard to food-need results in the destruction of the organism. Perception of non-food objects as edible, and of food as inedible, means suicide. Such a perceptual constancy, as regards sex, may be extremely uncomfortable—and yet, as the patient sees it, more acceptable than the apparent alternative. It seems likely that neurotic equilibria becomes stabilized only with regard to conflicts which do not violate the most comprehensive constancy of all—the maintenance of the total organism as a going concern.

Ego-Constancy and Ego-Motivation

Let us now return to the problem raised in an earlier passage, the problem of the dominance of social constancies over biological constancies. This is the problem raised by exceptions to the suggestion made earlier, that biological demands finally control perception and behavior. How can homeostatic theory deal with the artist who starves in a garret to express his ideas, the martyr who prefers physical pain to an abandonment of his beliefs?

The solution to this problem seems to depend upon the evolution of a new perceptual object, the self or ego, and the establishment of a perceptual constancy with regard to it. The theory of the development of the ego as an object of perception has been presented adequately elsewhere (23, 2, 32). The tendency toward perceptual constancy will operate to hold constant the self-image. Since the ego will be repeatedly perceived as part of a total situation involving the restoration of biological equilibrium, physical constancy and social uniformity, it can become a highly-valued cue-object for the maintenance of all needed equilibria. The possibilities of mutual reinforcement (by different inner tensions) and of overvaluing the ego as object are therefore obvious.

The maintenance of ego-constancy may involve physical, social or individual uniformities. The child may seek to maintain himself in relation to physical patterns of security or symbols of prestige, such as toys, clothing, etc.; or he may focus on dominance or submission, exhibitionism or withdrawal, as social patterns; or he may try to act out verbal labels attached to him by adults, such as studious, "bad boy," artistic, or stupid.

The self-image (including the relation of self to environment) so evolved represents a "constant state" which the organism seeks to preserve. As such it may dominate the motor system and may even prevent homeostatic action based on earlier physical or social constancies. The person defending his ego-system of percepts and values may accept social ostracism or even physical disequilibrium. The mature ego, therefore, has its own constancy function; it tends to render the personality more independent of random changes in the physical or social milieu.

In this connection it should (unfortunately, perhaps) be emphasized that only a modest percentage of people really come to value ego-constancy as highly as often-cited examples would suggest. Thus, we need only look at Germany, where most people, even in the professional classes, abandoned valued portions of the self-image in order to preserve biological, physical and social constancies under the Nazi regime.

We suggest, however, that in some individuals a modification of the schema shown in Fig. 1 is necessary. For these persons the self or ego becomes a perceptual object, the constancy of which is highly valued. It may dominate over the social milieu, as when a person suffers ostracism for his ideals; or even over the physical environment, as in the man who indulges in hazardous activities for ego-gratification.

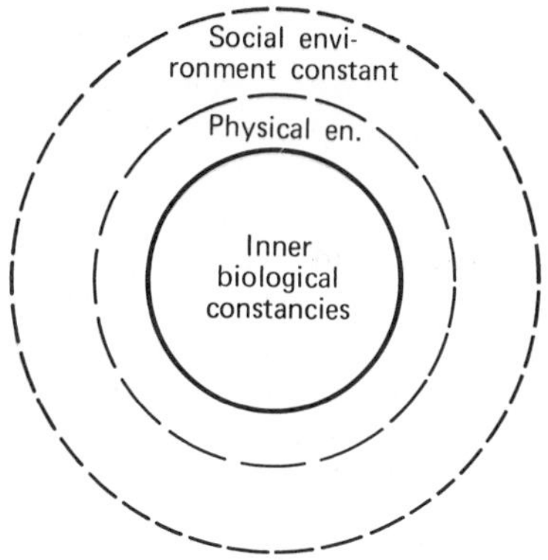

Fig. 1. The inner tissue constancies are most resistant to disturbance, and mobilize maximum energy to restore equilibrium. The physical environment is maintained constant by perceptual and functional activities, as is the social environment. Individuals differ in the extent to which physical or social constancies will be defended.

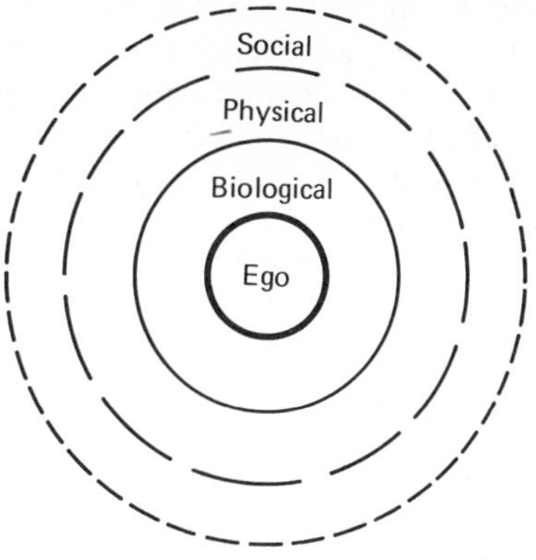

Fig. 2. In some personalities, ego-constancies come to dominate the motor system even to the exclusion of biological constant states.

Finally, in extreme forms, it may be represented as in Fig. 2, where the individual actually is more disturbed by loss of ego integrity than by hunger or pain.

The motivational potency of threats to the ego will depend, then, on the pattern of constancies an individual is trying to maintain, and upon their relative dominance. In everyday life this is likely to be ascertained by observing the types of disequilibrating stimuli which are most effective in mobilizing his energies. Thus we may find John (a viscerotonic, in Sheldon's schema) concerned mostly with his vegetative functions; he lives to eat, and is most profoundly disturbed by any stimulus which interferes with his visceral peace. Harry, on the other hand (perhaps an Adlerian case), may be concerned primarily with status equilibrium; his motivation is ego-centered, and any stimulus perceived as a threat to status sets off a violent reaction. Tom (studied by a Freudian, hence an anal-erotic) has an equilibrium based on order, scheduling and precision of physical arrangement; any interference with these patterns may be profoundly disturbing to him. Obviously, any number of such illustrations could be offered.

For the purposes of clinical personality study, it is more fruitful to investigate the particular *pattern of perceptual constancies* most characteristic of the person, rather than to hunt for behavioral constancies. Thus the orthodox analytic procedure is likely to determine father-figures, mother-figures, situations symbolizing traumatic (disequilibrating) stimuli, and so on. The non-directivists are concerned to obtain knowledge of the client's self-image, as well as his perception of reassuring and threatening social objects.

Action, of course, is directed by perception, not by the "physically real" stimulus. Under most conditions this is adaptive; it is, indeed, our justification for the survival value of the perceptual constancies. When the physically presented stimulus is so contrived as to give a perception of a radically different object (as in certain of the Ames demonstrations), behavior is governed by the percept, not by the intellectually known reality.

Clinical psychologists are, of course, familiar with this phenomenon. The patient perceives a harmless situation as involving a drastic threat to his ego. He may rationally know the threat to be non-existent; it may be demonstrated logically or even empirically to be non-threatening. Nevertheless, as long as the perception holds, the behavior is governed by perception, not by knowledge.

The importance of this point for social psychology was developed by Kurt Lewin (25) in a penetrating essay. Rational, intellectual education against prejudice, in favor of new ways of dealing with human-relations problems, is doomed to failure unless it is accompanied by education for a new way of perceiving the situation. If minority groups continue to be perceived as having undesirable characteristics, behavior toward them will be discriminatory. We may even say that, within this restricted frame of reference, prejudice is rational; if the physically real minority group member had these traits, it would be proper to discriminate. The same, of course, can be said of the neurotic; a man would be a fool if he were not defensive when surrounded by the terrifying dangers which people the neurotic's environment. It is only by undermining the "unreal" perception that we can make progress.

In social relationships, behavioral constancy also reinforces perceptual constancy. If a man enters a group and perceives the other men as aggressive toward him, he will probably behave in such a way as to evoke aggression. A woman who attends a tea expecting to be snubbed may stay away from others and thus elicit non-accepting responses; she then concludes that her original perception of the situation was correct. There is, consequently, a major difference between the homeostatic process in the perception of physical and of social situations. Erroneous perceptions of physical constancies are automatically selfcorrecting; in the quest for need-gratification, behavior based on inadequate perceptions will fail of reinforcement. Because of the mechanism just sketched, behavior based on erroneous perceptions of social situations may be reinforced; thus an artificial constancy of the perceived environment is perpetuated.

According to the work of Frenkel-Brunswik (15) and her collaborators, intolerance of ambiguity is in itself a major personality variable. The secure individual is not seriously disturbed by unclear physical percepts or equivocal emotional relationships. Certain insecure personalities, on the other hand, seem to be quite upset by any deviation from clearly defined structures, either perceptual or emotional. This quest for security through rigidity may be a function of having change and uncertainty forced upon the child before he is mature enough, or the ego-system well enough organized, to accept them. Many neurotics are capable of normal functioning in a constant environment, but they are thrown into panic by even minor changes. Clearly, in these cases, ego-constancy has *not* been successfully developed to replace physical and social constancies.

Projective Tests

Projective tests reveal the inner personality to the extent that they expose perceptual constancies. If, in a series of Rorschach blots, the person repeatedly perceives objects in disturbed motion, or if he seems able to see only minute, carefully delineated forms, the clinician is provided with supposedly valuable information. When a series of TAT productions gives repeated characterizations of father-figures as stern, punishing and repressive, we feel that something of importance has been ascertained. The relative value of specific tests is largely a function of the extent to which they tap important percepts, particularly if the characteristics of these percepts are, for one or another reason, not available to conscious report.

Projective tests are more useful than reality situations for diagnostic purposes. The percept in the latter case is likely to be a compromise between a value corresponding to true "constancy" and that dictated by the physical stimulus.[5] Even the neurotic does not perceive all social situations as equally threatening. While his "constancy" hypothesis may be that all adult males are threatening, the smile, voice, etc., of a specific male acquaintance may give him some reassurance. The ambiguous projective situation thus gives a more valid insight into this inner determinant of behavior than many reality situations.

Therapy

The purpose of therapy, of course, is to help the patient achieve a realistic equilibrium in place of the unstable neurotic pattern he has evolved. Behavior aimed at the achievement of realistic need-gratifications and inner homeostasis is blocked by a pattern of inappropriate perceptual constancies. Therapy, then, must operate by modifying these perceptions of the self and the environment (*cf.* 33). Just as suggestion from a person of prestige may modify the perception of a social object (5), so suggestion from the respected therapist may induce modification of a perceived personal relationship. In the analytic situation, reactivation of infantile emotions without punishment and without rejection often leads to restructuring of percepts involved. This is not accomplished without extensive disturbances of equilibrium, and profound tensions within the patient.

As with projective tests, it is apparently possible in therapy (specifically, in the transference relationship) to evoke relatively "pure" emotions freed of reality factors. That is, if the therapist succeeds in keeping himself unclearly structured, the patient may project onto the therapist his image of one or more emotion-arousing figures; and the patient's experienced emotion in this case is uncomplicated by the reality features of the immediate situation. Since this makes an excellent opening for the therapist to demonstrate the projective character of the patient's perceptions, it offers an optimal chance for corrective work.

The modern trend in therapy calls for guided efforts at reality-testing by the patient (1, pp. 87–94). It is important that this be done if therapeutic gains are to transfer to everyday life, but it is futile to urge reality experimentation prior to insight and perceptual modification. Indeed, the neurotic at the onset of therapy will claim that he has tested reality and found it wanting. What he does not realize is that he never actually contacted reality; he perceived only his own projected universe of constant threats and frustrations. Thus a change in perception of the self and the environment is a necessary preliminary to practice of new patterns.[6]

Implicit in the foregoing is the notion that therapy, in the early stages, leads to a disturbance of equilibrium. Neurosis is homeostatic in character; the neurotic has established his stable environment, with some dependable need-gratifications; even a painful symptom serves its purpose in the psychic economy. Phobias, compulsions, paralyses and other psychopathologies aid in the preservation of a precarious balance between gratification and threat.

If therapy is to be successful, this stable environment must be restructured. The patient immediately reacts to this as a threat, with consequences familiar to all clinicians. As Bergler (6) has noted, "what neurotics fear most" is a disturbance of this formula, or "basic fallacy," which we have shown to be a form of perceptual constancy. It should not be surprising, furthermore, if modes of perceiving practiced for twenty or thirty years cannot be modified overnight.

[5] This happens also in the laboratory. *Cf.* particularly the studies cited by Woodworth (36, pp. 605–621).

[6] It is perhaps worth noting that the same symptomatic pattern of constancies can be produced by quite divergent series of events. Let us consider (a) a young woman who felt rejected by her parents, although she was in fact physically secure; who developed a fantasy of being orphaned, of being punished for some mysterious but enormous guilt; and who in consequence perceived herself as inadequate and worthless. Contrast (b) a young woman who was in fact orphaned, treated brutally by a family with whom she was placed, and indoctrinated with feelings of sin and guilt in a religious orphanage. The perceptual constancies which characterize the two personalities may be superficially quite similar; but in case (b) they have been reinforced so much more regularly and intensely that the therapeutic task is vastly harder. Even years of life under relatively secure economic and domestic conditions may fail to modify these constancies.

Motivation is necessary if this restructuring is to be achieved. A person comes for therapy only when he is aware of a discrepancy between the equilibrium he has attained and that formerly possessed, or that believed to be attainable. There is nothing about the concept of homeostasis that is defeatist in character. While it is true that some pathological equilibria seem so stable as to defy therapeutic intervention (schizophrenias), it is generally possible to set up for the patient a fantasied new situation with a more favorable balance than he has achieved. Such phenomena as the positive transference can be utilized to provide some gratification, counterbalancing the painful effects of disequilibration as therapy proceeds. As therapy approaches its conclusion, many patients also show symptoms of disturbance as this new equilibrium must in turn be abandoned. Only the presence of these motivational factors makes possible the therapeutic modification of perceptions; the neuromuscular system is subservient to the vegetative system.

Summary

Homeostasis is accepted as a general biological law. Since personality is developed on a biological foundation, it must follow homeostatic principles to some extent. Actually, these principles recur in many aspects of the psychology of personality.

Considering personality as a universal, we find the maintenance of constant states not only at the microscopic level (tissue conditions) but also at macroscopic levels (objects in the physical environment, and persons in the social environment). Physical and social constancies are shown to function in the service of tissue constancies. Disturbances at these macroscopic levels set off vigorous energy mobilizations comparable with those induced by disequilibrium on the tissue level. Constancies may be perceptual (uniform percept with varying "real" stimuli) or functional (manipulation of the "real" environment to reduce variation).

With reference to personality as a unique individual phenomenon, it is suggested that the homeostatic approach is useful in several ways. (1) The personality is characterized by the particular equilibria, disturbance of which gives rise to maximum energy mobilization, and by the particular perceptual constancies, especially social and ego constancies, which have been developed. (2) Neurotic, unrealistic equilibria can develop with reference to needs not directly involved in organismic survival, *e.g.*, sex. Such unrealistic equilibria involve perceptual constancies not appropriate to the "real" situation, but often reinforced because resultant behavior seems to lead to confirmation of the constancy hypothesis. (3) Projective tests may give a more adequate picture of these constancies than would result from observation in "real" situations. (4) Therapy involves disturbing the neurotic equilibrium, restructuring the unrealistic percepts, and evolving a new equilibrium providing more need-gratification.

REFERENCES

1. Alexander, F., & French, T. M. *Psychoanalytic therapy*. New York: Ronald Press Co., 1946.
2. Allport, G. W. *Personality: a psychological interpretation*. New York: Henry Holt & Co., 1937.
3. Ames, A., Jr. Some demonstrations concerned with the origin and nature of our sensations (what we experience). Hanover, N. H.: The Hanover Institute, 1946 (mimeo.).
4. Angyal, A. *Foundations for a science of personality*. New York: Commonwealth Fund, 1941.
5. Asch, S. E., Block, H., & Hertzman, M. Studies in principles of judgments and attitudes. I. *J. Psychol.*, 1938, **5**, 219–251.
6. Bergler, E. What neurotics dread most—loss of the "basic fallacy." *Psychoanal. Rev.*, 1946, **33**, 148–153.
7. Bruner, J. S., & Goodman, C. C. Value and need as organizing factors in perception. *J. abnorm. soc. Psychol.*, 1947, **42**, 33–44.
8. Cannon, W. B. *The wisdom of the body*. New York: W. W. Norton, 1932.
9. Cantril, H. *Understanding man's social behavior (preliminary notes)*. Princeton: Office of Public Opinion Research, 1947.
10. Edwards, A. L. Political frames of reference as a factor influencing recognition. *J. abnorm. soc. Psychol.*, 1941, **36**, 34–50
11. Eysenck, H. J. *Dimensions of personality*. London: Kegan Paul, Trench, Trubner & Co., 1946.
12. Fletcher, J. M. Homeostasis as an explanatory principle in psychology. PSYCHOL. REV., 1942, **49**, 80–87.

13. Franklin, J. C., Schiele, B. C., Brozek, J., & Keys, A. Observations on human behavior in experimental semistarvation and rehabilitation. *J. clin. Psychol.*, 1948, **4**, 28–45.
14. Freeman, G. L. *Energetics of human behavior.* Ithaca, N. Y.: Cornell Univ. Press, 1948.
15. Frenkel-Brunswik, Else. Intolerance of ambiguity as an emotional and perceptual personality variable. *J. Personality*, 1949, **18**, 108–143.
16. Freud, S. *Beyond the pleasure principle.* Vienna: International Psychoanalytical Press, 1922.
17. Hastorf, A. H. Influence of suggestion on relationship between stimulus size and perceived distance. *J. Psychol.*, 1950, **29**, 195–217.
18. Hebb, D. O. *Organization of behavior.* New York: John Wiley & Sons, 1949.
19. Helson, H. Adaptation level as a frame of reference for prediction of psychological data. *Amer. J. Psychol.*, 1947, **60**, 1–29.
20. Ichheiser, G. Misunderstandings in human relations. *Amer. J. Sociol.*, 1949, **55**, Part 2.
21. Jacobson, E. Effect of disappointment on ego and superego formation in normal and depressive development. *Psychoanal. Rev.*, 1946, **33**, 129–147.
22. Katz, D., & Braly, K. Racial stereotypes of 100 college students. *J. abnorm. soc. Psychol.*, 1933, **28**, 280–290.
23. Koffka, K. *Principles of Gestalt psychology.* New York: Harcourt, Brace & Co., 1935.
24. Leeper, R. W. Study of a neglected portion of the field of learning—the development of sensory organization. *J. genet. Psychol.*, 1935, **46**, 41–75.
25. Lewin, K., & Grabbe, P. Conduct, knowledge and acceptance of new values. *J. soc. Issues,* 1945, **1**, 53–63.
26. Mowrer, O. H., & Ullman, A. D. Time as a determinant in integrative learning. *Psychol. Rev.*, 1945, **52**, 61–90.
27. Murphy, G. *Personality: a biosocial approach to origins and structure.* New York: Harper & Bros., 1947.
28. Plant, J. S. *Personality and the cultural pattern.* New York: Commonwealth Fund, 1937.
29. Raney, E. T., & Carmichael, L. Localizing responses to tactual stimuli in the fetal rat in relation to the psychological problem of space perception. *J. genet. Psychol.*, 1934, **45**, 3–21.
30. Rappaport, D. Principles underlying projective tests. *Character & Pers.*, 1942, **10**, 213–219.
31. Richter, C. P. Animal behavior and internal drives. *Quart. Rev. Biol.*, 1927, **2**, 307–343.
32. Sherif, M., & Cantril, H. *Psychology of ego-involvements.* New York: John Wiley & Sons, 1947.
33. Snygg, D., & Combs, A. W. *Individual behavior.* New York: Harper & Bros., 1949.
34. Stagner, R. *Psychology of personality.* New York: McGraw-Hill Book Co., 1948.
35. ———, & Osgood, C. E. Impact of war on a nationalistic frame of reference. I. *J. soc. Psychol.*, 1946, **24**, 187–215.
36. Woodworth, R. S. *Experimental psychology.* New York: Henry Holt & Co., 1938.
37. Young, P. T. Food-seeking drive, affective process, and learning. *Psychol. Rev.*, 1949, **56**, 98–121.
38. ———, & Chaplin, J. P. Studies of food preference, appetite and dietary habit. III. Palatability and appetite in relation to bodily need. *Comp. Psychol. Monogr.*, 1945, **18**, 1–45.

Mathematical Aspects of General Systems Analysis

ANATOL RAPOPORT

"General system theory" subsumes an outlook or a methodology rather than a theory in the sense ascribed to this term in science. The salient feature of this outlook is, as its name implies, an emphasis on those aspects of objects or events which derive from general properties of systems rather than from the specific content. Clearly, then, the power and the scientific fruitfulness of general system theory depends on whether in fact there exist properties common to all systems, and if so whether important consequences can be derived from these properties. This, in turn, depends on the way "system" is defined or, in a pragmatic sense, on what portions of the world one chooses to regard as systems.

The system-theoretic point of view received its impetus from two sources: first, a realization of the inadequacy of "mechanism" as a universal model; second, a tendency to counteract the fractionation of science into mutually isolated specialties. A radical critique of the mechanistic outlook was voiced already in the 1920's by Alfred North Whitehead (in *Science and the Modern World*). A principal thesis in that book was a warning that the store of fundamental ideas on which the then contemporary science was based (the "intellectual capital," as Whitehead called it) was becoming depleted. The implication was that unless a new source of ideas were tapped, science would face a dead end. Whitehead suggested that the concept of "organism," hitherto neglected in physical science, might be a source of new ideas.

Actually the concept of organism has always been fundamental in biology. Its exclusion from physics marked the beginning of modern physical science. This exclusion was necessary in order to free physics from the dead hand of Aristotelian philosophy with its emphasis on teleological goal-seeking determinants of motion. In this framework of thought, philosophers sought to explain the falling of stones by the "nature" of stones and the rising of smoke by the "nature" of smoke. The "nature" of an object or a substance was supposed to prescribe for it its proper or natural position, and so motion was explained by the supposed striving of each object or substance to attain its natural position.

This teleological conception of motion proved to be sterile and was rejected by Galileo and his successors in favor of the mechanistic conception. In this conception, it was not some final sought-after state of affairs, but the combination of forces acting on a body at a given moment, that determined its motion, namely via instantaneous changes of velocity. The observed motion was a sequence of these instantaneous changes. In this scheme, the "nature" of the moving body and of its "proper" position has no place.

The phenomenal success of classical physics (which was nurtured entirely on the mechanistic view) attests to the fruitfulness of this view. The difficulty of incorporating in it the behavior of living systems attests to its limitations. Both the strength and the limitations of the mechanistic outlook reside in the mathematical methods used in the construction of mechanistic theories. The fundamental tool of this method is the differential equation which is essentially a precise statement about how certain quantities and their rates of change are related. For example, the law of motion of a particle in a gravitational field is expressed by a relationship involving the acceleration suffered by the particle and the strength and direction of the field at a particular time in a particular place. But the strength and direction of the field depend on the position of the particle, and its acceleration involves the second derivatives (the rates of change of the rates of change) of the position coordinates. In other words, a law of motion is expressed by a differential equation. The solution of such a differential equation gives the position of the

From *The Sciences of Man: Problems and Orientations*, Unesco/Mouton & Co., n.v., The Hague, 1968. Reprinted by permission of Unesco.

particle for all time to come, once the initial position and velocity and the nature of the gravitational field are known. The immense predictive power of celestial mechanics derives from this deterministic character of the differential equation.

If several bodies are involved, the gravitational field associated with each of them affects the accelerations of all of them. Their motions would then be described by a *system* of differential equations in which the relations between the positions and the accelerations are all interwoven by a network of interdependencies. Now if the differential equations comprising a system are linear, i.e., if the variables and their rates of change appear at most in the first degree, the same general methods of solution apply regardless of how many equations are involved. However, the differential equations describing motions of bodies in the gravitational field associated with them are not linear (since the gravitational forces are inversely proportional to the squares of distance, between the bodies). Consequently the equations are not solvable by the known general methods.

Fortunately for the success of the mechanistic method, the solar system, with which classical celestial mechanics was concerned, constituted a special, tractable case of several bodies in motion. The sun is so huge compared even to the largest of the planets that the mutual gravitational forces among the planets can be neglected in the first approximation. That is to say, the motion of each planet can be calculated with good approximation as if it and the sun were the only two bodies in the universe. This is the so-called two-body problem, which can be solved by classical methods. To obtain better approximations, the mathematicians of the eighteenth and nineteenth centuries made use of the so-called perturbation method, in which the influences of the other planets were superimposed on the solutions of the separate two-body problems. The success of these methods was assured by the weakness of interdependence among these separate two-body problems. Had these interdependencies been strong (if, for example, the masses of the planets were comparable to that of the sun), the mathematicians would have been faced with an N-body problem, which has not been solved in the general form to our day.

Thus the specific nature of the solar system had both a stimulating and an inhibiting effect on the development of applied mathematics. On the one hand, the success of mathematical methods made the physicists supremely confident in the power of these methods and led to the creation of mathematical physics, which to this day remains *the* model of completely rigorous science. On the other hand, the successful methods became "fixated" in the minds of workers in applied mathematics, who sought to formulate problems in ways which made them tractable by those methods. Consequently, many phenomena remained outside the scope of mathematized (i.e., completely rigorous) science.

The most important of these phenomena are those involving instances of "organized complexity." Mathematically an "organized complexity" can be viewed as a set of objects or events whose description involves many variables, among which there are strong mutual interdependencies, so that the resulting system of equations cannot be solved "piece-meal," as in the case of classical celestial mechanics, where perturbations can be imposed on two-body problems.

In our experience, the living organism is the most obvious example of "organized complexity." Attempts to represent the living organism as a mechanism have been unsuccessful except in extremely limited contexts, usually quite tangential to the central problem, that of describing the living process (including behavior) in mechanistic terms. Awareness of this limitation propelled some philosophers (for example, Bergson) and some biologists (for example, H. Driesch) toward vitalism, which excludes the prospect of eventually explaining living processes in terms of known physical and chemical processes. The vitalists postulated special "vital forces" to account for phenomena associated with life. Other philosophers, while avoiding the refuge of ad hoc concepts like "vital force," emphasized the necessity of re-organizing or extending the conceptual repertoire of science in order to bring "organized complexity" within its scope. This was the meaning of A. N. Whitehead's warning that the intellectual capital accumulated in the seventeenth century (i.e., the mechanistic method of analysis) was becoming depleted.

The mechanistic method of analysis can be understood in a sense broader than that of classical mechanics. It includes all forms of analysis which seek to explain the working of a whole in terms of the working of its parts. Such an approach characterizes not only classical celestial mechanics (in which the behavior of the solar system emerges from the behavior of individual "point masses" which comprise it) but also the methods of physiology in which the life process is viewed in terms of sequences of chemical reactions; the method of behavioristic psychology which conceives of behavior as a totality of "responses to stimuli"; classical market economics, which pictures the economic process as a totality of actions of individuals motivated to buy or to sell by the fluctuations of supply and demand, etc. In short, in a broader sense the mechanistic outlook is an extension of the Laplacian idea that the universe (or any portion of the universe singled out by our attention) can be explained if the laws governing its constituent atomic units are known. Roughly speaking, it is a view which holds the whole to be the sum of its parts. The often cited negation of this view, "The whole is greater than the sum of its parts," should be regarded not as a denial of a well known tautology but rather as an expression of the inadequacy of the mechanistic view.

An antithesis to the mechanistic outlook is a view which makes some "whole" the starting point of investigation. According to this view, the laws governing the behavior of the whole are taken as primary. To the extent that one is interested in the behavior of the parts, one seeks to deduce them from the laws governing the behavior of the whole. Thus one would seek to deduce the behavior of individuals from the roles they play in an institution or a society, which is supposedly governed by laws relevant to *that* level of organization. In this approach, the problem of synthesizing the behavior of the whole from that of the parts is by-passed. This view, which can be called the organismic, still prevails in certain areas of biological and social science. For example, when a physiologist explains the action of an organ in terms of its contribution to the survival of the organism, or when a cultural anthropologist of the "functionalist" school explains a practice or belief in terms of how it fits into a "culture pattern," each is using the organismic approach.

The organismic approach brings into focus the "whole," which often eludes the methods of the mechanistic approach. The weakness of the organismic approach stems from its tendency toward teleological explanation, which, as we have already seen, had led pre-Galilean physical science into an impasse.

General system theory, or at least its mathematical aspect, can be viewed as an effort to fuse the mechanistic and the organismic approaches so as to utilize the advantages of each. A system is not merely a totality of units (particles, individuals), each governed by laws of causality operating upon it, but rather a totality of *relations* among such of these units. The emphasis is on organized complexity, i.e., on the circumstance that the addition of a new entity introduces not only the relation of this entity to all others but also modifies the relations among all the other entities. The more tightly interwoven is the network of relations, the more organized is the *system* comprised by the relations. *Degree of organization*, then, becomes the central concept of the system-theoretic view. Theories engendered by this view have been called (among other things) contributions to general system theory.

A second impetus to general systems theory came, as we have said, from a perceived need to counteract the excessive specialization in science which had been threatening to sever all communication among scientists in different fields, or even different subfields of the same field, for want of a common technical language. This view was forcefully voiced by Norbert Wiener in his book, *Cybernetics*.[1] Cybernetics is an example of a discipline which cuts across the established disciplines of science and by doing so provides opportunities for communication among scientists from different disciplines.

While the organismic view, proposed by Whitehead and other philosophers of similar

[1] The singling out of authors as proponents of views does not imply priority. Thus L. Bertalanffy, to whom, incidentally the term "general system theory" is credited, anticipated Wiener in pointing out the necessity of counteracting the fractionation of science. We mention Wiener in order to emphasize the importance of cybernetics in providing a framework of concrete ideas which have stimulated recent developments in general system theory.

persuasion, was hardly more than an expression of awareness of the problem posed by the inadequacy of the mechanistic view, cybernetics became a concrete example of how the system concepts could be developed without departing from the standards of rigor demanded in physical science. For cybernetics is a mathematical method specifically developed to describe "organized complexity."

Cybernetics has been defined as the science of communication and control. It first developed in the context of problems associated with the development of complex weapons systems equipped with automatic guidance and control devices. Similar problems arose also in the design of communication systems and of high speed computers. Almost simultaneously, Wiener, a pioneer in cybernetics, and Claude E. Shannon, who first formulated rigorously the foundations underlying the mathematical theory of communication, recognized the cardinal principle involved in all of these problems, namely that of "amount of information." The concept of information is as central in cybernetics and communication engineering as the concept of energy is in classical physics.

Energy had been the unifying concept underlying all physical phenomena involving work and heat. Information became the unifying concept underlying the working of organized systems, i.e., systems whose behavior was under control so as to achieve some pre-set goals. This control is accomplished by processes involving the coding, the storage, and the transmission of information. In this way the organismic, "teleological" notions of goal-seeking behavior were reintroduced into the theory of physical processes. In this modern version, however, these notions are derived not from metaphysical speculations on the "nature" of the behaving entities but from the mathematical structure of systems characterized by organized complexity.

Since "amount of information" is defined in purely mathematical terms, this concept is applicable to the analysis of all phenomena in which organized, specifically goal-seeking behavior is involved. Thus the ideas of cybernetics have served not only in extending rigorous mathematical methods to the study of organized complexity but also as a source of concepts cutting across the disciplines. In this way the ideas of cybernetics have been instrumental in counteracting the alienation between scientists who had become isolated from each other by virtue of the barriers set up by specialized technical language.

An example of this integrating function of cybernetics is seen in the fusion of biological and physical concepts which cybernetics has stimulated. The concept of "the amount of information" has played an important part in this fusion. "The amount of information" required to describe some state of affairs is roughly related to the average (expected) amount of guessing required to guess the actual state of affairs among all the possible ones. Thus, if I ask you to guess the number which I have arbitrarily selected from the numbers between one and one million, it will take you (on the average) more guesses to determine this number than if I had selected it from one to one hundred. (A "guess" is understood as a question which can be answered by "yes" or "no.")

It can be easily seen that a number from one to one hundred can always be guessed in seven guesses, while a number from one to a million can always be guessed in twenty guesses. To do this one needs to make guesses in such a way as to eliminate one half of the remaining range. In the case of a million one starts with "Is it less than 500,000?" If yes, "Is it less than 250,000?" If no, then "Is it less than 375,000?" etc. Since one million is less than 2^{20}, it will take at most 20 such dichotomies to determine the number.

So far we have assumed that the selection of each number in the range is equally probable. If this is not the case, the "amount of information" is reduced. Specifically, let p_n be the probability that the number n has been selected from the range $1 \leq n \leq N$. Then it can be shown that $H(n) = -\sum_{n=1}^{N} p_n \log_2 p_n$ is the average number of guesses required to guess the number. Accordingly, $H(n)$ is defined as the amount of information associated with the situation.

Now Wiener has noted that this expression of "the amount of information" was formally identical (as a mathematical expression) with the formula which designates the *entropy* of a physical system. In this interpretation, p stands for the probability that the system is in a particular "molecular state," as defined by the configuration of its molecules and of their velocities. This formula was derived in statistical mechanics and provided a link between the kinetic theory of gases and classical thermodynamics. The concept of entropy had been developed in the latter discipline in connection with the formulation of its so-called Second Law. The Second Law of Thermodynamics states that if a physical system (in this context, simply a portion of the physical universe) is isolated from its environment, then the amount of entropy in the system can only increase toward a maximum (never decrease). *Physically*, this means that although the total amount of energy in the system will remain constant (a consequence of the First Law of Thermodynamics), the amount of so-called "free energy" (i.e., energy which can do work on the environment) can only decrease. To put it in another way, the tendency in an isolated system is for its energy to be "degraded," i.e., to become heat energy, which becomes unavailable for "useful work" (i.e., work upon the environment). *Statistically* this means that isolated systems tend to drift from less probable configurations to more probable ones, or, which is the same thing, from more "organized" states to more "chaotic" ones.

For a while the vitalists cited the Second Law in support of their contentions. It appeared to them that living organisms violated the Second Law; for, at least in the process of embryonic development, an organism becomes *more* organized, not less. Only after death does the process of disorganization set in, until the organism disintegrates and gradually becomes undifferentiated from the environment. The vitalists sought, therefore, to explain the entropy-reducing capacity of living organisms by a vital principle outside the scope of physical law.

It did not take long to point out the basic error in the vitalists' conclusion. The Second Law of Thermodynamics applies only to *isolated* systems. An isolated system cannot be a living system (at least not for long). Therefore an argument based on the supposed circumvention of the Second Law by living systems collapses. However, the vitalists' argument, although it was in itself unsound, served a constructive purpose in calling attention to a fundamental aspect of the living process previously unnoticed, namely that the food ingested by living organisms serves not only as a source of energy but also as a source of *free* energy, which compensates for the increase of entropy associated with physical and chemical processes in accordance with the Second Law. As E. Schroedinger put it picturesquely, "life feeds on negative entropy." Food ingested by animals and sunlight absorbed by plants are rich in "negative entropy" (free energy), and this supplies the living organisms not only with energy used in maintaining the living process, but also with means to maintain and even to increase the "organized complexity" which characterizes them as living systems and so to resist the trend toward disorganization inherent in the operation of the Second Law.

Wiener's insight into the meaning of the mathematical connection between entropy and information provides further clarification of the fundamental principle of the living process. Increase of entropy can be viewed as "destruction of information." Conversely, information can be used to reduce entropy. A simple analogy will serve to illustrate this principle. Consider a deck of playing cards as it comes from the factory, i.e., arranged in perfect order. If we know the order, we can name with certainty the card which follows any given card. Putting it in another way, knowledge of what card has been picked gives us much information about what card follows. Let now the deck be shuffled by repeated cuttings of the deck. After only a few cuttings we can still frequently guess what card follows a given card (if the two happened not to have been separated by a cutting). However, as the number of cuttings increases, we shall make more and more errors in our guesses. Eventually the cuttings will completely "randomize" the deck and so we shall guess the card following a given card with no more than chance frequency (once in fifty-one times). That is, all the information provided by a given card about the next card has been destroyed by the shuffling. This process is analogous to the operation of the Second Law of Thermodynamics. The deck goes from an ordered (improbable) state to a chaotic (probable) state. We cannot reverse this process by continued shuffling: the original order will almost certainly not be restored.

We can, however, restore the original order by "feeding information" into the deck. This can be done in the following manner. Imagine a position assigned to each card according to the original order, i.e., 1–52. Look at each successive card of the shuffled deck; and if it has moved forward from its original position, move it one position backward, and vice versa. In doing so we are "injecting" information (in the form of either-or decisions) into the deck. Eventually the original order of the cards will be restored. In other words, a process analogous to a reversal of the Second Law may well occur if interventions in the form of decisions are allowed.

This way of looking at the Second Law of Thermodynamics led Clerk Maxwell to formulate an interesting idea, namely that a being with perceptions sufficiently keen to observe and control the positions and velocities of single molecules (Maxwell's Demon), could reverse the process of increasing entropy (disorder) even in an isolated system. To an outside observer, such a system would appear to be violating the Second Law of Thermodynamics.

Maxwell's argument, however, contains a basic fallacy. If the demon is placed inside the system, the processes going on within *him* must also be taken in to account in computing the total change in entropy. It was subsequently shown by L. Szilard and later by L. Brillouin that the processes within the demon (whether he is a mechanism or an organism) must be such that the decrease in entropy effected by his intervention is at least compensated (in general, over-compensated) by an increase of entropy in the demon. If, on the other hand, the demon intervenes from outside the system, then the system can no longer be considered to be isolated, and the Second Law does not apply.

It was this fundamental distinction between isolated and non-isolated systems that led L. Bertalanffy to formulate his approach to general system theory. The distinction, argued Bertalanffy, leads to a crucially important insight into the nature of life.

The most fundamental property of a living organism is its ability to maintain its "organized" state against the constant tendency toward disorganization implied by the operations of the Second Law of Thermodynamics. We have seen that this ability is inherent in the fact that a living organism is an open (non-isolated) system. Therefore, biology must be rooted in the theory of such systems. In particular, the characteristic properties of living organisms—for example, the maintenance of steady states (homeostasis), the principle of equifinality (the attainment of final states, irrespective of initial conditions), the apparently purposeful behavior of organisms, etc.—ought to be derivable from general properties of open systems.

To the extent that such general properties of systems are describable in a language independent of the specific nature of the systems, general system theory can provide the framework for integrating the specialized disciplines and in this way alleviate the estrangement between workers in fields separated by over-specialized language.

The language of mathematics is eminently qualified to serve as the language of general systems theory, precisely because this language is devoid of content and expresses only the structural (relational) features of a situation.

As an example, consider a system of chemical reactions in which the rate of change of concentration of each of the substances involved is a linear function of the concentrations of all of the substances. The behavior of such a system is described by a system of first order linear differential equations of the following form:

$$\frac{dx_i}{dt} = \sum_{j=1}^{n} a_{ij}\, x_j + b_i \quad (i = 1, 2 \; . \; . \; . \; n), \qquad (1)$$

where x_i is the concentration of the i-th substance, and a_{ij} represents the effect of substance j upon the rate of change of substance i. This effect is facilitating if a_{ij} is positive, and inhibitory if negative. The constant b_i represents an outside source of the i-th substance (if positive) or a sink (if negative).

Suppose now we are interested in a steady state of the system, i.e., a state of affairs in which all of the rates of change are zero. We can obtain such a steady state if we set the lefthand side of every equation equal to zero and solve for the x_i, thus obtaining the concentrations which guarantee a steady state. Suppose first, that the system is isolated, i.e., has neither sources nor sinks. Mathematically this means that all the b_i are zero. The resulting system of equations is then a *homogeneous* system of n linear equations in n unknowns. It is known that the only unique solution of such a system is $x_i = 0$. In other words, the only steady state which is uniquely determined by our conditions would be the trivial one, where all the concentrations are zero. However, we have omitted an important condition if we are speaking of a real physical system, namely the fact that the total mass of all the substances must remain the same (the law of conservation of mass). Mathematically this law is expressed by the condition.

$$\sum_{i=1}^{n} \frac{dx_i}{dt} = 0. \qquad (2)$$

But if the condition holds, we get only $n - 1$ independent equations when we set $dx_i/dt = 0$. Such a system has an infinity of solutions. A *unique* solution can be obtained only if an additional condition is imposed. If the system is isolated, this additional condition must be a statement concerning the total mass (or the sum of the concentration) of the substances, e.g.,

$$\sum_{i=1}^{n} x_i = C \text{ (a constant)}. \qquad (3)$$

Now the b_i are not all zero; the system of what this steady state is depends on C, i.e., on the sum of the initial concentrations.

Suppose now, on the contrary, that the system is open, i.e., contains sources and sinks. Now the b_i are not all zero; the system of equations is non-homogeneous and (except in some very special cases) has a unique steady state solution. This steady state does *not* depend on the initial concentrations. Consequently, if we tamper with the system, i.e., increase or decrease various concentrations, it will nevertheless tend to the *same* steady state as soon as we leave it alone. This steady state will depend only on the a_{ij} and on the b_i, that is, on the *relations* within the system and between the system and the ouside world. Such a system will exhibit "equifinality," i.e., will seem to an observer to "seek" a final state "appropriate" to it. A naive observer may be induced to invoke teleological notions or to attribute purposeful behavior to a system of this sort, whereas mathematical analysis shows that the apparently purposeful behavior of the system is a consequence strictly deduced from the fact that it is open, not closed.

The question of the existence of a steady state independent of initial conditions is only one of many questions one can ask with reference to the behavior of a system. Other important questions relate to the stability of steady states, if they exist. A steady state is stable if small departures from it result in an ultimate return of the system to the same steady state. If, however, small departures tend to be "magnified" so that the system moves even further away, the steady state is unstable. Next, there may be several steady states if the differential equations describing the system are not linear. The number and stability of the steady states, as well as the behavior of the system in moving over intermediate states toward or away from the steady states, are thus completely determined by the structure of the *mathematical model* which describes the system.

Mathematical aspects of general system theory are those that concern the structure of mathematical models which describe the systems. The shift of attention from the specific nature of systems (physical, biological, social) to their mathematical structure makes possible a rigorous definition of "system," suggests ways of linking the organismic view with the mechanistic, and opens excellent opportunities for bridging the gap between specialized disciplines.

A system from a mathematical point of view is any portion of the world which at any given time can be described by ascribing specific values to a number of variables. The totality of these values constitutes a *state* of the system. A static or structural theory of a system is the totality of assertions which relate the values of these variables to each other, when the system is in some state singled out for attention (for example, an equilibrium or steady state). A dynamic theory of a system is one which indicates how changes in the values of some of the variables depend on the values or on the changes in the values of other variables. Thus a dynamic theory is the totality of assertions from which the behavior of the system, as it goes from state to state, can be mathematically deduced.

The system is the more complex, the more variables are required to describe a state of the system. The system is the more organized, the more it is equipped to resist disturbances in "pursuing a chosen goal." The phrase in quotation marks is to be understood metaphorically. No conscious striving for goals needs to be ascribed to a system. A "goal" in its general sense is simply some end state to which a system tends by virtue of its structural organization (as was made clear in the chemical reaction example above).

Organization and complexity are correlated. For example, the essence of automation is the capacity of machines to adjust to changing conditions (as in an automated oil refinery). The adjustments require "sense receptors" (which take readings from the environment), communication networks, correction devices, etc. All of these make for greater complexity, since the state of each device is an additional variable in the state of the system.

As has been pointed out, the system-theoretic view provides a link between the mechanistic view, which does not encompass the workings of a complex system as a whole, and the organismic view, which relies on ad hoc teleological notions and often sacrifices rigor in the interest of suggestive descriptions of system behavior. The most important advantage of the mathematical system-theoretic view, however, is in the natural integrative function of mathematical theory.

From the standpoint of a mathematical theory, two systems are the more closely related the more structural similarity there is between the mathematical models that describe them. As an example, consider the following systems of differential equations,

$$\frac{dx_i}{dt} = \sum_{j=1}^{n} \sum_{k=1}^{n} a_{jk}^{(i)} x_j x_k + \sum_{j=1}^{n} b_{ij} x_j + C_i \qquad (i = 1, 2 \ldots n). \tag{4}$$

This system is of the second degree, since products of pairs of variables appear on the right, in addition to the variables themselves and the constant terms. This system of equations is a reasonable description of a system of chemical reactions in which reactions occur as a consequence of collisions between molecules of the different substances involved. The frequencies of such collisions are roughly proportional to the products of the corresponding concentrations, as reflected in the quadratic terms. The linear terms represent the monomolecular reactions, while the constant terms represent, as in the previous example, sources and sinks. However, there is nothing about these indications that suggests an interpretation in terms of chemical reactions. The variables might well represent populations of several species of organisms in an ecological system. If the members of such populations prey on each other, then the rates of population increase or decrease may well depend on the frequencies with which individuals "collide," since a collision between a predator and its prey may result in the demise of the prey and in an increase in the mass of the predator. Similarly, reproduction depends upon meetings of members of the same species of opposite sex. Therefore equations (4) may represent a rough model of an ecological system as well as of a chemical one.

Finally, consider a population of human beings divided into groups, each characterized by a certain behavior pattern or a complex of opinions or beliefs (i.e., members of subcultures, religions, political parties, and the like). Contacts between members may result in shifts or modifications of behavior patterns, beliefs, or the like, consequently in increases or decreases of the sub-populations. Thus equations (4) may be imagined to be also a model of some social process.

How accurately a mathematical model can describe a real system is an important question but is not central to a general system theory. In order to answer this question, an intensive empirical study is required of the system in question. Such a study is centered on the *content* of the events examined. General system theory, however, is primarily concerned with the *structures* of systems as defined by the relations which the parts of a system have to each other, in the way these relations determine the dynamic behavior of the system (its passage from state to state), and with the history of the system, i.e., its own development as a result of the interactions between it and its environment.

A mathematical general system theory provides descriptions of these three aspects of systems, namely structure, behavior, and evolution, in abstract mathematical language. A typology of systems, accordingly, becomes a mathematical typology. Two systems are identical if the mathematical structures of their respective models are identical (or *isomorphic*, to use the mathematical expression). The degree of similarity between the systems is estimated by the degree in which their mathematical models are related.

The shift of emphasis from the content to

the structure of events helps in the resolution of many controversies of questionable fruitfulness. For example, in the light of the organismic approach to a theory of social systems, many analogies suggest themselves. An institution can be easily imagined to be an organism. Its organizational structure can be thought to correspond to "anatomy," its modus operandi to "physiology" or "psychology," its history to the development of the organism; while the history of the *type* of institution can be compared to the evolution of the organism. The analogy may be extremely suggestive, but suggestiveness is not an index of reliability. One does not know the limits to which the analogy can be pushed; nor how to answer those who decry any theory inspired by "mere analogy." After all, an institution is *not* a biological organism, and the resemblance brought out by the analogy may be as spurious as the resemblance of some cloud formations to animals, or of thunder to an angry outburst.

Another familiar example of a heated controversy concerning the validity of analogy is that raging around the question of whether the "the brain is a computer." This controversy is obscured by clashing philosophical convictions. There are people who relish the idea of reducing all phenomena, including mental operations and emotions, to physical events; and there are others who are repelled by this idea. The general system theorist bypasses this issue. He is interested in the *extent* to which the operation of a brain can be likened to that of a computer. The answer to this question is not to be found in what a brain and a computer "are" (such questions are vestiges of prescientific metaphsics), but rather in what brains and computers *do*. *To the extent* that certain operations of the brain can be represented as the behavior of a system having some hypothesized structure and dynamic properties, and *to the extent* that such a system can be simulated by a computer, both the brain and the computer appear to be realizations of a certain general system type. [Note that this is not the same as saying that the brain "is" a computer.] The actual extent to which this analogy can be carried out becomes an empirical question rather than a metaphysical one. Clearly, any such re-statement of a problem facilitates a meaningful search for new knowledge both in the realm of automated information processing (computer technology) and in the realm of brain physiology. In this context, the concept of "amount of information," discussed above, serves the function of binding together theoretical frameworks of widely different content but of similiar structure.

Still another example of how putting system-theoretic ideas into a mathematical framework clarifies certain issues of long standing is seen in the recent mathematical approaches to certain aspects of international relations. The idea of balance of power has been for a long time important in the conceptualization of international relations. The idea clearly derives from an analogy with physical equilibria. As such it is open to all the objections raised against analogical thinking. It is, however, possible to construct various mathematical models of power relations among states. The aim is to see what theoretical consequences can be rigorously (e.g., mathematically) drawn from the various models. We have already seen how mathematical analysis brings out crucial distinctions between stable and unstable equilibria (steady states). The property of stability is a general system property. If the totality of relations among states vying with each other for power constitutes a system, then this system too has certain properties of stability or instability, depending on the parameters of its dynamics.

Economic systems are also characterized by degrees of stability or instability in certain phases of their existence. To the extent that certain aspects of an economic system (fluctuation of production levels, prices, or investment capital) can be cast into a mathematical model, questions about equilibria and their stability can be answered by rigorous mathematical deduction rather than by intuitive guesses.

It would be rash to draw definitive conclusions about the stability of the economic or international system from the properties of various hypothetical systems offered as models. However, an examination of these purely theoretical consequences cannot fail to be instructive in the sense of enlarging the conceptual repertoire of the theoreticians. Mathematical models bring to our attention aspects of phenomena which might not otherwise have occurred to us.

In recent years increasing emphasis has been put upon probabilistic or stochastic aspects of processes. The corresponding models are based on the assumption that the transitions of a system from state to state are governed by probabilities. The question arises whether a system so defined is still an instance of "organized complexity," since one ordinarily thinks of organization in terms of well-defined contingencies of events rather than in terms of events determined by chance. To this one can reply along two lines. First, the distinction between deterministic and probabilistic contingencies is not sharp. Probabilities tend toward certainty as the probability of one of the possible events approaches one. Therefore a probabilistic system theory provides a useful intermediate theoretical framework between chaos and organization. Indeed, the degree of organization of a system can be conveniently defined in terms of the departure of the observed behavior from a base line, determined by purely chance events. Second, in a large population of systems, probabilities become frequencies, and so determinism is in a sense re-established in the observed distributions of system characteristics.

The introduction of probabilistic and stochastic models to describe systems puts the entire conceptual apparatus of the theory of stochastic processes at the disposal of general system theory. Like all other mathematical concepts, those derived from the theory of stochastic processes are content-free and therefore provide additional opportunities for integrating theories of widely different content. The statistics of accidents, of divorces, of strikes, of elections, etc., are all derivable from appropriate stochastic models. The parameters of these models constitute the corresponding system characteristics. These parameters are structural parameters independent of content, and therefore are suitable building blocks of corresponding unified theories cutting across the special concepts derived from special contents.

In calling attention to the methodological advantages of general system theory, particularly of its mathematical formulations, one should not, of course, forget the limitations of this approach. Conclusions about structural similarities between two or more systems are valid only if the corresponding mathematical models are sufficiently faithful representations of the systems. As a matter of fact, however, the formulation of a mathematical model is often an extremely difficult task. Some systems defy all attempts at mathematical descriptions. So far, all the suggestions for constructing mathematical models of a brain have remained merely suggestions. No such model exists; nor does one seem feasible, if by a model one means more than a description in mathematical terms of some very special features of neural functioning.

Too strong confidence in mathematical general system theory, therefore, may have one of two unfortunate consequences. First, far from adequate models may be taken too seriously, for want of better models which remain tractable. Second, effort may be wasted in trying to subject to mathematical analysis systems so complex that they cannot possibly yield to such analysis, with the consequent neglect of other approaches, for example, the purely organismic approach which, after all, has been considerably successful in classical biology. It would be wise, therefore, to consider mathematical general system theory as an important addition to the conceptual repertoire of the scientist rather than a method destined to drive all the older methods into obscurity.

REFERENCES

Bertalanffy, L. von. "General System Theory, a Critical Review." *General Systems*, Vol. 7, pp. 1–22 (1962).

Brillouin, L. "Life, Thermodynamics, and Cybernetics." *American Scientist*, Vol. 36, pp. 554–568 (1949).

Schroedinger, E. *What Is Life?* New York: The Macmillan Co., 1945.

Shannon, C. E. and Weaver, W. *The Mathematical Theory of Communication*. Urbana, Ill.: University of Illinois Press, 1949.

Szilard, L. "Über die Entropieverminderung in einen thermodynamischen System bei Eingriffen intelligenter Wesen." *Zeitschrift für Physik*, Vol. 1, 53, pp. 840–856 (1924).

Whitehead, A. N. *Science and the Modern World*. New York: Pelican Mentor Books, 1948.

Wiener, N. *Cybernetics*. New York: John Wiley & Sons, 1948.

The Architecture of Complexity

HERBERT A. SIMON*

A number of proposals have been advanced in recent years for the development of "general systems theory" which, abstracting from properties peculiar to physical, biological, or social systems, would be applicable to all of them.[1] We might well feel that, while the goal is laudable, systems of such diverse kinds could hardly be expected to have any nontrivial properties in common. Metaphor and analogy can be helpful, or they can be misleading. All depends on whether the similarities the metaphor captures are significant or superficial.

It may not be entirely vain, however, to search for common properties among diverse kinds of complex systems. The ideas that go by the name of cybernetics constitute, if not a theory, at least a point of view that has been proving fruitful over a wide range of applications.[2] It has been useful to look at the behavior of adaptive systems in terms of the concepts of feedback and homeostasis, and to analyze adaptiveness in terms of the theory of selective information.[3] The ideas of feedback and information provide a frame of reference for viewing a wide range of situations, just as do the ideas of evolution, of relativism, of axiomatic method, and of operationalism.

In this paper I should like to report on some things we have been learning about particular kinds of complex systems encountered in the behavioral sciences. The developments I shall discuss arose in the context of specific phenomena, but the theoretical formulations themselves make little reference to details of structure. Instead they refer primarily to the complexity of the systems under view without specifying the exact content of that complexity. Because of their abstractness, the theories may have relevance—application would be too strong a term—to other kinds of complex systems that are observed in the social, biological, and physical sciences.

In recounting these developments, I shall avoid technical detail, which can generally be found elsewhere. I shall describe each theory in the particular context in which it arose. Then, I shall cite some examples of complex systems, from areas of science other than the initial application, to which the theoretical framework appears relevant. In doing so, I shall make reference to areas of knowledge where I am not expert—perhaps not even literate. I feel quite comfortable in doing so before the members of this society, representing as it

---

From *Proceedings of the American Philosophical Society*, Vol. 106, No. 6, December 1962, pp. 467–482. Reprinted by permission of the author and the publisher the American Philosophical Society.
* The ideas in this paper have been the topic of many conversations with my colleague, Allen Newell. George W. Corner suggested important improvements in biological content as well as editorial form. I am also indebted, for valuable comments on the manuscript, to Richard H. Meier, John R. Platt, and Warren Weaver. Some of the conjectures about the nearly decomposable structure of the nucleus-atom-molecule hierarchy were checked against the available quantitative data by Andrew Schoene and William Wise. My work in this area has been supported by a Ford Foundation grant for research in organizations and a Carnegie Corporation grant for research on cognitive processes. To all of the above, my warm thanks, and the usual absolution.

[1] See especially the yearbooks of the Society for General Systems Research. Prominent among the exponents of general systems theory are L. von Bertalanffy, K. Boulding, R. W. Gerard, and J. G. Miller. For a more skeptical view—perhaps too skeptical in the light of the present discussion—see H. A. Simon and A. Newell, Models: their uses and limitations, in L. D. White, ed., *The State of the Social Sciences*, 66–83, Chicago, Univ. of Chicago Press, 1956.

[2] N. Wiener, *Cybernetics*, New York, John Wiley & Sons, 1948. For an imaginative forerunner, see A. J. Lotka, *Elements of Mathematical Biology*, New York, Dover Publications, 1951, first published in 1924 as "Elements of physical biology."

[3] C. Shannon and W. Weaver, *The Mathematical Theory of Communication*, Urbana, Univ. of Illinois Press, 1949; W. R. Ashby, *Design for a Brain*, New York, John Wiley & Sons, 1952.

does the whole span of the scientific and scholarly endeavor. Collectively you will have little difficulty, I am sure, in distinguishing instances based on idle fancy or sheer ignorance from instances that cast some light on the ways in which complexity exhibits itself wherever it is found in nature. I shall leave to you the final judgment of relevance in your respective fields.

I shall not undertake a formal definition of "complex systems." [4] Roughly, by a complex system I mean one made up of a large number of parts that interact in a nonsimple way. In such systems, the whole is more than the sum of the parts, not in an ultimate, metaphysical sense, but in the important pragmatic sense that, given the properties of the parts and the laws of their interaction, it is not a trivial matter to infer the properties of the whole. In the face of complexity, an in-principle reductionist may be at the same time a pragmatic holist.[5]

The four sections that follow discuss four aspects of complexity. The first offers some comments on the frequency with which complexity takes the form of hierarchy—the complex system being composed of subsystems that, in turn, have their own subsystems, and so on. The second section theorizes about the relation between the structure of a complex system and the time required for it to emerge through evolutionary processes: specifically, it argues that hierarchic systems will evolve far more quickly than non-hierarchic systems of comparable size. The third section explores the dynamic properties of hierarchically-organized systems, and shows how they can be decomposed into subsystems in order to analyze their behavior. The fourth section examines the relation between complex systems and their descriptions.

Thus, the central theme that runs through my remarks is that complexity frequently takes the form of hierarchy, and that hierarchic systems have some common properties that are independent of their specific content. Hierarchy, I shall argue, is one of the central structural schemes that the architect of complexity uses.

Hierarchic Systems

By a *hierarchic system,* or hierarchy, I mean a system that is composed of interrelated subsystems, each of the latter being, in turn, hierarchic in structure until we reach some lowest level of elementary subsystem. In most systems in nature, it is somewhat arbitrary as to where we leave off the partitioning, and what subsystems we take as elementary. Physics makes much use of the concept of "elementary particle" although particles have a disconcerting tendency not to remain elementary very long. Only a couple of generations ago, the atoms themselves were elementary particles; today, to the nuclear physicist they are complex systems. For certain purposes of astronomy, whole stars, or even galaxies, can be regarded as elementary subsystems. In one kind of biological research, a cell may be treated as an elementary subsystem; in another, a protein molecule; in still another, an amino acid residue.

Just why a scientist has a right to treat as elementary a subsystem that is in fact exceedingly complex is one of the questions we shall take up. For the moment, we shall accept the fact that scientists do this all the time, and that if they are careful scientists they usually get away with it.

Etymologically, the word "hierarchy" has had a narrower meaning than I am giving it here. The term has generally been used to refer to a complex system in which each of the subsystems is subordinated by an authority relation to the system it belongs to. More exactly, in a hierarchic formal organization, each system consists of a "boss" and a set of subordinate subsystems. Each of the subsystems has

[4] W. Weaver, in: Science and complexity, *American Scientist,* 36:536, 1948, has distinguished two kinds of complexity, disorganized and organized. We shall be primarily concerned with organized complexity.

[5] See also John R. Platt, Properties of large molecules that go beyond the properties of their chemical sub-groups, *J. Theoret. Biol.* 1:342–358, 1961. Since the reductionism-holism issue is a major *cause de guerre* between scientists and humanists, perhaps we might even hope that peace could be negotiated between the two cultures along the lines of the compromise just suggested. As I go along, I shall have a little to say about complexity in the arts as well as in the natural sciences. I must emphasize the pragmatism of my holism to distinguish it sharply from the position taken by W. M. Elsasser in *The Physical Foundation of Biology,* New York, Pergamon Press, 1958.

a "boss" who is the immediate subordinate of the boss of the system. We shall want to consider systems in which the relations among subsystems are more complex than in the formal organizational hierarchy just described. We shall want to include systems in which there is no relation of subordination among subsystems. (In fact, even in human organizations, the formal hierarchy exists only on paper; the real flesh-and-blood organization has many inter-part relations other than the lines of formal authority.) For lack of a better term, I shall use hierarchy in the broader sense introduced in the previous paragraphs, to refer to all complex systems analyzable into successive sets of subsystems, and speak of "formal hierarchy" when I want to refer to the more specialized concept.[6]

Social Systems. I have already given an example of one kind of hierarchy that is frequently encountered in the social sciences: a formal organization. Business firms, governments, universities all have a clearly visible parts-within-parts structure. But formal organizations are not the only, or even the most common, kind of social hierarchy. Almost all societies have elementary units called families, which may be grouped into villages or tribes, and these into larger groupings, and so on. If we make a chart of social interactions, of who talks to whom, the clusters of dense interaction in the chart will identify a rather well-defined hierarchic structure. The groupings in this structure may be defined operationally by some measure of frequency of interaction in this sociometric matrix.

Biological and Physical Systems. The hierarchical structure of biological systems is a familiar fact. Taking the cell as the building block, we find cells organized into tissues, tissues into organs, organs into systems. Moving downward from the cell, well-defined subsystems—for example, nucleus, cell membrane, microsomes, mitochondria, and so on—have been identified in animal cells.

[6] The mathematical term "partitioning" will not do for what I call here a hierarchy; for the set of subsystems, and the successive subsets in each of these defines the partitioning, independently of any systems of relations among the subsets. By hierarchy I mean the partitioning in conjunction with the relations that hold among its parts.

The hierarchic structure of many physical systems is equally clear-cut. I have already mentioned the two main series. At the microscopic level we have elementary particles, atoms, molecules, macromolecules. At the macroscopic level we have satellite systems, planetary systems, galaxies. Matter is distributed throughout space in a strikingly non-uniform fashion. The most nearly random distributions we find, gases, are not random distributions of elementary particles but random distributions of complex systems, i.e., molecules.

A considerable range of structural types is subsumed under the term hierarchy as I have defined it. By this definition, a diamond is hierarchic, for it is a crystal structure of carbon atoms that can be further decomposed into protons, neutrons, and electrons. However, it is a very "flat" hierarchy, in which the number of first-order subsystems belonging to the crystal can be indefinitely large. A volume of molecular gas is a flat hierarchy in the same sense. In ordinary usage, we tend to reserve the word hierarchy for a system that is divided into a *small or moderate number* of subsystems, each of which may be further subdivided. Hence, we do not ordinarily think of or refer to a diamond or a gas as a hierarchic structure. Similarly, a linear polymer is simply a chain, which may be very long, of identical subparts, the monomers. At the molecular level it is a very flat hierarchy.

In discussing formal organizations, the number of subordinates who report directly to a single boss is called his *span of control.* I will speak analogously of the *span* of a system, by which I shall mean the number of subsystems into which it is partitioned. Thus, a hierarchic system is flat at a given level if it has a wide span at that level. A diamond has a wide span at the crystal level, but not at the next level down, the molecular level.

In most of our theory construction in the following sections we shall focus our attention on hierarchies of moderate span, but from time to time I shall comment on the extent to which the theories might or might not be expected to apply to very flat hierarchies.

There is one important difference between the physical and biological hierarchies, on the one hand, and social hierarchies, on the other. Most physical and biological hierarchies are described in spatial terms. We detect the organelles in a cell in the way we detect the raisins in a cake—they are "visibly" differentiated substructures localized spatially in the larger structure. On the other hand, we propose to identify social hierarchies not by observing who lives close to whom but by observing who interacts with whom. These two points of view can be reconciled by defining hierarchy in terms of intensity of interaction, but observing that in most biological and physical systems relatively intense interaction implies relative spatial propinquity. One of the interesting characteristics of nerve cells and telephone wires is that they permit very specific strong interactions at great distances. To the extent that interactions are channeled through specialized communications and transportation systems, spatial propinquity becomes less determinative of structure.

Symbolic Systems. One very important class of systems has been omitted from my examples thus far: systems of human symbolic production. A book is a hierarchy in the sense in which I am using that term. It is generally divided into chapters, the chapters into sections, the sections into paragraphs, the paragraphs into sentences, the sentences into clauses and phrases, the clauses and phrases into words. We may take the words as our elementary units, or further subdivide them, as the linguist often does, into smaller units. If the book is narrative in character, it may divide into "episodes" instead of sections, but divisions there will be.

The hierarchic structure of music, based on such units as movements, parts, themes, phrases, is well known. The hierarchic structure of products of the pictorial arts is more difficult to characterize, but I shall have something to say about it later.

The Evolution of Complex Systems

Let me introduce the topic of evolution with a parable. There once were two watchmakers, named Hora and Tempus, who manufactured very fine watches. Both of them were highly regarded, and the phones in their workshops rang frequently—new customers were constantly calling them. However, Hora prospered, while Tempus became poorer and poorer and finally lost his shop. What was the reason?

The watches the men made consisted of about 1,000 parts each. Tempus had so constructed his that if he had one partly assembled and had to put it down—to answer the phone say—it immediately fell to pieces and had to be reassembled from the elements. The better the customers liked his watches, the more they phoned him, the more difficult it became for him to find enough uninterrupted time to finish a watch.

The watches that Hora made were no less complex than those of Tempus. But he had designed them so that he could put together subassemblies of about ten elements each. Ten of these subassemblies, again, could be put together into a larger subassembly; and a system of ten of the latter subassemblies constituted the whole watch. Hence, when Hora had to put down a partly assembled watch in order to answer the phone, he lost only a small part of his work, and he assembled his watches in only a fraction of the manhours it took Tempus.

It is rather easy to make a quantitative analysis of the relative difficulty of the tasks of Tempus and Hora: Suppose the probability that an interruption will occur while a part is being added to an incomplete assembly is p. Then the probability that Tempus can complete a watch he has started without interruptio n is $(1-p)^{1000}$—a very small number unless p is .001 or less. Each interruption will cost, on the average, the time to assemble $1/p$ parts (the expected number assembled before interruption). On the other hand, Hora has to complete one hundred eleven subassemblies of ten parts each. The probability that he will not be interrupted while completing any one of these is $(1-p)^{10}$, and each interruption will cost only about the time required to assemble five parts.[7]

[7] The speculations on speed of evolution were first suggested by H. Jacobson's application of information theory to estimating the time required for biological evolution. See his paper, Information, reproduction, and the origin of life, in *American Scientist* 43:119–127, January, 1955. From thermodynamic considerations it is possible to estimate the amount of increase in entropy that occurs when a complex system decomposes into its elements. (See, for example, R. H. Setlow and E. C. Pollard, *Molecular Biophysics*, 63–65, Reading, Mass., Addison-Wesley Publishing Co., 1962, and references cited there.) But entropy is the logarithm of a probability, hence information, the

Now if p is about .01—that is, there is one chance in a hundred that either watchmaker will be interrupted while adding any one part to an assembly—then a straightforward calculation shows that it will take Tempus, on the average, about four thousand times as long to assemble a watch as Hora.

We arrive at the estimate as follows:

1. Hora must make 111 times as many complete assemblies per watch as Tempus; but
2. Tempus will lose on the average 20 times as much work for each interrupted assembly as Hora [100 parts, on the average, as against 5]; and
3. Tempus will complete an assembly only 44 times per million attempts ($.99^{1000} = 44 \times 10^{-6}$), while Hora will complete nine out of ten ($.99^{10} = 9 \times 10^{-1}$). Hence Tempus will have to make 20,000 as many attempts per completed assembly as Hora. $(9 \times 10^{-1})/(44 \times 10^{-6} = 2 \times 10^4$. Multiplying these three ratios, we get:

$$1/111 \times 100/5 \times .99^{10}/.99^{1000}$$
$$= 1/111 \times 20 \times 20{,}000 \sim 4{,}000.$$

Biological Evolution. What lessons can we draw from our parable for biological evolution? Let us interpret a partially completed subassembly of k elementary parts as the coexistence of k parts in a small volume—ignoring their relative orientations. The model assumes that parts are entering the volume at a constant rate, but that there is a constant probability, p, that the part will be dispersed before another is added, unless the assembly reaches a stable state. These assumptions are not particularly realistic. They undoubtedly underestimate the decrease in probability of achieving the assembly with increase in the size of the assembly. Hence the assumptions understate—probably by a large factor—the relative advantage of a hierarchic structure.

Although we cannot, therefore, take the numerical estimate seriously the lesson for biological evolution is quite clear and direct. The time required for the evolution of a complex form from simple elements depends critically on the numbers and distribution of potential intermediate stable forms. In particular, if there exists a hierarchy of potential stable "subassemblies," with about the same span, s, at each level of the hierarchy, then the time required for a subassembly can be expected to be about the same at each level—that is proportional to $1/(1-p)^s$. The time required for the assembly of a system of n elements will be proportional to $\log_s n$, that is, to the number of levels in the system. One would say—with more illustrative than literal intent—that the time required for the evolution of multi-celled organisms from single-celled organisms might be of the same order of magnitude as the time required for the evolution of single-celled organisms from macromolecules. The same argument could be applied to the evolution of proteins from amino acids, or molecules from atoms, of atoms from elementary particles.

A whole host of objections to this oversimplified scheme will occur, I am sure, to every working biologist, chemist, and physicist. Before turning to matters I know more about, I shall mention three of these problems, leaving the rest to the attention of the specialists.

First, in spite of the overtones of the watchmaker parable, the theory assumes no teleological mechanism. The complex forms can arise from the simple ones by purely random processes. (I shall propose another model in a moment that shows this clearly.) Direction is provided to the scheme by the stability of the complex forms, once these come into existence. But this is nothing more than survival of the fittest—i.e., of the stable.

Second, not all large systems appear hierarchical. For example, most polymers—e.g., nylon—are simply linear chains of large numbers of identical components, the monomers. However, for present purposes we can simply regard such a structure as a hierarchy with a

---

negative of entropy, can be interpreted as the logarithm of the reciprocal of the probability—the "improbability," so to speak. The essential idea in Jacobson's model is that the expected time required for the system to reach a particular state is inversely proportional to the probability of the state—hence increases exponentially with the amount of information (negentropy) of the state.

Following this line of argument, but not introducing the notion of levels and stable subassemblies, Jacobson arrived at estimates of the time required for evolution so large as to make the event rather improbable. Our analysis, carried through in the same way, but with attention to the stable intermediate forms, produces very much smaller estimates.

span of one—the limiting case. For a chain of any length represents a state of relative equilibrium.[8]

Third, the evolution of complex systems from simple elements implies nothing, one way or the other, about the change in entropy of the entire system. If the process absorbs free energy, the complex system will have a smaller entropy than the elements; if it releases free energy, the opposite will be true. The former alternative is the one that holds for most biological systems, and the net inflow of free energy has to be supplied from the sun or some other source if the second law of thermodynamics is not to be violated. For the evolutionary process we are describing, the equilibria of the intermediate states need have only local and not global stability, and they may be stable only in the steady state—that is, as long as there is an external source of free energy that may be drawn upon.[9]

Because organisms are not energetically closed systems, there is no way to deduce the direction, much less the rate, of evolution from classical thermodynamic considerations. All estimates indicate that the amount of entropy, measured in physical units, involved in the formation of a one-celled biological organism is trivially small—about -10^{-11} cal/degree.[10] The "improbability" of evolution has nothing to do with this quantity of entropy, which is produced by every bacterial cell every generation. The irrelevance of quantity of information, in this sense, to speed of evolution can also be seen from the fact that exactly as much information is required to "copy" a cell through the reproductive process as to produce the first cell through evolution.

The effect of the existence of stable intermediate forms exercises a powerful effect on the evolution of complex forms that may be likened to the dramatic effect of catalysts upon reaction rates and steady state distribution of reaction products in open systems.[11] In neither case does the entropy change provide us with a guide to system behavior.

Problem Solving as Natural Selection. Let us turn now to some phenomena that have no obvious connection with biological evolution: human problem-solving processes. Consider for example, the task of discovering the proof for a difficult theorem. The process can be—and often has been—described as a search through a maze. Starting with the axioms and previously proved theorems, various transformations allowed by the rules of the mathematical systems are attempted, to obtain new expressions. These are modified in turn until, with persistence and good fortune, a sequence or path of transformations is discovered that leads to the goal.

The process usually involves a great deal of trial and error. Various paths are tried; some are abandoned, others are pushed further. Before a solution is found a great many paths of the maze may be explored. The more difficult and novel the problem, the greater is likely to be the amount of trial and error required to find a solution. At the same time, the trial and error is not completely random or blind; it is, in fact, rather highly selective. The new expressions that are obtained by transforming given ones are examined to see whether they represent progress toward the goal. Indications of progress spur further search in the same direction; lack of progress signals the abandonment of a line of search. Problem solving requires *selective* trial and error.[12]

[8] There is a well-developed theory of polymer size, based on models of random assembly. See for example P. J. Flory, *Principles of Polymer Chemistry*, ch. 8, Ithaca, Cornell Univ. Press, 1953. Since *all* subassemblies in the polymerization theory are stable, limitation of molecular growth depends on "poisoning" of terminal groups by impurities or formation of cycles rather than upon disruption of partially-formed chains.

[9] This point has been made many times before, but it cannot be emphasized too strongly. For further discussion, see Setlow and Pollard, *op. cit.*, 49–64; Schrodinger, *What Is Life?* Cambridge Univ. Press, 1945; and H. Linschitz, The information content of a bacterial cell, in H. Quastler, ed., Information Theory in Biology, 251–262, Urbana, Univ. of Illinois Press, 1953.

[10] See Linschitz, *op. cit.* This quantity, 10^{-11} cal/degree, corresponds to about 10^{13} bits of information.

[11] See H. Kacser, Some physico-chemical aspects of biological organization, Appendix, pp. 191–249 in C. H. Waddington, *The Strategy of the Genes*, London, George Allen & Unwin, 1957.

[12] See A. Newell, J. C. Shaw, and H. A. Simon, Empirical explorations of the logic theory machine, *Proceedings of the 1957 Western Joint Computer Conference*, February, 1957, New York: Institute of Radio Engineers; Chess-playing pro-

A little reflection reveals that cues signaling progress play the same role in the problem-solving process that stable intermediate forms play in the biological evolutionary process. In fact, we can take over the watchmaker parable and apply it also to problem solving. In problem solving, a partial result that represents recognizable progress toward the goal plays the role of a stable subassembly.

Suppose that the task is to open a safe whose lock has ten dials, each with one hundred possible settings, numbered from 0 to 99. How long will it take to open the safe by a blind trial-and-error search for the correct setting? Since there are 100^{10} possible settings, we may expect to examine about one-half of these, on the average, before finding the correct one—that is, fifty billion billion settings. Suppose, however, that the safe is defective, so that a click can be heard when any one dial is turned to the correct setting. Now each dial can be adjusted independently, and does not need to be touched again while the others are being set. The total number of settings that has to be tried is only 10×50, or five hundred. The task of opening the safe has been altered, by the cues the clicks provide, from a practically impossible one to a trivial one.[13]

A considerable amount has been learned in the past five years about the nature of the mazes that represent common human problem-solving tasks—proving theorems, solving puzzles, playing chess, making investments, balancing assembly lines, to mention a few. All that we have learned about these mazes points to the same conclusion: that human problem solving, from the most blundering to the most insightful, involves nothing more than varying mixtures of trial and error and selectivity. The selectivity derives from various rules of thumb, or heuristics, that suggest which paths should be tried first and which leads are promising. We do not need to postulate processes more sophisticated than those involved in organic evolution to explain how enormous problem mazes are cut down to quite reasonable size.[14]

The Sources of Selectivity. When we examine the sources from which the problem-solving system, or the evolving system, as the case may be, derives its selectivity, we discover that selectivity can always be equated with some kind of feedback of information from the environment.

Let us consider the case of problem solving first. There are two basic kinds of selectivity. One we have already noted: various paths are tried out, the consequences of following them are noted, and this information is used to guide further search. In the same way, in organic evolution, various complexes come into being, at least evanescently, and those that are stable provide new building blocks for further construction. It is this information about stable configurations, and not free energy or negentropy from the sun, that guides the process of evolution and provides the selectivity that is essential to account for its rapidity.

The second source of selectivity in problem solving is previous experience. We see this particularly clearly when the problem to be solved is similar to one that has been solved before. Then, by simply trying again the paths that led to the earlier solution, or their analogues, trial-and-error search is greatly reduced or altogether eliminated.

What corresponds to this latter kind of information in organic evolution? The closest analogue is reproduction. Once we reach the level of self-reproducing systems, a complex system, when it has once been achieved, can be

grams and the problem of complexity, *IBM Journal of Research and Development*, 2:320–335, October, 1958; and for a similar view of problem solving, W. R. Ashby, Design for an intelligence amplifier, 215–233 in C. E. Shannon and J. McCarthy, *Automata Studies*, Princeton, Princeton Univ. Press, 1956.

[13] The clicking safe example was supplied by D. P. Simon. Ashby, *op. cit.*, 230, has called the selectivity involved in situations of this kind "selection by components." The even greater reduction in time produced by hierarchization in the clicking safe example, as compared with the watchmaker's metaphor, is due to the fact that a random *search* for the correct combination is involved in the former case, while in the latter the parts come together in the right order. It is not clear which of these metaphors provides the better model for biological evolution, but we may be sure that the watchmaker's metaphor gives an exceedingly conservative estimate of the savings due to hierarchization. The safe may give an excessively high estimate because it assumes all possible arrangements of the elements to be equally probable.

[14] A. Newell and H. A. Simon, Computer simulation of human thinking, *Science*, 134:2011–2017, December 22, 1961.

multiplied indefinitely. Reproduction in fact allows the inheritance of acquired characteristics, but at the level of genetic material, of course; i.e., only characteristics acquired by the genes can be inherited. We shall return to the topic of reproduction in the final section of this paper.

On Empires and Empire-Building. We have not exhausted the categories of complex systems to which the watchmaker argument can reasonably be applied. Philip assembled his Macedonian empire and gave it to his son, to be later combined with the Persian subassembly and others into Alexander's greater system. On Alexander's death, his empire did not crumble to dust, but fragmented into some of the major subsystems that had composed it.

The watchmaker argument implies that if one would be Alexander, one should be born into a world where large stable political systems already exist. Where this condition was not fulfilled, as on the Scythian and Indian frontiers, Alexander found empire building a slippery business. So too, T. E. Lawrence's organizing of the Arabian revolt against the Turks was limited by the character of his largest stable building blocks, the separate, suspicious desert tribes.

The profession of history places a greater value upon the validated particular fact than upon tendentious generalization. I shall not elaborate upon my fancy, therefore, but will leave it to historians to decide whether anything can be learned for the interpretation of history from an abstract theory of hierarchic complex systems.

Conclusion: The Evolutionary Explanation of Hierarchy. We have shown thus far that complex systems will evolve from simple systems much more rapidly if there are stable intermediate forms than if there are not. The resulting complex forms in the former case will be hierarchic. We have only to turn the argument around to explain the observed predominance of hierarchies among the complex systems nature presents to us. Among possible complex forms, hierarchies are the ones that have the time to evolve. The hypothesis that complexity will be hierarchic makes no distinction among very flat hierarchies, like crystals, and tissues, and polymers, and the intermediate forms. Indeed, in the complex systems we encounter in nature, examples of both forms are prominent. A more complete theory than the one we have developed here would presumably have something to say about the determinants of width of span in these systems.

Nearly Decomposable Systems

In hierarchic systems, we can distinguish between the interactions *among* subsystems, on the one hand, and the interactions *within* subsystems—i.e., among the parts of those subsystems—on the other. The interactions at the different levels may be, and often will be, of different orders of magnitude. In a formal organization there will generally be more interaction, on the average, between two employees who are members of the same department than between two employees from different departments. In organic substances, intermolecular forces will generally be weaker than molecular forces, and molecular forces than nuclear forces.

In a rare gas, the intermolecular forces will be negligible compared to those binding the molecules—we can treat the individual particles, for many purposes, as if they were independent of each other. We can describe such a system as *decomposable* into the subsystems comprised of the individual particles. As the gas becomes denser, molecular interactions become more significant. But over some range, we can treat the decomposable case as a limit, and as a first approximation. We can use a theory of perfect gases, for example, to describe approximately the behavior of actual gases if they are not too dense. As a second approximation, we may move to a theory of *nearly decomposable* systems, in which the interactions among the subsystems are weak, but not negligible.

At least some kinds of hierarchic systems can be approximated successfully as nearly decomposable systems. The main theoretical findings from the approach can be summed up in two propositions: (a) in a nearly decomposable system, the short-run behavior of each of the component subsystems is approximately independent of the short-run behavior of the other components; (b) in the long run, the behavior of any one of the components depends in only an aggregate way on the behavior of the other components.

Let me provide a very concrete simple example of a nearly decomposable system.[15] Consider a building whose outside walls provide perfect thermal insulation from the environment. We shall take these walls as the boundary of our system. The building is divided into a large number of rooms, the walls between them being good, but not perfect, insulators. The walls between rooms are the boundaries of our major subsystems. Each room is divided by partitions into a number of cubicles, but the partitions are poor insulators. A thermometer hangs in each cubicle. Suppose that at the time of our first observation of the system there is a wide variation in temperature from cubicle to cubicle and from room to room—the various cubicles within the building are in a state of thermal disequilibrium. When we take new temperature readings several hours later, what shall we find? There will be very little variation in temperature among the cubicles within each single room, but there may still be large temperature variations *among* rooms. When we take readings again several days later, we find an almost uniform temperature throughout the building; the temperature differences among rooms have virtually disappeared.

We can describe the process of equilibration formally by setting up the usual equations of heat flow. The equations can be represented by the matrix of their coefficients, r_{ij}, where r_{ij} is the rate at which heat flows from the ith cubicle to the jth cubicle per degree difference in their temperatures. If cubicles *i* and *j* do not have a common wall, r_{ij} will be zero. If cubicles *i* and *j* have a common wall, and are in the same room, r_{ij} will be large. If cubicles *i* and *j* are separated by the wall of a room, r_{ij} will be nonzero but small. Hence, by grouping all the cubicles together that are in the same room, we can arrange the matrix of coefficients so that all its large elements lie inside a string of square submatrices along the main diagonal. All the elements outside these diagonal squares will be either zero or small (see Figure 1). We may take some small number, ε, as the upper bound of the extradiagonal elements. We shall call a matrix having these properties a *nearly decomposable matrix*.

	A1	A2	A3	B1	B2	C1	C2	C3
A1	—	100	—	2	—	—	—	—
A2	100	—	100	1	1	—	—	—
A3	—	100	—	—	2	—	—	—
B1	2	1	—	—	100	2	1	—
B2	—	1	2	100	—	—	1	2
C1	—	—	—	2	—	—	100	—
C2	—	—	—	1	—	100	—	100
C3	—	—	—	—	2	—	100	—

Fig. 1. A hypothetical nearly-decomposable system. In terms of the heat-exchange example of the test, A1, A2, and A3 may be interpreted as cubicles in one room, B1 and B2 as cubicles in a second room, and C1, C2, and C3 as cubicles in a third. The matrix entries then are the heat diffusion coefficents between cubicles.

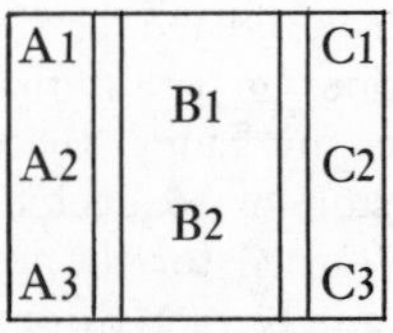

Now it has been proved that a dynamic system that can be described by a nearly decomposable matrix has the properties, stated above, of a nearly decomposable system. In our simple example of heat flow this means that in the short run each room will reach an equilibrium temperature (an average of the initial temperatures of its offices) nearly independently of the others; and each room will remain approximately in a state of equilibrium over the longer period during which an over-all temperature equilibrium is being established throughout the building. After the intraroom short-run equilibria have been reached, a single thermometer in each room will be adequate to describe the dynamic behavior of the entire system—separate thermometers in each cubicle will be superfluous.

[15] This discussion of near-decomposability is based upon H. A. Simon and A. Ando, Aggregation of variables in dynamic systems, *Econometrica* 29:111–138, April, 1961. The example is drawn from the same source, 117–118. The theory has been further developed and applied to a variety of economic and political phenomena by Ando and F. M. Fisher. See F. M. Fisher, On the cost of approximate specification in simultaneous equation estimation, *Econometrica* 29:139–170, April, 1961, and F. M. Fisher and A. Ando, Two theorems on *Ceteris Paribus* in the analysis of dynamic systems, *American Political Science Review* 61:103–113, March, 1962.

Near Decomposability of Social Systems. As a glance at Figure 1 shows, near decomposability is a rather strong property for a matrix to possess, and the matrices that have this property will describe very special dynamic systems—vanishingly few systems out of all those that are thinkable. How few they will be depends, of course, on how good an approximation we insist upon. If we demand that epsilon be very small, correspondingly few dynamic systems will fit the definition. But we have already seen that in the natural world nearly decomposable systems are far from rare. On the contrary, systems in which each variable is linked with almost equal strength with almost all other parts of the system are far rarer and less typical.

In economic dynamics, the main variables are the prices and quantities of commodities. It is empirically true that the price of any given commodity and the rate at which it is exchanged depend to a significant extent only on the prices and quantities of a few other commodities, together with a few other aggregate magnitudes, like the average price level or some over-all measure of economic activity. The large linkage coefficients are associated, in general, with the main flows of raw materials and semi-finished products within and between industries. An input-output matrix of the economy, giving the magnitudes of these flows, reveals the nearly decomposable structure of the system—with one qualification. There is a consumption subsystem of the economy that is linked strongly to variables in most of the other subsystems. Hence, we have to modify our notions of decomposability slightly to accommodate the special role of the consumption subsystem in our analysis of the dynamic behavior of the economy.

In the dynamics of social systems, where members of a system communicate with and influence other members, near decomposability is generally very prominent. This is most obvious in formal organizations, where the formal authority relation connects each member of the organization with one immediate superior and with a small number of subordinates. Of course many communications in organizations follow other channels than the lines of formal authority. But most of these channels lead from any particular individual to a very limited number of his superiors, subordinates, and associates. Hence, departmental boundaries play very much the same role as the walls in our heat eaxmple.

Physico-Chemical Systems. In the complex systems familiar in biological chemistry, a similar structure is clearly visible. Take the atomic nuclei in such a system as the elementary parts of the system, and construct a matrix of bond strength between elements. There will be matrix elements of quite different orders of magnitude. The largest will generally correspond to the covalent bonds, the next to the ionic bonds, the third group to hydrogen bonds, still smaller linkages to van der Waals forces.[16] If we select an epsilon just a little smaller than the magnitude of a covalent bond, the system will decompose into subsystems—the constituent molecules. The smaller linkages will correspond to the intermolecular bonds.

It is well known that high-energy, high-frequency vibrations are associated with the smaller physical subsystems, low-frequency vibrations with the larger systems into which the subsystems are assembled. For example, the radiation frequencies associated with molecular vibrations are much lower than those associated with the vibrations of the planetary electrons of the atoms; the latter, in turn, are lower than those associated with nuclear processes.[17] Molecular systems are nearly decomposable systems, the short-run dynamics relating to the internal structures of the subsystems; the long-run dynamics to the interactions of these subsystems.

A number of the important approximations employed in physics depend for their validity

[16] For a survey of the several classes of molecular and inter-molecular forces, and their dissociation energies see Setlow and Pollard, *op. cit.*, chapter 6. The energies of typical covalent bonds are of the order of 80–100 k cal/mole, of the hydrogen bonds, 10 k cal/mole. Ionic bonds generally lie between these two levels, the bonds due to van der Waals forces are lower in energy.

[17] Typical wave numbers for vibrations associated with various systems (the wave number is the reciprocal of wave length hence proportional to frequency):

steel wire under tension—10^{-10} to 10^{-9} cm^{-1}
molecular rotations—10^{0} to 10^{2} cm^{-1}
molecular vibrations—10^{2} to 10^{3} cm^{-1}
planetary electrons—10^{4} to 10^{5} cm^{-1}
nuclear rotations—10^{9} to 10^{10} cm^{-1}
nuclear surface vibrations—10^{11} to 10^{12} cm^{-1}

on the near-decomposability of the systems studied. The theory of the thermodynamics of irreversible processes, for example, requires the assumption of macroscopic disequilibrium but microscopic equilibrium,[18] exactly the situation described in our heat-exchange example. Similarly computations in quantum mechanics are often handled by treating weak interactions as producing perturbations on a system of strong interactions.

Some Observations on Hierarchic Span. To understand why the span of hierarchies is sometimes very broad—as in crystals—sometimes narrow, we need to examine more detail of the interactions. In general, the critical consideration is the extent to which interaction between two (or a few) subsystems excludes interaction of these subsystems with the others. Let us examine first some physical examples.

Consider a gas of identical molecules, each of which can form covalent bonds, in certain ways, with others. Let us suppose that we can associate with each atom a specific number of bonds that it is capable of maintaining simultaneously. (This number is obviously related to the number we usually call its valence.) Now suppose that two atoms join, and that we can also associate with the combination a specific number of external bonds it is capable of maintaining. If this number is the same as the number associated with the individual atoms the bonding process can go on indefinitely—the atoms can form crystals or polymers of indefinite extent. If the number of bonds of which the composite is capable is less than the number associated with each of the parts, then the process of agglomeration must come to a halt.

We need only mention some elementary examples. Ordinary gases show no tendency to agglomerate because the multiple bonding of atoms "uses up" their capacity to interact. While each oxygen atom has a valence of two, the O_2 molecules have a zero valence. Contrariwise, indefinite chains of single-bonded carbon atoms can be built up because a chain of any number of such atoms, each with two side groups, has a valence of exactly two.

Now what happens if we have a system of elements that possess both strong and weak interaction capacities, and whose strong bonds are exhaustible through combination? Subsystems will form, until all the capacity for strong interaction is utilized in their construction. Then these subsystems will be linked by the weaker second-order bonds into larger systoms. For example, a water molecule has essentially a valence of zero—all the potential covalent bonds are fully occupied by the interaction of hydrogen and oxygen molecules. But the geometry of the molecule creates an electric dipole that permits weak interaction between the water and salts dissolved in it—whence such phenomena as its electrolytic conductivity.[19]

Similarly, it has been observed that, although electrical forces are much stronger than gravitational forces, the latter are far more important than the former for systems on an astronomical scale. The explanation, of course, is that the electrical forces, being bipolar, are all "used up" in the linkages of the smaller subsystems, and that significant net balances of positive or negative charges are not generally found in regions of macroscopic size.

In social as in physical systems there are generally limits on the simultaneous interaction of large numbers of subsystems. In the social case, these limits are related to the fact that a human being is more nearly a serial than a parallel information-processing system. He can carry on only one conversation at a time, and although this does not limit the size of the audience to which a mass communication can be addressed, it does limit the number of people simultaneously involved in most other forms of social interaction. Apart from requirements of direct interaction, most roles impose tasks and responsibilities that are time consuming. One cannot, for example, enact the role of "friend" with large numbers of other people.

It is probably true that in social as in physical systems, the higher frequency dynamics are associated with the subsystems, the lower frequency dynamics with the larger systems. It is generally believed, for example, that the relevant planning horizon of executives is longer the higher their location in the organizational hierarchy. It is probably also true that both the average duration of an interaction between

[18] S. R. de Groot, *Thermodynamics of Irreversible Processes,* 11–12, New York, Interscience Publishers, 1951.

[19] See, for example, L., Pauling, *General Chemistry,* ch. 15.

executives and the average interval between interactions is greater at higher than at lower levels.

Summary: Near Decomposability. We have seen that hierarchies have the property of near-decomposability. Intra-component linkages are generally stronger than intercomponent linkages. This fact has the effect of separating the high-frequency dynamics of a hierarchy—involving the internal structure of the components—from the low frequency dynamics—involving interaction among components. We shall turn next to some important consequences of this separation for the description and comprehension of complex systems.

The Description of Complexity

If you ask a person to draw a complex object—e.g., a human face—he will almost always proceed in a hierarchic fashion.[20] First he will outline the face. Then he will add or insert features: eyes, nose, mouth, ears, hair. If asked to elaborate, he will begin to develop details for each of the features—pupils, eyelids, lashes for the eyes, and so on—until he reaches the limits of his anatomical knowledge. His information about the object is arranged hierarchicly in memory, like a topical outline.

When information is put in outline form, it is easy to include information about the relations among the major parts and information about the internal relations of parts in each of the suboutlines. Detailed information about the relations of subparts belonging to different parts has no place in the outline and is likely to be lost. The loss of such information and the preservation mainly of information about hierarchic order is a salient characteristic that distinguishes the drawings of a child or someone untrained in representation from the drawing of a trained artist. (I am speaking of an artist who is striving for representation.)

Near Decomposability and Comprehensibility. From our discussion of the dynamic properties of nearly decomposable systems, we have seen that comparatively little information is lost by representing them as hierarchies. Subparts belonging to different parts only interact in an aggregative fashion—the detail of their interaction can be ignored. In studying the interaction of two large molecules, generally we do not need to consider in detail the interactions of nuclei of the atoms belonging to the one molecule with the nuclei of the atoms belonging to the other. In studying the interaction of two nations, we do not need to study in detail the interactions of each citizen of the first with each citizen of the second.

The fact, then, that many complex systems have a nearly decomposable, hierarchic structure is a major facilitating factor enabling us to understand, to describe, and even to "see" such systems and their parts. Or perhaps the proposition should be put the other way round. If there are important systems in the world that are complex without being hierarchic, they may to a considerable extent escape our observation and our understanding. Analysis of their behavior would involve such detailed knowledge and calculation of the interactions of their elementary parts that it would be beyond our capacities of memory or computation.[21]

[20] George A. Miller has collected protocols from subjects who were given the task of drawing faces, and finds that they behave in the manner described here (private communication). See also E. H. Gombrich, *Art and Illusion,* 291–296, New York, Pantheon Books, 1960.

[21] I believe the fallacy in the central thesis of W. M. Elsasser's *The Physical Foundation of Biology,* mentioned earlier, lies in his ignoring the simplification in description of complex systems that derives from their hierarchic structure. Thus (p. 155): "If we now apply similar arguments to the coupling of enzymatic reactions with the substratum of protein molecules, we see that over a sufficient period of time, the information corresponding to the structural details of these molecules will be communicated to the dynamics of the cell, to higher levels of organization as it were, and may influence such dynamics. While this reasoning is only qualitative, it lends credence to the assumption that in the living organism, unlike the inorganic crystal, the effects of microscopic structure cannot be simply averaged out; as time goes on this influence will pervade the behavior of the cell 'at all levels.' "

But from our discussion of near-decomposability it would appear that those aspects of microstructure that control the slow developmental aspects of organismic dynamics can be separated out from the aspects that control the more rapid cellular metabolic processes. For this reason we should not despair of unravelling the web of causes. See also J. R. Platt's review of Elsasser's book in *Perspectives in Biology and Medicine* 2:243–245, 1959.

I shall not try to settle which is chicken and which is egg: whether we are able to understand the world because it is hierarchic, or whether it appears hierarchic because those aspects of it which are not elude our understanding and observation. I have already given some reasons for supposing that the former is at least half the truth—that evolving complexity would tend to be hierarchic—but it may not be the whole truth.

Simple Descriptions of Complex Systems. One might suppose that the description of a complex system would itself be a complex structure of symbols—and indeed, it may be just that. But there is no conservation law that requires that the description be as cumbersome as the object described. A trivial example will show how a system can be described economically. Suppose the system is a two-dimensional array like this:

A	B	M	N	R	S	H	I
C	D	O	P	T	U	J	K
M	N	A	B	H	I	R	S
O	P	C	D	J	K	T	U
R	S	H	I	A	B	M	N
T	U	J	K	C	D	O	P
H	I	R	S	M	N	A	B
J	K	T	U	O	P	C	D

Let us call the array $\left|\begin{matrix}\mathrm{AB}\\\mathrm{CD}\end{matrix}\right|$ *a*, the array $\left|\begin{matrix}\mathrm{MN}\\\mathrm{OP}\end{matrix}\right|$ *m*, the array $\left|\begin{matrix}\mathrm{RS}\\\mathrm{TU}\end{matrix}\right|$ *r*, and the array $\left|\begin{matrix}\mathrm{HI}\\\mathrm{JK}\end{matrix}\right|$ *h*. Let us call the array $\left|\begin{matrix}\mathrm{am}\\\mathrm{ma}\end{matrix}\right|$ *w*, and the array $\left|\begin{matrix}\mathrm{rh}\\\mathrm{hr}\end{matrix}\right|$ *x*. Then the entire array is simply $\left|\begin{matrix}\mathrm{wx}\\\mathrm{xw}\end{matrix}\right|$. While the original structure consisted of 64 symbols, it requires only 35 to write down its description:

$$S = \begin{matrix}\mathrm{wx}\\\mathrm{xw}\end{matrix}$$

$$w = \begin{matrix}\mathrm{am}\\\mathrm{ma}\end{matrix} \qquad x = \begin{matrix}\mathrm{rh}\\\mathrm{hr}\end{matrix}$$

$$a = \begin{matrix}\mathrm{AB}\\\mathrm{CD}\end{matrix} \qquad m = \begin{matrix}\mathrm{MN}\\\mathrm{OP}\end{matrix} \qquad r = \begin{matrix}\mathrm{RS}\\\mathrm{TU}\end{matrix} \qquad h = \begin{matrix}\mathrm{HI}\\\mathrm{JK}\end{matrix}$$

We achieve the abbreviation by making use of the redundancy in the original structure. Since the pattern $\begin{matrix}\mathrm{AB}\\\mathrm{CD}\end{matrix}$, for example, occurs four times in the total pattern, it is economical to represent it by the single symbol, *a*.

If a complex structure is completely unredundant—if no aspect of its structure can be inferred from any other—then it is its own simplest description. We can exhibit it, but we cannot describe it by a simpler structure. The hierarchic structures we have been discussing have a high degree of redundancy, hence can often be described in economical terms. The redundancy takes a number of forms, of which I shall mention three:

1. Hierarchic systems are usually composed of only a few different kinds of subsystems, in various combinations and arrangement. A familiar example is the proteins, their multitudinous variety arising from arrangements of only twenty different amino acids. Similarly, the ninety-odd elements provide all the kinds of building blocks needed for an infinite variety of molecules. Hence, we can construct our description from a restricted alphabet of elementary terms corresponding to the basic set of elementary subsystems from which the complex system is generated.

2. Hierarchic systems are, as we have seen, often nearly decomposable. Hence only aggregative properties of their parts enter into the description of the interactions of those parts. A generalization of the notion of near-decomposability might be called the "empty world hypothesis"—most things are only weakly connected with most other things; for a tolerable description of reality only a tiny fraction of all possible interactions needs to be taken into account. By adopting a descriptive language that allows the absence of something to go unmentioned, a nearly empty world can be described quite concisely. Mother Hubbard did not have to check off the list of possible contents to say that her cupboard was bare.

3. By appropriate "recoding," the redundancy that is present but unobvious in the structure of a complex system can often be made patent. The most common recoding of descriptions of dynamic systems consists in replacing a description of the time path with a description of a differential law that generates that path. The simplicity, that is, resides in a constant relation between the state of the system at any given time and the state of the system a short time later. Thus, the structure of the sequence, 1 3 5 7 9 11 . . . , is most simply expressed by observing that each member is obtained by adding 2 to the previous one.

But this is the sequence that Galileo found to describe the velocity at the end of successive time intervals of a ball rolling down an inclined plane.

It is a familiar proposition that the task of science is to make use of the world's redundancy to describe that world simply. I shall not pursue the general methodological point here, but shall instead take a closer look at two main types of description that seem to be available to us in seeking an understanding of complex systems. I shall call these *state description* and *process description*, respectively.

State Descriptions and Process Descriptions. "A circle is the locus of all points equidistant from a given point." "To construct a circle, rotate a compass with one arm fixed until the other arm has returned to its starting point." It is implicit in Euclid that if you carry out the process specified in the second sentence, you will produce an object that satisfies the definition of the first. The first sentence is a state description of a circle, the second a process description.

These two modes of apprehending structure are the warp and weft of our experience. Pictures, blueprints, most diagrams, chemical structural formulae are state descriptions. Recipes, differential equations, equations for chemical reactions are process descriptions. The former characterize the world as sensed; they provide the criteria for identifying objects, often by modeling the objects themselves. The latter characterize the world as acted upon; they provide the means for producing or generating objects having the desired characteristics.

The distinction between the world as sensed and the world as acted upon defines the basic condition for the survival of adaptive organisms. The organism must develop correlations between goals in the sensed world and actions in the world of process. When they are made conscious and verbalized, these correlations correspond to what we usually call means-end analysis. Given a desired state of affairs and an existing state of affairs, the task of an adaptive organism is to find the difference between these two states, and then to find the correlating process that will erase the difference.[22]

Thus, problem solving requires continual translation between the state and process descriptions of the same complex reality. Plato, in the *Men*, argued that all learning is remembering. He could not otherwise explain how we can discover or recognize the answer to a problem unless we already know the answer.[23] Our dual relation to the world is the source and solution of the paradox. We pose a problem by giving the state description of the solution. The task is to discover a sequence of processes that will produce the goal state from an initial state. Translation from the process description to the state description enables us to recognize when we have succeeded. The solution is genuinely new to us—and we do not need Plato's theory of remembering to explain how we recognize it.

There is now a growing body of evidence that the activity called human problem solving is basically a form of means-end analysis that aims at discovering a process description of the path that leads to a desired goal. The general paradigm is: given a blueprint, to find the corresponding recipe. Much of the activity of science is an application of that paradigm: given the description of some natural phenomena, to find the differential equations for processes that will produce the phenomena.

The Description of Complexity in Self-reproducing Systems. The problem of finding relatively simple descriptions for complex systems is of interest not only for an understanding of human knowledge of the world but also for an explanation of how a complex system can reproduce itself. In my discussion of the evolution of complex systems, I touched only briefly on the role of self-reproduction.

Atoms of high atomic weight and complex inorganic molecules are witnesses to the fact that the evolution of complexity does not imply self-reproduction. If evolution of complexity from simplicity is sufficiently probable, it will occur repeatedly; the statistical equilibrium of the system will find a large fraction of the elementary particles participating in complex systems.

If, however, the existence of a particular

[22] See H. A. Simon and A. Newell, Simulation of human thinking, in M. Greenberger (ed.), *Management and the Computer of the Future*, 95–114, esp. pp. 110 ff., New York, Wiley, 1962.

[23] *The Works of Plato, B. Jowett, trans.*, 3:26–35, New York, Dial Press.

complex form increased the probability of the creation of another form just like it, the equilibrium between complexes and components could be greatly altered in favor of the former. If we have a description of an object that is sufficiently clear and complete, we can reproduce the object from the description. Whatever the exact mechanism of reproduction, the description provides us with the necessary information.

Now we have seen that the descriptions of complex systems can take many forms. In particular, we can have state descriptions or we can have process descriptions; blueprints or recipes. Reproductive processes could be built around either of these sources of information. Perhaps the simplest possibility is for the complex system to serve as a description of itself—a template on which a copy can be formed. One of the most plausible current theories, for example, of the reproduction of deoxyribonucleic acid (DNA) proposes that a DNA molecule, in the form of a double helix of matching parts (each essentially a "negative" of the other), unwinds to allow each half of the helix to serve as a template on which a new matching half can form.

On the other hand, our current knowledge of how DNA controls the metabolism of the organism suggests that reproduction by template is only one of the processes involved. According to the prevailing theory, DNA serves as a template both for itself and for the related substance ribonucleic acid (RNA). RNA, in turn, serves as a template for protein. But proteins—according to current knowledge—guide the organism's metabolism not by the template method but by serving as catalysts to govern reaction rates in the cell. While RNA is a blueprint for protein, protein is a recipe for metabolism.[24]

Ontogeny Recapitulates Phylogeny. The DNA in the chromosomes of an organism contains some, and perhaps most, of the information that is needed to determine its development and activity. We have seen that, if current theories are even approximately correct, the information is recorded not as a state description of the organism but as a series of "instructions" for the construction and maintenance of the organism from nutrient materials. I have already used the metaphor of a recipe; I could equally well compare it with a computer program, which is also a sequence of instructions, governing the construction of symbolic structures. Let me spin out some of the consequences of the latter comparison.

If genetic material is a program—viewed in its relation to the organism—it is a program with special and peculiar properties. First, it is a self-reproducing program; we have already considered its possible copying mechanism. Second, it is a program that has developed by Darwinian evolution. On the basis of our watchmaker's argument, we may assert that many of its ancestors were also viable programs—programs for the subassemblies.

Are there any other conjectures we can make about the structure of this program? There is a well-known generalization in biology that is verbally so neat that we would be reluctant to give it up even if the facts did not support it; ontogeny recapitulates phylogeny. The individual organism, in its development, goes through stages that resemble some of its ancestral forms. The fact that the human embryo develops gill bars and then modifies them for other purposes is a familiar particular belonging to the generalization. Biologists today like to emphasize the qualifications of the principle—that ontogeny recapitulates only the grossest aspects of phylogeny, and these only crudely. These qualifications should not make us lose sight of the fact that the generalization does hold in rough approximation—it does summarize a very significant set of facts about the organism's development. How can we interpret these facts?

One way to solve a complex problem is to reduce it to a problem previously solved—to show what steps lead from the earlier solution to a solution of the new problem. If, around the turn of the century, we wanted to instruct a workman to make an automobile, perhaps the simplest way would have been to tell him how to modify a wagon by removing the singletree and adding a motor and transmission. Similarly, a genetic program could be altered in the course of evolution by adding new pro-

[24] C. B. Anfinsen, *The Molecular Basis of Evolution,* chs. 3 and 10, New York, Wiley, 1959, will qualify this sketchy, oversimplified account. For an imaginative discussion of some mechanisms of process description that could govern molecular structure, see H. H. Pattee, On the origin of macromolecular sequences, *Biophysical Journal* 1:683–710, 1961.

cesses that would modify a simpler form into a more complex one—to construct a gastrula, take a blastula and alter it!

The genetic description of a single cell may, therefore, take a quite different form from the genetic description that assembles cells into a multi-celled organism. Multiplication by cell division would require, as a minimum, a state description (the DNA, say), and a simple "interpretive process"—to use the term from computer language—that copies this description as part of the larger copying process of cell division. But such a mechanism clearly would not suffice for the differentiation of cells in development. It appears more natural to conceptualize that mechanism as based on a process description, and a somewhat more complex interpretive process that produces the adult organism in a sequence of stages, each new stage in development representing the effect of an operator upon the previous one.

It is harder to conceptualize the interrelation of these two descriptions. Interrelated they must be, for enough has been learned of gene-enzyme mechanisms to show that these play a major role in development as in cell metabolism. The single clue we obtain from our earlier discussion is that the description may itself be hierarchical, or nearly decomposable, in structure, the lower levels governing the fast, "high-frequency" dynamics of the individual cell, the higher level interactions governing the slow, "low-frequency" dynamics of the developing multi-cellular organism.

There are only bits of evidence, apart from the facts of recapitulation, that the genetic program is organized in this way, but such evidence as exists is compatible with this notion.[25] To the extent that we can differentiate the genetic information that governs cell metabolism from the genetic information that governs the development of differentiated cells in the multi-cellular organization, we simplify enormously—as we have already seen—our task of theoretical description. But I have perhaps pressed this speculation far enough.

The generalization that in evolving systems whose descriptions are stored in a process language, we might expect ontogeny partially to recapitulate phylogeny has applications outside the realm of biology. It can be applied as readily, for example, to the transmission of knowledge in the educational process. In most subjects, particularly in the rapidly advancing sciences, the progress from elementary to advanced courses is to a considerable extent a progress through the conceptual history of the science itself. Fortunately, the recapitulation is seldom literal—any more than it is in the biological case. We do not teach the phlogiston theory in chemistry in order later to correct it. (I am not sure I could not cite examples in other subjects where we do exactly that.) But curriculum revisions that rid us of the accumulations of the past are infrequent and painful. Nor are they always desirable—partial recapitulation may, in many instances, provide the most expeditious route to advanced knowledge.

Summary: The Description of Complexity. How complex or simple a structure is depends critically upon the way in which we describe it. Most of the complex structures found in the world are enormously redundant, and we can use this redundancy to simplify their description. But to use it, to achieve the simplification, we must find the right representation.

The notion of substituting a process description for a state description of nature has played a central role in the development of modern science. Dynamic laws, expressed in

[25] There is considerable evidence that successive genes along a chromosome often determine enzymes controlling successive stages of protein syntheses. For a review of some of this evidence, P. E. Hartman, Transduction: a comparative review, in W. D. McElroy and B. Glass (eds.), *The Chemical Basis of Heredity*, Baltimore, Johns Hopkins Press, 1957, at pp. 442–454. Evidence for differential activity of genes in different tissues and at different stages of development is discussed by J. G. Gall, Chromosomal Differentiation in W. D. McElroy and B. Glass (eds.), *The Chemical Basis of Development*, Baltimore Johns Hopkins Press, 1958, at pp. 103–135. Finally, a model very like that proposed here has been independently, and far more fully, outlined by J. R. Platt, A "book model" of genetic information transfer in cells and tissues, in Kasha and Pullman (eds.), *Horizons in Biochemistry*, New York, Academic Press, 1962. Of course, this kind of mechanism is not the only one in which development could be controlled by a process description. Induction, in the form envisaged in Spemann's organizer theory, is based on process description, in which metabolites in already formed tissue control the next stages of development.

the form of systems of differential or difference equations, have in a large number of cases provided the clue for the simple description of the complex. In the preceding paragraphs I have tried to show that this characteristic of scientific inquiry is not accidental or superficial. The correlation between state description and process description is basic to the functioning of any adaptive organism, to its capacity for acting purposefully upon its environment. Our present-day understanding of genetic mechanisms suggests that even in describing itself the multicellular organism finds a process description—a genetically encoded program—to be the parsimonious and useful representation.

Conclusion

Our speculations have carried us over a rather alarming array of topics, but that is the price we must pay if we wish to seek properties common to many sorts of complex systems. My thesis has been that one path to the construction of a non-trivial theory of complex systems is by way of a theory of hierarchy. Empirically, a large proportion of the complex systems we observe in nature exhibit hierarchic structure. On theoretical grounds we could expect complex systems to be hierarchies in a world in which complexity had to evolve from simplicity. In their dynamics, hierarchies have a property, near-decomposability, that greatly simplifies their behavior. Near-decomposability also simplies the description of a complex system, and makes it easier to understand how the information needed for the development or reproduction of the system can be stored in reasonable compass.

In both science and engineering, the study of "systems" is an increasingly popular activity. Its popularity is more a response to a pressing need for synthesizing and analyzing complexity than it is to any large development of a body of knowledge and technique for dealing with complexity. If this popularity is to be more than a fad, necessity will have to mother invention and provide substance to go with the name. The explorations reviewed here represent one particular direction of search for such substance.

PART TWO

Systems Properties of Organizations in the Steady State

P A R T   T W O

WE HAVE REVIEWED some of the basic writings and ideas of general systems. However, the study of General Systems is not the study of organization, for while organizations possess General Systems properties they are, at the same time, both more and different from General Systems. To continue one of our early analogies, the study of Newtonian physics is not the study of astronomy. Astronomy is the study of planets, part of which is aided because certain aspects of the subject exhibit properties that can be explained with the aid of Newtonian physics. Throughout this book, and particularly in the remaining portions of this volume, we are attempting to examine organizational phenomena that reveal General Systems characteristics. In this part, we are particularly concerned with identifying and clarifying some of the relationships of organizations in the steady state. As a general guide, we shall use the ten characteristics of systems identified in the preceding part. Since these, however, were the characteristics of open systems, some will not be significantly applicable in this section.

Some Characteristics of Organizations as Systems

What, then, are some of the things we look at when we study organization and hope to explain with systems concepts? Some general ones are:

1. Some of the components in an organization are animals, more particularly, human beings.
2. Decisions that will control actions within the organization will be spread over two or more people or groups.
3. Functionally distinct groups will be aware of each other's behavior through communication.
4. As a unit, the organization has some freedom of choice in both the ends to be achieved and the means by which they will be realized (Ackoff).
5. Organizations are in part contrived entities (as noted in Volume I). Organizations spring not only from the needs and desires of men but also have other aspects

that come about as the result of deliberate planning.

6. An organization must accomplish two different functions or deliver two different products. One is to satisfy the needs and desires of its members, and the other is to accomplish some technical or economic result of use to the environment.
7. The organization's existence is not dependent on the life or tenure of each individual component. While it is very dependent on certain functions being performed, the specific element that performs them may change. This is one of the unique functions of organizations as contrasted to the systems found in areas such as biology or physiology. If a person's lungs were to cease operation, the whole body dies. If a president of a corporation dies, the firm goes on with a new person filling his function. Hence, organizations can and have survived long after all the original physical components have changed.

Before continuing, it would be well to examine one of the things this set of characteristics suggests, namely, the unique relationship between people and organization. As Homans pointed out, the dilemma of man is that he can live neither with nor without organization.[1] He needs the products or organizations: the food, the clothing, the protection and, indirectly, the leisure time, but while these are being produced, man must sacrifice opportunities at having his "humanness" adequately cared for. Hence, man enters organizations with two different and often conflicting needs: those that will be satisfied through the organization in attaining wages, automobiles, houses, prestige, etc., and those that will be attained through association with other human beings *in* the organization. It suggests that since there is no way of maximizing both simultaneously, man will seek continually for the most adequate combination or balance between these two factors.

The same may be suggested as being true for the organization itself. It must continually attempt to accomplish its purpose and yet also to maintain itself in part by satisfying the needs of its members. These two functions are not possible of simultaneous maximization, and the organization, therefore, can be conceived as attempting to reach some satisfactory balance between them. We might, therefore, add an eighth characteristic: organizations perform several noncompatible functions, among which there is continual search for a balance.

[1] George C. Homans, *Some Elementary Forms of Social Organization*, New York, Harcourt, Brace and World Co., 1961 (see, for example, Chapter 18).

Systems Characteristics of Organizations in Steady State

In this part, we shall look at some of the ways in which the systems properties of organizations are manifest. It is not sufficient to say that there is an interrelatedness of elements. In particular, we have to examine what is interrelated and the particular way the interrelation occurs. We shall identify only a small fraction of these. The intent is to illustrate rather than exhaustively to treat these aspects. To guide us, we shall use a list of characteristics identified in the preceding part.

Interrelatedness

When discussing interrelatedness, we frequently and easily talk about the interrelatedness of things. Parents are related to their children, superiors have a particular relationship with their subordinates, an individual may have a particular relationship with a machine he operates. We have also cited the interrelation of events in identifying the serial relationship of events in a production operation, suggesting not only which events must occur but also their order. What is not as easily obvious, but is at the same time more important, is that we are primarily interested in the relationship among attributes. To illustrate, let's return to our astronomy analogy. To recognize that the earth has an interrelationship with the sun is important, but not too clarifying. If we are to understand this interrelationship more effectively, we must understand what it is about the sun and the earth that are involved. Is it the fact that the earth has mountains and oceans, that the sun gives off light? Not really. There are many things about the sun and the earth that, in any direct or immediate sense, are irrelevant in understanding and explaining their interrelationship. What is important is that they exert forces on each other, and the magnitude and direction of these forces is determined by the particular attributes of their mass and their velocity. To discuss the movement of the earth in regard to the sun, all we need is very limited and precisely stated information concerning these attributes.[2] Hence, in the study of organizations, to recognize that we are concerned with the interrelationships of people is a start. If we are going to explain adequately their various movements in regard to each other, we must determine what attributes are peculiarly involved with this interrelatedness.

The Strength of the Interrelationship

In organizations, the interrelatedness comes about because the attributes of the parts or elements draw something from each other. Furthermore, they produce something that can feed still other elements of the organization. For example, an individual has a personality that can be described as quiet, friendly, nonassertive, and methodical, and we have a position, such as that of a bank teller, where it is necessary for the public to be treated quietly, to have their problems handled competently and discreetly, and to have the detailed records kept reliably; then we would have an important and meaningful interrelationship between the attributes of the person and the requirements of the job (Argyris). The fact that this occurs opens several other things. For example, the job is performed well so that the bank can be successful in fulfilling its responsibility to society. But since the person's particular set of needs will be well-handled by the position, other needs, such as monetary ones, may not be as strong, and the individual may prefer to settle for a lower salary, permitting the bank also to operate economically. Hence the economic requirements of the bank, as well the technical aspects of the job, need that type of person.

Needless to say, there are many attributes involved in an organization. Furthermore, it is very difficult to identify them readily. Perhaps one of the most useful ways to begin is by focusing on an activity and asking, "What functions does this activity fill for the various elements in the organization?" Not all elements will have a function filled by a particular activity, but those that do will be those that are interrelated, and we shall now be able to say what the nature of this interrelationship is. This is a complex process, but it can be done, and the paper by Argyris on the organization of a bank is an excellent illustration of this form of analysis.

Wholism

To talk about the wholistic properties of an organization, one must first have some idea of what constitutes the organization under discussion. One striking difference between organizations as systems and other entities with system properties, such as plants or animals, is the absence of any sharp boundaries for organizations. If an organization is made up of people, one of the questions we might well ask is what set of people constitute the organization. Is it merely those on the payroll? In a business firm, might it also be stockholders? How about customers? Furthermore, do those who are within the boundary all have equal weight, or are some quite important and others hardly considered? Various aspects of this problem are explored by Dent and Argyris.

Goal Seeking—Equilibrium

One characteristic of organizations is that they behave as if they are attempting to achieve a goal or, more accurately, goals, for it is commonly observed that organizations have multiple goals (Bales). The collection and arrangement of these goals will be dependent upon the membership of the organization (Dent).

In attempting to achieve several goals, organizations frequently encounter the problem that all cannot be achieved, or at least maximized, simultaneously. Bales gives a very interesting description of how, within a group that

[2] At first glance this might appear to be a return to the search for properties of things previously identified as an unprofitable direction for research. It is not, however, since it is a search for the elements in the earth-sun system and not for the unique characteristics of the earth or the sun.

has an objective of both completing a task and satisfying certain social needs of members, an initial effort to work on the task creates a situation in which social needs are less satisfied. As a result, groups then make the effort to correct this and overcome the negative aspects of task efforts, sometimes even by holding back those efforts. He finds a regular sequence of events or behaviors in a group directed to restarting the disturbed balance between the two organizational or group goals.

Although regulation is going to be more thoroughly treated in later parts, we see a number of interesting illustrations of how it occurs in organizations. Bales, in reporting that he regularly finds a particular sequence of phases following the disturbance of balance between task and social needs of a group, gives a good illustration of regulation by adjustment. Argyris gives interesting examples of where learning occurs in organization and new patterns emerge as a consequence.

Hierarchy of Systems

Several authors in this part, among them Argyris, Herbst, and Kaufman, explicitly analyze systems that exist within larger systems in an organization and some of the many ways in which this phenomenon occurs.

Entropy

Many differing conditions can cause entropy to occur in organizations. One of the more important general patterns is described by Kaufman in which he analyzes the problems encountered in the forest service when making the performance of its various members fit into an integrated pattern, rather than permitting their behavior to go in many different and unrelated directions. The problems are many and so, as he points out, are the actions that can be taken to counter them.

Differentiation

Both Herbst and Bales give interesting descriptions of how differentiation occurs in organizations in order to permit the organization to function more adequately. Herbst identifies the failure of intrinsic coordination as the casual factor leading to the rise of a managerial function to provide extrinsic coordination. Bales analyzes the reason why the leadership functions become more specialized and go into the hands of several parties.

In short, in these few selections we find many illustrations of the systems properties of organizations. Not all characteristics of systems, however, are to be found here, but will be covered in later sections.

Systems, Organizations, and Interdisciplinary Research

RUSSELL L. ACKOFF

When the announcement was made of the establishment of a Systems Research Center at Case, a number of my associates in operations research asked me how the activity of the Center was to differ from that of the Operations Research Group at Case. My colleagues in the Control (or Systems) Engineering Group at Case were asked similar questions concerning the relationship of their group to the Center. The question could be answered by saying that the Center is designed to facilitate cooperative research and educational activities among the Operations Research Group, the Control Engineering Group, and other systems-oriented activities at Case, particularly the Computing Center.

This answer may satisfy the curiosity of some and discourage probing by others. It is not enough, however, to satisfy or discourage probing by those of us who have some responsibility for the development of this Center. Much more than good will among men is required to make this Center play a significant role in research and education. Part of what is required is a philosophy and a program. A philosophy and program for the Center cannot be expected to spring into existence in a mature state; it must evolve out of proposals, discussion, reformulations, and experience. I should like here to formulate an initial philosophy and program which I hope will lead to constructive discussion, not only at this conference, but afterwards in other cells in which the systems movement is taking shape. There is no doubt in my mind that centers such as we are forming here at Case will develop in profusion in other academic institutions and in industrial and governmental organizations.

From *Systems: Research and Design*, Eckman (ed.). New York: Wiley, 1961, pp. 26–36. Reprinted by permission of the publisher.

I will use my own interdiscipline, operations research, as my springboard. But before I take the leap I would like to make some general observations about the systems movement.[1]

First, I believe the systems movement will reach its fruition in an interdiscipline of wider scope and greater significance than has yet been attained. I should like to emphasize that my concern is not with what systems research is, but rather with what we can make of it. I consider operations research an intermediate step toward this fruition, a step away from traditional science. Correspondingly, I take systems engineering to be an intermediate step toward the same objective, a step away from traditional engineering. I believe systems engineering and operations research are rapidly converging. What more fitting title for the convergence than systems research.

Operations research is concerned with increasing the effectiveness of operations of organized man-machine systems. A complete understanding of the significance of this too brief characterization requires at least definitions of *systems*, *operations*, and *organization*. I shall deal with the first two very lightly, only enough for my immediate purposes.[2] I shall, however, deal with the concept of organization in more detail because I shall use it as the key to the philosophy and program which I hope to develop. It is in the context of organized man-machine systems, I believe, that we find the most comprehensive demands for departure from the existing content and structure of science and technology. Now, to the task.

[1] I am deeply indebted to Vernon C. Mickelson for the use of his mind and ears in the preparation of this chapter.

[2] For a more detailed discussion of "systems" and "operations" see "The Meaning, Scope, and Methods of Operations Research," Chap. 1 in *Progress in Operations Research*, Vol. I, edited by R. L. Ackoff, John Wiley & Sons, New York, 1961.

Systems and Operations

The term "system" is used to cover a wide range of phenomena. We speak, for example, of philosophical systems, number systems, communication systems, control systems, educational systems, political systems, and weapon systems. Some of these are conceptual constructs and others are physical entities. Initially we can define a system broadly and crudely as *any entity, conceptual or physical, which consists of interdependent parts.* Even without further refinement of this definition it is clear that in systems research we are interested only in those systems which can display activity, i.e., *behavioral* systems.

It is also apparent that systems research is only concerned with behavioral systems which are subject to control by human beings. Consequently, the solar system—although it may be on the verge of becoming so—is not yet a part of the subject matter of systems research. The relevant domain of such research, then, is controllable behavioral systems.

The essential characteristics of a behavioral system is that it consists of parts each of which displays behavior. Whether or not an entity with parts is considered as a system depends on whether or not we are concerned with the behavior of the parts and their interactions.

A behavioral system, then, is a conceptual construct as well as a physical entity since such a system may or may not be treated as a system, depending on the way it is conceptualized by the person treating it. For example, we would not normally think of a man who starts a car as a system because we do not distinguish the parts of the man involved in the component acts. We may, however, consider man as a biological system when studying the metabolic process. A physical entity is considered a system if the outcome of its behavior is conceptualized as the product of the interactions of its parts. Therefore, many entities may be studied either as elements or as systems; it is a matter of the researcher's choice.

The behavior displayed by a system consists of a set of interdependent acts which constitute an *operation.* An operation is a complex concept which I do not want to deal with in detail here. Loosely put, a set of acts can be said to constitute an operation if each act is necessary for the occurrence of a desired outcome and if these acts are interdependent. The nature of this interdependence can be precisely defined. Both the relevant outcome and acts involved in an operation may be defined by a set of properties which can be treated as variables. The acts are interdependent relative to the outcome if the rate of change of any outcome variable affected by change in any variable describing one of the acts depends on (i.e., is a function of) all the other relevant act variables. Therefore, if all the variables can be represented by continuous quantities, the derivative of an outcome variable with respect to any act variable (if it exists) is a function of all other act variables. In ordinary language, then, an outcome is the product of a set of interdependent acts if it is more than the sum of (or difference between) these acts.

Organization

An organization can be defined as an at least partially self-controlled system which has four essential characteristics:

1. *Some of its components are animals.* Of particular interest to us, however, are those systems in which the animals are human beings. Wires, poles, switchboards, and telephones may constitute a communication system, but they do not constitute an organization. The employees of a telephone company make up the organization that operates the communication system. Men and equipment together constitute a more inclusive (man-machine) system that we can refer to as organized. Since most organizations utilize machines in a significant way in order to achieve their objectives, the discussion here will be directed to organized man-machine systems.

2. *Responsibility for choices from the sets of possible acts in any specific situation is divided among two or more individuals or groups of individuals.* Each subgroup (consisting of one or more individuals is responsible for one or more choices of action and the set of choices is divided among two or more subgroups. The classes of action and thus the subgroups may be individuated by a variety of types of characteristics, for instance:

(a) *by function* (e.g., the departments of production, marketing, research, finance, and personnel of an industrial organization),

(b) *by geography* (e.g., areas of responsibility of the Army), and

(c) *by time* (e.g., waves of an invading force).

The classes of action may, of course, also be defined by combinations of these and other characteristics.

It should be noted that the individuals or groups need not carry out the actions they select; other human beings or machines may perform the actions, which are programmed or controlled in order that the desired objective is accomplished. It should also be noted that the equipment involved and the subgroups may also be considered as systems, i.e., as subsystems.

3. *The functionally distinct subgroups are aware of each other's behavior either through communication or observation.* In many laboratory experiments, for example, subjects are given interrelated tasks to perform and are rewarded on the basis of an outcome which is determined by their collective choices. The subjects, however, are not permitted to observe or communicate with each other. In such cases the subjects are unorganized. Allow them to observe each other or communicate and they may become an organization. Put another way, in an organization the human subgroups must be capable of responding to each other either directly or indirectly.

4. *The system has some freedom of choice of both means (courses of action) and ends (desired outcomes).* This implies that at least some parts have alternative courses of action under at least some possible sets of conditions. The simplest type of system, the *binary* type, has only two possible states: "off" and "on" (e.g., a heating system in a home). More complex *adaptive* systems can behave differently under different conditions, but only in one way under any particular set of conditions (e.g., a ship operated by automatic pilot). Still others are free to choose their means to an end but have no choice of this end (e.g., a computer programmed to play chess). Finally, there are those which are free to choose *how* they will act in any situation (means-free) and *why* (ends-free). To be sure, such systems are usually constrained in their choices by larger systems which contain them (e.g., government restrictions on a company's behavior). Their efficiency is also affected by either the behavior of other systems (e.g., competition in industry) or natural conditions (e.g., weather).

The four essential characteristics of an organization, then, can be briefly identified as content, structure, communication, and decision-making (choice) procedures.

Design and Operation of Organized Man-Machine Systems

Now we want to consider the significance of these characteristics to one who wants either to create an effective organized system or to improve the operation of an existing one. He has four basic types of approach to organizational effectiveness and combinations thereof. The basic types of approach correspond to the four essential characteristics of organizations.

Content. The content (men and machines) of an organization can be changed. The study of organizational personnel—their selection, training, and utilization—has come to be the domain of *industrial psychology*.[3]

Three fundamentally different approaches to personnel problems have developed within industrial psychology. The first, *personnel* psychology, is primarily concerned with selecting the right man for a specified job. Its principal activity, therefore, is directed toward specifying the relevant characteristics of a job, determining which individual properties are related to its performance, and selecting those individuals who are best equipped for the job. The personnel psychologist, therefore, takes the task to be done as fixed and varies the men.

The personnel psychologist is also interested in modifying man so that he is better capable of performing the task. He attempts such modification through education and training. Here he partially overlaps with the *industrial engineer*, who tries to modify the behavior of man more directly. On the basis of time and motion

[3] For a very penetrating review of this field see Mason Haire's "Psychology and the Study of Business: Joint Behavioral Sciences," in *Social Science Research on Business: Product and Potential*, Robert A. Dahl, Mason Haire, and Paul F. Lazarsfeld, Columbia University Press, New York, 1959.

studies the industrial engineer attempts to find those movements which optimize the individual's operations. The industrial engineer, therefore, is preoccupied with manual operations, whereas the personnel psychologist tends to concentrate on communication and decision making.

The second psychological approach is that of the *human engineer*. The human engineer tries to modify the job to be done so that it can be done better by the people available to do it. Here the men are taken to be fixed and the task is taken to be variable. Hence, human engineers, like industrial engineers, are concerned with the acts to be performd, but they try to modify them through the design of the equipment involved in these tasks. It is only natural, therefore, that there has been an increasing convergence of these two approaches.

A third psychological approach takes both the man and the job to be fixed, but the psychological and social environment to be variable. This type of approach yields studies of motivation, incentive systems, interpersonal relationships, group identification or alienation, and the like and the effect of such variables on human productivity, job satisfaction, and morale. These studies are essentially *social-psychological* in nature and are epitomized by the early work of Mayo and Roethlisberger and Dickson. Studies of the social environment frequently consider the effect of the noncontent aspects of organization (structure, communication, and control) on human performance. For example, the effect of various types of communication networks on the performance of an individual in the network has been extensively explored. Clearly, such studies are related to those directed at structure, communication, and control, but the emphasis of most of them is on the *individual's* performance rather than on the performance of the organization as a whole.

The other part of the content of man-machine systems is equipment. We have already observed that human engineers are concerned with modifying equipment so that it can be better operated by available personnel. They seldom, however, completely design this equipment. Normally they collaborate with representatives of the traditional branches of engineering in design activity so that the latter can take the capabilities of the operators into account more effectively. Human engineers, therefore, do not replace, they supplement, the traditional engineer in his design function.

The individual piece of equipment can frequently be studied as a system. Engineers have increasingly tended to so regard the machine and the weapon. In equipment incorporating automatic controls the systems approach is almost inescapable. In addition, engineers have become increasingly concerned with the interactions of equipment in machine and weapon complexes and so they have become concerned with larger and larger equipment systems. Out of this concern the interdiscipline of *systems engineering* has emerged. The engineer, of course, can no more ignore the human operator than the personnel psychologist can ignore the machine to be operated. The variables which they manipulate, however, remain distinct.

Structure. The second major approach to organizational effectiveness is through its structure, i.e., to the way that the necessary physical and mental labor is divided. Although political scientists, economists, and sociologists have concerned themselves with organizational structure, there is as yet no organized body of theory or doctrine of practice on which a unified disciplinary or interdisciplinary applied-research activity can be based. As a consequence most studies of organizational structure, such as those leading to reorganization of a system, are generally done by managers or management consultants whose approach involves more art and common sense than science.

Within the last few decades there has been increasing experimental study of organizational structure. More recently, there has begun to appear a body of mathematical theory of organizational structure. Haire has pointed out, however, that as yet

> We do not have much in the way of systematic behavioral data collected for the purpose of testing hypotheses or quantifying variables used in models. For example, we have models dealing with the cost of decentralized decision-making in abstract terms, but we know nothing about the information and decision load that can be supported, or how individuals vary along this dimension. . . . We know little about the effect of various communication structures

and practices on alternative forms of organizations and their cohesiveness. . . . We should be just on the brink of a period of exciting systematic data collection (1959, p. 72).

We may have reached that brink in a provocative new development: operational gaming.[4] In operational gaming organized groups are given problems analogous to real ones, usually with a collapse of the time dimension, and are observed under controlled conditions. We appear to be developing a way of experimenting quantitatively with at least small organizations under conditions which appear to be relevant to actual operations.[5] Difficult problems remain concerning inferences from the game to the real situation, but there is little doubt that within the next few years a significant reduction of these difficulties will occur.

Communication. The effectiveness of an organization depends in part on its having "the right information at the right place at the right time." The study of organizational communication is in much the same stage of development as the study of organizational structure. It has no organized body of theory, but it has been developing a doctrine of practice. *Systems and procedures analysts,* stimulated by the numerous installations of automatic data-processing systems, have been perfecting techniques of qualitative analysis of information and its flow. It may seem peculiar that this work is predominantly qualitative in light of the highly developed mathematical theory of communication, based to a large extent on the work of Claude Shannon, and its pervasive application to the design of physical communication and information-processing systems.

This theory, however, concerns itself exclusively with the physical aspects of communication and has no relevance to problems involving the meaning of the communication. In Shannon's theory, for example, the measure of information contained in a message is a function of the number of distinct physical messages that could have been sent and the probability associated with the selection of each. The measure makes no reference to the content or significance of the message.

The same thing has been said very well by Haire in his discussion of an article by Rapoport:

> He [Rapoport] points out that in dealing with communication among linked individuals we have tended to use the information theory developed by the communications engineer. Such a formulation is useful for determining channel capacity . . . but it is not maximally useful for studying decision-making in groups. Here one needs a model of the cognitive aspects of communication theory—a way to indicate the potential of bits for reducing uncertainty about a real state of affairs. Such an approach contrasts with the definition of information in terms of the probabilities of selecting a certain class of messages from a source with given statistical characteristics (1959, p. 7).

There is a growing body of experimental work on the effect of different types of communication networks on organizational (rather than individual) performance, particularly on small groups. Such experimentation has been stimulated to a large extent by the pioneering work of Alex Bavelas. In addition, the body of special theories is rapidly expanding so that we may well be on the verge of a major breakthrough in this area. This work is very effectively summarized in the recent work of Colin Cherry.

Beginnings toward the construction of a behavioral theory of communication have been made at Case. This theory has two essential characteristics. First, it does not equate the transmission of information with communication but recognizes three types of message content: information, instruction, and motivation. Information is defined and measured in terms of the effect on the receiver's possibilities and probabilities of choice. Instruction is defined and measured in terms of the effect on the efficiency of the receiver's action, and mo-

[4] For a detailed discussion of the product and potential of this technique see Clayton J. Thomas and Walter L. Deemer, Jr., The Role of Operational Gaming in Operations Research, *Operations Research,* Vol. 5, Feb. 1957, pp. 1–27. For illustrative applications see Harold Guetzkow, The Development of Organizations in a Laboratory, *Management Science,* Vol. 3, July 1957, pp. 380–402.

[5] For some work along these lines performed at Case see D. F. Clark and R. L. Ackoff, A Report on Some Organizational Experiments, *Operations Research,* Vol. 7, May–June, 1959, pp. 279–293.

tivation in terms of the effect of the message on the values which the receiver places on possible outcomes of his choices. A single message may combine all three types of content.

The second essential aspect of this theory is that it provides separate measures of the amount and value of information, instruction, and motivation contained in a message. It therefore distinguishes between information and misinformation, effective and ineffective instruction, and motivation.

A theory with these characteristics, whether the ones developed at Case or another, increases the possibility of useful quantitative treatment of organizational communication problems.

Decision-Making Procedures. The last type of approach to organizational problems involves its decision-making procedures. An organization with good personnel and equipment, and an effective structure and communication system, may still be inefficient because it does not make effective use of its resources. That is, the operations of the organization may not be efficiently controlled. Control is a matter of setting objectives and directing the organization toward them. It is obtained by efficient decision making by those who manage the operation.

Study of the effective utilization of economic resources in industrial and public organizations is a well-established domain of interest to that splinter group in economics which concerns itself with *micro-economics* and *econometrics.* In the last decade it has produced a rapidly expanding body of theory and research techniques. Concurrent with this development there has been another which deals with a broader class of resources than do the economists alone and, consequently, with a wider variety of organizational decision problems. This broader interdisciplinary approach to organizational control has come to be known as *operations research.*

The essential characteristics of this interdisciplinary activity lie in its methodology. Out of an analysis of the desired outcomes, objectives of the organization, it develops a measure of performance (P) of the system. It then seeks to model the organization's behavior in the form of an equation in which the measure of performance is equated to some function of those aspects of the system which are subject to management's control (C_i) and which affect the desired outcome, and to those uncontrolled aspects of the system (U_j) which also affect the outcome.

Thus the model takes the form:

$$P = f(C_i, U_j)$$

From the model, values of the control variables are found which maximize (or minimize) the measure of the system's performance:

$$C_i = g(U_j)$$

The solution, therefore, consists of a set of rules, one for each control variable, which establishes the value at which that variable should be set for any possible set of values of the uncontrolled variables. In order to employ these rules it is necessary to set up procedures for determining or forecasting the values of the uncontrolled variables.

It will be recognized that this procedure is one by which equipment systems should be ideally designed. In design one should also develop a consolidated measure of system performance, and identify the variables which the designer can control as well as those uncontrolled aspects of the system or its environment which will affect its performance. Unfortunately, in many cases such a model of a desired equipment system cannot be constructed because of our ignorance. For example, I have not yet seen a good single consolidated measure proposed for the performance of an aircraft. Nor is there sufficient knowledge to relate any of the less perfect available measures of performance to the large number of design variables of such craft. As a consequence, design is currently accomplished by a combination of scientific analysis, intuition, and aesthetic considerations. It should be recognized, however, that current design procedures are only an evolutionary stage which will be replaced as rapidly as possible by effective modeling and the extraction of solutions from the resulting models.

REFERENCES

1. Claude E. Shannon and Warren Weaver, *The Mathematical Theory of Communication,* University of Illinois Press, Urbana, 1949.

2. See, e.g., A. Bavelas, Communication Patterns in Task-oriented Groups, *Journal of Acoustical Society of America*, Vol. 22, 1950, pp. 725–730.
3. Colin Cherry, *On Human Communication*, Technology Press and John Wiley & Sons, New York, 1957.
4. R. L. Ackoff, Toward a Behavioral Theory of Communication, *Management Science*, Vol. 4, Apr. 1958, pp. 218–234.
5. C. West Churchman and Russell L. Ackoff, *Psychologistics* (mimeographed), University of Pennsylvania Research Fund, 1947.

Selections from Organization of a Bank

CHRIS ARGYRIS

Theoretical Preconceptions

These postulates and theorems and hypotheses derived from them govern the design of the present research herein reported.

The set of categories that we shall use have the following advantages:

1. They are derived logically from a definition of organization.[1]
2. They are therefore logically interrelated. It is possible to see exactly how one can move through logical paths from one construct to another.
3. They serve as a basis from which theorems are derived. These theorems form the hypotheses of the research. If confirmed, they have the advantage of being empirically as well as logically valid.

Hypotheses About the Nature of Organization. Below, we propose five hypotheses [2] about the fundamental nature of social organization. One of the objectives of this research is to test the validity of these hypotheses

1. Men have needs to fulfill and goals to achieve. Many of these needs cannot be fulfilled and many of the goals cannot be achieved unless they join groups and pool their abilities and energies. The moment people join forces to achieve some goal, the first necessary step toward an organization has been taken.

2. All social organizations, therefore, are created by people to accomplish some goal or set of goals that they have in mind. We picture an organization as people's creative attempt to establish some order in their world so that they will be able to fulfill their needs and achieve their goals. In other words, people create organizations and then permit those organizations to coerce them into behaving in a specific manner. They permit this coercion *not* because organizations are superhuman entities, but because the people creating them want to be coerced in order to fulfill their needs and achieve their goals. This is not unlike the streets we pave in our communities which, once put into operation, tell us, so to speak, where to drive.

3. On the other hand, and this constitutes our third hypothesis, the parts of a social organization, unlike the streets in the example above, are *not* static entities. They are dynamic, everchanging processes, or sequences of activities.[3] To be sure, they manifest stable properties or a stable pattern. But in doing so, these parts are continuously in movement, acting, interacting, and transacting with each other in order to maintain this stable pattern. Much of the behavior in organizations exists in order that the organization may remain stable. In short, stability is as important a phenomena in a dynamic system as is change.

Viewing an organization as being basically constituted or processes may suggest to some that we are not considering the *form* or *structure* of organization; this is not so. Structure or form is definitely an important problem for us to consider. We believe that it is not fruitful to look at structure as being something discrete from process. Basically, organizational structure is simply organizational processes in a stable state. Thus, *the organizational structure is the organizational processes viewed in a stable state and the organizational processes are the organizational structure viewed in fluid state.*

This view, we suggest, is more in keeping with the recent findings in the study of other forms of organization. In embryology and

From *Organization of a Bank,* New Haven: Labor and Management Center, Yale University, 1954, pp 7–10; 51–69; 77–80; 86–92; 97–102. Reprinted by permission of the publisher.

[1] The actual steps of logical derivation are presented in Appendix A, B, and C *Organization of a Bank.*

[2] These are called hypotheses since they are derived from reading the literature and not from a systematic theory.

[3] See below p. 9, for definition of the processes.

biology, for example, structure and process are viewed as being "heads and tails" of the same phenomena.[4] Similarly, modern physics and chemistry view structure as being basically activity (e.g., a set of molecular particles in continuous motion).

4. A fourth basic hypothesis is that organization is to be conceived as an open system rather than as a closed system. Bertalanffy defines an open system as one where there is an inflow and an outflow and therefore movement in the components of the system.[5]

5. A fifth basic hypothesis related to the characteristics of an open system is that the final state of the system cannot be determined simply by knowing the initial conditions. Open systems are not like the mechanical "closed system" models where knowledge of the state of the system at time t_1 permits one to predict the state of the system at time t_2. One reason for this is that the final state of the system can be reached from different initial conditions and in different ways.[6]

Postulate 1: Organization. The following conceptual properties of "organization" are postulated. An organization is:

1. any aggregate of parts,
2. in a hierarchical order
3. coexisting
4. and interrelated in such a unique manner
5. that the parts can be maintained as agents only through this unique interrelatedness
6. and simultaneously these parts work together in order to achieve resultants of the characteristic dynamic tendencies of the organization
7. and to achieve numbers 5 and 6 by adapting, within limits, to any external influences, thereby
8. maintaining the characteristic interrelated state of these parts (i.e., maintaining organization).

[4] Alexis Carrel, "Physiological Time", *Science*, Vol. 74, No. 1929, p. 620; and G. E. Coghill, "The Neuro-Embryologic Study of Behavior: Perspective and Aim," *Science*, Vol. 78, No. 2016, August 18, 1933, p. 137.

[5] Ludwig von Bertalanffy, "Problems of General System Theory," *Human Biology*, Vol. 23, December 1951, No. 4, pp. 302–312.

[6] *Ibid.*

What empirical properties are coordinated to the concept, "parts?" The answer is that this is dependent upon what sort of organization is being studied and from what viewpoint. Thus, in the case of a social organization one can coordinate "people," "jobs," "role," or "bonds of organization" to the concept "parts." In the derivation of the theorems which follow, it is assumed that "people" are included as "parts" of organization.

Theorems I–VI: Organizational Processes. By applying deductive reasoning, the following "organizational processes" may be derived from Postulate I as being necessary if an organization is to exist. A process is defined as any course or sequence of behavior accomplishing a necessary purpose. A purpose is simply an intended consequence.[7]

The processes must exist in a specific relationship to each other which has been called "interdependence." Interdependence is defined as the simultaneous independence-dependence relationship of each process to all the other processes.

THEOREM I. There must be a Workflow Process to define the behavior sequence that the parts of the organization must accomplish to achieve results in the form of a product or service (e.g., in a shoe factory, a series of behavior sequences must be set up which people must perform in order to produce shoes).

THEOREM II. There must be an Authority Process in order to direct behavior in the interests of the organization and its participants.

THEOREM III. There must be a Reward and Penalty Process to induce people to behave in a way required by the interests of the organization and its participants. (In other words, the Reward and Penalty Process "taps" human motivation by rewarding or penalizing according to the acceptability of the actions performed.)

THEOREM IV. There must be a Perpetuation Process to maintain and replenish the quantity and quality of the participants plus the resources they utilize.

THEOREM V. There must be an Identification Process to develop a concept of the wholeness, uniqueness, and significance of the organization. This is usually accomplished by efforts to select and define clearly understood, emotion-

[7] I am indebted to Dr. R. D. Schwartz, Yale University, for this definition of purpose.

ally toned symbols, concepts, or other such factors which will help individual participants identify the uniqueness of the organization as a whole, which in turn automatically helps to define the uniqueness of the organization in the larger environment in which it is embedded.

THEOREM VI. There must be a Communication Process to provide for the exchange of information, ideas, and values, etc., utilized in all activities.[8]

The Steady State of the Bank's Processes of Organization

In the previous chapter we defined the fusion process as being basically concerned with the interaction of peoples' personalities with the organization. We are concerned with finding out how much expression peoples' personalities obtain in the organization. We are also concerned with finding out how much expression the organization obtains through the personalities and activities of its individual participants. In order to do this, we must give content to the word "organization."

This is the task we have set before us in this chapter. We will describe as accurately as we can the relevant activities in each of the organizational processes in the bank as a whole and show how each process is intimately interrelated with the others. Once this "steady state" of the organizational processes is understood we will have a picture of the content of the organizational as a whole.

A. *Workflow Process.* The workflow process includes all the behavioral activities and their concomitant codes and specifications which must be accomplished if the organization's objective is to be achieved.

1. MULTI-OBJECTIVES LEAD TO MULTI-WORKFLOWS. Generally speaking, the organization's objective comes under the category of "services." It does not produce a product. More concretely, the organization actually has more than one objective. In fact, there are at least ten "sub" objectives that can be observed in the activities of people in the bank:

(a) Receiving and protecting deposits, checks, currency, and coin.

(b) Providing customers (the public) with cash and change; cashing coupons and other items.

(c) Maintaining deposit facilities; in other words creating and servicing a medium (the bank check) which is used in place of actual cash.

(d) Paying out funds on the customer's order—by checks, by transfer of funds by wire, or by payment of funds upon his written direction.

(e) The bookkeeping of the customer's financial transactions—a direct result of the operation of a checking account.

(f) The collection of checks and other items which are payable at the bank itself or at other local banks or at banks in any part of the United States or abroad.

(g) The making of loans to businesses qualified for credit—for the production of materials in manufacturing, in agriculture, in transportation, and in every other phase of American business life.

(h) The making of loans to individuals for a vast variety of purposes—to assist in the purchase of homes, household goods, and automobiles, in the payment of existing obligations, and for a myriad of other purposes that are worthy of credit.

(i) The handling of funds for others—trust services and the holding and administering of property for the owners.

(j) A large number of more or less related services—credit information, foreign transactions, safe deposit facilities, savings or investment facilities, general collection facilities, the servicing of government and other securities (including purchases, sales, and redemptions) and many specialized services to

[8] Bakke suggests that an Evaluation (status) Process may also be logically derived as one of the basic processes of organization. This process establishes criteria for and defines levels of utility and value for people, materials, and ideas and which rates them and allocates them to these levels. Although the writer agrees that an evaluation process does exist, he is not certain that it is as basic as the other processes. (See footnote, Appendix B.)

meet the financial requirements peculiar to particular communities.[9]

The first important characteristic of the workflow process, therefore, is that it is not simply one, but many discrete, interconnected processes.

2. THE CRITICAL ACTIVITY OF EACH WORKFLOW PROCESS IS ACCOMPLISHED AT THE BEGINNING. In other words, the critical point at which the consumer "buys" or "receives" the service is near the beginning of the series of activities which constitute the process.

The workflows of industrial organizations are usually characterized by sequences of behavior leading to the production of some objection. (e.g., the production of shoes, cars, etc.) As such, every step in the workflow process is critical, since a failure in one can upset the entire workflow and result in non-achievement of the objective.

The workflow of a bank seems to have somewhat different characteristics. The bank's primary objective, we recall, is to render specific services to customers. Secondary to this objective is that of keeping sound records of the services rendered. Because the rendering of services is the primary objective, the steps in the workflow leading directly to this objective are viewed by all employees as being much more important than the steps in the workflow which record the services rendered. We call these steps "critical" simply to emphasize their importance. For example, when a customer deposits money, cashes a check, makes a loan, or initiates a trust account, two sets of behavior sequences occur in the workflow. First is the behavior that includes the actual rendering of the service. Second is the behavior which *records* the rendering of the service. The first are "critical" workflow activities; the latter are not. This does not mean of course that the latter are unimportant.

The critical activities in the workflow processes studied at the bank come at the *beginning* of the process. This fact has an immediate bearing on the evaluation process described below. The employees report that this tends to give highest status to the people at the beginning of the workflow processes. Thus, receptionists, private secretaries, and officers, in terms of workflow, have high status, with the last having the highest. The employees who are behind the tellers, loan officers, or trust officers in the workflow handle material that has, so to speak, already been sold. Their reported status is less. This is not to say the many record keepers, clerks, bookkeepers are not important; they are very important. They can cause the loss of customers if they make too many errors.

3. WORKFLOW PACE IS NOT WHOLLY CONTROLLED BY PEOPLE FROM WITHIN. Again, unlike manufacturing organizations, the pace of the workflow processes for the most part is not controlled by people within the organization.[10] The pace is primarily controlled by the customers and the amount of business they bring to the organization.

Although the workflow pace varies according to the number of customers, it does not mean that certain patterns are not discernible. The employees clearly know that Mondays and Fridays, lunch hour on all days, days after holidays, and finally the first and last day of each month are "heavy periods." They expect to work harder on those days and they do. But it is the decision of customers rather than of bank officers which produces this workflow pace.

One by-product of the fact that the workflows are not controlled by management is that the employees realize that they cannot find rational reasons to blame management for "speedups." Conversely, management realizing that the workflow pace cannot be kept constant is careful about complaining of lack of industry among employees.

4. THE WORKFLOW HAS A DISTINCTLY HUMAN QUALITY. Functions (jobs) along the workflow process, especially in manufacturing organizations, traditionally contain highly fractionized, highly specialized, and highly mechanical tasks.

Again the bank differs. The employees who deal with the customers deal with human beings. Thus, their interactions may be full of

[9] J. Stanley Brown, *You and Banking*, American Institute of Banking, Section of American Bankers Association, 1951, p. 10.

[10] The Bookkeeping department (Dept. D) is one of the important exceptions. Interestingly enough, it has a low status among the employees and officers and is perceived by many as being the "factory department."

emotionally toned, human experiences. This is especially true in the case of loans, trust, and mortgage personnel who deal with people usually having problems and needing help. (More of this later.)

Many of the employees who do not deal with customers personally experience the "human touch" in their functions through interactions with customers by letters and telephones. Another possibility available to them is to identify with the "human problem" information that they read in the many confidential reports and bank forms that pass through their hands. For example, one typist was observed to be crying as she typed a loan rejection form.[11]

5. THE INTER-RELATEDNESS OF THE WORKFLOW WITH THE OTHER PROCESSES

(*a*) *Authority, rewards and penalty, identification, and perpetuation processes.* In most industrial organizations, the employees who work on the actual workflow process usually have few, if any, formal authority, reward and penalty, or perpetuation tasks in their functions, save to respond to initiating activities of others. Functions with initiating tasks representing these processes are usually limited to supervisory personnel.

This is not the case in the bank. Because of the nature of the human contact, the employees have "inherent" in their functions to initiate authority, reward and penalty, perpetuation, communication, and identification tasks. These tasks are related to their interactions with customers. Thus they are observed to direct customers in what to write, or what to borrow or what to invest, etc. They can reward or penalize customers in the sense that they can compliment, praise, or flatter them. Similarly, they can penalize them (albeit, diplomatically) in many different ways. Finally, their interaction with the customer can be crucial as to whether or not the customer remains a participant, or in our technical language, is perpetuated. Much of the power that employees have to express authority, reward and penalty, or perpetuation activities stems directly from legal laws (state and national) which clearly define what are acceptable and non-acceptable transactions and methods for these transactions. Thus, the source of the authority lies outside the organization and in institutions that have power over the organization.

The control over or direction of customers places a great responsibility on the employees. The management of the organization realizes that the employees could legitimately use this inherent power in their customer contacts in such a manner that the customer might become displeased. It tries to minimize the use of this power by emphasizing to the employee the importance of such identification symbols as "friendly bank," "courteous personnel," "tactful employees," etc. Thus, the identification process is brought to bear upon and keep within bounds any feelings of freedom that the individuals might feel they have for the use of the power inherent in their function.

(*b*) *The customer in relation to the employee.* The customer is also perceived by the employees and the organization[12] as having authority, reward and penalty, and perpetuation tasks of an initiating sort. These tasks are perceived as assigned by the organization to the customer. For example, a customer may demand speedier service. He may request special favors. He may criticize the employee or he may praise the employee. He may even raise such a fuss that the employee's tenure, that is his perpetuation is questioned.

This is an unusual situation, for here is an example of people who are not formally employees, but who are permitted to perform organizational tasks. Their control over activities of these processes stems not only from the organization's basic need for the customer but from their continuous contacts with the regular employees. Clearly, without customers the organization would collapse and without their frequent appearance on the scene, the employees' tasks could not be performed. Data of this type confirm our assumption that organizations are open systems and are affected by others outside them.

Analyzing the situation in this manner indicates that not only does the customer buy and receive a service provided by the organization, but he is also given certain privileges and responsibilities which place him high on the organizational ladder of control over employ-

[11] Not all employees experience these human contacts. The situation is different for employees in the Bookkeeping Department. (See Part III.)

[12] When we say "perceived by organization," we mean "perceived by those *agents* who control the formal activities of the organization."

ees. In fact, as we shall see, the customers actually express many more authority, reward and penalty, any perpetuation activities toward the employees than do the officers.

Whereas such identification symbols as "friendly bank," "courteous personnel," and "tactful employees" have the effect of regulating and even *minimizing* the employees' expression of their inherent authority, reward and penalty, and perpetuation activities, the same symbols affect the customers differently. As far as the customers are concerned, these same identification symbols help *maximize* or emphasize the use of *their* authority, reward and penalty, and perpetuation activities in relation to the employees.

The employee is therefore placed in a position of being dependent upon both the customers and the officers for initiating authority, reward and penalty, and perpetuation activities. Like the foreman in industry, he becomes the "person in the middle." The difference is that in this case the interests of the customer are usually the interests of the officer. Thus the employee tends to feel that he is between two people who have similar interests rather than divergent interests as is the case of the foreman in industry. In line with this, it is interesting to note that if customers "become difficult," the employees are instructed to refer them to the officers. Such a policy again helps minimize the possible expression of initiating authority, and other tasks by the employees.

6. OFFICERS ARE IN THE WORKFLOW PROCESSES. Unlike many industrial situations, the supervisory as well as the non-supervisory personnel are an integral part of various workflow processes. In a manufacturing organization, for example, a supervisor usually supervises production. He may or he may not help to produce the product. However, in the bank the workflows are such that the officers are on the production line, so to speak, as are the employees. The supervisors are continually serving the public.

7. THE WORKFLOW TIES EMPLOYEES TO THE CUSTOMERS RATHER THAN TO OTHER EMPLOYEES. Descriptions of workflows in industrial organizations illustrate how the workflow process throws employees together and thus ties them together to produce the product.

In the bank the situation is different. The employees who deal with customers are bound by the workflow with the customers rather than with each other. In Part III we shall find that the employees find most of their expression in their interactions with customers. This seems to result in almost no need for informal activities in the departments. This lack of informal activities, in turn, results in few friendships being made among employees. Thus 65% of the employees report that they have no close friends in the bank. Of the remaining 35% who state that they do have close friends, 2/3 come from two departments whose workflow processes tie them with each other and not with the customer.

Also partially as a result of this unique workflow characteristic, there exists little basis for the formation of an active informal organization to represent employees. In other words, as a result of the structure of the workflow processes there do not exist any patterns for cooperative interactions among employees.

From this, we can hypothesize that a union would have difficulty in being established. It is interesting to note that an "employees' association" (definitely not a "union," insist the employees) as formed years ago primarily for the purpose of raising salaries. Once this was accomplished, the association eventually became a "social club." Today the organization is mostly active in the social areas. It is management conscious. In fact, many of its presidents have become bank officers. More about the employees' association later on.

8. THE WORKFLOW PROCESSES DEAL WITH CONFIDENTIAL INFORMATION. We mentioned above that by their very nature, the services sold at the bank automatically includes the communication of important and personal information. Not only is this information personal, but in many cases it provides knowledge of major economic and even social changes in the community. Employees who deal with the special confidential information (e.g., mortgages, loans, and trusts) acquire information about families and industries rarely known to many people. This adds to the importance of the work performed and to the perceived status of the workflows that deal with confidential information.

Many employees (69%) for example, mention that they like working in the bank because, "it is the center of things"—"you know a lot about what is going on in this town."

B. *Authority Process.* The authority process includes all those behavioral activities (and their concomitant codes and specifications) where people are coordinating and directing others in the organization. The authority process has both formal and informal activities.

1. SUPERVISORY PERSONNEL HAVE AUTHORITY TASKS, BUT INFREQUENTLY EXPRESS THEM.[13] Perhaps the most striking characteristic of the authority activities between officers and employees is that, according to both, they are infrequently expressed. More concretely, 24% report that they are contacted by, or they contact officers "very frequently" for authority activities.[14] None report a moderate number of contacts. Only 5% report one contact a day. The remaining 71% report contacts less than once a day (e.g., once or twice a week or month). There are a few exceptions who report relatively high numbers of authority contacts. These are mostly trainees in the organization.

Although there seems to be a minimal amount of overtly expressed authority, this is not to be interpreted to mean that people do not know that their officer supervisors have authority. "They may not breathe down our necks, but we still know who is the boss," is a typical statement. These results indicate that even with a minimal overt expression of authority, the employees in this organization still realize who is boss. There is in the authority process, as suggested by our theory, a basic relationship of dependence of the subordinate on the leader.

Similar conclusions may be drawn in the employee-customer relations. Fifty-five per cent of the employees report that they have authority tasks in their relationship with the customers. But, due to the identification symbols, they add the overt expression of authority is greatly minimized. The same number of employees also report that they believe that the customers have authority over them.

2. THERE EXISTS A "GAP" BETWEEN THE OFFICERS AND EMPLOYEES AND MULTIPLE SUPERVISION. As we shall see later on when we deal with the total relationship between employee and officer (i.e., not only the authority relationship) there is a social gap between employees and officers within and without the organization. Partially as a result of this gap the organization tends to be divided into two groups, namely, the members of the official family (i.e., the officers) and the employees.

As far as the authority process is concerned, this tends to make the officers feel free to direct in more departments than their own. As members of the official family, they are responsible for the organization. It is not unlike the armed services where a captain or colonel simply because they are officers feel free, if necessary, to direct soldiers' activities in other units than their own.

Some employees are in positions where they are forced to interact with several different officers for workflow purposes. Although these officers may not express overt authority toward them, the employees *feel* that the officers *do* have authority over them. It isn't long before these employees *feel* that they are reporting to more than one boss. This feeling results from the perceived fact on the part of the employees that anyone who is in the "officer group" is a boss. It is reenforced by the fact that their own officer rarely expresses overt authority, and thus behaviorally he is like all the other officers.

3. FEELINGS OF SELF-RESPONSIBILITY ARE CLEARLY EVIDENT. Most of the employees spontaneously mention in their discussions of the authority process that they are their own boss, that is they exercise authority over themselves. They cherish the possibility of working "without someone breathing down their necks." They like the idea of not working under pressure. They are quick to point out that this is one reason why they would not like to leave the bank. Thus, "I am my own boss," was the second most frequent reason given as to why they stay in the bank."

The people emphasize the fact that the

[13] Unless otherwise noted, a reference to any sort of task will mean it is one initiating activity.

[14] Many of these come from the bookkeeping department and the trust department.

The operational criteria for the "degree of frequency" is as follows:

VF	Very Frequent (5–10 contacts a day)
M	Moderate (2–5 contacts a day)
I	Infrequent (1 or less contacts a day, but at least 1 a week)
PN	Practically never (less than 1 contact a week)

"weak" [15] authority process (as they refer to it) is to be explained by the fact that the organization trusts them and feels they are responsible individuals.[16]

The feeling on the part of the employees that "we're responsible" individuals requires some clarification. As far as we can see, it may be accounted for as follows:

Since the organization minimizes the expression of authority tasks, by officers, the expression of authority is left up to the individual. He must direct himself. This requires the individual to create authority *acts* to take the place of the authority tasks. Thus, in actuality, a "weak" authority process encourages individuals to use and therefore to express their own personality and to become their own "policeman." It provides personality expression in an area crucial to most people (i.e., control over one's self). Might it not be that what the employees mean by "self responsibility" is the degree to which they are able to substitute personality created acts for organizationally defined tasks? [17]

The question arises as to whether people might take advantage of this situation. For example, would they work as hard as they would if they were continually directed?

The people respond ambivalently. On the one hand they insist that this would not be a cue for them to "ease up" on the work (72%). On the other hand, they also admit that they do not work extremely hard (48%). The reason for any laxity in the work, the employees' state, is due to the poor reward policies and not to a weak authority process. The writer hypothesizes that both processes are relevant. The poor rewards provide the employees with a rational reason to "goldbrick" and the "weak" authority process provides the opportunity.

4. THE INTER-RELATEDNESS OF AUTHORITY WITH THE OTHER PROCESSES

(a) The first possible reason for the "weak" authority process is that it is a compensatory adjustment for an unsatisfactory reward and penalty process. The people feel that the financial rewards are low. Too low. Seventy-nine per cent believe that the wages are "poor" or "terrible." Only 7 per cent suggested the wages are satisfactory. Thus they believe that these reward activities at least are unfair.

They also believe that one way they make up for their low wages is by having unusually good working conditions. One "good working condition" is a "weak" authority process. The officers realize this and act accordingly. They do not express authority too often. This provides a "feedback" action to help maintain a "weak" authority process. Furthermore, the officers reenforce the employees' beliefs by "explaining" low wages and infrequent substantial raises as being off-set by the easy work and by the lack of pressure from the authority process.

(b) The degree of autonomy in many stages of the workflow enters into the picture as the second reason for a "weak" authority process. We mentioned previously that the workflow processes are unique in that they do not tie the employees together. Most employees have relatively discrete jobs. Thus, there is not as much need for coordinating and controlling activities of the various employees.

The third reason is also related to the workflow process. The inherent power and possible consequent pressure which customers are able to express also help to account for the minimal expression of authority. Thus the officers realize that the employee has enough potential pressure (i.e., from customers) upon him, and therefore they (officers) should minimize the expression of their authority. This reason seems especially likely when we examine the personality type that tends to be perpetuated by the organization.[18] People with that type

[15] "Weak" refers operationally to two complimentary criteria. The first is to the perceived quality of the relationship as defined by the employees. The second is to the frequency of the employees' experience of authority.

[16] Believing that they are trusted leads the employees to act in a reciprocal fashion. Thus, one day an officer checked certain departments as to tardiness. He found that a certain number of employees were late arriving on the job. He checked an hour later to see if the employees lied about the time they "signed in." In all cases, the employees signed in late.

[17] As we shall see, the above holds true for the reward and penalty process. The people are permitted to create reward and penalty acts to take the place of the lack of reward and penalty tasks. Thus, the scope of "self-responsibility" is increased.

[18] See pages 67 to 80 in this chapter.

of personality would find difficulty in coping with much pressure. A weak authority process appears therefore to minimize negative effects that may arise from the employee being dependent on both the customers and the officers. It does this by minimizing the dependence of the employees upon the officers.

A fourth reason is that the officers are busy with their own workflow duties. Many of the officers must spend much of their time (70%-85%) interacting with customers. Thus they actually have little time for authority activities.

(c) The fifth possible reason for a "weak" authority process is related to both the perpetuation process and the reward and penalty process. We will note when we discuss the reward and penalty and perpetuation processes that most of the officers have few of the important reward and penalty and perpetuation tasks in their functions. They cannot directly fire or hire, upgrade or downgrade, give vacations or other similar things. Thus the officers sense that they have little with which to back up their authority. In other words, as indicated in our theory, since the organizational processes are mutually dependent, an authority process that is not reenforced by the reward and penalty and the perpetuation process is bound to be "weak."

(d) The perpetuation process also dovetails with the weak authority process in another way to present us with a sixth reason for a "weak" authority process.

When we discuss the perpetuation process we will see that there is a general type of person that gravitates to and is hired by the bank. This personality type is such that a strong self-controlling authority process is already built-into its structure (i.e., strong super-ego). Thus the individual who tends to be perpetuated in the bank is, from a personality point of view, ideally suited for a "weak" authority process. It permits him to express his relatively strong internalized authority process. In fact, one would guess that if the expression of the authority process is for some reason greatly increased, it might have serious effects upon the individuals.[19]

(e) The identification process provides a seventh reason for the minimal expression of authority process. The bank continually creates emotionally toned symbols for its employees to identify with which lead them to expect that a "good bank leader does not actively utilize his authority tasks."

(f) Still another (i.e., eighth) reason is related to the unique authority process assigned to the auditing department. The organization has a department whose primary objective is one of control. It is continually checking the other departments to make certain their work is accurate and up to the organization's standards. Thus, the officers in each department tend to feel a lesser need continually to check their own department's work themselves.

5. Finally, all these phenomena feed back and help create a set of codes and specifications in the authority activities which might be summarized as "passive leadership." This, then, becomes the norm. The employees guide their expectancies and the officers their behavior by these codes.

Thus we see how the other processes plus the personality of the individuals in the bank dovetail to maintain a "weak" authority process.

C. *Reward and Penalty Process.* The reward and penalty process includes all the behavioral activities (and their concomitant codes and specifications) which influence people to behave in a way the organization requires, and in a way making possible continued association of the people involved. As there are formal and informal organizational requirements, there are also formal and informal reward and penalty activities.

1. REWARD AND PENALTY ARE HARDLY EVER DISTRIBUTED BY THE MAJORITY OF OFFICERS. The officers dispense few rewards and few penalties. Thus only 19 per cent of the employees report having "very frequent"[20] reward and penalty contacts with their superiors. Only one reports "moderate" and none report "hardly ever." Six per cent report less than one reward or penalty contact a day. The remainder report that rewards and penalties are "practically never" distributed by the officers.

Like the authority tasks, reward and penalty tasks are inherent in the function of employees

[19] This phenomenon provides us with another possible reason as to why people stay in the bank in spite of low pay.

[20] Again the bookkeeping department reports the majority of these contacts.

who deal with customers. Fifty-two per cent of them report "very frequent" reward and penalty contacts in their relationships with the customers.

But, the employees do not feel that their supervisors are able to reward and penalize them in terms of financial rewards and penalties. These, as we mentioned above, are largely in the hands of the person who controls the personnel perpetuation process. Thus, although the people feel dependent upon their superiors for some reward and penalty, this is not necessarily the case for the important economic rewards and penalties. But the employees do realize that they are dependent upon someone for economic rewards (i.e., the director of personnel perpetuation). More of that when we discuss that process. Thus, the notion derived in our theory of a built-in state of dependency between subordinate and leader is again confirmed. The only difference is that the employees perceive their dependency in this instance to be with an officer above their own immediate superiors.

2. FEELINGS OF SELF-RESPONSIBILITY ARE USUAL. As in the case of the authority process, the employees view the lack of expression of penalties as a sign of "self-responsibility" since they substitute reward and penalty acts for tasks, thereby obtaining personality expression. They also approve a "weak" reward and penalty process since it helps keep pressure at a minimum.

3. WAGES ARE NOT SATISFACTORY. As we noted before, seventy-five per cent describe the wages as "poor" or "terrible". Four per cent suggest the wages are "poor" for the older employees and good for the younger employees. The same percentage believe that the wages are poor for the men employees and good for the female employees. Seven per cent suggest that the wages are better than they used to be, but there is always room for improvement. Only seven per cent describe the wages as satisfactory.

Wages are important in the employees' lives. They represent the chance of having a decent standard of living. Moreover, employees like most human beings in our culture, view wages as an indication of their "worth" to the organization and thus as an indication of how much the organization thinks of and about them.

One employee voices some of the often mentioned problems related to wages as follows:

> Well naturally everybody's looking for more money and I'd say that people around here feel that they are not getting paid well. I think a big complaint that people have is that there is too big a spread between the officers and the clerks. There's too big a gap. A lot of us, you know if you look at it, we're not making too much more than some of the newcomers, maybe a couple of dollars more. Of course I realize times are hard and it's hard to get employees, but still you feel that here I am, I've been here for 29 years, you'd think they'd give me some recognition for service. I realize that not all of us can be officers but if those of us that can't and we've been doing a good job, I should think they would recognize that. Many of the other gentlemen's wives work here because they couldn't make ends meet if they didn't, but I would say that, as I told one officer, well the officers seem to be getting the cream and we are getting the skimmed milk.

Thus the older employees who are not periodically being upgraded feel that they are "forgotten men." They are bitter about this, especially since, according to them, the codes of the organization keep saying, as it were, "Work hard, have patience, you'll be advanced." Their bitterness is increased when they learn that newly appointed employees either begin at the same salary level or just a few dollars less a week. This is especially resented since they know it has taken them many years of hard work to arrive at their present level. To make matters even more difficult, the older men are the ones who tended to come into the organization because of its status in the community. Thus these are the individuals who presumably would do their best to "keep up" the external signs of a standard of living equal to the perceived status of the organization. This creates problems since the status these older people have in mind tends to be higher than they can afford.

The younger employees, on the other hand, who have come into the organization after the war, do not view the organization as having any unusually high community status. As a result, the older employees are faced with the fact that the employees who do not come to the bank because they really want to work in the bank are the employees who salary-wise are favored.

4. OTHER REWARDS THE ORGANIZATION OFFERS TO THE EMPLOYEES

(a) Fifty-five per cent cited "benefits" as being the most important reason for staying in the organization despite the low wages. Included in the benefits are (1) the pension plan, (2) insurance, (3) medical benefits, and (4) vacations with pay. It is primarily these items that people seem to think of when they discuss the importance of "security" in the bank. One item that is omitted but must be included under the notion of "security" is the organization's policy of never firing an employee in times of depression, or even when he is judged incompetent. We will see that the need for security is especially important, generally speaking, for the type of personality that tends to be perpetuated in the bank. Thus the perpetuation process comes to the aid of the reward and penalty process.

(b) Fifty per cent state that they remain in the organization because "no one breathes down their neck." They are their "own-boss." Thus the weakness of the authority system is rewarding.

(c) Working conditions which include physical working conditions, clean work, and hours accounts for twenty-three per cent of the reasons given for staying with the bank.

(d) "People" who are "nice because they let you alone" is next. This reason also expressed in answer to other questions is indicative of the characteristics we speak about in the workflow process. The people work pretty much by themselves with a minimal of interaction with other employees.

(e) Only six per cent suggest that working in their organizations provide them with a sense of prestige. Even these admitted the prestige isn't what it used to be.[21]

(f) Twenty-five per cent of the employees (mostly the older ones) do not honestly know why they stay in the organization. After some discussion they usually place the reason as one of a combination of the reasons we are discussing. The fact that they find it difficult to verbalize why they stay in the organization leads the writer to believe that the reasons may be related to their personality needs. These needs are not easily verbalized. Data to support this belief will be presented in the next section.

5. INTER-RELATEDNESS OF REWARD AND PENALTY WITH THE OTHER PROCESSES

(a) As was mentioned previously, perhaps one organizationally related reason for the apparent non-action of the employees about their low wages is related to the "weak" authority and reward and penalty processes. A sense of self-responsibility seems to arise as employees substitute authority and reward and penalty tasks for similar acts. These acts are important to the employees and they are willing to give up a certain amount of money for the possibility of expressing them.

(b) The security of a job (perpetuation) is also very important in helping the employees to accept their low wages.

(c) The personality type selected and maintained by the perpetuation process, helps to make the reward system workable. The kind of person perpetuated in the organization, we suggest, is not likely to be aggressive enough to complain or agitate actively. This is not to infer that the employees like low wages. They do not. We are only saying that, in spite of their unhappiness, but partially due to their personality, they will not tend to become active and do something about them.

(d) The autonomous character of many tasks in the workflow process also has effects. A weak reward and penalty process may be possible because of the relative independence of the jobs and the lack of pressure from the officers associated with the jobs. The fact that many of the jobs provide a basis for human contacts which helps employees to have an unusual amount of opportunity for personality expression may also minimize the needs for other types of rewards and penalties.

The officers' perception of the customers' inherent power to express reward and (particularly) penalty activities might lead them to minimize the expression of their own. This has the effect of minimizing the difficulties inherent in the double dependence of the employee upon the officer and the customer.

(e) Finally, the identification process tries to get employees to identify with such con-

[21] For those interested, the following reasons are also given as to why people stay in the bank. (1) Too old to move. Too much seniority invested. (20%). (2) Fear of unemployment (6%).

cepts as "security," "banks are slow in moving you upwards—but they are steady," "bank employees must have many years of experience before they become officers, etc."

D. *Perpetuation Process.* The perpetuation process includes all the behavior activities (and their concomitant codes and specifications) which maintain and replenish in quantity and quality the people, materials, and ideas utilized in the organization.

1. SUPERVISORY PERSONNEL HARDLY EVER EXPRESS PERPETUATION ACTIVITIES. The perpetuation process has characteristics similar to the authority and reward and penalty processes. First of all, the perpetuation process is used minimally as far as the immediate officer-employee relationships are concerned. Only twenty per cent of the employees state that they experience "very frequent" perpetuation contacts with the officers, and most of these respondents are in one department. No employees report perpetuation contacts in the "moderate" and "hardly ever" categories.

As in the case of the reward and penalty process, the perpetuation process is primarily in the hands of a few officers. The employees know that even if they request "a few days off" or "sick leave" or "a vacation," their supervisor must clear it with the individual in charge of personnel perpetuation. This fact plus the already mentioned fact that the organization bends backwards before it discharges anyone tends to minimize the employees' sense of dependency upon their immediate supervisor. However, the employees still feel dependent for the perpetuation process upon the direction of that process.

The picture is different if we examine the employee-customer relationships. Here, at least forty-six per cent of the employees report "very frequent" perpetuation contacts and an equal amount report in the "moderate" and "hardly ever" categories. Similarly, they perceive that all the customers have inherent perpetuation activity in their functions, e.g., the customer could "cause trouble" which may lead to their being discharged.

2. FEELINGS OF SELF-RESPONSIBILITY ARE USUAL. As in the case of the other processes, a "weak" perpetuation process seems to help enforce the already established notion that the employees are "responsible people." The informal code that no one is discharged even if he is not as capable as the bank desires, also tends to reenforce this belief.

3. PERPETUATION OF PEOPLE ACTIVITIES ARE CENTRALLY CONTROLLED. The individual primarily responsible for perpetuation of the number and quality of employees holds a tight reign over the process. Although he consults with other interested officers, nevertheless in most cases he still makes the final decisions. Let us examine this phenomenon and some of its effects.

(a) Why is there a "central" control?

The first reason is related to the director's belief that there are officers who are not as capable as they should be in perpetuation matters. He quickly adds that the organization is working hard to rectify the situation and he feels that it is succeeding.

The second reason is that the director fears that there might be inequities if there isn't central control. One officer could give high raises, and another low ones. Or, one officer could be more lenient than another.

A third possible reason is related to the informal organizational code that everybody's salary is a private, in fact secret, matter. Most of the employees (95%) and officers agree that there is an organizational code that "salaries are not discussed." The director believes this code may be more easily followed if only one individual controls the process.

The final possible reason is related to the importance the organization places in hiring the "right person." Most industrial organizations place their emphasis on an individual's abilities to work at the job for which he applies. Little emphasis is made on examining the total personality characteristics.

This is not the case in this organization. Due to the fact that the organization's primary workflow processes are related to customers, it is important that the organization look for the "right type" of personality as well as ability. The director feels especially responsible for making certain that the new employees fit into the already accepted personality type in the organization. Under these circumstances, he feels safer if he does the choosing of employees.

The fact that one or perhaps two individuals

make the initial choices leads to the existence of a homogeneity of personality types. To put it another way, the director and his assistant have definitely defined restricted tolerances of the type of person they will accept to work in the bank.[22] It is our assumption that the central control of the perpetuation process helps to assure the maintenance of this clearly defined "personality type."

The discussion to date has been primarily on the organizational level. We now turn to the individual (psychological) level to analyze the kind of person that tends to be perpetuated in the bank. Although the theory permits easy locomotion from the organizational to the individual level of analysis by the use of the same categories, some scientists may wish we kept these discussions separate. In terms of logical clarity, their wish has substantial merit. However, we would like to suggest that it is useful to analyze phenomena in a sequence which mirrors reality even if this sequence is not logically clear. Clinicians have long ago learned that the analysis of emotions requires different logic. The same may be true for the analysis of organizational process. Perhaps we may have to think in terms of circular processes on all levels of analyses (organizational, individual) which feed back and reenforce one another. This seems to be the case here. We will now see how the individual level of analysis is influenced by and in turn influences the organizational level of analysis.

From all this material, it is possible to make further inferences and thereby deepen our picture of the "right type." The writer infers that some of the more latent characteristics of the "right type" are:

A strong desire for security, stability, predictability in their life.

A strong desire to be left alone and work in relative isolation.

A dislike of aggressiveness and/or hostility in themselves and others.

If these inferences are valid, then we can begin to understand why the people have little difficulty in being retiring, polite, courteous, tactful, conventional, etc. Behaving in this manner tends to minimize any chances of overt difficulties with others. This in turn minimizes the possibility of experiencing aggression from others and/or expressing aggression towards others.

Unfortunately, it is difficult, even in this organization, for people to live together and work together. The very nature of the organization, we shall see, creates some of the conflict. Real difficulties arise when the employees experience tension and conflict and find it difficult (for organizational and personality reasons) to express their feelings. It is our inference that they usually respond by "bottling up" their feelings and placing a tight lid on their expression.[23] In other words, they internalize these tensions. We know from research that people can do this only up to a certain point.[24] After that point is reached, some expression must take place or the pent-up feelings may be converted into work inefficiency, behavior difficulties, and physiological difficulties, i.e., stomach trouble. It takes a long time to reach this stage. Most people, especially the newer employees, are probably not affected in this manner.

But, we believe most of the people are affected in the following manner: As the feelings are bottled up inside, the individuals become increasingly careful not to become careless and "blow their top." Such an occurrence would release the trigger to the expression of feelings pent up for many years. This, as we have seen, is not permitted by the organization, nor is it desired by the people. This may be another reason why "everybody is nice in the bank—they leave each other alone."

Consequently, the people become increasingly polite to make certain that they do not get into any difficult human relationships. This behavior is not only accepted, but it is also reenforced by the organization's identification process. (i.e., Nice people in the bank are people who are non-aggressive.) People also become increasingly careful not to become too personal in their relationship because personal relationship may lead to expression of personal

[22] To be sure, they don't seem to be able to find the "right type" as often as they desire.

[23] This inference logically follows from the previously mentioned personality characteristics (e. g., dislike of aggressiveness and/or hostility in themselves and others).

[24] The exact point varies with different people and with the same person as the situation varies.

feelings. They begin to desire to work by themselves with a minimal amount of interaction with others. This, we believe, partially accounts for the fact that the majority of the employees, although they admit human relations abilities are important, would under no circumstances discuss or explain "proper" human relations in the organization to a newcomer. This also helps account for the fact that "nice" people in the organization are people who are "polite and leave you alone."

A word of explanation about "nice people." In answer to the question, "If wages are low, what other reasons might there be for remaining here," one of the most often mentioned reasons is that the organization has "nice" people. Careful prodding and questioning suggests that "nice" people are not, in the majority of cases, a specific class of people—although this phrase is used. "Nice people" are those who are "quiet, friendly people who mind their own business and do their work." Other data helping to confirm this are found in the fact that 93% of the people state they have no close friends in the organization. Another bit of datum is related to the fact that 75% of the people believe that the motto "The Friendly First" is much more true for the employee-customer relationship than for the employee-employee relationship.[25]

These data help to explain why the caste-like system between officers and employees may have adaptive value, as far as both the parties are concerned. It helps maintain "peace" by minimizing interactions.

Also, if these inferences about personality are correct, we can see why the employees are willing to sacrifice high wages for security and stability in life. To personalities of this type, "security and stability are more crucial." Thus, the benefits are continually emphasized as being important. The ones mentioned most often are the retirement plan, and the regulation that the bank continues the employee's salary during illness. This latter benefit is especially important for people of the "right type." It frees them from constant worry if they are ever ill.

Another benefit often mentioned by the employees is the organization's refusal to fire people even if they do not meet all the desired standards. One would guess that this is also especially important to people who place security and stability in life over social mobility and economic wealth.[26]

[25] These figures do not include one atypical department.

Before we leave the discussion of the "right type," it seems useful to anticipate a few effects that it might have upon the total organization.

The most important effect is related to defining such a narrow band of "acceptable" personality characteristics. This tends to make the organization highly homogeneous. The homogeneity of personality leads to "sameness in thinking," and "inflexibility," and "near rigidity." These in turn lead to high resistance to new ideas and to change. Eighty-nine per cent of the employees state that "sameness" and "organizational rigidity" is an important problem. "We do things in a certain way simply because they've always been done that way."

The narrowness of the acceptable range of personality is compounded by the type which is selected. Conservative, retiring, conventional, cautious, and non-aggressive people themselves lead to and reenforce the organizational homogeneity and rigidity.

We have, therefore, a phenomenon where a particular type of personality gravitates to the organization. The organization, in turn, perpetuates this type of personality and the personality, the organization. In this way they act as a feedback for each other. Thus, we have an important basis for fusion since, according to our definition, fusion is facilitated as personality and organization are congruent.

In summary, we may say that central control of the perpetuation of materials leads the employees to feel (1) less responsible for making cost conscious decisions, (2) that the organization through Mr. —— is "tight." And (3), both officers and employees are aware of another limitation on the leaders' departmental control.

E. *Identification Process.* The identification process includes all the behavioral activities and their concomitant codes and specifications which define emotionally toned phrases and symbols that enable employees to identify with

[26] All these results do not apply completely in some departments. The departments in which they do not apply are those that are called the "factory departments." These exceptions are discussed individually in the subsequent chapters.

the organization. The identification process also points out the uniqueness of the organization in the community. As in all the other processes, there are formal and informal activities in the process.

1. THE SUPERVISORY PERSONNEL EXPRESS FEW IDENTIFICATION ACTIVITIES. Few formal identification activities are expressed in the supervisory-employee relationship, according to the employees. Only 20 per cent report any formal identification activities and 18 per cent of these are in one department. Although few identification activities are expressed, the employees definitely understand the "things the organization is supposed to stand for." Thus, as in the case of the other processes, the fact that there is infrequent overt expression of these activities does not mean that the people do not know of their existence. These symbols definitely influence their behavior. In fact as we shall see later on, the identification process seems to contain key words to the "organization's idea" (formal and informal) of the ideal aspects of the steady state among the processes.

On the other hand, the employees emphasize their very frequent performance of identification tasks in their contacts with customers (46%) Thus, as in the case of the other processes, there is more overt daily expression of identification activities in the employee-customer relationship than in any other single relationship.

2. THE SLOGANS AND PHRASES IDENTIFYING THE BANK. Below are listed and discussed some of the most important slogans and phrases created by, and used in the performance of identification activities.[27]

(a) "THE FRIENDLY FIRST." The motto of the organization is the "Friendly First." Forty-eight per cent of the employees state that "friendly first" is more true for the customer-employee relationship than for the employee-employee relationship. If, for a moment, we include only those employees who have primary contacts with customers, the percentage goes up to 64 per cent. This, according to the employees, operationally means that no matter how difficult relationships become between customer and employee, the employee should bend over backwards to satisfy the customer. This phenomenon leads the employees to add to the operational meaning of the motto. "Friendly First employees" means to them that they must be patient, tactful, diplomatic, and polite employees. Thus, 55 per cent of the employees spontaneously list "tact and diplomacy" as the most often required ability in their formal work. The next most often listed ability, "accuracy," has two-thirds less votes. When at another point the employees are asked to state "the most important ability required by the job, from the job's point of view," "tactfulness and diplomacy" again is most often chosen. It is interesting to note in connection with these results that the same ability is mentioned most often (receives as many votes as all others combined) in response to the question, "From your own personal point of view, thinking of your whole life, what if any ability is the most important to you?" These results provide us with another overall clue as to the fusion between personality and organization.

Returning to the motto, "friendly first," we find that the officers give it even more meaning. They believe, and therefore expect their employees to believe that the motto includes initiative, adaptability, cooperation, accuracy, efficiency, prompt service and honesty. These characteristics the officers believe are part and parcel of every function. Although the employees would probably agree that the officers believe this, they do not mention these characteristics with any great frequency. They seem to prefer to identify with such informal identification symbols as "easy place to work," "no one breathes down your neck," "little pressure," "easy-going supervisors who let you alone," and "good hours coupled with many vacations."

The reader may recall that the identification process defines the uniqueness of the organization in the community. We find an interesting phenomenon arises. The employees (officers and non-officers) when they interact with customers or potential customers *outside* the organization, emphasize the formal slogans, quoted by the officers (i.e., accuracy, efficiency, honestly, etc.). But when they interact with prospective employees, they "sell" the organization on the basis of the informal slogans (easy place to work, no pressure, good hours, etc). These informal characteristics are

[27] As Bakke has pointed out in *Bonds of Organization,* such phrases are important ingredients in the "Organizational Charter" of the organization.

especially attractive to the "right type" personality. Thus we see how the identification process helps prospective employees decide whether they should choose the organization as a place to work.

(b) THE "RIGHT TYPE." As we imply above, the perpetuation of the "right type" is reenforced and facilitated by the identification process. The employees call the "right type" simply a "nice person," or "proper" person. A closer understanding leads to such characteristics as submissive, passive, meek, quiet, conservative, cautious, etc.

(c) "PASSIVE LEADERSHIP." This has been discussed in the authority process. Suffice to say that the authority process is helped by the identification process in maintaining passive leadership.

(d) "STEADY, STABLE PLACE TO WORK WITH EXCELLENT BENEFITS." The organization is known in the community to provide security (i.e., steady work) and excellent benefits. The community according to the employees, knows that the wages are low. Thus, those who come do know this in the beginning. This helps to point up that although the word "security" is defined by many of the employees as "always having work," it also has another meaning which they do not readily verbalize. This is the meaning of psychological security, which they require and are able to obtain in their work.

(e) "YOU WORK WITH PEOPLE," "NO ONE BOTHERS YOU WHEN YOU WORK," AND "NICE CLEAN WORK." These three phrases find their bases in the workflow process where, because of the nature of the work, the tasks performed are primarily (according to the employees) (1) in relation with people, (2) discrete and independent, and (3) clean. These phrases are all a part of the bank's "Organizational Charter" produced by the identification process.

Thus the identification process "picks up" its emotionally toned symbols by "sensing" the highlights of the other processes and how these dovetail to form one interwoven steady state.

F. *Communication Process.* The communication process includes all those behavioral activities and their concomitant codes and specifications which define and implement ways, methods, and media of communication. There are formal and informal activities in this process.

The communication process along with the identification process obtains much of its content from the other processes, since its very job is to communicate the content of the other processes.

1. EVERYONE HAS SOME COMMUNICATION TASKS. The communication process is one of the most equally distributed processes in the organization. Almost everyone communicates something to someone else. In some cases, where the function does not contain formal communication tasks, the people define informal ones.

Statistically, the picture is as follows. Eighty-nine per cent of the employees report formal communication tasks. Ten per cent report they do not have formal communication tasks. (These people perform for the most part, machine work, so actually of course, they are performing communication (accounting) tasks for the organization.)

The communication process, like the workflow process, helps to maintain a formal tie between the employees and their supervisors. Thirty-four per cent report they communicate "very frequently" with their supervisors. Eleven per cent report "moderate" communication and 65 per cent report "hardly ever."

2. COMMUNICATIONS ARE OVERTLY "FRIENDLY." As might be expected the people to communicate with each other and with the customers in a manner that is congruent with the organization's values and their own personality requirements. For the most part,[28] the communications are in a polite, formal, cautious manner. People smile and always remember the "friendly first." Thus, on the surface, the communication process is as serene as one will probably ever observe in an organization.

3. COVERTLY COMMUNICATIONS ARE NOT TOO FRIENDLY. People cannot, however, entirely hide their underlying attitudes. They communicate them through feelings. Thus many people report that individuals aren't honest with each other. "They don't tell you what they really think," is a representative comment, "People are two-faced," is a rather aggressive

[28] Excepting the bookkeeping and block departments.

description while "most people are friendly." "They never try to hurt you," is a complimentary way of describing the same phenomenon.

The fact that people sense a difference between what others say and how they feel is crucial. It indicates that communications are open, but not on the overt level. As one employee states it, "You can feel what people want better than you can hear it." Sensing this helps to maintain "peace in the family," since people are able to sense when they might hurt someone and when they might not. As we indicated previously, we believe that this general type of personality dislikes and fears hurting others.

Although such a communication process might have disadvantages in the employee-employee relationships, it has important advantages in the employee-customer relationships. It is advantageous for an organization to have employees who are able to be sensitive to customers' feelings as well as to their verbal communications. This is especially important in the loan, trust, and credit and mortgage work of the organization.

4. COMMUNICATION WITH OFFICERS ARE OFFICER-CENTERED. Due to the dependency the employee feels upon his supervisors, he tends to communicate that which he believes the supervisor wants to hear. The employees obtain their cure of "proper" communication content and methods from noting the supervisors' behavior and finding out their sentiments about the codes of the organizational processes.

This tends to provide the leader with a relatively "skewed" picture of the employees' world. Thus, the majority of the leaders are not able to provide an accurate description of th employees' world. This is especially true regarding the employees' feelings about (a) wages, (b) benefits, (c) human problems, (d) the supervisors, and (e) individual problems. In connection with this, it is interesting to note that there are a few officers who are able to describe accurately the employees' world. All these are described by the employees as excellent officers. It is also interesting to note that these officers sense their own warm relationships, but become overtly embarrassed when the researcher discusses it with them.

5. THE INTER-RELATEDNESS OF COMMUNICATION WITH THE OTHER PROCESS

(a) The structure of the workflow plays a crucial role in defining communication patterns. For example, the commercial and savings tellers, loan officers, and trust officers report that they spend the greatest percentage of the time communicating with customers rather than with themselves. The second most frequent area of communication reported by these same people is defined by the employee-officer relationship. The communication is also due to the nature of the workflow. For example trust employees are continually communicating technical information to their superiors necessary for these supervisors to make proper investment decisions.[29] Similarly, employees in the loan department are continually communicating workflow information to the loan officers (e.g., credit record of borrower). Commercial tellers and savings tellers must have certain types of checks or deposit slips initialed by officers before they may be processed. This requires communication activities.

In short, the structure of the workflow is a crucial variable in determining the network of communication relationships.

On the other hand, we do not mean to imply, as some writers do, that the influence of the workflow structure on communications is so great that it cannot be changed or modified. We have found numerous examples where the employees do create communication patterns which are vastly different from and in some cases, antagonistic to the workflow structure. When the desire to communicate becomes great enough, employees simply by-pass the natural workflow links. For example, in the bookkeeping department, the girls are so placed in workflow positions that they are only able to easily communicate with their own bookkeeping partner who sits next to them. However, these bookkeepers report, and they are frequently observed, to get up from their place of work and go over to talk to one of their girlfriends. Or, groups of them may leave their machines for a five minute talk-fest and "smoke." Still others have been observed to shout to a friend a few "machines" away.

(b) The "weak" formal authority, reward and penalty and perpetuation processes have an interesting effect upon communication. As would be expected, the employees report al-

[29] See Chapter V for details concerning this communication.

most no communication between themselves and their officers about matters related to these three processes. Interestingly, this seems to influence informal communication patterns. Thus over 75 per cent of the employees report that "salary," "psychological rewards" (commendations, etc.) "psychological penalties" and "activities related to being hired, discharged or transferred" are considered highly confidential and not the proper subject for conversation among employees. This in turn leads to a "black market" type communication about these matters where the employees secretly exchange information concerning these activities. In fact it may not be incorrect to hypothesize that one may find that the "degree of cohesiveness" between two people could be measured by the kind of information they are willing to communicate to each other.

(c) The perpetuation process, we note previously, affects the kind of communication in another way. Primarily because of the "right type" we find that covert communications are not too friendly.

(d) The identification process, on the other hand, acts to make the content of *overt* communication "friendly." Thus we find that such slogans as "Friendly First," "the customer is always right" act as cues for the proper manner and content of employee communication.

Summary

1. The behavioral content and the codes of each organizational process has been described. Also, the necessary connections among the processes are defined.

2. We note that each process is to a certain extent both independent of and dependent upon the other processes. In this organization, the communication and identification processes are dependent upon them, and upon each other.

3. The processes dovetail so that they form a steady state where each process reenforces and helps maintain the others. This steady state, we note, is characterized by frequent participation and overt activity in the workflow, communication, and identification processes. The authority, reward and penalty, and perpetuation processes lack frequent participation, and are called "weak" by the employees. This "weakness" is desired and required by the personality type that tends to be perpetuated. Thus, the individual personalities find opportunity for expression or actualization, because of the nature of these three processes.

It is within and with this overall "steady state" that the departments and individuals must fuse. Therefore, the next step is to examine the steady state of some of the departments and see how they fuse with the whole organization. This will lay the proper groundwork for ascertaining individuals' fusion scores in these departments. But before we do, let us make a few comments on the results to date.

Some Implications of the Results

It is useful to pause for a moment to see if the data in the previous chapter confirm or contradict the relevant theoretical preconceptions and hypotheses presented at the outset. The data, we suggest, do provide evidence for the sorts of ideas about the nature of organization that we discussed primarily on a theoretical level.

Steady State of the Processes

1. The theory suggests that the organization's processes must exist in such a way that they maintain a steady state. Note that the theory, at the moment, states nothing as to what this specific steady state *should* be in any given organization. The only thing that it does suggest is that the unique steady state of the processes is the organization's "answer"—so to speak—to how it is going to maintain itself internally while trying to achieve the objective of adapting to the external environment.

We also suggest that the notion of steady state implies that the dynamic nature and position of each process will vary as is necessary to be in balance with the other processes. Each process may be described as having a certain "strength" or "power," in relation to the other processes. This "strength" or "power," in relation to the other processes. This "strength" or "power" may be measured in terms of the employees' perceptions (i.e., "weak" or "strong") and/or in terms of frequency of activity in each process. The strength or power of each process at the point of balance among the processes is supposedly the optimum strength. In other words, when a steady state is achieved, we assume that the strength of each process is at its most favorable point. By "favorable" point we mean that point where the organizational processes are such that the best possible results are being obtained under the particular given conditions.

It follows from above that the "strength" of any given process in the organization that we study may only be understood in terms of the strength of the other processes at the point of steady state.

2. A review of the data in the previous chapter suggests that we do find conditions in this organization. There is continual organizational activity to maintain a specific steady state of balance among the organizational processes. This steady state, we note, is accounted for by describing each process and showing how it interacts with and is acted upon by the other processes.

For example, we may recall that in this organization, "weak" authority, reward and penalty, and perpetuation processes on the *organizational* level are balanced by a "strong" identification, workflow, and communication process. On the small group or departmental level, in cases where there are "weak" authority, reward and penalty, and perpetuation processes, informal group activities are almost non-existent. Thus, the lack of adaptive informal activities lessens the necessity for the need for "strong" formal authority, reward and penalty, and perpetuation processes.

In this way the balancing of the organizational processes goes on at three discrete but intrically inter-related levels of activity, the overall organization, the small groups (i.e., department) and the individual. Each level serves to reenforce the other and to help maintain its own position. We have, therefore, as we suggest in Chapter I, a network of circular activities going on among the organizational processes within each level of analysis and between the levels of analysis. This circularity permits us to begin our analysis of a set of variables at any given point. We will necessarily be led to an examination of all the other inter-related variables within the organization. We will know when we are finished by noting when we arrive at the beginning point.

To put all this in slightly different words, we may say that there are multiple, co-existing, inter-related feedback processes. Each feedback process has at least two reasons for existing. One is to maintain itself. The other is to reenforce and help maintain the other processes of the organization.

The feedback processes in this organization are such that the authority, reward and penalty, and perpetuation processes are "weak" while the workflow, communication, and identification processes are "strong." This specific steady state, on the organizational level, is balanced by the feedback processes related to the individual level. On the individual level we have a fusion process going on which desires just such a steady state on the organizational level. As a result of this, there is a relatively high degree of fusion between the organization and the individual. This in turn affects the small group level by minimizing the necessity for active informal group activities.

Organizational Correlates of the Goals of Business Managements

JAMES K. DENT [1]

This paper presents the goals of business managements as expressed by the chief executives or deputy chiefs of 145 business establishments. The goals most frequently expressed by management are profits, public service in the form of good products, and employee welfare. But other goals are also important such as growth, efficiency, meeting competition, and operating the organization.

Managers of large businesses more often speak of public service than do managers of small businesses, probably because they are relatively secure and because they are in the public eye. If they are unionized, large businesses show more interest in the welfare of their employees than do small businesses. If nonunion, the relationship is reversed. The explanation of these findings regarding expressed interest in employee welfare is probably complex, involving the psychological distance between manager and employee, the varying nature of collective bargaining, and the ideologies of owners and professional managers.

The higher the proportion of white-collar employees, the fewer the managers who mention profits. Similarly, the higher this proportion the more managers mention growth as a goal (but still not more than the number mentioning profits). These findings appear to reflect the varying cultural milieu of white-collar and blue-collar establishments. The finding becomes all the more important in view of the long-term trend toward greater upgrading and professionalization of labor.

Managers of "successful" growing businesses, like large businesses, more frequently speak of good products than do managers of declining businesses. They are also more interested in meeting and staying ahead of competitors. Their orientation is outward; they express less interest in such internal matters as running the organization. Although these findings do not directly contradict the position of Adam Smith that the public interest is best served by the pursuit of "own self-interest," they do suggest that the success of the business itself is furthered not by the pursuit of own self-interest but by the pursuit of public service in the form of good products. On the other hand, there is no evidence in the present data that the managers' pursuit of broader social responsibilities, such as employee or community welfare, furthers the growth of the business.

These data suggest that understanding and

From *Personnel Psychology*, Vol. 12, Autumn 1959, pp. 365–393. Reprinted by permission of the publisher.

[1] The author is Assistant Professor of Psychology at Wayne State University and Research Associate in the Institute of Labor and Industrial Relations, University of Michigan-Wayne State University.
This research was fully supported by the Institute.

The author wishes to thank the Co-Directors of the Institute, Ronald W. Haughton and Russell A. Smith, for their encouragement and continued interest in the study.

A special debt is owed to my wife, Vivian E. Dent. In her roles as research assistant, editor, and critic, she has made a considerable contribution. The data for the analysis are from a study directed by the author while he was a member of the staff of the Survey Research Center, Institute for Social Research, University of Michigan. Robert L. Kahn, Program Director, under whom the original study was conducted, contributed valuable suggestions to the design.

The present analysis is derived in part from the author's doctoral dissertation. As adviser and committee chairman, Professor Daniel Katz was a source not only of guidance but of intellectual stimulation.

The author has had the benefit of many valuable suggestions and criticisms from the following persons who read the manuscript: C. G. Browne, Chester E. Evans, Ronald W. Haughton, Robert L. Kahn, Daniel Katz, Arthur Kornhauser, and Ross Stagner. Responsibility for interpretations presented must be assumed by the author.

evaluation of organizations and institutions require a consideration of their broad functions and characteristics. It is the characteristics of the total organization and of all its members that determine its goals. If it has a function outside its membership, it is this function that must be given attention, rather than the rewards it offers its leaders, its owners, or its members.

During the past century profound changes have been occurring in American industrial society. Among these changes are the advent of big business, the separation of ownership and management accompanied by the professionalization of managers, the growth of large labor unions, the expanding role of government, and the ever greater specialization of knowledge and skill. There has been considerable interest in the nature and effects of these changes. Allen (1952) has written of "the big change," and Berle (1954) of "the 20th century capitalist revolution," to mention only two examples. Attention has been focused on the large corporation. This relative newcomer to the economic scene is a kind of curiosity, particularly since it was both rejected and doomed by the early classical economists. Questions have been raised as to whether its power is exercised in a responsible fashion, and to whom it is answerable. The literature of the area is vast and no effort will be made to summarize it here. For a summary of "managerial" theory, see Mason (1958). For a summary and bibliography of the literature of business ethics, the reader is referred to the *Harvard Business Review* (1958a, 1958b).

Although observers are not in agreement about the effects of various industrial changes, several recurring themes can be found in the literature. It is argued that big business is more socially responsible. It has a greater concern for its customers, its employees, and the public. The reasons for this are ascribed to big business ideology and to the intervention of other institutions such as government and labor unions. Similarly, it is argued that big business is less concerned with making profits. Frequently, it is held that big businesses are run, not by their owners, but by professional managers who have little personal stake in profits since they do not have a large ownership equity.

Definitive proof of the effect of industrial changes would require systematic observations over a long period of time. Such studies are quite expensive and slow. An alternative method (superior only in that it is cheaper and faster) is to compare various kinds of businesses at a point in time. Although there are dangers involved in longitudinal extrapolation of correlational findings, nevertheless the latter provide important insights into the meaning of such variables as size of business, professional vs. owner management, and so forth.

The present paper reports an empirical analysis of the goals of 145 business managements. It would be of considerable interest merely to describe the goals of business managements. However, the primary purpose here is to determine how various goals are related to the size of the business, the nature of ownership, unionization, and the composition of the labor force. Do big businesses show more or less interest in their employees, or in their customers, than small ones? Do professional managers express less interest in profits than owner managers? A second purpose is to evaluate various goals by describing the orientations of "successful" growing businesses.

The Stated Aims of Managements

The analysis is derived from the interview responses of 145 chief executives in business (or their deputies) to a single question: "What are the aims of top management in your company?" [2] This was the second question in the interview (preceded only by an even more general question concerning the activities of the organization). Interviewers were instructed not to probe this question, but to

[2] This question was included in a study conducted for the Occupational Health Program of the U.S. Public Health Service. The purpose of the study was to ascertain managerial attitudes toward the provision of preventive health services for employees, i.e., the regular services of a doctor or nurse, not simply for the treatment of injuries, but also for such preventive activities as physical examinations, the control of hazards, and so forth. For the methods of this study, see Dent and Griffith (1957). In addition, there is an appendix to the present article, available from the author on request, which considers the design of the larger study in relation to the purposes of the present analysis and reports a number of supplementary analyses.

accept whatever answer was given by the respondent. If he gave a single goal, this was recorded. If he gave a large number of goals (and some gave as many as eight or nine) the interviewer tried to record them as nearly verbatim as possible.[3]

For descriptive purposes, the data presented in Table 1 can not be considered to be representative of American business in any precise sense. In the first place, the 145 establishments included in this analysis are only those where the respondent for the interview was the chief executive or his deputy. More specifically, an interview is included if the respondent was the president or executive vice president (if the establishment was a complete company) or the general manager, assistant general manager, or superintendent (if the establishment was part of a multiple-unit company).[5]

Table 1. Aims of Managements in Five Cities and for Three Cities Separately

	PERCENTAGE OF MANAGERS GIVING VARIOUS AIMS				
	ALL FIVE CITIES		1ST THREE AIMS		
AIMS OF MANAGEMENT	1ST AIM	1ST 3 AIMS	CITY A	CITY B	CITY C
To make money, profits, or a living	36	52	49	75	39
To pay dividends to stockholders	1	9	9	12	2
To grow	12	17	14	5	22
To be efficient, economical	4	12	16	15	—
To meet or stay ahead of competitors	5	13	12	5	15
To operate or develop the organization	9	14	7	15	17
To provide a good product; public service	21	39	47	20	49
To contribute to the community; community relations	—	3	5	—	2
To provide for the welfare of employees: a good living, security, happiness, good working conditions	5	39	51	22	32
Miscellaneous other aims	7	18			
Total	100	*	*	*	*

* Adds to more than 100% because many executives gave more than one goal.

Table 1 presents the goals to which the 145 managers subscribe. The first column indicates the percentage of managers who mentioned the specified goal first; the second column presents the percentage of managers who gave a particular goal among their first three "mentions." One-fourth of the managers gave only one goal. One-sixth mentioned more than three goals.[4]

[3] The interview responses were coded by a group of five trained in content analysis. About one-fifth of the interviews were check-coded, that is, the material was recoded by a different person and the two codings were compared. The coders were in agreement in nine out of ten instances.

[4] In the analysis to be presented, the first three goals are combined. Analysis of only the first goal would have been unfair to those respondents whose second and third mentions were about as important to them as their first mention. Analysis of more than three responses would have given considerable weight to those managers who mentioned a large number of goals. The second and third goals mentioned tend to be different from the first one. For example, employee welfare is more likely to be mentioned as a second or third goal. For this reason, the three mentions were analyzed separately; it was found that the relationships to be presented are similar for each of the mentions.

[5] The study included 262 establishments of employment. Of these, 49 were non-profit general hospitals excluded from the present analysis because their goal orientations are quite different from businesses. For example, whereas two-fifths of the business managers express a concern for public service, all of the hospital administrators give this as a goal.

Also excluded from the present analysis are 68

Secondly, although the sample is a probability sample, it is not a representative one. The establishments were selected from among *all* types of industry, and all size groupings greater then 50 employees in five communities: Bridgeport (Conn.), Philadelphia, Cleveland, Houston, and San Francisco. The reader can imagine a matrix of cells which would result from a cross tabulation of several communities by several size groups by several broad industry groupings. Probabilities of selection were varied from cell to cell in such a manner as to yield a constant number of interviews in each cell. The three variables, community, size, and industry, were thus "held constant" simultaneously. This means that for the three cities presented in Table 1, the size and industrial distributions are similar. There is a great variation in the goals expressed by managers in these three cities, and this variation can not be explained by variation in the size of the business or by variation in industrial classifications. This wide variation in managerial goals in the three cities indicates that a representative sample of cities would be necessary to describe business goals in the United States. The communities included in this study are characterized by a diversity of industry. It is possible that a single-industry community would vary more from them than they do from each other.[6]

It can be seen from the first two columns of Table 1 that managers mention profits, a good product, employee welfare, and growth more frequently than other aims. Slightly more than half mention profits. One is tempted to conclude that nearly half of them are not interested in profits. Such an interpretation depends upon what meaning can be attached to their responses. It could be argued that their interest in a good product is really a concern for profits, or that their attention to employee welfare is with a view to increasing their profits. It is logically possible to reduce any aim to any other aim. Such a reduction would not be very acceptable to the manager who said: "I know what the economics text books say about this, but we are interested in being of service to our customers." The fact that many managers give several aims suggests that the various aims are not synonymous in their minds. Moreover, the reduction of aims to other aims does not seem to be very useful, except perhaps to satisfy the individual personality needs of those who are committed to a kind of 20th-century, social-psychological alchemy. Moreover, such a reduction ignores the fact that motives are frequently in conflict.

More important is the question of whether managers *can* and *will* report their real goals in an interview. People tend to express motives which are socially acceptable. The profit motive is not as socially acceptable as is public service in the form of good products.

There are several reasons for assuming that

---

businesses where the interview respondent held a staff position: industrial relations or personnel executive, treasurer, legal counsel, etc. In those establishments where the deputy chief was the respondent, the goals of management are similar to those where the chief executive was interviewed. However, in establishments where the respondent occupied a staff role, the expressed goals differ from those of chief executives and deputies. The nature and significance of the differing orientations are discussed in the appendix referred to in footnote 2. Browne (1950) found systematic differences in the perceptions of goals by respondents occupying various positions in a business.

[6] Within cells of the experimental matrix, businesses were selected at random from the files of the Federal Bureau of Old Age and Survivors Insurance for businesses with 100 employees or more, and from the files of the state employment services for businesses with 50 to 99 employees. The sample contained two submatrices, two of the communities being represented in only one of these. For these two communities, the number of cases is small and they are not presented in Table 1. Because of the large variation in goals in the several communities, the analyses to be presented were done separately for each of the three communities where the number of cases was sufficiently large. The relationships were found to be similar for each community. Thus it is unlikely that the findings presented are a function of community variation in goals. In cities A, B, and C, there are 43, 40 and 41 cases respectively.

Interviews were secured in 86 per cent of the sampled establishments. Nine per cent of the sample refused to make an appointment when the interviewer called; one per cent had been flooded by a hurricane (fall of 1955). The remaining four per cent, where interviews were not obtained, are multiple-unit companies that requested that the interview be conducted in the home office of the company, a procedure which did not fit the design of the study.

the responses are reasonably valid for our present purposes. In the first place, it should be noted that these respondents were not talking "for the record." They had been assured "that the interview will be held in complete confidence with no names of individuals or companies being used in any reports of this study." One company president responded: "Our aim is to make a profit; this is no philanthropy." Had he been making a public speech, he might have stated the company aims less bluntly. There is no evidence anywhere in the interviews of distortion, and in many instances the respondents were quite willing to divulge matters of a very confidential nature. For example, this respondent discussed fully his company's plans to relocate, a matter which at that time was known only to the directors.

Not only is there no evidence of distortion, there is evidence of surprising frankness. Anticipating results to be presented later, it will be noted in Chart 2 that none of the managers of nonunion businesses with more than 10,000 employees mentioned employee welfare as a goal. Such businesses are much in the public eye and in the eye of the union organizer. A public statement of company goals would certainly include some mention of the employees.

A second reason for accepting the data for present purposes is that we are not primarily concerned with description of managerial goals but with the relation of those goals to various characteristics of the enterprise. The findings are invalid only if there is differential distortion upon the part of managers of varying types of businesses. Although differential distortion can not be ruled out, it seems less likely than a constant distortion resulting from the general values of our culture.

Finally, it can be noted that the ultimate test of the validity of goals is in the behavior of managements. The interview provides material about managerial decisions regarding employee health services such as the provision of a regular doctor or nurse, periodic physical examinations, pre-employment physical examinations not simply for hiring but also for placement, the use of accident and sickness records to reduce accidents and sickness, inspections of the premises, etc. In establishments where there are none of these activities, only five per cent of the managers mentioned employee welfare as a goal. Where there were four or more of these activities, fifty per cent of the managers gave employee welfare as a goal. The relationship is statistically significant (tau is .23, p is .03).[7] It is significant, too, because these activities are rarely the result of government or union pressure and only occasionally due to pressure from insurance companies. In other words, these activities usually represent a voluntary decision on the part of management. Thus the expressed aims appear to be valid in the area where behavioral measures are available.

Prediction

Can we predict the manager's orientation if we know the characteristics of his business? Of particular interest are those characteristics which have been changing so much, namely: the size of the business, the nature of corporate stock ownership, unionization, and the proportion of employees who are white collar, professional, or supervisory. Each of these characteristics was studied in relation to each of the major goals: profits, growth, meeting competition, operating the organization, good products, and employee welfare. If no relation is reported between a particular characteristic and a particular goal, the reader can assume that no relation was found in analysis.[8]

[7] Kendall's tau is a coefficient of correlation which assumes only that the data are in ordered classes (rank correlation with ties in both ranks). As compared with the Pearsonian product-moment coefficient it yields a figure considerably lower when applied to the same data. It has an exact test of significance. The expression "p is .03" is for the hypothesis that tau equals zero (two-tailed test). The preventive health services are also related to whether the manager mentions good products as a goal (tau is .20, p is .03). For the goal, profits, tau is negative but not significant (—.12 at .10). The other goals do not relate to the preventive health services.

[8] Certain other charactersistics showed no relation to any of the goals. The amount of education the respondent has had is not a useful predictor; the relationship is slightly positive for the goal "good product," but falls far short of statistical significance (p is .30). Although seven of ten of these respondents have had some college education, their field of specialization in college is not related to the aims of the business. Managerial goals are not related to the age of the company (how long ago

Size and Ownership. The limited liability corporation has made it possible for a large business organization to come into being. It is very doubtful that individuals or groups of individuals in partnership could ever have amassed the capital required to build the continental railroads, nor could they have afforded to assume the risks that were involved. Moreover, the limited liability corporation has resulted in a separation of the functions of ownership and of management. Along with this has come a professionalization of managers. This change is variously interpreted, but for most observers it means at least that management is no longer identified with ownership. It has a role of its own in striking a fair balance between the claims of customers, stockholders, and employees. Most observers feel that the professional manager is more concerned with volume of production, with service, and with social responsibilities. He is less concerned with maximizing profits (although he is concerned that profits be satisfactory).

A large portion of the literature of managerial ideology has dealt with the joint effect of increasing size of businesses and increasing professionalization of management. Generally speaking, no separation has been made between these two variables, it being assumed that big businesses are run by professional managers. Although this is correct, there seems to be no inherent reason why increasing size of organization should have the same effect as the professionalization of its managers. The two characteristics are discussed together chiefly because the existing literature makes few distinctions between them. Each of the major goals will be considered in the light of what various authorities have written about them and the degree to which these ideas are confirmed by the present data.

Most observers feel that large businesses are less interested in profits than are their smaller owner-managed counterparts. Since the managers of big business usually have a very small ownership equity, they do not have a direct personal stake in profits. This is the position taken by Griffin (1949, pp. 96–104), Maurer (1955, pp. 77–78) and Sutton, Harris, Kaysen, and Tobin (1956, pp. 57–58). These authors do not hold that profits are of no significance to the professional manager of a large corporation. Rather they take the view that the manager regards profits as a symbol of success, or as a means to other ends, e.g., growth.

Against this view is that of Katona (1951, p. 197) who argues that a salaried executive, because of his strong personal identification with the firm, will be just as interested in profits as are owner managers. As a result of long service, the executive identifies his own success with that of the company, and profits are an important test of company progress. Still another line of reasoning is conceivable: since the profit record of the professional manager is published while that of the owner manager is not, one could argue that the professional manager is more interested in profits. He must answer not only to the stockholders but to the entire business community.

In the present data, professional managers of "publicly-held" businesses mention profits as a goal just as frequently as do the owner managers of privately-held and family-held companies. Similarly, managers of large businesses seem to be just as interested in profits as are managers of small ones.[9] It can be noted that one of the subclassifications of the profits category, "to make a living," is mentioned more frequently by managers of small businesses, suggesting that the significance of profits may be different for owner managers. Since the sample is small, and since other variables may be interfering with the relationship, we can

the company was established). Nor are they related to whether the establishment is part of a multiple-unit company or is a complete company in itself.

The relationships found between goals and organizational characteristics are presented in Charts 1 through 5 below. The number of cases for the size groups presented in Chart 1 are as follows: 28, 28, 26, 31, 20, not ascertained as to size of company 12. These numbers of cases are divided in Chart 2 as follows: union: 6, 16, 14, 22, 12, not ascertained 7; nonunion: 22, 12, 9, 8, not ascertained 5. For Chart 3: 17, 32, 27, 14, 11, 23, not ascertained 21. For Charts 4 and 5: 12, 19, 20, 28, 20, not ascertained 46 (see footnote 13).

[9] As would be expected, there is a positive correlation between the size of the establishment and the size of the company of which it is a part. The two variables are related to managerial goals in essentially the same way; that is, if one predicts a certain goal the other one does also. In the case of "employee welfare" the correlations with size of company are somewhat better than with size of establishment.

draw only a tentative conclusion that business growth and the professionalization of managers has not led to a declining interest in profits.

Turning now to the goal "growth," Griffin (1949, p. 98) has emphasized the professional managers' interest in the growth of the business. He observes that a manager's salary is more closely related to the size of the business than to its profits. In the present data, professional managers are slightly more interested in growth than are owner managers but the relationship is not statistically significant (tau is .13, p is .14). There is no relationship between a manager's subscribing to growth as a goal and the size of his business. Pending further data from a larger sample, it appears possible that managers' interest in growth is increased as a result of professionalization, but not as a result of size.

It might be expected that large businesses would be more interested in efficiency, "the best product at the lowest price." The "dynamic logic of mass production" is to increase volume by lowering costs and prices (Allen, 1952, pp. 112–120; Maurer, 1955, pp. 55–57). This logic is sometimes considered to be the integrating principle of the large corporation. The analysis shows no relationship between this goal and size of the business or the nature of ownership. Several writers have suggested that the large business is less troubled by competition. Again, this hypothesis is not confirmed by present data. It is probable that the difference in competition for large and small firms is one of kind rather than degree.

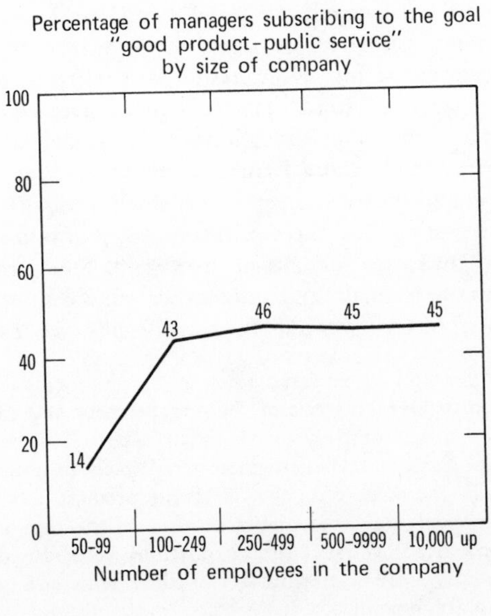

Chart 1

Since the peculiar function of management is to manage, it is reasonable to expect that professional managers of publicly-held corporations would be more interested in the sheer mechanics of operating and developing the organization. The data suggest that this may be true, but the relationship is not statistically significant (tau is .14 p is .11).

There is considerable concern about the purposes to which corporate power is directed and this concern is evidenced by a large volume of literature about the "social responsibilities" of the business man. These responsibilities are variously considered to extend to the community, to the nation both economically and politically, and to international affairs (Berle, 1954; Bowen, 1953; Levitt, 1958; Lauterbach, 1954, pp. 8–11). As a basic minimum, the term "social responsibilities" includes responsibility to the public to provide a good product, and responsibility for the welfare of employees. Presumably, because of its great power, the large corporation would be expected to show greater responsibility in these areas than would the small one.

Chart 1 shows the relationship between the managers' subscription to the goal "good product—public service" and the size of the company. This relationship if significant (tau is .22, p is .003). Of interest is the fact that the curve levels off for businesses with more than 100 employees. Feelings of responsibility to provide a good product are by no means confined to the nation's largest corporations.

There are a number of possible explanations for this finding. It might be argued that professionalization is the chief reason since the professional manager is not so closely identified with ownership. The fact that there is no relationship between the type of ownership and the managers' references to this goal (even though professional managers are found more frequently in large corporations) indicates that professionalization is not an adequate explanation.

A more plausible explanation is that the sheer size of the business focuses public attention upon it. This fact has been emphasized by Allen (1952, p. 240) who writes "a goldfish has got to be good."

There is yet another explanation for this finding which does not make use of the concept "social responsibility." Katona (1951, pp. 204–207) contrasts the orientation of managers under two different types of circumstances. The first circumstance is that of a precarious business, perhaps a new firm or one which is struggling to stay in business. The second circumstance is that of a well-established firm operating under prosperous conditions. In the first case the business firm has a short-range view point and is interested in quick profits and liquidity. It can not be concerned with nonpecuniary motives. The well-established firm, on the other hand, is likely to have a longer time perspective and to engage in activities which may not bring in any returns for a number of years. It is likely to become interested in the good will of the firm and even in such broad objectives as full employment and the avoidance of depression. Since a larger company is more likely to be in such a secure position than a small one, this in itself may explain why more managers of large firms give public service as a goal.

Katona extends the range of interest of the prosperous firm to still other fields. He feels that it is more likely to be concerned with community betterment and employee welfare. In the present data, large businesses do not mention the community more frequently than small businesses, but the number of managers who mention this goal is too small to provide reliable evidence. When union and nonunion businesses are taken together, there is no relationship between the size of the business and the managers' interests in employee welfare. Similarly, in the next section of this paper, it will be seen that growing businesses express more interest in good products than declining ones, but they do not show more interest in community and employee welfare. These data are not a fair test of Katona's hypothesis since he is concerned with the relationship between *financial* affluence and goals. Insofar as size and growth are measures of affluence, his hypothesis does not explain the findings of this study. Thus, the public service orientation of large businesses is explained not so much in that they can afford to be public-spirited, but in that they must be public-spirited because they are more visible. It is probable that public demands in the area of good products are far greater than in the areas of community betterment and employee welfare.

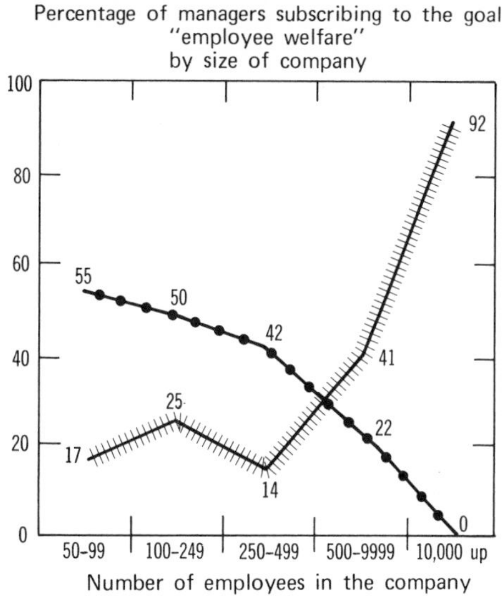

Chart 2

Chart 2 presents the relationship between managers' subscription to the goal "employee welfare" and the size of the company for union and nonunion businesses separately. It can be seen that large businesses in which employees are organized are more likely to mention the welfare of their employees than are small ones; among the nonunion businesses the relationship is reversed. (For union businesses tau is .38, p is .004. For nonunion businesses tau is -.30, p is .009). Here again there are several possible explanations.

The negative slope of the nonunion curve may be explained by the hypothesis that as a business grows larger the manager loses touch with employees and consequently loses his personal interest in them (Stagner, 1956, pp. 317–318). A contrary hypothesis is that, as a business becomes larger, it becomes more welfare conscious because of the greater threat of unionization. Both hypotheses can be reconciled with the present findings if we assume that managers of large nonunion businesses view employee welfare as a means to other ends (productivity, forestalling unionization, etc.) rather than as an end in itself.[10]

[10] As would be expected, union businesses were found to be generally larger than nonunion businesses. Of businesses with 50 to 100 employees, 22% have a union, while of businesses with 10,000 employees, 60% are unionized. There is little evidence in the study that nonunion businesses regard the forestalling of unionization as an important goal. A few managers in retail trade refused to answer questions having to do with unions, and

The converse of this explanation would be that unionization requires a manager to take a genuine interest in his employees. Why then do so few managers of small unionized businesses mention employee welfare? It might be argued that this is the reason why they are unionized, that causation runs from goals to unionization rather than the reverse. Here again we are confronted with a problem, for large unionized businesses do mention their employees. It is possible that the positive slope of the curve for unionized businesses arises out of the varying nature of the collective bargaining relationships. Many small businesses complain that they do not have much to say about the contents of the collective agreement; rather they must accept a pattern which has been established by large companies. In some industries, bargaining is done by an employers' association. It is possible that small businessmen feel that the matter of employee welfare has been taken out of their hands. Large businesses may feel that they actively participate in establishing matters that affect the welfare of employees.

The relationship between the employee-welfare goal and the nature of ownership is similar to that for size of company. If unionized, more professional managers of publicly-held companies mention employee welfare than do owner managers of privately-held and family-held companies; for nonunion businesses, the reverse is found. The relationships are not as sharp and are not statistically significant. (For union businesses tau is .21, p is .07. For nonunion businesses tau is -.22, p is .10.)

The fact that there is any relationship at all suggests the possibility of another explanation of the variation in managers' interest in employee welfare. The owner manager of a small business feels that the business belongs to him; he may have similar attitudes towards his employees provided they are not members of a union. If they are organized, he may feel that the union has trespassed upon his property. By contrast the professional manager probably does not feel this sense of ownership. Many writers (Griffin, 1949; Maurer, 1955; Berle, 1954; Allen, 1952) have pointed out that the professional manager is likely to view his role as that of mediating the interests of the shareholder, the employee, and the public. Unionization may actually enhance his role in dealing with the directors.

Looking back over all the relationships presented so far, it can be seen that there are significant relationships with size of company and unionization, but the relationships with type of ownership are weak or nonexistent.[11] Immediately below it will be seen that the goals of management are related to the nature of the labor force. Size, unionization, and the nature of the labor force are characteristics of the total business, whereas the nature of ownership is a characteristic of management. The fact that this latter does not predict well, while the former characteristics do, *suggests* the possibility that the formal goals of business are related more closely to the broad characteristics of the business than to the characteristics of its managers.

Proportion of Employees who are White-Collar, Professional, or Supervisory. One might think that the nature of the labor force is an irrelevant consideration in understanding the aims of businessmen. The literature of managerial ideology contains few references to the occupational distribution of the labor force. Two goals of management are significantly related to the nature of the labor force; these results are presented in Chart 3. It can be seen that fewer managers of white-collar establishments mention profits than do managers of blue-collar establishments (tau is -.20, p is .02). More white-collar managers talk about growth than do blue-collar managers (tau is .22, p is

some even refused to answer questions in the area of employee relations generally. But these are only four in number. Among the nonunion businesses with more than 10,000 employees, there is a disproportionately large number of establishments in retail trade.

[11] The relationship between unionization and the goals of management appears to be only in the area of employee welfare, and then only in complex interaction with the size of the business (Chart 2). Comparing the distribution of responses in union and nonunion businesses, the proportion of managers giving various goals is surprisingly similar. This is true even when the several communities are considered individually. All of the analyses were conducted for union and nonunion establishments separately. Again, except for the relationship between size and the goal, employee welfare, all of the relationships presented in this article are similar in union and nonunion establishments.

.01). However, even when the proportion of white-collar workers exceeds fifty per cent, the number of managers mentioning growth does not exceed that mentioning profits. Further, it should be noted that the relationship applies to the white-collar range from zero to fifty per cent rather than to the range of fifty to one-hundred per cent.[12] In other words, the relationship reflects not simply the expressed goals of such businesses as retail trade, insurance, and banks, but also businesses which are half blue-collar such as engineering, utilities and so forth.

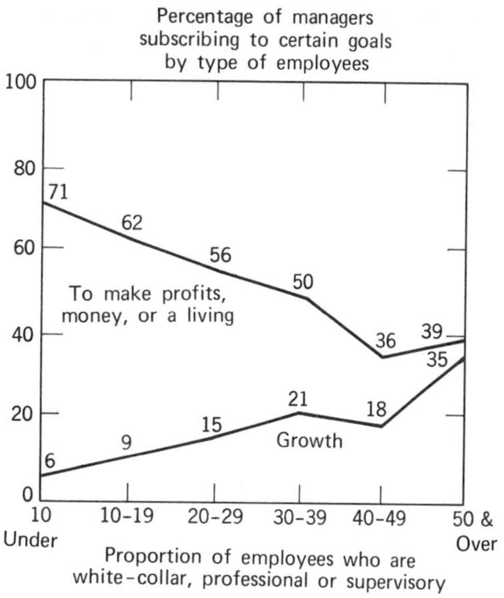

Chart 3

In speculating about the meaning of these findings, it seems highly probable that the goals of management are conditioned by the "cultural milieu" of the entire business. Are we to assume that the cultural milieu of a blue-collar establishment (managers and employees alike) is oriented more toward money than that of a white-collar establishment? The evidence for this is sketchy and not completely in agreement. In the present study managers were asked: About your employees and what they expect to get out of their jobs, to what extent are they interested in the money they take home, and to what extent are they interested in other things about the job? Managers who mention profits as a goal are much more likely to see their employees as interested primarily in money than are managers who do not mention profits as a goal. Moreover, more of the managers of blue-collar establishments see their employees as primarily interested in money than do managers of white-collar establishments. This evidence, then, is consistent with a hypothesis that the cultural milieu of a blue-collar business is oriented more toward money. However, these findings are explained more parsimoniously if we simply assume that managers project their own motives onto their employees. Unfortunately, there were no interviews with employees in the present study, and we do not know whether blue-collar workers would see themselves as more interested in money than would white-collar workers. If we turn to other studies that have been done, the evidence is not completely consistent. The author knows of no study which shows that blue-collar workers are *less* interested in money than white-collar workers. There are several studies which show no difference between blue-collar and white-collar workers. (Centers, 1948; Jurgenson, 1947; Hersey, 1936; Stagner, 1956, p. 125; Institute for Social Research, 1952a, 1952b). There is one summary of nine studies, which shows that blue-collar workers rate wages second, while white-collar workers rate it fifth in a list of factors (Herzberg, Mausner, Peterson, and Capwell, 1957, p. 53). On one matter most studies are in agreement, namely, that white-collar workers derive more intrinsic satisfaction from their jobs than do blue-collar workers (Katz, 1954, p. 93). However, any conclusions concerning the money orientations of

[12] In the range zero to fifty per cent white-collar, average wages of employees rise. Above this range average wages decline. Average wages does not predict the goals of management. The observed relationships appear to be a white-collar rather than a wage effect. In union establishments, the proportion of employees who are union members declines as the proportion of white-collar employees increases (tau is —.51 with a critical ratio of 20). The proportion of employees who are union members predicts the expressed goals in the same way as the proportion of employees who are white-collar. However, since the relations with white-collar are found also in nonunion establishments, the effect is probably not due to the degree of unionization. For a comparison of the "fact" of unionization with the "degree" of unionization in predicting managers' perceptions of their employees, see Dent (1958).

these two types of establishments must necessarily be tentative in view of the paucity and conflict of evidence.

Variations in the cultural milieu may explain why managers of white-collar establishments mention growth more frequently than do managers of blue-collar establishments. There is considerable evidence that white-collar workers attach greater importance to promotion than do blue-collar workers. (Centers, 1948; Hersey, 1936; Stagner, 1956; Herzberg, *et al.* 1957). A manager who sees his employees as having high needs for promotion may perceive growth as a means of meeting these expectations. However, it should be noted that there is no relation between a manager's mentioning growth as a goal and whether his establishment is growing in fact. Nor is there any relation between the actual growth of the business and the proportion of employees who are white-collar. Thus, assuming that the cultural milieu of a white-collar business is one of promotion through growth, there is little evidence that this happy state is in fact achieved.

In appraising the validity of the cultural-milieu hypothesis we can not rule out the possibility that some other common factor like technology or competition is responsible for the managers' orientations. Nevertheless, the relationships presented in Chart 3 are quite stable and strong, and there is at least some external evidence to support this hypothesis.

Summary. The data presented in this section indicate that three characteristics are related to the goal orientations of managers: the size of the business, unionization, and the nature of the labor force. As company size increases from 50 to 250 employees, more managers mention good products as a goal. Managers' subscription to employee welfare as a goal increases over the entire range of size if the business is unionized but it decreases if the business is nonunion. The professionalization of management does not seem to be so important to managerial goals. Professional managers are not less interested in profits than are owner managers. Much more important, it seems, than the professionalization of management is the professionalization of employees, for as the proportion of white-collar employees increases fewer managers mention profit as a goal. Again, as this proportion increases more managers talk about growth. Although we can not be certain about the direction of causation, the findings are consistent with explanations which assume that the goals derive from the characteristics of the business.

The ultimate significance of these findings depends upon the validity of extrapolating longitudinally from a correlational study. If it is legitimate to project these differences into the future, certain trends in managerial ideology seem reasonably certain. We cannot be certain of the future course of unionization; this depends largely upon the attitudes of white-collar workers and the ability of management to satisfy their needs. Nor does it seem likely that the concentration of industry in big business will increase greatly, if past trends can be projected (Adelman, 1951). But it is certain that the proportion of white-collar workers in industry will increase due to the greater demands of technology and logistics and to occupational shifts to service industries. For this reason it seems likely that growth will be an increasingly important feature of the ideology of managers, and that profits will be of declining importance. But it is doubtful that businessmen's interest in growth will ever exceed that in profits.

Evaluation

The problem of evaluation involves the choice of a criterion. Ideally, a number of criteria would be available so that the importance of various factors could be assessed against various criteria simultaneously. The only criterion of success available in this study is the growth of the business. This was measured by the average annual per cent increase in employment for the period 1947 to 1955.

As a criterion it has a narrow frame of reference. The business may have grown at the expense of other businesses, and even at the expense of the public and of its employees. We are therefore evaluating managerial goals in terms of a commonplace definition of the success of the business, as a business. We are not evaluating managerial goals in terms of the broad social contribution of the business or of the success of the economy as a whole.[13]

[13] There are many possible criteria of success of a business. The social theorist is concerned with broad social responsibilities, or, at least with a con-

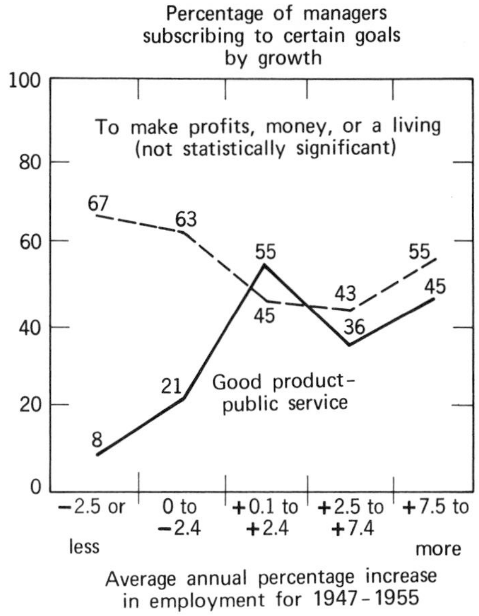

Chart 4

The results of the analysis are presented in Charts 4 and 5. Chart 4 shows the relationship between the actual growth of the business and the manager's expression of profits and public service as goals. The relationship with profits is not statistically significant (tau is − .11, *p* is .26); it is presented for comparison with the curve for "good product—public service." This latter relationship is statistically significant (tau is .21, *p* is .03). Thus, not only do larger businesses subscribe to public service more than small ones, but growing businesses likewise mention public service more frequently than declining ones.[14] Chart 4 shows

sideration of social costs and products which do not appear in current accounting procedures. For the businessman, the level of profits is the most common criterion of success. In this study, this criterion was rejected for methodological reasons. Many small businessmen are unwilling to divulge profits even though confidentiality is pledged. Large multiple-unit businesses frequently do not know the profits of individual establishments. Even if these problems can be solved, there remains the difficulty that profit ratios vary by industry and over time quite independently of the success of the business. To deal with this it would be necessary for the sample to be large enough so that each business could be compared with others in the same line. Profit ratios generally decline with size because of reduced risk and some allowance would be necessary for this. It is for these reasons that profits are frequently compared with profits for the previous period. The ratio has little meaning in an absolute sense.

Using growth in employment as a measure of success also has some limitations. Even though employment were stable, the output of a business might be expanding with technological change. However, it is very likely that those businesses which are expanding their employment are expanding output more rapidly than those which have stable employment. One final limitation in the criterion is that about one-third of the firms did not furnish the necessary data. This large proportion is due mainly to the fact that two of the fifteen interviewers did not understand how these data were to be collected. Since interviews are assigned to interviewers at random, it is doubtful that the large proportion not ascertained caused any systematic bias in the results.

As in the previous section, the results presented were studied and found to be similar within the following subgroups of the sample: union and nonunion; single unit and multiple-unit companies; first, second, and third "mentions"; three communities.

[14] Considering all businesses together there is no relationship between the size of the business and the growth of the establishment. However, when the union and nonunion businesses are separated there is an interaction; the larger nonunion businesses are growing faster than the small ones, while the small union businesses are growing faster than the large ones. No explanation of these phenomena has been found in the data.

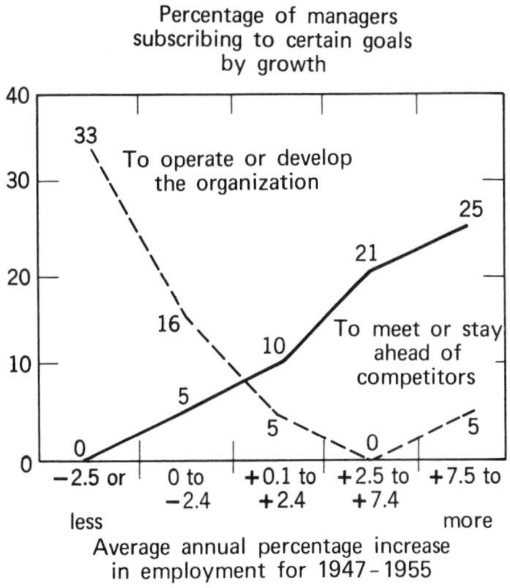

Chart 5

that managers of *growing* businesses keep profits and public service in perspective; that is, profits and good product are mentioned with about equal frequency. More managers of declining businesses mention profits than good product.

Chart 5 shows the relationship between the growth of business and manager's interest in organization and in competition. Both relationships are significant (taus are − .26 and .25 respectively, both significant at the .01 level). Managers of growing businesses are not primarily concerned with their organizations but they are concerned with competition. The fact that managers of successful businesses are concerned with public service and with competition suggests that their orientations are outward towards the environment of the business rather than inward towards the business itself.[15]

In summary, managers of growing businesses show less concern with the business itself than do managers of declining ones. Managers of growing businesses express *more* concern with competition and good products. To be concerned with competition does not fit Katona's hypothesis about the long-range perspective of the well-established firm, although the good-product orientation does fit his hypothesis. We would also expect the growing firm to express more interest in employee welfare and community contribution than the declining firm, if this were the explanation, and such relationships are not found in the data. An alternative explanation is that, although competition today is different from that described by Adam Smith and the classical economists, it still has effect; the successful business must reckon *consciously* with its environment and its chief social function—to provide a product. Pursuit of "self interest" may not be enough. Sounder conclusions can be drawn when data are available relating these orientations to such things as product development, productivity increases and market practices.

Discussion

These data raise a number of questions regarding business organization and organizational theory in general. First, businesses have a number and variety of goals. The complex way in which these goals relate to various organizational characteristics raises a question of whether the search for a single unifying principle is any more likely to be successful than was the alchemists' search for the "philosophers' stone." It may be more fruitful to proceed, as did the early chemists, with a systematic study of the characteristics of the elements, with the idea that an integrated theory will be built by a synthesis of detailed findings.

Profits seem to be the most salient single goal of business. But the data suggest that the profit motive is declining. If there has been a decline, it is not due so much to the "professionalization" of managers, as to that of labor generally. In keeping with recent interest in the "situational factors in leadership," the findings suggest that to understand managerial ideology we must do more than study managers. We must know the nature of the entire organization and the needs and aspirations of all its members. The fact that managers of white-collar businesses are more concerned with growth than managers of blue-collar businesses is compatible with the findings of many other studies that white-collar workers are primarily interested in their opportunities for promotion.

Probably of more importance than the question of what motive *is* prime for businessmen, is the question of what motive *should be* foremost. If the actual growth in employment is taken as a criterion, this study suggests that managers should be at least as interested in having a good product as in profits. As compared with managers of declining businesses, managers of growing businesses do not express more nor less interest in profits, or in growth; but they do express a greater interest in good products. This may confirm the belief that the

[15] Drucker (1958) has advanced the hypothesis that a business must be concerned with a variety of needs in order to survive. With this in mind the present data were examined to see if growing businesses give more goals than declining ones. No such relationship was found. However, this does not constitute a fair test of Drucker's hypothesis since the goals presented here are not in correspondence with those he lists. An analysis of the pattern of goals given by managers (the combination of goals mentioned) yielded no conclusions beyond those in Charts 4 and 5.

prime function of a social institution is to serve a social purpose rather than to serve its owners, its leaders, its members, or even itself.

Again, using growth as a criterion, there is no evidence that the success of the business is furthered by an interest in such broad social responsibilities as employee welfare or community betterment. This suggests that a "feeling of social responsibility" is not a unitary variable. There is no evidence in this study that managers who are interested in serving their customers are likewise interested in serving their employees, or the public in a broad social sense.

In any event, it is probable that a business responds to forces both within and without itself. The complex way in which the managers' orientations toward employee welfare relate to the size and unionization of the business suggests that the internal and external forces are in interaction. An integrated theory will have to deal with both sets of forces in combination.

To take another example, consider the curve presented in Chart 1. Here it is observed that more managers of businesses with over 100 employees mention good products as a goal than do managers with 50 to 100 employees. The explanation of the greater concern for good products might be (a) internal—the greater security that comes with size enables the firm to turn its attention to such things as good will, or (b) external—the greater public visibility of such firms result in their paying greater attention to their function. If these are the explanations, why does the curve not rise continuously instead of leveling off? Could it be that the relationship between this goal and security is an inverted "U," that interest in good products rises as the firm becomes more secure, but falls off when the firm becomes very secure? Perhaps the leveling off is a result of "over-security" forces and public visibility forces cancelling each other. Whatever the explanation, it seems likely that both internal and external forces are at work.

In the face of these complexities and unanswered questions, the present data provide a rather large measure of satisfaction and hope. Although more questions are raised than are answered, the findings indicate that the questions will yield to systematic empirical exploration.

REFERENCES

Adelman, M. A. "The Measurement of Industrial Concentration." *Review of Economics and Statistics*, XXXIII (1951), 269–296.

Allen, F. L. *The Big Change, America Transforms Itself, 1900–1950*. New York: Harper & Brothers, 1952.

Berle, A. A. *The 20th Century Capitalist Revolution*. New York: Harcourt Brace, 1954.

Bowen, H. R. *Social Responsibilities of the Business Man*. New York: Harper & Brothers, 1953.

Browne, C. G. "Study of Executive Leadership in Business: III. Goal and Achievement Index." *Journal of Applied Psychology*, XXXIV (1950), 82–87.

Centers, R. "Motivational Aspects of Occupational Stratification," *Journal of Social Psychology*, XXVIII (1948), 187–217.

Dent, J. K. "Managerial Leadership Styles: Some Dimensions, Determinants and Behavioral Correlates." Unpublished Ph.D. thesis, University of Michigan, 1958.

Dent, J. K. and Griffith, R. G. *Employee Health Services, A Study of Managerial Attitudes and Evaluations*. Ann Arbor: Institute for Social Research, 1957. (Also available from the U.S. Public Health Service.)

Drucker, P. F. "Business Objectives and Survival Needs: Notes on a Discipline of Business Enterprise." *Journal of Business*, XXXI (1958), 81–90.

Griffin, C. E. *Enterprise in a Free Society*. Chicago: Irwin, 1949.

Harvard Business Review. "Looking Around." *Harvard Business Review*, XXXVI, No. 2 (1958), 139–153. (a)

Harvard Business Review. "In this Issue." *Harvard Business Review*, XXXVI, No. 5 (1958), 5–12. (b)

Hersey, R. B. "Psychology of Workers." *Personnel Journal*, XIV (1936), 291–296.

Herzberg, F. Mausner, B., Peterson, R. O. and Capwell, D. F. *Job Attitudes: Review of Research and Opinion*. Pittsburgh: Psychological Service of Pittsburgh, 1957.

Institute for Social Research. *Report I, Attitudes and Opinions of Nonsupervisory Employees*. Ann Arbor: Author, 1952. (a)

Institute for Social Research. *Report III, Attitudes and Opinions of Office Employees*. Ann Arbor: Author, 1952. (b)

Jurgensen, C. E. "Selected Factors Which Influence Job Preferences." *Journal of Applied Psychology*, XXXI (1947), 553–564.

Katona, G. *Psychological Analysis of Economic Behavior*. New York: McGraw-Hill, 1951.

Katz, D. "Satisfactions and Deprivations of Industrial Life." In Kornhauser, A., Dubin, R. and Ross, A. M. (Ed.), *Industrial Conflict.* New York: McGraw-Hill, 1954.

Lauterbach, A. *Man, Motives and Money.* Ithaca: Cornell University Press, 1954.

Levitt, T. "The Dangers of Social Responsibility." *Harvard Business Review,* XXXVI, No. 5 (1958), 41–50.

Mason, E. S. "The Apologetics of 'Managerialism.'" *Journal of Business,* XXXI (1958), 1–11.

Maurer, H. *Great Enterprise.* New York: Macmillan Company, 1955.

Stagner, R. *Psychology of Industrial Conflict.* New York: John Wiley & Sons, 1956.

Sutton, F. X., Harris, S. E., Kaysen, C. and Tobin, J. *The American Business Creed.* Cambridge: Harvard University Press, 1956.

Measurement of Behaviour Structures by Means of Input-Output Data[1]

P. G. HERBST

There are two methods by which a system, no matter what kind, may be studied. We may study it directly by inspection, find out what its component parts are and how they are dynamically interrelated; or we may without interfering with its internal functioning find out how the system transforms a given set of inputs into outputs, and use the input-output relationships found to infer the internal structure. The latter method is of particular relevance in both the biological and the behavioural sciences, either because it is not feasible or in some cases not possible to get inside the system, or simply because input-output data are frequently more easily available.

In the present paper, which is exploratory in nature, an attempt will be made to show by means of an essentially simply model how data on input, output, and size of a behaviour system may be used to obtain measures of its internal structure. The diagnostic technique will be applied to group and organizational functioning and illustrated by data on the relationship between social structure and economic functioning of retail establishments.

The term behaviour system is used to refer both to individuals and to social organizations in the sense that both can be defined within a behavioural frame of reference as boundary-maintaining units of interdependent activities and activity-control functions both with respect to internal and external relationships. By a boundary is meant any critical value of system variables beyond which a change in structure occurs. In the special case where going beyond the critical value leads to disintegration or dissolution of the system, we have an external boundary.

From *Human Relations,* Vol. 19, 1957, pp. 335–345. Reprinted by permission of the publisher.

[1] Paper read at the International Congress of Psychology, Brussels, August 1957.

A characteristic shared by all behaviour systems is that, in order to maintain themselves, they have to set up some form of reciprocal relationship with their environment. More specifically, the input they obtain is dependent on the output that they supply to environmental units with which they are linked. Within the system itself intake and output are linked by internal processes of distribution and transformation. Before going on to a discussion of the model in more detail, it will be necessary to consider whether concepts of this type can be used to represent the process of group functioning.

In the case of human organizations the internal processes and interactions with the environment can be looked at in terms of three distinct aspects. There are first of all:

1. Social interactions within the group and relations of the group to the behavioural environment within which it is located. Social interactions include transformation processes in the form of assimilation and learning; distribution processes in the form of assignment of tasks, status, and responsibility; intake-output processes with respect to group members and the control of social processes both within the group and with respect to the relation of the group to its environment.

The second aspect concerns:

2. Techno-ecological processes within the group and techno-ecological relations to the environment. Here we include the technological and ecological facilities available to the group; the structure of the operations system which includes both the transformation and distribution structure; the control of transformation and distribution processes; and the import and export of materials, tools, and ecological facilities.

Thirdly we have:

3. Economic processes that concern the valuational aspects of both the social and the technological intakes, outputs, and internal operations. The value of some activities and exchange operations is measured in terms of an objective currency standard. Currencies of one type or another may be looked at as technical inventions that facilitate exchange through frequently used channels. It should be stressed, however, that economic behaviour is not limited to the use of currencies but that in practice all behaviour has a valuational or economic aspect.

A human organization may, then, be looked at as a system of behaviour which has social, technological, and economic aspects. We speak of different aspects, since a group is not a system of activities some of which are social and others economic or technological, but rather every activity may be analysed with respect to any one of these frames of reference.

Take, for instance, the sales activity in a retail store. This may be looked at from the point of view of the interaction between the customer and sales girl, and the impression each forms of the other. It may be looked at from the point of view of an operations sequence consisting of the receipt of an order by the sales girl, the girl looking for and transporting the article to the sales desk, wrapping up the article, writing out a bill, etc. Finally, we may study the activity by recording that the price of articles is fixed and not subject to bargaining, the transaction is one of cash in exchange for goods, we may note the cost of time spent by the sales girl with the customer against the value of goods sold, and the cost of material and sales operations in relation to the sales price. In each case we are looking at the same activity within a different frame of reference.

It may be noted that in the study of physical phenomena we proceed in a rather similar way. The physical object may be studied in terms of its weight, its colour or its temperature. Technically this process may be described as filtering. Each time for the purpose of description and measurement we use a filter which lets through a certain range nd type of data as significant and rejects other types of data. In the above example it is known that each aspect represents for practical purposes an independent dimension, that is, we can change the colour of an object without affecting its weight, or change the temperature up to a certain point without affecting the colour of the object. This, however, is not always the case. It is known for instance that the pressure, volume, and temperature of a gas are interdependent, so that for the study of these phenomena we need to obtain simultaneous measures of all three characteristics, or keep one or the other constant, if we want to study change phenomena.

In the study of human organizations we face a similar problem. We can filter out information about the social, technical, and economic aspects of the process of group functioning. These however are found to be interdependent with one another.

Let us again take as an example the sales activity in a retail store. Suppose we change the shop from over-the-counter selling to self-service, which represents a technological change. The customer now selects the goods she wants to buy and takes them to the cashier's desk, where they are wrapped up and paid for. The technological change alters the interaction process between customer and assistant, and also changes the economic valuation of the assistant's activities. Or suppose we change over from fixed-price sales to bargaining. This will evidently modify the interaction process between customer and assistant. The effect on the technological process is more complex. It may be noted that an increase in size of a retail store beyond a certain point is as a rule possible only by a switching over from bargaining to fixed-price sales. A change of this type may thus turn out to be incompatible with the existing socio-technical system.

In the study of human organizations we therefore need to consider the whole network of social, technical, or economic processes, or attempt to keep one or the other constant for the purpose of comparative study. Methods and concepts for studying the relation between social and technical organization have been developed by E. L. Trist (8) and A. K. Rice (6). The illustrative data that will be discussed in the following sections are based on relationships found between the social structure and economic functioning, keeping the technological structure constant so far as possible.

Table 1.

SYSTEM MODEL	GROUP FUNCTIONING
I = input	W = amount paid in wages in £'s
I_{min} = minimum boundary value of input	W_{min} = minimum boundary value for wages
U = output	S = sales turnover in £'s
N = size of system	N = number of persons in the organization
N_{min} = minimum boundary value for size of system	N_{min} = minimum boundary value for number of persons
G = size of integrating unit	A = number of persons exclusively in managerial and administrative roles

SIMPLE SYSTEM

Type of Function	
input-output $I = a_1 U + I_{min}$	$W = a_1 S + W_{min}$ (1)
output-size $N = a_2 U + N_{min}$	$N = a_2 S + N_{min}$ (2)
$\therefore I = \dfrac{a_2 I_{min} - a_1 N_{min}}{a_2} + \dfrac{a_1}{a_2} N$	
but if $N = 0, I = 0$, so that	
input-size $\dfrac{I}{N} = k$	$\dfrac{W}{N} = k$ (3)
efficiency $\dfrac{U}{N} = \dfrac{1}{a_2}\left(1 - \dfrac{N_{min}}{N}\right)$	$\dfrac{S}{N} = \dfrac{1}{a_2}\left(1 - \dfrac{N_{min}}{N}\right)$ (4)

COMPLEX SYSTEM

$G = b_1 N + b_2 N^{1+\alpha} - b_3$ where 'α' is the degree of complexity of the system which varies between 0 and 1	$A = b_1 N + b_2 N^{1+\alpha} - b_3$ (5)
output-size function $U = f(N,G)$ $= f(N, N^{1+\alpha})$	$S = c_1 N - \dfrac{1}{c_2 N^{1+\alpha}} + c_3$ (6)
efficiency $\dfrac{U}{N} = f(N, N^{1+\alpha})/N$	$S = c_1 - \dfrac{1}{c_2 N^{1+\alpha}} + \dfrac{c_3}{N}$ (7)
	where 'α' is the degree of complexity of the system

Levels of Organization

We may distinguish between three levels of organization, which will be referred to respectively as an assembly, a simple system, and a complex system. An *assembly* is defined as a set of elements whose output is proportional to the number of elements and the amount of input supplied. We can use this as a base-line model.

A *simple system* has the following additional properties:

1. It has minimum boundary values, both with respect to size and input required, below which it will cease to function.

2. The input that it obtains is linked to and dependent on the output supplied to one or more environmental units.

As the size of the simple system increases, and depending also on the extent of both its internal and external linkages, more and more work has to be carried out on the coordination of component functioning, so that a critical boundary value with respect to size is reached, beyond which intrinsic regulation breaks down. An increase in size beyond this point will become possible by differentiating out a separate *integrating unit*, which takes over the function of both control and coordination of component units, thus leading to a transition from a simple to a *complex system*. The point at which intrinsic regulation breaks down will be determined by the effectiveness of the organizational structure. The less efficient the organizational structure happens to be, the earlier the point at which intrinsic regulation breaks down.[2]

Let us consider first the characteristics of a simple system. The variables we are concerned with are measures of a given input, measures of a corresponding output, and an appropriate measure of system size.

Characteristics of Simple Systems. In the simple system the input obtained is dependent on the output supplied to one or more environmental unit. However, even if the system ceases to be output producing, there is some minimal input quantity that is required if the system is to survive. This is stated by the input-output function shown in Equation 1 (Table 1).

The output achieved will depend on the size of the system. An increase in the output accepted by environmental units will lead to increased size; and a decrease in the output accepted, i.e. a decreased demand for whatever is produced will lead to a reduction in size. Again there is a minimal boundary value, in this case with respect to size, below which the system cannot maintain itself in existence. This is shown by the output-size function in Equation 2.

From the above two relationships one interesting consequence follows, namely, that the ratio of input to size will be a constant. This is perhaps the most sensitive test of whether a unit studied constitutes a simple system.

The illustrative material is based on data obtained from small shops forming part of a retail chain and very similar to one another with respect to their technological structure. The measure of system size used is the number of persons employed in each shop. Output is measured by the sales turnover achieved, and input is measured by the total amount paid in wages.

Figure 1 shows that the total amount paid in wages increases at a linear rate with the sales turnover achieved. However, even if the shop were to make no sales whatever, then some minimum amount still has to be paid out in wages to the shop personnel.

Figure 2 shows that sales turnover increases at a linear rate with the size of the shop in terms of the number of persons employed. If there is an increased demand and sales turnover increases, more men are employed. If demand decreases, fewer men are employed, so that an equilibrium is maintained between shop size and sales turnover. However, even if no sales are made at all, there is still a minimum number of persons, in this case one person, required if the shop is to maintain itself in existence. It is interesting to note that in this context a single individual constitutes in a very real sense a group consisting of one member. In the case of manufacturing industries, which employ a more complex technology, the mini-

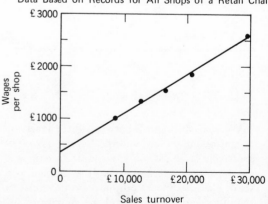

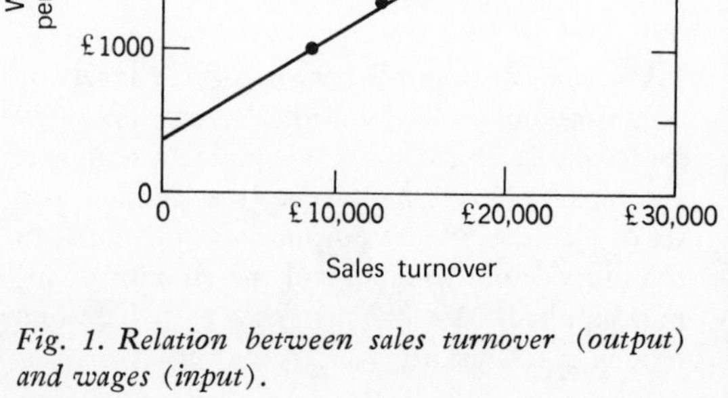

Fig. 1. Relation between sales turnover (output) and wages (input).

[2] Findings by A. R. Luria (5) are of interest in this connection. He reports that, under conditions of stress in the form of increased demand placed on children and also under pathological conditions, self-regulating behaviour is replaced by regressed behavior in the form of more extrinsic behaviour control. From the point of view of system functioning, this corresponds to the breakdown of self-regulation in groups under conditions of excessive demand load or faulty organization.

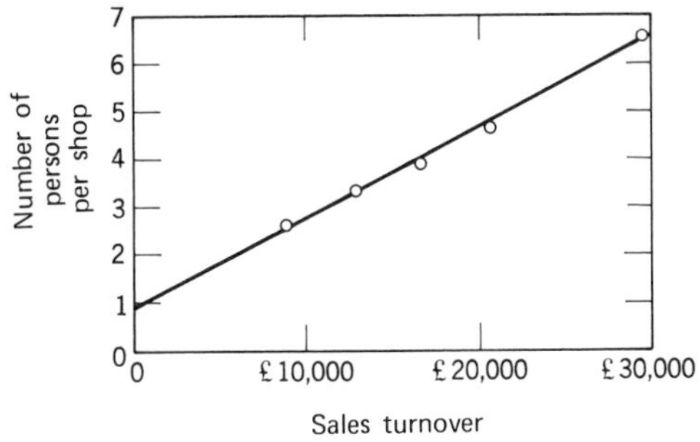

Fig. 2. Relation between sales turnover and size of shop.

mum size of the organization is likely to be much larger.

Figure 3 shows that the average wage per shop, that is, the ratio of total wages paid divided by the number of men employed, is practically a constant.

The data thus show that these shops have the characteristics of a simple system. In this specific case we may conclude from the findings that they constitute groups in which all members participate in productive functions and as yet no separate administrative component has been differentiated out. Before we go on to consider how the input-size-output functions are altered if an administrative unit is present, we shall need to consider first of all what are the conditions under which intrinsic regulation breaks down, and an extrinsic integrating unit takes over the function of control and coordination.

Size of the Integrating Unit. As an organization increases in size, a critical point is reached where an administrative unit is set up, that is, one or more persons who are concerned exclusively with the control and coordination of activities of their subordinates and whose contribution to output thus becomes indirect. An analogous problem in biology might be the conditions under which an organism develops a recognizable brain structure.

Let us suppose that the components of a system are independent of one another or very nearly so, then the amount of work required for control would be proportional to the number of components (n) of the system, so that the

$$\text{amount of control work} = b_1 n$$

If the component parts are interconnected, then the amount of work required additionally for the coordination of components may be taken to be a function of the number of interconnections between components. The maximum number of interdependence links between n components is $\frac{n(n-1)}{2}$ so that in the simplest case

$$\text{maximum coordination work} \simeq b_2 n^2$$

If we compare the amount of work in the form of control and integration in the case where there is complete independence between component parts with that where there is a complete linkage between components, we find that this is a function of n (the number of components) in one case and of n^2 in the other. The size of the integrating unit may then be taken to be a function of the size of the system raised to the power $1 + \alpha$, where α may be taken as a measure of the degree of complexity of the system in terms of the degree of connectedness between its components.

In so far as the integrating unit is concerned with both control and coordination, its size should be related to the size of the system by a function of the form shown in Equation 6 (Table 1). If α is zero, then the relationship becomes linear, which would indicate that the system consists either of productive components that are functionally undifferentiated or of a set of independent simple systems with a common control unit. If α is unity, this would imply that it consists of components that are functionally differentiated, each having an interdependence link with every other.

The equation discussed shows that apart

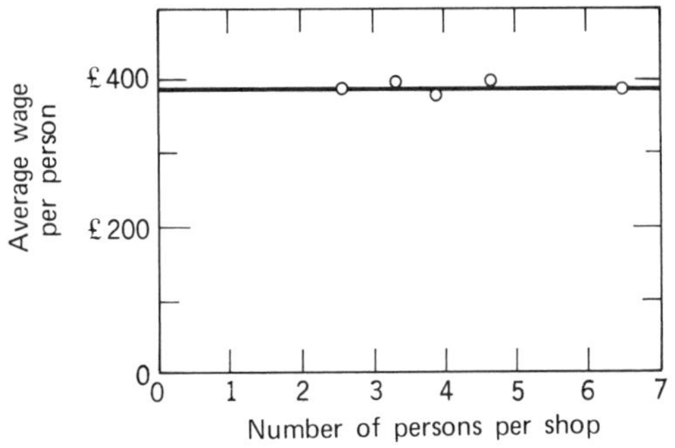

Fig. 3. Relation between size of shop and average wage of shop members.

from the size of the organization there are three factors that determine the proportion of personnel in management and administrative roles. These are the complexity of the organization, the extent or rate at which the organization reacts to a given degree of complexity of its operations by installing extrinsic control and coordination, and the critical point with respect to size at which intrinsic regulation breaks down and transition to a complex system occurs.

Some relevant data are reported by F. W. Terrien and D. L. Mills (7) in a study of the size of the administrative component in elementary and high school districts. The administrative staff is taken to include the superintendent, his assistants, and intermediate staff, principals, business managers, and the like. Students were excluded.

For elementary schools the relationship between the size of the administrative component and the size of the organization is a linear one, which would indicate a low level of functional differentiation. In the case of high school districts, the size of the administrative component rises at an increasing rate, from which it may be concluded that organizations of this type are functionally differentiated with some degree of interdependence between sub-units.[3] The report further shows that in school districts that consist of less than 10 persons, no separate administrative component had been differentiated out. Four hundred and sixty-eight out of 732 elementary school districts were of this type. However, only 4 out of 250 high school districts of this type were found, showing that the greater the complexity of the organization, the earlier the critical size at which intrinsic regulation breaks down.

In a survey study of industrial firms, A. W. Baker and R. C. Davies (2) present a large variety of data on the relation between various types of indirect and direct workers. Some of the data could be fitted to a linear function. Non-linear relationships were fitted to a parabolic function. In spite of the fact that they were not able to separate out different types of industries, reported correlations obtained with the curve of best fit range from ·83 to ·99, supporting the assumption that the size relationships between different component parts of an organization have lawful characteristics.

A finding of some interest is that the number of top-management executives rises at a decreasing rate rather than the increasing of constant rate found for other functions, showing that beyond a certain point the type of work in which top management is engaged is not materially affected by increasing size of the organization.

If we turn to the type of processes found in biological development, we find not only similar stages of development but also similar types of relationship in the size of functionally differentiated parts of the organism, the so-called allometric relationships, suggesting that we are dealing here with very general system characteristics (3).

Characteristics of Complex Systems. If the system contains only a control unit, then its presence may not be easily detectable by input-output measurement by itself, in so far as the size of the control unit varies at a linear rate with the size of the system. If, on the other hand, the system contains an integrating unit concerned with the coordination of on-going processes, then this should be detectable by means of any one of the input-size-output functions.

If an integrating unit is differentiated out this implies that some components are withdrawn from output-producing functions, so that there should be a relative decrease in output obtained. If the creation of an integrating unit should lead to reduced efficiency, then large complex systems would not come into being, so that the loss of output resulting from the withdrawal of components from productive functions must be at least compensated for by an increase in output capacity of components that are retained in output-producing functions.

Figure 4 shows the data obtained for the relationship between the size of retail establishments and output measured in terms of sales turnover for all retail establishments in Great Britain (9). It will be seen that with increased size, up to about 5 persons, retail establishments retain the characteristics of simple systems. At this point there is a definite break in the curve and a transition is found to occur to the formation of complex systems.

[3] I am indebted to Dr. Terrien for additional data from their study.

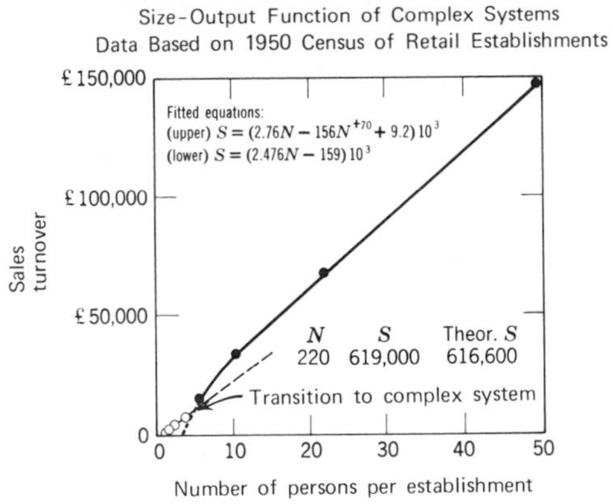

Fig. 4. Relation between sales turnover (S) and size of establishment (N).

A good fit to the data is obtained by the function shown in Equation 7 (Table 1), which states that the presence of an administrative unit concerned with the coordination of on-going activities increases the rate at which sales turnover increases with size of the organization, and that the loss incurred by withdrawing personnel from production tasks decreases as the organization becomes larger. From this relationship between size of the organization and sales turnover achieved, a value of ·70 is obtained from the data for the degree of complexity of independent retail establishments. The corresponding data for retail chains show complete linearity for the whole range, showing that these consist of simple systems that function independently of one another but are linked to a common control unit.

The efficiency of a system may be measured by the ratio of output relative to its size. In the case of retail establishments, the efficiency measure becomes the amount of sales turnover achieved, divided by the number of persons in the organization. Figure 5 shows the relative efficiency of simple and complex systems for the same data, fitted to Equation 4 and 7, respectively.

It will be seen that in shops with up to 5 persons intrinsic regulation is the more efficient form, and in practice the only possible one, since, as the data show, the group has to achieve at least this size before it can support an administrative apparatus. It is found, in fact, that in shops around this size the manager acts as a working leader and participates with his employees in the work that is carried out. As the shop becomes larger, the manager withdraws from production tasks and becomes more exclusively occupied with supervision and administration. At this point the transition to a complex system is found to lead to a considerable increase in efficiency and reaches a peak when the shop consists of around 8–9 persons. From there on efficiency begins to decline but ultimately reaches a constant value.

It is of interest to note that while in the case of independent shops an administrative staff is differentiated out when the size of the shop is around 5 or more persons, shops that form part of the retail chain maintain the characteristics of a simple system with up to about 9 persons in the shop. This suggests that the size of a working group can be increased without the need for developing a separate supervisory and administrative unit, provided that service activities and the supply of some technical inputs are taken over by the larger organization within which the shop operates. This would be supported by the discovery, in the course of a study at present being carried out of socio-technical organization in the coalmining industry, of a working group consisting of 48 men working with practically no external supervision, and possessing no internal directive leadership roles whatsoever. In this case, both the supply of service activities for the group and the distribution of coal output obtained are

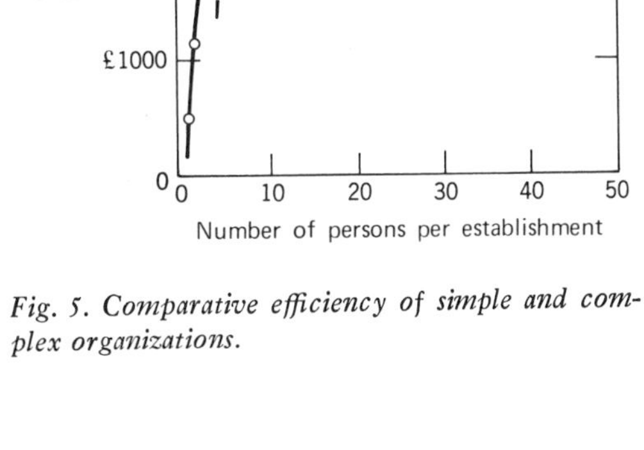

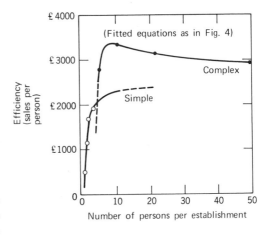

Fig. 5. Comparative efficiency of simple and complex organizations.

taken over by the large organization of which this group forms a part.

Summary

The possibility is explored of constructing a method to measure the level of organization of behaviour systems by the analysis of the relationship found between their input, size, and output. The diagnostic technique at the present stage may be summarized as follows. Assuming that the unit study does not contain input-consuming components that make no direct or indirect contribution to output:

1. If both size of unit and input have a minimum boundary value when output approaches zero, then the unit studied has the characteristics of a system rather than that of an assembly.
2. If a minimum boundary value with respect to size exists and the relationship is linear, then the unit has the characteristics of a simple system. It may consist of components that are functionally undifferentiated or of a set of independent simple systems that are linked to a common control unit.
3. If the relationship diverges from linearity, then the unit has the characteristics of a complex system in which component units are functionally differentiated and have some degree of interdependence with one another.

In the latter case we may go one step further and use the divergence from linearity to obtain a measure of the complexity of the system in terms of the degree of interdependence of its component units. The method is illustrated by data on group functioning which provide the opportunity of checking findings obtained by direct measurement. Finally, some of the conditions are discussed under which a group can maintain self-regulation.

The present method cannot be regarded as more than a first approach to a problem that is likely to become of increasing importance in behaviour studies. Among the major problems on which further research is needed is the extent to which different structures may give similar input-size-output functions. Eventually it should be possible to develop more sensitive sequential testing methods by which the range of possible structures is gradually narrowed down until correct identification has been made.

REFERENCES

1. Ashby, W. R. *An Introduction to Cybernetics.* London: Chapman & Hall, 1956.
2. Baker, A. W., and Davis, R. C. *Ratios of Staff to Line Employees and Stages of Differentiation of Staff Functions.* Bureau of Business Research, Ohio State Research Monograph 72, 1954.
3. Bertalanffy, L. von. "An Outline of General System Theory." *Brit. J. Philos. Sci.*, Vol. I, pp. 134–65, 1950.
4. Herbst, P. G. "Situation Dynamics and the Theory of Behavior Systems," *Behavioral Science*, Vol. 2, No. 1, pp. 13–29, 1957.
5. Luria, A. R. *Experimental Analysis of the Development of Voluntary Action in Children.* University of Moscow, p. 10, 1957.
6. Rice, A. K. *Productivity and Social Organization: The Ahmedabad Experiment.* London: Tavistock Publications (in press).
7. Terrien, F. W., and Mills, D. L. "The Effect of Changing Size upon the Internal Structure of Organisations." *Amer. Sociol Rev.*, Vol. 20, No. 1, pp. 11–13, 1955.
8. Trist, E. L., and Bamforth, K. W. "Some Social and Psychological Consequences of the Longwall Method of Coal-Getting." *Hum. Relat.*, Vol. 4, No. 1, pp. 3–38, 1951.

The Equilibrium Problem in Small Groups[1]

ROBERT F. BALES

The purpose of this paper is to present certain empirical findings from the program of observation of small groups at the Harvard Laboratory of Social Relations and to discuss their relevance to the theory of equilibrium developed elsewhere in this collection of working papers.

Method

Some of these findings have been published previously, and the reader is referred to these earlier articles for details omitted here.[2] It will also be assumed that the reader is familiar with the method of observation, recording, and analysis used in the direct study of the interaction process as it takes place in our small laboratory groups.[3] The observation categories are shown in Chart 1. Certain aspects of their theoretical grounding in the general theory of action have been discussed earlier in this collection of papers.

Conditions of Observation

A number of different types of groups have been observed, in natural as well as laboratory settings, and some of the generalizations to be discussed were obtained before the present observational series was begun. For purposes of exposition, however, it will be simpler to confine the description of the conditions under which the generalizations hold best to the series of groups now under observation since these groups were specifically set up to epitomize the appropriate conditions.

Groups of sizes two through ten are under observation in the present series. Data for sizes three through six have been gathered. The groups are experimental discussion groups, each group meeting for four meetings. The subjects are all males, Harvard undergraduates, who are obtained through the Harvard employment service and typically do not know each other prior to the first meeting. In each of its four meetings, the group examines and discusses a "human relations case". A different case is used for each of the four meetings. Each case is a summary of facts, five pages in length, about a person in an administrative setting who is having some kind of

From *Working Papers in the Theory of Action,* by Parsons, Bales, and Shills (eds.). Glencoe; Free Press, 1953, pp. 111–115; 140–161. Reprinted by permission of the publisher.

[1] The research reported in this paper was facilitated by the Laboratory of Social Relations, Harvard University. The funds for the observation project now in progress are provided by the RAND Corporation, Santa Monica, California. I am indebted to Philip E. Slater, Research Assistant in the Laboratory of Social Relations, especially for work on the latter parts of this paper on problems of role specialization, and more generally for the many stimulating discussions we have had on the research as a whole. Similarly, I owe much to Christoph Heinicke, Social Science Research Council Fellow, for initial insights on the nature of the status struggle as it appears through the series of meeting of our groups. This phenomenon will be described in later papers.

[2] Bales, Robert F., "A Set of Categories for the Analysis of Small Group Interaction," *American Sociological Review,* Vol. XV, No. 2, April, 1950, pp. 257–263.

Bales, Robert F., and Strodtbeck, Fred L., "Phases in Group Problem Solving," *Journal of Abnormal and Social Psychology,* Vol. 46, No. 4, October, 1951, pp. 485–495.

Bales, Robert F., Strodtbeck, Fred L., Mills, Theodore M., and Roseborough, Mary, "Channels of Communication in Small Groups," *American Sociological Review,* Vol. 16, No. 4 August 1951, pp. 461–468.

Bales, Robert F., "Some Statistical Problems of Small Group Research," *Journal of the American Statistical Association,* Vol. 46, No. 255, September 1951, pp. 311–322.

[3] Bales, Robert F., *Interaction Process Analysis, A Method for the Study of Small Groups,* Cambridge, Massachusetts, Addison-Wesley Press, 1950.

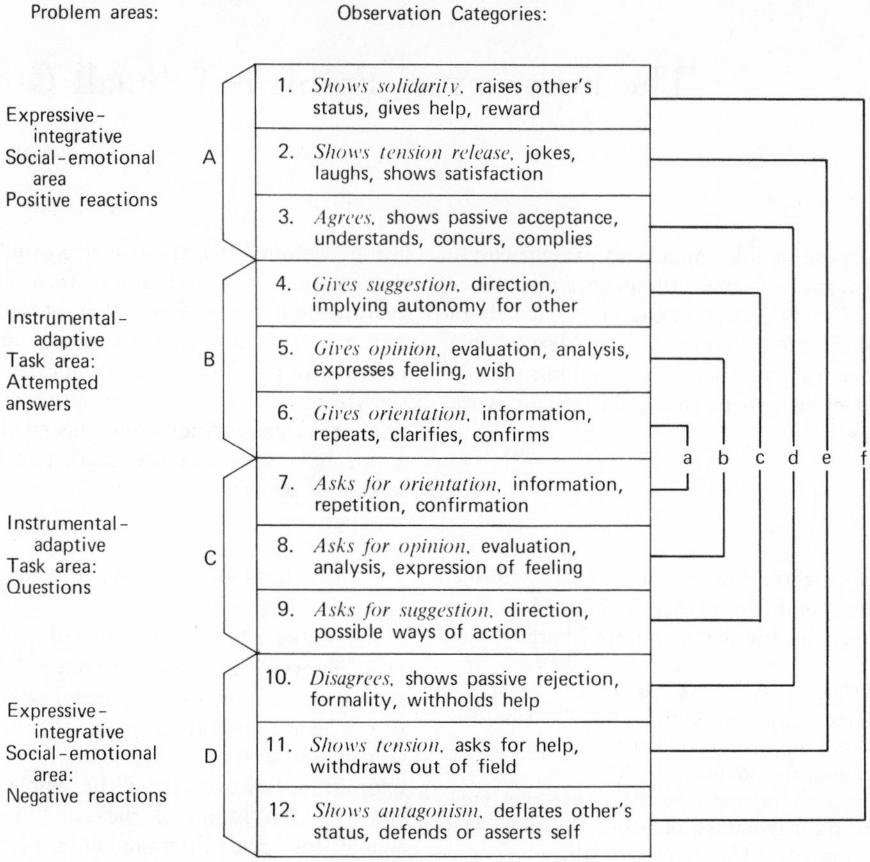

Chart 1. Set of categories used for direct observation of the interaction process. A subclassification of system problems to which each pair of categories is most relevant. a, ***Problems of orientation.*** b, ***Problems of evaluation.*** c, ***Problems of control.*** d, ***Problems of decision.*** e, ***Problems of tension-management.*** f, ***Problems of integration.***

difficulty with the men under him, and has some superior putting pressure on him to get some technically important job done. The summaries for a given case discussion are distributed separately to the subjects. After each member has read his summary the actual typed copy of the case is collected from each by the experimenter. The manner of presentation is such that the subjects are made specifically uncertain as to whether or not they possess exactly the same facts, but are assured that each does possess an accurate, though perhaps incomplete, factual summary.

The subjects are asked to consider themselves as members of the administrative staff of the central person in the case. He has asked them to meet and consider the case. He wishes an answer to two questions: (1) why are the persons in the case behaving as they do, and (2) what should he do about it. The members of the discussion group are asked to come to their decision in forty minutes. No leader is appointed. The host experimenter leaves the room. The discussion is observed through a one-way mirror and sound recorded. The interaction is observed and recorded in the categories shown on Chart 1. After the meeting the members fill out a questionnaire asking certain questions about their reactions, their satisfaction, their relations to each other, and their opinions about their discussion group.

Under each mode of analysis discussed below some of the main uniformities of behavior we have found will be compactly stated. Space does not permit the presentation of the evidence in detail. In general, the patterns described and illustrated can be understood to refer to approximate or average uniformities in aggregates of large numbers of group meetings under randomly varying external conditions, and in addition, they can be understood to hold more uniformly and in particular under the full-fledged conditions of the standard diagnostic task described above.

The Profile of Activity and the Equilibrium Problem

One of the interesting characteristics of interaction is the distribution of total number of acts among the twelve categories, according to quality. A distribution of this kind in percentage rates based on the total is called a profile. An illustrative comparison of group profiles of two five-man groups working on the standard diagnostic task is shown in Table 1.

In the present illustration the "satisfied" group attained a higher rate of suggestions, more often followed by positive reactions and less often by negative reactions and questions than did the "dissatisfied" group.

The profiles produced by groups, however, are not completely and radically different from each other. The profile produced by the average of these two illustrative groups is more or less typical of averages of larger aggregates under laboratory standard conditions. Attempted Answers, that is, giving orientation, opinion, and suggestion, are always more numerous than their cognate Questions, that is, asking for orientation, opinion, or suggestion. Similarly, Positive Reactions, that is agreement, showing tension release, and solidarity, are usually more numerous than Negative Reactions, i.e., showing disagreement, tension, and antagonism. Intuitively one would feel that the process would surely be self-defeating and self-limiting if there were more questions than answers and more negative reactions than positive.

On the average, for groups we have examined, the relations of amounts by Sections are about as they are in the illustration. The relations between the amounts can be viewed as the final result of a repetitive series of cycles, each of which consists of: (*1*) an initial disturbance of the system (precipitated by the intro-

Table 1. Profile of a "Satisfied" and a "Dissatisfied" Group on Case Discussion Task

	MEETING PROFILES IN PERCENTAGE RATES			
TYPE OF ACT:	SATISFIED *	DISSATISFIED †	AVERAGE OF THE TWO	AVERAGE RATES BY SECTIONS
1. Shows solidarity	.7	.8	.7	
2. Shows tension release	7.9	6.8	7.3	25.0
3. Agrees	24.9	9.6	17.0	
4. Gives suggestion	8.2	3.6	5.9	
5. Gives opinion	26.7	30.5	28.7	56.7
6. Gives orientation	22.4	21.9	22.1	
7. Asks for orientation	1.7	5.7	3.8	
8. Asks for opinion	1.7	2.2	2.0	6.9
9. Asks for suggestion	.5	1.6	1.1	
10. Disagrees	4.0	12.4	8.3	
11. Shows tension	1.0	2.6	1.8	11.4
12. Shows antagonism	.3	2.2	1.3	
PERCENTAGE TOTAL	100.0	100.0	100.0	100.0
RAW SCORE TOTAL	719	767	1486	

* The highest of sixteen groups. The members rated their own satisfaction with their solution after the meeting at an average of 10.4 on a scale running from 0 to a highest possible rating of 12.

† The lowest of sixteen groups. Comparable satisfaction rating in this group was 2.6.

duction of a new idea, or opinion, or suggestion into the group) followed by (2) a "dwindling series of feedbacks" and corrections as the disturbance is terminated, equilibrated, or assimilated by other parts or members of the system. Attempted Answers, or as one might call them for the moment, "Initial Acts," account for a little over half (or 57 percent) of the total activity, with Positive and Negative Reactions and Questions accounting for the other half, roughly.

Looking at the *Reaction* side alone, and assuming it to be 50 percent of the total, about half the reactions (or 25 percent of the total) are Positive and presumably terminate the disturbance introduced by the initial action. The other half of the time the Reaction fails to terminate the disturbance. Of this non-terminating portion again, about half (or 12 percent of the total) are Negative Reactions, which typically precipitate another Attempted Answer, thus beginning a repetition of the cycle. Of the remaining hypothetical 13 percent or so, about half (or 7 percent) are Questions, which also typically precipitate another Attempted Answer. If about 7 percent of Attempted Answers are in direct response to Questions, these might well be called "Reactions," thus leaving the relation of "Initial Acts" to "Reactions" about 50–50, as assumed above. One might say that quantitatively (as well as qualitatively, by definition) interaction is a process consisting of action followed by reaction. The balance of action with reaction is one of the equilibrium problems of the system.

Phase Movement and the Problem of Equilibrium

Changes in quality of activity as groups move through time in attempting to solve their problems may be called phase patterns. The pattern of phases differs in detail under different conditions. However, these changes in quality seem to be subject to system influences which produce similarities from group to group. An increase of task-oriented activities in the early parts of a meeting, that is, Questions and Attempted Answers, seems to constitute a disturbance of a system equilibrium which is later redressed by an increase in social-emotional activities, that is, both Positive and Negative Reactions.

Part of our observations prior to the development of the standard diagnostic task were kept by time sequence. Each available meeting was divided into three equal parts, and the amount of each type of activity in each part of each meeting was determined. The meetings were divided into two kinds: those which were dealing with full-fledged problems (essentially problems of analysis and planning with the goal of group decision as described for the standard diagnostic task), and those dealing with more truncated or specialized types of problems. Those groups dealing with full-fledged problems tended to show a typical phase movement through the meeting: the process tended to move qualitatively from a *relative* emphasis on attempts to solve problems of *orientation* ("what is it") to attempts to solve problems of *evaluation* ("how do we feel about it") and subsequently to attempts to solve problems of *control* ("what shall we do about it"). Concurrent with these transitions, the relative frequencies of both *negative reactions* (disagreement, tension, and antagonism), and *positive reactions* (agreement, tension release, and showing solidarity), tends to increase. Chart 2 presents the summary data for all group sessions examined in the phase study.

The underlying theory as to why the phase

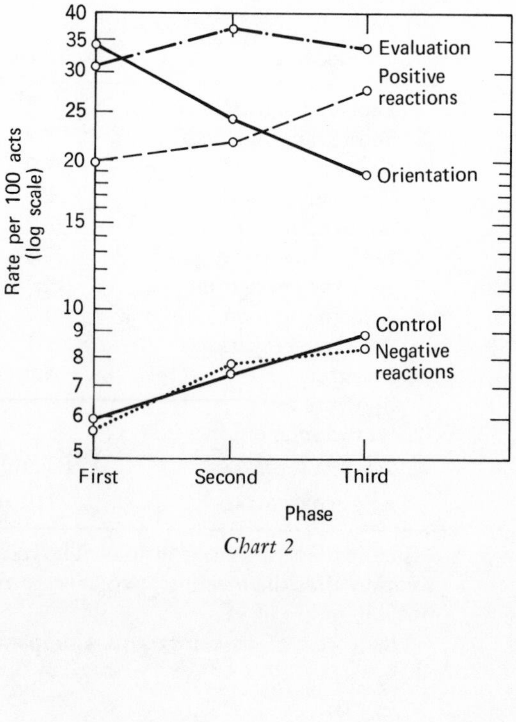

Chart 2

movement just described is characteristic of full-fledged conditions is again a system-equilibrium rationale. An individual may be cognitively oriented to a situation and speak of it to others in cognitive terms without committing himself, or the other when he agrees, either to evaluation of it, or an attempt to control it. But in speaking to the other in evaluative terms he attempts to commit both himself and the other to some assumed previous orientation, and further, if he suggests a way to control the situation by joint cooperative action, he assumes both previous orientation and evaluation. When the problems of arriving at a common orientation and evaluation of the situation have not been substantially solved by the group members, attempts at control will meet with resistance on the part of the others and frustration on the part of the person attempting to exercise the control. Probably generally, unless there are contrary cultural, personality, or group organizational factors, the interacting persons tend to avoid or retreat from this frustration-producing type of interaction by "back-tracking" toward orientation and evaluative analysis until the prior problems are solved.

In addition to their task problems, the members of any cooperating group have problems of their social and emotional relationships to each other to solve and keep solved. Efforts to solve problems of orientation, evaluation, and control as involved in the task tend to lead to differentiation of the roles of the participants, both as to the functions they perform and their gross amounts of participation. Both qualitative and quantitative types of differentiation tend to carry status implications which may threaten or disturb the existing order or balance of status relations among members. Disagreement and an attempt to change existing ideas and values instrumentally may be necessary in the effort to solve the task problem but may lead, nevertheless, to personalized anxieties or antagonisms and impair the basic solidarity of the group.

This impairment, or the threat of it, we may assume, tends to grow more marked as the group passes from emphasis on the less demanding and more easily resolved problems of cognitive orientation on to problems of evaluation, and still more acute as it passes on to its heaviest emphasis on problems of control. It will be recalled that this notion appeared earlier in the examination of act-to-act tendencies. This assumption seems to be a more generalized way of stating the findings of certain other studies. For example, Lippitt [4] found negative reactions to autocratic control or leadership in boys' clubs under certain conditions, while Rogers [5] and his associates tend to find a minimization of negative reactions on the part of clients when the counselor confines himself to nondirective (or, in our categories, orienting rather than evaluating or controlling) types of activity. The present assumption may be regarded as a generalization of this connection between degree of control and negative reactions, so that it is viewed as applying to different points in the process of the same group, not simply to differences between groups. Thus, a series of changes in the social-emotional relationships of the members tend to be set in motion by pressures arising initially from the demands of the external task or outer situation. These social-emotional problems tend to be expressed in overt interaction as they grow more acute—hence the increasing rate of negative reactions.

However, at the extreme end of the final period, assuming that the members' attempts at control over the outer situation and over each other are successful and a final decision is reached, the rates in Categories 1, 2, and 3 also rise to their peak. In other words, one might expect the successfully recovering group to confirm its agreement and to release the tensions built up in its prior task-efforts, repairing the damage done to its state of consensus and social integration. We note joking and laughter so frequently at the end of meetings that they might almost be taken as a signal that the group has completed what it considers to be a task effort, and is ready for disbandment or a new problem. This last-minute activity completes a cycle of operations involving a successful solution both of the task problems and social-emotional problems confronting the group. The apparent incongruity of predicting

[4] Lippitt, R., "An Experimental Study of Authoritarian and Democratic Group Atmospheres." *Stud. Topolog. Vector Psychol.*, No. 1, Univ. Ia. Stud. Child Welf. 1950, 16.

[5] Rogers, C. R., *Counselling and Psychotherapy: New Concepts in Practice* Boston, Houghton Mifflin, 1942.

a peak for both negative and positive reactions in the third phase is thus explained. Negative reactions tend to give way to positive reactions in the final part of the crudely defined third phase.

Changes in Role Structure and the Equilibrium Problem

We now consider a series of role changes which take place on "the next rung up" the ladder of microscopic-to-macroscopic contexts in which the general theory of action systems can be applied. Changes in quality of act from one act to the next are on a very microscopic level as to time span involved. Changes in rates of acts of various types through the course of a single meeting are on a more macroscopic level. As we have seen, very much the same sort of general system theory can be applied to both, with proper allowance for changes in conditions which will surely be characteristic of any shift up or down on the microscopic-macroscopic ladder. We now proceed up another rung of the ladder to consider changes that take place from meeting to meeting in a time span of four meetings. And for the present analysis, we shift from a primary emphasis on consideration of interaction rates to a consideration of more "generalized" or partially "structured" roles as reflected in post-meeting ratings and choices of members by each other. Much more detailed treatment of changes within the four meeting time span, using interaction rates as well as post-meeting measures will be given in later publications.

The essential rationale for the ratings and choices we ask members to make at the end of meetings is rooted back in the four types of system problems discussed in the other papers of this collection as the "dimensions" along which system changes takes place—the instrumental, adaptive, integrative, and expressive. For present purposes we link the instrumental and adaptive dimensions together to obtain one "pole" of specialization: the instrumental-adaptive pole. On the other side we link the integrative and expressive dimensions together to obtain the integrative-expressive pole.

Toward the instrumental-adaptive pole we distinguish two types of roles: The first is a role emphasizing specifically task-oriented achievement addressed to the problems of the external situation confronting the group. In terms of the type of task we give our groups, this role appears to be fairly well defined operationally by answers to the question: "Who contributed the best ideas for solving the problem? Please rank the members in order. . . . Include yourself." The second type of instrumental-adaptive role we distinguish is one which emphasizes regulation or management of the group process in the service of task oriented achievement—a role approximating that of "chairman" or perhaps in a more general sense that of "executive", (as contrasted with that of "technical specialist" which is the first type of role above). We attempt to get at the second type of role by the question: "Who did the most to guide the discussion and keep it moving effectively? Please rank the members in order. . . . Include yourself."

Toward the integrative-expressive pole we also distinguish two sub-types of roles, but this time according to a "positive-negative" distinction rather than according to an "external-internal" distinction as above. The questions we ask here are fairly orthodox sociometric choice questions—essentially "Who do you like in rank order" and "Who do you dislike in rank order", although we ask them in a somewhat more complicated way that would take unnecessarily long to describe here. Detailed description of scoring methods will also be omitted—by inverting ranks it is possible to obtain high scores for top ranking men and low scores for low ranking men. This is done for greater intuitive ease in grasping the meaning of the data. I shall refer to high ranking men as "receiving the most votes," sacrificing accuracy a bit to convenience.

Now, according to the line of thought embodied in the sample statistical model for reproducing the matrix, and its "rationalization," one might make the following sorts of inferences: Since a man may receive agreement for advancing ideas which appeal to other members, or for making neutral suggestions with procedural content rather than task content, or simply because people like him emotionally, and since agreement tends to encourage a man to go ahead and talk more, we might suppose that such men would tend to have high rates of participation. Conversely, since disagreement tends to discourage a man from talking, and since disagreement is often a manifestation of dislike, we might suppose that dislikes would tend to center around men with low rates of participation. And since the model makes no assumptions about the incompatibilities of these various roles (excepting the incompatibility of Liking and Disliking) we might suppose that the same man—"The Leader"—might receive the most votes on all three roles—Best Ideas, Guidance, and Best Liked, and that another man—"The Scapegoat"—at the bottom of the heap might receive the fewest votes on all three of these virtuous roles, but the most on Dislikes. The simplest assumption is that the votes on each of these roles will grade according to Basic Initiating Rank—the rank on total amounts of participation given out. Such a group we might call a "simply organized group", meaning that no matter what criterion of status were chosen, it would place the men in the same rank order of relative status. Now those who are acutely aware of the lack of such perfect integration of various criteria of status in larger social systems will be likely to suspect that small groups will not be so "simply organized" either. Nevertheless, we had evidence of some appreciable degree of positive correlation of these various status criteria with Basic Initiating Rank, and the hypothesis of the "simply organized group" was adopted as a working hypothesis for the first ordering and examination of the data.

Our first major insight with regard to what we now regard as a basic problem of role structure was obtained from a tabulation of data from twelve meetings of five-men groups (twelve instead of sixteen because of absences in four meetings). No distinction was made as to which meetings in the series of four were represented. The identity of men was not preserved from meeting to meeting. We simply took each meeting, listed the men in rank order of total amounts of participation given out, and recorded "the number of votes received" on each role. Then the data for all rank one men on total acts initiated were pooled, and so for all rank two men, and so on for the five. The fact that Joe Smith might have been rank one man in the first meeting, rank two man in the second, and so on, was ignored. The data are represented in Chart 3.

First it may be noted that there is a general gradation of votes on Best Ideas and Guidance by Basic Initiating Rank as expected by the

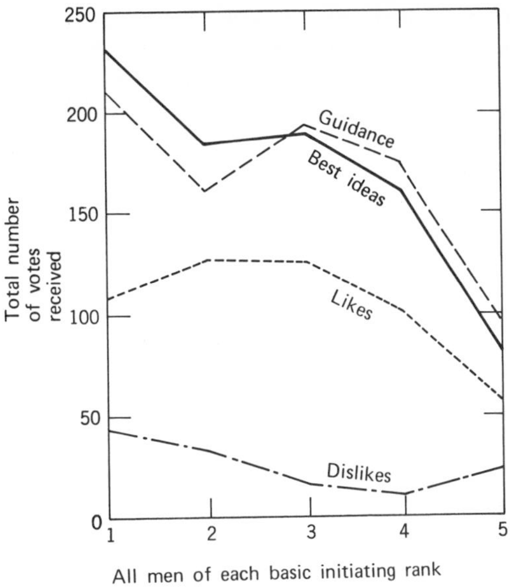

Chart 3. "Total Number of Votes Received" on each of four roles, pooled for men of each basic initiating rank as of each meeting. (Data from twelve assorted meetings of four five-man groups).

working hypothesis. Second, note that these two curves are very close together and move in the same way, indicating the relative lack of segregation of these roles from each other. But there is a departure from the prediction of the working hypothesis; on both curves the second man is unaccountably low.

But a more serious departure from the prediction is in terms of the curve on Likes. There the top man is unaccountably low, and the second man is highest in the group—by an insignificant margin, but still enough to give birth to the idea: can there be any connection between the fact that the second man, who is unaccountably low on Best Ideas and Guidance, is also Best Liked? Can it be that he is avoiding too heavy participation in the instrumental-adaptative area? Can it be that the man who is participating most heavily and is receiving the most votes on Best Ideas and Guidance is provoking dislikes and losing likes? Here we note the Dislike curve. Contrary to the prediction of the working hypothesis the top man receives *most* Dislikes, and they grade down by rank—until we come to the bottom man, and here the curve shows an upturn. The upturn is consistent with the scapegoat hypothesis.[6] Looking again at the Like curve, we note that although the second man is receiving more likes than the top man, actually both are depressed in terms of an expectation of an evenly graded curve. The new hypothesis is strengthened: there must be something about high participation and specialization in the technical and executive directions which tends to provoke hostility.

Here I think it can be seen that we are dealing with the same equilibrium problem encountered before in attempting to understand the uniformities of the profile, the matrix, and the phase movement. Movement in the instrumental-adaptive direction tends to upset the equilibrium of the system, and recovery mechanisms must be worked out of the system is to turn full cycle and regain equilibrium. The more "directive" and "constricting" the quality of activity, the more likely it is to arouse negative reactions. If a man begins to specialize noticeably in this direction, the negative reactions tend to be centered on him. The displacement of hostilities on a scapegoat at the bottom of the status structure is one mechanism, apparently, by which the ambivalent attitudes toward the instrumental-adaptive specialist—the "top man"—can be diverted and drained off. The centering of positive affect on a secondary man is another mechanism by which the solidarity of the group—its integration as a collectivity of persons—can be reestablished. Such a man can be warm, receptive, responsive, and rewarding, can "conciliate" and "bind up the wounds", without diverting the movement of the system too far from the kind of movement in the instrumental-adaptive direction which is also felt to be necessary. He can do this because he does not assume the "responsibility" for the movement of the system in these directions, but leaves this to the technical or executive specialist.

But suppose the best liked man is not willing to do this? Suppose that his perceptions of the likes of others "goes to his head" and encourages him to begin to "take over" from the technical or executive specialist? He is in a position to command considerable support, and the "top man" is in a vulnerable position because of the latent or overt hostility centered on him. Or suppose, on the other hand, that the top man is emotionally unable to stand the hostility, or is unable to tolerate the fact that not he, but another, is best liked? The top man is under strains, we might suppose, to try to "undercut" his nearest rival. Here are the seeds of a fundamental status struggle, exceedingly damaging, in potentiality, both for the instrumental-adaptive achievement of the group, and for its affective integration. This, as I see it now, is the core of the status struggle we see our groups go through in the course of their four meetings. The first meeting is typically rather cautious and tentative, and such "simply organized groups" as we do find, tend to be found at the end of this meeting. With the second meeting, the role structure which has crystallized, if at all, in the first meeting, is challenged in a status struggle which may result in either confirmation of the first structure, or an exchange of status positions between the top two or three men. If the original structure "holds up", the group may begin to "level out", and the status struggle slacks off. If a new man comes to the top, the *new* structure is challenged in the third meeting. Some groups apparently arrive at a fairly stable differentiated structure, others never do. Things go "from bad to worse", with a last meeting that breaks records for disagreement, antagonism, tension, perhaps tension release, and other signs of serious strains and an inability to achieve an equilibrated role structure.[7] However, the stable structure is never, in our data, a "simply organized" one. It is rather one in which differentiated roles have appeared, in which one specialist "undoes" the disturbance to equilibrium created by another, and in turn is dependent upon another to remove the strains he himself creates—the total constellation of specialists being one which allows or aids the system to establish a full orbit in its dimensions of necessary movement.

There is some reason to believe that one possible arrangement by which the status struggle between the top instrumental-adaptive leader and the best liked man can be prevented or stabilized is the formation of a kind of "coalition" between them, such that the two tacitly agree, as it were, not to undercut each

[6] Similar curves are found in 3 and 4-man groups. The 6-man groups introduce a special complication at a level of subtlety which is inappropriate to these preliminary generalizations.

[7] This discussion of structure changes by meetings is based upon findings which will appear in a separate paper.

other, which is to say, not to be "seduced" into attempting to form a coalition with lower status members in order to displace each other. If such a coalition can be formed, it becomes quite difficult for lower status members to revolt, unseat the top men, or develop the norms of the group in any different direction.

The findings for our five-man groups (Chapter 3) prompted an investigation into our data on comparable groups of other sizes. In this investigation we made use of all the data available at that time, i.e., 61 group meetings. This represents 14 completed groups (four meetings each), and 2 uncompleted groups (two and three meetings respectively). Five of the completed groups were 6-man groups, four were 5-man, four were 4-man, and one was a 3-man group. Both of the uncompleted groups were 3-man groups.

Our analysis deals with five roles, hypothesized as having leadership potentialities, and capable of being simply derived from our data. These are:

1. The Top Initiator, i.e., the man who initiates the most interaction, as determined by the "who-to-whom matrix." This role will be designated hereinafter as "TI."
2. The man who *receives* the most interaction (designated RM), as determined by the who-to-whom matrix.
3. The man who "has the best ideas" (designated BI), as determined by the rankings made by the members in the post-meeting questionnaires.
4. The man who "does the most to guide the discussion" (designated G), as determined by post-meeting questionnaire rankings.
5. The man who is best liked (designated L), as determined by the sociometric ratings in the post-meeting questionnaires.[8]

The question now arises, which of these roles represents "The leader"? Our findings suggest, I think, that this question is in one sense meaningless, since all of these roles are "leadership" roles. To think in terms of "*a* leader" is, however, not only traditional, but useful, and a partial answer to the question can be found. A section is included in the questionnaire at the close of the last meeting of each group, asking the subjects to rank each other in terms of whom they considered to be the leader of the group, taking all four meetings into consideration. With these rankings as a base we should be able to get a rough notion as to which of the five roles are considered *by the subjects* to be most closely related to overall "leadership."

Table 2. Subject's Concept of Leadership (10 Cases)

ROLE TYPES	NUMBER OF GROUPS IN WHICH PERSON DESCRIBED AS "LEADER" PLAYED THE ROLE MOST CONSISTENTLY OVER THE FOUR MEETINGS
TI (Top Initiator)	5.3
RM (Received Most)	5.5
BI (Best Ideas)	7.5
G (Guidance)	7.5
L (Liked)	2.0

Unfortunately, the available data on this question are rather inadequate, since we have only ten separate groups who gave usable "leader" rankings. Table 2, however, shows the results, which are at least suggestive. The figures represent the number of cases in which the chosen "leader" corresponded with the man who played the role in question most often during the four meetings. The decimals are created by ties in the role rankings, the incidence of which is, in our data, statistically small but methodologically provoking.

Table 2 suggests that the Best Ideas and Guidance roles are most closely associated in the subjects' minds with leadership, and that the Best-Liked role is *least* closely associated with leadership. Additional confirmation for this hypothesis may be found in the fact that in *no* case was the "leader" *neither* the Idea man *nor* the Guidance man. That the Best-Liked role was associated at all with leadership may therefore have been due to the fact that these two instances were also the *only* ones in which the Best-Liked role and either the Guidance or Idea roles were played by the same man.

The five-man group data indicated some specialization of role, in that the Best-Liked role was differentiated from the others by actor. Table 3 shows the degree of role specialization among all of the five roles. The

[8] It should be emphasized that in all of the presentation which follows we are dealing only with "top" men on each of these criteria.

figures here represent the number of cases (in percentages) in which any pair of roles were played by the same man. Once again it is apparent that the Best-Liked role is the most specialized, in the sense that the man playing this role is least likely to play another role simultaneously. The two roles most closely associated, in the minds of the subjects, with "leadership"—Ideas and Guidance—are played by the Best Liked man only 30 percent and 27 percent of the time, respectively.

Table 3. Matrix of Role Correspondence. Percentage of Meetings in which Each Type of Two-Role Combination Was Performed by the Same Man (61 Cases)

	TI	RM	BI	G	L
TI		62.3	60.3	44.6	25.4
RM	62.3		45.6	35.6	37.7
BI	60.3	45.6		54.9	30.0
G	44.6	35.6	54.9		27.0
L	25.4	37.7	30.0	27.0	
Totals	192.6	181.2	190.8	162.1	120.1

It is rather surprising that all of the figures are as low as they are, since presumably there is a tendency, in those roles determined by subjects' rankings (BI, G, and L), toward carryover from one ranking to another. For example, it seems likely that if subject A likes subject B best, and rates him most highly on Guidance, he will be somewhat inclined to rate him highly on Best Ideas. Be that as it may, the closest correspondence among these three roles is that between BI and G, which is only 54.9 percent, while the highest figure in the entire matrix is 62.3 percent (TI and RM).

The totals in Table 6 provide a crude measure of the degree to which each role is likely to be associated with others, or conversely, the degree to which it is specialized. Once again the Best-Liked role shows the least correspondence with other roles.

The Best-Liked role is not only differentiated by actor from the other roles in the overall picture, but also shows *increasing* differentiation over time. This is especially true vis-a-vis the two "leadership" roles, the

Table 4. Changes over Time in the Percentage of Cases in which the "L" Role Coincides with the "B" and "G" Roles (61 Cases)

MEETING NUMBER	I	II	III	IV
L with BI	64.4	18.8	23.3	10.7
L with G	40.6	35.6	12.0	17.9

Idea and Guidance roles. Table 4 shows the trend over time of correspondence between the Best-Liked and Idea roles and between the Best-Liked and Guidance roles. The percentages indicate the number of cases in which such correspondence occurred, by meetings, and Chart 4 represents these trends graphically.

Since the Idea and Guidance roles are equally "leader" roles, yet to a considerable degree differentiated by actor, it would perhaps be useful to average the two sets of fig-

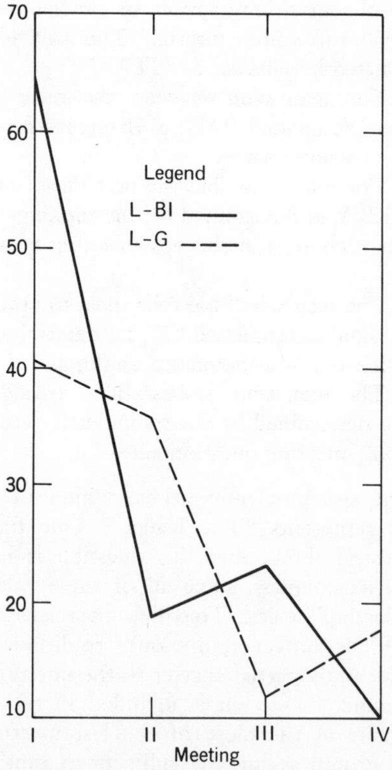

Chart 4. Change over time in percentage of cases in which best-liked man played other roles (by meeting).

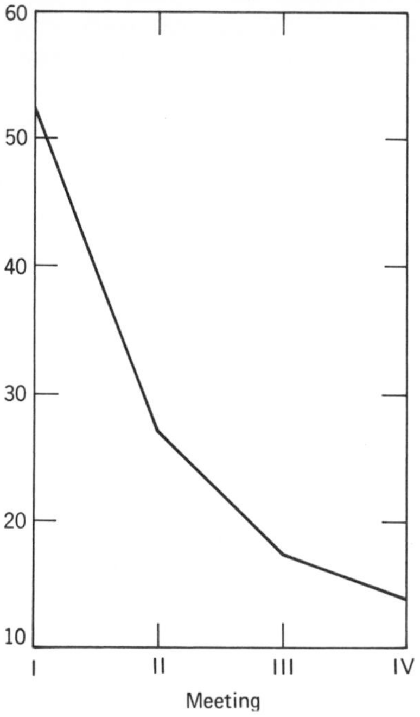

Chart 5. Change over time in percentage of cases in which best-liked man played "leader" roles (Bl and G), average of two curves in Chart IV (by meeting).

ures. That is, the merely moderate degree of correspondence between Ideas and Guidance means that when Best-Liked is associated more with one, there will be a partial lessening of its association with the other. This is apparent in Chart 4, in which the two curves show a strong tendency to diverge at each point.

When the two sets of figures are averaged, the curve in Chart 5 is obtained. This curve might be said to represent the change in correspondence over time between the Best-Liked role and the "leader" role (as suggested by Table 2). This is perhaps the most striking presentation we have given of the incompatibility of these two roles. At the end of the first meeting the man regarded as "Leader" has about a 50 per cent chance of also being Best Liked. From then on his chances drop regularly and precipitously, until at the end of the fourth meeting he has only a 14 per cent chance, and his chances are still decreasing.

One further bit of data may be presented bearing on the question: What is the *overall* degree of role specialization in these groups, and how does it change over time? Table 5(A) shows the number of cases (in percentages) in which the five roles were performed by one, two, three, four, and five persons, respectively, and the average for the 61 cases. Table 5(B) shows how this distribution changed over time, and Chart 6 shows the average trend over time.

Table 5(A). Allocation of Roles Among Personnel (61 Cases)

NUMBER OF PERSONS	PERCENTAGE OF CASES IN WHICH THE FIVE ROLES WERE DISTRIBUTED AMONG THE DESIGNATED NUMBER OF MEN
1	8.2
2	39.3
3	45.9
4	4.9
5	1.6
2.52	Average number of men playing five roles

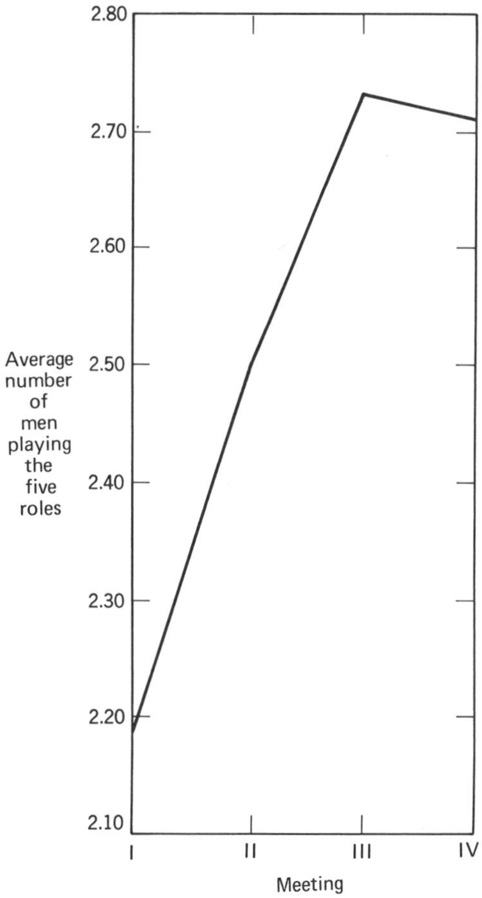

Chart 6. Index of role specialization (by meeting).

Table 5(B). Changes over Time (by Meeting)

NUMBER OF PERSONS	I	II	III	IV
1	25.0	6.3	—	—
2	37.5	43.8	33.3	42.9
3	31.3	43.8	60.0	50.0
4	6.3	6.3	6.7	—
5	—	—	—	7.1
Average number of men	2.19	2.50	2.73	2.71

The average number of persons playing the five roles was 2.52, but this average tended to increase over time, showing an increase in role specialization. To be sure, the change illustrated in Chart VI is a small one, but interestingly enough, it is considerably greater than the change by size, which appears in Table 6.

Table 6. Index of Role Specialization by Size (61 Cases)

SIZE GROUP	AVERAGE NUMBER OF MEN PLAYING THE FIVE ROLES
3-Man	2.50
4-Man	2.50
5-Man	2.50
6-Man	2.59

We can conclude from these findings that some degree of role specialization is the rule in groups of this kind, and that such specialization tends to increase over time. The "simply organized group", in which one "leader" plays all five roles, is a comparatively rare occurrence in our data, and where it does appear, it tends to break down, in time, as Chart 7 illustrates.

The implications of these preliminary findings are important in making distinctions between different types of leadership situations. We might tentatively advance the proposition that the traditional sociometric methods of determining "leaders" are appropriate only to situations where there is no specific and well-defined instrumental task. As soon as such a task is introduced there arises a demand for the performance of the new roles which the task creates. Initially the best liked man may perform these roles, but as time goes on, a dissociation takes place: either (1) someone else who can perform these new roles more successfully comes to the fore, or (2) the sociometric leader becomes a task leader and ceases to be best liked.

Essentially, it appears, we are dealing with the same problem of equilibrium that helps us understand the more microscopic levels of the profile, who-to-whom matrix, and phase movement. There we noted that as the quality of action moves from orientation to evaluation to control, negative reactions increase. Each transition, we may even say each instrumental *act*, disturbs to some degree the equilibrium which the system has achieved. The larger the disturbance, the more pronounced the negative reactions will become (thereby intensifying the need for reëquilibrating acts to occur). The Idea man is the one most prone to equilibrium-disturbing acts through his constant movement toward the instrumental goal, and hence he is most likely to arouse hostility. The value of the

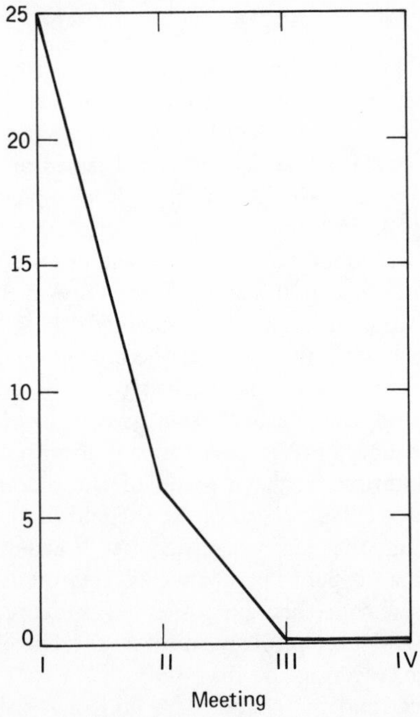

Chart 7. Changes over time in percentage of cases in which one man played all five roles (by meeting).

role he plays is so great for the group, however, that there are severe limitations on the amount of hostility which can be directed toward him, and as a result much of it may be displaced onto someone with low status. But at the same time this hostility places a strain on the friendly feelings of the group toward the Idea man, thereby lowering his sociometric position.

Table 7. Number of Cases in which Man Playing Both "BI" and "L" Roles in First Meeting Drops "L" Role or "BI" Role or Both in Second Meeting (10 Cases)

DROPS "L" ROLE	DROPS "BI" ROLE	DROPS BOTH ROLES
0	9	1

This tendency toward incompatibility between sociometric stardom and instrumental leadership can be handled, as we have said, in two ways. The only available data on the relative frequencies of these alternatives appear in Table 7, which deals with ten cases in which the same man played the Idea and Best-Liked roles in the first meeting, but was involved in some role change in the second meeting. These figures suggest that an individual is unlikely to give up his high popularity position in order to become an instrument leader. We might even guess (although this is a rather big jump) that some fundamental inability to "take" hostility was the origin of his striving for sociometric leadership in the first place. We appear to have arrived at a place where research on personality factors can be integrated most effectively with small group research.

We have begun to develop a systematic picture of the constellation of dynamically related roles that the group process tends to generate as a result of its equilibrating tendencies. We should now like to know more about the personality factors which cause particular individuals to seek to attain, or withdraw from given types of roles in this constellation.

Challenges to Unity

HERBERT KAUFMAN

General Instructions versus Specific Situations

Necessarily, the federal statutes under which the Forest Service operates are framed in general terms. This applies to the more than eighty laws applicable to the Service and the national forests specifically as well as those that govern the whole federal establishment—laws on personnel, budgeting, purchasing, contracting, and other staff services.

Similarly, the directives of the Secretary of Agriculture and the instructions from the Washington office of the Forest Service are couched in rather sweeping terms, for they must be drafted in sufficiently broad language to apply to all the different conditions obtaining in the far-flung national forests. Even the issuances of the regional and supervisors' offices cannot be too specific, for the regulations of the smallest region apply to seven national forests, and the largest region encompasses twenty-six, while most national forests contain four to six Ranger districts, and one has eleven.

Consequently, unless higher authorities were disposed to write individual instructions for each Ranger district—which would require them to know the details of the situation on each field unit, a manifest impossibility—they would seem to be compelled to allow considerable latitude for independent judgment on the part of the field officers with regard to the interpretation and application of the more general statements. Under these circumstances, personal and local factors assume substantial proportions in the management of the districts, increasing the likelihood of significant variations in policy as it emerges concretely on each such unit.[1]

Inconsistent Directives

Furthermore, the instructions field officers are called upon to execute are not always easily reconciled. While the Forest Service, as seen by the Chief or by the casual outside observer, assumes the form of a traditional administrative pyramid, it appears to the individual Ranger as an inverse pyramid with himself at the apex. For as he looks upward at the organization from his position in the field, he sees a forest supervisor aided by several staff assistants and perhaps by an assistant supervisor, all of whom send him communications and instructions (frequently over the name of the supervisor, but often, too, over the assistants' signatures). Above them is a regional forester with a more numerous and narrowly specialized group of assistant regional foresters with aides of their own in their divisions; the Rangers know that a good deal of what reaches them through the supervisors and staff assistants originates with these specialists. At the top, the organization burgeons out into the elaborate, highly specialized branches and divisions serving as staff to the Chief. To switch metaphors for a moment, the Forest Service seen from the level of the district Ranger looks like a vast funnel with the Ranger at the throat of it; all the varied elements and specialties above him pour out materials which, mixed and blended by the Ranger, emerge in a stream of action in the field.

What creates a problem for the field man is the fact that the materials sometimes require mutually exclusive courses of action on his

---

From *The Forest Ranger*. Baltimore: Johns Hopkins Press, 1960, pp. 66–87. Reprinted by permission of the publisher and Resources for the Future, Inc.

[1] For an interesting illustration of this problem, see J. Hersey, *A Bell for Adano* (New York: Alfred A. Knopf, 1944), pp. 13–15. Here a civil affairs officer on duty in a small town in Italy during World War II "took the sheets of instructions [from higher headquarters] up from his desk and tore them in half, tore the halves into quarters, and crumpled up the quarters and threw them into a cane wastebasket under the desk. . . . Plans for this first day were in the wastebasket. They were absurd. Enough was set forth in those plans to keep a regiment busy for a week."

part. The specifications for roads, for example, are generally predicated on engineering premises alone, but roads built to those specifications may conflict with the demands of watershed management or recreation management or timber management specialists. Rigid adherence to timber management or range management program goals can generate public criticism that provokes objections from information and education specialists. Emphasis on recreation that gratifies recreation officers may disturb fire control officers. What looks like adequate concern for the grazing uses of the national forests may seem like indifference to wildlife management from the perspective of those who specialize in this function. Administrative assistants call for greater attention to office routines and procedures and paperwork, while other functional specialists deplore expenditures of Ranger time in the office rather than in the woods. Despite the general consensus on the desirability of multiple-use resource management, it is not always clear what this indicates in specific instances.

The problem appears to be endemic in large-scale organizations.[2] It means field men must resolve conflicts in their own ways. As a result, there is always a strong possibility that there will be not one, but many policies.

Distance

Distance is used here in two senses: sociologically, to describe status, linguistic, and attitudinal barriers that divide components of organizations; and physically, to refer to the geographical spaces that separate members of organizations from one another.

Status distance—essentially, differences in rank and in the deference accorded people of different rank—operates as a devisive element in many organizations by filtering and distorting communications upward and downward.[3] On the one hand, people sometimes tend to tell their superiors only what they think their superiors want to hear: "most executives are very effectively insulated from the operating levels of the organization." Moreover, many leaders are not receptive to ideas put forth by their subordinates: "a suggestion coming from a person of low status will not usually be treated with the same respect and seriousness as one coming from a person of high status." On the other hand, casual remarks, inquiries, and tentative observations of high-status individuals are often emphasized and reinterpreted and applied in ways those who make the statements never actually intended. That is why one expert student of organization talks about the pathology of status systems, and of their disruptive tendencies.[4]

Linguistic barriers often arise as consequences of the unique universes of discourse that spring up in connection with occupational specialties and functional differentiations in organizations. Special meanings are attached to common words, special vocabularies emerge, special modes of expression evolve. Often, these serve as a shorthand method of communication among the members of each in-group. Sometimes they permit greater accuracy of expression, eliminating ambiguities for those who understand the jargon. Nevertheless, however useful these practices may be for the intiates, they frequently make it difficult for the various specialists to discourse with one another. The specialists use the same words in different ways and completely misunderstand each other, or they are unable to decipher each other's communications.[5]

Attitudinal barriers appear when people have totally different frames of reference. The same facts then appear in different perspectives, and lead to different conclusions. "The stimuli that fall on a person's eyes and ears are

[2] See, for example, how it appears in a work relief agency in A. W. Macmahon, J. D. Millett, and G. Ogden, *The Administration of Federal Work Relief* (Chicago: Public Administration Service, 1941), Chapter 11; in the conduct of foreign affairs in A. W. Macmahon, "Function and Area in the Administration of International Affairs," in L. D. White, et al., *New Horizons in Public Administration* (University of Alabama Press, 1945); and in the administration of a city health department in H. Kaufman, *The New York City Health Centers* (New York: The Inter-University Case Program, 1952.

[3] H. A. Simon, D. W. Smithburg, and V. A. Thompson, *Public Administration* (New York: Alfred A. Knopf, 1950), p. 236. The quotations in the above paragraph are from the same source.

[4] C. I. Barnard, *Organization and Management* (Cambridge: Harvard University Press, 1948), Chapter IX, especially pp. 231 ff.

[5] Simon, Smithburg, and Thompson, *op. cit.*, pp. 229–32.

screened, filtered, and modified by the nervous system before they even reach consciousness—and memory makes further selections of the things it will retain and the things it will forget." [6] Many things go into shaping mental sets, and no two individuals are likely to be identical in this respect. Moreover, even people who come to an agency with very similar attitudes and values will often develop divergent points of view according to the places they come to occupy and the functional specialties with which they become associated.[7] Thus, there are often wide discrepancies between what members of organizations *intend* to communicate to each other and what they *actually* convey.

Social distance in this fashion can easily lead to the pursuit of many different policies in an organization allegedly having only one. It produces grave distortions in the communications network, permitting officials throughout the hierarchy to strike out on a profusion of unrelated paths.

If this problem is vexing because of distortions of communication, it must obviously be even more troublesome where spatial distance reduces the frequency and length of contacts. In an agency as scattered as the Forest Service, this is far more than a hypothetical difficulty.

Modern techniques of communication and transportation have shrunk geographical distances, it is true. Few field installations of the Forest Service in continental United States cannot be reached from Washington in twenty-four hours or so, and in proportionally less time from regional and supervisors' offices. Federal, state, and local highways, as well as roads and highways constructed by the Forest Service itself, now make almost every Ranger station accessible by automobile, and virtually all field stations (as well as higher headquarters) are equipped with one or more vehicles for official use. Where commercial telephone lines have not yet reached, the Forest Service has strung its own lines to connect Ranger stations with lookout towers and made other improvements. The Service has been making increasing use of FM radio links (including transmitters and receivers in its vehicles). Planes have been added to the fire detection and suppression facilities, and smoke jumpers now arrive in hours at blazes that once would have taken days and even weeks to reach.

Nevertheless, many field stations are inconvenient to reach even though this can be done fairly quickly. If a trip takes the better part of a day, one way, members of the Service will not shuttle back and forth casually; they have neither time nor money for so much travel, and accumulate whatever business must be transacted in person to be handled in as small a number of trips as can be managed. In fact, even forest supervisors do not make a habit of running out to their Ranger districts with every little matter that comes up, nor do the Rangers rush in to the supervisors with every question, for even on a small national forest, a round-trip journey of this kind is apt to consume the better part of half a day. Commercial telephone rates are just high enough to discourage field officers from making toll calls (and thus using up their communications funds) for minor issues, and Forest Service telephone lines generally run from Ranger stations to the field rather than between Ranger stations or from Ranger stations to higher headquarters. (While many national forests employ their radio transmitters to establish communication links among these offices, the range and reliability of FM connections are still limited, and do not seem yet to have spanned the gaps entirely.)

To be sure, the Rangers are far from isolated today compared to what they were only a generation ago; [8] the volume of contacts with superiors and with other Rangers has unquestionably increased many times in recent years. Yet they are still forced to make many decisions and resolve many doubts without reference to those above them; they are thrown back on their own resources to a larger extent than most bureaucrats. As a means of co-ordination, "the device of propinquity, the juxtaposition of offices in the same building or city, and reliance on ordinary

[6] *Ibid.*, pp. 232–35.

[7] H. A. Simon, *Administrative Behavior* (New York: The Macmillan Co., 1947), p. 214 n., records a perfect illustration, in which a bureau chief, serving as acting department head for his absent superior, disapproved a number of proposals he himself had initiated as bureau chief. "From up here," he is reported to have explained, "things don't look the same as they do from down there."

[8] Cf. pp. 84–85.

daily contact,"[9] is for all practical purposes denied the Forest Service. Geographical dispersion is thus a powerful centrifugal factor here.[10]

Behavioral Norms of Face-to-Face Work Groups. A voluminous literature has grown up in recent years describing the characteristics of small groups in face-to-face contact—"primary" groups.[11] Among the results of these studies is the accumulation of strong evidence that groups of this kind tend to develop norms of their own, norms governing procedures and relationships among personnel and work output, to which the members adhere. In general, the norms evolve without conscious or systematic effort on anyone's part; indeed, it sometimes appears the individuals controlled by them could not articulate them if they were asked to, although the observer can see quite plainly that the standards determine what personnel do and decide. Unconsciously the members act in the group-prescribed way because that is simply "the way things are done." Sometimes, it is true, those who violate these informal standards are subjected to sanctions of many kinds by their fellows. Most of the time, however, the norms take effect without many people being at all aware that the process is operative.

If the leaders of an organization are fortunate, these informal norms will coincide with formally promulgated regulations. Often, however, conflicts develop. Output is then restricted by the workers, methods are adopted that are at odds with prescribed procedures, changes in modes of operation or in established relationships are resisted.[12] What work groups actually do may consequently be quite different from what the leadership intended or anticipated.

This presents a challenge in the Forest Service because most Ranger districts employ nonprofessional workers, under the Rangers and assistant Rangers, who remain on the districts for many years, in contrast to the professional men, who change frequently because of Forest Service transfer and promotion policies (discussed in later chapters). These permanent personnel are usually not many in number, varying from one or two on districts having short field seasons to as many as ten or fifteen on districts where long field seasons justify the maintenance of a year-round work force. (Temporary employees engaged as seasonal labor fill out the work force during the months of mild weather.) But they come to know the districts and the local people intimately, and the frequently-transferred executives over them depend heavily on them in the management of district resources and programs.

Considering what sociologists have found in their studies of large-scale organizations and of small groups, it might be expected that the local standards would gradually impress them-

[9] L. Gulick, "Notes on the Theory of Organization," in L. Gulick and L. Urwick (eds.), *Papers on the Science of Administration* (New York: Institute of Public Administration, 1937), p. 36.

[10] That distance is still a factor in communication in the Forest Service is indicated by the general agreement among the personnel interviewed that the more accessible forests and districts are more frequently visited and inspected by representatives of higher levels than are the more remote areas. For this reason, some field men prefer the more distant stations.

[11] Comprehensive surveys of this literature are contained in A. P. Hare, E. F. Borgatta, and R. F. Bales, *Small Groups* (New York: Alfred A. Knopf, 1955); *The American Sociological Review,* Vol. XIX, No. 6 (December, 1954); D. Cartwright and A. Zander, *Group Dynamics* (Evanston: Row, Peterson and Co., 1953); and G. C. Homans, *The Human Group* (New York: Harcourt, Brace and Co., 1950). Of particular relevance to the discussion here is Part Three of the Cartwright and Zander book.

[12] F. J. Roethlisberger and W. J. Dickson, *Management and the Worker* (Cambridge: Harvard University Press, 1939), Chapters XXII, XXIII, XXIV; S. B. Mathewson, *Restriction of Output among Unorganized Workers* (New York: The Viking Press, 1931); B. B. Gardner and D. G. Moore, *Human Relations in Industry* (Chicago: Richard D. Irwin, Inc., 1950), Chapter 18 and pp. 372 ff; B. M. Selekman, "Resistance to Shop Changes," *Harvard Business Review,* Vol. 24, No. 1 (Autumn, 1945), pp. 119–32; R. N. McMurry, "The Problem of Resistance to Change in Industry," *Journal of Applied Psychology,* Vol. 31, No. 6 (December, 1947), pp. 589–93; L. Coch and J. R. P. French, Jr., "Overcoming Resistance to Change," in S. Hoslett (ed.), *Human Factors in Management* (New York: Harper and Brothers, 1951), pp. 242–68 (especially at pp. 265–66).

selves on the Rangers, that the norms of conduct prevailing locally would occasionally clash with the official requirements of the agency, and that some Rangers would consequently deflect in some respects from those requirements. And there is some evidence that they do—for example, in whether or not they wear the Forest Service uniform regularly, insist on formal training sessions for their subordinates, or follow work-planning "guidelines" to the letter, the Rangers seem to be influenced by habits and reactions of local groups of employees. (National forests as entities also tend to fashion rather special ways of doing things; one, for example, handled its budgeting in a way quite at variance with regulations, a departure from prescribed practice no one on the supervisor's staff or among the Rangers realized had occurred or thought to check; the "common-sense" procedures evolved on that forest simply became the customary and accepted method of financial planning.)

The formation of "informal" groups with parochial patterns of behavior sometimes in conflict with official regulations is a phenomenon with which relatively compact organizations are compelled to deal. The problem in an agency as scattered geographically as the Forest Service, whose component face-to-face groups are comparatively isolated, is especially acute, and constitutes a particularly serious challenge to the cohesion of the organization.

"Capture" of Field Officers by Local Populations. "Where considerable authority is devolved upon field officials," observes one eminent student of government, "there is always the danger . . . that policy will be unduly influenced by those private individuals and groups who are in closer and more intimate contact with the field than are the superior officers . . . Localized influence, . . . if carried to any great lengths, is likely to beget such differences of policy between field offices that national policy will be a fiction."[13] Clearly, considerable authority is indeed devolved upon the field officials of the Forest Service, and the danger noted is therefore substantial.

The danger is really twofold. On the one hand, there is the risk that field men, regarded by their chiefs as emissaries sent to live among local populaces and represent the agency to the people, become so identified with the communities in which they reside that they become community delegates to headquarters rather than the reverse.[14] On the other hand, there is the possibility that the field men, though devoted to their leaders, might be cowed by local pressures.

The first aspect of this danger arises in the Forest Service because so much emphasis is placed on the local roots of the field units;[15] Rangers are encouraged to take as active a part as they can in community service, social, and fraternal organizations. Slowly, they absorb the point of view of their friends and neighbors. One, for example, reported that he found himself tending to "look the other way" and to delay investigation as long as he reasonably could when he had reason to believe the chamber of commerce of the town in which he lived, and to whose executive committee he belonged, was operating a resort area without the rather expensive liability insurance required by the terms of its special-use permit. Another argued vigorously in favor of disposing of timber through many small sales instead of fewer large ones (preferred by his superiors because the large ones are more economical, simpler to administer and police, and make the achievement of management goals easier to attain); though he did not deny the administrative advantages of larger sales, he contended they attract large "outside" companies able to outbid the local operators whose interests he sought to defend.

Also, in a couple of instances, Rangers decided against termination of grazing permits for small herds better removed (from the

[13] D. B. Truman, *Administrative Decentralization* (Chicago: University of Chicago Press, 1940), pp. 14–15.

[14] The process is described amusingly in J. Patrick, *The Teahouse of the August Moon* in L. Kronenberger, *The Best Plays of 1953–54* (New York: Dodd, Mead and Company, 1954); here, the inhabitants of an Okinawan village succeed in making Okinawan villagers of American officers sent to bring them American culture. In I. Stone, *Lust for Life* (New York: The Modern Library, 1939), pp. 26–83, the same theme is treated tragically as a missionary to a Belgian mining town becomes indistinguishable in outlook and behavior from the miners whose lives he was to enrich through religious teaching and practice.

[15] See the remarks of the Chief of the Forest Service quoted on pp. 190–191.

technical standpoint) from their districts, and of no importance to the local economy, just because they felt such action would work some hardship on the families who owned the cattle. The people the Rangers sought to protect were not influential enough to cause the Rangers any difficulty had the Rangers not fought for their welfare; it was not anxiety of this kind that moved the forest officers. Rather, it seems to have been a genuine concern for the individuals involved, a sense of community with them. Men who thought only in terms of their organizations rather than in terms of their friends and neighbors doubtless would have been less sensitive to the latter's personal needs and desires.

The second aspect of the danger is that many local interests are in positions to bring considerable pressure to bear on the field man. Sometimes it is exerted on him directly—to convince him of the wisdom and justice of the local demand, if possible; to compel him to accede to the demand, whatever his convictions, if necessary. They can visit him repeatedly in his office and home, argue with him at meetings of civic and fraternal associations, talk with him at gatherings of church groups. News reports and editorials in the local press and on the air ventilate local grievances and aspirations. (Incendiarism has been employed in some areas as a coercive measure against the Forest Service, and one Ranger was threatened with violence by an armed man in the backwoods of West Virginia when the Ranger was investigating a possible timber trespass, but these, of course, are not the ordinary modes of persuasion and protest.) Even the most devoted forest officer might understandably yield to these constraints now and then; on a large scale, the results could gravely undermine the unity of agency policy.

Sometimes the pressure is directed over the head of the Ranger and exerted on his superiors. Statutes and regulations of the Department of Agriculture establish regular procedures for the handling of appeals from administrative decisions, and a person affected by a Ranger's action (or inaction) may file formal requests for hearings and redress with the forest supervisor, and carry his case to the regional forester, the Chief, the Secretary of Agriculture, and ultimately to the courts if he is so minded. More commonly, aggrieved individuals simply write informally to higher headquarters and pray for relief; in most cases, this is sufficient to precipitate an inquiry into a field officer's decision.[16] Many people get in touch with their United States Representatives or Senators, whose queries to the Chief on behalf of their constituents ordinarily get prompt attention and cause reverberations throughout the hierarchy of the Forest Service. From time to time, individuals approach the functionaries of the political parties for help (but it appears the functionaries then contact Members of Congress because party officers carry less weight than Congressmen with Forest Service field personnel). By one means or another, then, citizens seeking to obtain or overturn a ruling by a Ranger fight to get their way, and they sometimes succeed.

Every Ranger and former Ranger interviewed in the course of this study has been involved in appeals cases of some kind. It is accepted as one of the hardships of doing public business in a democratic government and is not ordinarily treated as a discredit, even if a field officer is eventually overruled. Yet it is a bother, at best—a distraction from the more "productive" labors of the members of the Forest Service, a cause of additional paperwork, a generator of inspections and inquiries from higher levels. And it is certainly true that, at worst, a Ranger whose constituency is *constantly* restive and rebellious is likely to stimulate some doubts about his judiciousness and skill. So Rangers prefer to avoid them if they can, and are often confronted with a delicate choice between the annoyance and risk of continuous skirmishing with local interests on the one hand, and conceding away elements of the Forest Service program (perhaps to save the remainder) on the other.

Sometimes they make concessions. When his forest supervisor wanted to spray herbicides on stands of commerically undesirable species of trees (in order to destroy the valueless trees and make way for more merchantable growth), one Ranger persuaded him to delay the project indefinitely because the Ranger anticipated that hunting and fishing clubs and other associations of wildlife enthusiasts would raise a hue and cry about the alleged injury to birds, small game, and fish. In another case, a plan to require grazing permittees to put ear tags on their cattle because the Ranger discov-

[16] See pp. 153–155.

ered they were running more animals than their permits allowed was deferred when the permittees organized resistance to the program. Another Ranger elected not to press for the termination of a special-use permit under which a small town within the boundaries of his district used national forest property for a town dump; although the dump was an eyesore and a potential fire hazard, he thought the town officials could muster enough support to defeat such a move. On one district, the Ranger was trying to eliminate grazing from some high-altitude, snow-covered, water storage areas, but only slowly and cautiously, so as to minimize the opposition this would provoke. On another, protests by nature lovers concerned about songbirds and game forced deferral of spraying designed to eliminate the highly destructive spruce budworm.

In every instance, to have pressed forward regardless of local sentiment unquestionably would have cost far more in the long run than was gained in the short run; tactically, the concessions were certainly sound. But these examples do indicate how local pressure can influence the behavior of field officers, slowing or modifying what actually happens on the ground as compared with what is mandated from central headquarters.

Thus, a needed step is not taken here, an undesirable permit is issued there, a measure is recommended in order to avoid trouble—and an agency-wide policy can be eroded. From the standpoint of this study, it does not matter whether acquiescence by field officers in the demands of local special interests results from the assimilation of Service personnel into the communities in which they live or from the overwhelming nature of the pressure brought to bear upon them; the erosive impact on policy is the same. Nor does it matter that no single action, as the illustrations demonstrate, is likely by itself to have much effect on policy; multiplied many times, over long periods, in large numbers of Ranger districts, the cumulative impact could be considerable. Unity does not demand uniformity, but it does require consistency and co-ordination. It is in this sense that "capture" of the men "on the firing line" is a challenge to the unity of the Forest Service, as it is to the unity of any large organization.[17]

Personal Preferences of Field Officers. Men do not enter organizations devoid of opinions, values, preferences, and their own interpretations of the world. Nor do they shed all these once they become members. True, these things may be modified by organizational experience. But job experience is only part of a person's total experience; many of the predilections each man brings with him to his work are reinforced elsewhere and therefore persist even when they are not in harmony with the objectives or desires of his organization's leaders. Since personal predilections and prejudices are presumably among the determinants of behavior, they can produce actions that clash with the proclaimed policies of the organization. This possibility is not confined to the field levels of any agency, of course, but it is especially problematical there because the leadership opportunities to manipulate individual outlooks by personal contact are more limited, and because so many other factors at the lower levels also generate centrifugal forces.

The top offices of the Forest Service were reminded of this when, in the immediat post-World War II period, they adopted a firm position in favor of public regulation of timber cutting on privately owned lands. This has been a controversial question among foresters for two generations; with three-quarters of the forest acreage of the country held by private owners, it is clear that the public forests alone cannot safeguard the nation's forest resources, but many foresters, while recognizing this, share the ideological opposition of many other citizens to expansion of governmental regulatory powers. Nevertheless, advocacy of such a program became official Forest Service policy, and communiques went out from the Washington office requesting field officers to encourage grassroots support by taking every opportunity to explain it, analyze it, and justi-

[17] Even higher officers are vulnerable in this respect. In 1933, the leaders of the Department of Agriculture under a new administration looked over the Forest Service and "thought that the Washington headquarters had fallen into a rut, being content to relay the legislative demands of the district foresters [now called regional foresters] who in turn were caught in complexes of local interests," (A. W. Macmahon and J. D. Millett, *Federal Administrators* [New York: Columbia University Press, 1939], p. 346.) Consequently, there was a fairly sweeping reorganization in both the regions and in Washington. (See *Report of the Chief of the Forest Service, 1936*, pp. 4 ff.)

fy it. Apparently, these activities were conceived as a prelude to a campaign for enactment of the necessary legislation.

There are many reasons why the effort made little headway, but one of them was certainly the indifferent response of many field men to the request that they press the issue. Some were hostile, most cared little. A number made token moves to satisfy minimum requirements, many did nothing at all. The change of administrations in 1953, the enactment of regulatory laws by a number of states, and the improvement of private industrial practices in response to rising stumpage values of timber diminished the urgency of such a program and might have doomed it in any event, but the attitudes of the men virtually assured its downfall. The personal values of Forest Service personnel helped defeat it.

Similarly, it has taken considerable effort by Forest Service leaders to overcome the objections of some of their subordinates to "controlled burning" as an effective and economical way of encouraging new growth in some kinds of forested areas. According to one school of thought, fires deliberately set and controlled to clear away underbrush speed the germination of seeds and the growth of seedlings; for a long time, another school of thought argued that the heat injures seeds, destroys seedlings, and devastates the soil, and that the risk of fires getting out of control is very great. Even to experiment with the technique, the Forest Service had to engage in a large-scale program of information and education for its own men, to sell them on the utility of at least *testing* it, and to overcome the overwhelming fear and hatred of fire instilled in them in their training. The program could not be instituted at once by fiat; the attitudes of many men had to be changed gradually before it made much progress.

To cite a third instance, when a change of administration brought about a change in land acquisition policy—a contraction of the boundaries of the "purchase units" in which further purchases of property for addition to the national forests takes place, requiring the disposal by exchange of parcels lying beyond the new boundaries—one Ranger, reluctant to see acreages reduced, deliberately concentrated his land exchange program only on plots too small and too isolated to manage effectively, and made little effort to dispose of larger holdings located outside the diminished territory. Since he did not subscribe to the philosophy of diminishing the number and scale of federal business enterprises, and anticipated that the policy would change again one day, he "dragged his feet" on carrying it out.

That is not to say that Rangers run their districts as personal fiefs. But they are not just instruments of the agency leaders either, without wills of their own. While their wills may often coincide with the desires of the leadership, conflicts also develop, and the result is the attenuation or distortion of facets of announced agency policy. A comprehensive national policy may dissolve into a host of different policies in the actual work in the field if such developments are not corrected or prevented.

The Ideology of Decentralization. The Forest Service has made decentralization its cardinal principle of organization structure, the heart and core of its "administrative philosophy." "The Forest Service," says the *Forest Service Manual*, "is dedicated to the principle that resource management begins—and belongs—on the ground. It is logical, therefore, that the ranger district constitutes the backbone of the organization." A former assistant chief described "The constant effort to decentralize and delegate authority to the tree and grass roots," and declared, "Most of the responsibility for national forest work is delegated down to the forest supervisors and the forest rangers." The Ranger, he added, "is checked closely against policies and regulations and must conform, but because it is a fundamental national policy that the forest take its place locally as a contributor to community prosperity, the Chief of the Forest Service insures that the ranger's authority is protected and that no one above him sabotages his planning or action. In other words, he has his job and is protected in it." [18] Field personnel share this attitude, and speak of Rangers as "their own bosses," men who "run their own show," "kings of their own domains" who make "90 to 95 per cent of the decisions made on their districts." At higher levels, Forest Service officials often reminisce nostalgically, and rather proudly, of their days in the field. The doc-

[18] E. W. Loveridge, "The Administration of National Forests," in U.S. Department of Agriculture, *Yearbook of Agriculture, 1949*, pp. 376–377.

trine is widely accepted—indeed, almost sanctified.

It has a long tradition. It was first propounded in a letter from the Secretary of Agriculture to the Chief when the Forest Service was established in 1950: [19]

> In the management of each reserve [now called national forests] local questions will be decided upon local grounds . . . General principles . . . can be successfully applied only when the administration of each reserve is left largely in the hands of local officers, under the eye of thoroughly trained and competent supervisors.

In the context of the times, such a philosophy was almost inescapable. In the first place, the back areas of the reserves were highly inaccessible, unserved by roads or railroads, unsettled, and without means of communication; a man went into the woods and was virtually isolated for days and weeks on end. One of the earliest United States Forest Rangers was sent out with instructions

> to take horses and ride as far as the Almighty will let you and get control of the forest fire situation on as much of the mountain country as possible. And as to what you should do first, well, just get up there as soon as possible and put them out.[20]

With little more than their orders and water buckets, rakes, axes, shovels, maps and badges, almost alone in the forests, the first Rangers went out to execute national policy. There was no real alternative to decentralization.

Moreover, Gifford Pinchot, the first Chief, was determined to avoid the scandals that had discredited the General Land Office, from which the Forest Service took over the administration of the forest reserves. The Division had been beset by fraud, bribery, and laxity; [21] it had also been centralized, authoritarian, and led by men unfamiliar with field conditions:

> The abysmal ignorance of the Washington Office about conditions on the ground was outrageous, pathetic, or comic, whichever you like. Division P ordered one Supervisor to buy a rake for himself and another for his Ranger and rake up the dead wood on the Washington Forest Reserve—a front yard of a mere three and a half million acres, where the fallen trees were often longer than a city block and too thick for a man to see over. And that was no case by itself. Another Supervisor got a similar order for the Lewis and Clark Reserve. But that was only three million acres.
>
> Said Major F. A. Fenn . . . who became one of the very best forest officers the West has ever produced: "For an officer in the field to question the policy outlined in the regulations on any point no matter how trivial, or to suggest that a change in regulation would be beneficial to the [Government] Service or conducive to better administration, was almost equivalent to religious heresy." And when out of his practical experience Major Fenn ventured to suggest certain changes in the regulations, he got this reply: "It is the duty of forest officers to obey their instructions and not to question them." [22]

Pinchot therefore set out to prevent these faults by building an organization that was composed of professional foresters, co-operative as well as hierarchical, and, inevitably, decentralized.

So decentralization became one of the commandments of the Forest Service from the very start. The idea has been affirmed and reaffirmed, over and over again, for every generation of foresters. It is now part of the dogma of the agency.

Men indoctrinated with this philosophy, it seems reasonable to infer, will probably display a good deal more independence of judgment and readiness to challenge higher authorities than those trained in an ours-not-to-reason-why environment or in the Prussian kind of total military submissiveness that allegedly led Frederick the Great to remark his system was still not perfect because it did not control his soldiers' breathing. To be sure, a

[19] Dated February 1, 1905; reproduced in *Forestry Directory* (Washington: American Tree Association, 1943) pp. 108–110. The letter bears all the earmarks of having been drafted by Gifford Pinchot for the Secretary's signature.

[20] B. M. Huey, "The First U. S. Forest Ranger," *Journal of Forestry*, Vol. 45, No. 10 (October, 1947) p. 765.

[21] L. D. White, *The Republican Era: 1869–1901* (New York: The Macmillan Co., 1958), pp. 205–8.

[22] G. Pinchot, *Breaking New Ground* (New York: Harcourt, Brace and Co., 1947), p. 162.

Ranger district could not be successfully administered by such docile individuals; performance of the job demands a relatively high degree of personal autonomy. At the same time, the emphasis on decentralization places a high value on assertion of independence, willingness to make decisions and to act without consulting superior officers, and defense of personal and local points of view. It generates centrifugal drives. It builds up the sense of local command. It proclaims that a high degree of self-containment is prized. Thus, it adds to the tendencies toward fragmentation.

Conclusion: The Impulse toward Disintegration. Were the Forest Service not as large and complex as it is, had its massive responsibilities not been imposed on it all at once, did it not depend so heavily on its officers in the field to make the kinds of decisions that translate its enunciations of policy into tangible actions and accomplishments, it would still have to contend with powerful forces drawing the Rangers along many different paths. For there are many influences besides the top policy pronouncements shaping their behavior. The customs and standards of the groups they work with, the values and attitudes and pressures of the communities in which they reside, and the preferences and prejudices they bring with them from their extra-organizational experiences and associations may lead them in a variety of directions. And the problems of internal communication make the task of directing them a complicated and difficult operation, leaving them vulnerable to the fragmentative influences.

Unchecked, these influences could produce such diverse Ranger district programs as to dissolve the Forest Service into an aggregate of separate entities, destroying it as an integrated, functioning organization.

But they are not unchecked. They are overcome, or at least neutralized. The remainder of this volume is an analysis of the techniques by which integration is achieved.

PART THREE

Organizations as Open Systems

PART THREE

RECOGNIZING that organizations must be viewed as open rather than closed systems greatly complicates our problem of understanding them. Within organizations, these elements are connected not in short, simple cause-effect chains but in highly interconnected webs. Even if we could examine them arrested, in a static picture, they would be exceedingly difficult to study. Opening all this to the environment would seem to make it necessary to include a limitless number of elements that cannot be considered in any fixed or stable relationship but, as we have already noted, exist only in a dynamic, changing relationship. To study such a phenomenon is quite beyond the more familiar approaches. We are only beginning to develop tools molded in a systems orientation and utilizing the strengths of mathematics. In this book, we do nothing more than brush these developments. Some developments permit us to orient ourselves better to the problem and to simplify it without excessive distortion, and these are covered in the remaining parts of this volume. In Part Three, we examine some basic ideas of how we may view the organization embedded in an environment.

We have already noted that open systems are, in part, characterized by having inputs and outputs and some means of transforming the throughput from one to the other. In Volume I, it was noted that once the internal operations of the organization grew above a basic size, they needed a differentiated managerial system that provided an extrinsic coordination for the unit (Herbst, Volume I). Further transformation is achieved by using a technology which, to become rational, needs to be separated and buffered from the environment (Thompson, Volume I). One of the key managerial efforts in an organization is concerned with seeing that the technical work involved with the transformation is efficiently carried out. But inputs (such as raw materials) and outputs (such as finished products) are not automatically taken care of. In fact, the processes for this are often complex and, because they are at the interface between the organization and its environment, must bridge two different settings. These processes too must be managed. This managerial effort is of a different sort, with different concerns and different bases than that of the technical or transformation system. This managerial system is concerned with integrating the organization into its environment in a very basic way. But there is still another way in which the organization must be integrated into its environment. In the social work at least, the environment is concerned not only with the basic output of the technical or transformation system but also with the way that system operates or the way the transformation is carried out. In our society, for example, we cannot use children of ten or twelve in mines or textile mills even though it might permit production of lower-priced goods. There is an enormous array of points on which an organization must be adequatedly intergrated or compatible with the standards of society other than those that are directly concerned with output. This area of concern also has to be managed. It also is a different type of managerial concern. It is much broader and more pervasive than the others. It has elements of trust or fiduciary responsibility to society or parts of the society in which the organization operates. Organizations then have at least three different concerns that have to be handled by different managerial systems. These managerial systems can be arrayed in a hierarchial fashion in the reverse order discussed (Parsons).

This gives us a framework of basic systems in an organization when the basic relationship of the organization to its environment is taken into account. It does not tell us very much about how these processes work or the ways they influence each other, for it is a static model. Other writers, whom we shall examine shortly, present us with more dynamic models. First, however, we shall review some other concepts on how to study organizations as open systems.

Any area of intellectual enquiry has ways of simplifying the problems or items of study. In Part One, it was established that the methods of simplifying questions or problems in the physical sciences, where the assumption of the closed system is possible, is not a workable strategy for other scientific disciplines when they must assume as open system. One of the basic concerns of General Systems is to develop a different and more workable strategy. The starting point of the developing strategy is that the study of open systems must begin with the study of the whole and then move progressively into its subparts. If one were to use this approach to diagnose a system that was not operating correctly, one would not proceed to search for a malfunctioning part and then ask what was wrong with it. The systems concepts assumes that the functioning of any part is dependent upon the other elements in the system; hence the malfunctioning of a part is not a characteristic of the part but of the system it is in. One, therefore, analyzes the malfunctioning system.

Systems are defined by the function they fill or the purpose they satisfy. Since there are many of these in an organization, there is always a degree of arbitrariness in selecting a system. Is this sound? Does it open pitfalls because of the very common human tendency to gradually forget this arbitrariness? It has been shown that any open system can be represented as a closed system consisting of units (Herbst). This opens up many possibilities for analyzing open systems and also gently reminds us of the necessary artificiality of our approach.

Another basic strategy to develop a way of simplifying the questions to be studied is to simplify the elements by being able to differentiate among them. With open systems, we discuss the organization and its environment. However, we cannot study organizations nor do organizations function meaningfully with a large, vague, undifferentiated thing called an environment. Organizations must relate specific actions or functions to specific aspects of an environment. Ultimately, we may be able to identify these specific aspects. As a start, we are beginning to see that an environment is really made up of many environments and that the organization responds differently to each.

But how are environments to be differentiated? One approach would be to find the characteristics unique to each. But, unfortunately, while this may make the environments thus identified easy for our minds to grasp and differentiate, it is almost sure to be the case that this scheme of categorization will not help us in studying organizational questions. It is as if we decided to differentiate male youths on the basis of the color of their hair. It helps us separate them if all we want to do is to differentiate. However, if we are studying the relationship between an organization such as a draft board and one of its important environments, male youths, it does not help us very much to divide this environment into subenvironments distinguished by color of hair. We must differentiate in terms meaningful to the organization or system about which we are concerned. Differentiation should be on the basis of deduction, not of convenience. We begin by picking some function, phenomenon, or attribute important to the organization or system. We can then classify the environment according to the amount or form of the differentiating characteristic each of the environments possesses. We could, for example, differentiate the environments of the firm as scientific, market, technical resources and find that, by chance, these mean something. We could also differentiate environments on the speed with which they feed back information into the organization, which we can demonstrate to be variable for influencing organization performance. It so happens that the scientific, market, and technical-resource environments have different speeds of feedback. It is the fact that these environments have different speeds of feedback that makes it meaningful to differentiate among them, not the fact that one deals with science, another with selling, etc. The study of organizations is littered with useless typologies for environments, organizations people, etc., which are based on convenience or a search for unique characteristics.

What are the characteristics of environments that are meaningful in organization analysis? One observation is that environments differ in the number of their customers. A firm may be dealing with many buyers, each of whom may take relatively small amounts of its products, and it may be competing against many other small manufacturers. Or a firm may have a very few or perhaps an only buyer and it may compete with only one or two other firms. Variations in the gross structuring or texture of the set of users of the organization's output and the set of conditional elements extant differentiate environments (Emery and Trist). However, the structure or texture of the environment is but one aspect of importance. The pattern of inputs from the environment, such as precision of feedback, speed of feedback, etc., also defines different types of environments and requires different forms of organization structure and operations to achieve adequate performance (Lawrence and Lorsch). With such differences in environments and internal structure and operation, the transactions involved with boundary spanning flows will also differ. Examination discloses that there are different types of transactions, each of them of considerable complexity.

Implicit in many theories of organization is the assumption that the organization as an entity has a precarious autonomy, always subservient to the requirements of its environment. Closer examination suggests three general states are possible. The organization has substantial autonomy, neither being influenced by nor influencing the environment. The organization has a weak or easily subverted autonomy, where it can be molded to the benefit of the environment or important elements in it. Or the organization can exert influence on the environment to change it to suit its own needs and conditions (Eisenstadt).

Considering organizations as open systems does greatly complicate our study of them, but as even these few studies show, it is possible to find ways of approaching the subject and making some progress in our understanding. Having taken these steps, the study of organizations should be able to make further and more elegant advances.

Some Ingredients of a General Theory of Formal Organization

TALCOTT PARSONS

Most of the recent literature in the field of formal organization has tended to deal with internal structure and processes: such problems as line authority, staff organization, and the process of decision-making. I have therefore selected for comment three fields which have been less in the center of attention. The first of these is the set of differences which arise at various levels in the hierarchy of control and responsibility in systems of organization. The second concerns analysis of the *external* relations of organizations to the situations in which they function, and the third is the variation in *types* of organization which is related, on the one hand, to their technical functions, on the other, to variations in their external relations. These three problem areas are closely interdependent. It would not be useful to deal with them entirely independently; it will be necessary to interweave them. But I would like to build the main structure of the paper on the distinctness of these three themes and at the same time their interdependence.

The theory of "bureaucracy" has been so strongly influenced by the conception of "line" authority that there has been a tendency to neglect the importance of what in some sense are qualitative breaks in the continuity of the line structure. There is much sound observation and comment on many relevant problems but little direct attempt to analyze them in a more formal way. I would like to suggest a way of breaking down the hierarchical aspect of a system of organization—of examining, for example, the line within a school system that runs all the way from the chairman of the school board to the teacher of most junior status, or even to the non-teaching employee in the humblest position. I make this breakdown according to three references of function or responsibility, which become most clearly marked in terms of the external references of the organization to its setting or to the next higher order in the hierarchy. These three may be called, respectively, the "technical" system, the "managerial" system, and the "community" or "institutional" system.

Three Levels in the Hierarchical Structure of Organization

In the first place, every formal organization has certain "technical" functions. In an educational organization these are the actual processes of teaching; in a government bureau, the administrative process in direct relation to the public (e.g., tax collecting by the Bureau of Internal Revenue); in a business firm, the process of physical production of goods, etc. There is, then, always a type of suborganization whose "problems" are mainly those of effectively performing this "technical" function—the conduct of classes by the teacher, the processing of income tax returns and the handling of recalcitrants by the bureau, the processing of material and supervision of these operations in the case of physical production. The primary exigencies to which this suborganization is oriented are those imposed by the nature of the technical task, such as the "materials"—physical, cultural, or human—which must be processed, the kinds of co-operation of different people required to get the job done effectively.

I assume, however, that on the level of social differentiation with which we are here concerned, there is another set of "problems" which becomes the focus of a different order of organizational setup. In the area where parents teach their own children, for example, to speak their language, there is no problem of the selection and appointment of teachers, or even of their qualifications; the status of par-

From *Structure and Process in Modern Society*, Glencoe: Free Press, 1960, pp. 59–96. Reprinted by permission of the publisher.

ent *ipso facto* makes him the appropriate teacher. But in a school system teachers have to be especially appointed and allocated to teach particular classes. Moreover, classrooms have to be provided; the teacher does not automatically control adequate facilities for performing the function. Furthermore, while it is taken for granted that a child should learn to speak the language of his parents, what should be taught in what schools to what children is by no means automatically given.

In a complex division of labor, both the resources necessary for performing technical functions and the relations to the population elements on whose behalf the functions are performed have become problematical. Resources are made available by special arrangements; they are not simply "given" in the nature of the context of the function. And who shall be the beneficiary of what "product" or "service" on what terms is problematical; this becomes the focus of organizational arrangements of many different kinds.

When the division of labor has progressed beyond a certain point, decisions that pertain to this division must take precedence over those on the "technical" level. Thus it does not make sense to set up classrooms without having decided what children should be taught what things by what kinds of teachers, or without knowing whether specific teachers and specific physical facilities can be made available. Similarly, the Bureau of Internal Revenue does not just "collect taxes" in general; it collects specific taxes assessed by a higher authority, from specific categories of persons. And the plant does not just produce goods without anyone's worrying about how the materials will be procured, who will do the actual work on what terms, and who wants the goods anyway—again on what terms. In the case of a subsistence farm family there is no problem: its members have to eat; they have access to soil, seeds, and some simple equipment; and they work to produce their own food. But this is not the typical case for a modern society.

We may say then that the more complex technical functions are performed by suborganizations controlled and serviced—in various ways and at a variety of levels—by higher-order organizations. The higher-order organization is sometimes called an "administration." In the business case it is usually called the "firm," whereas the technical organization is called the "plant." In the field of government, "bureaus" are mainly technical organizations, while the "political" parts of government are, literally, the "policy-making" parts (in our system, principally legislative [1] and higher executive). Perhaps a good name for this level of organization is, as suggested above, a "managerial" system.

The relations between such a managerial system and the technical system can be divided into two categories: mediation between the organization and the external situation, and "administration" of the organization's internal affairs. Both involve the "decision-making" processes which have been the center of so much recent attention.

At the level I have in mind, there are two main foci of the external reference and responsibility. The primary one is to mediate between the technical organization and those who use its "products"—the "customers," pupils, or whoever. The second is to procure the resources necessary for carrying out the technical functions (i.e., financial resources, personal, and physical facilities).

In one set of connections, decisions made in the management system control the operations of the technical system. This is certainly true for such matters as the broad technical task which is to be performed in the technical system—the scale of operations, employment and purchasing policy, etc. But, as in other cases of functional differentiation, this is by no means simply a one-way relation, for managerial personnel usually are only partially competent to plan and supervise the execution of the technical operations. The managers present specifications to the technical subsystem, but vice versa, the technical people present "needs" which constitute specifications to the management; on various bases the technical people are closest to the operating problems and know what is needed. Perhaps the most important of these bases is the technical *professional* competence of higher personnel in technical systems, a professional competence not often shared by the administrative personnel who—in the line sense—are the organizational superiors of the technicians.

[1] The legislative function may, however, be placed mainly at the still higher level, which I call "institutional" and which will be discussed below.

In its external relations, the managerial system is oriented to the "markets" for the disposal of the "product" and for "procurement" of the resources required by the organization to perform its functions. But those "lateral" external relations do not exhaust the "external" problem foci of a managerial system. The organization which consists of both technical and managerial suborganizations never operates subject only to the exigencies of disposal to and procurement from other agencies (which stand on an approximately equal level) as "customers" or as sources of supply. There is always some "organized superior" agency with which the organization articulates.

A formal organization in the present sense is a mechanism by which goals somehow important to the society, or to various subsystems of it, are implemented and to some degree defined. But not only does such an organization have to operate in a social environment which imposes the conditions governing the processes of disposal and procurement, it is also part of a wider social system which is the source of the "meaning," legitimation, or higher-level support which makes the implementation of the organization's goals possible. Essentially, this means that just as a technical organization (at a sufficiently high level of the division of labor) is controlled and "serviced" by a managerial organization, so, in turn, is the managerial organization controlled by the "institutional" structure and agencies of the community.

The ways in which the managerial system fits into the higher-order institutional system vary widely according to the character of the managerial system's functions and the organization's position on both the "lateral" and the "vertical" axes of the larger social system. But it is a cardinal thesis of this analysis that no organization is every wholly "independent." In terms of "formal" controls it may be relatively so, but in terms of the "meaning" of the functions performed by the organization and hence of its "rights" to command resources and to subject its "customers" to disciplines, it never is wholly independent.

As noted, this third level of organization, which articulates with the managerial, may take many forms. In the educational field, for instance, I would put school boards with their representative functions in the local community in this category; similarly with trustees of the various types of private, non-profit organizations and indeed, under the fully-developed corporate form, with the boards of directors of business corporations.[2] These, and possibly other agencies, are the mediating structures between the particular managerial organization—and hence the technical organization it controls—and the higher-order community interests which, on some level, it is supposed to "serve."

Without attempting to be more circumstantial and formal at this stage, I may merely suggest that the foci of these higher-level controls which stand "over" the managerial organization are of three main types, which often appear in combination. One control is universal: the operation of the organization is subjected to generalized norms, valid throughout a wider community. These range from the rules formally codified in the law to standards of "good practice" informally accepted. So far as control is of this type, the distinctive thing is that no organized agency continually supervises the managerial organization; intervention is likely only when deviant practice is suspected—such control is exerted, for example, through litigation or by law-enforcement agencies, trade and professional associations, and relevant "public opinion."

The second type of control mechanism is some formal organization which is interstitial between the managerial structure and a more diffuse basis of "public interest." The fiduciary board which supervises the typical private non-profit organization is the type case, though in many respects the directors of business corporations also belong in this category.

Finally, the third type is that which brings the managerial organization directly into a structure of "public authority" at some level. In our society this is usually "political" authority, i.e., some organ of government; but in the past, religious authorities have also performed this function, and even now, for example, the Catholic school system should be treated as belonging to this type. The relation to superior authority may in turn be "administrative" or "regulative."

[2] For the business case one may thus designate the three organizational levels as plant, firm, and corporation. The "central office" may be thought of as the "plant" of the administrative organization of the firm.

The Points of Articulation between the Three System-Levels

I have emphasized these *three* different levels of the organization hierarchy because at each of the two points of articulation between them we find a qualitative break in the simple continuity of "line" authority. School boards, boards of directors, or trustees and political superiors do not, in the nature of the case, simply tell the people at the next level down "what to do." This is essentially because the people "lower down" typically must exercise types of competence and shoulder responsibilities which cannot be regarded as simply "delegated" by their "superiors." This again is because the *functions* at each level are qualitativley different; those at the second level are not simply "lower-order" spellings-out of the "top" level functions.

In the case of the technical organization, I illustrate this by the case of the higher level technical functions. When the personnel of the technical organization reach a full professional level of competence, a crucial problem of organization appears. For no matter how far removed these professionals may be from certain levels of concrete "operations," they must necessarily have the last word in planning and evaluating these operations (i.e., setting the *criteria* of effective operation in technical terms), simply because their managerial superiors are seldom, if at all, equally competent in the technical field. Organizational arrangements are extremely varied; sometimes such people have important positions in the "firm" or other managerial organization, and they should be regarded, like the foreman, as interstitial. In any case, their position cannot be a simply "line" position. Nor, indeed, is it adequate to assign them to the "staff" and say that their function is to "advise" the "lay" executive. This implies that it is the executive who *really* makes the decisions. But this is not correct. The technical expert must, in the nature of the case, *participate* in the technically crucial decisions. He does not simply lay the alternatives with their consequences before his "boss" and say, "Take *your* choice." The technical expert takes responsibility for *his* judgment, and when the decision has fallen a given way, he must assume his share of responsibility for the consequences. Hence, if he feels that he cannot take this responsibility, his recourse is to resign, exactly as in the case of an executive. A decision is arrived at not by the executive's deciding in the light of the expert's advice but by a process of weighing the considerations for which each is responsible and then reaching some kind of a balance of agreement. Because of the functions of the managerial organization, the executive has some kind of "last word." But this is a veto power, not a capacity to implement, because the executive is powerless to implement or plan implementation without the competence of the expert. The most the executive can do is to fire one expert and hire another in his place.

This leads to another crucial point. The technical expert at the professional level may be a member of the managerial organization, and of the technical system under it, but his allegiance is never exhausted by these two. Though degrees of formal organization vary greatly, the expert is typically a member of one or more collectivities of specialists sharing a type of competence which cuts across the structure of managerial and specific technical organizations. Thus no one industrial firm employs all the engineers, nor one hospital all the doctors, nor one school system all the teachers. The "reference group" to which the expert looks in connection with his competence and the definition of its standards is not his "managerial" boss but his professional peers and colleagues.

Similar considerations apply at the point of articulation between the managerial and the institutional system. But the qualitative break in line authority at this point is obscured because we have tended to describe organizational situations according to one of two extreme types. One is exemplified by the business firm where the "top man" is thought of as beholden to no one; he is "on his own." He is thought of as responsible only to his own conscience, and everyone else in the organization is under his orders. The other type of organization is that in which the managerial unit is incorporated in a "political" structure, so that the nominal head of the unit is thought of merely as a subordinate of his political superiors.

The essential focus of the qualitative break in line authority I have in mind here is the managerial *responsibility* assumed by the executive and the managerial organization which he, in many cases, heads. This also is not a mere "delegation" where the executive is commissioned to carry out the "details" while his superiors decide all the "policies." This is because it is not possible to perform the functions of focusing legitimation and community support for the organization and at the same time act as the active management of it—that is, when the differentiation of function in the structure has gone far enough. The "board," or whatever structural form it takes, is a mediating structure between the affairs of the organization at the managerial level and its "public." It can become absorbed in the managerial structure only at the expense of its primary function.

Of course the degree to which legitimation and support are essential functions varies from case to case. In some cases, most nearly approached but by no means reached in the business world, the "automatic" institutional controls constitute the main regulatory mechanism. Perhaps near the extreme in the other direction is the case of the school board in a community where a great many issues touching the operation of the school system are politically "hot." Then the superintendent may be sorely in need of a buffer between himself and various "pressure groups" in the community, but by the same token the board itself may be "bent" by the pressure of these groups. Its failure to protect the "professional"[3] element in the school system is not, however, an adequate measure of its dispensability.

Not least of the reasons why the board does not merely delegate functions to the managerial executive is the type of relation the latter must maintain with the technical personnel. The same holds, however, for the executive's external responsibilities. The essential point is that the executive must perform his functions by coming to terms with categories of other people—experts, customers, and resource people—who are in a position (within limits) to exact their own terms independently. Therefore, to be effective, the executive must have considerable freedom to use his own judgment as to what terms are good for the organization. He can be reasonably bound by broad policies and rules laid down from above, but these cannot be too restrictive. Certainly he cannot be regarded as the mere implementing agent of other people's decisions. Furthermore, he must be in a position to present *his* problems to his board and to negotiate with them from a position of relative strength, not just to go to them for "instructions."

[3] Note the ambiguity of the term "professional." Ordinarily I use the term in a sense denoting *technical* competence. When used otherwise, I shall put it in quotation marks.

I may generalize about the nature of the two main breaks in line authority which I have outlined by saying that at each of the two points of articulation between subsystems there is a *two-way* interchange of inputs and outputs. What has to be "contributed" from each side is qualitatively different. Either side is in a position, by withholding its important contribution, to interfere seriously with the functioning of the other and of the larger organization. Hence the *institutionalization* of these relations must typically take a form where the relative independence of each is protected. Since, however, there is an actual hierarchy, since in some sense the "higher" authority must be able to have some kind of "last word," the problem of protection focuses on the status of the lower-order element. Accordingly, we find that such institutions as tenure serve, in part at least, to protect professional personnel from pressures exerted by management—pressures that are often passed on down from board levels.

The Disposal and Procurement Functions

Let us now take a brief look at the second main topic in my outline: the relation between each of these systems—the technical, the managerial, and the community—and the "lateral" elements of the society with which they have to deal. First, what I have called a "technical" process must be carried out in relation to some "materials" or to an environmental situation; facilities are required to do this, and many of these resources must be secured from outside the organization.

With respect to what I have called materials, the first important distinction is whether they are or are not "physical" objects whose "motivations" do not need to be taken into account. Physical production in the sense of modern technology is the type case involving the physical object. Complex organized co-operation is generally necessary to carry out the technical process of production, but it is not necessary to secure the "co-operation" of the raw materials or of the partly finished products at any stage. Nor is it necessary to get the consent of the finished product to dispose of it to users outside the organization in any stage. Nor is it necessary to get the consent of the finished product to dispose of it to users outside the organization in any way the management sees fit. In economic terms this is the type case of a "commodity."

In another very large class of cases the "materials" on which technical operations must be performed are human individuals, or collectivities. This is pre-eminently true of education, but also of health services, of the practice of law, and of "administration," which may be defined as the processes by which persons and collectivities and categories of them may be brought actually to fulfill the obligations imposed by the decision of a "legitimate authority"—e.g., paying taxes, teaching the classes assigned, or observing traffic regulations. Here the conditions under which the "objects" of the technical process will co-operate satisfactorily and the kind of social relationship structure required under these conditions become matters of paramount importance.[4]

The important point to which I wish now to call attention is that the second case, where the object is a "social" object, necessitates a special link at the managerial level between the technological process and the disposal process. In the physical cases the technical production process can be completed, and then, quite independently, those responsible for sales can take over; the customer need have no relation at all to the technical production process, though of course there are cases of "custom" production where he supervises phases of it quite closely.

In the case of the social object, however, a *prior* relation to the recipient or beneficiary of the "service" is a prerequisite for undertaking the technical process at all. Teaching presupposes pupils in the school, and therefore settlement of the terms on which pupils go to school is a prerequisite for the teaching process. Similarly with the practice of medicine and law—there have to be patients or clients "on whom" to practice, and there has to be a basis on which they have "come to" the doctor or lawyer. In the case of administration, finally, the law or policy which has to be administered must designate the categories of persons or collectivities to which it applies, and only when this has been specified can the administrative agency even *begin* to administer.

Even within the category where the object of processing is a "social" object, a wide range of variation is found. At one extreme is the case where a rule simply forbids certain actions; then the administrative agency is involved only when the prohibition is violated; its only "customers" are offenders. At the other extreme is the case where the organization or agency, must establish a long-continuing and in some sense "intimate" relation which affects the most vital interests of the recipients of the organization's service. Education belongs in this category. There must be a long-standing relation between a pupil and a succession of teachers, and both the structure of the pupil's personality and his future position in the community depend heavily upon the process of education.

In this type of case it is common for the recipient of the service to be taken into an important kind of *membership* in the technical organization which provides the service. The school class is a social system with an important degree of integration between teacher and pupils. Teaching cannot be effective if the pupil is simply a "customer" to whom the "commodity" of education is "turned over" without any further relation to its purveyor than is required for settlement of the terms of transfer—as in the case of the typical commercial transaction. An even further stage of variation is given by the case of the boarding school or residential college where the main focus of the recipient's everyday living is brought within the organization. The same is true of hospitals, but of course for periods of different duration.

From one point of view, the *technical* neces-

[4] There is a third category, namely, where the technological problem concerns attainment of results in a cultural realm, the solution of scientific problems through research being a type case. The valued result is in this case neither a physical object or class of them, nor a state of social objects, i.e., of persons or collectivities, but an addition to the body of *knowledge,* which is a cultural object. This may, of course, impose very special exigencies upon the technical process. For simplicity's sake I shall ignore this third case in the discussion which follows.

sity of establishing a prior and special link between the organization and its recipients imposes an important set of constraints on the managerial system. It is not free to "bargain" with its "customers" in ways which might jeopardize the conditions essential for carrying out the technical functions of the organization. Circumstances such as these strengthen the position of the technical personnel vis-à-vis the managerial, because the former are in a position to insist upon the conditions they think essential for doing the job adequately if management, in turn, *wants* it done adequately.

Looked at from a slightly different point of view, the performance of "services" requires the *co-operation* of the recipient of the service. This co-operation cannot always be taken for granted; it has to be motivated. Witness, for example, the problem of truancy in schools, to say nothing of passive resistance to learning and the commonness with which patients leave hospitals contrary to medical advice. Since sheer coercion is not adequate, the service-performer must *offer* something to induce adequate co-operation, and the readiness to do this has to be included in the terms by which the co-operative relationship is set up in the first place. But the physical producer does not have to offer his raw materials anything.

This difference between the processes of physical production and various types of "service" has much to do with the fact that the *products* of physical technology in our society tend to be disposed of through the process of commercial marketing, while services—with many variations, of course—are much more frequently purveyed within different kinds of non-profit contexts.

These problems also have an important relation to the problems of "payment" for the products of organization function, and hence to the procurement side at the level of financing the operations. Again it is no accident that it is the business firm—an agency most frequently concerned with physical production—which is expected, in the long run, to finance its operations *wholly* from the sales of its products—in the long run, because borrowing for investment purposes is common and essential. Some services are provided on this same basis, but examples range from these cases to those where the service is provided to the recipients entirely without charge, and the organization must therefore be financed from other sources, notably private contributions or taxation.

One aspect of the "meaning" of the payment emerges from the above discussion: in the commercial case, all the "contribution" to the process of production has been made by the producing organization; the customer has typically "done nothing" to make the result possible. But in cases like education, the pupil and his parents have obviously done a great deal; without their co-operation, the result would not have been possible at all. Probably along with the problems of equality in access to benefits, this is the principal reason why "full payment" is not expected for many services. If payment is expected, it may well be a matter of "noblesse oblige," as in the case of medical patients at the upper end of the sliding scale paying considerably *more* than the service costs to provide. They are contributing to a worthwhile societal function in proportion to their financial capacity to do so.

The Managerial Contribution to Social Function

If there is a meaningful set of interchanges between the output of "technical product" and what is in some sense "compensation" for that output—on the model of the sale of the commodity and full payment for it—we may now ask whether this account of things is adequate to account for the importance of the *managerial* level of organizations in its relation to the lateral aspect of its external situation. Is the managerial organization, then, nothing more than a "facilitator" of the process of technological production?

I am conceiving the problem in direct relation to its formulation for purposes of economic theory. It has seemed possible on the levels already dealt with to relate the prototypical economic case to others in a fairly specific way, and I should like to attempt this for the managerial level. Here the point of reference is the "double interchange" which has served as a central paradigm for treating problems of equilibrium in the economy and hence in its suborganizations.

One of these two interchanges is the one just reviewed, the output of commodities or goods in exchange for money payment. In the case of the business firm, this payment is expected—in the long run—to cover the whole cost of production. But in the economic paradigm there is a second interchange, that of the wage output of the firm for labor input from outside. In part this duality is necessitated by the division of labor and is facilitated by the monetary mechanism. The typical customer of a firm is not also an employee.

But there is not merely a difference of agency; there is also a difference of level. We might say that the firm "pumps" purchasing power into the market system. This is not an instrumentality of consumers "want-satisfaction" but of *control* in the allocation of resources within the community. In return, the firm receives a share of an essential societal resource—what in technical terms I have called the "performance capacity" of the community. Some economists have called it "labor power." This performance capacity represents the human agent's commitment—within the limits of his competence and skill—to co-operate in the productive process. By treating performance capacity as an input to the firm, we mean that *this* firm has been allocated this share of commitment through the contract of employment.

The next question is whether the firm's output of purchasing power in the form of wage payments is more than an instrumentality for securing an indispensable facility for its operations. Of course it *is* such a facility, but it is also more. It is a contribution to the total pool of purchasing power in the community. The firm "makes money" in a double sense; it is the recipient of the proceeds of sales, but it also contributes to the flow of commodities and to the community's purchasing power. This is the main mechanism for the *generalization* of facilities, for increasing the community's level of economic effectiveness. This has been a commonplace to economists since Keynes.

In the system as a whole there must, of course, be a balance between the flow in marketing commodities and the output of purchasing power; imbalance in one direction results in deflation; in the other, inflation. But the main point here is that the output of purchasing power is not merely an "instrumentality" for purchasing labor; it is an essential part of the functional *contribution* of the firm, and of course the same is true on the consumers' side. The famous oversaving is the counterpart of undue hesitancy about production commitments.

The output of commodities is primarily the work of the technical subsystem of the organization—of the plant. But the output of purchasing power is the work of the managerial organization. Hence this distinction of "levels" in the structure of organizations corresponds to the differentiation between the two interchange processes which have figured so prominently in economic theory.

This set of relationships is not peculiar to organizational contexts where the primary technical output is commodities. In many respects education is the antithesis of the commodity case. Here the technical output is the change in the character, knowledge, and skill levels of *individual* pupils. But the school *system* may be treated as responsible for another category of output: its contribution to the general level of performance capacity in the community. Just as "wealth" is not a simple aggregate of physical commodities but one which includes the specifically *economic* element of generalized disposability through the mechanisms of purchasing power, so the capacity of a community to get valued things done is not, so far as it depends on the performances of individuals, simply an aggregate of the individual qualities of its members; it includes a factor of allocation relative to need and generalized disposability—through the "labor market." Through such decisions as what to teach to what categories of pupils, the school system decisively influences this pool of usefully disposable performance capacity in the community; it adapts the technical education process to the conditions of the community, how effectively is, of course, an empirical question in the individual case. These decisions are the result of "ideas" and "plans" on the part of school authorities and of the "demand" for trained performance capacities in the community—not, of course, only an an economic sense of demand.

The "input" at this higher level from the community may be said to consist in the community's *support* for education as a function, in its commitments to the maintenance or improvement of the capacity-level of its population. Here, in a sense parallel to the economic case, the effectiveness of a particular individual's education is a function not only of what he has acquired in the process but also of the educational *level* of the community as a whole. Hence various units in the community, but particularly families and interest groups oriented to educational goals, are concerned with this *level*. What I am speaking of here is a set of relationships focused not on the community as a whole, but rather on those members who are direct "clients" of the educational system. But this is one of the essential foci of responsibility for the managerial subsystem in education. This should be distinguished from the superordinate (e.g., "political") support of education to be discussed later.

A few words about the parallel in the political field may extend the picture a little. Here the technical process is the administrative implementation of "decisions" reached at higher levels. "Compliance" or the necessary "cooperation" is perhaps the relevant input category. This compliance must, however, be "motivated" by some sort of "demands" in the community that the measures in question be carried out; if this is in deficit, the administrative process runs into all sorts of difficulties (such as, shall we say, tax evasion) which coercive powers alone are often not adequate to cope with. But there is also a higher-level output of political systems which may be called the assumption of leadership responsibility. This is the system's contribution to the community's general level of political effectiveness; this involves more than satisfying particular interests and demands for decisions.

For this generalized contribution to take place, there must be a counter-input to the political organization from outside. The primary mechanism seems to be that the citizen, especially through his vote but in other ways also, contributes to the *generalized support* without which effective leadership in the political system would be impossible. In a democratic system this operates above all through the mechanism of parties. Only a party supported by a majority of the electorate can take the leadership responsibility required for making important decisions and can implement them over a wide enough range. The support on which a party depends cannot be specific to a particular issue or interest, except in a limiting case. But without both generalized support (at least at the party level) and the assumption of leadership responsibility, the political system's capacity for effective action in the public interest is impaired.

The Procurement of Personnel

In discussing the functions of the "managerial" level of organization in mediating the organization's relations to the external social situation, I have concentrated on the "disposal" function. Its monetary aspects have necessitated some discussion of the "procurement" functions because of the relation between them. There is, however, one part of the procurement function which requires special discussion because it is so fundamental to all types of modern organization: namely, the procurement of personnel. It is fundamental to modern society that a large range of its functions are performed in *occupational* roles by persons who have no ascriptive or associational connection with the organization but are *employed* by it through a formal or informal contract of employment.

From one point of view, the contract of employment is a special case of the settlement of terms for the selling of a service. Its distinctive feature is that the service is performed in the context of organization, and the "customer" is the organization in a managerial capacity. Of course, the kind of contract and the expectations of the occupational role will vary enormously as a function both of the kind of organization and of the type of role within it. There is thus the closest sort of link between the procurement of personnel and both the technical functions and the internal organization of the employing unit. Very broadly indeed, it may be useful to distinguish three basic types of role, and hence of personnel: "operative" at the technical levels; "administrative" or "executive," having special responsibilities for the functioning of the organization at the managerial level; and "professional," characterized by some special competence which roots in a generalized cultural tradition focused outside the organization as such. These are "ideal types," and there are plenty of mixtures among them.

Economists have long discussed the standard of "marginal productivity" for determining the rewards available to an employee of an organization. Similarly, most economists tend to assume that the "reward-value" of a job will be exhausted in monetary terms.[5] This reference is to an equivalence between the economic value to the firm of an employee's contribution to its functioning and the value to the employee—which really means to this household—of the goods and services which can be purchased with his money wage. This also tends to go with a form of "contract" according to which the relation is terminable at will on both sides, with no "justification" needed for discharge or "laying off" other than that it does not seem profitable for the firm to continue the employment. Of course this actually is not the typical pattern for employment at operative levels by business firms, but it is more closely approximated there than elsewhere. Variations from this pattern may be looked at under three headings: first, the pattern of monetary reward itself—whether it focuses on what the service is "worth" in monetary terms; second, the balance between monetary and non-monetary components in the reward; and, third, the terms for continuance or termination of the relation.

The closest approach to this marginal-productivity, terminable-at-will patterns seems to be the operative technical role in the business firm, namely, the ordinary industrial worker or clerical employee. This seems in turn to be closely related to the fact that such firms to such a large extent produce commodities. This circumstance minimizes the non-economic element in the firm's relation with its customers and eliminates overlap between the customer role and the employee role. This relatively unobstructed orientation to the market facilitates internal cost accounting and exerts a pressure toward maximizing the use of cost critera in contracting for the factors of production (in terms of what he is *worth* to us, not of what we can afford). Accordingly, the terminability of the contract at will protects management's freedom to rationalize its employment procedures from a cost accounting point of view.

This pattern has been both an ideological ideal for the businessman and a highly convenient reference point for the economist; if this pattern were tenable, it would greatly simplify the economist's problems. But it has in fact been greatly modified, most conspicuously by the development of trade unions. The union seems to modify the situation in two directions. First, and most obviously, it greatly restricts the employer's freedom to hire and fire. Unions in general do not impose formal rules of tenure; "layoffs" are permissible for purely economic reasons, e.g., when the company, for market reasons, "needs" to cut down its scale of operations. But these cuts must be made according to well-formulated rules, not simply at the employer's discretion. Furthermore, the closed shop ideal of unionism would restrict hiring to members of the union or would at least require union membership of all who accept employment. The second main focus of the union's effect is to compress the spread of wage rates among its members, so that in unionized industries there is a greater concentration near the average.

The union seems to root in two circumstances that are predominantly non-economic in significance. The first of these is the power discrepancy between the employing organization and the individual employee, particularly when so much is at stake for the employee both as an individual and as the representative of his family. Here the union has not only acted on its own but has also been supplemented by the government in assuring workers a measure of "social security." The second context is the associational solidarity of union members, to some degree constituting a company of equals banded together for mutual benefit and protection. There is some inhibition on their differing too much from each other in individual performance or interest because of the impact this differentiation would have on the structure of the union. Of course, patterns such as strong emphasis on seniority also enter into union practice.

But the farther the function on an organization moves away from the production of commodities for a market, the more the pattern of employment and remuneration of "operatives" tends to move away from the "marginal productivity" standard. The largest-scale example of a very different type is provided by the civilian operative employees of governmental agencies. Here two patterns are particularly conspicuous, namely, the seniority principle and the institutionalization of tenure. More

[5] Alfred Marshall was an exception to this tendency, since he insisted on the importance of "activities" valued "for their own sake." See *Economy and Society*.

generally, there is regulation by a complicated civil service code. Within the limits of effectiveness, it may be said that one main emphasis is on security. Negatively, this seems to be associated with the virtual impossibility of effective cost accounting, since the value of the service provided by the agency is generally not measurable in money terms. Futhermore, the code protects a group in a weak power position from arbitrary action by administrative superiors and from "political" intervention. Positively, however, in a field where achievement cannot usually be very high, the code seems to be related to the need for enlisting loyalty to the employing organization by emphasizing the sense of "belongingness." In general, a direct appeal to "self-interest" does not accord well with the "public service" orientation of government.

It is of great importance that government stands in competition with private employment for personnel. There is, however, a persistent lag between the salary levels for civil servants and of those for comparable jobs in the business world. This may mean that there are non-financial components of the reward pattern in government which are not present in business in the same degree. Security is probably one of them, but the sense of contributing directly to the public welfare may well be more important than much of our current ideology would allow.

Among different types of organizations we find a wide range of policy about administrative personnel, especially in regard to remuneration and tenure. However, we can identify the practice in two main types of organizations. At one end of the range is the American business executive. Here the pattern is to emphasize very high financial rewards but to minimize anything like tenure. The executive assumes his responsibilities at his own risk, as it were. He is highly rewarded if he is regarded as successful, but he is subject to being cashiered if he fails to satisfy his organizational superiors. The other type is found in most non-profit organizational contexts, including government.[6] Here the pattern is one of very moderate financial reward, much less than in business and comparable to many professional levels. On the other hand, such positions generally contain elements of security which the business executive does not enjoy. This security is either explicitly recognized by the organization itself, or—as in the case of "policy" level political appointees—is provided by the cushion of the party's indebtedness to them, if not through tangible recognition of this indebtedness.

These two types of practice for administrative personnel—for the business executive and for the government executive—may be considered alternative reactions to the assumption of *responsibility* in the sense discussed above and to the meaning of its assumption for those agencies on whose "behalf" it is done. The relevant agencies are usually not "customers" but the superordinate organization on the institutional level; i.e., a business executive is "responsible" in the most direct sense to his board.

In the case of the managerial executive of a business firm, I think that his high salary-bonus remuneration is not to be interpreted mainly in terms of the marginal productivity of his services, as many economists would argue, and much business ideology too. Nor is it primarily entrepreneurial profit, e.g., in Schumpeter's sense. It is rather the "wages of responsibility," the symbolic recognition of the importance of executive responsibilities. Since the success of the firm tends to be measured in terms of its "profits," it is *symbolically* appropriate for managerial responsibility to be remunerated in terms cognate with the measure of the firm's success. This is not, in the sense that economists have used this concept with reference to entrepreneurial profit, primarily a reward for "risk-taking," since it is fundamental to the structure of modern business that the typical executive does *not* risk his personal property. He takes responsibility in situations where other people risk their property, which is a very different thing.[7]

The executive in a non-profit organization, on the other hand, receives a different order of

[6] Elective office is, however, too special a case to be considered here; it is not technically "employment."

[7] The aspect of executive remuneration I have just discussed cannot be the result of a sheer assertion of "power" on his part. There is a power factor in this as in all other cases of renumeration, but there is an institutionalized factor as well. Business executives as a group are far less organized than either operative employees or professional people; they are clearly neglecting an opportunity to assert their power.

financial remuneration in the first instance because profit is not the primary measure of the success of his organization, be it governmental or private. On the contrary, money to finance the organization's operations has to be "raised" in whole or in part. Hence it becomes a question of what remuneration, usually a salary, is "fair" in terms both of the resources of the organization and of the interests of the individual. (There interests include an adequate standard of living and status-dignity.) In this case there are other components of reward than the financial; recognition of service is in some sense a very important component. The nonprofit executive is also likely to have some form of tenure.

In the society as a whole there is a delicate balance between these high-remuneration and low-renumeration sectors of the administrative class. I think it likely that in recent times the balance has tipped unduly in favor of the business group and that a readjustment is likely to come, indeed is already in process.

In the case of professional services, a convenient point of reference is the sliding scale which typically operates in the situation of individual fee-for-service practice. Here the practitioner can cover his total expenses and make a good living from professional fees. But his patients or clients pay by "capacity," not by the value of the service as if it were a commodity. I have noted above that professional service very generally (not, for example, for engineering) involves establishing a cooperative solidarity between performer and recipient. From this point of view, the fee is a "contribution" to the *joint* performance of the valued function.

When professional services are performed in the context of organization, the sliding scale principle does not disappear, but it is typically moved up either one or two organizational levels in the focus of its application. This is to say that recipients pay the *organization*, not the practitioner, on a sliding-scale principle. Thus in the case of college or university, though there are standard tuition fees, "needy" students are given scholarships, and well-to-do alumni are expected to contribute to the college in some sort of proportion to their resources. Or, where support is by taxation, a still "higher" organizational level is involved, in which case the assessments to support the organization are made on a "progressive" principle. But in this instance the service is a public responsibility independent of whether the individual taxpayer is or has been a recipient of the particular service.

The professional practitioner in an organization, however, typically works on salary. Salary levels, then, are typically those prevailing in non-profit organizations and are usually below executive salaries, but not too much. Special problems are raised by professional personnel employed in business firms; there clearly is a tendency to lift their remuneration levels up toward those of executives in the same organization. But with the exception of this and of certain elite private-practice groups, the level of remuneration for the professional practitioner is similar to that for the non-business category. Again, this suggests the importance of a non-financial component in the rewards of professional workers.[8]

Along with government employees, professional workers in organizations—notably teachers—provide the type case of the institution of tenure. I interpret this, above all, as a mechanism for protecting these workers from pressures by the administrative authority to which they are necessarily subject. This gives them some assurance of professional independence and integrity.

The marginal productivity model of economic theory and the "liberal" idea of a contract of employment governed by simple mutual advantage of the moment ("freedom of contract" in one version) thus provide a convenient reference point. But this model is more nearly descriptive of an industrial than, say, of a feudal society. However, this pattern of employment is only approximated even for the operative employees in a business firm; as we go to other types of organization and to other types of occupational role that cut across organization types, we find increasing deviation from this pattern. It is a *limiting* type of contract of employment, not a model type for the general occupational structure, even within an industrial society.

[8] Some component of this kind must provide part of the explanation for the well-known findings of the North-Hatt study that professional occupations tend to outrank business in prestige in the community, with physicians ranked in the highest regular category of all. It also has something to do with the pressure by many marginal groups to secure recognition as "professionals."

Disposal and Procurement at the Institutional Level

To complete this review of the principal set of factors that account for differences between types of formal organizations, we need to examine further what happens at the "institutional" level. So far, I have dealt with this level mainly in its relation to the managerial level—particularly, I have noted how the institution or community provides legitimation and support to management and why management cannot secure this support through its relation with the recipients of its product—whether commodity or service—or through its relation with its resources of procurement. It should be clear that the importance of these legitimation and support functions mounts rapidly as we move from the case of the "pure" commodity to those categories of service which require a strategic, long-term relation of solidarity between performer and recipient.

It should also be clear that where financial resources must be "raised" in order to finance the function of the organization, the responsibility for this generally rests either at the institutional level or, as in the case of many tax-supported functions, at a still higher level in the organizational scale. In this respect, the administrative head of a non-profit organization (like a university) often has a key role in money-raising. However, a university president, like an industrial foreman or a non-commissioned officer in the military, occupies an interstitial position between two organizational system-levels. He is *both* the top executive of the managerial subsystem of the university *and* a member and representative of the trustees. In his role as money-raiser, he acts predominantly on behalf of the trustees, not as manager of the university.[9]

An institutional system, however, has not only vertical relations to the managerial subsystem for which it takes some order of responsibility but also lateral relations. It has a "product" to "sell," and it has procurement problems. Of course it also must be integrated with still higher levels of organization, of which just a word presently.

What order of "product" can an institutional organization be conceived to "sell" which is not already covered in the previous discussion? The answer lies in the proper use of the concept of function at different levels in the structure of society as a system. The economist's typical commodity is a contribution to the functional needs of the consuming unit, which is typically though by no means exclusively the household. The same is true of the types of service which have been reviewed above. For example, education, especially elementary, and medical practice are, at the *technical* levels, services to the family household. This is why there is a "parent-teachers' association" but no teacher-prospective employers' association of comparable significance, and why the doctor who is treating an adult male will often deal directly with the patient's wife but seldom, if ever, with his employer.

At the managerial level, I have argued that there is also a function, namely, contribution to the *generalized* capacity of the society to perform that category of function. For example, the economic process produces both commodities and wealth; the educational process, both character, knowledge, and skills of individuals, and generalized performance capacity at the societal level. However, the production, even of the generalized capacity to perform the relevant function effectively, does not settle the *position* of that function in the society, does not in itself determine the "public's" evaluation of it, nor the proportions of resources which are to be devoted to it in comparison with and hence in competition with other functions. It is in this sphere that the outputs or products of institutional organizations are to be found.

A striking example is the business corporation's policy on what proportion of income will be distributed in dividends and what proportion will be "ploughed back" into the company. This is a decision between two alternative uses of financial resources, consumption[10] or economic investment. In the classical theory of the corporation this was a decision made by the *owners* of the property rights in

[9] Similarly, it is significant that most universities have a treasurer or chairman of the finance committee who clearly acts as a member of the governing board, and this office is clearly distinguished from that of the bursar or comptroller, who is an *administrative* officer at the managerial level.

[10] Consumption refers to any use of funds *other* than investment. Of course, the stockholders are free to invest their dividends in other lines of production, too.

the business, but this position has become radically unrealistic. The decision has tended to become the responsibility of a *fiduciary* board who, to a degree, represent owners, but not simply in the sense of the owners' financial "self-interest." (Similarly, the *institution* of property itself is not, as one ideological version would have it, a simple matter of protecting the right of an individual to "do what he will with his own.") Insofar as individual owners have ceased to be primary,[11] these decisions have tended, in the "private" sector, to be shared between banks (and other fiduciary financial organizations) and producing corporations. But in the latter case it is above all at the board level that such decisions focus: they are not, in the sense of this paper, "managerial" prerogatives.

Cognate things can be said in the case of education. The teacher's role is primarily to educate in the *technical* sense. That of the school administration, i.e., the superintendent's office and the principal's, typically is to *organize* the educational process in the community, to make it, within the framework of community commitments to education, as effective as possible and thereby to contribute to the level of performance-capacity in the community. But the superintendent is not the focus for determining the community's commitments to education in relation to other competing demands on its total resources. In community terms this is a "political" problem. In organizational terms this problem focuses on the school board; in the case of the university, the trustees. In this context it is essential that the membership of such bodies should not consist predominantly of "professionals," meaning persons with a full occupational commitment to education, since their role is to *mediate* between the "professionals" and the more diffuse community. To constitute such boards principally of "professionals" would be to make the profession judge in its own case, a privilege which a pluralistic society obviously cannot grant as a general rule.

From this point of view, then, the primary "disposal" function of the institutional organization is to contribute to the *integration* of the higher-order system within which the function at the managerial level is placed. Its role is to mediate between the claims of this function on community resources and legitimation, and the exigencies of effective performance of the function on the "lower" levels. Of course, just as the university president is generally involved in financial responsibilities, so is the school superintendent involved in "politics," because he also occupies an interstitial status.

On the procurement side, something has been said of the financial responsibilities of institutional organizations. The salience of this responsibility is a function of the failure of "automatic" market mechanisms to provide for the problem through generating adequate proceeds. But even the business corporation is not, as I just tried to show, a case of full "automatization" because decisions have to be made about the allocation of proceeds—presuming the firm is "in the black"—between further investment and consumption, and the investment decisions of the board hence are—in our sense—procurement decision at the institutional level. On the other hand, where the financial question becomes too difficult, there is a tendency to shunt it to the next higher level of organization, as in the case of financing public education through taxation (but, it should be clearly noted, so far mainly through *local* taxation). In the middle is the case, typical of private non-profit organizations, where the proceeds, if any, are clearly inadequate to finance the essential services, and hence the responsibility for meeting the deficit rests squarely at the board or trustee level. The function here is essentially that of persuading those who control financial resources in the community that what the organization is doing is important enough to merit their financial support (this includes the self-persuasion of wealthy trustees). The number of dunning letters in the mail of persons who by no current standard could be considered wealthy is an index of the great importance of this factor in American society. There is almost as intensive a competition for the citizen's contributory dollar as there is, through advertising and other aspects of salesmanship, for this consumer's dollar.

The prominence of the financial aspect of the procurement responsibilities of institutional organizations is in the first instance a result of the fact that money is the generalized facility par excellence. It is also particularly prominent in a society so heavily oriented to economic values and functions (properly un-

[11] They have usually represented *kinship* property interests.

derstood) as the American is. But it is by no means the only relevant input at the institutional level. Perhaps second in importance in most cases is the factor of power, in a technical political sense which cannot be fully explained here. The essential point is the "subsumption" of organization goals under the more generalized goal-structure of the still higher-level social structure and therefore the explicit or implicit "authorization" to embark on the organizational activities in question and to "take them seriously" to the degree to which that is done. A very important aspect of what is sometimes called the struggle for power in a society consists in this competition for support and authorization among the many different organized interests of the society.

"Organized" here, as so often, has a double reference. One is to the organizations which have interests in their power position in the larger society. The other is to the ways and extent to which units with common interest in this sense have organized to promote their interests. I suggest two primary points about this situation. First, the unit of the *organization* of "interest groups" in the political sense is not the managerial system but the institutional system. The "board" must have the primary concern for the position of the *category* of organization for which it is responsible within the power system of the community as a whole. Second, the category of interest group is on quite a different level from that of economic interests; to identify them is the "Marxian fallacy." The Catholic church is an interest group par excellence, as is the National Association of Manufacturers. The point is that there is a problem of allocating power to *all* significant organized units in the society, *whatever* their primary functional significance. The assertion and mediation of the claims of this interest necessarily focus at what I have called the institutional level.

What I have said about wealth and power applies equally to other societal resources. To give only one more illustration, what above I have called performance capacity is a resource which has to be allocated among different fundamental functions in the society. Given a high level of differentiation, perhaps one of the worst tendencies of organizational practice is for trustees or boards to attempt to control specific appointments in the organizations under their trusteeship. This function rests between the managerial and the technical aspects of organization. But trustees *must* be concerned with the question of how far and under what conditions their organization (and, at the next level up, their type of organization) has access to the type and quality of performance capacity which is essential for the proper functioning of the organization. To take a current example, the concern of university trustees with faculty salaries is not a simple "financial" problem. Discrepancy between salary levels in the academic profession and those in other occupations in competition with it—and the same goes for teachers—can be a serious threat to access to the essential capacities without which the fiduciary responsibilities in question cannot be discharged. It is therefore important to distinguish two levels of the financial responsibilities of institutional organizations. The first of these is the responsibility for adequate financial resources to perform the function of the organization. The second is the policy about the kind and amount of performance capacity which, in the societal interest, *should* be made available for this function and hence the price, financially speaking, which *should* be paid for this performance capacity. For instance, thinking of university trustees only as "businessmen" interested in driving the best bargain they can in the labor market ignores the importance of the second financial responsibility. They cannot escape a responsibility for the *level* of faculty salaries as well as for the conservation of the university's necessarily limited funds.

It is directly in the logic of our whole analysis that the institutional organization, as well as the managerial and the technical, will necessarily have connections and interchanges "upward" as well as laterally and "downward." These "upward" connections fall above all in the area of legitimation and support. One context in which these problems have repeatedly come into the discussion here is where the function is treated as a "public" or political responsibility, most conspicuously, where the organization responsible is made an integral part of governmental structure itself. Here not only the responsibility but also conversely, the claim to legitimation and support is sharply focused for the collectively organized segment of the society—i.e., from local to national levels of government. So long as the responsibility is accepted as a *public* responsibility, there is an obligation on government to "do justice" to the exigencies of discharging it effectively. From this case, there is a shading-off to the ideal type of the purely laissez faire sectors of economic organization, where public responsibility is confined to protecting the freedom to produce for the market and reap the rewards, setting up the necessary regulatory system of legal rules, etc. This is clearly a limiting case and is really only approximated. But even here it is essential to note that this is a mode of organizing and institutionalizing societal responsibility for effective economic production. This case does not reflect the absence of any such responsibility. Else why should a President of the United States continually emphasize the duty of the government he heads to facilitate the functioning of a private enterprise economy? The clear implication is that the welfare of the society, not just of individual business men or firms, is thought to be dependent on this system.

The Variability of Organizational Types

Co-ordinate with the heavy emphasis on the unbroken continuity of "line" authority which I noted at the beginning of this chapter, there has been a tendency to think of "bureaucracy" as a kind of monolithic entity which can vary in degree of development but not significantly in type. A major purpose of the present discussion has been to question this assumption and to help lay the basis for a more sophisticated analysis of the variation we find in types of formal organizations and in the factors on which these variations depend. All the essential considerations I have in mind—at the present stage of development in my knowledge of the field—have already been brought up. However, it may be useful to try to pull some of these together in summary fashion.

Perhaps the appropriate type of organization will be determined by the type of function the organization performs in the system of which it is a part. But though true, this formula by itself is wholly inadequate, for it fails to discriminate the various levels of differentiation from subsystem to subsystem which inevitably exist in a complex society. What is by a conventional designation, like "economic" or "educational," the "same" function does not lead to the same type of organization at all levels. This is obvious—no one would seriously suggest that the United States Office of Education can be treated as if it were a classroom, though both this office and a classroom have educational functions—but the point is often overlooked. My distinction between technical, managerial, and institutional levels of formal organization has been designed to help make discriminations of this order in a useful fashion. I have argued that there are important uniformities which are primarily a function of the *level* at which the organization or suborganization operates but which are independent of the functional *content* of the organization at any level. In general, the theory of bureaucracy has concentrated at the managerial level and has emphasized the uniformities most appropriate to it, across the board.

Another equally important and independent set of considerations, however, are those which differentiate organizations according to their functional type. In a sense, the most obvious of these concern the technical functions themselves and the exigencies to which they are subject. But these considerations are so various that there is a great temptation to jump to the managerial level and talk as if the imperatives of good organization—whatever the function in technical terms—are always the same. I hope I have adequately indicated that this is not true; a good organization for the physical production of goods at the technical level would inevitably be a bad one for the educational process.

I have then attempted to show that organizations at all these levels are subject not only to technical exigencies but to those of disposal and procurement at each level and that these exigencies—even at the same level—are sources of profoundly significant differences in organizational type. Thus I think it safe to say that no organization dependent on highly trained professional personnel can employ them typically on the basis of a marginal productivity, terminable-at-will contract of employment. Or, on the other side, the organization which produces commodities for a market must be very different in structure from the residential college which takes its "customers" into a special type of membership status.

Next, I have emphasized the relative independence of the three level-types of organization, an independence that constitutes my main objection to the continous line-authority picture of formal organization. This relative independence means that there is, at each linkage point, a range of possible *different* types of articulation. Thus the professional personnel of military organizations are much more rigidly subjected to line authority than are those with the same professional qualifications in, let us say, the professional faculty of a university. There are limits to how far the military can press its professional personnel into the line pattern, but it does not follow that the university pattern is the only possible one. Similar considerations hold at the articulation point between managerial and institutional systems. An important special case of this problem is the very top of the three-stage hierarchy with which I have been working, namely, the articulation of the institutional system with the still wider society.

This is not the place to attempt a classification of types of formal organizations. If such were to be attempted, however, it would be necessary to build into it many of the distinctions that I have reviewed and illustrated here. Even within the same society—to say nothing about a comparative perspective—the range would be wide and the significantly different types numerous. Only along such a path as this, however, can even the structural aspect of a theory of organization reach a modicum of scientific maturity. And a sophisticated understanding of the range of structural variation is essential to any high-level attempt at analyzing the dynamic processes that take place within organizations.

I do not mean this last note to be one of discouragement. Much fine work has been done in this field. But its range has been rather severely limited. There are many insights which social scientists have developed in this field which can be highly useful to the practical administrator here and now. But the field is one of immense complexity at the scientific level and is only at the beginning of its scientific development. An immense amount of work will be required before we can have anything that deserves to be called a theory of formal organization. We have, however, made some very important beginnings. For administrators, the great importance of social science theory lies in the future, when these beginnings will have grown into a mature science.

The Analysis of Social Flow Systems [1]

P. G. Herbst

The introduction of changes in any component part of a social system generally results in complex changes and adjustments in other parts of the system. As a result it may happen that modifications introduced in a social organization with the aim of improving its functioning may ultimately result in the creation of new symptoms of malfunctioning or even in the reduction in its efficiency of functioning to a lower level. The apparently unpredictable effects of modifications which may be carried out in a social system would appear to represent one of the main obstacles in the way of providing a sound theory of social behaviour which could be used as a reliable guide in problems of diagnosis and social action.

The problem with which the present paper will be concerned is the determination of interdependence effects arising in the process of change in the location of individuals within a given social system. Provided that the system can be clearly differentiated into sub-units, the location of individuals is uniquely determined, and precise measurement of changes in location becomes possible. Phenomena of this type, such as the intake and loss of members by a social organization and the transfer of individuals within the organization, can be represented quite generally as processes within a flow system.

A *flow system* is defined as two or more bounded units each containing a set of elements which may enter or leave a unit without being modified in the process, in the sense that each element retains its identity. The units are connected, so that transfer of elements between units is possible either directly or via one or more intervening units. It will be assumed to begin with that all elements are of the same class, and independent. A flow system is said to be *closed* if its boundary is impermeable so that no elements can enter or leave the system. Flow will in this case be limited to the transfer of elements between units. The system is said to be *open* if, in addition to internal transfers, flow both into and out of the system may occur.

The units with which we are here concerned are social regions, so that flow or transfer will have the character of social locomotion. Intake and loss of members may be regarded as a universal property of social systems. Examples of phenomena of this type to which a flow model can be applied are

(a) Population movement between countries.

(b) Mobility within the hierarchy of a social organization.

(c) Locomotion of students through an educational institution.

(d) Transfer of workers between departments of a factory, and movement of workers between factories.

A considerable amount of empirical work has been carried out on the subject of population movement which has not however generally been brought into a form suitable for system analysis. In the study of labour turnover, on the other hand, a number of theoretically orientated studies have recently been carried out by Rice, Hill, and Trist (3, 4) which show that the rate of leaving by an entrant group into an institution can be described by a hyperbolic curve, and that differential leaving rates of entrants into a factory department from outside or inside the factory respectively can be used to determine the relative degree of independence of each department.

Similar types of phenomena have been studied in biology where a model of material transport between an organism and its environment, and the transformation of material within the organism has been developed by Bertalanffy (1) which demonstrates that open systems exist which are able to maintain a

---

From *Human Relations,* Vol. 7, 1954, pp. 327–336. Reprinted by permission of the publisher.

[1] The author wishes to acknowledge a number of valuable suggestions made by A. R. Jonckheere in the course of a discussion of the manuscript.

steady state in a variable environment. In economics, flow problems have been studied by means of an input-output model developed by Leontief (2) which deals with the cost and the distribution of goods between factories, and between factories and consumers.

I. Flow in a Closed System

In order to simplify the presentation, assume that we have three units between which transfer of individuals may occur (see Fig. 1). The units may be thought of as the departments of a factory, and the transfer as that of workers from one department to another. Let X_1 be the number of persons who leave unit 1 during a given period of time; of these a certain number x_{12} will go from unit 1 to unit 2, and x_{13} will go from unit 1 to unit 3.

Since the total outflow from each unit must equal the sum of component outflows from there to all the other units, it follows that the set of equations below must hold.

$$\left.\begin{aligned} -X_1 + x_{12} + x_{13} &= 0 \\ x_{21} - X_2 + x_{23} &= 0 \\ x_{31} + x_{32} - X_3 &= 0 \end{aligned}\right\} \quad (1)$$

Flow volumes for each unit will clearly be interrelated. If for instance the volume of flow x_{12} from unit 1 to unit 2 is increased, then in order to satisfy equality conditions either the total outflow from that unit must be increased or the value of x_{13} decreased. We may gain somewhat more information about the system by asking how many flow values can be freely varied and how many are dependent values. Since we have three equations, it follows that three flow rates will be dependent values. In other words, if six out of the nine flow rates are fixed, then the other three can be calculated and are therefore no longer free to vary.

The system so far is one in which no restraint exists on the size of units. This however is not generally the case. Social organizations which have a work function seek to maintain the size at an optimum level determined both by their social and technological structure and the characteristics of the environment within which they function. A different type of restraint operates in the case of ideological groups which may attempt to maximize their size, resulting in a situation which will be

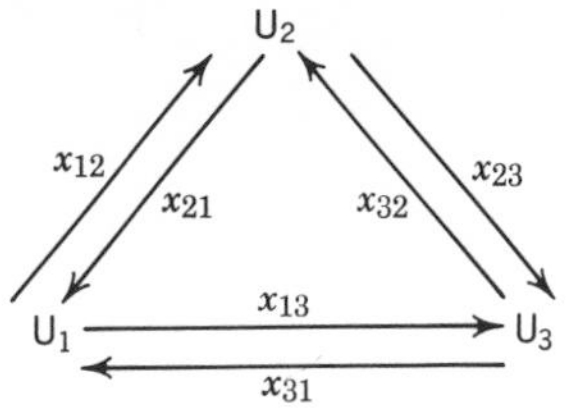

Fig. 1. A closed flow system consisting of three units, U_1, U_2 and U_3. The rate of flow from unit 1 to unit 2 is represented by x_{12}.

competitive to the extent that the system is closed since gain by one group is possible only through loss by another group.

We shall in the following pages consider the characteristics of a system which maintains the size of its units constant during a given period. The control of unit size may be either internal or external to the unit. A club or society may fix its membership to a certain number by means of a standing rule arrived at by vote of members. The size of departments in a factory, on the other hand, is generally determined by means of a control system which is external to the department concerned.

Closed Systems with Steady State of Units. A steady state of units implies that for each unit the total inflow must equal the total outflow. The set of equations will be identical with those of Equation 1 except that in the present case both rows and columns will add up to zero.

$$\left.\begin{aligned} -X_1 + x_{12} + x_{13} &= 0 \\ x_{21} - X_2 + x_{23} &= 0 \\ x_{31} + x_{32} - X_3 &= 0 \end{aligned}\right\} \quad (2)$$
$$=0 \quad =0 \quad =0$$

The system at this stage is said to possess four *degrees of freedom*, the values of not more than four variables being required for the state of the system to be completely determined, since the remaining five variables will have dependent values which can be calculated.

Suppose that for a given period of time the total outflows X_1, X_2 and X_3 from each unit are kept constant, then only one degree of freedom is left to the system. If we now fix the rate of flow for, say, x_{12} from unit 1 to unit 2, then the inter-unit flow rates between all other units of the system must each adjust to that

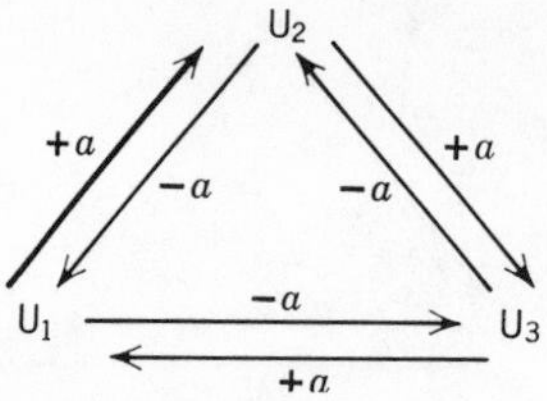

Fig. 2. An impressed increase in the rate of flow from unit 1 to unit 2 (shown by a heavy line) leads to changes in the rates of flow along other flow lines (shown by a light line) as a result of equilibrium conditions for the system.

value in order to satisfy the given equilibrium conditions.

We are therefore in a position to calculate the effect which a change along any flow line will have on the rest of the system. Let us for instance increase the rate of flow from unit 1 to unit 2 to the value $x_{12} + a$. Substituting in the above equation and equating both rows and columns to zero the resulting state of the system is found to be

$$\begin{array}{ccccccc} -X_1 & + & (x_{12}+a) & + & (x_{13}-a) & = & 0 \\ (x_{21}-a) & - & X_2 & + & (x_{23}+a) & = & 0 \\ (x_{31}+a) & + & (x_{32}-a) & - & X_3 & = & 0 \\ \hline =0 & & =0 & & =0 & & \end{array}$$

It will be seen that the rate of flow along all other flow lines has been changed. What has happened to the system is shown more clearly in Figure 2.

It is found that initiating an increased rate of flow from unit 1 to unit 2, creates a similar increase in the rate of flow from unit 2 to unit 3 and back to unit 1. At the same time a compensating decrease in flow is set up in the opposite direction. The *rate of turnover* of a unit of constant size may be measured by the sum of inflows plus outflows. It may be noted that changes which have occurred in the system may also be described by stating that the system has adjusted itself in such a way as to keep the rate of turnover of its units unchanged.

II. Flow in Open Systems

We shall in the following pages consider the most general type of open system, where entry into or exit from the system may occur through any of its units (see Fig. 3). The total outflow from each unit will in this case be equal to the sum of component outflows both to other units and to the environment. In addition we have an inflow E from the environment into the system which will be equal to the sum of component inflows to each unit. The rate of flow from the environment into, say, unit 1 will be represented by x_{E1} and similarly the flow from unit 1 to the environment will be represented by x_{1E}.

The following set of equations must hold for the open flow system consisting of three units.

$$\left.\begin{array}{r} -X_1 + x_{12} + x_{13} + x_{1E} = 0 \\ x_{21} - X_2 + x_{23} + x_{2E} = 0 \\ x_{31} + x_{32} - X_3 + x_{3E} = 0 \\ x_{E1} + x_{E2} + x_{E3} - E = 0 \end{array}\right\} \quad (3)$$

If the set of equations for an open system is compared with the corresponding set for the closed system, it will be observed that the equations for the open system consisting of three units are formally identical with those of a closed system consisting of four units. The following important theorem is thus demonstrated.

1. *An open flow system consisting of n units can always be represented by means of a closed system consisting of n + 1 units.*

The theorem can be generalized for any type of system for, let S be the system considered and E its effective environment, then if B is any behaviour characteristic of the system,

$$B = f(S, E) \quad (4)$$

If the behaviour characteristic is uniquely determined in this way, then the system together

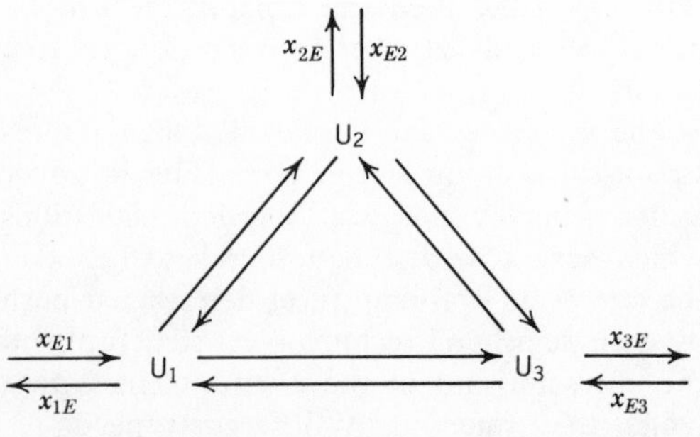

Fig. 3. An open flow system consisting of three units. The inflow from the environment into unit 1 is represented by x_{E1}.

with its environment can be represented by an equivalent closed or total system S_c so that

$$B = f(S_c) \qquad (5)$$

If we now take any component of the closed system, then the rest of the system represents its effective environment. As an illustration, consider the closed flow system consisting of three units. If we select unit 1 for study, then units 2 and 3 form its environment. Similarly, if we choose unit 3 for study, then units 1 and 2 form its environment.

From the point of view of system theory the preferred approach is to begin by studying the system as a whole, and then at a second stage to derive the properties of one or other component which may be of particular interest. Quite apart from the methodological advantages of this approach, it avoids the development into a rigid dichotomy of one or other of the many possible ways of differentiating a total system into referent and environment.

It was pointed out earlier that existing flow systems generally operate under a number of constraints, and that the introduction of such constraints is equivalent to a reduction in the degrees of freedom of the system. Before introducing a number of constraints into the open system under consideration, the following interrelation between steady states may be made explicit.

2. *If the units of an open system are kept in a steady state, then the inflow into the system must equal the outflow.*

For, suppose that the rate of inflow into the system does not equal the outflow, then one or other unit must either increase or decrease in size which contradicts the assumption. In view of *Theorem 1,* the equivalent statement for the closed system may be formulated as

3. *If n — 1 units of a closed system are kept in a steady state, then the nth unit must also be in a steady state.*

Suppose that in the open system under consideration all units are kept in a steady state. It has been shown that in this case the inflow into the system must equal the outflow, so that both rows and columns of Equation 3 will add up to zero. As before we shall let the outflow from each unit and, in addition, the outflow to the environment remain constant for the period of time under consideration. The resulting system will have five degrees of freedom.

Since we are interested in the effect which a change in any one component will have on the rest of the system, let us set up the following situation for analysis. Let an additional a elements enter unit 1 from the outside and to balance this let an equal number leave to the outside. Let us similarly increase the turnover of unit 3 with the outside. We now wish to know what would happen if we were to increase the rate of flow from unit 1 to unit 2 by an amount b.

Substituting these values in Equation 3, and calculating the values of the dependent variables by equating both rows and columns to zero, the resulting state of the system is found to be given by the set of equations below.

$$\begin{array}{ccccccccc}
-X_1 & + & (x_{12}+b) & + & (x_{13}-a-b) & + & (x_{1E}+a) & = & 0 \\
(x_{21}+2a-b) & & -X_2 & + & (x_{23}+b) & + & (x_{2E}-2a) & = & 0 \\
(x_{31}-3a+b) & + & (x_{32}+2a-b) & & -X_3 & + & (x_{3E}+a) & = & 0 \\
(x_{E1}+a) & + & (x_{E2}-2a) & + & (x_{E3}+a) & & -E & = & 0 \\
\hline
=0 & & =0 & & =0 & & =0 & &
\end{array}$$

The resulting changes in the system may be more clearly presented by means of Figure 4.

It will be noted that the increased turnover rates which were impressed on units 1 and 3 have led to a considerable drop in the turnover rate of unit 2 towards the environment. The direct causal effect can be tested by impressing the same increased turnover rates while keeping internal flow rates unchanged. Similarly, a decreased turnover rate which might have been achieved in any one unit would have led

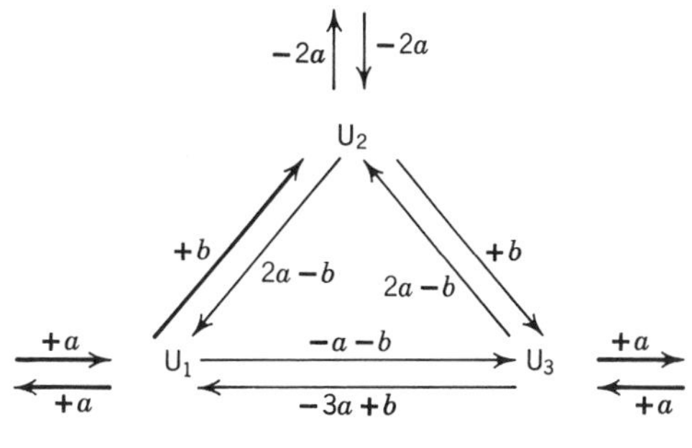

Fig. 4. Impressed increases of turnover with the environment of unit 1 and 3, and in the internal flow rate from unit 1 to unit 2 are shown by heavy lines. The resulting adjustments in the system in order to reestablish equilibrium conditions are shown by light lines.

to an increased turnover rate in one or more other units. The impressed increase of internal flow from unit 1 to unit 2 has led to more complex readjustments which are a function not only of the internal structure of the system, but also of its interrelation with the environment.

A characteristic which is shared by both the open and closed model is that changes in components immediately react on the characteristics of other components of the system, a phenomenon which we might describe as *over-reaction.* In practice a system may be unable to function efficiently if no changes could be made anywhere without immediate readjustments having to take place in all other components. In order to maintain efficient functioning in the process of readjustment, flow systems in their interaction with the socio-technical organization within which they function develop a certain amount of lag and decrease in sensitivity. By *lag* we mean the amount of time required before changes in one component are communicated or transferred to other components. *Sensitivity* refers to the relative amount of change which has to take place before it affects other dependent components. In the study of individual behaviour lag is related to the "reaction time" and sensitivity to the "threshold" for a person in a given situation.

The reason for the apparent over-reaction will be seen to be due to the fact that in the present model we have not as yet introduced a time dimension. A model of this type is generally described as *static* since its function is to determine the readjustments which will occur between the components of a system in order to reestablish equilibrium after a disturbance. The static model, in other words, enables us to determine the final steady state towards which the system will move, but can not be expected to give us any information with regard to its rate of change.

III. The Control Organization as a Function of System Structure

It was found that a flow system has only a limited number of degrees of freedom, which are determined by its structural characteristics. Only a limited number of demands can therefore be made on the system with regard to its flow rates and turnover. If the demands made exceed the number of degrees of freedom, then the system will be unable to satisfy them. The demands made on the system will in this case be said to be *incompatible*.

Let us again choose as an illustration the entry and loss of employees to a factory and their rate of transfer between departments. Among the types of decisions which need to be made are the following: to which department new entrants should be allocated; how and when they should be transferred; and what policies should be followed with regard to termination of employment. Suppose that each department has a supervisor who is autonomous in his decisions and concerned with maximizing the efficiency of his department. Situations would, in this case, arise when incompatible demands would be made on the flow system which, if not adjusted, would result in protracted malfunctioning or breakdown in the organization. Efficient system functioning thus requires the existence of a unit with the function of avoiding or adjusting incompatible demands, and balancing gains in efficiency which may arise out of a new policy for one department against possible decrease in the efficiency of other departments. The coordinating unit is said to belong to the upper level of a *control hierarchy*, which in this instance consists of two levels. Since the joining of a number of systems of this type into a larger organization would in turn lead to the development of a further higher level in the hierarchy, it will be seen that

4. *The joining of units to form systems will result in an upward growing control hierarchy.*

A more familiar development of a control organization occurs in the process of growth of a system. In its early stage, a factory may consist of a manager and a number of employees. As the organization grows, differentiation occurs into departments each of which may require a supervisor. With further growth beyond a certain point a further lower level in the control hierarchy will be added, so that quite generally

5. *The process of differentiation in the growth of a system will lead to a downward growing control hierarchy.*

The degree of separation of hierarchical functions may differ in practice. At one extreme we may find a complete separation of function into responsibility for component units, and responsibility by a higher level control unit for inter-unit adjustments. An example would be a factory in which each supervisor was given responsibility for his department, but responsibility for inter-departmental adjustments was placed with a higher authority. It appears likely that by taking inter-departmental policy out of the hands of departmental supervisors, one would tend to increase their concern with departmental interests as against interests in the efficient functioning of the organization as a whole. This type of pattern would, in this case, tend to generate or accentuate inter-departmental conflicts which the higher authority had been set up to avoid or adjust. The authority structure would therefore tend to be self-perpetuating. The resulting situation has a structural similarity to that of the family, where parent-child relationships tend to generate sibling rivalry. Non-separation of hierarchical functions may be said to exist if those responsible for component parts of the organization at the same time act as a group, generally in the form of a committee, in order to decide jointly on general policies and inter-unit relationships. A number of intermediate hierarchy relationships are possible. Their relative adequacy will need to be determined with respect to the context of the organization in which they function.

Summary

The characteristics of flow in both closed and open social systems has been considered. It was shown that an open system can always be represented by means of an equivalent closed system. Malfunctioning of a component part of a social organization can be due to changes in other components of the organization, and thus have the characteristics of a symptom which it would be ineffective to deal with directly. A satisfactory diagnosis can only be made of the basis of the specific interdependence structure of the system. It will generally be insufficient to determine the characteristics of a social unit with respect to its direct dependence on other social units. Instead, the total dependence structure in which the unit is embedded has to be studied. Social therapy may consist in the modification of the malfunctioning unit, modifications in dependent units or changes in the dependence structure of the system. Finally the characteristics of a control organization were discussed. It was shown that the structure of the system determines the hierarchical structure of its control organization, but does not determine the degree of functional separation between hierarchy levels.

REFERENCES

1. Bertalanffy, L. von. "The Theory of Open Systems in Physics and Biology," *Science*, 1950, Vol. 3, No. 1, 23–29.
2. Leontief, W. W. *The Structure of American Economy 1919–1929*. Harvard University Press, 1951.
3. Rice, A. K., Hill, J. M. M., and Trist, E. L. "The Representation of Labour Turnover as a Social Process," *Human Relations*, 1950, Vol. 3, No. 4, 349–371.
4. Rice, A. K. "The Relative Independence of Sub-Institutions as Illustrated by Departmental Labour Turnover," *Human Relations*, 1952, Vol. 5, No. 1, 83–90.

The Causal Texture of Organizational Environments

F. E. EMERY AND E. L. TRIST

Identification of the Problem

A main problem in the study of organizational change is that the environmental contexts in which organizations exist are themselves changing, at an increasing rate, and towards increasing complexity. This point, in itself, scarcely needs labouring. Nevertheless, the characteristics of organizational environments demand consideration for their own sake, if there is to be an advancement of understanding in the behavioural sciences of a great deal that is taking place under the impact of technological change, especially at the present time. This paper is offered as a brief attempt to open up some of the problems, and stems from a belief that progress will be quicker if a certain extension can be made to current thinking about systems.

In a general way it may be said that to think in terms of systems seems the most appropriate conceptual response so far available when the phenomena under study—at any level and in any domain—display the character of being organized, and when understanding the nature of the interdependencies constitutes the research task. In the behavioural sciences, the first steps in building a systems theory were taken in connection with the analysis of internal processes in organisms, or organizations, when the parts had to be related to the whole. Examples include the organismic biology of Jennings, Cannon, and Henderson; early Gestalt theory and its later derivatives such as balance theory; and the classical theories of social structure. Many of these problems could be represented in closed-system models. The next steps were taken when wholes had to be related to their environments. This led to open-system models.

A great deal of the thinking here has been influenced by cybernetics and information theory, though this has been used as much to extend the scope of closed-system as to improve the sophistication of open-system formulations. It was von Bertalanffy who, in terms of the general transport equation which he introduced, first fully disclosed the importance of openness or closedness to the environment as a means of distinguishing living organisms from inanimate objects. In contradistinction to physical objects, any living entity survives by importing into itself certain types of material from its environment, transforming these in accordance with its own system characteristics, and exporting other types back into the environment. By this process the organism obtains the additional energy that renders it "negentropic"; it becomes capable of attaining stability in a time-independent steady state—a necessary condition of adaptability to environmental variance.

Such steady states are very different affairs from the equilibrium states described in classical physics, which have far too often been taken as models for representing biological and social transactions. Equilibrium states follow the second law of thermodynamics, so that no work can be done when equilibrium is reached, whereas the openness to the environment of a steady state maintains the capacity of the organism for work, without which adaptability, and hence survival, would be impossible.

Many corollaries follow as regards the properties of open systems, such as equifinality, growth through internal elaboration, self-regulation, constancy of direction with change of position, etc.—and by no means all of these have yet been worked out. But though von Bertalanffy's formulation enables exchange processes between the organism, or organization, and elements in its environment to be dealt with in a new perspective, it does not deal at all with those processes in the environment itself which are among the determining conditions of the exchanges. To analyze these an additional concept is needed—*the causal texture of the environment*—if we may re-

---

From *Human Relations*, Vol. 18, August 1963, pp. 20–26. Reprinted by permission of the publisher.

introduce, at a social level of analysis, a term suggested by Tolman and Brunswik and drawn from S. C. Pepper.

With this addition, we may now state the following general proposition: that a comprehensive understanding of organizational behaviour requires some knowledge of each member of the following set, where L indicates some potentially lawful connection, and the suffix 1 refers to the organization and the suffix 2 to the environment:

$$L_{1\,1},\ L_{1\,2}$$
$$L_{2\,1},\ L_{2\,2}$$

$L_{1\,1}$ here refers to processes with the organization—the area of internal interdependencies; $L_{1\,2}$ and $L_{2\,1}$ to exchanges between the organization and its environment—the area of transactional interdependencies, from either direction; and $L_{2\,2}$ to processes through which parts of the environment become related to each other—i.e. its causal texture—the area of interdependencies that belong within the environment itself.

In considering environmental interdependencies, the first point to which we wish to draw attention is that the laws connecting parts of the environment to each other are often incommensurate with those connecting parts of the organization to each other, or even with those which govern the exchanges. It is not possible, for example, always to reduce organization-environment relations to the form of "being included in"; boundaries are also "break" points. As Barker and Wright following Lewin have pointed out in their analysis of this problem as it affects psychological ecology, we may lawfully connect the actions of a javelin thrower in sighting and throwing his weapon; but we cannot describe in the same concepts the course of the javelin as this is affected by variables lawfully linked by meteorological and other systems.

The Development of Environmental Connectedness (Case I)

A case history, taken from the industrial field, may serve to illustrate what is meant by the environment becoming organized at the social level. It will show how a greater degree of system-connectedness, of crucial relevance to the organization, may develop in the environment, which is yet not directly a function either of the organization's own characteristics or of its immediate relations. Both of these, of course, once again become crucial when the response of the organization to what has been happening is considered.

The company concerned was the foremost in its particular market in the foodcanning industry in the U.K. and belonged to a large parent group. Its main product—canned vegetable—had some 65 per cent of this market, a situation which had been relatively stable since before the war. Believing it would continue to hold this position, the company persuaded the group board to invest several million pounds sterling in erecting a new, automated factory, which, however, based its economies on an inbuilt rigidity—it was set up exclusively for the long runs expected from the traditional market.

The character of the environment, however, began to change while the factory was being built. A number of small canning firms appeared, not dealing with this product nor indeed with others in the company's range, but with imported fruits. These firms arose because the last of the post-war controls had been removed from steel strip and tin, and cheaper cans could now be obtained in any numbers—while at the same time a larger market was developing in imported fruits. This trade being seasonal, the firms were anxious to find a way of using their machinery and retraining their labour in winter. They became able to do so through a curious side-effect of the development of quick-frozen foods, when the company's staple was produced by others in this form. The quick-freezing process demanded great constancy at the growing end. It was not possible to control this beyond a certain point, so that quite large crops unsuitable for quick freezing but suitable for canning became available—originally from another country (the United States) where a large market for quick-frozen foods had been established. These surplus crops had been sold at a very low price for animal feed. They were now imported by the small canners—at a better but still comparatively low price, and additional cheap supplies soon began to be procurable from underdeveloped countries.

Before the introduction of the quick-freezing form, the company's own canned product—whose raw material had been specially grown at additional cost—had been the premier brand, superior to other varieties and charged at a higher price. But its position in the product spectrum now changed. With the increasing affluence of the society, more people were able to afford the quick-frozen form. Moreover, there was competition from a great many other vegetable products which could substitute for the staple, and people preferred this greater variety. The advantage of being the premier line among canned forms diminished, and demand increased both for the not-so-expensive varieties among them and for the quick-frozen forms. At the same time, major changes were taking place in retailing; supermarkets were developing, and more and more large grocery chains were coming into existence. These establishments wanted to sell certain types of goods under their own house names, and began to place bulk orders with the small canners for their own varieties of the company's staple that fell within this class. As the small canners provided an extremely cheap article (having no marketing expenses and a cheaper raw material), they could undercut the manufacturers' branded product, and within three years they captured over 50 per cent of the market. Previously, retailers' varieties had accounted for less than one per cent.

The new automatic factory could not be adapted to the new situation until alternative products with a big sales volume could be developed, and the scale of research and development, based on the type of market analysis required to identify these, was beyond the scope of the existing resources of the company either in people or in funds.

The changed texture of the environment was not recognized by an able but traditional management until it was too late. They failed entirely to appreciate that a number of outside events were becoming connected with each other in a way that was leading up to irreversible general change. Their first reaction was to make an herculean effort to defend the traditional product, then the board split on whether or not to make entry into the cheaper unbranded market in a supplier role. Group H.Q. now felt they had no option but to step in, and many upheavals and changes in management took place until a "redefinition of mission" was agreed, and slowly and painfully the company re-emerged with a very much altered product mix and something of a new identity.

Four Types of Causal Texture

It was this experience, and a number of others not dissimilar, by no means all of them industrial (and including studies of change problems in hospitals, in prisons, and in educational and political organizations), that gradually led us to feel a need for re-directing conceptual attention to the causal texture of the environment, considered as a quasi-independent domain. We have now isolated four "ideal types" of causal texture, approximations to which may be thought of as existing simultaneously in the "real world" of most organizations—though, of course, their weighting will vary enormously from case to case.

The first three of these types have already, and indeed repeatedly, been described—in a large variety of terms and with the emphasis on an equally bewildering variety of special aspects—in the literature of a number of disciplines, ranging from biology to economics and including military theory as well as psychology and sociology. The fourth type, however, is new, at least to us, and is the one that for some time we have been endeavouring to identify. About the first three, therefore, we can be brief, but the fourth is scarcely understandable without reference to them. Together, the four types may be said to form a series in which the degree of causal texturing is increased, in a new and significant way, as each step is taken. We leave as an open question the need for further steps.

Step One. The simplest type of environmental texture is that in which goals and noxiants ("goods" and "bads") are relatively unchanging in themselves and randomly distributed. This may be called the *placid, randomized environment*. It corresponds to Simon's idea of a surface over which an organism can locomote: most of this is bare, but at isolated, widely scattered points there are little heaps of food. It also corresponds to Ashby's limiting case of no connection between the environmental parts and to Schutzenberger's random field. The economist's classical market also corresponds to this type.

A critical property of organizational response under random conditions has been stated by Schutzenberger: that there is no distinction between tactics and strategy, "the optimal strategy is just the simple tactic of attempting to do one's best on a purely local basis." The best tactic, moreover, can be learnt only by trial and error and only for a particular class of local environmental variances. While organizations under these conditions can exist adaptively as single and indeed quite small units, this becomes progressively more difficult under the other types.

Step Two. More complicated, but still a placid environment, is that which can be characterized in terms of clustering: goals and noxiants are not randomly distributed but hang together in certain ways. This may be called the *placid, clustered environment*, and is the case with which Tolman and Brunswik were concerned; it corresponds to Ashby's "serial system" and to the economist's "imperfect competition." The clustering enables some parts to take on roles as signs of other parts or become means-objects with respect to approaching or avoiding. Survival, however, becomes precarious if an organization attempts to deal tactically with each environmental variance as it occurs.

The new feature of organizational response to this kind of environment is the emergence of strategy as distinct from tactics. Survival becomes critically linked with what an organization knows of its environment. To pursue a goal under its nose may lead it into parts of the field fraught with danger, while avoidance of an immediately difficult issue may lead it away from potentially rewarding areas. In the clustered environment the relevant objective is that of "optimal location", some positions being discernible as potentially richer than others.

To reach these requires concentration of resources, subordination to the main plan, and the development of a "distinctive competence", to use Selznick's term, in reaching the strategic objective. Organizations under these conditions, therefore, tend to grow in size and also to become hierarchical, with a tendency towards centralized control and coordination.

Step Three. The next level of causal texturing we have called the *disturbed-reactive environment.* It may be compared with Ashby's ultra-stable system or the economist's oligopolistic market. It is a type 2 environment in which there is more than one organization of the same kind; indeed, the existence of a number of similar organizations now becomes the dominant characteristic of the environmental field. Each organization does not simply have to take account of the others when they meet at random, but has also to consider that what it knows can also be known by the others. The part of the environment to which it wishes to move itself in the long run is also the part to which the others seek to move. Knowing this, each will wish to improve its own chances by hindering the others, and each will know that the others must not only wish to do likewise, but also know that each knows this. The presence of similar others creates an imbrication, to use a term of Chein's of some of the causal strands in the environment.

If strategy is a matter of selecting the "strategic objective"—where one wishes to be at a future time—and tactics a matter of selecting an immediate action from one's available repertoire, then there appears in type 3 environments to be an intermediate level of organizational response—that of the *operation*—to use the term adopted by German and Soviet military theorists, who formally distinguish tactics, operations, and strategy. One has now not only to make sequential choices, but to choose actions that will draw off the other organizations. The new element is that of deciding which of someone else's possible tactics one wishes to take place, while ensuring that others of them do not. An operation consists of a campaign involving a planned series of tactical initiatives, calculated reactions by others, and counter-actions. The flexibility required encourages a certain decentralization and also puts a premium on quality and speed of decision at various peripheral points.

It now becomes necessary to define the organizational objective in terms not so much of location as of capacity or power to move more or less at will, i.e., to be able to make and meet competitive challenge. This gives particular relevance to strategies of absorption and parasitism. It can also give rise to situations in which stability can be obtained only by a certain coming-to-terms between competitors, whether enterprises, interest groups, or governments. One has to know when not to fight to the death.

Step Four. Yet more complex are the environments we have called *turbulent fields*. In these, dynamic processes, which create significant variances for the component organizations, arise from the field itself. Like type 3 and unlike the static types 1 and 2, they are dynamic. Unlike type 3, the dynamic properties arise not simply from the interaction of the component organizations, but also from the field itself. The "ground" is in motion.

Three trends contribute to the emergence of these dynamic field forces:

1. The growth to meet type 3 conditions of organizations, and linked sets of organizations, so large that their actions are both persistent and strong enough to induce autochthonous processes in the environment. An analogous effect would be that of a company of soldiers marching in step over a bridge.
2. The deepening interdependence between the economic and the other facets of the society. This means that economic organizations are increasingly enmeshed in legislation and public regulation.
3. The increasing reliance on research and development to achieve the capacity to meet competitive challenge. This leads to a situation in which a change gradient is continuously present in the environmental field.

For organizations, these trends mean a gross increase in their area of *relevant uncertainty*. The consequences which flow from their actions lead off in ways that become increasingly unpredictable: they do not necessarily fall off with distance, but may at any point be amplified beyond all expectations; similarly, lines of action that are strongly pursued may find themselves attenuated by emergent field forces.

The Salience of Type 4 Characteristics (Case II)

Some of these effects are apparent in what happened to the canning company of Case I, whose situation represents a transition from an environment largely composed of type 2 and type 3 characteristics to one where those of type 4 began to gain in salience. The case now to be presented illustrates the combined operation of the three trends described above in an altogether larger environmental field involving a total industry and its relations with the wider society.

The organization concerned is the National Farmers Union of Great Britain to which more than 200,000 of the 250,000 farmers of England and Wales belong. The presenting problem brought to us for investigation was that of communications. Headquarters felt, and was deemed to be, out of touch with county branches and these with local branches. The farmer had looked to the N.F.U. very largely to protect him against market fluctuations by negotiating a comprehensive deal with the government at annual reviews concerned with the level of price support. These reviews had enabled home agriculture to maintain a steady state during two decades when the threat, or existence, of war in relation to the type of military technology then in being had made it imperative to maintain a high level of home-grown food without increasing prices to the consumer. This policy, however, was becoming obsolete as the conditions of thermonuclear stalemate established themselves. A level of support could no longer be counted upon which would keep in existence small and inefficient farmers—often on marginal land and dependent on family labour—compared with efficient medium-size farms, to say nothing of large and highly mechanized undertakings.

Yet it was the former situation which had produced N.F.U. cohesion. As this situation receded, not only were farmers becoming exposed to more competition from each other, as well as from Commonwealth and European farmers, but the effects were being felt of very great changes which had been taking place on both the supply and marketing sides of the industry. On the supply side, a small number of giant firms now supplied almost all the requirements in fertilizer, machinery, seeds, veterinary products, etc. As efficient farming depended upon ever greater utilization of these resources, their controllers exerted correspondingly greater power over the farmers. Even more dramatic were the changes in the marketing of farm produce. Highly organized food processing and distributing industries had grown up dominated again by a few large firms, on contracts from which (fashioned to suit their rather than his interests) the farmer was becoming increasingly dependent. From both sides deep inroads were being made on his autonomy.

It became clear that the source of the felt difficulty about communications lay in radical environmental changes which were confronting the organization with problems it was ill-adapted to meet. Communications about these changes were being interpreted or acted upon as if they referred to the "traditional" situation. Only through a parallel analysis of the environment and the N.F.U. was progress made towards developing understanding on the basis of which attempts to devise adaptive organizational policies and forms could be made. Not least among the problems was that of creating a bureaucratic elite that could cope with the highly technical long-range planning now required and yet remain loyal to the democratic values of the N.F.U. Equally difficult was that of developing mediating institutions—agencies that would effectively mediate the relations between agriculture and other economic sectors without triggering off massive competitive processes.

These environmental changes and the organizational crisis they induced were fully apparent two or three years before the question of Britain's possible entry into the Common Market first appeared on the political agenda—which, of course, further complicated every issue.

A workable solution was needed to preserve reasonable autonomy for the farmers as an occupational group, while meeting the interests of other sections of the community. Any such possibility depended on securing the consent of the large majority of farmers to placing under some degree of N.F.U. control matters that hitherto had remained within their own power of decision. These included what they produced, how and to what standard, and how most of it should be marketed. Such thoughts were anathema, for however dependent the farmer had grown on the N.F.U. he also remained intensely individualistic. He was being asked, he now felt, to redefine his identity, reverse his basic values, and refashion his organization—all at the same time. It is scarcely surprising that progress has been and remains, both fitful and slow, and ridden with conflict.

Values and Relevant Uncertainty

What becomes precarious under type 4 conditions is how organizational stability can be achieved. In these environments individual organizations, however large, cannot expect to adapt successfully simply through their own direct actions—as is evident in the case of the N.F.U. Nevertheless, there are some indications of a solution that may have the same general significance for these environments as have strategy and operations for types 2 and 3. This is the emergence of *values that have overriding significance for all members of the field*. Social values are here regarded as coping mechanisms that make it possible to deal with persisting areas of relevant uncertainty. Unable to trace out the consequences of their actions as these are amplified and resonated through their extended social fields, men in all societies have sought rules, sometimes categorical, such as the ten commandments, to provide them with a guide and ready calculus. Values are not strategies or tactics; as Lewin has pointed out, they have the conceptual character of "power fields" and act as injunctions.

So far as effective values emerge, the character of richly joined, turbulent fields changes in a most striking fashion. The relevance of large classes of events no longer has to be sought in an intricate mesh of diverging causal strands, but is given directly in the ethical code. By this transformation a field is created which is no longer richly joined and turbulent but simplified and relatively static. Such a transformation will be regressive, or constructively adaptative, according to how far the emergent values adequately represent the new environmental requirements.

Ashby, as a biologist, has stated his view, on the one hand, that examples of environments that are both large and richly connected are not common, for our terrestrial environment is widely characterized by being highly subdivided; and, on the other, that, so far as they are encountered, they may well be beyond the limits of human adaption, the brain being an ultra-stable system. By contrast the role here attributed to social values suggests that this sort of environment may in fact be not only one to which adaptation is possible, however difficult, but one that has been increasingly characteristic of the human condition since the beginning of settled communities. Also, let us not forget that values can be rational as well as irrational and that the rationality of their rationale is likely to become more powerful as the scientific ethos takes greater hold in a society.

Matrix Organization and Institutional Success

Nevertheless, turbulent fields demand some overall form of organization that is essentially different from the hierarchically structured forms to which we are accustomed. Whereas type 3 environments require one or another form of accommodation between like, but competitive, organizations whose fates are to a degree negatively correlated, turbulent environments require some relationship between dissimilar organizations whose fates are, basically, positively correlated. This means relationships that will maximize cooperation and which recognize that no one organization can take over the role of "the other" and become paramount. We are inclined to speak of this type of relationship as an *organizational matrix*. Such a matrix acts in the first place by delimiting on value criteria the character of what may be included in the field specified—and therefore who. This selectivity then enables some definable shape to be worked out without recourse to much in the way of formal hierarchy among members, Professional associations provide one model of which there has been long experience.

We do not suggest that in other fields than the professional the requisite sanctioning can be provided only by state-controlled bodies. Indeed, the reverse is far more likely. Nor do we suggest that organizational matrices will function so as to eliminate the need for other measures to achieve stability. As with values, matrix organizations, even if successful, will only help to transform turbulent environments into the kinds of environment we have discussed as "clustered" and "disturbed-reactive". Though, with these transformations, an organization could hope to achieve a degree of stability through its strategies, operation, and tactics, the transformations would not provide environments identical with the originals. The strategic objective in the transformed cases could no longer be stated simply in terms of optimal location (as in type 2) or capabilities (as in type 3). It must now rather be formulated in terms of *institutionaliaztion*. According to Selznick organizations become institutions through the embodiment of organizational values which relate them to the wider society. As Selznick has stated in his analysis of leadership in the modern American corporation, "the default of leadership shows itself in an acute form when *organizational* achievement or survival is confounded with *institutional* success." ". . . the executive becomes a statesman as he makes the transition from administrative management to institutional leadership."

The processes of strategic planning now also become modified. In so far as institutionalization becomes a prerequisite for stability, the determination of policy will necessitate not only a bias towards goals that are congruent with the organization's own character, but also a selection of goal-paths that offer maximum convergence as regards the interests of other parties. This became a central issue for the N.F.U. and is becoming one now for an organization such as the National Economic Development Council, which has the task of creating a matrix in which the British economy can function at something better than the stop-go level.

Such organizations arise from the need to meet problems emanating from type 4 environments. Unless this is recognized, they will only too easily be construed in type 3 terms, and attempts will be made to secure for them a degree of monolithic power that will be resisted overtly in democratic societies and covertly in others. In the one case they may be prevented from ever undertaking their missions; in the other one may wonder how long they can succeed in maintaining them.

An organizational matrix implies what McGregor has called Theory Y. This in turn implies a new set of values. But values are psychosocial commodities that come into existence only rather slowly. Very little systematic work has yet been done on the establishment of new systems of values, or on the type of critera that might be adduced to allow their effectiveness to be empirically tested. A pioneer attempt is that of Churchman and Ackoff. Likert has suggested that, in the large corporation or government establishment, it may well take some ten to fifteen years before the new type of group values with which he is concerned could permeate the total organization. For a new set to permeate a whole modern society the time required must be much longer—at least a generation, according to the common saying—and this, indeed, must be a minimum. One may ask if this is fast enough, given the rate at which type 4 environments are becoming salient. A compelling task for social scientists is to direct more research onto these problems.

Summary

(a) A main problem in the study of organizational change is that the environmental contexts in which organizations exist are themselves changing—at an increasing rate, under the impact of technological change. This means that they demand consideration for their own sake. Towards this end a redefinition is offered, at a social level of analysis, of the causal texture of the environment, a concept introduced in 1935 by Tolman and Brunswik.

(b) This requires an extension of systems theory. The first steps in systems theory were taken in connection with the analysis of internal processes in organisms, or organizations, which involved relating parts to the whole. Most of these problems could be dealt with through closed-system models. The next steps were taken when wholes had to be related to their environments. This led to open-system models, such as that introduced by Bertalanffy, involving a general transport equation. Though this enables exchange processes between the organism, or organization, and elements in its environment to be dealt with, it does not deal with those processes in the environment itself which are the determining conditions of the exchanges. To analyse these an additional concept—the causal texture of the environment—is needed.

(c) The laws connecting parts of the environment to each other are often incommensurate with those connecting parts of the organization to each other, or even those which govern exchanges. Case history I illustrates this and shows the dangers and difficulties that arise when there is a rapid and gross increase in the area of relevant uncertainty, a characteristic feature of many contemporary environments.

(d) Organizational environments differ in their causal texture, both as regards degree of uncertainty and in many other important respects. A typology is suggested which identifies four "ideal types", approximations to which exist simultaneously in the "real world" of most organizations, though the weighting varies enormously:

1. In the simplest type, goals and noxiants are relatively unchanging in themselves and randomly distributed. This may be called the placid, randomized environment. A critical property from the organization's viewpoint is that there is no difference between tactics and strategy, and organizations can exist adaptively as single, and indeed quite small, units.
2. The next type is also static, but goals and noxiants are not randomly distributed; they hang together in certain ways. This may be called the placid, clustered environment. Now the need arises for strategy as distinct from tactics. Under these conditions organizations grow in size, becoming multiple and tending towards centralized control and coordination.
3. The third type is dynamic rather than static. We call it the disturbed-reactive environment. It consists of a clustered environment in which there is more than one system of the same kind, i.e., the objects of one organization are the same as, or relevant to, others like it. Such competitors seek to improve their own chances by hindering each other, each knowing the others are playing the same game. Between strategy and tactics there emerges an intermediate type of organizational response—what military theorists refer to as operations. Control becomes more decentralized to allow these to be conducted. On the other hand, stability may require a certain coming-to-terms between competitors.
4. The fourth type is dynamic in a second respect, the dynamic properties arising not simply from the interaction of identifiable component systems but from the field itself (the "ground"). We call these environments turbulent fields. The turbulence results from the complexity and multiple character of the causal interconnections. Individual organiza-

tions, however large, cannot adapt successfully simply through their direct interactions. An examination is made of the enhanced importance of values, regarded as a basic response to persisting areas of relevant uncertainty, as providing a control mechanism, when commonly held by all members in a field. This raises the question of organizational forms based on the characteristics of a matrix.

(e) Case history II is presented to illustrate problems of the transition from type 3 to type 4. The perspective of the four environmental types is used to clarify the role of Theory X and Theory Y as representing a trend in value change. The establishment of a new set of values is a slow social process requiring something like a generation—unless new means can be developed.

Differentiation and Integration in Complex Organizations

PAUL R. LAWRENCE AND JAY W. LORSCH

Considerable attention has recently been devoted to understanding behavior in large organizational systems. Although some of this work has been based on research, it has more typically been general theorizing with little support from research data.[1] Our interest in examining complex organizations is to study more systematically and empirically their internal functioning in relation to the demands of the external environment on the organization and the ability of the organization to cope effectively with these demands, contributing to a theory of the functioning of large organizations based on empirical research.[2]

Basic Research Design

Major Concepts and Questions. The basic concepts used in this examination of the internal functioning of large organizations are *differentiation* and *integration*, the key research question being: What pattern of differentiation and integration of the parts of a large organizational system is associated with the organization's coping effectively with a given external environment? The concepts as used here in relation to organizational studies suggest a return to the central concern of early organizational theorists; i.e., the optimal division of labor given a general organizational purpose.[3] More recently, Miller has used these concepts in theorizing about complex organizations, and Rice has made use of them in the description of his work with an Indian textile firm.[4]

Although our use of these concepts is not new, it does represent an apparent break with some of the current and widely known approaches to the study of large organizations. March and Simon's work reflects a key concern with the issue of inducing contributions from organizational members and emphasizes rationality in organizations.[5] The writing of Likert and MacGregor reflects a central interest in organizational arrangements for releasing the underutilized energy of individual members.[6] Argyris' work emphasizes the impact of the organization on individual development.[7] All of these writers tend to start with

---

From *Administrative Science Quarterly*, Vol. 12, No. 1, June 1967, pp. 1–47. Reprinted by permission of the authors and publisher.

[1] For data-based studies see, for example, A. Rice, *The Enterprise and Its Environment* (London: Tavistock, 1963); or T. Burns and G. Stalker, *The Management of Innovation* (London: Tavistock, 1961). For examples of theorizing about behavior in complex organizations see P. Pugh, *et al.*, A Scheme for Organizational Analysis, *Administrative Science Quarterly*, 8 (1963), 289–315; V. Thompson, Bureaucracy and Innovation, *Administrative Science Quarterly*, 10 (1965), 1–20; and E. Miller, Time, Technology, and Territory, *Human Relations*, 7 (1959), 245.

[2] The exploratory study upon which this research is based is reported in J. Lorsch, *Organization and Product Innovation* (New York: Macmillan, 1965). This article is based on research supported in part by the Harvard University Program on Technology and Society under a long-term grant from the International Business Machines Corporation and in part by a grant from the Ford Foundation to the Division of Research, Graduate School of Business Administration, Harvard University.

[3] Some prominent exponents of this approach have been H. Fayol, *Industrial and General Administration* (London: Pitman, 1930); L. H. Gulick and L. Urwick (eds.), *Papers on the Science of Administration* (New York: Institute of Public Administration, Columbia University, 1937); J. D. Mooney and A. C. Reiley, *The Principles of Organization* (New York: Harper, 1939).

[4] E. Miller, *op. cit.;* A. Rice, *op. cit.*

[5] James G. March and Herbert A. Simon, *Organizations* (New York: John Wiley, 1958).

[6] R. Likert, *New Patterns of Management* (New York: McGraw-Hill, 1961); D. McGregor, *The Human Side of Enterprise* (New York: McGraw-Hill, 1960).

[7] C. Argyris, *Integrating the Individual and the Organization* (New York: John Wiley, 1964).

the individual as the basic unit of analysis and build toward the large organization, while we are proposing to start with larger, sociological entities—the entire organization and its larger subsystems. But, the divergence from this current literature is more apparent than real, and the return to the questions of classical organization theory is done with a difference. While this study selects sociological entities as the primary focus of analysis, it differs from the classical approach in being based on the premise that the individuals in organizations can best be viewed not as passive instruments of organization, but as feeling, reasoning, and motivated beings.

The importance of the concepts of differentiation and integration to the analytic scheme developed here can best be indicated by the definition of the primary unit of analysis in this study—the organizational system. An *organization* is defined as a system of interrelated behaviors of people who are performing a task that has been differentiated into several distinct subsystems, each subsystem preforming a portion of the task, and the efforts of each being integrated to achieve effective performance of the system. *Differentiation* is defined as the state of segmentation of the organizational system into subsystems, each of which tends to develop particular attributes in relation to the requirements posed by its relevant external enironment. Differentiation, as used here, includes the behavioral attributes of members of organizational subsystems; this represents a break with the classical definition of the term as simply the formal division of labor. *Integration* is defined as the process of achieving unity of effort among the various subsystems in the accomplishment of the organization's task. *Task* is defined as a complete input-transformation-output cycle involving at least the design, production, and distribution of some goods or services. By these definitions, the boundaries of organizations will not always coincide with their legal boundaries: some institutions, such as large corporations, encompass a number of organizations by our definition; while others, such as certain subcontractors, do not constitute a single complete organization.

It is helpful to look first at the relation between the development of specialized attributes of subsystems and the task of each subsystem in coping with the relevant segment of the external environment.[8]

The Organization and Its Environment. Since the primary concern was with the internal functioning of organizations, it appeared that one useful way to conceive of the environment of an organization was to look at it from the organization outward. This approach is based on the assumption that an organization is an active system which tends to reach out and order its otherwise overly complex surroundings so as to cope with them effectively. Then as the organization becomes differentiated into basic subsystems, it segments its environment into related sectors. As Brown has pointed out, industrial organizations usually become segmented into three essential major subsystems here termed basic subsystems to distinguish them from integrative subsystems. These are the sales subsystem, the production subsystem, and the research and development subsystem.[9] By the definition given, this segmentation indicates that the organization is undertaking a whole task. In this division of tasks, the organization is also ordering its environment into three sectors: the market subenvironment, the technical-economic subenvironment, and the scientific subenvironment.[10]

[8] It is important to emphasize that in this study, no attempt was made to distinguish between the real attributes of the environment and management's perception of these attributes. W. Dill (Environment as an Influence on Managerial Autonomy, *Administrative Science Quarterly*, 2 (1958), 409–433) has pointed out that there may be a discrepancy between these, but we attempted to minimize this gap by selecting as research sites organizations which were pursuing quite similar strategies in the same industry, the assumption being that similar strategies imply similar perceptions of the environment.

[9] W. Brown, *Explorations in Management* (London: Heinemann, 1960), pp. 143–145. This in no way denies that other functions such as finance and personnel are usually differentiated, do at times play critical roles, and have a concern for a sector of the organization's total environment.

[10] The term technical-economic subenvironment refers to the environmental sector of relevance to the production subsystem. Production systems are concerned with processing technology and with environmental changes in them; however, they need not search the environment for all developments of technical relevance, only for those that

It is readily apparent that each of these environments can range from highly dynamic to extremely stable. The importance of this variability can easily be obscured by the usual approach of thinking of an organization's environment as a single entity. Here, each major subsystem was seen as coping with its respective segment of the total external environment. It was hypothesized that each subsystem would tend to develop particular attributes which would be predictably related to characteristics of its relevant external environment.

It was hypothesized that four attributes of an organizational subsystem would vary with the relevant subenvironments. Although many other attributes of organizations could be related to the environment, prior research led to a special interest in structural attributes and the pattern of cognitive and normative orientations held by the members of each subsystem.

DEGREE OF STRUCTURE. Prior experimental and field studies indicated that an important attribute of any subsystem that could be expected to be related to its relevant environment was its degree of *formalized structure*. Structure here refers to those aspects of behavior in organizations subject to pre-existing programs and controls. We wanted to compare the degree of formalized structure in different organizations and subsystems, that is, the extent of pre-existing programs and controls. Leavitt, as well as other researchers working with experimental groups, found that groups working on relatively simple and certain tasks tend to perform the task better when the groups had more structure (i.e., preplanned and limited communication nets), whereas groups working on uncertain, more complex tasks tended to perform better with less structured communication nets.[11] In field studies, Burns and Stalker found that organizations that were profitably coping with uncertain, changing environments had a low degree of formalized structure ("organic"), instead of the higher degree of structure ("mechanistic") associated with financial success in more certain environments.[12] Woodward also found a relationship between the nature of the task and the structure, of the organization. More significantly she found that more profitable organizations tended to adopt structures consistent with the requirements of their technological environments.[13] Similarly, Hall found that departments with routine tasks tended to have a higher degree of bureaucracy (structure) than departments with less certain tasks.[14] These findings suggested that subsystems in any organization could be expected to develop different degrees of structure in relation to the certainty of their subenvironment. It was there fore, hypothesized that:

Hypothesis 1. The greater the certainty of the relevant subenvironment, the more formalized the structure of the subsystem.

ORIENTATION OF MEMBERS TOWARD OTHERS. Moment and Zalezink, and Leader suggested a second attribute of subsystems that could be expected to be related to the task of coping with different subenvironments.[15] This is a cognitive and affective orientation toward the objects of work, which is manifested in a person's interpersonal style. The objects can be either people or inanimate tools and instruments, and the concern of members with them tends to polarize along a task-social dimension. Subsystem members in their interpersonal relationships will be primarily concerned with either task accomplishment or with social relationships. Fiedler in studies of group effectiveness found task-oriented leadership associated

also meet a second criterion of economic relevance. These dual criteria are suggested by the name of the sector, since both can markedly alter the characteristics of this subenvironment.

[11] H. Leavitt, "Some Effects of Certain Communication Patterns on Group Performance," in E. Macoby *et al.* (eds.), *Readings in Social Psychology* (New York: Holt, Rinehart, and Winston, 1958), pp. 546–563.

[12] T. Burns and G. Stalker, *op. cit.*, pp. 1–10.

[13] J. Woodward, *Management and Technology* (London: Her Majesty's Printing Office, 1958), pp. 16–24.

[14] R. Hall, Intraorganizational Structure Variables, *Administrative Science Quarterly*, 9 (1962), 295–308.

[15] D. Moment and A. Zaleznik, *Role Development and Interpersonal Competence* (Boston: Graduate School of Business Administration, Harvard University, 1963); and G. Leader, "The Determinants and Consequences of Interpersonal Competence in a Bank Setting" (Unpublished D.B.A. thesis, Graduate School of Business Administration, Harvard University, June, 1965).

with effective task performance under the extreme conditions of high and low task certainty, while more socially oriented styles were associated with effective performance under conditions of moderate uncertainty.[16] Although Fiedler was focusing particularly on leadership behavior, whereas the interest here is in the wider interpersonal orientation of members of an organizational unit, his findings are relevant if one recognizes that leadership behavior is closely related to the interpersonal norms of the unit in which the leader functions. Based on these earlier findings it was hypothesized that:

Hypothesis 2. Subsystems dealing with environments of moderate certainty will have members with more social interpersonal orientations, whereas subsystems coping with either very certain environments or very uncertain environments will have members with more task-oriented interpersonal orientations.

TIME ORIENTATION AND MEMBERS. A third attribute of subsystems can best be understood by considering the definition of certainty used in conceptualizing the characteristics of the different subenvironments. Three indicators of subenvironmental certainty were used: the rate of change of conditions over time in the subenvironment, the certainty of information about conditions in the subenvironment at any particular time, and the modal time span of definitive feedback from the subenvironment on the results of subsystem behavior. It was predicted that structure and interpersonal orientation would be related to all three environmental indicators, while the members' time orientation, the third subsystem attribute, would be related to the timespan of definitive feedback. For example, a production subsystem that received feedback about its efforts on an almost daily basis, could be expected to have members with a short-term orientation, whereas a research unit coping with a subenvironment where feedback might occur only on the completion of a project lasting well over a year would be apt to have members with a more long-term orientation. It was hypothesized that:

Hypothesis 3. The time orientations of subsystem members will vary directly with the modal time required to get definitive feedback from the relevant subenvironment.

This attribute has apparently not been empirically studied in organizations, but it has been used as an important dimension of the comparative study of cultures.[17]

GOAL ORIENTATION OF MEMBERS. The fourth attribute that subsystems were expected to develop in relation to their subenvironments was the *goal orientation* of members. Following the empirical research done by Dearborn and Simon on this subject, it was hypothesized that:

Hypothesis 4. The members of a subsystem will develop a primary concern with the goals of coping with their particular subenvironment.[18]

Thus marketing managers could be expected to be more concerned with customer and competitor actions, while production executives would be more oriented toward the operation of equipment and the actions of suppliers.

One might question whether the development of these four different attributes in subsystems is not so obvious as to make it unnecessary to test for them. The testing can be sufficiently justified, however, on the grounds of establishing a factual base line for the testing of more debatable hypotheses to be described shortly. Furthermore other factors can be expected to counteract the tendency of subsystems to become differentiated in relation to their relevant subenvironment. The only counterforce to be dealt with formally in this study

[16] F. Fiedler, Technical Report No. 10, Group Effectiveness Research Laboratory, Department of Psychology, University of Illinois, May, 1960. While Fiedler in published studies has referred to this dimension as directive-permissive, in a recent private conversation with one of the authors, he has indicated that the task-social dimension is a more appropriate way to conceptualize his findings.

[17] F. Kluckholn and F. Strodbeck, *Variations in Value Orientations* (New York: Row, Peterson, 1961); W. Caudill, and H. Scarr, Japanese Value Orientations and Culture Change, *Ethnology*, 1 (1962), 53–91; C. McArthur, "Cultural Values as Determinants of Imaginal Productions," Unpublished Ph.D. thesis, Harvard University; abstract in *Journal of Abnormal and Social Psychology*, 50 (March 1955), 247–254.

[18] D. Dearborn and H. Simon, Selective Perception: a Note on the Departmental Identification of Executives, *Sociometry*, 21 (1958), 140–144.

is the tendency to reduce differences between subsystems to achieve integration between them. Finally, it needs to be emphasized again that the particular attributes selected for measurement and examination in this study are not the only ones related to differences in subenvironments. Other attributes were seriously explored for inclusion, but were excluded because of methodological problems. The first was the linguistic or semantic orientation of the subsystems. The specialized languages that develop around certain tasks and environments are reputed to complicate the relations between subsystems.[19] The second was concerned with supplementing the goal-orientation attribute with a measure of the more latent value orientation of the subsystems, since some studies indicate that various motivational orientations toward achievement, power, or social rewards are related to environmental characteristics.[20] The four attributes selected for this study however, were considered both operationally feasible and based on prior research.

Relation between Differentiation, Integration, and Organizational Performance. To understand the functioning of complex organizations, it is necessary not only to consider the state of differentiation in relation to properties of the environment, but also to understand the functioning of complex organizations, it is also necessary to understand the relationship between differentiation and integration, and how these are related to organizational performance. Ronken and Lawrence found that differences in assumptions (orientations) between grous were related to difficulties in achieving collaboration.[21] Miller suggested that as clusters of roles developed in relation to differentiated tasks, problems would result in achieving integration.[22] Both Seiler and Sherif reported findings that indicate a relationship between the degree to which members of two groups share norms, values, and/or superordinate goals, and the ability of the two groups to cooperate.[23] Similarly, March and Simon indicated that differences in goals and in perceptions of reality could be a condition for intergroup conflict.[24] On the basis of these prior studies its was predicted that the degree of differentiation between any pair of subsystems in the four measured attributes would be inversely related to the effectiveness of integration between them.

One other factor must be considered in examining the relationship between differentiation and integration within an organization, what March and Simon have identified as the "felt need for joint decision-making" or what is here termed the degree of" *requisite integration*";[25] that is, whether task characteristics make it possible for subsystems in an organization to operate independently of each other, or require continual collaboration in making decisions before a given subsystem may act? The greater the degree of requisite integration between two subsystems the more difficult it will be to achieve integration. Therefore only pairs of units with a similar degree of requisite integration were examined. It was hypothesized that:

Hypothesis 5. Within any organizational system, given a similar degree of requisite integration, the greater the degree of differentiation in subsystem attributes between pairs of subsystems, the less effective will be the integration achieved between them.

Several organizations were compared to gain some insight into the relationship between differentiation and integration, and the performance of an organization in a given industrial environment. Rice indicated that effective subsystem performance is related to the subsystem being well differentiated in relation to its "primary task."[26] This suggests that the performance of a subsystem will vary directly

[19] J. March and H. Simon, *op. cit.*, pp. 162–163.

[20] D. McClelland, *The Achieving Society* (Princeton: D. Van Nostrand, 1961), pp. 266–267.

[21] H. Ronken and P. Lawrence, *Administrating Changes* (Boston: Harvard University Graduate School of Business Administration, 1952), p. 203.

[22] E. Miller, *op. cit.*, p. 245.

[23] J. Seiler, Toward a Theory of Organization Congruent with Primary Group Concepts, *Behavorial Science*, 8 (July 1963), 190–198; J. Seiler, Diagnosing Interdepartmental Conflict, *Harvard Business Review*, 4 (September-October 1963), 121–132; M. Sherif, Superordinate Goals in the Reduction of Intergroup Conflict, *American Journal of Sociology*, 3 (1958), 356–394.

[24] J. March and H. Simon, *op. cit.*, pp. 121–129.

[25] *Ibid.*

[26] A. Rice, *Productivity and Social Organization* (London: Tavistock, 1958), pp. 227–233.

with the extent to which the subsystem realized the relationship hypothesized between its four internal attributes and the characteristics of its subenvironment; that is, subsystems in different organizations would vary in the *degree* to which they realize the predicted relationships, and it is this degree of congruence that is proposed as a predictor of subsystem performance. Moreover, it is clear that total organizational performance is also related to achieving the degree of integration between subsystems required for the overall organizational task of coping with the external environment. It was hypothesized, therefore, that:

Hypothesis 6. Overall performance in coping with the external environment will be related to there being a degree of differentiation among subsystems consistent with the requirements of their relevant subenvironments and a degree of integration consistent with requirements of the total environment.

This hypothesis, along with hypothesis 5, raises the question of how organizations confronted with environmental demands for high differentiation and close integration achieve both, if differentiation and integration are in fact antagonistic. This question was of particular interest, because the environment selected for this study made just such demands on the organizations studied.

Means of Achieving Integration. Much of the theorizing about integration has suggested that the achievement of integration is the task of top management. Barnard has indicated that this is one of the principal functions of an executive.[27] More recently, both Haire and Rice, among others, have made a similar point.[28] Although coordination is undoubtedly an important part of the top manager's job, there is considerable evidence that many organizational systems develop integrative devices in addition to the conventional hierarchy. Litterer recently suggested three main means of achieving integration: through the hierarchy, through administrative or control systems, and through voluntary activities.[29] It is our view that these "voluntary" activities, which managers at lower echelons develop to supplement the hierarchical and administrative systems, are becoming increasingly formalized. One has only to note the proliferation of coordinating departments (whether called new product, marketing, or planning departments), task forces, and cross-functional coordinating teams to find evidence that new formal devices are emerging to achieve coordination.

It was predicted that in the industry studied, the high degree of subsystem differentiation required and the environmental requirements for a high degree of integration between the differentiated subsystems would make integrative devices necessary for effective performance. Top managers in these organizations would not be able to deal with the many technical and market factors that had to be assimilated in making well-coordinated decisions. It was therefore hypothesized that:

Hypothesis 7. When the environment requires both a high degree of subsystem differentiation and a high degree of integration, integrative devices will tend to emerge.

The effectiveness of these integrative devices is questionable. Burns and Stalker reported that such devices observed in their study were effective.[30] However, if an organization was both highly differentiated and highly integrated, and yet these two processes are antagonistic, then these integrative devices would have to be functioning effectively. This raised another question: If the presence and effective functioning of these devices was necessary for high system performance, what were some of the determinants of the effectiveness of these devices? Before this question can be answered, it is necessary to consider the findings about the relationship between differentiation and integration, and the relation of these of the ability of the organization to cope with its external environment.

Research Findings

Research Setting. The six organizations studied were all operating in a chemical pro-

[27] C. Barnard, *The Functions of an Executive* (Cambridge, Mass.: Harvard University, 1938), pp. 136–137.

[28] M. Haire, *Modern Organization Theory* (New York: John Wiley, 1953), pp. 302–303; and A. Rice, *The Enterprise and Its Environment*, *op. cit.*, p. 35.

[29] J. Litterer, *The Analysis of Organizations* (New York: John Wiley, 1965).

[30] T. Burns and G. Stalker, *op. cit.*, p. 9.

cessing industry, which was characterized by relatively rapid technological change and product modification and innovation. According to top executives in these organizations, the dominant competitive issue confronting them was the development of new and improved products and processes in this rapidly changing environment. The organizations were selected for study because these environmental conditions, particularly the importance of innovation, seemed to require organizations to achieve a high degree of both differentiation and integration.[31]

SUBENVIRONMENTS. Since the six organizations were operating in the same environment, efforts to characterize this environment were limited to an examination of the requirements of the three subenvironments: the market subenvironment, the scientific subenvironment, and the technical-economic subenvironment. Data about these subenvironments were collected in interviews with the top executives in each organization.[32] From these interviews it was concluded that the certainty of these subenvironments could be measured by: (*1*) the rate of change in environmental conditions, (*2*) the certainty of information at a given time about environmental conditions, and (*3*) the time span of definitive feedback from the environment. The ranking of each of the subenvironments along these three dimensions is presented in Table 1. The total score obtained by summing the three columns provides at least a crude estimate of the relative certainty of these subenvironments; science being the least certain and the technical-economic the most certain.

Table 1. Ranking of Subenvironments along Three Dimensions

SUBENVIRONMENT	CERTAINTY OF INFORMATION	RATE OF CHANGE	TIME SPAN OF DEFINITIVE FEEDBACK	TOTAL
Science	1 *	1.5	1	3.5
Market	2	1.5	2	5.5
Technical-economic	3	3	3	9

* 1—least certain or longest in time span; 3—most certain or shortest in time span.

The scientific subenvironment was characterized by relatively uncertain information at any given time about the nature of the materials being investigated. This was further complicated by the rapid rate of change in knowledge; new materials and formulations continually being developed might antiquate present methods and products. Definitive feedback from this subenvironment was only secured after a project was entirely completed; only then was there concrete evidence to evaluate the success of the organizations in coping with its scientific subenvironment.

The rate of change in the market subenvironment was also relatively high; however, the executives seemed to feel somewhat more certain about market information than about scientific data. They indicated that they received feedback from the market subenvironment on a regular basis, and often as frequently as once a week.

In the technical-economic subenvironment, there was much more certainty about conditions in this subenvironment at a given time than in the others. Machine capacities, raw material specifications, and similar conditions could be accurately assessed. Also the rate of change was less rapid, since processes change

[31] Although this study was conducted in one environment, the authors are curerntly expanding this research into several other environments in an effort to discover how effective performance under different environmental conditions is related to differentiation and integration.

[32] While this was an admittedly crude method for characterizing these subenvironments, it seemed sufficient for this phase of the research. A more systematic method for obtaining data about the environment has since been developed in the form of a questionnaire. These data are being collected as part of the doctoral work of James S. Garrison and will be reported in his dissertation, now in progress. A preliminary analysis of these data strongly supports the findings about the environmental characteristics of this industry reported here.

only after thorough testing had indicated they were warrated economically as well as technically. Finally feedback from this subenvironment was very rapid; information about processing costs, quality, and the like, being available on a daily basis.

REQUISITE INTEGRATION. In addition to the characteristics of these subenvironments, interviews with the top executives also provided information on the requirements for integration in this environment. A high degree of integration was required primarily because of the necessity for developing new processes and products and constantly modifying old ones. The executives indicated that the requirement for effective integration was particularly acute between the sales and research subsystems and between the production and research subsystems, as well as between these units and the integrative departments intended to link them. Sales and research needed to maintain an effective liaison first, so that the sales subsystem could provide researchers with information about market needs and requirements; and second, so that the research subsystem could make sales and marketing managers aware of the characteristics of new products. In addition to this flow of technical information, a close bond was necessary to achieve relationships that motivated salesmen to sell new products and researchers to undertake scientific investigations to meet market requirements.

Similarly close collaboration was needed between production and research so that the researchers would be aware of processing capabilities and limitations as they developed new and modified processes, while production personnel would understand how to set up and maintain new and modified processes. Here too, collaboration was required to maintain close interpersonal ties between these groups, so that researchers would be motivated to investigate processing problems, and production personnel would be receptive to changes in production processes originating in the research subsystem.

All the organizations studied had segmented the research subsystem further into two subsystems: one for applied research and the other for more fundamental long-range investigations. Of these two units, the fundamental research subsystem, both because of the longer time span of definitive feedback and the less certain information with which it dealt, was coping with the least certain portion of the scientific subenvironment. Also, in each organization, a extra subsystem had been established to integrate the activities of the basic subsystems. These were one type of integrative device that was expected to emerge, and they will be discussed in more detail later.

The presence of two research subsystems and the integrative subsystem in each organization complicated the question of where high integration was required. In some of the organizations, the top executives indicated that integration was also required between the two research subsystems; in other organizations, this was not required. This depended largely on the function assigned to the integrative subsystem. Since we were interested in studying subsystems of equal requisite integration, attention was focused on the relationship between sales and applied research and between production and applied research, as well as the relation of these subsystems to the integrative subsystems, where high requisite integration was defined as necessary by all of the top executives. In determining which subsystems had comparable requisite integration with the fundamental-research subsystem, the special circumstances of each organization as defined by the top executives involved, served as a guide.

Attributes of Basic Subsystem and Requirements of Subenvironments. It was predicted that each of these basic subsystems would develop four attributes (structure, members' interpersonal orientation, members' orientation toward time, and members' orientation toward goals) in relation to the specific requirements of the relevant subenvironment, particularly its certainty.[33]

STRUCTURE. To measure the structure of the subsystems, dimensions suggested by Hall, Woodward, Evans, and Burns and Stalker that could be operationally measured were used: the span of supervisory control, number of levels to a supervisor shared with other subsys-

[33] The data for this study were gathered in interviews and questionnaires with 216 managers, engineers, and scientists in six organizations. The number of individuals in each organization ranged from 30 to 40.

Table 2. Scales of Structural Characteristics

STRUCTURAL CHARACTERISTICS	FORMALIZED STRUCTURE * 1	2	3	4
Average span of control	11–10 persons	9–8 persons	7–6 persons	5–3 persons
Number of levels to a shared superior	7 levels	8–9 levels	10–11 levels	12 levels
Time span of review of subsystem performance †	Less than once each month	Monthly	Weekly	Daily
Specificity of review of subsystem performance	General oral review	General written review	One or more general statistics	Detailed statistics
Importance of formal rules	No rules	Rules on minor routine procedures	Comprehensive rules on routine procedures and/or limited rules on operations	Comprehensive rules on all routine procedures and operations
Specificity of criteria for evaluation of role occupants	No formal evaluation	Formal evaluation—no fixed criteria	Formal evaluation—less than 5 criteria	Formal evaluation—detailed criteria—more than 5

* Scores from low to high formalized structure.
† Based on shortest review period.

tems, the specificity of review of subsystem performance, the frequency of review of subsystem performance, the specificity of review of individual performance, and the emphasis on formal rules and procedures.[34] The more levels to a shared superior, the tighter the span of control; the more frequent and specific the reviews, and the more emphasis given to rules, the higher the formalized structure of the particular subsystem. Data on these characteristics for each subsystem were gathered from organizational documents (organization charts, procedural manuals, and the like), or when these were not available, by interviewing subsystem managers about organizational practices.

A four-point scale, ranging from most controlling to least controlling, was developed for each structural characteristic (see Table 2), and a structural score was computed for each subsystem in all organizations by adding the scores on all six characteristics. While there was some variation within individual subsystems, scores for one characteristic were generally consistent with those for others. Although space precludes discussing all these scores in detail, the important finding was that subsystems within each organization did tend to rank from low to high structure in relation to the uncertainty of their subenvironments, as is apparent from Table 3.

Production, with a more certain subenvironment, tended to have the highest structure in all but one organization (IV). Fundamental-research subsystems tended to have the least structure. Sales subsystems with moderately certain tasks tended to be more structured than research subsystems, but usually less structured than production. Although these rankings were found within all organizations, it is important to emphasize (as the raw scores indicate), that the degree of structure varied considerably between organizations. For example, the fundamental research subsystems in organizations I, IV, and VI tended to be considerably less structured than the counterpart subsystems in the other three organizations. We will return to the significance of this point later.

These data indicate, as predicted, that subsystems tend to develop a degree of formalized structure related to the certainty of their relevant subenvironment. This also, of course, in-

[34] R. Hall, Intraorganizational Structural Variables, *Administrative Science Quarterly*, 9 (1962), 295–308; J. Woodward, *op. cit.;* T. Burns and G. Stalker, *op. cit.;* W. Evans, Indices of Hierarchical Structure of Industrial Organizations, *Management Sciences*, 9 (1963), 468–477.

Table 3. Subsystem Structure Scores Ranked from Low to High Structure *

	ORGANIZATIONS					
SUBSYSTEM	I	II	III	IV	V	VI
Fundamental research	(8)1	(13)1.5	(12)1	(8)1	(16)1.5	(8)1
Applied research	(16)2.5	(13)1.5	(13)2	(16)2	(16)1.5	(15)2
Sales	(16)2.5	(17)3	(17)3	(18)4	(19)3	(16)3.5
Production	(18)4	(22)4	(21)4	(17)3	(23)4	(16)3.5

* Number in parentheses structure score: Low score indicates low structure; high score indicates high structure. Other numbers are rank order.

dicates that the subsystems within each of these organizations were differentiated from each other in their internal structure.

INTERPERSONAL ORIENTATION. The interpersonal orientation of members of the several subsystems in these organizations was measured by using the Least Preferred Coworker instrument developed by Fiedler.[35] This semantic differential scale measures the respondent's interpersonal style on a continuum from primary concern with task accomplishment to primary concern with social relationships. The results are presented in Table 4.

Table 4. Subsystem Interpersonal Scores Ranked from Task Concern to Social Concern *

	ORGANIZATIONS						AVERAGE RANK ALL ORGANIZATIONS
SUBSYSTEM	I	II	III	IV	V	VI	
Sales	(103)2	(100)1	(90)2	(92)2.5	(118)1	(92)2	1.8
Applied research	(85)3	(96)2	(86)4	(99)1	(93)2.5	(98)1	2.3
Fundamental research	(112)1	(94)3	(87)3	(90)2.5	(88)4	(78)4	2.9
Production	(71)4	(83)4	(98)1	(83)4	(93)2.5	(90)3	3.1

* Numbers in parentheses are mean scores: high score indicates social concern; low score indicates task concern. Other numbers indicate rank order from social to task.

Although the interpersonal orientation of the various subsystems were generally differentiated in a direction consistent with their environmental tasks, the relationship was not as clear as in the case of structure. The sales subsystem, with a moderately certain subenvironment, did tend to have members who preferred a more socially oriented interpersonal style. The data also suggest that production personnel, whose task was most certain, preferred a more task-oriented style. In five organizations, fundamental-research personnel, confronted with a highly uncertain subenvironment, seemed to prefer a more task-oriented style, though less intensively than production personnel.

The findings for the applied-research subsystems are even less clear. In some organizations, members of these subsystems preferred a more social orientation; in others, a task orientation. The explanation may be because the applied-research task in the six organizations differed more than the tasks of any of the other basic subsystems. In some organizations, the applied-research subsystem was doing long-range research; in other organizations it was directly involved shortrange process development and technical service activities. This made it difficult to establish the subenvironmental requirements for applied research subsystems. It is also possible, as Fiedler has pointed out, that situational factors other than

[35] See note 16.

the nature of the task were also influencing the preferred interpersonal style in all of these subsystems.[36] Nevertheless, the findings about the interpersonal orientation of members of subsystems in these organizations appear to follow the curvilinear relationship consistent with their subenvironmental requirements, as interpreted by Fiedler's contingency model. The clearest evidence of this is seen in the average ranking of units for all six organizations.

Table 5. Dominant Time Orientation of Basic Subsystems *

SUBSYSTEMS	ORGANIZATIONS I	II	III	IV	V	VI
Sales	S	S	S	S	S	M
Production	S	M	S	S	S	M
Applied research	M	L	S	L	L	L
Fundamental research	L	L	L	L	L	L

* S = one month or less; M = one month to one year; L = one year to five years.

TIME ORIENTATION OF MEMBERS. The time orientation of members of the different units was measured with a question which asked for an estimate of the percentage of total time used working on activities affecting the organization's profits within a specific time period: less than one month, one month to one year, and one year to five years. The results (see Table 5 clearly support the prediction that the time orientation of members of each subsystem would be related to the time span of definitive feedback of the relevant subenvironment. Sales and production subsystems tended to have the shortest time orientations, consistent with the shorter time span of definitive feedback in the market and technical-economic subenvironments. The research subsystems tended to have a long-term time orientation, which was congruent with the longer time span of feedback in the scientific-subenvironment. The time orientation of the applied-research subsystems was somewhat less consistent than that of the fundamental-research subsystems, which, again, seemed to be due to the differences in the division of the research task within each organization. For example, in organizations I and III the applied-research subsystem worked primarily on immediate customer and process problems, whereas in the other organizations they focused on more complex applied problems. Thus, in organizations I and III the members of the applied research subsystems tended to have more short-termed time horizons.

[36] F. Fiedler, *op. cit.*

GOAL ORIENTATION OF MEMBERS. Finally, it was predicted that each subsystem would develop a goal orientation toward its relevant subenvironment. A list of ten criteria which managers might consider in making decisions relevant to product and process innovation was developed to measure this goal orientation. Three of these criteria related to factors in each of the three subenvironments; for example, competitive action (market), processing costs (technical-economic), and developing new knowledge (scientific). One criterion, which was related to the total environment, was not used in this analysis. The respondents were asked to select from these ten criteria the three most important considerations in making decisions, and then the next three most important.

Table 6. Goal Orientation of Basic Subsystems *

SUBSYSTEMS	ORGANIZATIONS I	II	III	IV	V	VI
Sales	M	M	M	M	M	M
Production	TE	TE	TE	TE	TE	TE
Applied research	S	TE	TE	TE	TE	TE
Fundamental research	S	TE	TE	S	TE	S

* M = market; TE = technical-economic; S = science.

The primary goal orientation of the sales and production subsystems (see Table 6) was as predicted. Sales personnel were more concerned with the market subenvironment, whereas production personnel were concerned primarily with the technical-economic subenvironment. In five of the organizations, however, the research personnel in the applied-research subsystems were concerned mainly with the technical-economic subenvironment. Among the fundamental-research subsystems the primary goal orientation was equally divided between the scientific subenvironment and the technical-economic subenvironment. This finding is not too surprising, since much of the activity of research subsystems was dealing with process improvements and modifications. However, where members indicated a primary goal orientation toward the technical-economic subenvironment, they also indicated a strong secondary orientation toward the scientific subenvironment. In goal orientations, then, the subsystems in these six organizations generally tended to develop a primary concern with their relevant subenvironment.

The basic subsystems were therefore differentiated in these four attributes, and the differentiation was generally in a direction consistent with predictions. Although these findings are not surprising, since they had been strongly suggested by earlier studies, they are important, because they suggest that these attributes within each subsystem are related to the particular requisites of the relevant subenvironment. They are also important because it was possible to measure these four attributes in each subsystem, at least crudely, so that the relationship of the differentiation in these four attributes to integration between the subsystems could be examined.

Differentiation and Integration within Organization. To test hypothesis 5, we measured the degree of differentiation in the four subsystem attibutes between the pairs of subsystems with high requisite integration by computing the differences in each attribute score for each pair of relevant units. The range of differences for all six organizations in each attribute was divided into quintiles. Each quintile was assigned a "unit of differentiation" score from one (least differentiated quintile) to five (most differentiated quintile). These five-point units of differentiation scores for each attribute made it possible to arrive at a rough measure of the relative differentiation between pairs by summing the score for each pair of subsystems in all four attributes.

The effectiveness of integration was measured by asking respondents for their evaluation of the state of interdepartmental relations between all the pairs of subsystems, the evaluation being made on a seven-point scale ranging from "sound, full unity of effort in obtaining innovations is achieved," (1) to "couldn't be worse—bad relations—serious problems exist in getting innovations, which are not being solved" (7). In general, the respondents in all organizations tended to use only the upper part of this scale. It was possible to check the validity of responses to this question in interviews and it was found that mean scores of 2.5 or more for a pair of relationships seemed to indicate that there were appreciable difficulties in achieving integration.

The rank orders of these integration scores are compared with the rank orders of units of differentiation for the appropriate pairs of subsystems within each organization in Table 7. In all six organizations a significant relationship was found (Spearman's coefficient of rank correlation) between the rank order of the units of differentiation and the rank order of the effectiveness of integration. The more highly differentiated pairs of subsystems were encountering more difficulty in achieving integration than the less highly differentiated pairs, thus strongly supporting the hypothesis. This relationship was found in all six organizations for the total units of differentiation, but was not consistent for the units of differentiation in any one attribute. This suggests that it may be the sum effect of differences in orientations and differences in formalized structure between any two subsystems that is related to achieving effective integration, and not just a large difference in one attribute. Even a cursory inspection of the data in Table 7 indicates variations in the extent to which these organizations were differentiated and integrated. These variations in differentiation and integration between organizations are now examined to determine if, as predicted, they are related to organizational performance.

Relation of Differentiation and Integration, to Organizational Performance. It appeared from hypothesis 6 that with the different demands of the several subenvironments in this study and the requirement for high interdependence between parts of the organizations, effective organizations would be both more highly differentiated and more highly integrated than less effective organizations.

The mean differentiation and integration scores for the pairs of subsystems in each or-

Table 7. Relationship of Differentiation and Integration of Subsystem Pairs in Six Organizations

	I		II		III	
SUBSYSTEM PAIRS	UNITS OF DIFFERENTIATION *	INTEGRATION SCORES †	UNITS OF DIFFERENTIATION	INTEGRATION SCORES	UNITS OF DIFFERENTIATION	INTEGRATION SCORES
Integrative–production	12(6)	2.47(4)	11(6)	2.60(4)	10(7)	2.78(5)
Integrative–sales	6(1)	1.91(1)	9(3)	2.19(3)	6(2)	2.32(2)
Integrative–applied research	7(2)	1.97(2)	4(1)	1.71(1)	4(1)	2.26(1)
Integrative–fundamental research	11(5)	2.72(6)	9(3)	2.80(6)	8(4.5)	3.00(6)
Production–applied research	10(3.5)	2.00(3)	10(5)	2.72(5)	9(6)	3.02(7)
Sales–applied research	10(3.5)	2.51(5)	9(3)	2.04(2)	8(4.5)	2.72(4)
Production–fundamental research	19(7)	2.95(7)	15(8)	3.05(7)	13(8)	3.04(8)
Sales–fundamental research	—	—	14(7)	3.07(8)	—	—
Applied research–fundamental research	—	—	—	—	7(3)	2.64(3)

	IV		V		VI	
	UNITS OF DIFFERENTIATION	INTEGRATION SCORES	UNITS OF DIFFERENTIATION	INTEGRATION SCORES	UNITS OF DIFFERENTIATION	INTEGRATION SCORES
Integrative–production	9(4.5)	2.82(4)	8(3)	3.10(3)	5(1)	3.15(3)
Integrative–sales	8(2.5)	2.47(3)	7(2)	2.78(2)	6(3)	2.90(2)
Integrative–applied research	8(2.5)	2.43(2)	6(1)	2.76(1)	6(3)	3.50(4)
Integrative–fundamental research	13(7)	3.41(7)	11(5)	3.32(5)	8(6)	3.65(6)
Production–applied research	7(1)	2.40(1)	9(4)	3.12(4)	6(3)	2.72(1)
Sales–applied research	9(4.5)	3.42(5)	13(6)	3.46(6)	7(5)	3.55(5)
Production–fundamental research	—	—	—	—	—	—
Sales–fundamental research	—	—	—	—	—	—
Applied research–fundamental research	10(6)	3.55(6)	—	—	11(7)	4.10(7)

* Low score indicates low degree of differentiation. Number in parentheses indicates rank order.

† Low score indicates effective integration. Level of significance of Spearman's coefficient of correlation between differentiation and integration is .05 for organization II and .01 for all others. Number in parentheses indicates rank order.

ganization with high requisite integration were used as an index of the total differentiation and integration in each organization. One difficulty with this procedure is the slight differences in the six organizations as to the subsystems having high requisite integration with the fundamental-research subsystems. Since this subsystem was highly differentiated in all the organizations, then including an extra pair relationship with it could cause a significant variation in the mean differentiation score for any organization. In computing the mean scores, therefore, only the pairs of subsystems common to all six organizations were included: applied research with sales, applied research with production, and the integrative subsystem with sales, production, applied research, and fundamental research. The mean differentiation and integration scores for the six organizations were then divided into high, medium, and low classes.

MEASURES OF PERFORMANCE. As Seashore and others have indicated, it is difficult to measure organizational performance.[37] In the organizations studied it seemed desirable to use the conventional financial data used by management as measures of performance. Since these six organizations were operating in the same environment, a profitable and growing operation should be good evidence of effective coping with the environment. Some managers, however, considered the data on the actual rate of profit too confidential, therefore actual profitability data were not provided. It was possible however, to secure other indices of performance, such as: change in profits over the five years prior to the study; change in sales volume over the same period and percentage of current sales volume accounted for by products developed within the last five years (a measure of past success in innovation, and also an indicator of probable future effectiveness in maintaining volume and profits). The six organizations were ranked in each of these indices. (see Table 8). These rankings were then totaled as a crude measure of the total performance of the organization.

As a check on the validity of these measures, the chief executive responsible for each organization was asked to indicate what percentage of an ideal 100 percent performance he thought his organization was achieving. These

Table 8. Organizational Performance *

ORGANIZATION	CHANGE IN PROFITS	CHANGE IN SALES VOLUME	NEW PRODUCTS DEVELOPED (% OF CURRENT SALES)	TOTAL RANKING †	CHIEF EXECUTIVES' SUBJECTIVE APPRAISALS †
I	2	3	1	6(2)	2.5
II	1	1	3	5(1)	2.5
III	3 ‡	2	4	9(3)	1
IV	6	4	2	12(4)	4
V	4	6	6	16(6)	6
VI	5	5	5 §	15(5)	5

* Data from past 5 years, ranked from high to low performance.

† Spearman's rank-order correlation between the ranking of index totals (in parentheses) and the ranking of chief executives' subjective appraisal was significant at .05 level (corrected for ties).

‡ Had been operating at or near the break-even point during 5-year period. A small increase in profit made this index rise unrealistically in relation to all other organizations, so the average of the other two indices was used.

§ All products had been introduced in the past 5 years because operating only 5 years, therefore the average of the rankings for the other two indices was used.

[37] S. Seashore, B. Indik, and B. Georgopoulos, Relationships Among Criteria of Job Performance, *Journal of Applied Psychology*, 44 (1960), 195–202.

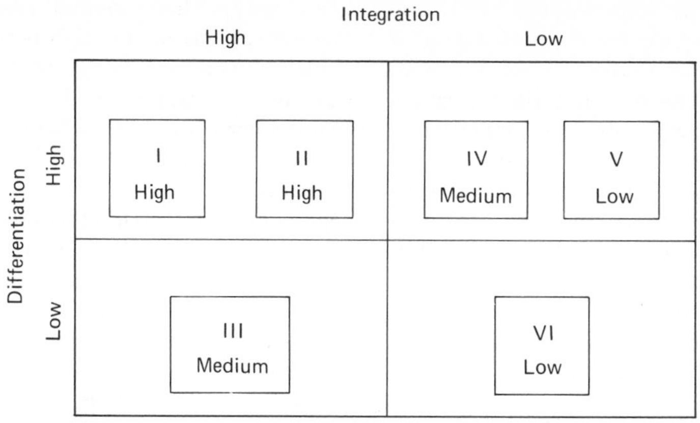

Fig. 1. Differentiation, integration, and performance in the six organizations. Performance rankings are given in cells.

data were also ranked for the six organizations (see Table 8). The rank-order correlation between the chief executives' subjective appraisal and the index of performance suggests that the salient dimensions of total organizational performance were being measured, at least crudely.

The only significant variation between the chief executives' subjective appraisal and the empirical performance index was in organization III, where the chief executive, pleased at the performance of his organization in finally achieving a consistent, if small, profit, ranked his organization's performance higher than the other chief executives ranked theirs.

As a further check on these performance measures, interviews were held with the top two or three executives including the chief executive, in each organization. Data collected in these interviews were consistent with those reported in Table 8. In organizations I and II the top executives were pleased with the past and current performance and felt the future looked even more promising. The top executives in organizations III and IV appraised the performance of their organizations more modestly. In organization III, the top executives indicated, that they had been through a difficult period, but in the current year the organization had begun an upward trend in performance, although they indicated a need for even greater improvement. Organization IV, according to its top executives had in the distant past (five to ten years before the study) been very effective and an industry leader. Its position had slipped in the ensuing years, but at the time of the study the executives felt the organization had reversed this unfavorable trend, although there was a need for greater improvement in performance. Organizations V and VI were both characterized by their top executives as having considerable difficulty in introducing and marketing new products. This together with other measures of performance gave the top executives a feeling of disquiet and a sense of urgency to find ways to improve performance.

Based on these evaluations and the data presented in Table 8, the organizations were divided into three performance categories: high (I and II), medium (III and IV), and low (V and VI). The organizations in each performance category were then compared in terms of their average differentiation and integration scores, as shown in Figure 1. It is clear from this figure that, as we had predicted, the two high-performing organizations had both the high differentiation and the high integration demanded by this environment.[38] The two

[38] Using orthogonal comparisons, differences in integration scores between the high-performing organizations (I and II) and the low-performing organizations (V and VI) are significant at .01. Differences in integration scores between high-performing organizations (I and II) and medium-performing organizations (III and IV) are significant at .05. Differences between the medium-performing organizations (III and IV) and the low-performing organizations (V and VI) are only significant at .10. Because of the nature of

medium-performing organizations (III and IV) were not achieving the required degree of differentiation or integration. Although organization IV had achieved high differentiation, it had relatively low integration. Organization III, which was achieving high integration, had the second lowest degree of differentiation. Organization VI, one of the two low performers had both the lowest degree of differentiation and the lowest degree of integration. The other low-performing organization (V) was achieving relatively high differentiation, but had very low integration.

RELATION OF SUBSYSTEM ATTRIBUTES TO SUBENVIRONMENTS. Despite this general support for the hypothesis about the relationship between differentiation, integration, and performance, it seemed of interest to get more details on the extent to which subsystems in the various organizations develop differential attributes that fit the demands of their subenvironments. In this analysis, it was necessary to exclude the applied-research subsystems, because of their variable function in the six organizations.

To determine whether the various subsystems met their subenvironmental demands in regard to structure, we trichotomized the structure scores for all subsystems. Fundamental-research subsystems were expected to fall in the lower third (less structured), sales subsystems in the middle third, and production subsystems the highest third. The interpersonal orientation scores were dichotomized: production and fundamental-research subsystems in the social half. As a test of whether the time and goal orientations of a subsystem were consistent with its subenvironmental demands, subsystems in the lower third of the range in orientation toward required time and goal dimensions were defined as not effecting a satisfactory fit.

The number of deviations from subenvironmental requirements in all four subsystem attributes was then calculated for subsystems in the high-performing organizations, which had 4 deviations and in the medium- and low-performing organizations, each of which had 10 deviations. The difference between the high and low performers and the high and medium performers is significant at $P = .05$ (Fischer's exact test). This provides further evidence that subsystems in the high-performing organizations were achieving differentiation that was more consistent with subenvironmental requirements than were subsystems in less effective organizations and that effective performance would be related to achieving both a degree of differentiation consistent with the requirements of the subenvironments and a degree of integration consistent with the requirements of the total environment. In this particular environment, this meant both high differentiation and high integration.

We are not suggesting, however, that other factors were not also influencing performance. Also no attempt was made to explore the causal influence of differentiation and integration on each other, yet some of the data gathered in interviews suggest that the interrelationship is complex. For example, in organization VI, which had both low differentiation and low integration, there was considerable evidence that certain subsystems (particularly the research subsystems) had such low differentiation that they were competing with each other in performing the same tasks. One interpretation would be that the competition resulting from the low degree of differentiation was contributing to the difficulties of achieving integration. Thus, in order to achieve higher integration this organization would first have to achieve clearer differentiation of the competing subsystems.

Most important, these findings confirm the importance of questions on how an organization can achieve both high differentiation and high integration when these are basically antagonistic states. Since the data supported the hypothesis that high differentiation between any pair of subsystems was related to low integration between them, the question arises as to how organizations I and II maximized both states simultaneously. There is considerable evidence that many, if not most industries, will be increasingly characterized by dynamic, heterogeneous environments, as scientific advances continue and as markets and technologies become more complex. If high performance in such environments is at least partially related to attaining both high differentiation and high integration, it is clear that to be effective, the organization will have to achieve integration between specialists, while simultaneously encouraging increased differentiation.

---

the differentiation scores, calculations of significance would not be meaningful.

Achieving Differentiation and Integration

Emergence of Integrative Devices. Hypothesis 7 predicted the emergence of integrative devices. As indicated, in all the organizations except organization II, there were integrative subsystems whose members had the function of integrating the sales-research and the production-research subsystems. In organization II there was also a formally established integrative subsystem, but it functioned somewhat differently from the others and might be termed an integrative role set.

In addition to these integrative subsystems, four of these organizations (I, IV, V, and VI) had integrating teams with representatives from each of the basic subsystems and the integrative subsystems. The function of the teams was to facilitate the coordination of these activities of the various subsystems by providing formal machinery for discussing and resolving mutual problems.

Thus the hypothesis that integrative devices would emerge in organizations with environments which required both high differentiation and integration was confirmed; however, we were interested in examining these devices to understand the factors related to their effectiveness in achieving integration in the face of varying degrees of subsystem differentiation. Preliminary and prior research pointed to several factors that might be partial determinants of the effectiveness of these devices, and these were investigated further.

Structure and Orientation of Integrative Subsystem. It was predicted that one partial determinant of effective integrative devices would be that the orientations of members of the integrative subsystem would be intermediate between those found in subsystems they were to coordinate. An effective coordinator working between research and sales, for example, could be expected to be oriented equally toward long-term problems (the requisite time orientation of researchers) and short-term problems (the requisite time orientation of sales personnel) and to have an equal concern with market goals and scientific goals. Similarly, it was expected that effective coordinators would have interpersonal orientations between those of the groups they were linking. Finally, it was expected that the structure of the integrative subsystem would be intermediate between those of the basic subsystems being linked. This determinant was derived from the work of Sherif and of Seiler.[39]

The methods used for measuring structure, and time, goal, and interpersonal orientations were also used for this analysis. The midpoint of the range of scores in each attribute was computed for the basic subsystems being integrated. The difference between the score for the integrative subsystem and the midpoint was then computed, to determine how closely the integrative subsystem approached an intermediate position.[40]

These difference scores indicate that the integrative subsystem in organization I was the only one to be intermediate in all four attributes, as indicated in Table 9. All other organizations, except organization V, appeared to be intermediate in two of the four attributes. Data gathered in interviews suggested that in all the organizations not intermediate in all four attributes (except organization II), the failure to meet this condition made it difficult for the members of the integrative subsystem to communicate effectively.

The time and goal orientations seemed to cause the most difficulty. Members of the basic subsystems in organizations III, V, and VI complained frequently that the members of

[39] J. Seiler, *op. cit.;* M. Sherif, *op. cit.*

[40] In structure and interpersonal orientation, where there was only a single mean score for each subsystem, this procedure was straightforward. However, since in time and goal orientations there were three dimensions to each attribute, the procedure was somewhat more complicated. In time orientation the differences in only short- and long-term orientations were considered, since these were the dimensions where the greatest differences existed in all six organizations. The differences in both dimensions were summed to get a single score. In goal orientation only those units which were concerned with a particular subenvironment were considered. For example, in orientation toward the marketing subenvironment, only the differences between the integrative unit and the sales and research subsystems were considered, since these were the units between which the integrative subsystem was providing a flow of marketing information. The differences in orientation toward the market, toward the scientific, and the technical-economic environment were then summed to get a single score.

Table 9. Intermediate Position of Integrative Subsystems *

	ORGANIZATION					
ATTRIBUTE	I	II	III	IV	V	VI
Structure	2.0(+)	4.5(−)	3.5(−)	0.0(+)	2.5(−)	1.0(+)
Interpersonal orientation	1.5(+)	7.8(−)	2.8(+)	13.0(−)	2.0(+)	6.5(−)
Time orientation	8.0(+)	19.0(+)	33.0(−)	22.0(+)	51.0(−)	34.0(−)
Goal orientation	.4(+)	.5(+)	.5(+)	.7(−)	.7(−)	.5(+)
Number of intermediate attributes	4	2	2	2	1	2

* The figures given are the differences between the midpoint of the range of basic subsystem scores in each attribute and the score of the integrative subsystem in each attribute. Since different scales have been used for each attribute, comparisons cannot be made between attributes; + indicates low difference in attribute as compared with other organizations; − indicates a high difference.

the integrative subsystems, who were not intermediate in time orientation, were too preoccupied with current problems to be helpful in coordinating long-range activities. Typical comments from sales, production, and research personnel in these organizations follow:

> I am no coordinator, but I can see that one of our troubles is that they [integrative] are so tied up in day-to-day detail that they can't look to the future. They are still concerned with '64 materials when they should be concerned with '65 markets.
>
> We get lots of reports from them [the integrative subsystem] and we talk to them frequently. The trouble is that all they present to us [in research] are short-term needs. They aren't the long-range things we are interested in.
>
> They [the integrative unit] only find out about problems when they find out somebody has quit buying our material and is buying somebody else's, and this keeps you on the defense. A lot of our work is catch-up work. We would like more future-oriented work from them.

Similarly members of the basic units in organization IV and V frequently complained about the lack of balance in the goal orientation of the members of the integrative subsystem:

> Our relations with them [the integrative subsystem] are good, but not as good as with research. They [integrative] are not as cost-conscious as the laboratory people. They are concerned with the customer.
>
> He [the integrator] is under a lot of pressure to work with the salesmen on existing products in our product lines. What he [the integrator] should be and often tries to act like is a liaison person, but in reality he is not. He is too concerned with sales problems.
>
> What's lacking is that they [the integrators] are so busy that they continually postpone working with research. They work closely with applied research on minor modifications, but the contact with basic research is minimal.

We are not implying that the other attributes (structure and interpersonal orientation) were unimportant, but only that they operated more outside the awareness of the members of the organization. In any case one can conclude from these data that organization I, with the most effective integration, had an integrative subsystem that was consistently intermediate in structure and orientation, whereas organizations II, III, IV, and VI had integrative subsystems that were only moderately intermediate, and organization V, a low-integration organization, had an integrative subsystem that was intermediate only to a very limited extent.

Influence Attributed to Integrative Subsystem. A second partial determinant of effective integrative devices was also derived from the work of Seiler, and from a preliminary analysis. Seiler reported that intergroup relations tend to be characterized by open collaboration when high-satus groups were initiating for lower-status groups.[41] Preliminary analysis suggested that many of the activities would be initiated by the integrative subsystem; therefore an effective integrative subsystem would be perceived to be legitimate in initiating activities for the basic subsystems. Seiler had discussed this legitimacy in terms of status, but the internal organizational status of a subsystem can be measured in terms of the influence attributed to members of that subsystem by members of the rest of the organization. We thus predicted that the members of effective integrative subsystems would be perceived by other organizational members as having high influence in decision making relative to the members of other subsystems.

To measure the influence of the several subsystems, members of each organization were asked, "How much say or influence do you feel each of the units listed below has on product-innovation decisions?" Each subsystem was included, and responses were made on a five-point scale ranging from "little or no influence" to "a very great deal of influence." The mean scores for each subsystem within each organization were then ranked.

The integrative subsystem was ranked first out of the five subsystems, in organizations I, IV, and VI; second in organizations II and V, and tied for first ranking in organization III. Since all integrative subsystems appeared to have relatively high influence, it was concluded that this particular determinant did not discriminate among these organizations and it was not used further in this analysis.

Basis of Influence. A separate but related partial determinant is that the basis for influence be appropriate to the task of achieving integration. Influence can be based either on professional expertise or on hierarchical authority. As Blau and Scott have pointed out, influence based on hierarchical position is not appropriate where professional judgment is required for decisions related to coordination.[42] In the organizations studied, where integration often had to be achieved around complex, unprogrammed problems involving technical issues, it was predicted that integrators whose influence stemmed from their professional competence would be more effective than those whose influence was based on their position in the organization.

Data about the basis of influence was collected in interviews from responses to questions about the role of the integrative subsystem. In organizations I and II, the integrative personnel were seen as having influence primarily stemming from their knowledge and competence in dealing with problems associated with the environment. In the other organizations the influence of the integrative personnel was almost entirely attributed to their position.

Typical comments made by personnel in the basic subsystems in organizations I and II are:

> He [the integrator] has a powerful job if he can get the people to work for him. A good man in that job has everybody's ear open to him. A good coordinator has to be thoroughly oriented to his market or to his process. Whichever area he is working in he has to be able to make good value judgments in his area.
>
> The way we operate we feel that we get suggestions rather than directions from him [the integrator]. In my relations with him there is 100 percent freedom of action. He may tell me what to work on, but in the day-to-day operations I am never really aware of it.
>
> We usually talk to him [the integrator] on the nature of two things. We are asking him that since we have such and such a material, how does it work as a new product? He might tell us what kind of product the market is looking for. We get a flow of information both ways.
>
> They [the integrators] are the kingpins. They have a good feel for our [research's] ability and they know the needs of the market. They will work back and forth with us and the others.
>
> It [the integrative subsystem] is on the border of research, so we work together closely. The integrative people are just a step away from the customer, so when I make a change in a material I let them know because they may have a customer who can use it. The good thing about our situation is that it [the integrative unit] is close enough to sales to know what they are

[41] J. Seiler, Organization Theory and Primary Group Concepts, *op. cit.*, 196–197.

[42] P. Blau and W. Scott, *Formal Organizations* (San Francisco: Chandler, 1962), p. 185.

doing and close enough to research to know what we are doing.

It is clear from these comments that the coordinators were seen as people who had knowledge about different aspects of the environment, and this knowledge appeared to be the basis of their high influence.

In the other four organizations, the comments about the integrator's role were quite different:

> We [in the integrative subsystem] are in the thick of activities here. We are in control of the experimental material. When we feel that things are ready, we can transfer to sales. In this respect we are in the driver's seat.
>
> We [in research] have to go by what they [the integrative subsystem] say. They have the upper hand. If we can't get their approval, we have to shut up.
>
> He [an integrator] will tell you what material he thinks will work, and if you don't agree there isn't much you can do except beat your head against the wall and continue to work. If you aren't getting anywhere, then eventually he may listen to you.
>
> We [the integrators] are staff men, but I like to feel we are line men. I take authority and initiative. If a salesman has a problem I go directly to him; then I tell his boss. When I talk to the laboratory director I like to feel I am his boss, even though the organization chart doesn't say so.
>
> In setting up a coordinator, what you have done is set up a staff position where [the general manager] is able to go to a man and beat him on the head to get information and get things done.
>
> A good coordinator is a guy with a red hot bayonet. He doesn't take no for an answer on anything. He also is in an enviable position since he reports to the general manager and he finds very little opposition to what he wants to do.
>
> Nobody wants to pull the wool over the coordinator's eyes, since he reports to the general manager. That would be disastrous. I don't think anybody could be a coordinator and have many friends. You have to be too aggressive.
>
> For a man to move into a coordinating role should be a big thing. But it isn't now. My guys can say "I know more than that guy [in the integrative subsystem]." People compare their skills and often the comparison is not favorable.
>
> He [the integrator] is supposed to know the field and he may think our product isn't any good. This is fine if you have confidence in him, but we have had a bad experience with some of them. As the knowledge of chemistry grows, his [the integrator's] knowledge of the market must grow. I guess I would appraise the situation this way: just because they [integrators] have had twenty years' experience doesn't mean they have twenty years of knowledge.

In these organizations, the coordinators were seen as having influence stemming from their positions, either because of the formal authority of their position or because of their close proximity to top management; the only comments about the knowledge and competence of the coordinators tended to be negative ones. These excerpts from interviews suggest that organizations I and II met the hypothesized condition for good integration and the other four organizations did not.

Perceived Basis of Rewards for Integrators. A third partial determinant of effective integrative devices was suggested by the work of Zander and Wolfe.[43] They found that members of groups conditioned experimentally to be concerned with group performance, "generated more emphasis on providing successful scores for others and less concern about personal rewards or costs involved, more motivation to achieve a good score, more trust in others, and less strain in interpersonal relations."[44] On this basis, it was predicted that integrative devices would be most effective when the integrators perceived themselves to be rewarded for the performance of the total set of activities they were integrating; that is, effective integrators were expected to perceive that they were being rewarded for the achievement *with* others of a superordinate goal.

One of the questions included in the questionnaire asked respondents to select from a list of possible criteria for evaluation, the three most important factors used by their supervisors to evaluate their performance. The cri-

[43] A. Zander and D. Wolfe, Administrative Rewards and Coordination, *Administrative Science Quarterly* 9 (1964), 50–69.
[44] *Ibid.*

teria used were: your own individual accomplishments, performance of your subordinates, performance of the product group, how well you get along with others in your own department, and how well you get along with members of other departments. The respondents were asked to rank their three choices: most important (1) second most important (2), and least important (3). The mean score for the integrators in each organization was then computed. The criteria by which personnel were being evaluated indicated to them the basis on which they were being rewarded; therefore, the basis of evaluation may be used as a measure of the perceived basis of rewards.

The data indicated that integrative personnel in the two least integrated organizations V (with a score of 2.5) and VI (with a score of 3) saw themselves as being significantly less rewarded for the performance of the product group with which they were associated than did the integrators in organizations II (with a score of 1.8) and III (with a score of 1.1). Organizations V and VI were significantly different from organizations II and III at the .01 level. Although the difference between organizations V and VI and organizations I and IV (both with a mean score of 2.0) was not significant, it was clearly in the predicted direction. The integrators in organizations V and VI also perceived themselves to be significantly more rewarded for their individual performance than did the integrators in organizations III and IV. In organizations V and VI, then, this determinant was not present. In organizations II and III, two of the high-integration organizations, it was clearly operating; while in organizations I and IV, this determinant was operating to a moderate extent. From this, one can conclude that this factor generally discriminated between the organizations which were lowest in achieving integration and the other organizations.

Total Influence in the Organizational System. The fourth partial determinant of effective integrative devices was derived from the work of Smith and Ari, who found a relationship between the total amount of perceived influence among organizational members and organizational effectiveness.[45] They concluded that, "The significant exercise of control by both members and leaders leads to a high degree of identification and involvement in the organization." Horwitz's findings about influence and hostility carried this point a step further.[46] Organizations with subsystem members who feel that they have high influence in the organization would be likely to feel that their point of view was being given adequate weight by other groups and therefore would not feel hostility toward the members of other subsystems. This suggested that another factor related to effective integrative devices would be a high total amount of perceived influence in the organization.

The question used to determine the relative influence of the integrative subsystem was also used to derive the data for this determinant. The scores ranged from "little or no influence" (1) to "a very great influence" (5). Organizations I, II, and IV had mean influence scores of 3.6; organization III, a mean influence score of 3.5. The two organizations with the lowest integration scores—V with a total influence score of 2.5, and VI with a total influence score of 3.1—had significantly less total influence than the other four organizations. These two organizations were significantly different from the other organizations at the .05 level using an orthogonal comparison and did not meet this determinant.

Locus of Influence in Subsystems. A fifth partial determinant of effective integrative devices was also suggested by Smith and Ari. In the same study they predicted that "democratic" influence (high influence at lower levels of the organization) would be associated with high organizational performance.[47] Although their findings in the organization they studied did not support their hypotheses, they concluded that:

> It is conceivable that a positively sloped distribution of control [high influence at lower echelons] might lead to a system of shared norms and consequently concerted action on the part of the organization in a different type of organization with different

[45] C. Smith, and O. Ari, Organizational Structure and Member Consensus, *American Journal of Sociology, 69* (May 1964), 623–638.

[46] M. Horwitz, "Hostility and Its Management in Classrom Groups," in W. W. Charters and N. L. Gage (eds.), *Readings in the Social Psychology of Education* (Boston: Allyn and Bacon, 1964), pp. 196–212.

[47] C. Smith and O. Ari, *op. cit.*, 623–638.

organizational conditions. This might occur in a "mutual benefit" type of organization such as some voluntary organizations where the interests and objectives of members and leaders are more widely shared, and where decision-making is of a judgmental nature.[48]

As these authors point out, Tannenbaum found that this condition was present in a voluntary organization.[49] Although the organizations we studied were not voluntary, they had managers and professionals at several levels of the organizational hierarchy whose interests and objectives might be more highly shared than in the organization studied by Smith and Ari. Furthermore, the environmental demands made it necessary to have the influence for decision making and conflict resolution at the management levels, where the knowledge about technical and market factors was available. We therefore predicted that another partial determinant of effective integrative devices would be the presence of a sufficient degree of influence to resolve interdepartmental conflicts at the level in each subsystem where the most knowledge about subenvironmental conditions was available; that is better integration would be achieved if the persons who had the knowledge to make decisions also had sufficient influence to do so.

Data about the locus of pertinent knowledge was obtained in interviews with top managers in all six organizations. There was widespread agreement that in both the fundamental- and applied-research subsystems, the knowledge required to make product decisions was found among personnel at the lower levels of the organizational hierarchy. In the sales and production subsystems, where the subenvironment was more certain, the required knowledge was at the upper levels of the hierarchy. In the integrative subsystems, the respondents indicated that the required knowledge was to be found among members at the lower levels of the hierarchy. Since in all six organizations, high influence in the integrative subsystems was at the lower levels, as consistent with the task requirements, the integrative subsystems were not considered in this analysis.

[48] *Ibid.*, 638.

[49] A. Tannenbaum, Control in Organizations: Individual Adjustment and Organizational Performance, *Administrative Science Quarterly*, 7 (1962), 236–257.

To measure influence in each subsystem, respondents were asked to indicate for their own subsystems, "How much say or influence each of the levels has on product innovation decisions?" The scale used was five points ranging from "little or no influence" to "a very great deal of influence." These data were analyzed to determine if the levels where influence was concentrated were also the levels with the required knowledge.

Organizations V and VI (the low-integration organizations) did not have the highest influence at the required level in two subsystems. In organization VI, influence was centered at too high a level in the applied-research subsystem and at too low a level in the production subsystem hierarchy.

In both the applied- and fundamental-research subsystems of organization V, the highest influence was too far up the organizational hierarchy. Organizations II, III, and IV each had one subsystem in which influence was not concentrated at the required level. In organization II influence was centered at too low a level in the production hierarchy. The concentrated influence in the applied research subsystem in organization III was at too high a level in the hierarchy, while in organization IV it was at too low a level in the sales hierarchy. In organization I the locus of high influence was consistent with the required knowledge in all four subsystems. Thus organization I, which achieved the highest integration, met this condition completely; organizations II, III, and IV met it partially, and organizations V and VI, with the lowest degree of integration, met it the least.

Modes of Conflict Resolution. The sixth determinant was suggested by the work of Blake and Mouton, who emphasized that the mode of conflict resolution used in organizations was an important variable in intergroup collaboration.[50] Initially they had identified five possible modes of resolving conflict: win-lose power struggle, smoothing over, withdrawal, compromise, or confrontation. They suggested that organizations placing greater emphasis on confrontation or problem-solving modes of conflict resolution would have effective intergroup relations.

In complex organizations having differen-

[50] R. Blake and J. Mouton, *The Managerial Grid* (Houston: Gulf Publishing Co., 1964).

tiated subsystems with different goals, norms, and orientations, it appeared that intergroup conflict would be an inevitable part of organizational life. The effective achievement of integration through the use of teams and other interpersonal contacts, therefore, would be closely related to the ability of the organization to resolve these conflicts. It was therefore predicted that the use of confrontation as the typical mode of conflict resolution would be an effective integrative procedure. The more confrontation and problem solving that occurred within an organization, the more effective would be its integrative procedures. Although this determinant is the last to be discussed it is not the least important. The differentiated subsystems often have quite different interests and objectives, so that the resolution of conflict between them may well be the most important function of integrative devices.

Limitations of space make it impossible to describe in detail the method used to measure the modes of conflict resolution, but a short description may be useful. The instrument to measure modes of conflict resolution used aphorisms or traditional proverbs, which described various methods of resolving conflict. It was assumed that these modes could be classified into the five types identified by Blake: confrontation, compromise, smoothing, forcing, and withdrawal, and the aphorisms were selected to match these modes.[51] Aphorisms were used, because they represent folk wisdom about the useful methods of handling conflict and because they avoided the use of biased phraseology and social science jargon.

Respondents indicated on a five-point scale (from "very typical behavior, usually occurs" to "behavior which never occurs") to what extent each of twenty-five aphorisms described typical ways of handling conflict in their organization. The data were factor analyzed using an orthogonal rotation. Three factors were identified and are presented in Table 10. Factor I described the forcing mode of conflict resolution while factor II described the smoothing mode and factor III described the confrontation mode. No other interpretable factors were present.

The scores for these three factors provide several important findings (see Table 11). Although all organizations used confrontation more than other modes, organizations I and II used confrontation to a significantly greater degree than the other organizations and organizations III and IV used it to a significantly greater extent than organizations V and VI. As

Table 10. Modes of Conflict Resolution

FACTOR AND APHORISM	FACTOR LOADING
I. Forcing	
Might overcomes right.	.56
The arguments of the strongest have always the most weight.	.47
He who fights and runs away lives to run another day.	.45
If you cannot make a man think as you do make him do as you think.	.39
II. Smoothing	
Kill your enemies with kindness.	.42
Soft words win hard hearts.	.41
Smooth words make smooth ways.	.41
When one hits you with a stone hit him with a piece of cotton.	.38
III. Confrontation	
By digging and digging the truth is discovered.	.57
Seek till you find and you'll not lose your labor.	.50
A question must be decided by knowledge and not by numbers, if it is to have a right decision.	.41
Come now and let us reason together.	.41

[51] R. Blake and J. Mouton, *op. cit.*

predicted, the effectiveness of each organization in achieving integration seemed to be clearly related to the extent that its members relied on problem-solving behavior to resolve conflicts.

Table 11. Modes of Conflict Resolution *

ORGANIZATION	FACTOR I. FORCING	II. SMOOTHING	III. CONFRONTATION
I	9.5	8.9	13.0 †
II	9.5	9.3	13.1 †
III	9.1 ‡	9.0	12.4 †
IV	9.7	9.8 ‡	12.0 †
V	9.8	9.0	11.7 †
VI	8.5	9.8 ‡	11.8 †

* Higher scores indicate more typical behavior.
† Pairs of organizations (I and II, III and IV, and V and VI significantly different from other organizations at .01 level (orthogonal comparison).
‡ Significantly different from other organizations at .01 level (orthogonal comparison).

These data also provide an interesting additional finding. Organizations IV and VI were doing significantly more smoothing than the other organizations. Organizations III and VI were using significantly less forcing behavior than the other organizations. This, together with the data about smoothing, suggests that a large amount of smoothing behavior or a small amount of forcing behavior can also hinder effective integration. For example, organization VI, with the lowest integration, was not only doing less confrontation than the more effective organizations, but was also doing more smoothing and less forcing. This suggests that while heavy reliance on controntation to handle conflict is important, it is also important to have a supporting mode of handling conflict which relies on some forcing behavior and a relative absence of smoothing behavior.

Summary. One of the main broad hypotheses of this study was that those organizations with integrative devices that more clearly met the six hypothesized partial determinants would be able to achieve both high integration and high differentiation, and that these in turn would be associated with high performance. All of the data relevant to this general hypothesis have now been presented and are summarized in Table 12. This indicates the extent to which organizations met the conditions for each of the six partial determinants. We have no adequate theory or empirical data at present to guide us in gauging the relative impact of each of these conditions on overall effectiveness of integration, nor on how these conditions affect one another. There certainly is no reason to think they are simply additive. However, the entire configuration of these conditions in relation to our measure of overall integration is highly suggestive of a close causal relationship. Experimental methods will probably be necessary to develop an understanding of these relationships further.

The relation between these six partial determinants and the degree of differentiation is not so clear. One can see by inspection that organizations I and II present patterns that fit the entire sequence of hypothesized relations very closely. They met most of the six conditions, achieved high differentiation as well as high integration, and were the two high companies in total system performance. This suggests that, as predicted, integrative devices that meet the six conditions tend to increase both overall integration and differentiation, which then leads to high performance in this industrial environment.

The data on organizations III and IV suggest that they achieved their medium level of overall performance by emphasizing different states. Organization III was the higher of the two in integration, but did not achieve a very high degree of differentiation. In contrast, organization IV seems to have emphasized achieving a fairly high degree of differentiation at the expense of integration. This kind of a potential exchange is, of course, consistent with our finding that these two states are essentially antagonistic.

The final pair (V and VI) were low in overall performance. Organization V achieved a higher degree of differentiation than is consistent with its failure to meet the six conditions and its level of performance, but its level of integration is consistent with these variables. This, along with the other data, suggests that integration is a better single predictor of

Table 12. Summary of Partial Determinants of Effective Integrative Devices Relative to Differentiation, Integration, and Performance

ORGANIZATION	INTERMEDIATE POSITION OF INTEGRATIVE SUBSYSTEM *	INFLUENCE OF INTEGRATORS DERIVED FROM TECHNICAL COMPETENCE *	INTEGRATORS PERCEIVE REWARDS AS RELATED TO TOTAL PERFORMANCE *	HIGH INFLUENCE THROUGHOUT THE ORGANIZATION *
I	H	H	M	H
II	M	H	H	H
III	M	L	H	H
IV	M	L	M	H
V	L	L	L	L
VI	M	L	L	L

ORGANIZATION	INFLUENCE CENTERED AT REQUISITE LEVEL *	MODES OF CONFLICT RESOLUTION	DEGREE OF DIFFERENTIATION	DEGREE OF INTEGRATION	SYSTEM PERFORMANCE
I	H	H	H(9.4)	H(2.3)	H
II	M	H	H(8.7)	H(2.4)	H
III	M	L	L(7.5)	H(2.7)	M
IV	M	L	H(9.0)	L(2.9)	M
V	L	M	H(9.0)	L(3.1)	L
VI	L	L	L(6.3)	L(3.3)	L

* High = high, M = medium, L = low; indicates relative extent to which each organization met this condition.

performance than differentiation alone. Organization VI presents a pattern that is again consistent with all hypothesized relationships. It failed to meet almost all of the conditions for integrative devices that were predicted to be associated with high integration and differentiation, and is, in fact, the lowest company on both of these scores.

Bureaucracy, Bureaucratization, and Debureaucratization[1]

S. N. EISENSTADT

In the literature dealing with bureaucracy we can often discern a continual shift between two points of view. The first point of view defines bureaucracy mainly as a tool, or a mechanism created for the successful and efficient implementation of a certain goal or goals. Bureaucracy is seen as an epitome of rationality and of efficient implementation of goals and provision of services.

The second point of view sees bureaucracy mainly as an instrument of power, of exercising control over people and over different spheres of life, and of continuous expansion of such power either in the interests of the bureaucracy itself or in the interests of some (often sinister) masters. This point of view tends mainly to stress the process of bureaucratization, i.e., the extension of the power of a bureaucratic organization over many areas beyond its initial purpose, the growing internal formalization within the bureaucracy, the regimentation of these areas by the bureaucracy, and in general a strong emphasis by the bureaucracy on the extension of its power.

This twofold attitude toward bureaucracy can be discerned, although in differing degrees, in most of the basic literature on the subject, whether that of the classical sociological approaches (Max Weber, Mosca, Michels) or that of public administration and the theory of organization. This twofold approach has in fact run through most of the discussions about bureaucracy since the end of the last century.[2]

Although the awareness of this problem of the twofold aspect of bureaucracy can be found in most of the literature dealing with bureaucracy, it is significant that these two points of view rarely converge. For those persons, as for instance the students of public administration, who see bureaucracy as a tool for implementation of goals, the power element is mainly seen as a stumbling block in the process of rational and efficient implementation of such goals. For those who see in bureaucracies mainly instruments of power and bearers of a continuous process of bureaucratization and of growing power of oligarchies, the implementation of the official or purported goals of the bureaucracy is but a secondary aspect, sometimes only an empty ideology.

And yet the very fact that these two points of view can be found in almost all the literature on bureaucracy seems to indicate that they are not two entirely separate and contradictory points of view, but rather that they point to various possibilities, all inherent in the very nature of bureaucracy. Thus the main problem seems to be not which point of view is right in itself, but rather the conditions under which each of these tendencies becomes actualized and predominant in any given bureaucratic organization.

It is the purpose of this paper, first, to show that both these tendencies are indeed inherent in the basic conditions of growth and development of any bureaucracy by its very nature as a social organization; and, second, to propose

---

From *Administrative Science Quarterly*, Vol. 4, December 1959, pp. 302–320. Reprinted with permission of the author and the publisher.

[1] This paper is a development of some of the analyses presented in a Trend Report on Bureaucracy and Bureaucratization, prepared by the writer for *Current Sociology*, 7 (1958), 99–163 (hereafter cited as Trend Report). I am indebted to the publishers, Messrs. Blackwell, Oxford, for permission to reprint some parts of the report. The reader will find in the Trend Report a more complete exposition of some of the points made here. The presentation here owes much to several discussions of this problem held during the fall of 1958 at the Universities of Oslo and Copenhagen and the Christian Michelsen Institute at Bergen. The general report has greatly benefited from the preliminary data of a research project on bureaucracy and new immigrants conducted at the Hebrew University under the supervision of Dr. E. Katz and the writer.

[2] For a fuller discussion of this problem and of the literature see Trend Report.

some preliminary hypotheses about the conditions under which each of these tendencies may become predominant in a given bureaucracy. In this way we hope to demonstrate that the convergence of various types of studies of bureaucracy and organizations that have developed recently can enable us to overcome the dichotomy developing between these two different points of view and some of the problems of the "metaphysical pathos" in the discussion of bureaucracy.[3]

Conditions of Development of Bureaucratic Organizations

We shall start with an analysis of the conditions of development of bureaucratic organizations and see to what extent these conditions can explain the existence of different inherent tendencies in their development and their patterns of activities.

Although since Weber, there have been relatively few systematic studies of the conditions responsible for the development of bureaucratic organizations and processes of bureaucratization that could serve as a basis for a systematic comparative analysis, there exist numerous concrete historical analyses of the development and functioning of different bureaucratic organizations.[4] On the basis of these materials and of current research it is possible to specify, tentatively, the conditions under which bureaucratic organizations tend to develop and which apply both to historical (Chinese, Byzantine, and Egyptian) bureaucratic societies and to modern societies or sectors of them.

The available material suggests that bureaucratic organizations tend to develop in societies when:

1. There develops extensive differentiation between major types of roles and institutional (economic, political, religious, and so forth) spheres.
2. The most important social roles are allocated not according to criteria of membership in the basic particularistic (kinship or territorial) groups, but rather according to universalistic and achievement criteria, or criteria of membership in more flexibly constituted groups such as professional, religious, vocational, or "national" groups.
3. There evolve many functionally specific groups (economic, cultural, religious, social-integrative) that are not embedded in basic particularistic groups, as, for example, economic and professional organizations, various types of voluntary associations, clubs, and so forth.
4. The definition of the total community is not identical with, and consequently is wider than, any such basic particularistic group, as can be seen, for instance, in the definition of the Hellenic culture in Byzantium or of the Confucian cultural order.
5. The major groups and strata in the society develop, uphold, and attempt to implement numerous discrete, political, economic, and social-service goals which cannot be implemented within the limited framework of the basic particularistic groups.
6. The growing differentiation in the social structure makes for complexity in many spheres of life, such as increasing interdependence between far-off groups and growing difficulty in the assurance of supply of resources and services.
7. These developments result to some extent in "free-floating" resources, i.e., manpower and economic resources as well as commitments for political support which are neither embedded in nor assured to any primary ascriptive-particularistic groups, as, for example, monetary resources, a relatively free labor force, and a free political vote. Consequently, the various institutional units in the society have to compete for resources, manpower, and support for the implementation of their goals and provision of services; and the major social units are faced with many regulative and administrative problems.

[3] See A. Gouldner, Metaphysical Pathos and the Theory of Bureaucracy, *American Political Science Review*, 49 (June 1955), 496–507

[4] Parts of this material are now being used by the writer in a comprehensive comparative study of the political systems of historical bureaucratic empires, and some of the hypotheses presented here are based on this work. A preliminary presentation of some of the problems of these historical societies can be found in S. N. Eisenstadt, Internal Contradictions in Bureaucratic Polities, *Comparative Studies in History and Society*, 1 (Oct. 1958), 58–75; and see also S. N. Eisenstadt, Political Struggle in Bureaucratic Societies, *World Politics*, 9 (Oct. 1956), 15–36.

The available material suggests that bureaucratic organizations develop in relation to such differentiation in the social system. Bureaucratic organizations can help in coping with some of the problems arising out of such differentiation, and they perform important functions in the organization of adequate services and co-ordination of large-scale activities, in the implementation of different goals, in the provision of resources to different groups, and in the regulation of various intergroup relations and conflicts. Such bureaucratic organizations are usually created by certain elites (rulers, economic entrepreneurs, etc.) to deal with the problems outlined and to assure for these elites both the provision of such services and strategic power positions in the society.

Thus in many historical societies bureaucratic administrations were created by kings who wanted to establish their rule over feudal-aristocratic forces and who wanted, through their administration, to control the resources created by various economic and social groups and to provide these groups with political, economic, and administrative services that would make them dependent on the rulers.

In many modern societies bureaucratic organizations are created when the holders of political or economic power are faced with problems that arise because of external (war, etc.) or internal (economic development, political demands, etc.) developments. For the solution of such problems they have to mobilize adequate resources from different groups and spheres of life.

Obviously, these conclusions have to be tested and amplified through detailed application to various societies and different institutional spheres.[5] But even at this preliminary stage of our analysis they are of interest in relation to tendencies of development inherent in bureaucratic organizations.

In sum, the development of bureaucratic organizations is related to certain social conditions, the most important of which are, first, the availability of various fluid, "free-floating" resources; second, the necessity for large-scale organizations; and, third, the development of several centers of power that compete for such resources. Thus two conclusions are indicated.

First, as a result of the very conditions that give rise to a bureaucratic organization, it is, almost by definition, obliged to compete for resources, manpower, legitimation within the society, general support and clientele, and, to some extent also, patrons and protectors.

The classical theories of bureaucracy recognized that a bureaucracy is always dependent on the outside world for its resources. Unlike traditional ecological, family, or kinship groups, the incumbents of its office do not receive direct remuneration from their clients nor do they own their means of production. But because many of these theories referred chiefly to governmental bureaucracies, they took the supply of the requisite resources for granted and only emphasized the fact that dependence on external resources assures the relative segregation and independence of the bureaucrat's role. In reality, however, the need to compete for legitimation and resources faces governmental departments also and can be considered as a basic aspect of every bureaucracy.

Thus from the very beginning a bureaucratic organization is put in what may be called a power situation, in which it has to cast its influence and to generate processes of power on its own behalf and in which it is under pressure from different centers of power in the society that would control it.

Second, this basic power situation in which a bureaucratic organization develops and functions is strongly underlined by the fact that any bureaucracy, not only implements different political and social goals and provides different services, but also necessarily performs regulatory and mediating functions in the society. This is because the rules governing implementation of goals and provision of services by a bureaucracy necessarily affect the distribution of power and allocation of resources to different groups in the society. These regulative and mediating functions enhance the potential power position of any bureaucracy, increase the competition of other groups for its services and for control over it, and generate many pressures both emanating from it and impinging on it.

Thus from its inception a bureaucratic organization is in a state of constant interaction with its environment and has to develop differ-

[5] A more complete exposition of this hypothesis will be presented in the forthcoming analysis of the bureaucratic empires.

ent ways of maintaining a dynamic equilibrium in this environment. The equilibrium results from adjustment of its own goals, structure, and interests in relation to the major forces in its social environment and to the power processes generated by each of them.

The Bureaucratic Organization as a Social System

To understand more fully how different types of equilibrium are developed by different bureaucratic organizations, it is necessary to examine more closely some of the major characteristics of the internal structure of bureaucracies. A systematic approach to this problem is facilitated by the extensive data in the literature dealing with the problems of bureaucracy and of organization.[6] The major insights to be gained from these materials and analyses seem to be as follows:

1. Any bureaucratic organization constitutes a social system of its own; therefore its internal division of labor is determined not only by the technical problems of implementation of goals, but also by other needs and problems. Since special roles and activities geared to the provision of these needs exist within it, there can be no purely rational bureaucratic organization free from personal, primary, or power elements. On the contrary, some such elements (like primary groups of workers or identification between different participants) perform functionally important tasks in the organization.

2. Each of the roles existing in any bureaucratic organization is systematically related to the outside world. The organization must manipulate several aspects of its external environment (e.g., directors must deal with boards of trustees and legislative committees, the sales managers with buyers and sellers, the manager with trade unions and labor exchanges. The necessary contact between the incumbents of such roles and parallel role incumbents in other organizations may establish professional, solidarity, or conflict relations and various reference orientations and identifications. The relations resulting from such contact may cut across any given organization and at the same time greatly influence the behavior of the incumbents in their organizations, consequently affecting the performance of these organizations. These contacts also distinguish the incumbents' bureaucratic roles within the organization from their other social roles in the family or community, especially the type of motivation for performance of their bureaucratic role that they bring from their social background. Finally, the relations with different types of clients and sections of the general public with which the incumbent of a bureaucratic role comes into selective contact might put him under pressure with respect to the performance of his bureaucratic roles. Such pressure may be exerted either by means of various professional or community roles and organizations in which both the bureaucrat and the client may participate, by specific organizations of the public or clients, or through direct interaction in the bureaucrat-client role.

3. Within each organization there develop various subgroups and subsystems (workmen, foremen, professional groups, departmental units, and so forth), and the organization is faced with the problem of co-ordinating these subgroups, of regulating their relations with each other and with the organization as a whole. Such subgroups may have different conceptions of and attitudes toward the organization's goals and needs, and these differences must be taken into account when studying the functioning of any bureaucratic organization.

4. Thus the interaction between the different subgroups or subsystems in any bureaucratic organization should be viewed as a continuous process of communication, of allocation of rewards, of mutual perception, a process by which some—but only some—fusion (the extent of which necessarily varies) is effected between the motives and goals of individuals and subgroups and the over-all organizational goals.[7]

5. The multiplicity of any organization's external relations and internal subgroups may lead to the development of many different types of activity that transcend the specific bureaucratic roles and relations both within and without the organization. Thus an organi-

[6] For a review of this literature see Trend Report.

[7] Conrad M. Arensberg and Geoffrey Tootell, Plant Sociology: Real Discoveries and New Problems, in Mirra Komarovsky, ed., *Common Frontiers of the Social Sciences* (Glencoe, Ill., 1957), pp. 310–337.

zation interested in improving its internal human and public relations may help its members and their families integrate their activities with those of other social groups—all this to improve performance of the bureaucratic. role.

Such activities, in turn, bring the incumbents of the bureaucratic role into various relations with other persons that may go beyond the basic relationship of the bureaucratic role. These might consequently lead (a) to development of new goal orientations by the organization and to processes of bureaucratization or debureaucratization; (b) to attempts on the part of the bureaucrats to impose the bureaucracy's conceptions and goals on these external activities and groups, or (c) to pressures of these groups on the goals of the organization and performance of the bureaucratic roles within it. These pressures may be directed toward changing or supervising the goals and activities of the bureaucratic organization, limiting their application, adding new dimensions to them, or taking over of the organization.

Here we are confronted with an aspect of the bureaucratic organization that is of major importance to our analysis, namely, the potential flexibility of its goals. We have seen that any bureaucratic organization evolves as a means of implementing a specific goal or goals. However, the very conditions responsible for its development, the multiplicity of its internal subgroups, its continuous dependence on external groups, and the numerous pressures to which it is subjected facilitate or perhaps even necessitate modification of at least some of its goals. Such flexibility is, as Thompson and McEwen have rightly stressed, almost a condition (especially in modern society) of the bureaucratic organization's survival.[8]

It is largely through incorporating new (mostly secondary) goals and attempting to assure the requisite resources for their implementation that a bureaucratic organization maintains its equilibrium with its environment. It thus exerts its influence on this environment, establishes various rules which influence the training of people aspiring to be enrolled into it, and indirectly may influence general educational standards and impose its own specific orientations on parts of its environment. It is through such processes, as well as those of competition for resources and power, that the different types of interaction and equilibrium between the bureaucratic organization and its social environment develop.

Bureaucratization and Debureaucratization

It is through such continuous interaction with its environment that a bureaucratic organization may succeed in maintaining those characteristics that distinguish it from other social groups. The most important of these characteristics, common to most bureaucratic organizations and often stressed in the literature, are specialization of roles and tasks; the prevalence of autonomous, rational, nonpersonal rules in the organization; and the general orientation to rational, efficient implementation of specific goals.[9]

These structural characteristics do not, however, develop in a social vacuum but are closely related to the functions and activities of the bureaucratic organization in its environment. The extent to which they can develop and persist in any bureaucratic organization is dependent on the type of dynamic equilibrium that the organization develops in relation to its environment. Basically, three main outcomes of such interaction or types of such dynamic equilibrium can be distinguished, although probably each of them can be further subdivided and some overlapping occurs between them.

The first type of equilibrium is one in which any given bureaucratic organization maintains its autonomy and distinctiveness. The basic structural characteristics that differentiate it from other social groups and in which it implements its goal or goals (whether its initial goals or goals added later) are retained and it is supervised by those who are legitimately en-

[8] J. D. Thompson and W. J. McEwen, Organizational Goals and Environment, *American Sociological Review*, 23 (Feb. 1958), 23–31.

[9] See, for instance, P. M. Blau, *Bureaucracy in Modern Society* (New York, 1956). Blau summarizes much of the available literature on this problem.

titled to do this (holders of political power, "owners," or boards of trustees).

The second main possibility is that of bureaucratization, as it has been already defined earlier. This is the extension of the bureaucracy's spheres of activities and power either in its own interest or those of some of its elite. It tends toward growing regimentation of different areas of social life and some extent of displacement of its service goals in favor of various power interests and orientations. Examples are military organizations that tend to impose their rule on civilian life, or political parties that exert pressure on their potential supporters in an effort to monopolize their private and occupational life and make them entirely dependent on the political party.

The third main outcome is debureaucratization. Here there is subversion of the goals and activities of the bureaucracy in the interests of different groups with which it is in close interaction (clients, patrons, interested parties). In debureaucratization the specific characteristics of the bureaucracy in terms both of its autonomy and its specific rules and goals are minimized, even up to the point where its very functions and activities are taken over by other groups or organizations. Examples of this can be found in cases when some organization (i.e., a parents' association or a religious or political group) attempts to divert the rules and working of a bureaucratic organization (school, economic agency, and so forth) for its own use or according to its own values and goals. It makes demands on the members of bureaucratic organizations to perform tasks that are obviously outside the specific scope of these organizations.

Each of these possibilities entails a specific development of the bureaucratic role in relation to other social roles with which it has to interact—whether other social roles of the incumbents of the bureaucratic roles or other "client," public, or similar roles. Thus in the maintenance of a bureaucracy's autonomy and of its goal and service orientation the bearers of the bureaucratic roles maintain their distinctiveness from closely related roles but at the same time fully recognize the distinctiveness of these other roles.

In the case of bureaucratization the bureaucratic roles tend to dominate the other roles (both of the incumbents and of those with whom they interact) and to impose on them the bureaucratic criteria, so as to minimize the autonomy and distinctiveness of these other roles and maximize their own power over them.

In the case of debureaucratization the various outside nonbureaucratic roles impinge on the bureaucratic role to an extent which tends to minimize the specificity of the bureaucratic roles and the relative autonomy of the bureaucratic rules in the implementation of goals and in the provision of services.

Each of these possibilities may also involve, in different ways and degrees, the bureaucracy's orientation to new goals, its incorporation of new goals, and its diversion of activities to the implementation of such new goals. Many overlappings between these various tendencies and possibilities may, of course, develop. The tendencies toward bureaucratization and debureaucratization may, in fact, develop side by side. Thus, for instance, a growing use of the bureaucratic organization and the extension of its scope of activities for purposes of political control might be accompanied by deviation from its rules for the sake of political expediency. The possibility of these tendencies occurring in the same case may be explained by the fact that a stable service-oriented bureaucracy (the type of bureaucracy depicted in the Weberian ideal type of bureaucracy) is based on the existence of some equilibrium or *modus vivendi* between professional autonomy and societal (or political) control. Once this equilibrium is severely disrupted, the outcome with respect to the bureaucracy's organization and activity may be the simultaneous development of bureaucratization and debureaucratization in different spheres of its activities, although usually one of these tendencies is more pronounced.

We thus see that the problem of what kind of equilibrium any bureaucratic organization will develop in relation to its environment is inherent both in the conditions of the development of a bureaucratic organization and in its very nature as a social system, in its basic components and its interrelation with the external environment in which it functions. Thus the dilemma of viewing a bureaucracy either as an instrument for the implementation of goals or as a power instrument is in a way resolved.

But this poses a new problem or question as

to the conditions that influence or determine which of these tendencies will become actualized or predominant in any given case.

Some Variables in the Study of Bureaucracy

It is as yet very difficult to propose any definite and systematic hypothesis about this problem since very little research is available that is specifically related to it.[10]

What can be done at this stage is, first, to point out some variables that, on the basis of available material and the preceding discussion, seem central to this problem, and then to propose some preliminary hypotheses, which may suggest directions in which research work on this problem may be attempted.

On the basis of those discussions we would like to propose that (a) the major goals of the bureaucratic organization, (b) the place of these goals in the social structure of the society, and (c) the type of dependence of the bureaucracy on external forces (clients, holders of political power, or other prominent groups) are of great importance in influencing both its internal structure and its relation with its environment. These different variables, while to some extent interdependent, are not identical. Each brings into relief the interdependence of the bureaucratic organization with its social setting from a different point of view.

The bureaucracy's goals, as has been lately shown in great detail by Parsons,[11] are of strategic importance, because they constitute one of the most important connecting links between the given organization and the total social structure in which it is placed. That which from the point of view of the organization is the major goal is very often from the point of view of the total society the function of the organization. Hence the various interrelations between a bureaucratic organization, other groups, and the total society are largely mediated by the nature of its goals. This applies both to the resources needed by the organization and to the products it gives to the society.[12]

But it is not merely the contents of the goals, i.e., whether they are mainly political, economic, cultural, and so forth, that influence the relation of the organization with its environment, but the place of the goals in the institutional structure of the society as well. By the relative place of the specific goals of any given bureaucratic organization within the society we mean the centrality (or marginality) of these goals with respect to the society's value and power system and the extent of legitimation it affords them. Thus there would obviously be many differences between a large corporation with critical products and a small economic organization with marginal products; between a political party close to the existing government performing the functions of a "loyal opposition" and a revolutionary group; between established churches and minority or militant sects; between fully established educational institutions and sectarian study or propaganda groups.

A third variable which seems to influence the bureaucracy's structural characteristics and activities is the extent and nature of its dependence on external resources and power. This dependence or relation may be defined in terms of:

1. The chief function of the organization, i.e., whether it is a service, market, or membership recruitment agency. (This definition is closely related to, but not necessarily identical with, its goals.)
2. The extent to which its clientele is entirely dependent upon its products, or conversely, the type and extent of competition between it and parallel agencies.
3. The nature and extent of the internal (ownership) and external control.
4. The criteria used to measure the success of the organization as such and its members' performance, especially the extent of changes in the behavior and membership affiliation of

[10] Thus, for instance, in existing literature there is but little distinction between conditions which make for the growth of bureaucracy and those conducive to increasing bureaucratization. Gouldner's polemics against those who foresee the inevitability of bureaucratization are to some extent due to the lack of this distinction in the available literature. See his Metaphysical Pathos and the Theory of Bureaucracy.

[11] See T. Parsons, Suggestions for a Sociological Approach to the Theory of Organization, I and II, *Administrative Science Quarterly*, 1 (June and Sept. 1956), 63–85, 225–239.

[12] For additional discussion of this problem see Trend Report.

its clients (as, for instance, in the case of a political party).

5. The spheres of life of its personnel that the activities of a given bureaucratic organization encompass.

6. The spheres of life of its clientele that the activities of a given bureaucratic organization encompass.

It is not claimed that this list is exhaustive, but it seems to provide some preliminary clues as to the possible direction of further research on the problem.

All these variables indicate the great interdependence existing between the bureaucratic organization and its social environment. Each variable points to some ways in which a bureaucratic organization attempts to control different parts of its environment and to adapt its goals to changing environment or to different ways in which groups outside the bureaucracy control it and direct its activities. The outcome of this continuous interaction varies continuously according to the constellation of these different variables.

Conditions of Bureaucratization and Debureaucratization

On the basis of the foregoing considerations and of current research like that of Janowitz,[13] of historical research on which we have reported already,[14] and research in progress on the relations between bureaucratic organization and new immigrants in Israel,[15] we propose several general hypotheses concerning the conditions that promote autonomy or, conversely, bureaucratization or debureaucratization. In these hypotheses we deal with the influence, first, of the structure, organization, and distribution of different goals in the bureaucracy's immediate social environment and, second, of the types of dependency of a bureaucracy on its clientele. As already noted, these are only preliminary hypotheses that do not, as yet, deal with all the variables previously outlined.

The first of these hypotheses proposes that the development of any given bureaucratic organization as a relatively autonomous service agency is contingent upon the following conditions obtaining in its social setting:

1. Relative predominance of universalistic elements in the orientations and goals of the groups most closely related to the bureaucracy.

2. Relatively wide distribution of power and values in the economic, cultural, and political spheres among many groups and the maintenance of continuous struggle and competition among them or, in other words, no monopoly of the major power positions by any one group.

3. A wide range of differentiation among different types of goals.

4. The continuous specialization and competition among different bureaucratic organizations and between them and other types of groups about their relative places with regard to implementation of different goals.

5. The existence of strongly articulated political groups and the maintenance of control over the implementation of the goals by the legitimate holders of political, communal, or economic power.

Thus a service bureaucracy, one that maintains both some measure of autonomy and of service orientation, tends to develop either in a society, such as the "classical" Chinese Empire or the Byzantine Empire from the sixth to the tenth century, in which there exist strong political rulers and some politically active groups, such as the urban groups, aristocracy, and the church in the Byzantine Empire, or the literati and gentry in China, whose aspirations are considered by the rulers.[16] It also tends to de-

[13] See M. Janowitz, D. Wright, and W. Delany, *Public Administration and the Public—Perspectives towards Government in a Metropolitan Community* (Ann Arbor, 1958), which is one of the few available works that have a bearing on this problem. We would also like to mention the work of J. A. Slesinger, who has worked with Janowitz, and who has recently proposed several hypotheses concerning some of the factors that might influence aspects of the development of bureaucracy that are of interest to us. See Slesinger, "A Model for the Comparative Study of Public Bureaucracies," Institute of Public Administration, University of Michigan, 1957 (mimeo.).

[14] See note 4 above.

[15] See E. Katz and S. N. Eisenstadt, Debureaucratization: Observation on the Response of Israeli Organizations to the New Immigrants (forthcoming).

[16] For a more complete discussion of some of the problems of these societies see the references in note 4.

velop in a democratic society in which effective political power is vested in an efficient, strong, representative executive. In both cases it is the combination of relatively strong political leadership with some political articulation and activity of different strata and groups (an articulation which necessarily tends to be entirely different in expression in historical empires from modern democracies) that facilitates the maintenance of a service bureaucracy.

In some societies a group may establish a power monopoly over parts of its environment and over the definition and establishment of the society's goals and the appropriation of its resources. This group may use the bureaucracy as an instrument of power and manipulation, distort its autonomous function and service orientation, and subvert some of its echelons through various threats or inducements for personal gratification. Historically the most extreme example of such developments can be found in those societies in which the rulers developed political goals that were strongly opposed by various active groups that they tried to suppress, such as in Prussia in the seventeenth and eighteenth centuries, in many conquest empires such as the Ottoman, or in the periods of aristocratization of the Byzantine Empire.[17] Modern examples of this tendency can be found in totalitarian societies or movements. Less extreme illustrations can also be found in other societies, and it should be a major task of comparative research to specify the different possible combinations of the conditions enumerated above and their influence on the possible development of bureaucratic organizations.

The development of a bureaucratic organization in the direction of debureaucratization seems to be connected mainly with the growth of different types of *direct* dependence of the bureaucratic organization on parts of its clientele. At this stage we may propose the following preliminary hypotheses about the influence that the type of dependency of the bureaucracy on its clients has on some of its patterns of activity. First, the greater its dependence on its clientele in terms of their being able to go to a competing agency, the more it will have to develop techniques of communication and additional services to retain its clientele and the more it will be influenced by different types of demands by the clientele for services in spheres that are not directly relevant to its main goals. Second, insofar as its dependence on its clients is due to the fact that its criteria of successful organizational performance are based on the number and behavior pattern of the organization's members or clients (as is often the case in semipolitical movements, educational organizations, and so forth), it will have to take an interest in numerous spheres of its clients' activities and either establish its control over them or be subjected to their influence and direction. Finally, the greater its *direct* dependence on different participants in the political arena, and the smaller the basic economic facilities and political assurance given by the holders of political power—as is the case in some public organizations in the United States and to some extent also in different organizations in Israel[18]—the greater will be its tendency to succumb to the demands of different political and economic pressure groups and to develop its activities and distort its own rules accordingly.

As already indicated, in concrete cases some overlapping between the tendencies to bureaucratization and debureaucratization may occur. Thus, for instance, when a politically monopolistic group gains control over a bureaucratic organization, it may distort the rules of this organization in order to give special benefits to the holders of political power or to maintain its hold over different segments of the population. On the other hand, when a process of debureaucratization sets in because of the growing pressure of different groups on a bureaucracy, there may also develop within the bureaucratic organization, as a sort of defense against these pressures, a tendency toward formalization and bureaucratization. This shows that the distinctive characteristics of a specific bureaucratic organization and role have been impinged upon in different directions, and one may usually discern which of these tendencies is predominant in different spheres of activity of the bureaucracy. It is the

[17] Hans Rosenberg, *Bureaucracy, Aristocracy and Autocracy: The Prussian Experience, 1660–1815* (Cambridge, Mass., 1958); A. Lybyer, *The Government of the Ottoman Empire in the Time of Suleiman the Magnificent* (Cambridge, Mass., 1913); and Eisenstadt, Internal Contradictions.

[18] See Janowitz *et al.*, *op. cit.*, pp. 107–114, and Katz and Eisenstadt, *op. cit.*

task of further research to analyze these different constellations in greater detail.

Conclusions

The hypotheses presented above are necessarily both very general and preliminary and have as yet to be applied in detail to different types of societies and to their institutional spheres. Nevertheless, they make it possible to identify at least some of the major variables responsible for the development of bureaucratic organizations and to relate them systematically to the factors that determine the internal structure of such organizations and to types of equilibrium developing between bureaucracies and their environment. The preceding discussion points out that the type of dynamic equilibrium established at a given time depends largely on the forces in the immediate environment of the organization on the one hand and the type of power processes it generates in its environment on the other.

The interaction between these forces and processes engenders the continuous development of bureaucratic organizations and of processes of bureaucratization and debureaucratization. Whether a given bureaucracy will maintain its relative autonomy, whether at the same time it will be subject to effective "external" control, or whether it will develop in the direction of bureaucratization or debureaucratization is not precisely predeterminable but is largely contingent upon the concrete constellation of these various forces.

It is hoped that the preceding discussion—although preliminary—indicates possible ways of investigating various structural aspects of bureaucratic organizations and the nature of the processes of bureaucratization and debureaucratization. It has shown that with the development, systematization, and convergence of different fields of research it is possible to avoid the dichotomy of viewing bureaucracy as a service instrument or viewing it as an instrument of power. It is also possible to identify the conditions under which the autonomy of a bureaucratic organization and its service orientation is maintained or the conditions under which processes of bureaucratization and debureaucratization develop, and to relate them systematically to the analysis of the structure of bureaucratic organizations.

PART FOUR

Equilibrium, Feedback, and Control

PART FOUR

ONE CHARACTERISTIC of systems or organizations is regularity or stability. It persists over time. Some elements appear to stay unchanged over time; others may change. Given that systems are open; then, since the environment in which they are immersed is changing, this stability or appearance of stability is not easily obtained.

Static and Dynamic Equilibrium

Let us explore this matter further by making some distinctions. If we envision a domino standing on its edge, it will in all likelihood stay that way, and we would describe it as being in equilibrium. It is in equilibrium because all the forces working on it are in balance. The push of the table holding the domino up is matched exactly both in magnitude and direction by the force of the domino on the table. This is a static situation, the forces stay the same, and the block does not move.

Contrasted with this is a condition of dynamic equilibrium. For example, when riding a bicycle, we stay in an upright position, but our position is not fixed or unchanging. If we were to look carefully, we would note that first we lean a little to one side, then move back to dead center, then move a little to the other side, and then back to dead center again. Furthermore, when we make a turn, we lean considerably to one side and could not be considered being vertical, yet nonetheless we still say we are "up" and that the bike is in equilibrium or under control. There are two important things to observe at this time. First, while the bicycle is seldom (and then for only a fleeting second) in an absolutely vertical position when it is off center, it tends to return to this position. Second, there are many motions or acts performed, although many are so subtle that we may not notice them at first, which are undertaken to bring the bike back to the vertical. In dynamic equilibrium, we have actions directed toward bringing a system back to equilibrium or to make it tend toward equilibrium.

Now an observer, looking at the efforts of the rider to keep his bicycle upright, might well be tempted to observe that the rider has an objective. On the other hand, the rider of the bike may say that his objective in riding the bike is to get to school. Both statements about objectives are true. When dealing with organizations, we would be remiss and greatly handicap our efforts if we restricted our analysis of equilibrium to those concerned with stated goals.

There is another dimension to dynamic equilibrium, the equilibrium point toward which performance is tending. The point can be fixed or it can be changing at some predictable rate. For example, we could say the population of a factory is in equilibrium when it remains stable at 1000 or, more accurately, tends to be around 1000, since it will probably be 998 one month and 1001 the next. Or it can be viewed as in equilibrium if it increases at a regular rate each month or year. If it increases at, say, ten percent a month but actually increases only from 1000 the previous month to 1090 the present month, in tending toward equilibrium next month it will go not to 1100 but to 1200.

Equilibrium for organizations is a very complex phenomenon to analyze. Organizations need people in them. As a minimum for survival in the steady state, they must replace those people who leave with new members. The balance here is between leavers and joiners. For the member, there is a different equilibrium consideration. He receives some things from organization membership, but he also gives things to be a member: effort, time, and a chance to do other things with his time and effort. The member also seeks, at the least, a balance between the inducements he receives and the contributions he makes (March and Simon). The inducements that a member receives directly or indirectly come from the contributions of other organization members. Thus an equilibrium of organization membership depends upon a balance of the set of contributions and inducements of all members.

Self-Regulation

That systems and organizations tend toward equilibrium or some objective is important, but it is equally important to note that the organizations in which we are interested themselves provide the necessary control. They are self-regulating, or self-controlling. Self-regulation occurs in many different entities: in organizations, physiological systems such as those that keep our body temperatures constant, machines such as automatic pilots, to name but a few. In all, however, the same elements appear, although of course the form they take may vary greatly. There is the performance of the system and a goal or standard toward which it is directed. There is information about the performance and whether it agrees with the standard. There is the transmission of this information to the controller of the performance. This feedback loop through which information about deviation from standard is transmitted to some mechanism for choosing a new or different action has received a great deal of attention from those interested in the science of Cybernetics. This feedback loop must exist whenever there is control. However, it does not always exist within the unit being controlled. Frequently, the feedback loop is made through some elements in the unit's environment. Self-regulation is possible only when all elements are within the same unit (Churchman et al.).

Control Systems of Organizations

Discussed in the abstract, control systems appear simple enough. However, when we examine actual control systems, for example in organizations, they turn out to be far more complex and more difficult to be explicit about. An actual control cycle may include many components. Within an actual control cycle, the elements may range from being as tangible as dollars or washers to such elusive things as the perception of beauty or a subordinate's feeling dependent on a superior. Furthermore, since each element in a control cycle is also an element in other systems, it is necessary to consider the other systems if one is going to describe a system performance completely. Of course, as we consider these other systems, we would recognize that they contain still further sets of elements, and so our collection of elements to be considered would be expanding rapidly, quickly becoming unworkable. As noted earlier, to study systems, one needs to limit arbitrarily what is to be included in the analysis. This is a matter of judgment, and there is little available to us to aid in making these judgments. The few suggestions that could be made are so basic and obvious that it would seem fatuous to mention them except that they are so often ignored.

Many control systems important to organizations have elements outside the organization as it is typically defined. For example, comparison of a company product with standards of acceptability may be made by users; actions to control the quality of raw materials will be taken by a supplier. If the definition of a control system stops at the boundaries of the firm as defined by ownership or employees, then the analysis of important control systems for a firm will be made impossible. As a minimal consideration, then, a system must be defined to include the basic elements, even though this may mean ignoring the formal or traditional organizational boundaries (Roberts).

Ultrastability

Thus far, our discussion of control or cybernetics has been restricted to a very simple form—the simple feedback loop that can be illustrated by the control of temperature in a room by a thermostat. With this type of control, the structure of the system is fixed, elements within the system being adjusted within limits that let the system structure persist. To put this differently, control is achieved by making adjustment within the resources or capacity of the system. The temperature in a house may stay at seventy degrees because the thermostat sends information or instructions that start the furnace when it is too cold and shut it off when the temperature gets to the desired level. However, if there is a cold wave, the instructions for the furnace to start and keep operating may be inadequate because even the continuous operating of the furnace may be inadequate to raise the room temperature to the proper level. This problem could be overcome by installing a larger furnace. Let us observe four very simple but important things. First, with a larger furnace, we have changed the structure of the system; yet the result is the same—a constant seventy degrees in the house. This capacity to persist even though the structure changes is called "ultrastability" (Cawallader). Second, for this new condition to come about, it was necessary that the inadequateness of the older set of elements and their possible adjustments be recognized, and a new arrangement sought and acquired. Third, the innovative or learning step was necessary for the unit to remain stable under unusual, or new or nonroutine, environmental conditions. Organizations, when giving evidence of ultrastability, can add new knowledge of how to do something, that is, to learn. For example, they develop new arrangements of tasks and departments such as when they change from a process to a product form of organization. Last, the restructuring of the initial system came about because another system came into operation, namely, the houseowner observed the inadequacy of the furnace and replaced it. Control in organizations, then, includes not only regulation of routine events but also innovation to adapt to the nonroutine or unusual and contains multiple control loops (Haberstroh).

Multiple Equilibriums

Organizations consist of many systems. Among the most important are production systems that are directly involved with accomplishing the unit's purpose and the maintenance systems concerned with preserving the organization through satisfying the needs of the organization members. The manager in his leadership capacity is concerned with seeing that both of these systems operate effectively. These two systems are also interdependent and, to some extent, mutually exclusive. One reason this condition arises is that the manager often can handle only one thing at a time. Hence, if he is involved with correcting some technical problem to improve production, he is not available to deal with some of the personal needs or problems of his subordinates. As a result, as has been reported in many studies, should a manager be concerned with maximizing one system, such as production, the other system will begin to function poorly, eventually reaching the point where it will interfere with the operation of the former. If he is aware of this, he can give attention to the second system before its operation is too impaired but, of course, he does this by neglecting the first system, and its performance will start to fall off. The manager is facing one of the more frustrating aspects of equilibrium in organizations (see Bales in Part Two). The many regulating systems have individual equilibrium points. However, the same conditions do not produce equilibrium in them all. On the contrary, the optimal conditions or stable conditions for one are unstable for another. Hence the experience of the manager reflects conditions for the organization in general. As one system takes action to bring itself into equilibrium, it upsets the equilibrium of another which, as it takes corrective action, upsets still other systems. The consequences are that organizations are continually churning internally as subsystems struggle for equilibrium against their reciprocally disturbing influences.

Information Overload

Central to the study of cybernetics is information. We need information about standards or goals, about performances, about the degree of difference between them, about what is to be done to change this, and many other things. How well control is realized depends upon how well information is handled. So closely are the two topics interrelated that to some investigators they are the same. Others would distinguish between them, but none would deny or ignore their close relationship.

In any information system we have a source of information, a coding operation in which the information is converted into a form that can be sent. There is also a need for some transmitting activity that actually sends the information out. But messages are directed to a destination through some sort of medium or channel, for example wires, air, etc. Before the destination can use the information it must first have some way of getting the message from the channel, a receiver; it must be able to decode the message so that it again becomes information.

In organizations, many problems are defined as communications problems. This often turns out to mean that the problems come from insufficient or inaccurate information which, if we take a sufficiently broad view, are essentially the same problem. A frequently heard proposal to improve organization performance is to "give people more information." There are a number of very interesting aspects to this proposal. One set concerns the ability of individuals to use this information, which opens many of the issues March and Simon have raised in their discussion of bounded rationality (See Vol. I, March and Simon). Another set concerns the capacity of the system to process the information. Does, for example, putting more information into one end of the system guarantee that more will come out at the destination, the same amount, or proportionally less? Any of the elements of a communication system mentioned above could control the proportion between inputs and outputs. One which has received considerable attention is the channel and the relation between its capacity for handling information and the amount of information that actually gets through. It has been found, for example, that as the information going into a channel increases toward the channel capacity, the performance of the unit under study also increases. However, when the amount of information being put in exceeds the channel capacity, the information delivered or the performance of the unit does not stay constant as might be expected, but actually decreases (Miller). Living systems seem to use one or more of a set of adjustive processes to cope with information overload: omission of information, error, queuing, filtering, approximation, use of multiple channels, decentralization, and escape (Miller). Each of these fulfill a function and, if a deliberate selection is made, it is possible to influence the shape of the curve of the relationship between information put in and organization performance.

The Theory of Organizational Equilibrium

JAMES G. MARCH AND HERBERT A. SIMON

The Barnard-Simon theory of organizational equilibrium is essentially a theory of motivation—a statement of the conditions under which an organization can induce its members to continue their participation, and hence assure organizational survival. The central postulates of the theory are stated by Simon, Smithburg, and Thompson (1950, pp. 381–382) as follows:

1. An organization is a system of interrelated social behaviors of a number of persons whom we shall call the *participants* in the organization.
2. Each participant and each group of participants receives *from* the organization *inducements* in return for which he makes *to* the organization *contributions*.
3. Each participant will continue his participation in an organization only so long as the inducements offered him are as great or greater (measured in terms of *his* values and in terms of the alternatives open to him) than the contributions he is asked to make.
4. The contributions provided by the various groups of participants are the source from which the organization manufactures the inducements offered to participants.
5. Hence, an organization is "solvent"—and will continue in existence—only so long as the contributions are sufficient to provide inducements in large enough measure to draw forth these contributions.

The theory, like many theoretical generalizations, verges on the tautological. Specifically, to test the theory, and especially the crucial postulate 3, we need independent empirical estimates of (*a*) the behavior of participants in joining, remaining in, or withdrawing from organizations; and (*b*) the balance of inducements and contributions for each participant, measured in terms of his "utilities."

The observation of participants joining and leaving organizations is comparatively easy. It is more difficult to find evidence of the value of variable (*b*) that does not depend on the observation of (*a*). Before we can deal with the observational problem, however, we must say a bit more about the concepts of inducements and contributions.

Inducements

Inducements are "payments" made by (or through) the organization to its participants (e.g., wages to a worker, service to a client, income to an investor). These payments can be measured in units that are independent of their utility to the participants (e.g., wages and income can be measured in terms of dollars, service to clients in terms of hours devoted to him). Consequently, for an individual participant we can specify a set of inducements, each component of the set representing a different dimension of the inducements offered by the organization. Thus, each component of the inducements can be measured uniquely and independently of the utilities assigned to it by the participants.

Inducement Utilities

For each component in the set of inducements there is a corresponding utility value. For the moment we will not be concerned with the shape of the utility function; but we do not exclude from consideration a step function. The utility function for a given individual reduces the several components of the inducements to a common dimension.

From *Organizations*, New York, Wiley, 1959, pp. 84–88. Reprinted with permission of the publisher.

Contributions

We assume that a participant in an organization makes certain "payments" to the organization (e.g., work from the worker, fee from the client, capital from the investor). These payments, which we shall call contributions, can be measured in units that are independent of their utility to the participants. Consequently, for any individual participant we can specify a set of contributions.

Contribution Utilities

A utility function transforming contributions into utilities of the individual contributor can be defined in more than one way. A reasonable definition of the utility of a contribution is the value of the alternatives that an individual foregoes in order to make the contribution. As we shall see below, this definition of contribution utilities allows us to introduce into the analysis the range of behavior alternatives open to the participant.

These definitions of inducements and contributions permit two general approaches to the observational problem. On the one hand, we can try to estimate the utility balance directly by observing the behavior (including responses to pertinent questions) of participants. On the other hand, if we are prepared to make some simple empirical assumptions about utility functions, we can make predictions from changes in the amounts of inducements and contributions, without reference to their utilities.

To estimate the inducement-contribution utility balance directly, the most logical type of measure is some variant of individual satisfaction (with the job, the service, the investment, etc.). It appears reasonable to assume that the greater the difference between inducements and contributions, the greater the individual satisfaction. However, the critical "zero points" of the satisfaction scale and the inducement-contribution utility balance are not necessarily identical. The zero point for the satisfaction scale is the point at which one begins to speak of degrees of "dissatisfaction" rather than degrees of "satisfaction." It is, therefore, closely related to the level of aspiration and is the point at which we would predict a substantial increase in search behavior on the part of the organism.

The zero point on the inducement-contribution utility scale, on the other hand, is the point at which the individual is indifferent to leaving an organization. We have ample evidence that these two zero points are not identical, but, in particular, that very few of the "satisfied" participants leave an organization, whereas some, but typically not all, of the "unsatisfied" participants leave (Reynolds, 1951).

How do we explain these differences? The explanation lies primarily in the ways in which alternatives to current activity enter into the scheme (and this is one of the reasons for defining contribution utilities in terms of opportunities foregone). Dissatisfaction is a cue for search behavior. Being dissatisfied, the organism expands its program for exploring alternatives. If over the long run this search fails, the aspiration level is gradually revised downward. We assume, however, that the change in aspiration level occurs slowly, so that dissatisfaction in the short run is quite possible. On the other hand, the inducement-contribution utility balance adjusts quickly to changes in the perception of alternatives. When fewer and poorer alternatives are perceived to be available, the utility of activities foregone decreases; and this adjustment occurs rapidly.

Consequently, we can use satisfaction expressed by the individual as a measure of the inducement-contribution utility balance only if it is used in conjunction with an estimate of perceived alternatives available. Speaking roughly, only the desire to move enters into judgments of satisfaction; desire to move *plus* the perceived ease of movement enters into the inducement-contribution utility measure. Many students of mobility (particularly those concerned with the mobility of workers) have tended to ignore one or the other of these two facets of the decision to participate (Rice, Hill, and Trist, 1950; Behrend, 1953).

Direct observation of the inducement-contribution utilities, however, is not the only possible way to estimate them. Provided we make certain assumptions about the utility functions, we can infer the utility balance directly from observations of changes in the inducements or contributions measured in nonutility terms. Three major assumptions are useful and perhaps warranted. First, we assume that the utility functions change only slowly. Second, we assume that each utility function is monotonic with respect to its corresponding inducement or contribution. Although we may not know what the utility of an increase in wages will be, we are prepared to assume it will be positive. Third, we assume that the utility functions of fairly broad classes of people are very nearly the same; within a given subculture we do not expect radical differences in values. Also, we can expect that if an increase in a given inducement produces an increase in utility for one individual, it will produce an increase for other individuals.

There are other reasonable assumptions about individual utility functions; some will be indicated below when we relate individual participation to other factors. These three assumptions, however, in themselves lead to a variety of estimation procedures. Under the first assumption the short-run effect of a change in inducements or contributions will be uncontaminated by feedback effects. By the second assumption (particularly in conjunction with the third) a host of ordinal predictions can be made on the basis of knowledge of changes in the inducements and contributions. The third assumption permits us to estimate some of the cardinal properties of the inducements-contributions balance, avoiding the problem of interpersonal comparison of utilities.

Assumptions such as those listed have some a priori validity, but it is more important that much of the evidence currently available on the behavior of participants is consistent with them. Thus, predictions are frequently and often successfully made by businessmen as to the feasibility of proposed organizational plans.

Consider the anlaysis of a businessman exploring the feasibility of a business venture. His first step is to construct an operating plan showing what activities and facilities are required to carry on the proposed business, including estimates of the quantities of "inputs" and "outputs" of all categories. In the language of economics, he estimates the "production function." In the language of organization theory, the production function states the rates of possible conversion of contributions into inducements (Simon, 1952–53).

His second step is to estimate the monetary inducements that will be needed to obtain the inputs in the amounts required, and the monetary contributions that can be exacted for the outputs—i.e., the prices of factors of production and of product. In estimating these monetary inducements, predictions are being made as to the inducements-contributions balances of various classes of participants. Let us give some hypothetical examples:

Salaries and Wages. Information is obtained on "going rates of wages" for similar classes of work in other companies in the same area. An implicit *ceteris paribus* assumption is made with respect to other inducements, or (if the work, say, is particularly unpleasant, if proposed working conditions are particularly good or bad, etc.) the monetary inducement is adjusted upward or downward to compensate for the other factors. If the problem is to attract workers from other organizations, it is assumed that a wage differential or other inducement will be required to persuade them to change.

Capital. Information is obtained on "the money market"—i.e., the kinds of alternative investment opportunities that are available, the weight attached to various elements of risk, and the levels of interest rates. It is then assumed that to induce investment, the terms (interest rates, security, etc.) must be at least equal to the inducements available in alternative investments.

The same procedure is followed for the inducements to other participants. In each case, information is required as to the alternative inducements offered by other organizations, and these establish the "zero level" of the net inducement-contribution balance. If nonmonetary factors are not comparable among alternatives, an estimated adjustment is made of the monetary inducements by way of compensation. Of course, the adjustment may just as well be made in the nonmonetary factors (e.g., in product quality).

If the planned inducements, including the monetary inducements, give a positive balance for all groups of participants, the plan is feasible. If the plan is subsequently carried out, a comparison of the actual operations with the estimates provides an empirical test of the assumptions and the estimates. If the outcomes fail to confirm the assumptions, the businessman may still choose which of the two sets of assumptions he will alter. He may interpret the result as evidence that the basic inducements-contributions hypothesis is incorrect, or he may conclude that he has estimated incorrectly the zero points of one or more of the inducements-contributions balances. The fact is, however, that such predictions are frequently made with substantial success.

The testing of the theory is not confined to predicting the survival of new enterprises. At any time in the life of an organization when a change is made—that (*a*) explicitly alters the inducements offered to any group of participants; (*b*) explicitly alters the contributions demanded from them; or (*c*) alters the organizational activity in any way that will affect inducements or contributions—on any of these occasions, a prediction can be made as to the effect of the change on participation. The effects may be measurable in terms of turnover rates of employees, sales, etc., as appropriate.

REFERENCES

Simon, H. A. *Administrative Behavior.* New York, 1947.

Simon, H. A. "A comparison of organization theories." *The Review of Economic Studies.* 1952–53, **20**, 40–48.

Simon, H. A., D. W. Smithburg, and V. A. Thompson. *Public Administration.* New York, 1950.

Analysis of the Organization

C. WEST CHURCHMAN, RUSSELL L. ACKOFF,
AND E. LEONARD ARNOFF

Basic Assumptions

During the late 1930's and the 1940's groups of physiologists, electrical engineers, mathematicians, and social scientists began to work on organizational problems. Many organizations, they found, had similar characteristics. For example, human beings seemed to suffer many faults in their nervous systems which were analogous to faults appearing in electric gun-control mechanisms. Diagrams (Fig. 1) which biologists and physiologists had drawn of the human nervous system even looked like electric circuit diagrams.

Groups of such scientists, working in Cambridge, Massachusetts, and elsewhere, soon saw the possibility of developing a generalized organization or control theory that would cut across scientific disciplines. Professor Norbert Wiener summarized the work of these mixed discipline groups in 1948. In his book *Cybernetics. Control and Communication in the Animal and the Machine*, he said that *communication* (or information transfer) and *control* were essential processes in the functioning of an organization. Professor Wiener used information as a general concept, meaning any sign or signal which the organization could employ for the direction of its activities. The information might be an electric impulse, a chemical reaction, or a written message; very generally, anything by which an organization could guide or control its operation.

Thus, the view of Cybernetics is that (*a*) organizations composed of cells in an organism, (*b*) organizations composed of machines in an automatic factory or electric communication network, and (*c*) organizations of human beings in social groups all follow the essential processes of communication and control in their operation.[1]

One can often analyze industrial or military organizations, even though they are complex, in the same communication and control terms. Such analysis can be directed toward the construction of a *communication (or control) model*[1] of the organization.

Some General Comments on the Communication Model

A communication model is not mathematical; it is not used for accurate predictions or calculations. It generally takes the form of a diagram. Such a diagram enables one to bring together, from various fields of research, knowledge about organizations. The diagram and other knowledge can be used to suggest points of attack upon organizational problems, to sort relevant information about an organization from the trivial, to suggest analogies and similarities among various kinds of organizations, and to suggest, for test, solutions to organizational problems.[1] These hints and guides are often sorely needed by Operations Researchers, particularly at the beginning of a new project.

Since communication models have this practical importance, we will stress their use rather than give a detailed discussion of their theoretical development. The chapter is therefore divided into three parts: (1) a simplified theoretical discussion of communication models; (2) a brief description of how to construct a communication model in practice; and (3) a discussion of the ways one can use the com-

From *Introduction to Operations Research*, New York, Wiley, 1957, pp. 26–42. Reprinted by permission of the publisher.

[1] K. W. Deutsch "On Communication Models in the Social Sciences," *Public Opinion Quarterly*, 16, 356–380 (1952). See also a discussion of the development of Cybernetic models in Deutsch "Mechanisms, Organizations and Society," *Phil. Sci.*, 230–252 (July 1951).

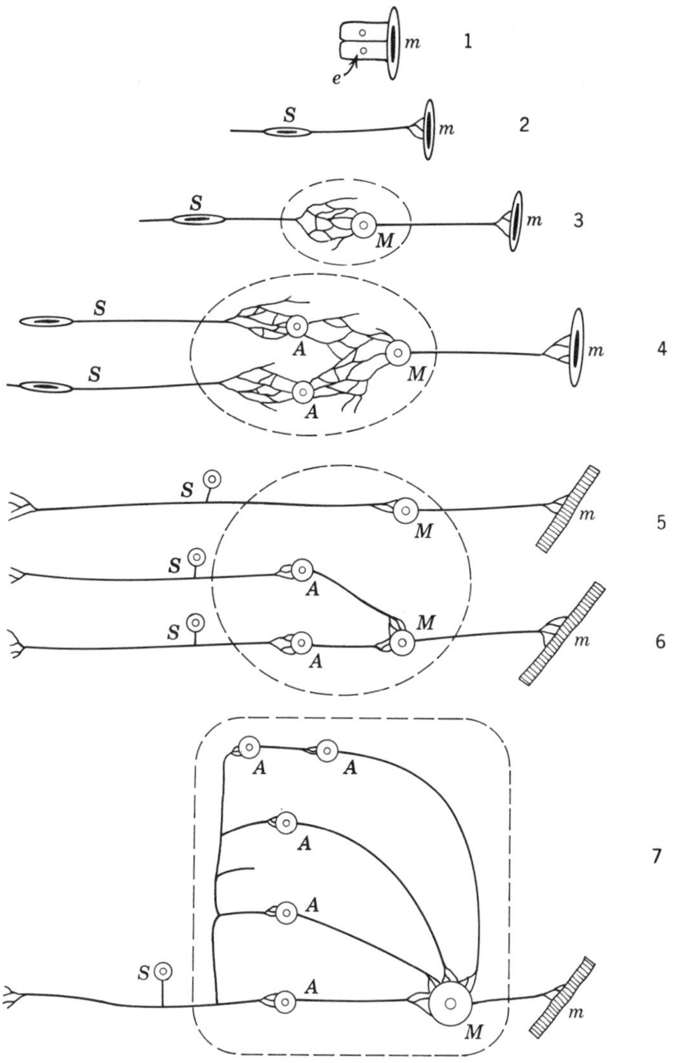

Fig. 1. The evolution of the nervous system. From Bayliss (Principles of General Physiology, N.Y. Longmans, Green, 1927, p. 468). Diagrams of the central nervous system drawn by physiologists look similar to electric networks drawn by electrical engineers. In general, any organization may be described as such an interconnection of parts. S, *Sensory neurone.* A, *Association neurone.* M, *Motor neurone.* e, *Epithelial cell.* m, *Muscle cell. The dotted lines indicate the boundaries of the nerve centers.* 1, *Sponge.* 2, *Sea anemone.* 3, *Simplest form in the earthworm.* 4, *Intercalation of association neurones in the earthworm.* 5, *Exceptional, simple, reflex arc in vertebrates. Possibly existing in the case of the knee jerk.* 6, *Usual type in vertebrates. The cell bodies of the sensory neurones are in the dorsal root ganglia, instead of in the receptor organs, except in the olfactory organ.* 7, *Addition of higher centers, consisting only of association neurones, some of which are inhibitory. They form, as it were, longer and longer parallel or alternative loops between the receptor and effector organs. These loops may be followed in Fig. 2.*

munication model, once it has been constructed. (References are provided at the end of the chapter for those interested in more detailed discussion of particular points.)

The communication model can be thought of as a glorified kind of fish net, spider's web, or network of nerves through which "information" passes or flows. The more formal material in later sections refers to a simple picture of this kind—in which various organizational characteristics are spoken of in terms of a communication network, of the information which passes through it, and of how both change with time.

Characteristics of Communication Models

It is worth noting here that a model is a miniature of, or compact representation of, an original. Usually models represent relevant points of interest in the original; these points can be combined so that the structure of the model and that of the original are similar. A set of rules may be included with a model to tell how it operates or how it can be manipulated.

The structure and points of interest used for a given model will change as the structure and points of interest in the original change. For example, if a road leading from one city to another is closed or abandoned, it may be eliminated from forthcoming editions of road maps of that area.

Development of a complete communication model follows similar lines. Knowledge of three kinds is required:

1. Knowledge of a communication network which exists at a given time (a collection of relevant points of interest and their connection).
2. Knowledge of existing control processes in the network (rules of operation of the network).
3. Knowledge of how existing network and control processes change with time.

For example, the physiologist may describe a nervous system and its evolution by a series of circles and interconnecting lines (as shown in Fig. 1). An increased complexity of organization of the nervous system will require increased or changing interconnection of the nerve centers (as shown in Fig. 2). Our development of the communication model will follow just this pattern.

The Communication Model Diagram

An organization can be thought of as a group of elements (divisions in a company, operating units in a machine, people in a social group) which are in some way tied together through their communication with each other, i.e., through their letters, their phone calls, a flow of material, their division of labor, personal conversation, and the like.

If a diagram is drawn showing how communication takes place between various elements of an organization (e.g., if written material orders are traced within a manufacturing organization as they are sent from one department to another), and if the diagram also indicates communication between the organization and the outside world (e.g., if one maps the pathways through which sales orders are solicited by the company and also maps the pathways through which orders are sent back), a picture results which describes, at least in part, what the organization is doing.

The communication diagram will look—on paper—like a road map or circuit diagram similar to Fig. 1. The lines represent the transmission of various pieces of paper, or information. The points (or boxes) represent places where the information is used, processed, or stored. One can get, very quickly, an idea of how complex the organization under study is just by looking at such a diagram. One can tell how the parts of the organization pictured are tied together.

The first thing to be determined about an organization is the existing structure of the communication network. The communication diagram will show this.

Internal Processes in the Organization: How It Is Controlled

Organizations—companies, groups of parts in a machine, the functional elements of the human body—operate together in a communication network, but they also exhibit another characteristic: the elements of an organization

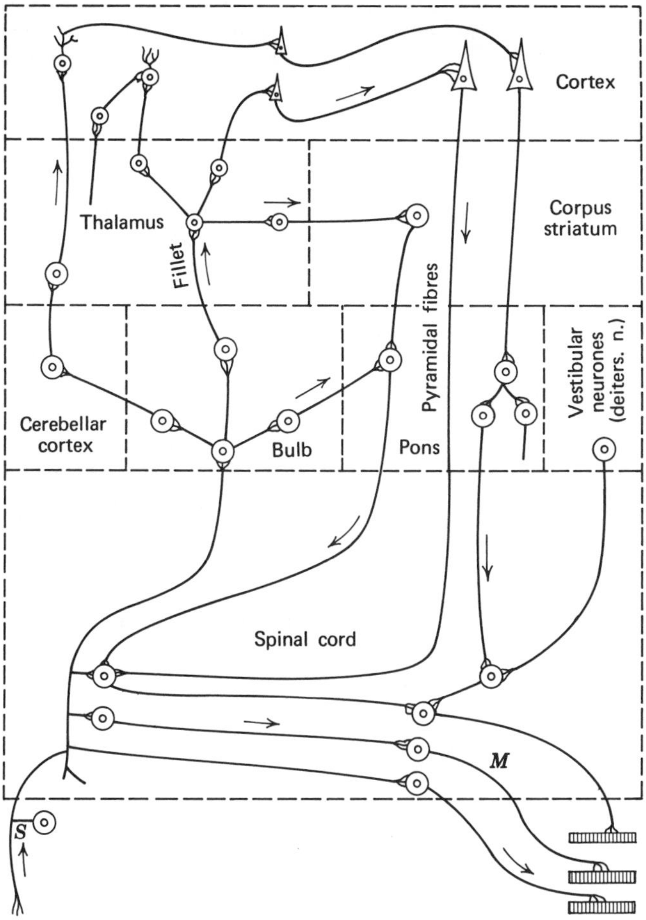

Fig. 2. Mammalian central nervous system, according to von Monakow and Mott. Shows the elaborate system of association neurones, arranged as parallel or alternative paths between the primary sensory neurones (S) and the final common paths (M). From Bayliss (Principles of General Physiology, N.Y. Longmans, Green, 1927, p. 478.) This is a further development of the diagrams shown in Fig. 1. Note the increased complexity of interconnection associated with the more refined nervous system.

operate together to reach or maintain an external goal (or its goal-image within the organization).[2] For the purpose of discussing com-

[2] The definition of goal used by Wiener is the one meant here. For a full and important discussion, see ref. 57. Quoting from this paper: If we divide behavior into active and passive, then "Active behavior may be subdivided into two classes: purposeless (or random) and purposeful. The term purposeful is meant to denote that the act or behavior may be interpreted as directed to the attainment of a goal—i.e. to a final condition in which the behaving object reaches a definite correlation in time or space with respect to another object or event. Purposeless behavior then is that which is not interpreted as directed to a goal." The important restriction involved in this definition of goal is stated later in the paper: ". . . We have restricted the connotation of teleological behavior by applying this designation only to purposeful reactions which are controlled by the error of the reaction—i.e. by the difference between the state of the behaving object at any time

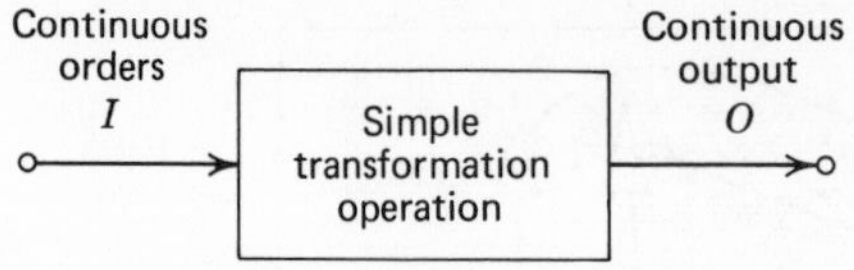

Fig. 3. A simple transformation unit. Continuous action is produced by a continuous series of orders. The unit has no goal of its own. An example: a gear train.

munication models (in a simplified manner), a goal may be defined as the operating standard in use by the organization at a given time. A goal is a bench mark one aims for or tries to keep close to at a given time. For example, a shop foreman is given a production goal for the week; the accounting department will set up standard costs, etc. Such goals are fairly simple. The organization may also have more complex goals, or a whole set of simple and complex goals. The simplicity, or complexity, of the operating goal or set of goals—and the way they are used by the organization—permits one to rank organizations by their ability to handle information and "make up their own minds."

The Simple Transformation Unit

The elementary organization has its directions given to it continuously from an external source. It can find no goal of its own, so it must be told what to do all the time; it cannot be left alone. Such organizations correspond to simple units of mechanical or electric transformation (gear trains, amplifiers, etc.) that might be shown diagrammatically as in Fig. 3. The three fundamental processes in the link are: (1) *reception;* (2) *conduction*, processing or transformation; and (3) *output transmission* (effector action). A simple industrial transformation takes place, for instance, when a sales order is transformed into an invoice.

The Simple Sorting System

Another elementary organization is the sorter, like a lemon grater or gravel sifter. A decision or sorting operation is built into the unit by its designer; the sorter also has to be fed continuously by an external operator. One input (say a load of gravel) can yield two or more different outputs (such as different sizes of gravel). A simple organization of this type might be diagrammed as in Fig. 4. It is similar to Fig. 3 but somewhat more complex. The most familiar sorting operation in business occurs in the mail room.

Note that the sorting unit, in effect, makes a decision, the criteria for which are built into the unit. The gravel sorter must have built into it different sizes of mesh for sifting.

Simple Goal-Maintaining Units: Control

The simplest type of organization which can, in some sense, control itself is characterized by its ability to monitor its own operation against an external goal. This type of unit is given one order and is left to carry that order out. An example of a purely mechanical goal-maintaining device is the governor of a steam engine (Fig. 5), which serves to regulate the engine's velocity under varying conditions of load. A desired velocity is set into the governor; the device seeks to maintain it.

In general, if an organization compares what

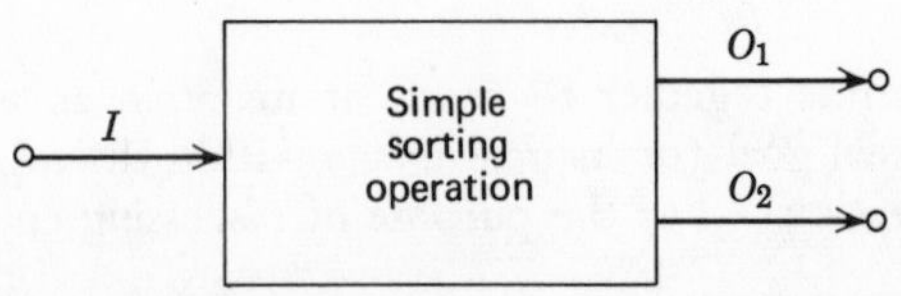

Fig. 4. A simple sorting unit. Two outputs are obtained from a single input. Rules for sorting (or decision) are built into the unit. The unit performs simple search and recognition operations common to more complicated processes.

---

and the final state interpreted as the purpose. Teleological behavior thus becomes synonymous with behavior controlled by negative feedback, and gains therefore in precision by a sufficiently restrained connotation."

Although this chapter will not discuss purposeful versus nonpurposeful behavior (or the philosophical issue of determinism versus free will), the subject was a fundamental one in the development of Cybernetics.

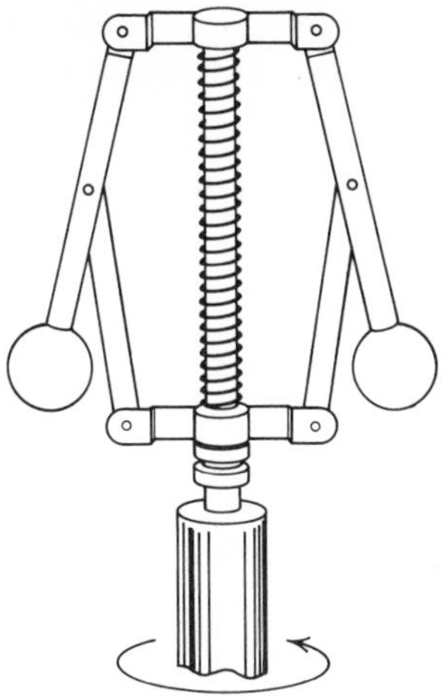

Fig. 5. A simple mechanical control unit, or governor, first treated by Clerk Maxwell. The governor seeks to maintain a steam-engine's velocity under changing load conditions.

it is doing with what its goal is, detects the error, if any, which exists between the two, and acts to reduce that error, then the organization *controls* its activities.

Feedback Necessary for Control

In order for an organization to determine if an error exists between what it is doing and what it intended to do to meet its goal, it must monitor its own activities: it must *feed back* a portion of its output for comparison with its input or standard. If the feedback tends to reduce error, rather than aggravate it, the feedback is called negative feedback—negative because it tends to oppose what the organization is doing. The steam governor is a *negative feedback* device, and in business the constant comparison of operating costs against standard costs (in order to keep operating costs in line) is a form of negative feedback.

One can explain the term "keeping up with the Joneses" in terms of negative feedback. The "Joneses" are what the sociologist calls a "reference group." Those of us who have such a reference group or goal (to equal the financial or social position of the Joneses) would constantly monitor our own financial and social position, detect the error or difference between our own position and the Joneses', and try to reduce the error, if possible, by appropriate action.

The nature of negative feedback is explicit if one takes an example from electrical engineering. Figure 6 represents a simple feedback circuit used in control devices called *servomechanisms.* Such devices can be used, for example, to actuate a radar antenna so that the position of the antenna matches the position set on a remotely located control box—in spite of wind resistance (load) at the antenna.

A certain position, or goal, can be set in the control box *A,* which in turn operates a motor or drive *B* to turn the antenna C. The actual position of the antenna, which may be different from the goal set because of, e.g., wind load, is fed back from C to *A,* and the error between the position of the antenna and the goal position set is detected at *A.* A signal in turn is sent to motor *B* to reduce the error.

Mathematically, the action of the circuit is described by the following relation (refer to Fig. 7)

$$E_2 = E_1 \left(\frac{K}{1-(-b)K}\right)$$

where E_1 is the input or standard set into the unit, E_2 is the output of the unit, K is the amplification factor or mechanical transformation factor of the unit, and $(-b)$ is the fraction of the unit's output E_2, used as negative feedback for error correction. In general, the greater the negative feedback, the greater the

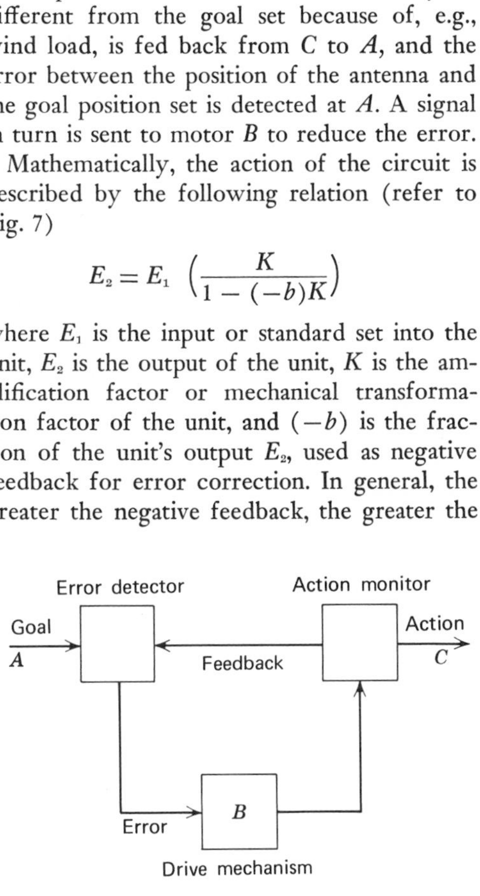

Fig. 6. The basic negative feedback circuit. The simplest organization which can control itself. Note the circularity of connection. A goal can be set at A, *then the feedback circuit left to maintain that goal on its own. The steam governor works like this.*

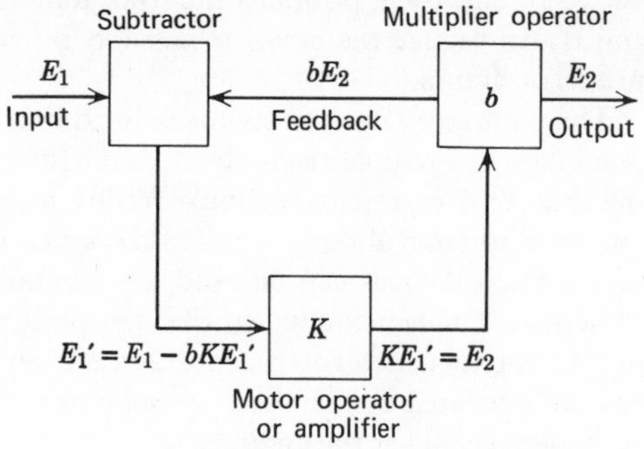

Fig. 7. The simple negative feedback circuit showing the mathematical relations which describe its operation.

error reduction or stabilization of the unit. The unit can be arranged so that, instead of negative feedback, *positive feedback* is obtained ($+b$). Error would then be aggravated when it occurred, oscillations would occur in the circuit's operation, etc. *Critical points for oscillation, stabilization, and error reduction are of particular interest to the control engineer, and although further discussion of feedback characteristics is beyond the scope of this chapter, the serious user of communication models should familiarize himself with feedback literature, such as that given in the bibliography.*

Control systems are in a sense circular in their operation, as can be seen from the circuit in Fig. 6. The feedback circuit and drive mechanism constitute a loop (or circle) of action. Systems which operate with negative feedback to maintain or reach a goal are said to be "goal-directed," and because of the circularity of action required by feedback such systems have also been called "circular causal systems."

The communications diagram can be studied for the presence of such circular feedback loops. This tells something about feedback and control in the organizations studied—the second point of interest. The Operations Researchers want to know, in particular, which processes are monitored, which are not; they want to obtain some idea of the efficiency of feedback loops, to determine if there is positive or negative feedback in these loops, to learn under what critical conditions negative (or positive) feedback may be useful or harmful. Scheduling and order processing systems, for example, deserve analysis with respect to stability, time lags, and feedback checks.

The Sorter with Feedback

If feedback can be applied to simple mechanical transformation systems (like the steam-engine governor) it is also applicable to the simple sorter. The various sorted outputs are then compared with standards for these outputs to determine if the sorter is, in fact, operating properly. The consistency and stability of the sorting operation is thereby improved. Figure 8 would be a diagram of such a system. The industrial inspection system of quality control, which checks various finished products against standards, sorting good and bad products into different piles, is an example of this kind of feedback sorter.

Combinations of Transformation and Sorter Units

To obtain a more complex organization that is more versatile, various combinations of transformation and sorting units (with or without feedback can be combined. This is roughly what happens when various parts or divisions of an organization are brought together. The most useful combination for a given job is usually not obvious, however, since the number of changes one could make in a many-part organization is inconceivably large.

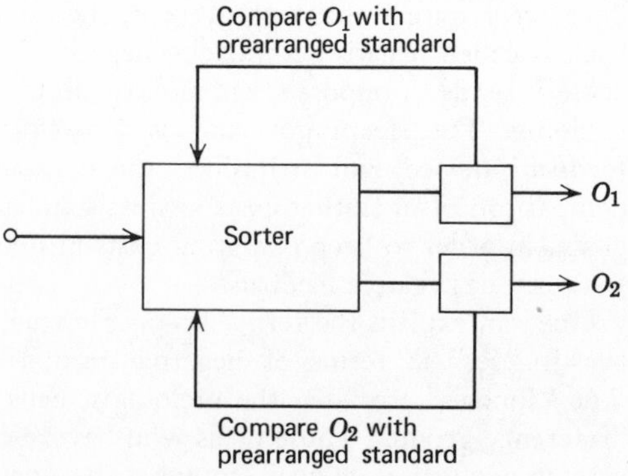

Fig. 8. The simple sorter with feedback applied. The output from the sorter is compared with the output desired (standard or goal) which has been built into the sorter mechanism.

Furthermore, the combination of various parts may have characteristics quite different from that of the parts themselves, particularly in industrial or human organizations. Professor Wiener, who was pressed by several of his social science friends to extend his mathematical theory of Cybernetics to the area of human organization, hesitated to do so because he realized that the rapidly changing conditions of social organizations, the necessity for short-run statistics, and the interaction of observers would make precise results difficult to obtain.

In other words, as stated on p. 191 of Professor Wiener's book, *Cybernetics. Control and Communication in the Animal and the Machine,* in the social sciences

> we have to deal with short statistical runs, nor can we be sure that a considerable part of what we observe is not an artifact of our own creation. An investigation of the stock market is likely to upset the stock market. We are too much in tune with the objects of our investigation to be good probes. In short, whether our investigations in the social sciences be statistical or dynamic—and they should participate in the nature of both—they can never be good to more than a very few decimal places, and, in short, can never furnish us with a quantity of verifiable significant information which begins to compare with that which we have learned to expect in the natural sciences. We cannot afford to neglect them; neither should we build exaggerated expectations of their possibilities. There is much which we must leave, whether we like it or not, to the unscientific, narrative method of the professional historian.

If the investigator is aware of these problems and he is looking only for fairly gross improvements in operations (as is often the case), some further discussion of complex organizations built up of the simple elements we have discussed may be helpful to the practical researcher.

The Automatic Goal-Changing Unit

If an organization has several alternatives prepared for action, and also has the rules set up for applying one or the other of them *when external conditions change* (i.e., can *predict* the best alternative for changing conditions), it can control its own activities more effectively than can a simple feedback system. Such action requires a second-order feedback and implies that a reserve or memory of possible alternatives exists within the organization.

An example of this type of organization—which can switch its standards for different courses of action—is the telephone exchange. The immediate goal of the telephone exchange is to search and find a specific number dialed by a subscriber. There may be many such numbers dialed during the day; the exchange must be prepared to receive different numbers and take different courses of action automatically for each one. (Figure 9 shows a simplified diagram of such a system, which is in fact a complicated sorting operation.) Another goal-changing example of similar type is the cat that chases the rat—not by following the rat's position at a given moment, but by *leading* the rat's position based on the cat's memory of how other rats ran in the past.

If an organization can control itself, particularly if it can change its goals, we call it an *autonomous* organization. The autonomy of the automatic goal-changing organization lies in its memory and ability to recall. The better the memory and the faster the recall, the more autonomous the organization is likely to be.

The storing up of information, which allows the organization to prepare various alternatives

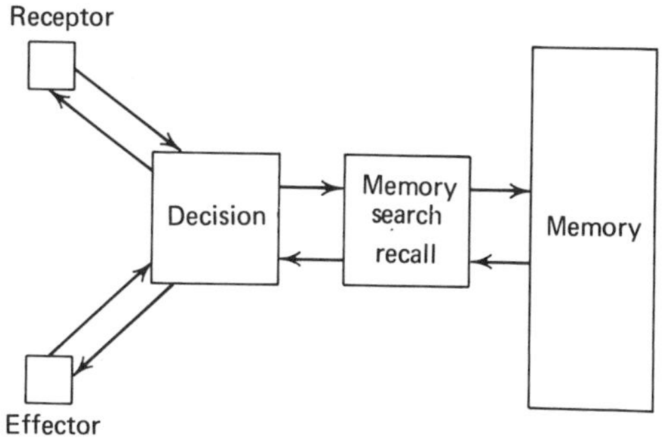

Fig. 9. Feedback circuit with memory device. By adding a memory and more complicated feedback loops, an organization can have more control over its own activities. In this case a series of alternatives for action is built into the system if external conditions (detected by the receptor) change. An example is the automatic switching of a telephone exchange.

for action, is a process of *learning*. Learning may result in a reconfiguration of the internal channels of the organization, or communication network. The learning organization's structure changes with time. For example, the circuits in a telephone exchange can be expanded to include the "numbers" of more subscribers by rewiring part of the telephone exchange. Increased memory reserves generally require greater complexity of interconnection in the communication network. In terms of physiology, more memory means a greater interconnection of nerve cells. For a librarian, more memory means a greater cross referencing of index cards.

Thus, after we have found out what the existing communication and control processes in an "automatic" goal-changing organization are, we ask: How do these processes change with time? How do the inner channels of communication in the organization develop? Fall into disuse? Maintain themselves? Where is the memory of the organization located? What kind of information is put into the memory? By what manner is it stocked? What kind of information is taken out of the memory? What is the *content* of the memory; how does it change? Is the organization learning anything? Is it forgetting properly or improperly? What can it *predict* from its memory?

The operation of a system with a memory also means that certain messages have greater priority of transmission into and out of the memory than others. The possible courses of action have different priorities or *values* for application in different situations, and the researcher wants to know about these values to understand the action of the system. Again, reasoning in terms of the telephone exchange is useful. When ten telephone calls are received at once, the exchange must decide which to answer first.

The Reflective Goal-Changing Unit

If an organization can collect information, store it in a memory, and then reflect upon or examine the contents of the memory for the purpose of formulating new courses of action, it will have reached a new level of autonomy. The mechanism that considers various goals and courses of action can be called the *consciousness* of the organization. Reflective decision-making takes place in such third-order feedback systems. The action of the organization begins to approach what we would expect of an actual industrial or human organization. See Fig. 10.

To get a concrete picture of what consciousness is, imagine a person sitting back, relaxed in an overstuffed chair, speculating on what he will do next—on how he might improve his lot by completion of a certain type of research or sale of an invention, or on how his wife told him to put a new washer in the bathroom because the faucet leaks. He decides to please his wife rather than his pocketbook. He would then be using his reflective goal-changing circuits, or consciousness.

Conscious learning can be selective and take, from a wide range of external information sources, that information relevant to the organization's survival or other major goals. The consciousness may redirect the *attention* of the organization; make it *aware* of some happenings and unmindful of others. It can *initiate or cease courses of action*, based on incoming information; *investigate* network conditions in the organization; *search* the organization's memory; and *pick up deviations* between various actions and the goals which direct them—to name but a few of the activities of this third-order control center.

By taking such actions, the organization with a consciousness can direct its own *growth*. The possibility of *recognizing* valuable information received by the organization, or valuable combinations of information in the memory, permits the organization to practice *innovation*. Such abilities are highly desirable for most organizations and so, as an industrial investigator, the Operations Researcher would be interested in the consciousness of the organization (what the executives do or do not do).

Reflective goal-changing is of interest in the field of electronic computers, too. For example, computers and mechanisms which repair themselves must be conscious of their internal circuit faults. The action of such a machine "consciousness" would be like this: The consciousness circuits would become aware that other parts of the organization (e.g., parts or tubes) had broken down or been superseded by a more efficient design. The consciousness circuits would then direct replacement of the broken or outmoded parts with new or im-

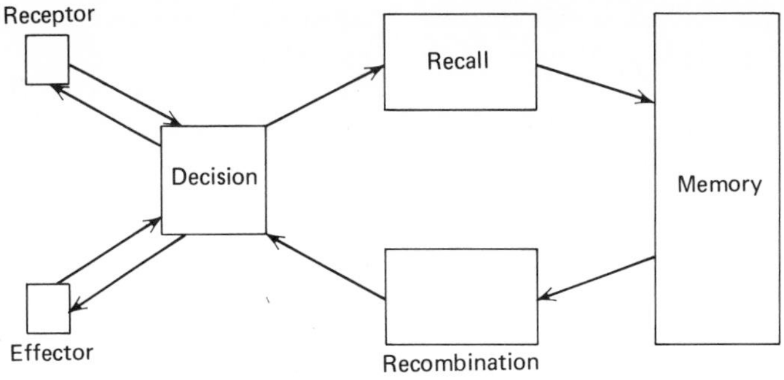

(a)

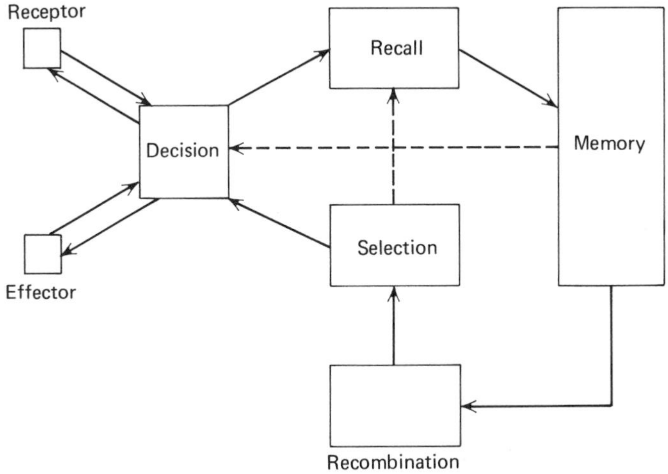

(b)

Fig. 10. (a) *Additional memory refinements. If information in the memory can be recombined and new alternatives produced for action (by the machine or organization itself), the unit becomes more versatile and autonomous. This device makes simple predictions.* (b) *Additional memory refinements: development of a consciousness. If many memories can be combined, and if from the many combinations a few can be selected for further consideration, further recombination, etc., the unit will have reached a still higher level of versatility or autonomy. The dashed lines indicate comparisons of what is going on with what has happened in the past and what might occur in the future (second- and third-order predictions). In many organizations, these comparisons are poorly made.*

proved ones. Such action lies in the realm of possibility for computers—but industrial organizations do it every day!

The consciousness could be expected to show all the faults, in its operation, that we might find in humans or in executive groups which run organizations: delusions, faulty direction, misinterpretation of messages, lack of awareness of new opportunities, poorly defined operating goals, and the rest. Such faults are the subject of the last half of this chapter. However, another example here may be illuminating.

Consider a computer which could repair itself. It would have consciousness circuits to direct the repairs. Now if the consciousness circuits themselves were faulty and directed indiscriminate repairs to be made on the properly working machine, disaster would result. Let a drunken repairman run through a local telephone exchange and randomly unsolder relay connections, and the result would be similar. It would become virtually impossible to find all the newly created faults. The unreliability of electronic components and circuits limits the application of "self-repair" or consciousness functions in computing machines today. Similarly, executives in industrial organizations can cause disaster if they get out of commission easily.

The O.R. team should make the most use of organizational knowledge brought together by Cybernetics in the analysis of complex organizations with a memory and a consciousness. One of the functions of O.R. with its mixed discipline teams is to increase an organization's memory—by bringing in a collection of knowledge different from that of the organization's routine—and to aid its consciousness (the executives) in developing and evaluating alternatives for action.

A Composite Communication Model

Figure 11 will serve to tie together these various ideas on communication and control in organizations. The diagram was proposed by K. W. Deutsch as a general communication model which might be used to describe complex organizations.[3] For the sake of discussion, it might be considered as a block diagram of a radar input gun-control mechanism which contains a memory device.

Column I of Fig. 11 contains circuits which operate as a simple feedback system with a fixed goal. The circuits consist of a receptor and an effector, e.g., the radar equipment for spotting planes and the gun-postioning and firing mechanisms. When a plane is picked up by the receptor device, the gun-effector devices are directed to follow the plane, or goal, and to track the position of the plane as accurately as possible.

The addition of memory and goal-changing circuits, located in Column II, allows the gun control to predict where the plane will be—to anticipate the plane's position rather than follow its position slavishly—and thus increases the number of hits the device can secure. Column II circuits are essentially *automatic goal-changing circuits;* the rules for changing goals are designed into the device by the communications engineer. So that action of the gun-control device can be changed (by the device itself) depending upon the type of aircraft observed, weather conditions, the predicted quality of the pilot, etc.

Column III, the consciousness, contains *reflective goal-changing circuits.* These were sketched in so the reader can see the development of the whole system, from the simple receptor and effector circuits to the complicated feedback circuits a consciousness would require. The consciousness circuits are dashed, because they are not yet part of normal electronic computers.

Again, for the sake of comparison, *analogies with industrial organizations* have been included in Fig. 11. Column I corresponds to the production-line–order-department combination which receives orders and fills them in a routine manner. Column II represents the domain of staff personnel, the file department, the semiautomatic or tactical goal-changing responsibilities of the executive vice-president. Column III represents the long-range planning functions of the president or the board of directors in a normal organization.

The purpose of this description of some characteristics of internal communication and control in organizations has been to give an idea of the *elaboration* that one can make on the communication diagram in order to indicate some of the analogies that can be made by using the diagram. The arrangement of receptor, effector, and processing circuits in Fig. 11 is also a fairly standard method of drawing communication networks. The receptor and effector circuits are to the left in the diagram, the processing circuits to the right.

Before continuing, it may be helpful to summarize what we have to work with in a communication model.

[3] Figure 11 is adapted from K. W. Deutsch (op. cit.). The Deutsch diagram may prove applicable to any level of social integration, including the individual.

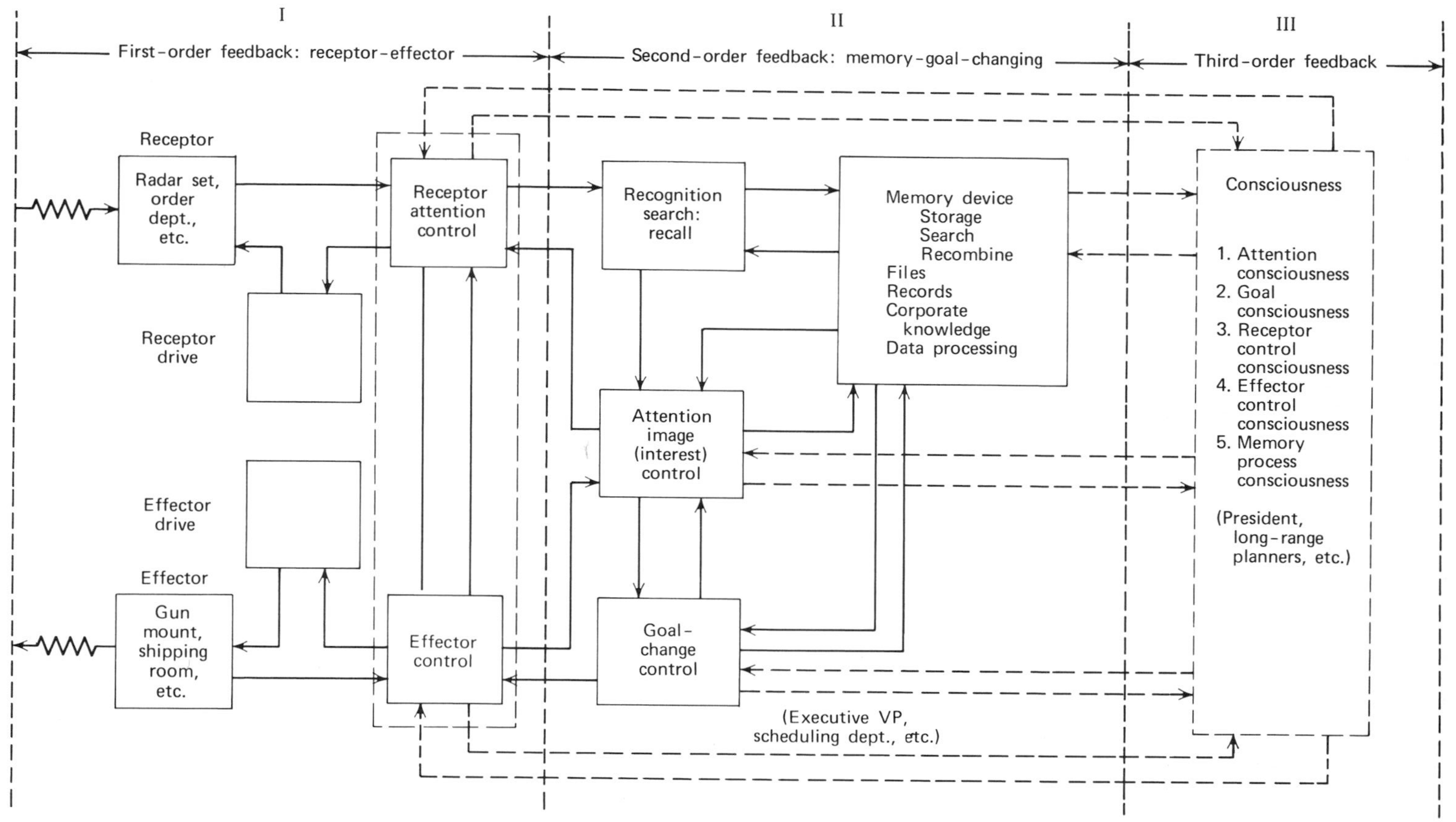

Fig. 11. Block diagram of a three-level feedback control system. Adapted from Deutsch (Models of Communication and Education, Unpublished). For explanation of the figure, see text. Note that this diagram is a build-up of simpler units shown in Figs. 4-3 through 4-10.

Summary of Communication Model Characteristics

The communication model should provide:

1. A map of the communication network of the organization.
2. Knowledge of the goal-maintaining or goal-directing processes of control in organization.
3. In complex goal-directed organization, some knowledge of goal-changing processes. The processes of innovation, growth, learning, the functions of memory and consciousness, and the concept of autonomy occur here.

In each of these categories, the Operations Researchers will be interested in the kind or content of information transmitted and received.

So, the complete communication model consists of a series of network pictures similar to Fig. 11 (in which the inner channels of the organization will change with time), plus accumulated knowledge on the processes of communication and control taken from various disciplines. This knowledge can be coordinated by use of the diagram.

Industrial Dynamics and the Design of Management Control Systems[1]

EDWARD B. ROBERTS

I. The Organization as a Control System

Every organization is a control system. Each has direction and objectives, whether explicit or implied. Each has beliefs as to its current status. Each has policies and procedures whereby it reaches decisions and takes actions to attain its goals more closely. Every organization actually contains a myriad of smaller control systems, each characterized by the same goal-striving, but not necessarily goal-attaining behavior.

The organization as a whole or any one its component subsystems can be represented by the feedback process shown in Exhibit 1. Four characteristics of this diagram are noteworthy. First, the transformation of decisions into results takes place through a complex process which includes a basic structure of organizational, human, and market relationships; this structure is sometimes not apparent because of its numerous sources of noise or random behavior and due to its often lengthy time delays between cause and effect.

The second aspect to be noted is the distinction between the achievements that are apparent in the organization and those which are real. The real situation is translated into the apparent through information and communication channels which contain delays, noise, and bias. These sources of error may be the inadvertent features of an organization's communication system, or they may result from the chosen characteristics of a data-processing system which sacrifices accuracy for compactness. In any event, however, the bases of actual decisions in an organization may be assumptions which bear but little reaction to fact.

The third feature of the diagram is that the decision-making process is viewed as a response to the gap between objectives of the organization and its apparent progress toward those objectives. Although both the objectives and achievements may be difficult to define precisely and measure accurately, such goal-seeking behavior is nonetheless present in all organizations and in every subsystem of the organizations. At any level of an organization, many similar decisions are being made. The real problem of the management control system designer is to recognize these multiple decision loops and their interrelationships, and to develop policies and an organizational structure that will tie these activities into progress toward total organization objectives.

The fourth characteristic of Exhibit 1 is the continuous feedback path of decision-results-measurement-evaluation-decision. It is vital to effective system design that each element of this feedback path be properly treated and that its continuous nature be recognized. Whether the decision in the system is made by the irrational actions or logical deductions of a manager or by the programmed response of a computer, the system consequences will eventually have further effects on the decision itself.

From *Management Controls* by Bonini, Jaedicke, and Wagner (eds.). Copyright 1964 by McGraw-Hill, pp. 102–126. Reprinted by permission of the McGraw-Hill Book Company.

---

[1] This article is based on studies supported principally by a grant of the Ford Foundation, which has sponsored Industrial Dynamics Research at M.I.T., and in part by a grant of the National Aeronautics and Space Administration to sponsor research on the management of research and development. The computer simulations were carried out at the M.I.T. Computation Center. The writer is grateful to Professors Donald C. Carroll, Jay W. Forrester, and Donald G. Marquis for their many helpful comments.

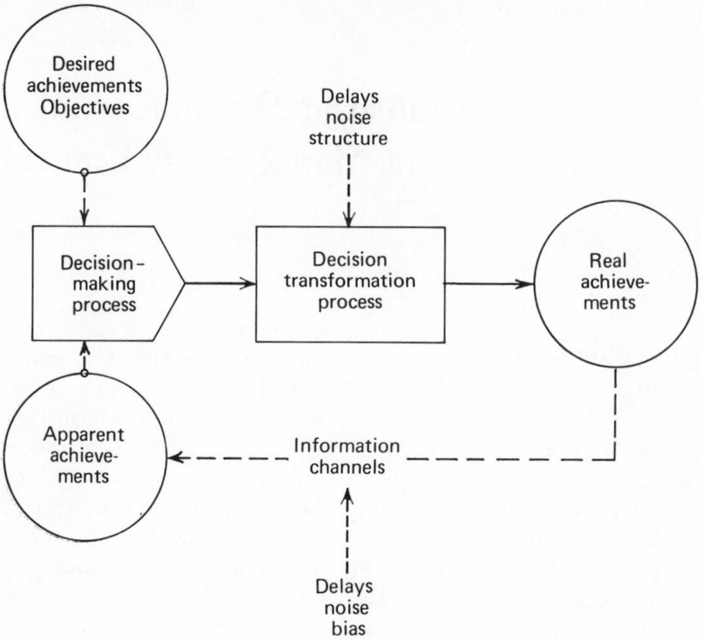

Exhibit 1. Control system structure of organization.

II. Industrial Dynamics—Philosophy and Methodology for Control System Design

Industrial Dynamics is a philosophy which asserts that organizations are most effectively viewed (and managed) from this control system perspective. It is also a methodology for designing organizational policy. This two-pronged approach is the result of a research program that was initiated and directed at the M.I.T. School of Industrial Management by Professor Jay W. Forrester. The results of the first five years of this program are described in Professor Forrester's book, *Industrial Dynamics*, which also discusses a variety of potential applications to key management problems.[2]

Industrial Dynamics recognizes a common systems base in the flow structure of all social-economic-industrial-political organizations. This perspective ties the segmented functional aspects of formal organizations into an integrated structure of varying rates of flow and responsively changing levels of accumulation. The flow paths involve all facets of organizational resources—men, money, materials, orders, and capital equipment—and the information and decision-making network that links the other flows.

Industrial Dynamics views decisions as the controllers of these organization flows. Such decisions regulate the rate of change of levels from which the flows originate and to which they are sent. In the flow diagrams drawn as part of an Industrial Dynamics study, decisions are even represented by the traditional control valve symbol of the engineer. Exhibit 2 shows such a decision, based in part on information about the contents of the source level, controlling the rate of flow to the destination level.

The system structures and behavioral phenomena that are studied by the Industrial Dynamics methodology are present at all levels of the corporation. The top management of the firm is involved in a system that can be studied and aided in the same manner as the middle management of the organization, and again in the same fashion as the physical operating system of the plant. The potential payoff from changes derived from systems studies increases

[2] Jay W. Forrester: *Industrial Dynamics*, Cambridge, Mass.: M.I.T., 1961.

greatly, however, as the study is focused higher up in the organization. For all studies the pattern of forming a dynamic verbal theory, developing mathematical equations, computer simulation of the model, and derivation of improved policies is followed. The problems encountered in these phases do not significantly change as we move from the bottom to the top of an organization. Only during the final stage of implementation of system change does the problem complexity get significantly greater the higher the level of organization involved. But the impact of improved corporate-level policy on company growth, stability, and profitability can readily justify this added effort to renovate top management policy making.

III. Problems of Management Control Systems

The preceding discussion has focused on the nature of organizational problems as management control system problems, and on the intended applicability of Industrial Dynamics to these problems. Observation of several different types of management control systems and a survey of the literature in this field lead to a belief that a new attack on control system design is needed. The traditional approaches to management control systems have mushroomed in number and sophistication of applications as operations research and electronic data processing have developed during the post-war era. Although these systems have made significant and successful inroads, many fail to cure the problems for which they were designed; other management control systems even amplify the initial difficulties or create more significant new problems. All this is taking place even as we derive enhanced but misplaced confidence in the systems.

Several examples will help to illustrate these problems and lead us to some findings about the design of management control systems.

Systems Inadequate for Their Problems. Sometimes the management control system is inadequately designed for the problem situation. In such a case the control system may improve performance in the trouble area, but be far short of the potential gains. At times the limited effectiveness may transform a potentially major benefit to the company into but a marginal application.

A PRODUCTION-INVENTORY-EMPLOYMENT CONTROL SYSTEM. As an example, let us take the case of an industrial components manufacturer who initially has no formal production-inventory-employment control systems. Such a firm operates by its response to current problems. It follows the example of the firemen trying to use a leaky hose—as soon as one hole is patched up, another leak occurs elsewhere. A company operating in this manner does not keep sufficiently close tabs on changes in sales, inventories, backlogs, delivery delays, etc. Rather, when customer complaints build up on company delivery performance, people will be hired to increase the production rate and repair the inventory position. Similarly, when a periodic financial report (or the warehouse manager's difficulties) shows a great excess in inventory, workers will be laid off to reduce the inventory position. Despite the obvious faults, the majority of our manufacturing firms have these problems. The dynamic be-

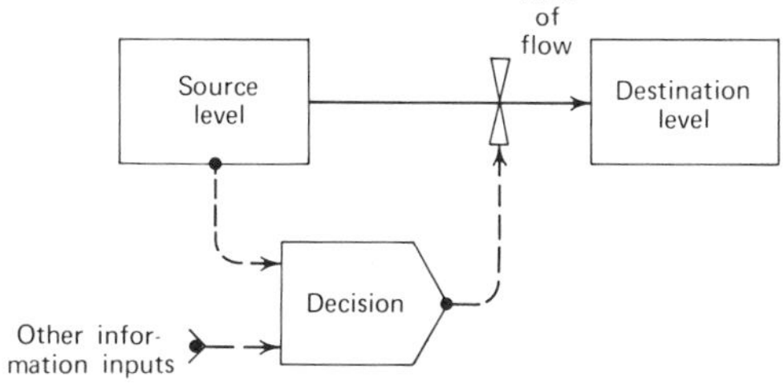

Exhibit 2. The decision as a controller.

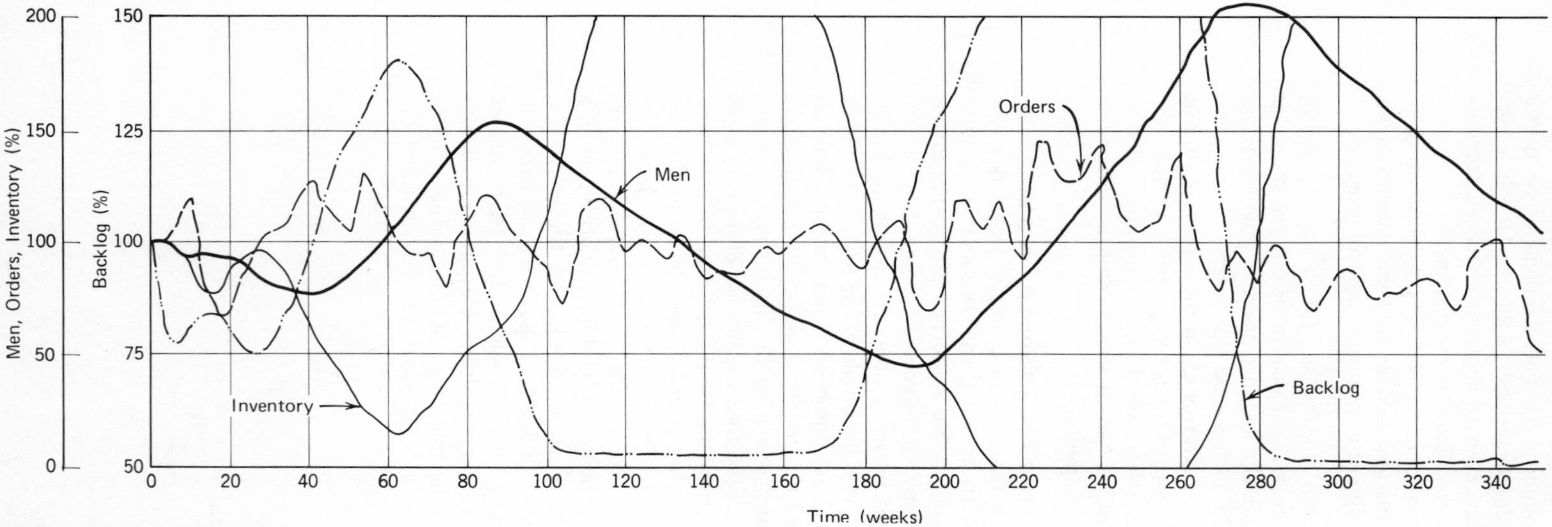

Exhibit 3. Management by crises.

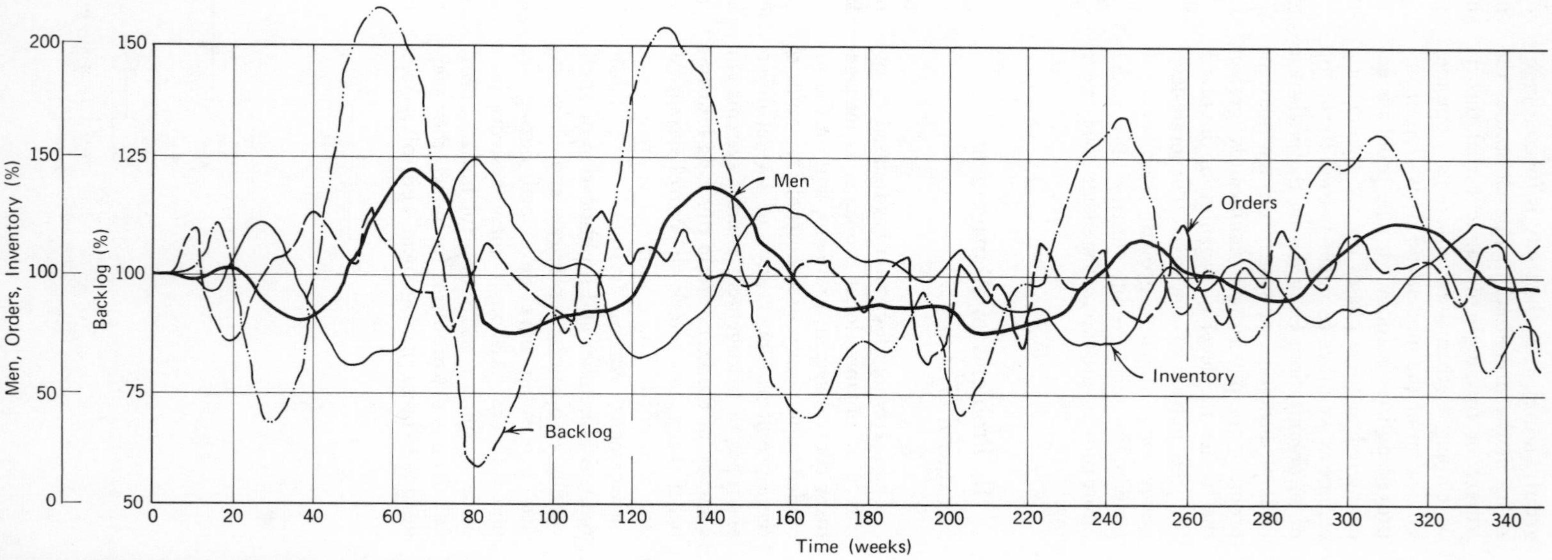

Exhibit 4. Effects of management control systems.

havior of such firms (as here illustrated by simulation results of an Industrial Dynamics model) has the appearance of Exhibit 3, with wide swings in sales, inventories, employment, order backlog, and, correspondingly, in profitability. The potential for a well-designed management control system in such a firm is enormous.

The traditional approach (some may prefer calling it the "modern approach") to the design of a control system for such an organization will recognize that: (1) better information on sales is necessary; (2) such information should properly be smoothed to eliminate possibilities of factory response to chance order-rate variations, (3) inventories should be periodically (perhaps even continuously) checked, and reorders generated when needed to bring stocks into line with target inventories; (4) order backlogs should not be allowed to drift too far from the normal levels; and (5) work force should be adjusted to meet the desired production rate that stems from consideration of current sales volume and the manufacturing backlog situation. Using our earlier company model, we can readily build into the model a management control system that incorporates all these features. The modeled company would then be a leader in its use of management control techniques. And, as Exhibit 4 illustrates, the company would have benefited by this approach. With the new control systems installed, fluctuations in the business have in general been reduced in magnitude as well as periodicity. Yet the basic dynamic pattern observed in the earlier diagram is still present —periodic fluctuations in sales, larger ones in inventories, and corresponding variations in production rate and work force. The latter situation is similar in character to that which we encountered at the Sprague Electric Company, at the beginning of our Industrial Dynamics

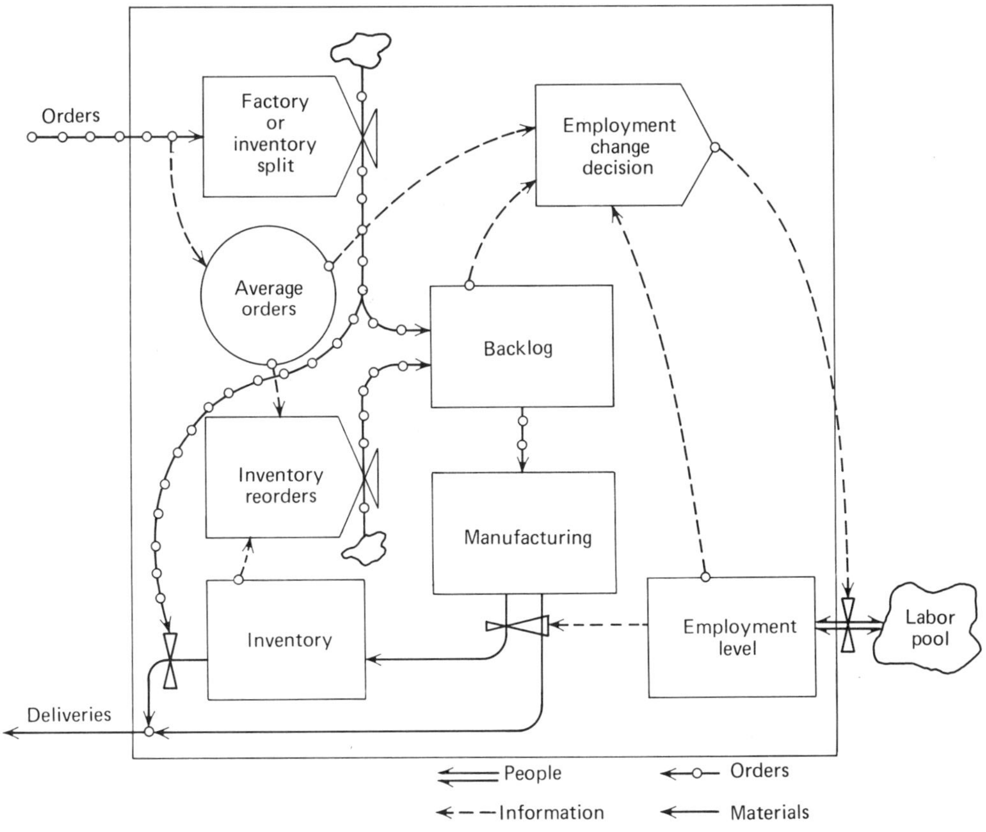

Exhibit 5. The manufacturer's organization structure.

study program with them several years ago.

Let us briefly review their case. The Sprague Electric Company is a major producer of electrical components, with an annual sales volume of approximately 75 million dollars. The particular product line which was selected for Industrial Dynamics research is a relatively mature industrial component, developed by Sprague several years ago and now past its market introduction and major growth phases. The principal customers of the product are manufacturers of military and high-grade consumer electronic systems. The industry competition is not price-based, but is rather dependent on product reliability and delivery time.

The work structure of the company, including its inventory and manufacturing control aspects, is diagrammed in Exhibit 5. Orders arrive from the customers, and a determination is made as to whether or not they can be filled from existing inventories. Orders for those catalogue items not ordinarily stocked, or for those which are currently out of stock, enter into the backlog of manufacturing orders. The customer orders for which inventory is in stock are processed and shipped from inventory.

The inventory control system of the company attempts to maintain a proper inventory position for the product line. Target inventories are adjusted to take into account average sales, and inventory reorders are generated to reflect the shipping rate from inventory and the desired inventory corrections. The orders for inventory replacements enter into the manufacturing backlog.

Production rate in the company is determined by the level of employment, with manufacturing output being sent to the customers or to inventory in reflection of the relative production order backlogs. Control of both backlog size and employment level is attempted by means of the employment change decision of the company.

As the curves of Exhibit 4 demonstrated, inventory, backlog, and employment all had sizable fluctuations, despite the existing controls in these areas. They seemed to reflect, with some amplification, the variability in incoming orders. Given this situation of fluctuating sales, the traditional management control designer would either express satisfaction with the system performance or perhaps seek additional improvement by parameter adjustment. Neither approach would get at the source of the difficulties, and this source is not the fluctuations in incoming customer orders.

To determine the real system problem, let us examine our next diagram (Exhibit 6). Here we have duplicated the manufacturer's organization of Exhibit 5 and added a representation of the customer sector of the industry. The customers receive orders for military and commercial electronic systems. These are processed through their engineering departments, resulting in requirements for components. Customer orders for components are prepared and released as demanded by the delivery lead time of the component manufacturers. Delivered components enter into the system manufacturers' component inventories and are used up during production of the systems.

Having added this sector to our diagram, we now discover the presence of another feedback loop in the total company-customer system: Changes in the company delivery delay will affect the customer release rate of new orders, which in turn will influence the company delivery delay. This loop amplifies the system problems of the company, being able to transform slight variations in system orders into sustained oscillations in company order rate, producing related fluctuations in company inventories, backlog, employment, and profits.

Let us follow through a possible dynamic sequence that will illustrate the full system interactions. If, for any reason, system orders received by the customers temporarily increase, the customers will soon pass this along to the component supplier as an order increase. Since, even under ordinary circumstances, weekly fluctuations in order rate to the component manufacturer are sizable, some time will elapse before this order rate change is noticed. In the meantime, the component manufacturer's inventory will be somewhat reduced, and the order backlog will be increased. Both of these changes tend to increase the delivery delay. The smaller inventory allows fewer incoming orders to be filled immediately; the larger backlog causes a longer delay for the now increased fraction of orders that must await manufacture. As the customers become aware of the longer lead time, they

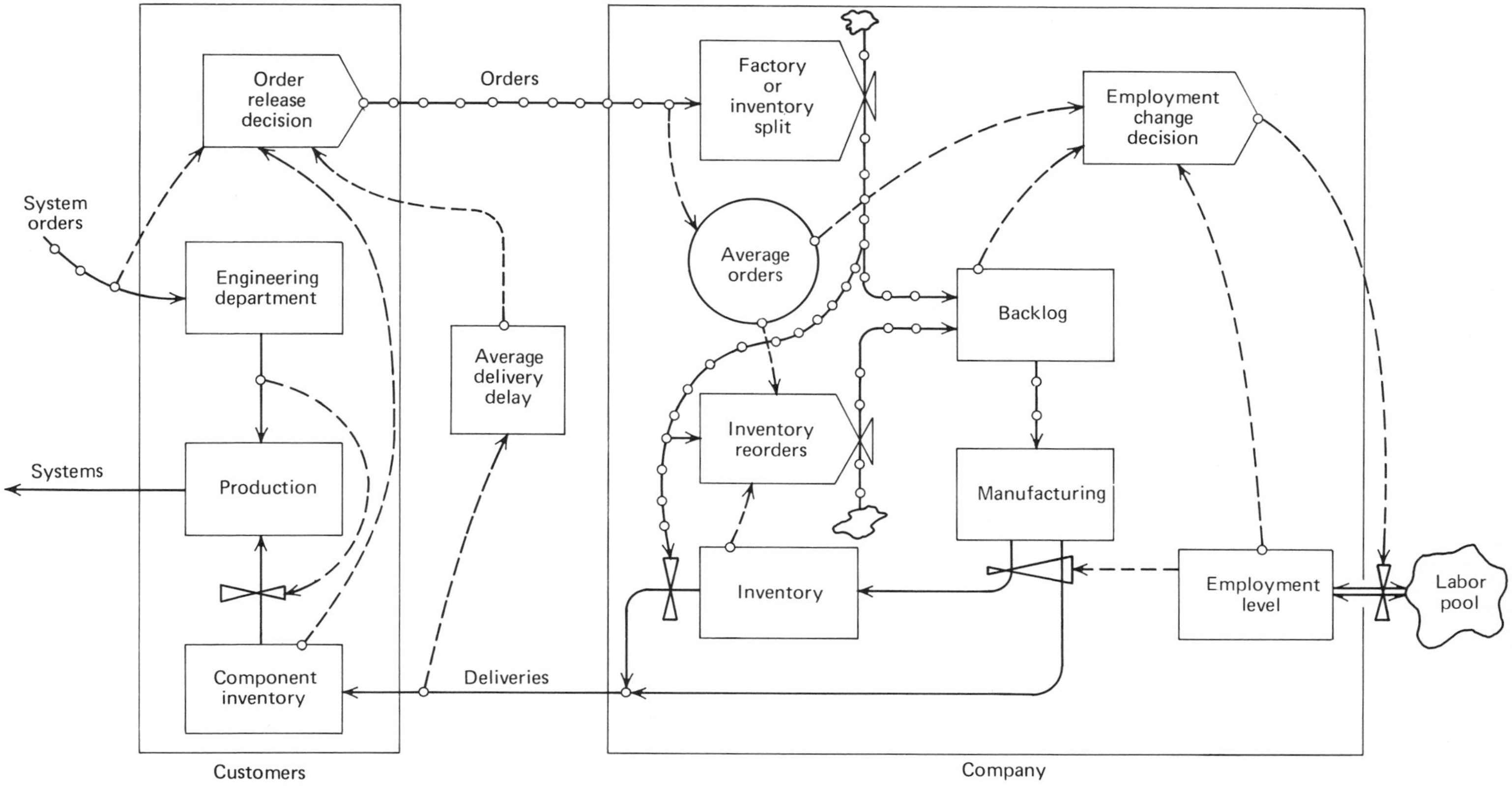

Exhibit 6. Company-customers system.

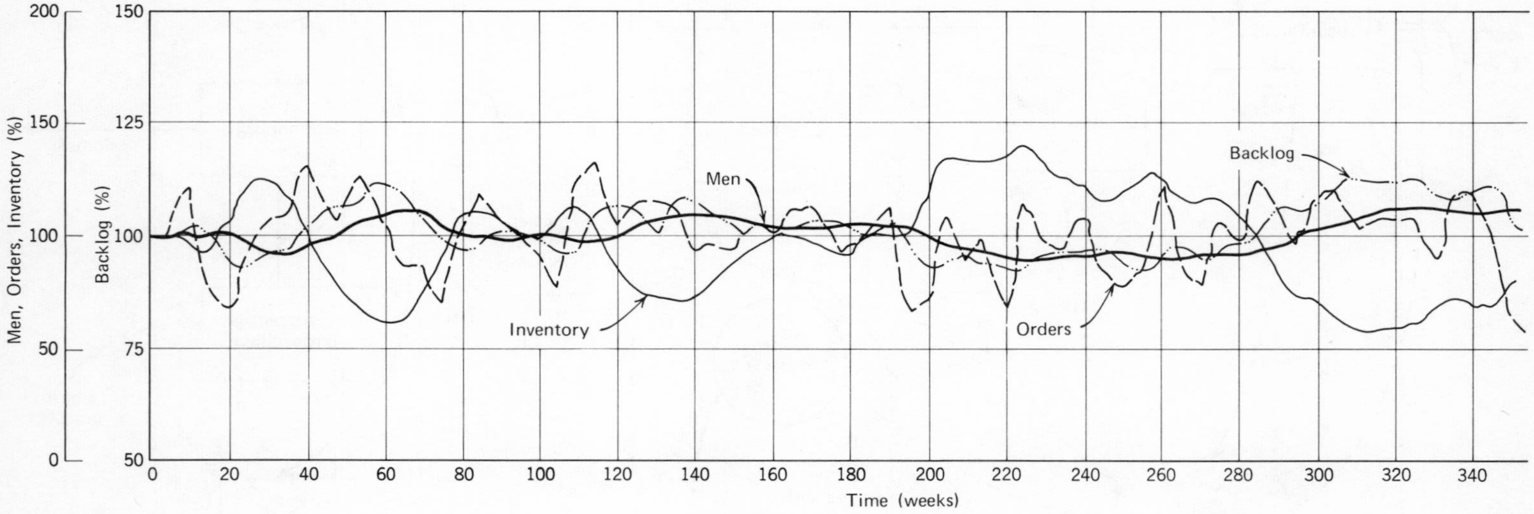

Exhibit 7. Effects of industrial dynamics policies.

begin to order further ahead, thus maintaining a higher order rate and accentuating the previous trend in sales.

Eventually, the component manufacturer notes the higher sales, larger backlog, and lower inventory, and begins hiring to increase his factory employment. The employment level is set higher than that needed to handle the current customer order rate, so that backlog and inventory can be brought into line. As the increased work force has its gradual effect on inventory and backlog, the changes tend to reduce the delivery time. The information is gradually fed back to the customers, lowering the order rate even below the initial value. This set of system interactions can produce order rate fluctuations unrelated to the basic demand pattern for the customers' products.

To dampen the fluctuations in customer order rate, the component manufacturer must control not inventory or backlog or employment, but rather he must stabilize the factory lead time for deliveries. This can readily be accomplished once the nature of the need is recognized. System behavior can also be improved to a great extent when the component manufacturer becomes aware that his inventory control system does not really control inventory, but it does contribute to production overshoots of any change in orders received.

The details of the Sprague case, the model for its study, and the new policies now being implemented at Sprague are discussed fully in chapters 17 and 18 of *Industrial Dynamics*.[3] It is sufficient for our purposes to show the effects of the new policies applied to the same situation shown earlier in Exhibit 4. The curves shown on the next graph (Exhibit 7) demonstrate a higher degree of stability achieved in all variables except inventory, which is now being used to absorb random changes in sales. In particular, the employment swings have been dampened significantly. The simulation results forecast significant benefits to the company deriving from the application of this new approach to management policy design. Our experiences during the past year of system usage at Sprague seem to support the initial hypotheses, and the product line is currently benefiting from higher productivity, improved employment stability, higher and smoother sales, and lower inventories.

THE CONTROL OF RESEARCH AND DEVELOPMENT PROJECTS. Another area in which the traditional approach to control system design has proven inadequate is the management of research and development projects. The intangibility, lack of precise measurements, and un-

[3] *Ibid.*

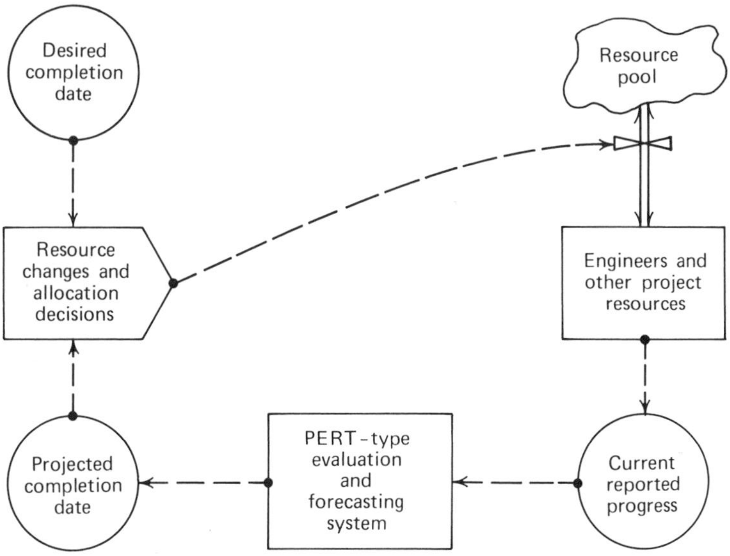

Exhibit 8. Assumed basis of current R and D project controls.

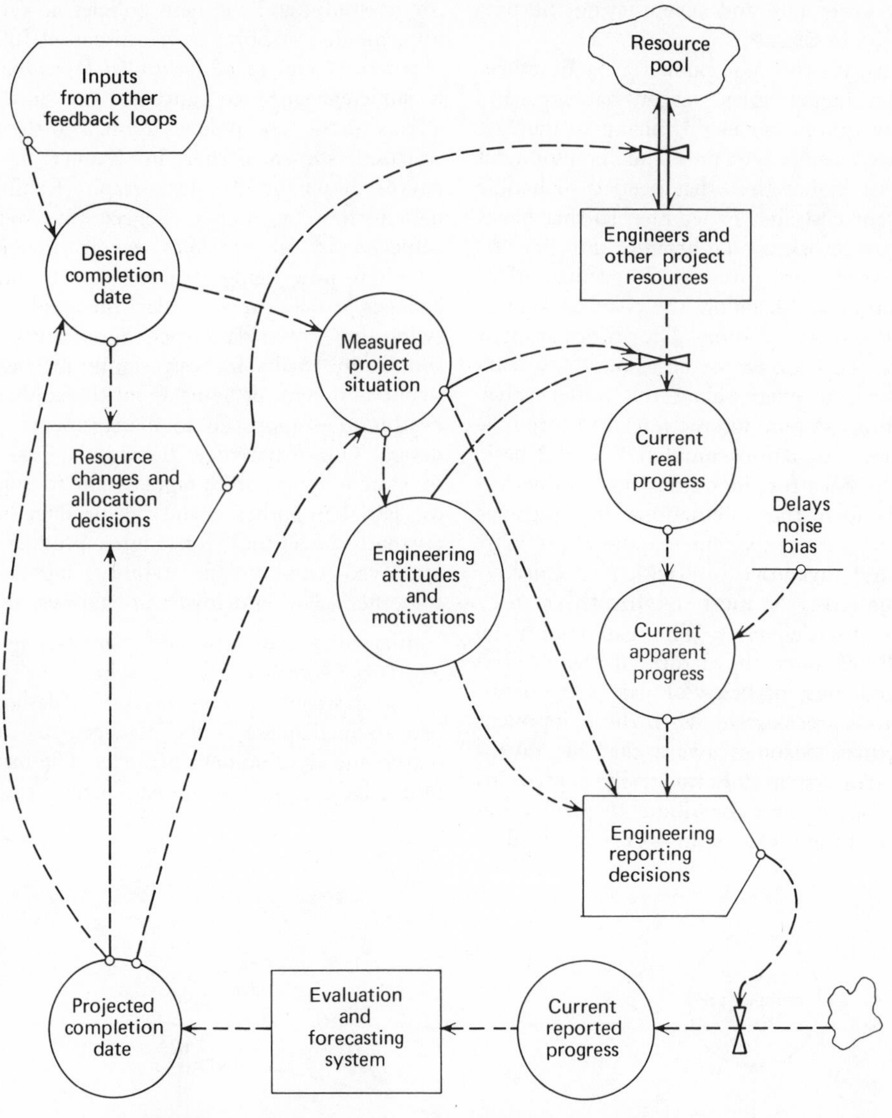

Exhibit 9. More complete representation of R and D system.

certain character of R and D results are partly responsible for this failure. But a more basic lack of system understanding has implications of even greater significance. All systems of schedule or budget controls that have been tried till now have failed to achieve success in R and D usage. These techniques have included Gantt charts, milestone schedules, and computerized systems of budgetary and manpower control.

The latest approaches to control of research and development projects are based on PERT (Program Evaluation Review Technique) or PERT/COST. The management control systems implied by the methods used can be represented by the diagram of Exhibit 8. As shown here, the basis for the current sophisticated methods is a single-loop system in which the difference between desired completion date and projected completion date causes decisions to change the magnitude or allocation of project resources (manpower, facilities, equipment, priorities). As these resources are employed, they are assumed to produce the progress that is reported during the project. These reports are processed through a PERT-type evaluation and forecasting system to create the projected completion time.

But the design of a management control system based on such a set of assumptions is doomed to failure, since some of the most vital aspects of the real system have been excluded from the underlying analysis. For example, the lack of tangible, precise measurement sources is entirely ignored. Yet these factors contribute much of the error between the *real* situation in the project (its true scope and actual progress to date) and that which is *apparent* to those doing the engineering work.

Another part of the real system which appears to be ignored by current R and D control system designers is the human element in the project actions and decisions. The attitudes and motivations of the engineers and managers, their knowledge of the schedules and current estimates in the project, the believed penalty-reward structure of the organization—all affect the progress and problems that are reported upward in the organization. Furthermore, these same factors even affect the rate of real progress toward project objectives. All systems of measurement and evaluation (in R and D, manufacturing, government, universities, or what-have-you) create incentives and pressures for certain actions. These interact with the goals and character of individuals and institutions to produce decisions, actions, and their results. For example, a system which compares "actual to budgeted expenditures" creates an incentive to increase budgets, regardless of need, and to hold down expenditures, regardless of progress; one which checks "proportion of budget spent" creates pressures on the manager or engineer to be sure he spends the money, whether or not on something useful. The presence of such factors in research and development ought to be recognized in the design of systems for R and D control.

Adding these two additional sources of system behavior to the earlier diagram produces the more complete representation of a research and development system that is pictured in Exhibit 9. But even this is an incomplete representation of the complex system which interrelates the characteristics of the product, the customer, and the R and D organization. A proper characterization of research and development projects must take into account the continuous dynamic system of activities that creates project life cycles. Such a system will include not just the scheduled and accumulated effort, costs, and accomplishments. Rather, it will encompass the full range of policies and parameters that carry a research and development project from initial perception of potential need for the product to final completion of the development program. The

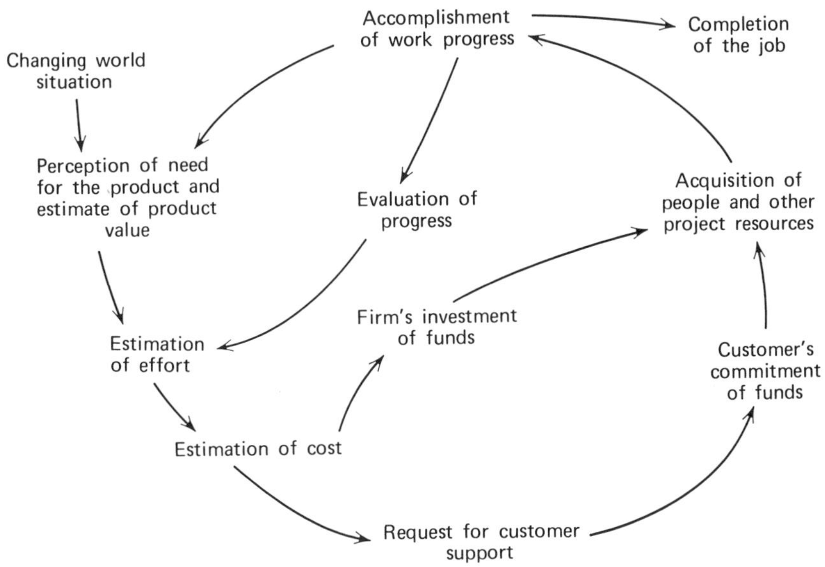

Exhibit 10. Dynamic system underlying R and D projects.

fundamental R and D project system is shown in Exhibit 10, from which we have developed an Industrial Dynamics model of research and development project dynamics.

Some of the results of simulation studies of this model are of particular interest to designers of management control systems. They demonstrate the importance of taking cognizance of the complete system structure in attempting to create and implement methods of system control. For example, one series of simulations of the general project model was conducted in which only the scheduled project duration was changed in the various runs. Within the model the effort allocation process *attempts* to complete the project during this scheduled period. However, the actual completion dates of the projects seem only remotely responsive to the changes in desired completion time.

Exhibit 11 demonstrates the nature of this response, using the data of four model simulations. The horizontal axis is an index of the scheduled project duration as a percentage of the maximum schedule used; the vertical axis shows actual completion time in a similar percentile manner. If changes in schedule produced corresponding changes in actual completion dates, the curve of results would have followed the diagonal "perfect response" line;

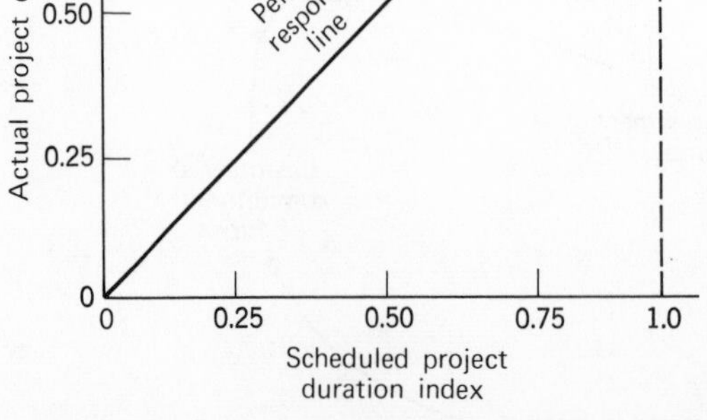

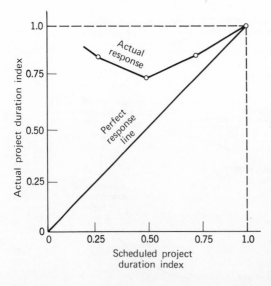

Exhibit 11. Scheduled versus actual project durations.

that is, a 50 percent reduction in scheduled duration should produce a 50 percent reduction in actual duration, if control is *perfect*. But the actual response is far from perfect; a 50 percent schedule change effects only a 25 percent actual change. And at the extreme, the actual change is even in the opposite direction, taking longer to complete the urgent crash project because of the resulting organizational confusion and inefficiencies. Of course, this response curve does not present the data on the manpower instability, total project cost, and customer satisfaction changes that also accompany shifts in the project schedule.

Some of the implications of Exhibit 11 are more clearly presented by the next curve (Exhibit 12). Here the slippage in project schedule is plotted as a function of the scheduled duration, the points on the curve coming from the project model simulations. A completion time slippage of 242 percent of schedule was incurred in the crash project, with a rapid decrease in this percentage completion date overrun as the schedule is dragged out. When the project is slowed too much, the slippage increases again as lack of enthusiasm induces further stretchout during the project life.

The principal point made by these two illustrations is that many factors other than desired schedule determine the resultant actual schedule of research and development projects. *Control systems for R and D which resort to schedule and effort rate control without full understanding of the system structure of projects are bound to be ineffective.* The current PERT-based project control systems seem guilty of this error in design philosophy. In fact, many aspects of our government contracting program suffer similar faults of inadequate system understanding, producing ill-conceived policies with attendant poor results. For example, increased risk-taking (i.e., greater willingness to invest company funds prior to contract receipt) and higher bidding integrity by R and D companies would act in the best interests of the government customer of research and development. However, our simulation studies show that neither policy is in the short-term best interests of the R and D companies, under existing government regulations and practices. Thus the contracting policies, a government control system for R and D procurement, act to the detriment of national objectives by inducing company behav-

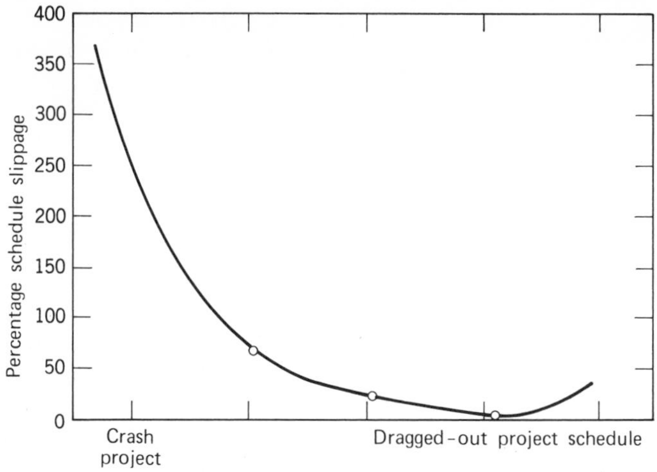

Exhibit 12. Schedule slippage as a function of schedule.

ior which produces unsatisfactory project outcomes.[4]

The proper design of research and development control systems, for both company and customer, should take into account three things: (1) the source of internal action, information, and control in a project is the individual engineer; measurement and evaluation schemes and the internal penalty-reward structure must be designed with him in mind, (2) the total results of research and development projects are created by a complex dynamic system of activities, which interrelates the characteristics of the product, the customer, and the R and D firm; control systems which ignore vital aspects of these flows cannot succeed; (3) institutional objectives of R and D companies (profits, growth, stability) can be aligned with the objectives of government customers; procurement policies constitute the system of control which can effect or destroy this alignment.

Systems Creating New Management Problems. The two control system areas discussed above were intended to demonstrate that many management control systems are designed in a manner that makes them inadequate to cope with the underlying problems. In each example, however, certain aspects of the systems were described which actually aggravated the existing problems. In the Sprague case, the inventory control system amplified sales changes to create wider swings in production and employment than actually existed in orders received from the customers. Our discussion of research and development project control indicated that government contracting policies often create resulting behavior that is contrary to the government's own interests. Other examples can be presented which have similar effects: the attempt to achieve management control leads to situations in which initial difficulties are amplified or significant new problems are created.

PROBLEMS OF LOGISTICS CONTROL. One apparent instance of this type occurs in the Air Force Hi-Value Logistic System. This inventory control system was developed over a long period of time at great government expense by some of the nation's most sophisticated control system designers. The Hi-Value System is intended to provide conservative initial procurement and meticulous individual item management during the complete logistic cycle of all high-cost Air Force material. Yet an Industrial Dynamics study of this system by a member of the M.I.T. Executive Development Program

[4] A general theory of research and development project behavior, a model of the theory, and extensive simulation studies of parameters and policies influencing R and D outcomes are reported in the author's book, *The Dynamics of Research and Development*, to be published later this year by Harper and Row.

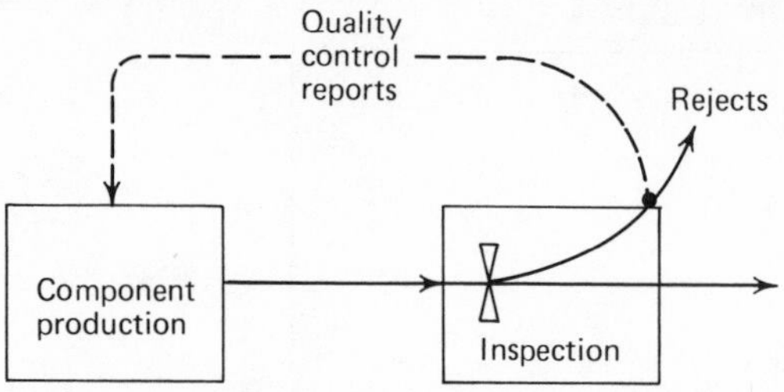

Exhibit 13. Theoretical quality control system.

concluded that the system behavior can result in periodic overstatement of requirements, excess procurement and/or unnecessary repair of material, followed by reactions at the opposite extreme.[5] These fluctuations produce undesirable oscillations in the repair and procurement work loads and in the required manpower at Air Force installations, supply and repair depots. The study recommended changes in policy and information usage that tend to stabilize the procurement system behavior.

QUALITY CONTROL SYSTEMS. A commonly utilized management control system has as its purpose the control of manufacturing output quality. The feedback system apparent to the designers of such quality control systems is pictured in Exhibit 13. Component parts are produced by a process that has a certain expected quality or reliability characteristic. The parts are inspected for flaws and rejects discarded or reworked. Statistically designed control charts determine when the production process is out of control, and reports are fed back to production to correct the problem sources.

The effectiveness of such quality control systems becomes questionable when we view the performance curves generated by a tropical system. Exhibit 14 plots component production rate and inspection reject rate over a period of two years. Wide periodic swings in reject rate produce violations of the control system tolerance limits which cause machine adjustments in production and temporarily lower production rates. But what causes the oscillations in the reject rate? Its periodic nature suggests seasonal fluctuations in production quality, often strangely encountered in many manufacturing plants. The manager has almost no way of checking the validity of such an assumption. Therefore, since the explanation seems reasonable, it would probably be accepted under most circumstances.

This situation illustrates one of the key problems in quality control—the lack of an objective confirming source of information. We are in a more favorable position to understand the phenomenon, however, since the results were produced by a computer simulation. The surprising fact is that the actual production quality was held constant, without even random variations, throughout the two years of the run. This means that the oscillations of reject rate and production shown in Exhibit 14 are not responses to outside changes, but rather are internally created by the behavioral system.

Let us examine a more complete picture of the total factory system, as shown in the next diagram (Exhibit 15). Components are produced, then inspected, rejects being discarded. The accepted components are forwarded to an assembly operation, where they enter into the manufacture of complete units. In an electronics plant, for example, the component production and inspection might correspond to a grid manufacturing operation, with the assembly operation putting together complete electronic tubes. When the tube is put through a life test, tube failure and the source of failure are far more obvious than are the grid imperfections during the component inspection. Should too many imperfections get through component inspection, eventual tube failure rate will produce complaints by the assembly manager to the quality control manager. As these complaints continue to build, the quality control manager puts pressure on his inspectors to be more careful and detect more of the poor grids. In response to this pressure, the inspectors reject far more grids. Without an objective measure of grid quality, the reject rate tends to be a function of subjective standards and inspection care. Under pressure from the manager, the inspectors will reject any grid which seems at all dubious, including many which are actually of acceptable quality. As the rejects rise, fewer poor grids enter the assembly process, thus causing fewer tube fail-

[5] Marx K. Kennedy: "An Analysis of the Air Force Hi-Value Logistic System; An Industrial Dynamics Study," unpublished S. M. thesis, M.I.T. School of Industrial Management, 1962.

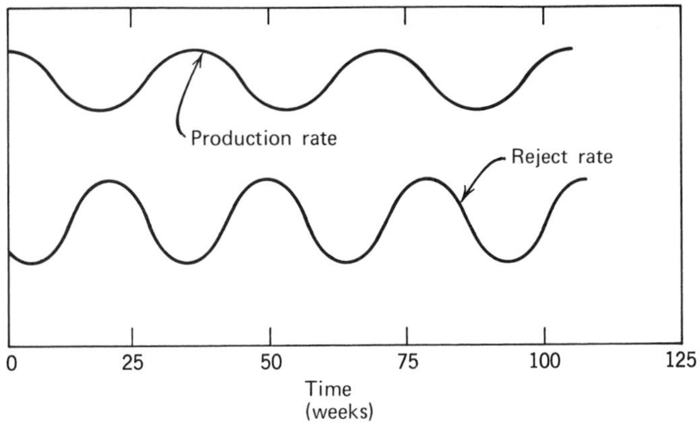

Exhibit 14. Quality control system performance.

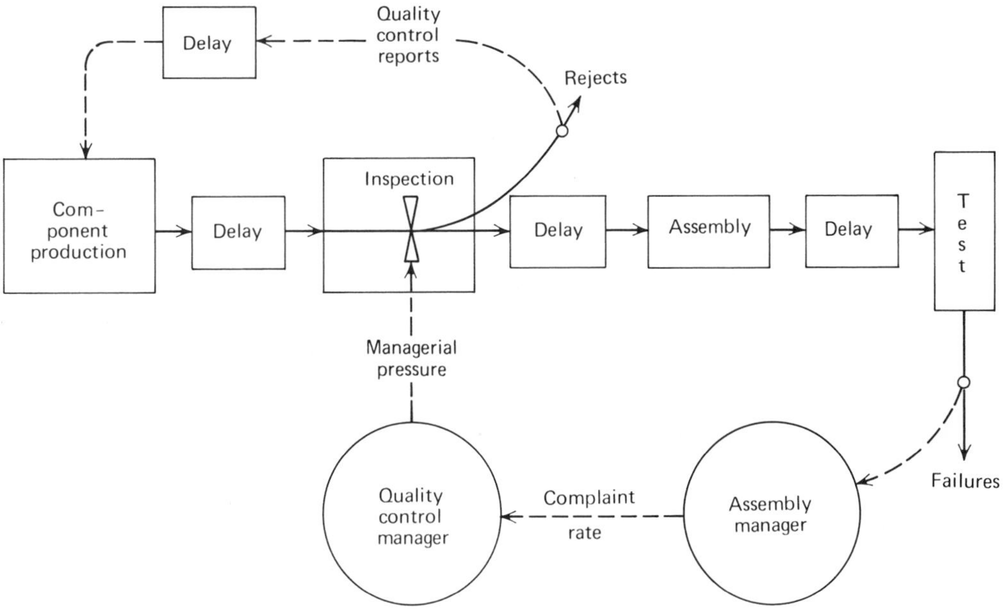

Exhibit 15. More complete representation of quality control system.

ures in test. The assembly manager's complaints drop off and, in fact, soon switch to a concern for getting more grids for his assembly operation. Without pressure from the quality control manager and with counterpressure to get more grids to the assembly operation, the grid inspectors tend to slacken gradually their care and their reject standards. Eventually, the number of rejectable grids getting into the tube assembly creates the problem of tube failures again, and the cycle repeats. Given normal delays in such a process, the entire cycle takes on a seasonal appearance. Thus, a system intended to assure control of product quality actually creates serious fluctuations of rejects, component production, and tube failures, all attributed to unknown factors "out of our control."

The consequences of such a situation are even more serious when the inspection output

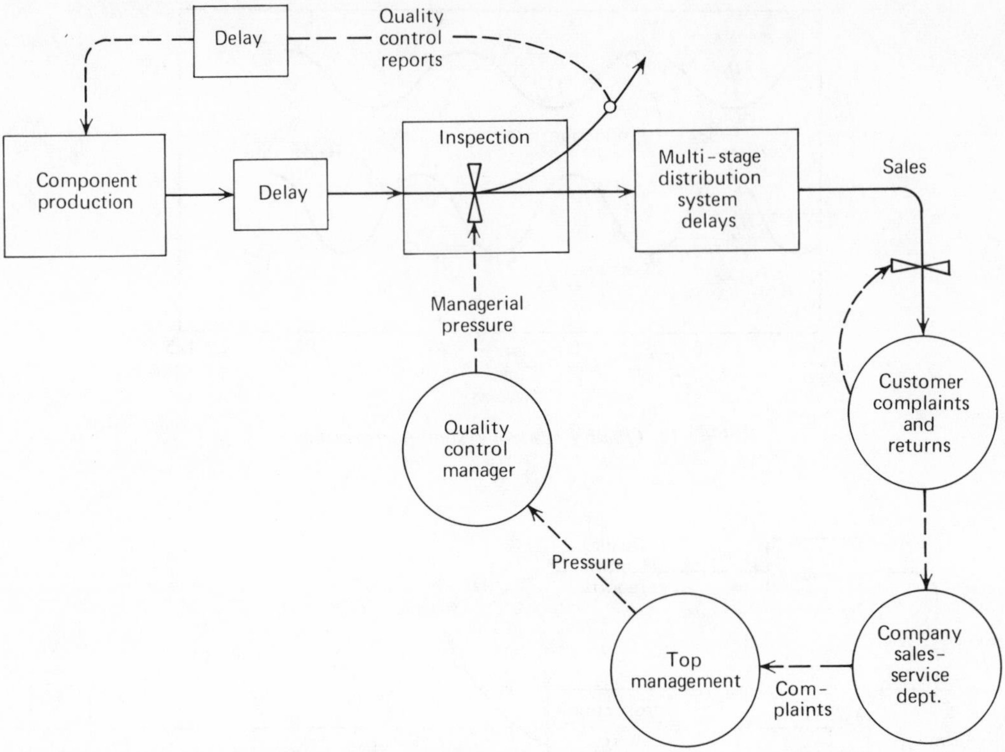

Exhibit 16. Total quality control system.

is distributed to eventual customers through the normal multi-stage distribution system. In this case the customer complaints and store returns also affect sales. These influences combine after a long delay to produce significant top management pressure on the quality control manager in reflection of a situation which existed many months before. In both Exhibits 15 and 16, the quality control manager's response is a key to system behavior. Here the manager of the formal quality control system is himself the most important aspect of the total system of quality and production control.

IV. Some Principles of Management Control System Design

The examples discussed represent a wide range of management control systems. Study of these applications produces some general principles of management control system design.

1. The key to effective control often lies outside the boundaries of *conventional* operational control systems; in fact, it is sometimes outside the *formal* boundaries of the company organization.

Too many organizations give up altogether too soon the battle for mastering a management problem caused by factors apparently "out of our control." The cyclic swings in customer orders in the production-inventory case, government changes in project funding of research and development, seasonal variations of product reject rate in the quality control problem are all examples of such factors. Yet in each case successful control system management rests within the access of company policy.

In the Sprague case the system requiring control included the ordering decisions of the customer, certainly not part of Sprague's formal organization. But the basis for system control exists in the stabilization of the input to the customer decision, the component delivery delay. Again, project success in R and D is strongly influenced by company integrity and risk-taking. Yet customer, not company, policy can be redesigned to achieve desirable company behavior. And the key to quality control involves recognition of the total system of product flow to assembly (or to customers) and the resulting feedback of complaints and pressures.

The boundaries of a management control system design study must not be drawn to conform with organizational structure merely because of that structure. System boundaries cannot ignore vital feedback channels for information and action if the system is to be effective.

2. The proper design of management control systems often requires inclusion of the effects of intangibles; in particular, the role of decision makers who are part of the total system of control must be treated carefully.

Control system designers who are working with computers often have as their end product a computer model for calculating (or searching for) an optimal control decision. Yet while being willing to model a decision for a machine, they seem unwilling to include in their studies any models of man—of human decision-making within the control loops. In the production-inventory control case, the modeling of aggregate customer decision-makers is a vital part of the system. Our second example emphasized that a properly designed R and D control system should be based on models of engineer and manager decision-making in both the company and customer organizations. Finally, we observed that the decision-making and responses of both managers and inspectors are crucial aspects of the quality control case.

These illustrations emphasize the usual failure to recognize and cope with the nature of human response in organizations. The decision-makers, single or aggregated—their motivations, attitudes, pressures, modes of response—must be included in management control system design. *The man (and manager) is part of the system of control, and management control system design must be viewed as a form of man-machine system design.*

3. A true understanding of total system basis and system behavior can permit effective design of both operational control systems and top management policy, without differences in philosophy or methodology of approach. In fact, most significant control system applications inherently require supra-functional or multi-departmental organization.

In the Sprague case, for example, successful control involved consideration of such aspects as customer service (marketing), inventory and production rate (manufacturing), and employment policies (personnel). Thus what often gets treated as a middle-management problem becomes resolvable only at the top policy-making level of the firm. The important elements in research and development tend not to be middle-management concerns for schedules, but rather top management policy affecting investment planning, customer relations, and company-wide attitudes. Management control systems can therefore seek to achieve the major goals of the organization as a whole, and not just the sub-optimizing aims of individual segments. A great present hazard, in fact, is the common planning and programming of control systems at the wrong level of the company, by people who lack total system perspectives and the authority to achieve broad system integration.

The Industrial Dynamics program has demonstrated the possibilities of examining and treating system problems of great variety and scope of complexity. We have dealt with many situations in which stabilization was needed and more recently with other cases in which balanced growth was the objective of the policy design efforts. The potential advantages to companies who pioneer in this work are significant and may become the basis of our future industrial competition. In this regard, it seems fitting to close with the implied advice of the Japanese scholar who said: "When your opponent is at the point of striking you, let your mind be fixed on his sword and you are no longer free to master your own movements, for you are then controlled by him." [6]

[6] Takawan, as quoted by Charles H. Townes: "Useful Knowledge," Technology Review, p. 36, January, 1963.

The Cybernetic Analysis of Change in Complex Social Organizations

MERVYN L. CADWALLADER

In the view of the general agreement about the fundamental role of communication in human life, it might be assumed that any major breakthrough in the scientific study of communication phenomena would be hailed as an event of considerable significance for sociology.[1] This has, indeed, occurred, but with the rapid development of information and cybernetic theory, most sociologists have remained unaware of it.

Cybernetic theory has been extensively applied in electronics, telecommunications, automation, and neurology. Some first attempts at the application of cybernetics in experimental psychology are reported in *Information Theory in Psychology*.[2] Communication theory has been slower in gaining attention among the social scientists interested in large social systems. The pioneers include economist Kenneth E. Boulding and electrical engineer Arnold Tustin, who have suggested a variety of empirical applications to the problems of economic analysis.[3] Karl W. Deutsch has undertaken a cybernetic analysis of the emergence of nationalism in political communities.[4] The work of these men demonstrates that cybernetics can be employed as a theoretical system in social analysis. The present essay sketches how some of the concepts and principles of cybernetics might be used in the analysis of change in formal social organizations.

The Ultrastable System

The fundamental theme of cybernetics is always regulation and control in open systems. It is concerned with homeostasis in organisms and the steady states of social organizations. Its orientation is the source of considerable misunderstanding because many of the sociologists who are interested in the subject of social change object to the use of all concepts of equilibrium, homeostasis, or stability, arguing that to include such ideas as a central part of social theory is to preclude the possibility of dealing with change.[5] They seem to believe that stability and change are not only contradictory ideas but that the processes themselves are totally incompatible. The difficulty here is not merely semantic: some kinds of stability do negate certain kinds of change. What has been overlooked is that at least one category of stability depends upon and is the consequence of change. Just this kind of stability is of prime interest to cybernetics.

From the *American Journal of Sociology*, Vol. LXV, September 1959, pp. 154–157. Reprinted by permission of the University of Chicago Press.

[1] "Advances in communications theory in the last few years give the appearance of an important scientific breakthrough. They provide principles for translating into similar terms and quantitative units communication interactions both among human beings and among machines, as well as between men and machines. *They also suggest aspects of a more inclusive theory of organization*." Richard L. Meier, "Communications and Social Change," *Behavioral Science*, I (January, 1956), 43. (Italics mine.)

[2] Henry Quastler (ed.), *Information Theory in Psychology* (Glencoe, Ill.: Free Press, 1955).

[3] Kenneth E. Boulding, *The Organizational Revolution* (New York: Harper & Bros., 1953); Arnold Tustin, *The Mechanism of Economic Systems* (Cambridge, Mass.: Harvard University Press, 1953).

[4] Karl W. Deutsch, *Nationalism and Social Communication* (New York: John Wiley & Sons, 1953).

[5] Such objections can be found in the following: Wayne Hield, "The Study of Change in Social Science," *British Journal of Sociology*, V (March, 1954), 1–11; David Lockwood, "Some Remarks on 'The Social System,'" *British Journal of Sociology*, VII (June, 1956), 134–46; and Barrington Moore, "Sociological Theory and Contemporary Politics," *American Journal of Sociology*, LXI (September, 1955), 107–15.

An open system, whether social or biological, in a changing environment either changes or perishes. In such a case the only avenue to survival is change. The capacity to persist through a change of structure and behavior has been called "ultrastability." [6] If a complex social organization is to survive critical changes in its environment, it can do so only by changing its structure and behavior. That Great Britain has survived through medieval, mercantile, and capitalist periods means that as a national state it has ultrastability. Any industrial corporation, such as International Business Machines or General Electric, that has survived the last fifty years of social change in the United States has done so through a process of self-transformation and not through the continuation of original organizational and operational patterns. Therefore, the concept of ultrastability will aid in distinguishing between systems that achieve stability under specific constant conditions and those that can learn or evolve new structures and behavior so as to remain stable under changing conditions. The latter is the focus here.

Another way of expressing the above is to say that some classes of open systems adapt to a fluctuating environment through processes of learning and innovation. There is nothing new in such a statement if the reference is to biological organisms. The novelty here lies in the proposal that complex formal social organizations, such as industrial corporations, armies, churches, and so on, be regarded as learning and innovating systems. Or, to put it another way, large-scale formal organizations are treated as open problem-solving systems, studied with a variety of theoretical problem-solving models, i.e., as learning and innovating systems.

By common convention we are used to thinking in terms of individual human beings as inventing or innovating, but not of social groups. But it is valid to talk about innovations produced by a social organization taken as a whole, and this is not to deny the fact of individual innovation. Any such system capable of purposeful problem-solving behavior and of learning from the past and innovating for the future is an ultrastable system.

Cybernetics and the Analysis of Ultrastable Organizations

From the point of view of cybernetics, any large scale formal social organization is a communication network. It is assumed that these can display learning and innovative behavior if they possess certain necessary facilities (structure) and certain necessary rules of operation (content).

First, consider the structure of the system—as it might be represented in the language of cybernetics. Any social organization that is to change through learning and innovation, that is, to be ultrastable, must contain certain very specific feedback mechanisms, a certain variety of information, and certain kinds of input, channel, storage, and decision-making facilities. This can be stated in the form of an axiomatic proposition: that complexity of purposeful behavior is a function of the complexity of the communication components or parts of the system. More specifically, every open system behaving purposefully does so by virtue of a flow of factual and operational information through receptors, channels, selectors, feedback loops, and effectors. Every open system whose purposeful behavior is predictive, and this is essential to ultrastability, must also have mechanisms for the selective storage and recall of information; it must have memory. Does the social organization under scrutiny behave purposefully, does it solve problems, and does it forecast future events? If the answers are in the affirmative, then one must find in it certain kinds of communications, information, and control mechanisms.

In addition to the requisite structural components mentioned above, the communication net must contain or acquire information that makes learning and innovating behavior possible. This is a "program." That is to say, it must acquire or discover rules of behavior, instructions regarding internal mechanisms and processes—all of which will result in performance to be identified as learning, problem-solving, and innovating.

Innovation by any system is subject to the limitations and possibilities established by the quantity and variety of information present in

[6] For a full discussion of this concept see W. Ross Ashby, *An Introduction to Cybernetics* (New York: John Wiley & Sons, 1956), pp. 82–85; H. S. Tsein, *Engineering Cybernetics* (New York: McGraw-Hill Book Co., 1954), pp. 253–67.

it at a particular time and by the information available to it from the environment. Something cannot be created from nothing, much less something new. Therefore the range of possible new combinations that may be formed by an innovating system depends upon the possible range of output, the range of available information stored in the memory, and the operating rules (program) governing the analysis and synthesis of the flow of information within the system. In order to innovate, the system must be able to analyze information, that is, it must separate it into constituent parts. In a social system this is a consequence of certain explicit operating rules about what can and should be done, by whom, when, and why.

The utilization by a system of a particular part of its fund of information as an output for the solution of an environmental problem is not usually determined by pure chance, unless the system, in dealing with a totally unfamiliar situation, is trying completely random outputs.[7] In the long run there must emerge an organization of the trial process in any open system capable of storing information about past behavior. Purposeful and predictive behavior depends upon memory, whether the system is organismic or social. Continuing behavior is modified by the results of specific acts. This is one kind of negative feedback and one which introduces a bias into the program of the system which changes the probabilities of various kinds of future acts in terms of present and past successes and failures.

If the problem-solving output of the system is organized solely in terms of past successes and failures, a point would be reached in its development at which it would not try anything new: all obstacles would be attacked with the techniques which had already proved successful. Innovation depends, therefore, on preventing such a freezing of the behavior of the system in old patterns. This is accomplished in a variety of ways. "Mistakes" in the identification, analysis, and synthesis of information may be the source of novel behavior. The loss of information (forgetting) about the past countermands the freezing process, to some extent, in all open systems complex enough to learn. In addition, the program of the system may contain specific instructions preventing the synthesis of all information into old familiar patterns and explicitly supporting certain kinds and amounts of novel action. Whenever novel behavior is successful, a negative feedback of information reinforces the creation and use of novelty. Not only will the system innovate, but it will remember that the act of innovating enabled it to circumvent obstacles and reach its goals. It will have discovered that a technique which worked in the past can be improved upon. Finally, in doing so, the system will have achieved the state of ultrastability which, for an open system, is the optimum road to survival.

[7] The randomized strategy of certain games as described in game theory is one example. However, it is assumed that goal-seeking behavior is guided by random trial-and-error process during the early history of such systems.

The Elements of a Model, Empirical Indicators, and Sample Hypotheses.[8]

One of the main tasks which a theoretical model performs for the scientist is the selection of relevant variables and significant hypotheses from the infinite number of possibilities. A cybernetic model would focus the investigator's attention on such things as the following: (1) the quantity and variety of information stored in the system; (2) the structure of the communication network; (3) the pattern of the subsystems within the whole; (4) the number, location, and function of negative feedback loops in the system and the amount of time-lag in them; (5) the nature of the system's memory facility; (6) the operating rules, or program determining the system's structure and behavior.

The operating rules of the system and its subsystems are always numerous. Relevant for the present problem are (1) rules or instructions determining range of input; (2) rules responsible for the routing of the information through the network; (3) rules about the identification, analysis, and classification of information; (4) priority rules for input, analysis, storage, and output; (5) rules governing the feedback mechanisms; (6) instructions for stor-

[8] The reader who is unfamiliar with the terminology of cybernetics will find a general discussion of the discipline in Colin Cherry, *On Human Communication* (New York: John Wiley & Sons, 1957); Norbert Wiener, *The Human Use of Human Beings* (Boston: Houghton Mifflin Co., 1950).

age in the system's memory; (7) rules regarding the synthesis of information for the output of the system—especially those concerned with the matter of usual or novel output.

It is now possible to suggest a few cybernetic propositions determining the presence, absence, and nature of innovative processes in complex communications systems. For example, it can be said that: (1) the rate of innovation is a function of the rules organizing the problem-solving trials (output) of the system; (2) the capacity for innovation cannot exceed the capacity for variety or available variety of information; (3) the rate of innovation is a function of the quantity and variety of information; (4) a facility, mechanism, or rule for forgetting or disrupting organizing patterns of a high probability must be present; (5) the rate of change for the system will increase with an increase in the rate of change of the environment (input). That is, the changes in the variety of the inputs must force changes in the variety of the outputs or the system will fail to achieve "ultrastability." [9]

While no exact mathematical relationship between the elements of such a system has been specified, it is assumed that this is possible in principle but that its realization must wait for the results of actual experimentation and field tests. The use of mathematical devices for the measurement of information and the representation of networks will be a necessary and crucial first step in research programs designed to test hypotheses derived from the above theory.[10] Research might be carried out along the following lines: (1) the volume of mail, telegrams, telephone calls, and memos could be sampled at input terminals, output terminals, and at crucial points in the network; (2) the volume of printed and written materials stored in the libraries and files of the system could be measured; (3) tracer messages would enable the observer to map channel connections, one-way couplings, two-way couplings, and to locate relatively independent subsystems; (4) the time taken by regular or tracer messages to move through a feedback loop would give information on time-lag; (5) the many techniques already in use by the social scientist for measuring values and attitudes will be useful tools for the detection and measurement of implicit operating rules. The techniques of content analysis could be put to use for the abstraction of critical operating rules contained in the official documents of the formal organization, in order to isolate and index those parts of the program of the system which constrain and determine the range, routing, identification, analysis, storage, priority, feedback, and synthesis of information. Above all else, the rules supporting the synthesis and use of unusual as against usual patterns of action would be of special concern in a description and analysis of the ultrastable system in the process of change, or of a system with a certain potential for purposeful change.[11]

[9] For a sophisticated development of this idea see W. Ross Ashby, "The Effect of Experience on a Determinate System," *Behavioral Science*, I (January, 1956), 35–42.

[10] The Shannon-Wiener concept of information is quantitative. However, there is some question as to whether it can be applied in macrosocial analysis at the present stage in the development of sociology. A qualitative concept may have to suffice for a time.

[11] It is assumed that there are distinctly different kinds of social change exhibited by different kinds of social systems. For a discussion of this problem see Mervyn L. Cadwallader, "Three Classes of Social Change," *Pacific Sociological Review*, I (May, 1958), 17–20.

Control as an Organizational Process

CHADWICK J. HABERSTROH

The study of self-regulating systems, now generally known as cybernetics, explores the ways in which some output of a dynamic system can be maintained in a more-or-less invariant equilibrium, or steady state, in the face of disrupting external forces.[1] The most general answer to this question is that the system must somehow be supplied with information about the disrupting forces that is used to offset their effect. A common way of supplying this is by means of a feedback of information on the deviations of the output from equilibrium. This information flow causes the equilibrium to be restored in some appropriate manner.

Even assuming that one does know the feedback channel used and understands the laws through which the feedback restores equilibrium, he still has a right to ask how it is that the system exists at all, and why it tends to an equilibrium at that particular value and not some other. In the case of engineering control systems the answer to this question is simple and direct: the designer intended them to perform in the way they do. Thus, there is a purposive element in these control systems resulting from an a priori selection of the equilibrium to be obtained. If one asks the same question, however, about naturally self-regulating systems, such as homeostatic mechanisms, in the living organism or ecological balances in a community of organisms, the answer is neither simple nor direct. The equilibria found and the mechanisms for attaining them have come about by the process of natural selection in the context of a particular environment. If we put the same question in the case of organizational systems, the answer is even less direct and more complicated, involving as it does a multitude of designers each consciously striving to realize his own objectives, in the context of an environment and of selection pressure arising from the limitation of resources as well.

In organizations the conscious intentions of the participants are an important factor. In order to explain the gross behavior of an organization, these intentions must be measured and brought into relation with the other aspects of the organization's functioning. The existence of stable organization implies a degree of harmony and co-ordination among the participants, a sharing of intention. In order to secure this, participants communicate with each other and in doing so construct a common symbolic picture of the goals they have set for the organization and the means by which they intend to attain the goals. This picture, or representation, of the means and ends of organization (the "task model") is implicit in the verbal communication inside the organization. It can be measured by the use of content-analysis techniques. I have attempted to apply these techniques to a sample of communication from an integrated steel plant operated by one of the American companies.[2] This case will be used as an example in exploring organization purposes and other organizational characteristics affecting control processes.

Goal formation is influenced by the intentions of the individual participants and by the environmental constraints under which they operate. Both can be sources of conflict. The emergence of stable, enduring patterns of organization is in part a process of conflict res-

From *Management Science*. Vol. 6, January 1960, pp. 165–171. Reprinted by permission of the publisher.

[1] N. Wiener, *Cybernetics* (New York: Wiley, 1948; W. R. Ashby. *An Introduction to Cybernetics* (New York: Wiley, 1956).

[2] This research was carried out at the Graduate School of Industrial Administration, Carnegie Institute of Technology, under a grant from the Ford Foundation for research on human behavior in organization. A full report of the methods and the results of this investigation, as well as a more thorough discussion of the topic of the present paper, is contained in my doctoral dissertation, *Processes of Internal Control in Firms*, University Microfilms, Inc. (Ann Arbor, Michigan, 1958).

olution. The necessity of reducing conflict to manageable bounds tends to direct the organization's efforts toward a small number of goals and a small number of means activities for achieving them, relative to the number of alternatives that might be conceivable. It is to be expected, therefore, that the number of independent goals turned up in the task model will be rather small. Conflict reduction is facilitated if these goals are formulated in terms of acceptable levels, rather than in terms of optima,[3] and if the criterion of goal achievements is external and objective, rather than subjective and open to dispute. If members measure goal achievement objectively and perceive means to attain them, the goals are termed "operative."

In the case of Integrated Steel, four goals were discovered. These relate to cost reduction, production level, safety, and medical care. The safety and production goals are formulated in terms of acceptable levels set by an external office. Performance is measured in terms of tonnage produced and frequency of injuries, and an elaborate technology exists for goal achievement. In the case of safety, this task model was measured in detail. The goal of providing adequate medical care was departmentalized in a plant hospital; and a standard cost system and various cost reduction programs were in operation. Neither the hospital nor the cost system was investigated, however.

If the process of goal formation results in a small number of operative goals, as it did at Integrated Steel, the basis for a feedback of information on deviations of performance from the established goals is already apparent. To affirm the existence of a control system we need only verify that this information is reported to executive centers and that the executives respond so as to achieve the goals. The task model comprises a program of means activities understood by the participants to lead to goal achievement. One way of responding would be to adjust the level of resource use in these means activities. Let us refer to this as "routine control." Another way of responding would be to look for a better way of achieving goals. This type of activity could take the form of inventing new means activities or of altering the system of executive organization (i.e., changes in personnel or in allocation of functions). It might be expected that this type of activity would occur only in a case of extreme or repeated failure. Let us call this "nonroutine control." Sufficient pressure might even lead to modification of goals in order to assure survival of the organization. Normally, however, the evolved structure of goals and means activities determines what the participants do; communication channels carrying information on performance influence when and how much they do.

In the case of Integrated Steel's safety program the type of means activities which have been developed to implement the safety objective are accident investigations, safety conferences with workmen, implementation of safety work-orders, special inspections, clean-up work, etc. The execution of each of these activities is in some way conditional on the occurrence of injuries in the plant. Other activities are also carried on which are independent of the occurrence of accidents. These include routine inspections, training and screening procedures for new employees, safety clearance of engineering proposals, job analysis, publicity campaigns, etc.

The formal communication channels on safety performance begin with injury reports made by the plant hospital. This information is collated and distributed daily throughout the plant's executive organization in detail and in statistical summary. This information cues the line supervision to investigate injuries; alerts the plant safety staff to inspect for similar hazards and to assist in accident investigations; and, in summary figures, provides the basis for broader types of corrective action such as the study of classes of jobs for hazards, the issuance of special instructions to employees, and evaluation of supervisors. The same reports when aggregated into divisional and plant injury frequencies serve as an indicator of the plant's over-all performance relative to its safety goals.

The routine control processes discussed above are not the only, or even the most important, means of control used at Integrated Steel. The nonroutine control processes, changes in personnel and in the institutional structure within which the participants operate, take precedence. The very nature of the accident process (i.e., the importance of human failure, rare events, conjunction of cir-

[3] H. A. Simon, *Models of Man* (New York: Wiley, 1957), p. 241.

cumstances, and the randomness of occurrence of injuries) make for a different degree of reliability on the technological side from that encountered in connection with, for instance, production matters. Because the coupling between the program of means activities and the degree of safety performance is not fully determined, there is a need for relatively tight control over the programs themselves. This is achieved by response of the top plant management to deviations of the plant and departmental injury frequencies from the objectives set for them at the beginning of the year. These yearly objectives are set by company officers above the plant level, although the plant management has discretion to aim at a more difficult target it if chooses.

Figure 1 is a block diagram of the control structure discussed above. The input (I) is the annual safety objective which is compared with the performance of the plant (O) by top management. The result of the nonroutine control functions at the top executive organization (X_1) may be expressed as the two parameters of the routine control system: the intensity of response to injuries (μ) and the level of independent safety activity (η). A complete model of the top executive function was not constructed, although there seems to be evidence[4] that it responds to changes in the degree of error (a differentiating operator). Other than that it appears possible to say only that its effects are intermittent, rather than continuous, and respond only to error in excess of a certain threshold. It is therefore a nonlinear operator. In the case of the routine control function (X_2), however, a linear model seems appropriate. Executives appear to proportion their influence on the injury rate to the magnitude of that rate plus a constant. The "program" operator (P) relates the control activities to the actual performance of the plant, adding and integrating the safety efforts ($\mu O + \eta$) and the exogenous load of new hazards (β).

Table 1 contains data on injury rates, safety objectives, and innovations in the safety program for a 10 year period. The changes in organization made by top management in year 7 did not take effect until year 9. Thus, during the period beginning with year 3 and ending with year 8, the routine control system operated with constant parameters μ and η. Under this assumption, the injury rate this assumption, the injury rate ($O(t)$) is given by

$$(1) \qquad O(t) = \int [\beta - \eta - \mu O(t)]dt$$

or equivalently

$$(2) \qquad O'(t) = \beta - \eta - \mu O(t).$$

Solving this differential equation,

$$(3) \qquad O(t) = \frac{\lambda}{\mu} + \left[\hat{O} - \frac{\lambda}{\mu}\right] e^{-ut}$$

[4] Compare columns 4 and 11 in Table 1.

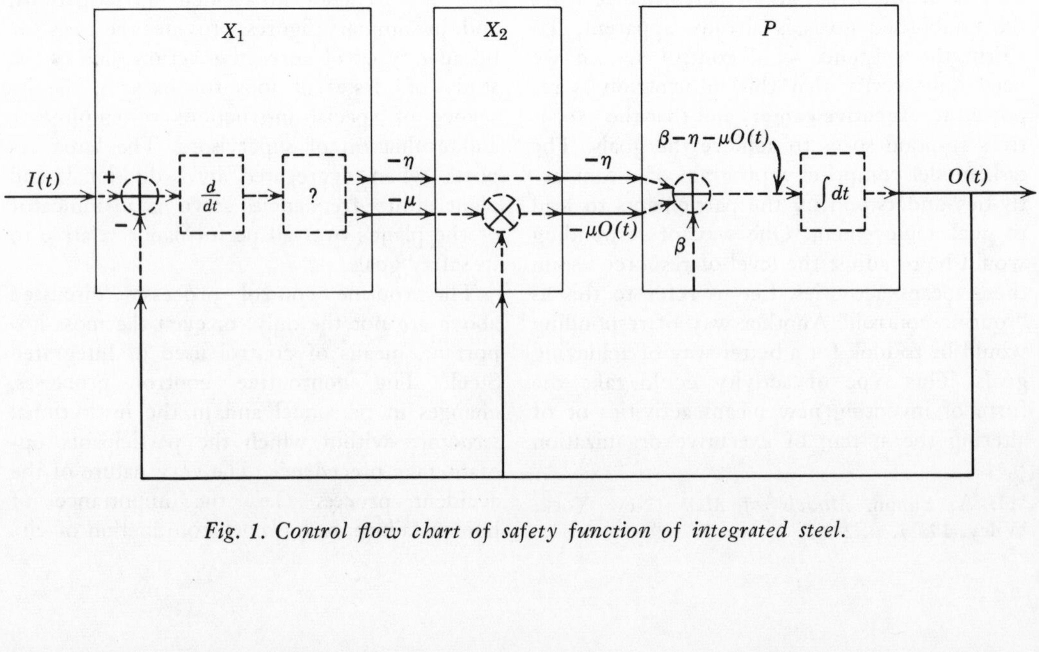

Fig. 1. Control flow chart of safety function of integrated steel.

Table 1. Innovation † and Performance at Integrated Steel

	DISABLING INJURIES						TOTAL INJURIES			
YEAR	AVERAGE ALL PLANTS	ERROR	Δ ERROR	PLANT PERFORMANCE	ERROR	TARGET	PLANT PERFORMANCE	ERROR	TARGET	INNOVATION †
1	5.29	.98	.98	6.17			357			moderate
2	4.95	.13	—.85	5.08			422			none
3	5.41	1.77	1.64	7.18			407			heavy
4	4.66	1.24	—.53	5.90			302			none
5	3.66	.67	—.57	4.33			244			none
6	3.55	.65	—.02	4.20	.46	3.74	210	0	238	light
7	3.00	.83	.18	3.83	.50	3.33	196	0	210	moderate
8	2.38	.81	—.02	3.19	.72	2.47	183	11	172	light
9	2.07	.63	—.18	2.70	.54	2.16	133	0	168	none
10 *	1.93	.91	.28	2.84	.80	2.04	128	0	133	heavy

* At time major decisions were taken.

† Level of innovation in the plant-wide safety program was rated by the author on the basis of a survey of plant safety files. The information found consisted of a description of the innovations made. This information is briefly summarized below.

In the first year studied the safety staff recommended and received management approval of a job analysis program which was to provide the basis for strict enforcement of safe working procedures. They also requested regular physical examinations for all employees.

In year 2, no safety innovations were discovered.

In year 3, one of the plant manager's top staff assistants announced to division managers the inauguration of an extensive program of job analysis and indoctrination of workmen in safe procedures. He also urged the division managers to inaugurate the practice of having foremen make thorough investigations of all minor injuries as a basis for corrective action. This was to be coupled with a program of training foremen in the responsibilities which would be placed upon them in these two programs, and also the formation of division safety committees at top division management level to expedite safety recommendations. He also announced inauguration of a plant-wide safety committee.

In years 4 and 5 no new activity was discovered.

In year 6 a proposal was made by the safety staff for transfer of some functions so as to improve the coordinating service of the safety staff and shift more executive responsibility on to the line organization. There was a new program of statistical reporting of injuries classified by types of accident.

In year 7 management inaugurated a revised system of job analysis, appointed a new plant-wide advisory committee, inaugurated an annual conference of all division managers for the purpose of setting objectives and reviewing the safety program, and also ordered the universal replacement of a hazardous type of crane controller in use through most of the plant.

In year 8 a new statistical basis for the reporting of injuries was inaugurated.

In year 9 no innovations were discovered.

In year 10 a revised and greatly expanded program of job analysis was instituted, with a number of executives re-assigned to safety responsibilities exclusively. Procedures for top level reporting and evaluation of safety performance were revised to place greater emphasis upon safety.

where $\lambda = \beta - \eta$ and O is the initial level of injury rate.

This equation implies that first differences in injury rates tend to decrease by a constant ratio from year to year. The performance data for years 3 to in Table 1 is fairly consistent with this.

Another principle of control, important in the case of organization, is that of factorization. Ashby has shown[5] that if trial-and-error changes are relied upon for control (compare the operator X_1 at Integrated Steel), a large system cannot practicably be stabilized unless its output can be factored into a number of independently controlled information sources.

[5] W. R. Ashby, *Design for a Brain* (New York: Wiley, 1952).

At Integrated Steel, the safety objective was broken down by divisions and injury rates were reported on that same basis. Part of the nonroutine control activity occurred at the division level. Innovation in divisional programs initiated by division management was correlated with the division's performance error.

This, of course, bears on the subject of decentralization in organizations. Meaningful decentralization is probably impossible without a resolution of the goals into nonconflicting, operative subgoals so that these can be placed under independent control. On the other hand, there is probably a size for organizations at which goal attainment becomes impossible without factorization, even though the method used may not resemble current definitions of "decentralized authority." The plant production, cost, and safety goals at Integrated Steel appear to represent just such a factorization of the company goals.

In summary, the characteristics postulated by cybernetic theory for self-regulating systems have their correlates in human organizations. In the case of Integrated Steel, the theory points up the influence of information feedbacks upon the actions of the executives in attempting to realize the organization objectives. Of particular importance are the role of the higher echelons of executives in controlling the mode of response of the lower echelons and the use of multiple feedbacks in the design of the executive system.

Adjusting to Overloads of Information [1]

JAMES G. MILLER

The response of living systems to overloads of information has interesting similarities whether the system in question is a neuron or a human group. With all their obvious differences, both are organizations of genetically linked protoplasm. They exist in the earthly environment, which requires similar, very specific characteristics of everything that survives in it. And they find their places in a hierarchy of systems which, composed of nonliving molecules, increase in complexity from cells through organs, organisms, groups, social organizations and societies, to supranational institutions. The units of each are systems of the next lower order.

Each of these may be regarded as a level which has its own special characteristics. At each level there are differences among the species and among the individual examples of each species. Over the whole range of living systems, however, there are some characteristics which are common to all.

They are all, for instance, open systems which maintain themselves in a changing environment by regulating inputs and outputs of matter or energy and information and by preserving internal steady states of critical variables by governance of subsystems.

A representative of the level upon which interest is focused at a given time is referred to as a "system." Those at lower levels are subsystems or subsubsystems and those at higher levels, suprasystems or suprasuprasystems. Each subsystem carries out a specific function.

From *"Disorders of Communication,"* Vol. XLII, *Research Publications, A.R.N.M.D.* Copyright 1964 by the Association for Research in Nervous and Mental Disease. Printed in United States of America.

[1] Supported in part by grants from Project MICHIGAN of the United States Army and from the Carnegie Foundation. The author wishes to thank Dr. William Horvath, Dr. Stanley Moss, Mr. Kent Marquis, Mr. Bertram Peretz and Dr. Paul Halick for their assistance in this research.

It may be localized in a single component or member of the system or dispersed to several of them. Sometimes a single component may carry out a number of subsystem functions.

Unless a living system exists in parasitism or symbiosis with another system, it must carry out for itself certain critical subsystem functions. Some of these involve information, some matter-energy processing. A free-living cell, like an ameba, has subsystems which perform all these essential processes, while a cell which is part of an organ may depend for some of them upon other specialized cells. An isolated group, like a roving gypsy family, will be found to have all the critical subsystems, while groups which are parts of social organizations often do not.

The Critical Subsystems

Table 1 lists the subsystems which a living system must have in order to survive and provide for the continuance of its species.

A system possessing all of these subsystems can be called totipotent. Of course, matter-energy and information never flow separately, but it is the energy in an intravenous injection of glucose and the information in his doctor's conversation which affect the patient. It is on this basis (which aspect of them affects the receiver) that matter-energy flows are distinguished from information flows. Three subsystems process both matter-energy and information, and the others transmit only one or the other. Because all living systems must be open to both matter-energy and information, the *boundary* provides for the passage of both. The *decider*, as the central controlling subsystem, must regulate both matter-energy and information transmissions, though the former are usually governed by information feedbacks. The *reproducer* is largely concerned with the information transmitted in the genes, but this must travel and divide and grow in a matter-energy substrate.

Within a system a subsystem function may be dispersed to subsubsystems or even lower levels. The reproductive function, for example, is carried on in animal species by a dyad, a mating pair of organisms, or by an individual organism. Levels of systems above the organism or group arrange that the reproductive function is carried out by enough of their units (the "household sector" in human societies) to assure the continuation of the larger system, but they do not themselves reproduce.

Table 1 shows that there are a number of rough parallels in the subsystem handling of matter-energy and information. The way a given function is carried out may be very different at different levels. The *ingestor*, for example, which takes required matter-energy into the system, may be an opening in the boundary of a cell, a mouth in an organism, a group of supply personnel in an organization or a set of agricultural, mining and importing organizations in a society. The input *transducer* has a parallel function to the ingestor, bringing information into the system and passing on these patterns to other subsystems. A sense organ does this for an organism, a scout does it for an army and an embassy does it for a nation. The *internal* transducer receives and passes on information which arises within the system. This the proprioceptors do in an animal and the organizations which discover attitudes of individuals and groups do within a society.

The *distributor* carries matter and energy about the system to the places where they are needed. Information is comparably transmitted among the parts of a living system by a *channel and net* subsystem which may be a nerve net in an organ, an entire nervous system or an elaborate set of communication devices used by individuals in a community and operated by an organization of communication specialists. The word "channel" is used two ways in electronics without confusion. It may refer only to the flow route for information or it may include along that route as well components of various sorts which alter the character of that flow. We follow the second usage because the noise, distortions and transformations of these components are factors of great importance in the communications of living systems.

Table 1. The Critical Subsystems

MATTER-ENERGY PROCESSING SUBSYSTEMS	SUBSYSTEMS WHICH PROCESS BOTH MATTER-ENERGY AND INFORMATION	INFORMATION PROCESSING SUBSYSTEMS
	Boundary	
Ingestor		Input transducer
		Internal transducer
Distributor		Channel and net
Decomposer		Decoder
Producer		Learner
Matter-energy storage		Memory
	Decider	
Excretor		Encoder
Motor		Output transducer
	Reproducer	

The parallel is not so close between the *decomposer*, which breaks down input energy and raw materials into simpler forms that meet the specific internal needs of the system, and the *decoder*. Every system, however, has an internal language or languages which differ from the languages of its suprasystem, and the decoder alters messages from the external form to a code which can be used internally.

The *producer* unites decomposed inputs to fabricate particular substances required for the internal operation of that particular system. These may (like an organism's protein molecules) differ somewhat from products synthesized by any other system. Perhaps slightly parallel is the function of the *learner*, which establishes reliable and enduring associations (by conditioning, imprinting or learning) between certain elementary information inputs and other elements of information from outside or inside the system, to "synthesize" items of knowledge that will be especially useful to that particular system.

Both energy and information are stored in living systems. *Matter-energy storage* may be in the form of fat, glucose or adenosine triphosphate in a cell, in body fat depots in an animal and in reservoirs and warehouses in a society. The information storage or memory of an animal is in the brain; of a group, perhaps in books kept by a secretary; and of a nation, in libraries and filing cabinets maintained by multitudes of librarians and file clerks.

Beyond the central decider of the system, matter-energy and information are prepared for output. Unneeded materials and energy are outputted by an *excretor,* so that the system will not become glutted as more inputs arrive. The information output from a living system is changed by the *encoder* from the system's internal language into a language used in the suprasystem.

The *motor,* by which all or part of a system moves in space, may in a nation be a different set of organizations (armies, navies, merchant marines) from the *output transducer* (radio broadcasters, writers, diplomats) which sends information out across system boundaries, although the matter-energy available to the society is used by both. In organisms, however, very comparable nervous and muscular apparatuses are both motor (hands, feet) and output transducer (larynx, face, hands, feet).

It is usually possible in organisms to show by anatomical and physiological studies what structures perform the subsystem functions relating to the use of energy and materials. This is not true, at least at present, for all the information-processing subsystems. Some of these, like the input transducer (all the external sense organs taken together) have been identified and studied with care. It is possible to specify such characteristics of sense organs as transducers, as their bandwidths, channel capacities, signal-to-noise ratios, distortions and response lags. Many, but not all, channels over which input and output information flows are also known. If, however, an experimenter wanted to use electrodes to study the functional characteristics of the decider, he would not know where in the nervous system to place them. The literature also makes it clear that the structures and physiological processes related to learning and memory cannot yet be definitely identified. We do have some evidence that the various "speech areas" of the cortex mediate language encoding and output transducing in human beings.

The Individual Organism as a Channel

Without precise knowledge about the relationship of structure to information processing in the brain, it becomes necessary to conceptualize the human organism in a communication situation as a "black box," whose inputs and outputs can be observed and measured, but not the different flows through specific components with their particular delays, distortions and breakdowns. Experimental controls can sometimes be used in a psychological research with human subjects when instructions are given so that it seems possible to study an aspect of function of a single information-processing subsystem holding constant all other subsystems. For instance, in complex reaction-time experiments one can calculate accurately the amount of time which is added to the response by a choice. Among alternate behaviors, in a situation where the muscular response time remains constant, this decision-time falls to zero as the task is better practiced and the choice becomes automatic (1). Again, Brown and Lenneberg (2) have demonstrated that encoding time is longer when subjects are naming unusual colors than when they are naming common ones.

One can look upon an individual as a single channel, as Broadbent has done (3). His information-flow diagram of the organism, which is based upon research in perception, learning, memory and other aspects of information processing, includes the sense modalities, a short-term memory store, a selective filter, a channel of limited capacity, a "store of conditional probabilities of past events," a "system for varying output until some input is secured" (an example of which is the continued appetitive behavior of an animal until it is able to reduce its drive) and effectors. The orderly progress of information processing in such a system can be delayed or disrupted by any of the components or by functional difficulties in any of their connecting links. The capacity of the short-term memory is limited. These may be retrieval problems from long-term stores. It may be necessary to establish new, learned input-output relationsships. The motor task required of the subject may be difficult and so it may slow his responses. It is also possible to present the system, whether it is a cell, an organism, or any other living system, with underload (sensory deprivation) or overload of input information, both of which may lead to pathological function.

Information Input Overload

In our information input overload research (4), the living system is regarded as a single channel whose capacity can be exceeded. The responses to various rates of information input up to and beyond the maximum rate which the system can process, and the ways of adjusting to overloads have been studied for different levels of living systems.

Quastler and Wulff (5) have experimented upon the upper limits of a human being's capacity to process information. Their tasks were designed so that neither peripheral input nor peripheral output handling ability were limiting factors. Rates were calculated for information transmission by reading, typing, playing the piano, doing mental arithmetic, glancing at displays of letters and playing cards, scales or dials. They found that people are able to make up to five or six successful associations per second, assimilate about 15 bit at a glance and process 22 bits per second in piano playing, 24 in reading aloud and 24 in mental arithmetic.

Our Iota Research

We have measured the channel capacity and studied the responses of individuals to overloads by the use of especially built equipment, known as the IOTA (Information Overload Testing Aid). This apparatus consists of a ground-glass screen about 3 by 4 feet in size, upon which stimuli are presented. The subject responds by pushing buttons arrayed before him. The stimuli are thrown on the back of the screen by a projector, known as a Perceptoscope, which is capable of showing moving picture film at rates of from 1 to 24 frames per second. The program for this experiment presents black arrows in one of eight angular positions, like clock hands, on a white background. These appear in from one to four of four 2-inch wide vertical slots, made up of 12 squares superimposed on one another, which run down the screen. There is a set of eight buttons, corresponding to the eight possible positions of the arrows, for each of the slots being used. A subject can see stimuli in a maximum of four slots at once, and therefore has 32 buttons. If an arrow in position A appears in slot 2, the correct response is to push button A for slot 2, and any other response is an error. A lack of response is an omission. The subject can control the number of squares with slots which are open by using a foot pedal. At the beginning of each test, only the top square in each slot is open. He can open all 12, or close as many as he wishes. As the film is run, an arrow in position B which first appears in slot 3 in frame 1 goes to the next lower square and then to the next lower, until it has gone through all 12 positions. While this stimulus is passing through the lower squares, others appear at the top of the same slot or in other slots. By pushing the pedal, the subject gives himself more time to respond before an arrow disappears.

With this apparatus the amount of information presented can be controlled in several different ways: first, it is possible to change the number of alternate positions of the arrows from two (1 bit) to eight (3 bits); second, the movie can run more or less rapidly; third, more or less slots can be used simultaneously; and fourth, the regularity or randomness of the presentations can be changed.

In the original study, two male college students were our subjects. A kymograph record of their button pushes was made, and this was compared with the program of arrows which had been presented to them. These data were fed into a computer which calculated the input and output rates in bits per second, using the Shannon information statistic.

The channel capacity of our subjects was about six bits per second (Figure 1). This is lower than maximum capacities which have

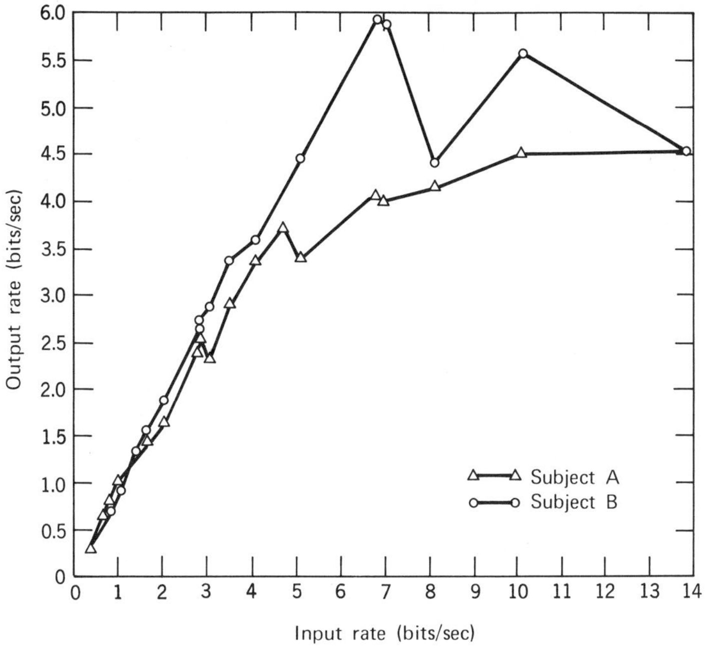

Fig. 1. Performance curves for Subject A and Subject B.

been found by others in other situations, but the subjects had less training; their task was more difficult in this problem, and it has relatively high stimulus-response incompatibility.

A review of the literature had yielded a curve which we believed might be demonstrated at all levels of living systems as characteristic of response to information input overload. We also were able to identify several adjustment processes which appeared at various levels and which, while perhaps not exhaustive, seemed to be the fundamental adjustments possible to this type of stress. These included: (1) omission, which is not processing information if there is an overload; (2) error, processing incorrectly and failing to correct for it; (3) queuing, delaying responses during heavy load periods and catching up during any lulls that occur; (4) filtering, systematic omission of certain types of information, usually according to a priority scheme; (5) approximation, a less precise response given because there is no time for details; (6) multiple channels making use of parallel subsystems if the system has them at its disposal; (7) decentralization, a special case of multiple channels; (8) escape, either leaving the situation or taking other steps which cut off the input of information.

For the purposes of our experiment, we trained the subjects to know how to make all these adjustments on the IOTA. Omissions and errors appeared without training and this fact was pointed out to the subjects. Queuing is possible because a subject can keep more squares open in a slot and see the arrows longer as they move down the openings, giving himself more time to make the required response. Of course, new stimuli keep appearing at the same time. A subject could filter with this apparatus by disregarding arrows in certain positions or paying attention to only certain of the slots. He could approximate by pushing all the buttons corresponding to right-hand positions of the arrow, if he had observed only that the arrow pointed to the right and not the exact position, or pushing all the buttons for a slot if he did not know the direction or position of the arrow but did know the slot. An ambidexterous subject could use multiple channels by working with both hands at the same time. Escape would occur if the subject refused to continue.

At slow rates of transmission our subjects

used few adjustment processes. At medium rates they attempted them all. At higher rates filtering was preferred, but as the maximum channel capacity was reached, both subjects used chiefly omission (Figure 2).

The curve which had been hypothesized after study of the literature showed the output rising as a more-or-less linear function of input until channel capacity is reached, then leveling off and finally decreasing as breakdown or confusion occurs. Data from these subjects produced curves of the general shape we had expected when information input is plotted against information output in bits per second. However, within the range that was used there was no breakdown or confusion. We probably had not raised the input rate sufficiently. Klemmer and Muller (6), in a comparable study, did find overload (Figure 3).

We also tested two three-man groups with the IOTA apparatus and found they had similar performance curves, with lower channel capacities of about 3 to 4 bits per second. The groups used adjustment processes in generally similar ways. A social organization made up of three echelons of three-man groups (an air raid warning system simulation at Systems Development Corporation) gave similar results.

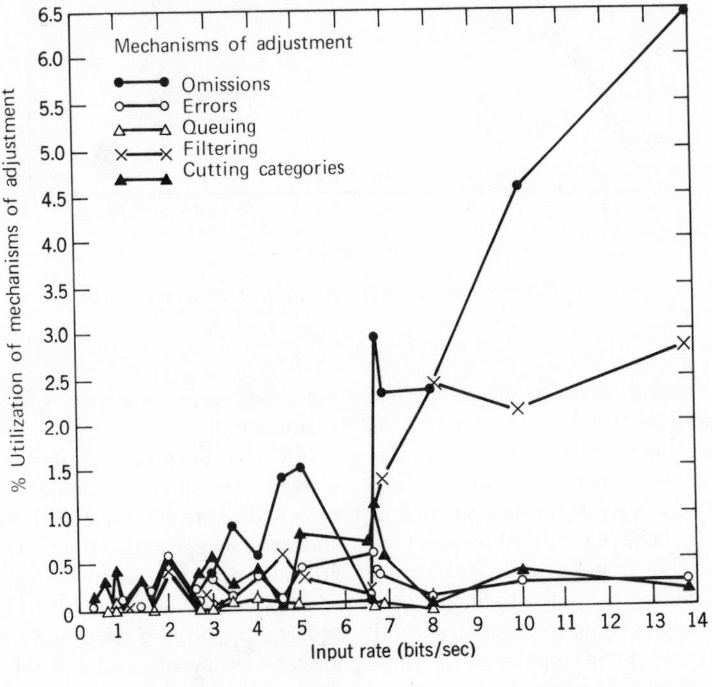

Fig. 2. Mean utilization of adjustment processes by both subjects at various input rates.

Our Pulse-Interval Code Research

The IOTA apparatus conveys its information by a code based upon presentation of different symbols from an ensemble or alphabet of arrow positions rather than upon different temporal intervals between its signals. It is a code founded on the nature of its signal pulses rather than its pulse intervals. Evidence is increasing, however, that pulse-interval codes are common, if not universal in the nervous system. If we wish to study true formal identities in information channel capacities across several levels of living systems, from cells to social institutions, therefore, we must employ pulse-interval codes rather than the type used in the IOTA apparatus. We have done this by constructing equipment which delivers pulses or signals at different intervals to systems at various levels (7).

At the level of the cell, we built an electronic stimulator which delivered two or more pulses at various brief intervals through electrodes attached to single fibers of the sciatic nerve of the frog. The interval between the input and output pulses, obtained through microelectrodes on the axons of the same fiber, was measured with an accuracy of one microsecond. This was repeated enough times to determine the variance in the latency (time between stimulus and response). This, together with the absolute refractory period or dead time, enabled us to calculate the theoretical maximum possible channel capacity of the neuron by a formula developed by Rapoport and Horvath (8). The curve obtained is the top one in Figure 4. The output curve rises rapidly to peak at a maximum slightly over 4000 bits per second and then declines gradually as pulse input rate increases.

A similar procedure was used at the organ level. Pulses at different intervals were delivered to the optic nerve of a rat, and the resultant evoked potentials were registered through a microelectrode on the optic cortex. The Rapoport-Horvath formula was applied to the data and, consequently, a curve of similar shape was obtained, peaking at about 55 bits per second (Figure 4).

Ten individual human subjects were presented with light flashes at differing intervals and were instructed to push a lever to respond to each flash. The intervals of the responses were compared with those of the flashes, and an average curve obtained from the 10 subjects' data was calculated, using the Rapoport-Horvath formula. It, of course, had the same general form and peaked at a maximum theoretical channel capacity of about 5.75 bits per second (Figure 4).

The face-to-face group level was studied using three separate groups of three members each. In each group subject A saw the first light flash and subject B saw the second. Each pushed a lever when he saw his light. Each of

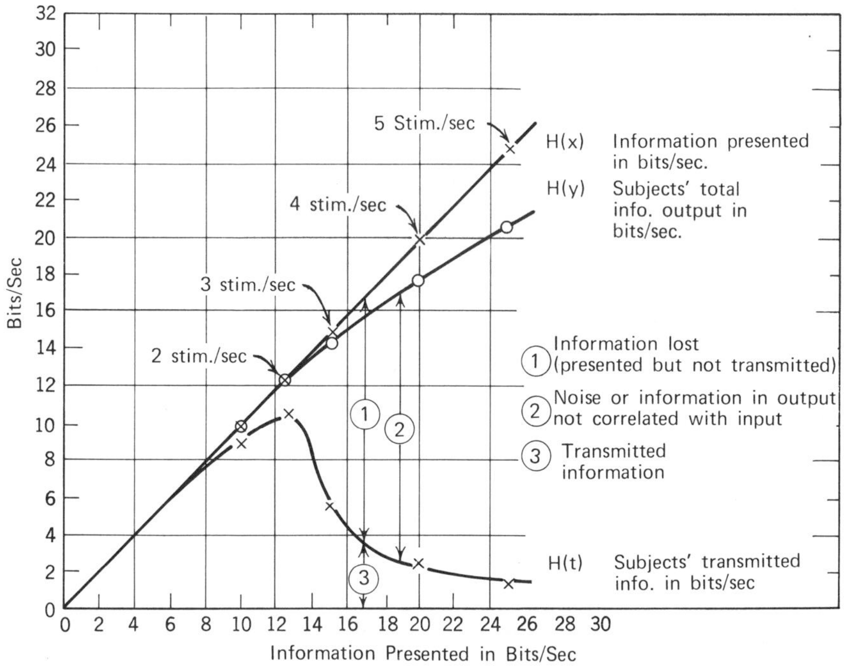

Fig. 3. Subjects' total information output and transmitted information as functions of input rate [from Klemmer and Muller (6)].

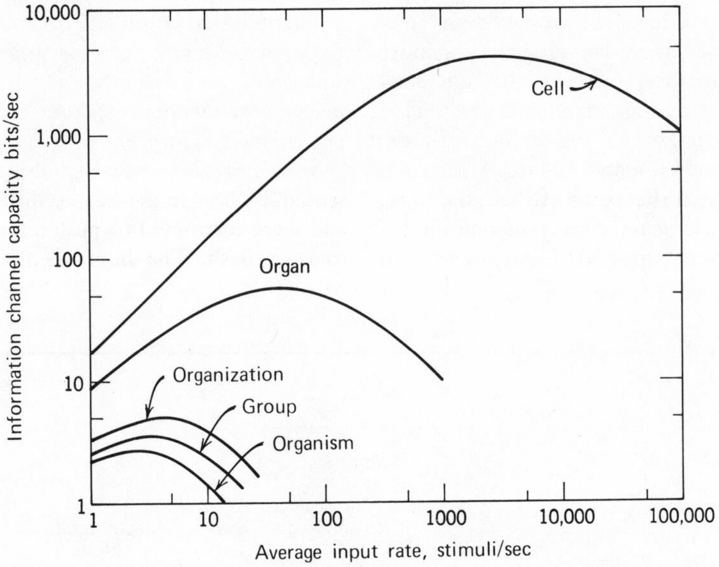

Fig. 4. Performance curves for five levels of systems calculated from pulse-interval data.

these lever pushes flashed a light before subject C, who responded to each flash by pushing a similar lever, creating the system output signals. Calculations using the same formula produced a comparable output curve peaking at about 3.75 bits per second (Figure 4).

A small multiechelon social organization has also been subjected to a similar experiment. It was made up of a primary input echelon of two groups of two subjects each, a secondary echelon of one group of two subjects each and a tertiary, output echelon of one subject—a total of seven subjects. Each subject in the first group saw the first of a pair of two flashes with differing intervals between them and responded as rapidly as possible with his lever. Each subject in the second group of this echelon (which was physically separate from the first group) responded similarly to the second flash when he saw it. One of the two subjects in the second echelon saw the two flashes caused by the lever pushes of the subjects in the first group, and responded when he saw both. The other subject in this echelon—physically separate from the first—did the same thing for the two flashes from the second group. (This echelon responded only after seeing *two* flashes from the input echelon, and so corrected for any erroneous extra pushes of a member of the input echelon—but not for erroneous omissions.) The one subject in the third echelon pushed his lever each time he saw a flash from either member of the second echelon. His signals were the output from the organization. The same formula applied to these data yielded a similar curve peaking at about 2.5 bits per second.

Thus, a formal identity of theoretical maximum channel capacity and over-all performance curves to increasing information input rates were found from experiments on five levels of living systems—cell, organ, organism, groups and organizations. These reached maxima descending heirarchically from about 4000 bits per second for the cell to about 2.5 for the multiechelon organization (Figure 4). Apparently the more components there are in a channel, the lower is its channel capacity. This probably is because no channel is faster than its slowest component, and the more components a channel has, the more likely it is to have a slow one. Also, some information is lost in the recoding process which must occur at the boundary of each component. These are probably explanations for findings by Roby and Lanzetta (9) that work groups which deployed their personnel so that a minimum number of communication links were required, performed their tasks best.

Psychopathology of Information Overload

Information input underload (sensory deprivation) is believed by many to be capable of producing psychopathology (10). Overload probably does also. We have received personal communications from clinicians concerning patients who appeared to break down in their performances on the job and in psychotherapy from information input which reached them faster than they could handle it.

More objective evidence is available. Incorrect associative responses have been emphasized by clinicians as characteristic of the thought deviations of schizophrenics (11–14). Stressful conditions which can produce such thinking in normals have been reported to include brain damage, centrally active drugs, oxygen deprivation, distraction, fatigue, interruption of ongoing activity, environmental changes and emotional excitement (15). Flavell *et al.* (16) used a word-association test to compare differences between schizophrenic and normal responses, with differences between normals who set their own rates of response and normals under time pressure. They found the responses of the last group to be more like those of schizophrenics than the responses of normals under no time pressure.

A well-controlled study by Usdansky and Chapman (17) also is highly relevant. To 28 apparently normal college student subjects, they presented a task of associating given words with one of three alternate words. The given word was on a card which the subject was instructed to put in one of three trays, each of which had a different alternate word displayed behind it. For each new card to be sorted, a new set of three alternate words appeared behind the trays. One of these three alternatives was always a "correct" conceptual response, one was an "associative distractor" and one an irrelevant response. For instance, to the word "gold" the conceptual response was "steel," the "associative distractor" was "fish," and the irrelevant response was "typewriter." "Fish" was considered an associative distractor because of the commonly experienced contiguity of the words "gold" and "fish." Other distractors were based on commonly experienced contiguity of objects (*e.g.*, "hat"—"head") or on rhymes (*e.g.*, "dragon"—"wagon"). Each subject sorted 45 cards under self-paced conditions (average sorting time 220 seconds) and 45 cards under forced-paced conditions, seeing how fast they could get through them while still trying to be correct (average sorting time 114 seconds). Half the subjects did the forced-pace task first, and half did the self-paced task first. Both the irrelevant and the associative errors increased significantly under the fast, force-paced conditions, just as errors increased in our research at rapid input rates. Associative errors, moreover, increased significantly more than irrelevant errors. Because, in a previous study, Chapman (18) had found the excess of associative errors over irrelevant errors to be much greater for schizophrenics than for normals, Usdansky and Chapman (17) concluded that increasing the speed of response (in our terms, the rate of information processing) in normals increased a kind of error characteristic of schizophrenic thought. One might speculate from such findings, and from ours reported above, that schizophrenia (by some as-yet-unknown process, perhaps a metabolic fault which increases neural "noise") lowers the capacities of channels involved in cognitive information processing. Schizophrenics consequently have difficulties in coping with information inputs at standard rates like the difficulties experienced by normals at rapid rates. As a result, schizophrenics make errors at standard rates like those made by normals under fast, forced-input rates.

Summary

Living systems at several levels process energy and information through a number of critical subsystems essential for their survival. Characteristic functions of these critical subsystems are discussed. The total human being may be viewed as an information-processing channel with a maximum channel capacity. As information input rates to such channels increase, output rates increase, then level off at the channel capacity and then decrease. Adjustment processes are employed at the higher input rates which serve to maintain output as information arrives even faster. Two sorts of research are reported, measuring individual human information processing performances under various input rates. In one sort the information is coded in discrete symbols; in the other it is coded in terms of the durations of interpulse intervals. These studies demonstrate how performance peaks and then declines and how adjustment processes are used as inputs to single human subjects get faster. Similarities in information processing characteristics of cells, organs, organisms, groups and multiechelon organizations are investigated in these researches. Their possible relevance to psychopathology, including schizophrenia, is discussed.

REFERENCES

1. Mowbray, G. H. and Rhoades, M. V.: On the reduction of choice reaction times with practice. Quart. J. Exper. Psychol., *11:* 16–22, 1959.
2. Brown, R., and Lenneberg, E.: A study in language and cognition. J. Abnorm. & Social. Psychol., *49:* 454–462, 1954.
3. Broadbent, D. E.: Perception and Communication, pp. 297–301. Pergamon Press, Inc., New York, 1958.
4. Miller, J. G.: Information input overload and psychopathology. Amer. J. Psychiat., *116:* 695–704, 1960.
   Miller, J. G.: The individual as an information processing system. *In* Information Storage and Neural Control, by Fields, W. S. and Abbott, W., pp. 1–28. Charles C. Thomas, Publisher, Springfield, Ill., 1963.
5. Quastler, H. and Wulff, V. J.: Human Performance in Information Transmission. Report R-62, Control Systems Laboratory, University of Illinois, Urbana, 1955.
6. Klemmer, E. T. and Muller, P. T., Jr.: The rate of handling information: key pressing responses to light patterns. H.F.O.R.L. Memo Report No. 34, March, 1953.
7. Miller, J. G.: Living systems and mechanical systems. Preprint 112. Mental Health Research Institute, University of Michigan, Ann Arbor, Michigan, 1963.
8. Rapoport, A., and Horvath, W. J.: The theoretical channel capacity of a single neuron as determined by various coding systems. Information and control, *3:* 335, 1960.
9. Roby, T. B. and Lanzetta, J. T.: Work group structure, communication, and group performance. Sociometry, *19:* 105, 1956.
10. Lilly, J.: *In* Illustrative Strategies for Research on Psychopathology in Mental Health, pp. 13–20. Group for the Advancement of Psychiatry, Symposium No. 2, June, 1956.
11. Kraepelin, A.: Dementia Praecox and Paraphrenia. E. & S. Livingstone, Ltd., Edinburgh, 1919.
12. Jung, C. G.: The psychology of dementia praecox. Nerv. & Ment. Dis. Monogr. Series, No. 3, 1936.
13. Bleuler, E.: Dementia Praecox or the Group of Schizophrenias. International Universities Press, Inc., New York, 1950.
14. Arieti, S.: Interpretation of Schizophrenia. Brunner, New York, 1955.
15. Cameron, N. A., and Margaret, A.: Behavior Pathology. Riverside Editions, Cambridge, Mass., 1951.
16. Flavell, J. H., Draguns, J., Feinberg, L. D., and Budin, W.: A microgenetic approach to word association. J. Abnorm. & Social. Psychol., *57:* 1–8, 1958.
17. Usdansky, G. and Chapman, L. J.: Schizophrenic-like responses in normal subjects under time pressure. J. Abnorm. & Social Psychol., *60:* 143–146, 1960.
18. Chapman, L. J.: Intrusion of associative responses into schizophrenic conceptual performance. J. Abnorm. & Social Psychol., *56:* 374–379, 1958.

PART FIVE

Adaptation, Growth, and Conflict

P A R T F I V E

The Decision to Innovate

To say that organizations change by permitting them to adapt to new circumstances or to grow is to face a new direction of vast proportions and confusing content. On the surface, change would seem simple enough. For any number of reasons, performance is not what is desired. The existing behavior is inadequate and a decision maker or controller in our cybernetic system issues instructions that a new set of behaviors be performed. If we view organization change as nothing more than a choice between behaviors or programs of instructions for behavior, it is, in truth, simple. In real organizations, however, we have to face a tedious problem of acquiring the knowledge of what specific behaviors will improve performance, and we have to possess the capacity to perform them. Programs to guide behavior and the resources needed are costly to acquire. Hence the decision to change behavior to improve performance must consider both the costs of acquiring the new programs and resources and the costs already incurred for the existing programs and resources that will now be abandoned. The unwillingness to incur these costs explains much of the so-called inertia in existing organizations (March and Simon).

Awareness of the cost of innovation leads to other things that have to be taken into account in the study of change. Organizations to change need surpluses such as cash reserves or slack (e.g., organization members are getting more from being in the organization than is needed to keep them there) that can be used to cover the costs of change (March and Simon). To put it another way, a "lean" organization that is just breaking even, that has no "fat," is doomed the next time change is required.

If we couple with this costliness of innovation an assumption that organizations act to minimize costs (and by cost, it should be clear that we mean all inputs such as psychological energy as well as money), then the order or process by which new programs are developed becomes understandable. There is first an attempt to find a program that will improve performance from among the available or known programs. The cost here is the cost of the search through existing knowledge. Should this fail to disclose a satisfactory program, the next effort is to create or invent a new one. This can be a costly and also a risky process, for an adequate new program may not be found. Should this occur, then the only other way to reduce the gap between performance and standard is to change the standard or goal (March and Simon). Goal definition, then, is a stage in the general process of change.

Goal Definition

Goals have been discussed frequently in these volumes. We have primarily considered their place in a control system and, to some extent, the occasions upon which they arise or may be revised. Thus far, however, we have not considered how they come into being. We are, of course, concerned with the actual goals that the organization seeks to achieve, not the stated or ideal goal. (They may of course be the same.) If we were to ask what are the real goals of an organization such as a business firm we might be told that they are whatever the owners or stockholders want them to be. Thus a conversation with the president might find him saying, "I know the stockholders would like such and such. However, we can't do that but must actually do this and that." "This" and "that" probably contain some of what the stockholders want but also some of what the president wants the goals to be. The chances are that closer observation would find that, in addition to the things the president stated, the organization was also working toward goals of interest to customers, other goals of interest to the unions, and still others of interest to the immediate community. The set of goals that the organization actually has are thus a mixed bag containing some things of interest to each party, which makes them willing to contribute their money, skills, or orders to the organization. It has been proposed that organizations be considered as coalitions of people who have agreed to join together in return for satisfaction of certain of their objectives. This agreement is arrived at by a process of bargaining and is recorded in the organization structure, the budgets, the policies (Cyert and March). Such a view permits us to account for many important things. Principal among them is the fact that decisions can be made only by a mind, and only individuals have minds; groups or organizations do not (although, for convenience, we often say that the organization decided to do so and so). It helps explain the number and diffuse nature of organization goals, and it makes clear how closely linked goals and structure are.

Adaptation through Changing the Basis for Goal Definition

Organization goals are served by the acts of members. For people to be members, for them to contribute effort to these acts, they must be involved with or committed to the organization. We have earlier observed that people become and stay committed to organizations because they find intrinsic or extrinsic satisfactions in the things they do in the organization. Organizations face a serious dilemma when people whose talents or resources are needed do not find the goals or activities of the organization sufficiently attractive to make them committed to the organization. Two general solutions might be considered: to change the goals or activities of the organization, or both, so that those needed can become committed. Another alternative is to influence the objectives and values of people so that they are more consistent with those of the organization. This latter alternative was discussed in Volume I (Mooney, Etzioni, Peabody). The former would mean admitting people who are currently outsiders into the central decision making of the organization to permit them to work with existing organization members on new goals and purposes. This process is called cooptation (Selznick) and is one where adaptation leads to increased integration of organization members.

Why should a group within an organization begin to develop goals at variance with those established? Why should the different ideas of groups be more potent or more seriously considered at one time than at another? One obvious answer is that the environment of the organization changes, and some groups may see before the rest of the organization that the organization must act differently to survive or that the organization can improve itself through modified objectives. It is the deviating group's *awareness of what the organization needs* for survival or advancement that gives the group its potency. But even if the environment does not change, the organization will. The needs of a newly formed organization are different from the established one, which is the effort to become efficient, and it, in turn, is different from the organization that has learned to become efficient but faces the problems of full maturity. As the organization goes through its own life cycle, the potency, influence, or power of individuals or groups changes as they becomes more or less able to define and facilitate solutions for the changing problems of the organization (Perrow).

Needless to say, as the needs of an organization change, increasing the potency of one group (because of its ability to define and implement organization), other groups will offer strong resistance to the changed relationship. If the situation involved only a single goal or problem for the organization or if the solution of the problem could be wholly contained within one group, then the clash between the two groups could be relatively simply solved. However, the reality in an organization is that, while several groups have and share power and their relative positions change, the change rarely leads to the complete exclusion of anyone. The matter is further complicated in that those who define the problem in large organizations are not often the people who have the technical capacity to solve them. Consequently, there is built into modern organizations conditions that breed continuing and increasing conflict between groups and individuals.

Conflict within organizations appears undesirable, at least at first glance. One of the few common assumptions of both the classical school of organization theory and the human relations school was that conflict is bad and should always be reduced if it could not be eliminated. Were this so, we would be in serious trouble, for other investigations have shown that there are important sources of conflict other than those mentioned above (Smith). Investigation also shows that organizations can tolerate considerable conflict without disastrous consequences and that there are clearly identifiable leadership patterns and structural arrangements that can be used to reduce conflict to tolerable levels. Perhaps most interesting, however, is the observation that conflict can be useful and constructive (Smith). Conflict can motivate behavior, and it can often lead to a search for new programs or objectives that bring about important innovation.

Growth and its Consequences

One of the fascinating similarities that organizations have with biological entities is that they grow; they change size, they add capacities, they fill different roles. Often, growth is explained by saying that an organization seizes opportunities available in its environment, that its growth is environmentally determined. However, it is also constrained, as we noted earlier in this section, by the availability of unused internal resources. Both of these, however, explain more of what is possible than why growth occurs. Occasionally, the explanation can be given that some external authority wills the growth, such as when Congress directs the expansion of the army or the forest service. However, our real concern has been with a view of organizations that sees them as self-regulating, self-directing. For our needs, the explanation of the impulses to grow must be located within the organization (Penrose).

Growth typically leads to greater efforts to rationalize the work of the organization which, in turn, usually means a finer division of work, greater psychological distances between people, and increasing interdependency, resulting in lower morale and increased friction and hostility.[1] Need this always occur? Is it possible to provide structure adequate for the larger scale of operations that will provide jobs which will have meaning and interrelationships which are constructive and supportive? The answer is hardly clear, but an interesting, important tentative "yes" is contained in some studies in this book (see, for example, Lawrence and Lorsch in this volume and Drucker and Litterer in Vol. I).

Structuring for and Bringing about Change

How organizations respond to change or the need for change depends largely on what type of organization structure prevails. One of the impulses to initiating or continuing the development of an organization is to increase the predictability of output to increase efficiency. We have already noted many ways in which

[1] See, for example, Walker and Guest in Volume I.

the organization can be molded to do this. There are also, as has been noted, serious costs. Some of these costs as noted above, are human. Others are that the organization can operate only under stable circumstances. In brief, an organization form called mechanistic, relying on increased structure, can be efficient provided that certain conditions prevail and certain costs can be accepted. Contrasted with this mechanistic organization is the organic organization, perhaps not as technically efficient, but more adaptive to change, more capable of innovating for change and, often, providing vastly different social environments (Burns and Stalker). To have an organization that can innovate in order to cope or respond to changes in the environment, one needs an organization structured in a special way.

Central to any question of organizational change is that of how do people change their objectives, their commitments to organization goals, their willingness to accept others as leaders or colleagues and themselves as subordinates and peers. We return to this issue once more, since it is important and the answers are hardly complete. Some have observed that no one is ever completely satisfied with a collective effort. The goals of the organization may not be exactly what a person wants. He may like his superior as a person but may be somewhat unsure as to his technical capacity to direct the organization in accomplishing its goal or vice versa. Hence, in reality, people have to be able to accept the idea that the arrangement under which they are to proceed is the best possible or available at the moment. Bringing people to this position is described as a political activity. People are asked to accept a leader or a plan because he or it is the best way of accomplishing what they collectively want. If this view holds, then organization development depends, in part, on political processes.

Planning and Innovation in Organizations

JAMES G. MARCH AND HERBERT A. SIMON

In Chapter 6 (not included here) we found it useful to contrast the concept of rationality that has been employed in economics and statistics with a theory of rationality that takes account of the limits on the power, speed, and capacity of human cognitive faculties. This contrast helped us understand the mosaic of programs that constitutes the great bulk of human behavior in organizations.

At a number of points in the chapter, we found it necessary to allude to unprogrammed activity, and activity directed toward the creation of new programs, but our attention was directed toward the organizational "steady state" rather than toward change in organizations. There still remains, therefore, the task of analyzing more completely how the cognitive limits on rationality affect the processes of organizational change and program development. In the present chapter we shall try to fit this remaining piece into the picture.

The Concept of Initiation

Theories of rational choice generally have not made a distinction between continuation of an existing program of action and change in the program of action. In these theories, the chooser is simply confronted with two (or more) alternatives of action and required to select the better of the two. There is no need to designate which, if either, of these actions continues the existing program.

In such formulations there is one way, however, in which the distinction between persistence and change can be given formal representation, and can be made to influence the choice. We exclude sunk costs when computing the costs of persisting in a going program. A great deal of the inertia of "going concerns" can be explained on the basis of the sunk costs doctrine. A simple example is the decision whether to move a factory to a new location. Unless the present facilities can be sold for an amount that tends to compensate for the cost of constructing or acquiring new facilities, the new location will be severely disadvantaged in the comparison, and only rarely will a change in location prove preferable to remaining in the present location.

We may also regard the costs of discovering and developing a possible program of action as sunk costs, for these costs must be incurred if there is to be a shift to a new program of action, but not if the organization persists in its present program. Hence, even if there are no tangible sunk costs, like factory buildings or specialized equipment, there will almost always be associated with a change in program a number of sunk *costs of innovation.* Costs of innovation, whatever their origin, will tend to produce *program continuity*.

Although tangible sunk costs often can be and sometimes are evaluated in monetary terms, it is seldom possible to make accurate estimates of the costs of innovation, and even in situations where it is possible, such estimates are seldom made. Individuals and organizations give preferred treatment to alternatives that represent continuation of present programs over those that represent change. But this preference is not derived by calculating explicitly the costs of innovation or weighing these costs. Instead, persistence comes about primarily because the individual or organization does not search for or consider alternatives to the present course of action unless that present course is in some sense "unsatisfactory." The amount of *search* decreases as *satisfaction* increases. Where search for new alternatives is suppressed, program continuity is facilitated.

The importance of this proposition to participation decisions has already been shown in Chapter 4 (not included here). Its main consequence is that, in a theory of choice, we should distinguish between the alternative of

---

Chapter 7 from *Organizations*, New York, Wiley, 1959, pp. 172–199. Reprinted by permission of the publisher.

continuing and alternatives of change, and should not treat these symmetrically as is done in most existing theories.

A theory of this kind does not attribute the persistence of behavior to any particular "resistance to change," but simply to the absence of a vigorous search for new alternatives under circumstances where the existing program is regarded as satisfactory. If a new alternative, which is superior in some or all respects to the current program, somehow presents itself to the choosing individual or organization, the theory does not predict that the program will remain unchanged; but a theory of choice without a theory of search is inadequate.

In general, we hypothesize that the *type of influence process* involved in decision-making will be a function of the *type of choice problem.* When a choice problem takes the form of selecting one course of action from a set of alternatives, influence processes operate by making one alternative more attractive relative to the others. When the choice, however, is one of change versus persistence, a great part of the influence process will consist in initiation—particularly, in suggesting alternatives of action where none existed before, either (*a*) to solve a problem for which there was not a solution, or (*b*) to improve the present program even when it was accepted as satisfactory. Hence, by observing the influence processes we can distinguish pretty clearly between choice situations where the main problem is to select one out of several alternatives and choice situations where a new program is being proposed that deviates from the existing program. Most research on interpersonal influence has focussed on the former situation. The results may be substantially irrelevant to the case where the alternatives are not specified in advance (March, 1955a).

One final qualification: not every change in behavior qualifies as initiation or innovation as those terms are used here. In the last chapter, an inventory and production control system was used to illustrate how, through the construction of a strategy, change could take place within the framework of a well-defined performance program. We would not regard a change in the operating level of a factory from one month to another as involving initiation or innovation.

Initiation and innovation are present when change requires the devising and evaluation of new performance programs that have not previously been a part of the organization's repertory and cannot be introduced by a simple application of programmed switching rules. The extent to which behavior in an organization can change without involving either initiation or innovation is limited only by the complexity of the strategies and switching rules that are imbedded in its performance programs. If we could describe for a particular organization what its program was, including its programmed switching rules, we would be in a position to distinguish ordinary programmed changes in behavior from changes that represent the initiation of new performance programs.

Action and Inaction. We need a theory that distinguishes between persistence and change; we need also a distinction between action and inaction. Just as most theories of choice fail to distinguish between persistence and change, they also fail to distinguish between doing something and doing nothing. "Doing nothing," in such theories, is simply a particular alternative of behavior that may be chosen or rejected in exactly the same way as "doing a particular something."

Consider a system having a set of criteria to determine what constitutes a "satisfactory" situation. For an organism, these criteria may include the requirements that it not be hungry, that no danger be present, and the like. For a business concern, the demands of "satisfaction" may be a particular profit level, market share, and liquidity position. It may happen that certain of these criteria are satisfied by activities that are compatible with a wide variety of other activities. Animals, for example, require oxygen, but breathing is compatible with the simultaneous performance of a large number of other activities. Thus, an animal that is only breathing is described as "inactive." Formally, we describe an activity as "action" or "inaction" relative to a set of alternative activities. Less formally, we recognize certain activities as conspicuous cases of "inaction" in the general environment in which we live, and we need not quibble about how to classify borderline cases.

The distinction between action and inaction is clearly relevant to the everyday world of organizations as we know it. There is ordinarily little or no limit to the amount of inaction an organization can "undertake"; inaction does not absorb resources. At the same time, the distinction is more important in some situations than in others. It is more significant for organizations or individuals that satisfice than for those that optimize. For the former can reach their goals by action programs that, taken collectively, satisfy the criteria in question; they need consider action only when inaction does not achieve this, and only in the specific directions in which action relates to particular criteria. If, for example, there is no safety problem (i.e., the present safety record is accepted as satisfactory), there need be no safety action.

The significance of the action-inaction distinction also depends on characteristics of the environment. Consider a world that is mainly "empty"—in which most events are unrelated to most other events; causal connections are exceptional and not common. In a world largely empty, a theory of rational action does not have to regard each choice as affecting each component of a "utility function"—everything connected with everything else. Instead, particular action programs have few consequences except for the criteria they were undertaken to satisfy. Hence, we suggest that the greater the *use of acceptable-level decision rules* and the less the *complexity of the environment*, the greater the *use of local changes in programs.* The picture (or perhaps, nightmare) of planning as the solution of almost unimaginable numbers of simultaneous equations can be replaced by a picture of planning as the construction of a series of unrelated action programs.

"Unrelated" is perhaps too strong a term; "loosely coupled" is a more appropriate one. Even in a mostly empty world there is one important connection among action programs that must be taken into consideration in planning: that they all draw upon the resources of the organization. Action, unlike inaction, incurs opportunity costs whenever the criteria that the organization must meet are (collectively) sufficiently stiff that meeting all of them simultaneously is not a trivial matter.

A Summary of the Planning Model. We can now summarize the essential characteristics of rational choice as we have described it, preparatory to a more detailed analysis of choice processes in organization.

1. We assume that the main requirement of the organizational program is to *satisfy* certain requirements or criteria, these criteria being subject to gradual change over time.
2. When, in the absence of an action program, one or more criteria are not being met, we predict that an *action* program will be initiated to remedy this condition.
3. A change in the program of an organization—whether by adding new activities or altering existing ones—involves not just a choice process, in the traditional sense, but requires also a process of *initiation* through which new program possibilities are generated and their consequences examined.
4. For the most part, particular action programs are connected with particular criteria, and the world is largely empty of complicated causal interrelations. Action programs are related to each other primarily through the demands they make on the scarce *organization resources* available for initiating and carrying on action.

The Process of Innovation

The innovative processes that are essential in initiating new programs in organization are closely related to the various intellective processes referred to by psychologists as "problem-solving," "productive thinking," "creative thinking," "invention," and the like. Our starting point will be to examine briefly what is known of the problem-solving process at the individual level, and then to introduce organiaztional considerations.

Memory and Problem-Solving. In virtually all human problem-solving, memory plays an enormous role. In the memory are stored both repertories of possible solutions to classes of problems that have been encountered in the past and repertories of components of problem solutions. The importance of such repertories—and their large magnitude—in difficult intellective activities like mathematical invention and chess-playing is amply documented. There can be little doubt that they are equally essential components of almost all kinds of everyday problem-solving (de Groot, 1946; Hadamard, 1945).

When problem-solving consists primarily in searching the memory in a relatively systematic fashion for solutions that are present there in nearly finished form, it is described as "reproductive." When the construction of new solutions out of more or less "raw" material is involved, the process is described as "productive." The *type of problem-solving* used, i.e., the extent to which productive elements are present, depends on both the characteristics of the problem and on the *past experience* of the problem solver.

Programmed activity generally involves a great deal of problem-solving of a rather routine and reproductive sort. That is to say, only under unusual circumstances is the detail of a program so stereotyped that it is stored in the memory as a series of specific instructions. On the contrary, in most situations the execution of a program involves a considerable amount of reconstruction of the program details, but without requiring extensive and difficult searches or computations. Contrariwise, the unprogrammed activity in innovation generally requires a great deal of "productive" problem-solving.

Basic Problem-Solving Processes. Our existing scientific knowledge of human problem-solving processes is incomplete. From what is known it is possible, however, to describe the general characteristics of these processes; and it is only these general characteristics that will be relevant for our analysis of organizational decision-making (Newell, Shaw, and Simon, 1958).

First, however complex the end products of these processes—however intricate the machine that is invented or however subtle and sophisticated the decision that is reached—the processes themselves are made up by aggregating very large numbers of elements, each element, taken by itself, being exceedingly simple. In an age of electronic computers this fact—if it is a fact—should not surprise us, for this is exactly the way in which a computer operates: it performs intricate and elaborate mathematical computations, but it performs them by executing sequences of enormous length of elementary steps, where each such step is no more complicated than adding 1 and 1 to get 2. We are not arguing that human brains are necessarily like computers, but simply that complex processes can be aggregated from simple elements (Plato, *Meno,* pp. 80–85).

Second, one large component of problem-solving consists of search processes. Search may be physical: finding a piece of correspondence in a file, or obtaining a customer by door-to-door canvassing; it may be perceptual: scanning the Patent Office Gazette to find items of relevance to a company's research activity; it may be cognitive: using associative processes to locate relevant information in the memory.

Third, another large component consists of screening processes. Items that are dredged up by search processes are examined to see whether they qualify as possible solutions to the problem at hand or possible components of such solutions. The screening of job applicants provides a simple example.

Fourth, the elementary components of the problem-solving process (the search and screening processes) are characterized by a great deal of "randomness." There is ordinarily considerable arbitrariness about the sequence in which problem-solving steps are taken, and in the order in which they are assembled. Running through the process, however, are two elements of organization that give it structure and that permit it to give rise to a highly organized product. These organizing processes are "programs" in the sense in which we have been using that term.

Two kinds of programs may be distinguished. On the one hand, although there is usually nothing inexorable in the sequence in which problem-solving steps are taken, and although many of these steps involve a great deal of search, certain broad *procedural* programs are recognizable in most problem-solving. Most of our descriptions of temporal pattern in problem-solving go back to John Dewey's analysis of the problem-solving process and to Gestalt theorizing about productive thinking. Empirical evidence generally supporting Dewey's phase hypotheses has been obtained by Bales and Strodtbeck (1951) in certain group problem-solving situations; and empirical evidence for some of the Gestalt hypotheses has been obtained, through "thinking aloud" techniques, by de Groot (1946) and others in individual problem-solving situations.

At the same time, there are *substantive* programs. By substantive programs are meant the structuring of the problem-solving process that comes about as a reflection of the structure of the problem to be solved. For example, a business policy problem of broad scope may be factored into its marketing aspects, its financial aspects, its production aspects, etc.; and at one stage in the solution process these several aspects may be dealt with separately—sequentially, or simultaneously—by the different parts of the organization.

Fifth, the programs, procedural and substantive, that govern problem-solving processes have generally a hierarchical structure. From a procedural standpoint this means that the problem goes through a sequence of broad phases (e.g., "problem formulation," "search for alternatives," "evaluation of alternatives," etc.), but that each of these phases may be made up, in turn, of similar phases at a more microscopic level of detail. On the substantive side a similar sequence of levels may be apparent: the problem is first analyzed in broad terms; each of its aspects becomes, in turn, a subproblem to be further analyzed in detail (Cyert, Simon, and Trow, 1956).

Some General Hypotheses about Process. We shall be concerned in the remainder of this chapter with propositions about the problem-solving and program-innovating processes as they occur in organizations. A few hypotheses are of such broad relevance that they are worth stating at the outset. Some of these have already been presented in earlier chapters; others are new.

In a search for programs of activity to achieve goals, the focus of attention will tend to move from one class of variables to another in the following general sequence. (1) Those variables that are largely within the control of the problem-solving individual or organizational unit will be considered first. There will be a serious attempt to elaborate a program of activity based on the control of these variables. (2) If a satisfactory program is not discovered by these means, attention will be directed to changing other variables that are not under the direct control of the problem solvers; for example, the program will be enlarged to include activities to be performed by other, independent, organizational units, or to include securing permission of courses of action not presently within the area of discretion of the problem solvers. (3) If a satisfactory program is still not evolved, attention will be turned to the criteria that the program must satisfy, and an effort will be made to relax these criteria so that a satisfactory program can be found.

In the search for possible courses of action, alternatives will be tested sequentially. That is to say, there will be no attempt at the first round of search to exhaust "all possible alternatives." Instead, as soon as a few possible alternatives have been found, these will be evaluated. If one proves satisfactory, when tested against the problem criteria, it will be accepted as a solution to the problem, and search will terminate. If all the alternatives discovered on the previous round of search prove unsatisfactory, this will initiate a new burst of search activity. If persistent search still fails to secure a satisfactory alternative, then the propositions listed above apply.

One higher-level procedural program that is constantly invoked in problem-solving is a search for substantive information by first instituting a higher-level search to determine the likely sources of information. That is, an important technique for obtaining information is to ask someone who has it rather than to search for it in a more painful fashion. But in order to do the former, a search may be needed to determine who has the requisite information. One important element of organization structure is a set of understandings and expectations among the participants as to what bodies of information repose where in the structure. This set of expectations and understandings is a major determinant of the use of communications channels.

Individual and Group Problem-Solving. Up to this point, we have not troubled to distinguish between problem-solving by individuals and problem-solving in groups. Most problem-solving and decision-making in organizations involves, at one stage or another of the proceedings, the participation of a number of persons. To what extent are the individual and the group problem-solving processes the same, and to what extent are they different?

Kelley and Thibaut (Lindzey, 1954), in their assessment of the literature on problem-solving in groups, observe that "most of the analyses of the group problem-solving process appear to derive by analogy from the stages or phases believed to exist in individual problem-solving." They cite Bales' hypotheses on phases in group problem-solving as examples of this. Moreover, a number of workers have assumed implicitly a considerable similarity of the two processes when they have suggested that group situations might provide better opportunities for the study of problem-solving than individual situations. In the group situation the process requires interpersonal communication, and hence many of the steps that would otherwise take place inside the individual brain become visible to the observer. But this point of view is valid, of course, only if the processes are more or less similar.

A substantial number of experiments have been performed to detect differences between the problem-solving performance of groups and individuals respectively. Kelley and Thibaut divide the effects of the group on the problem-solving process into two main types: (1) the effects of pooling a number of independent judgments, and (2) modifications in the problem solution produced by direct social influence.

Under the first heading, the pooling of independent judgments, they examine the following factors as possible explanations for the superiority of group over individual problem-solving capacities: (*a*) The scattering of errors. Since not all group members make the same errors simultaneously, the majority judgment is better than the average judgment of individual members (*b*) Extra influence of considered judgments. Not all proposed solutions will have equal weight with group members. Those proposals that appear to have the best basis will be the ones most likely to be accepted. Hence, again, the judgment accepted by the group will be better than the average of the group members. (*c*) Extra influence of confident judgments. Those members who are most likely to be correct are also most likely to be confident of their answers. Their confidence will attach extra weight to their judgments, and again this will improve the group judgment. (*d*) The division of labor. In handling some problems, the entire group need not deal with the whole problem, but may divide it up in some way and assign the parts to "specialists." This will almost certainly speed up the solution process and may also improve the quality of solutions.

Kelley and Thibaut examine the following kinds of "modifications produced by direct social influence." (*a*) The group members collectively will have available a larger number of possible solutions or contributions toward the solution than will any individual member. (*b*) There will be pressures upon individual group members tending to produce conformity to majority group opinion: (1) through effects on each member's confidence in his own judgment, (2) through needs for approval. (*c*) The group environment will increase or decrease motivation toward effort and task competition, as compared with an isolated individual. Cooperative and competitive groups will have strongly different behaviors in this respect. (*d*) The requirements of communicating ideas to others will force group members to sharpen and clarify their ideas. (*e*) In the combination or weighting of individual solutions in a group solution there will be effects from direct social pressure to conform and from self-weighting of proposals by degree of confidence expressed and by relative interest in the problem under consideration. (*f*) The group environment may produce varying amounts of distraction. (*g*) The group environment may encourage or inhibit initiation.

Since that task has already been performed by Kelley and Thibaut, we will not examine here the available evidence about the strength and significance of these variables. However, we wish to emphasize one feature of group problem-solving that we consider important. As Thorndike (1938) has noted, abilities to evaluate the correctness of proposed solutions are not necessarily the same as abilities to devise correct solutions. In fact, we generally assume that the latter abilities are somewhat less widely shared than the former. From this, Thorndike deduced the superiority of groups over indiviuals in some types of problems. This adds support to the general proposition that influence theory must deal with evoking phenomena as well as the evaluative phase of decision-making.

The Occasions of Innovation

When we treat persistence and change asymmetrically, we do not need to explain why an organization continues to carry out its present program of activity, but we do need to describe the situations in which innovation and change in program will take place. To explain the occasions of innovation is to explain why a program of action that has been regarded as satisfying certain criteria no longer does so.

Determinants of the Criteria of Satisfaction. The notion of criteria of satisfaction is closely related to the psychological notion of "aspiration levels," and we will argue that generalizations that have been found to hold for individual aspiration levels will continue to hold in the area of organizational behavior. The most important proposition is that, over time, the aspiration level tends to adjust to the level of achievement. That is to say, the level of satisfactory performance is likely to be very close to the actually achieved level of recent performance.

As we have noted earlier, this generalization about the adjustment of criteria to the *status quo* needs to be qualified in several important respects. First, adjustment of criteria is a relatively slow process, and cannot be indefinitely accelerated (Gaus and Wolcott, 1940, pp. 82–84). Second, when the situation is in a "steady state" over some period of time, aspiration levels do not remain absolutely constant but tend to rise slowly. Hence, even in the absence of environmental change, there is a continuous mild pressure toward innovation and change of program. Third, although past achievement provides a primary basis for adjusting aspirations to the achievable (or that which is thought to be achievable), other bases of comparison are used as well. Individuals adjust their criteria to the achieved levels of other individuals with whom they compare themselves, and to the levels that are established as norms by relevant reference groups. Organizations adjust their criteria to the levels achieved by other organizations. In general, awareness of a definite course of action that will yield substantially better results than the present program, or awareness that some other person or organization is achieving better results—even if the exact method is not known—will lead to revision of the standards of satisfaction (Cyert and March, 1956).

These postulates have been discussed in earlier chapters with respect to their effect on individual productive behavior and turnover. From them we can also predict variations in the *rate of innovation.* The rate of innovation is likely to increase when changes in the environment make the existing organizational procedures unsatisfactory. We would predict efforts toward innovation in a company whose share of market, total profits, or rate of return on investment had declined. We could predict which of these conditions would most likely induce innovation by determining which was attended to most carefully by the organization.

As a corollary to the first point, we would expect data in reports of operating statistics to trigger innovative effort when the data showed performance falling below present standards.

In the absence of significant environmental change, the gradual upward movement of criteria will lead to periodic demands for innovation, but to only moderately vigorous effort.

Some innovation will result from accidental encounters with opportunities. Stated otherwise, the rate at which opportunities for more satisfactory performance are encountered, whether by accident or design, will be one of the determinants of the rate of innovation.

The Concept of Optimum Stress. The hypotheses listed thus far attribute the parenthood of invention primarily to necessity and secondarily to opportunity. There is another common hypothesis, not derivable from these postulates, that innovation will be most rapid and vigorous when the "stress" on the organization is neither too high nor too low. By stress is meant the discrepancy between the level of aspiration and the level of achievement. According to this hypothesis, if achievement too easily exceeds aspiration, apathy results; if aspiration is very much above achievement, frustration or desperation result, with consequent stereotypy. In the first case, there is no motivation for innovation; in the second case, neurotic reactions interfere with effective innovation. Optimal "stress" results when the carrot is just a *little* way ahead of the donkey—when aspirations exceed achievement by a small amount.

The concept of optimal stress is central to Toynbee's theories of social progress. The same hypothesis is employed frequently in educational theory, in determining the difficulty of the successive tasks with which a learner should be confronted. It can be viewed as dealing with the same problem we noted in Chapter 3: that our model of "normal" motivated behavior requires a switching rule to allow it to accommodate the neurotic behavior sometimes observed.

The Institutionalization of Innovation. All these hypotheses about innovation rest on the assumption that the innovative process is not itself programmed. The stimuli to innovation, in this model, are external.

The "natural" stimuli to innovation—the failure of the existing program to attain satisfactory levels of the criteria—can be supplemented by additional programmed stimuli. There are at least two ways in which this can come about or can be produced in an organization. The criteria of satisfaction can themselves be stated in terms of *rates of change* (i.e., first derivatives) of performance. For example, the management of a business firm might aim at a certain annual percentage increase in sales or in profits. Then, if the existing program did not bring about such a rate of change, innovative activity would be induced in just the same way as by unfavorable environmental changes.

Second, the organization (or parts of it) can acquire criteria of satisfaction specifically stated in terms of rates of innovation. For example, if there is a formally organized research activity—a research and development department, say—the criterion that this unit might establish for itself could be a specified rate of introduction of new programs into the organization.

It should be possible to distinguish the patterns of innovation of organizations that have institutionalized the innovative process in one way or another from those that have not. For example, we would expect the rate of innovation to be less sensitive to environmental changes in the former than in the latter. On the whole, at least under conditions of a relatively stable environment, we would also expect the average rate of innovation to be higher the greater the *institutionalization of innovation.*

The Timing of Innovation. One cannot really draw a sharp line between the occasions of innovation and the timing of innovation. In both cases we are concerned with the kinds of innovative changes that take place and the rates at which they occur. But when we refer to the "occasions" of innovation, we are particularly interested in determining the circumstances that initially direct the attention of the organization to the need for or the possibility of changes in the current program. When we refer to "timing," we are particularly interested in determining the pace at which the subsequent steps—following upon the initial directing of attention—are taken.

What determines the type of activity that members of an organization—and here we are particularly concerned with members at a relatively responsible level—engage in? We can cite two factors that affect the *propensity of organization members to engage in an activity.* First, the greater the explicit *time pressure* attached to an activity, the greater the propensity to engage in it. The stimulus of deadlines tends to direct attention to some tasks rather than others (Gaus and Wolcott, 1940, pp. 68–69). Second, the greater the *clarity of goals* associated with an activity, the greater the propensity to engage in it. It is easier to attach rewards and penalties, internal as well as external, to completion of tasks with clear goals than to others.

These propositions lead to a prediction that might be described as the "Gresham's Law" of planning: Daily routine drives out planning. Stated less cryptically, we predict that when an individual is faced both with highly programmed and highly unprogrammed tasks, the former tend to take precedence over the latter even in the absence of strong over-all time pressure.

How, then, does unprogrammed activity ever take place? There are two general conditions (not necessarily exclusive) for bringing it about. They represent ways of affecting either goal clarity or deadlines attached to unprogrammed activity. The first is to allocate resources to goals requiring nonprogrammed activity, and to refuse to provide substitute or alternate goals that can be reached by programmed activity. In organizations, this means to create independently budgeted "planning" units that are kept out of the stream of day-to-day operating tasks (Lanzetta and Roby, 1956).

Deadlines provide the second condition for unprogrammed activity. One of the commonest forms of deadline is not usually regarded as such: the occurrence of a "case" that has to be settled, and that cannot be settled without deciding more general issues. Thus, the process of designing a new piece of equipment may be much accelerated if its immediate acquisition becomes essential because of the breakdown of the old one. Or, a company may develop a general vacation policy because a request by a particular employee for certain vacation privileges has to be granted or refused.

There are many other ways in which deadlines get set. They are commonly set by hierarchical superiors. In other cases they are undertaken voluntarily, but become definite commitments through the reliance of other persons upon them. The process of commitment is generally sequential. An initial commitment is a commitment primarily to undertake search activity. The outcome of the initial search process becomes itself a major determinant of how rapidly and with what resources the activity will continue to be pursued. Sometimes these sequential stages in the search process become formalized, and then are especially visible. They will be discussed further in the next section, when we come to a more detailed description of the processes of program elaboration.

Where an individual or organization unit is carrying on a number of unprogrammed activities, the priorities among these and the relative rates at which they proceed tend to be determined on highly fortuitous grounds. Stimuli that direct attention to one or another of the activities may have considerable short-run influence on the allocation of resources among them. Thus, such devices as tickler files may operate in much the same way, and with almost the same effect, as deadlines.

The Elaboration of Programs

In the present section, we examine in more detail the nature of innovative activity, and particularly the processes by means of which new programs of decision and action are discovered, developed, and put into effect.

Organization Resources for Innovation. The "Gresham's Law" propounded in the previous section implies that if all the resources of an organization are busily employed in carrying on existing programs, the process of initiating new programs will be slow and halting at best. Frequently, when a new program is to be developed, a new organizational unit is created and charged with the task first of elaborating the new program and then carrying it on when it has been elaborated. This procedure provides for a spurt of innovative, program-developing activity—a spurt that automatically diminishes as the program is elaborated and the task shifts gradually from one of planning to one of execution.

This two-phase process in the development of a new organization and a new program has often been commented upon by observers of organizations. For example, it is frequently observed that the initial stage of program elaboration is generally a period of excitement for the personnel engaged in it. They put in a great deal of overtime, and take much pride and pleasure in their work. As programmed activity begins to replace innovation, excitement wanes and feelings of anticlimax are often expressed.

Because such expectations are fairly common, it is often said that the creation of a new unit is the only way to secure innovation that is not excessively bound and hampered by tradition and precedent. Similarly, it is often claimed that the personality traits required of top executives during such an innovating phase are different from the traits required during the subsequent program-execution stage. The differences are in the obvious direction—"idea man" versus orderly bureaucrat.

A major consequence of this distinction between program elaboration and program execution is that decisions made during the former process are rarely re-examined during the latter. Selznick (1957) places great stress on the process of commitment during the program-elaboration stage, particularly as it affects, and is affected by, the power relations between the organization and its environment. More generally, we hypothesize that whatever relations are established in the initial phase will be relatively stable; hence the process of commitment is not reversible.

When an organization has slack money or manpower not committed to going programs, various specializations of function may arise with respect to commitment to new programs and program elaboration. In particular, there may be an "investing" function and an "entrepreneurial" function. The investor is in a position to make decisions on the allocation of resources, including decisions among competing claims; the entrepreneur is the source of program suggestions. The entrepreneur-investor distinction probably has broad significance in describing specialization in decision-making generally. We may distinguish those who are influential by initiating action proposals from those who are influential by being able to implement proposals that have been made. Most analyses of authority, particularly those that stress formal authority, have considered primarily the latter function.

There may be a third function—a "broker" function. Unless there are established channels for processing innovative proposals, the innovator is faced with a problem in discovering an investor who has available resources. Brokers serve to make investors visible to entrepreneurs, and to bring the innovative ideas of entrepreneurs to the attention of investors. By the manner in which he "filters" these communications, the broker can also share in the influence of entrepreneur and investor. In the next section of this chapter we will consider at what levels in the organization entrepreneurial, investment, and brokerage functions will be performed.

If investment decisions were made according to the classical theory of the firm, such considerations as these would be of little import. But when decisions are satisficing rather than optimizing decisions, *resource allocation* to new programs will depend substantially on the *communication structure* through which proposals are processed from entrepreneurs to investors and on the *order of presentation of alternatives*. Thus in this case, as in several others we have mentioned, organizational decisions depend at least as heavily on attention cues as on utility functions.

Sources of Program Ideas. In talking about the sources of program ideas, we need to draw a rough boundary around a unit that can be called the "organization." We need to do this because we wish to hypothesize that most innovations in an organization are a result of borrowing rather than invention. The borrowing may take the form of more or less direct imitation or it may be accomplished by importing new persons into the organization. In either case borrowing saves an organization many of the costs associated with innovation: (*a*) the costs of actual invention, (*b*) the costs of testing, (*c*) the risks of error in evaluation.

To the extent that innovation does occur through borrowing, both the rate of innovation and the *type of innovation* will be functions of exposure—thus of the communication structure of the organization.

With respect to the rate of innovation, we predict: When the environment has changed so as to create a new problem for a number of organizations (e.g., organizations in an industry where demand has shifted) there will be a period after awareness of the problem has spread during which actual innovation will be very slow. Once an acceptable solution to the problem has been invented and introduced in one such organization, it will spread rapidly to the others in the industry (Brown, 1957; Coleman, Katz, and Menzel, 1957). Innovation will be greatly increased for a short time if a group of new persons, from a subculture not previously strongly represented in the organization, is introduced into it.

The type of innovation depends on the specific exposure of the relevant unit in the organization. Thus we would predict a difference in product innovation between companies where research men have their greatest contact with the sales department and companies where research men have contact primarily with professional colleagues in other companies. Similarly, those units in contact with a particular clientele will be the source of innovation relating to the satisfactions of the goals of that clientele (Gaus and Wolcott, 1940, pp. 52–53, 82–84). Finally, program changes innovated in units that are not in direct contact with the outside environment will largely be resource-saving in character.

Selective filtering takes place not only at the boundary of the organization but at every stage in the transmission and elaboration of program proposals. We can think of each such stage as defining a new "boundary" (with varying properties of selective and nonselective permeability) that the proposed innovation must penetrate. The selective properties of each boundary will be functions of the kinds of *expertise* represented there. Since the points in the organization where uncertainty absorption takes place are the points of greatest discretionary judgment, the selective filtering of innovative proposals will be greatest at those points.

A special class of innovations are those that change the organization's model for representing the external world. Since comparison of the model with the world and awareness of discrepancies can occur only at points of uncertainty absorption, these will be the principal points where proposals of changes in the model originate.

Where an organization becomes aware of a problem, and a proposed solution does not accompany the communication of the problem awareness, repertories of problem solutions "stored" in the memories of organization members will be the principal source of solution proposals. As awareness of the problem is communicated through the organization, solutions will be evoked from these repertories and will become attached to it. The broader the problem, the more will the solution be affected by the numbers and diversity in the people among whom it is circulated. With the increase in the number of persons who become aware of the problem (without a corresponding increase in diversity) the number of solutions will increase, but at a negatively accelerated rate.

Check lists and repertories will be used both in finding innovative solutions to problems and also in checking the feasibility of proposed innovations. As a proposed solution is circulated through the organization, particular consequences will be checked by individuals and organization units in whose specialized province they lie. The propositions of the previous paragraph apply to this feasibility testing of ideas as well as to program innovation.

From the last two paragraphs we see that a good deal of the internal communication in an organization concerning new programs is aimed at a search of the organization's (collective) memory for relevant considerations—whether in the nature of program proposals or feasibility tests. The sequential order in which feasibility tests are applied is not particularly significant (although one sequence may be more efficient than another in amending proposals early and rejecting bad proposals promptly, provided the search is thorough).

The Hierarchical Structure of Programs. Most organizational programs, as we have seen in Chapter 6, are comprised of a complex structure of interrelated decisions. We appeal again to the principle of bounded rationality—to the limits of human cognitive powers—to assert that in the discovery and elaboration of new programs, the decision-making process will proceed in stages, and at no time will it be concerned with the "whole" problem in all its complexity, but always with parts of the problem.

It has often been observed that in the search for programs this simplification is achieved by factoring the problem in a hierarchical fashion. As Barnard has described the process (1938, p. 206):

> . . . the process of decision is one of successive approximations—constant refinement of purpose, closer and closer discriminations of fact—in which the march of time is essential. Hence those who make general decisions can only envisage conditions in general and vaguely. The approximations with which they deal are symbols covering a multitude of undisclosed details.

Means-End Analysis. In the present context we are discussing nonprogrammed decision-making, specifically, the process whereby new programs of action are discovered, elaborated, and instituted. Hence, we are concerned primarily with search activities and with processes for evaluating proposals. In the elaboration of new programs, the principal technique of successive approximations is means-end analysis: (1) starting with the general goal to be achieved, (2) discovering a set of means, very generally specified, for accomplishing this goal, (3) taking each of these means, in turn, as a new subgoal and discovering a set of more detailed means for achieving it, etc. (Haberstroh, 1957).

How far does this hierarchy of ends and means go in the direction of specifying detailed means? It proceeds until it reaches a level of concreteness where known, existing programs (generalized means) can be employed to carry out the remaining detail. Hence, the process connects new general purposes with an appropriate subset of the existing repertory of generalized means. When the new goal lies in a relatively novel area, this process may have to go quite far before it comes into contact with that which is already known and programmed; when the goal is of a familiar kind (e.g., a Red Cross disaster program in a particular area), only a few levels need to be constructed of the hierarchy before it can be fitted into available programmed sequences. (Metaphorically, we imagine a whole warehouse full of parts in various stages of prefabrication. The plan for the new structure must be carried to the point where it can be specified in terms of these stocked parts.)

Factorability. To carry out program elaboration by means-end analysis, two conditions must be satisfied. First, at each stage of the process, a feasibility judgment must be made: a judgment that when the time comes to specify the program in greater detail at a later stage, it will in fact be possible to discover such a detailed program. If it later turns out that this judgment was incorrect—no such program can be found—then it is necessary to return to a higher level of the means-end hierarchy and review that part of the process.

Second, each of the means, at any stage of the process, must be relatively independent of all the others. "Independence" here means two things: (a) that the means-end chain should be a genuine hierarchy, so that a given means does not affect to an important extent more than one end at the next higher level of generality; (b) that the feasibility of one of the means does not depend very much upon what other means are employed in the program. Where the conditions are violated, a means-end analysis may still be used to factor the problem into components, but additional steps will be needed in the approximation, so that the interactions among the parts of the program can be evaluated and a revised program developed that takes account of interactions.

Even when the conditions are absent that would make the end-means analysis simple and straightforward, it is still employed as the principal scheme for structuring the decision process. Where there are over-all consistency requirements, these are applied at a later stage in the process, and have only a very general influence on the initial means-end analysis.

A special case of broad practical significance is that in which the interaction among the various parts of the program can be summarized in one or a few conditions of the nature of "resource limitations." In this case, the means-end analysis may be paralleled by a sequence of allocative decisions that will guarantee the feasibility and consistency of the final detailed program.

In the simplest kinds of means-end hierarchy the relation of the specific, detailed means at the lowest level to the "payoff" or goal commonly takes one of two forms: (*a*) the payoff function is additive, i.e., it is a simple sum of partial payoffs attached to the individual means; (*b*) the payoff is all or none, and the specific means, taken collectively, constitute a set of sufficient conditions for the payoff.

Factorization and Group Problem-Solving. Some clues as to what is involved in analysis are provided by studies of problem-solving in small groups. This sort of study contrasts the coordinative techniques available to a group of persons with those of the individual organism. These studies show generally that interpersonal communication is a more primitive and limited coordinative mechanism than are the neural processes. Consequently, factorization of problems into semi-independent subparts is of more crucial importance for group than for individual problem-solving.

Modes of Factorization. There is little theory about the method of performing a means-end analysis. What determines the *type of factorization?* There grows up in any field a repertory of categories; for example, "to have a profitable company, you have to have a marketing process, a production process, and a financing process." How far does the end-means analysis reflect the intrinsic structure of the problem itself; and how far, alternatively, is it a relatively arbitrary, socially conditioned process? We can now add to the earlier discussions some propositions that derive from our present analysis.

When payoffs are additive, the components provide a basis for factorization of the problem. Frequently, this condition is approximately met when the problem involves a sequence of actions through time. Then payoffs in each time period are generally most dependent upon contemporaneous or neighboring actions, and not on more distant actions. Generalizing this, we may say that the intrinsic causal net, and the notions of local causation on which it rests, provide the element of the factorization that may be described as "intrinsic" in the problem. The remainder must be socially conditioned.

One important social influence on factorization is the existing *organizational division of labor.* Existing subunits may themselves be taken as the generalized means in terms of which the problem is to be solved (e.g., the sales department, the production department, the controller's department). In this case, the factorization of the problem will parallel the specializations that are incorporated in the division of work among these organizational units. At a still broader social level, the existing occupational specializations in society may partially dictate the factorization.

We may refer at this point also to the devices, mentioned in the previous chapter, for increasing the degree of independence among program segments by standardization and by inventory-holding. Although those devices refer to the content of programs, rather than to the process of program elaboration, we see that if the former can be factored, this permits the factorization of the latter.

In general, there is an order of temporal priority implicit in the means-end hierarchy. The general goal must be split up into major subgoals before consideration can be given to goals at a lower level. Hence, the mode of subdivision has an influence on the extent to which planning can proceed simultaneously on the several aspects of the problem. The more detailed the factorization of the problem, the more simultaneous activity is possible, hence, the greater the *speed of problem-solving.*

This indicates another respect in which individual problem-solving is to be distinguished from group problem-solving. The advantages of simultaneity in individual problem-solving are limited by the fact that the individual possesses only a single focus of attention, hence can only deal with one aspect of the problem at a time. In organizations, however, there is no limit to the number of attention centers that can be allocated to the parts of a problem. We conclude: (1) that there are important considerations other than the advantages of simultaneous processing for subdividing problems (otherwise factorization would not take place in individual problem-solving); (2) in group problem-solving it may be advantageous to introduce a greater degree of subdivision, even at some loss because of neglected interactions, in order to exploit the possibilities of simultaneous processing. This proposition parallels the corresponding proposition for programmed activities; the more rapidly changing the situation, the greater the degree of self-containment required for individual units.

Organization Level and Innovation

In the previous section, we devoted some attention to specialization of the function of innovation. In the present section we are particularly concerned with the significance of organization *levels* for the processes of innovation. At what levels does innovation take place, and why? Are there qualitative differences in the nature of participation in the innovation process as we move up and down the organization hierarchy? Are there differences in the types of innovation that are likely to be made at different levels?

Goal Structure and Organization Structure. As a first step toward answering these questions, we need to examine the relation between the goal structure in an organization and the hierarchy of organizational units. A means-end analysis of the objectives of an organization and of the activities directed toward these objectives reveals something like the following: (1) We can arrange the means and ends in some kind of hierarchy. The goals at the higher levels of this hierarchy are not, however, operational; i.e., there do not exist agreed-upon criteria for determining the extent to which particular activities or programs of activity contribute to these goals. (2) At lower levels of the means-end hierarchy, the goals are operational—we can measure the contribution of particular activities to these goals. (3) At some level of the hierarchy, a step or two below the highest level of operational goals, we can distinguish individual programs of action—each one contributing to some set of subgoals, and each one, in principle at least, a more or less independent set of activities that can be carried out without much reference to the other programs.

For example, the goal of "providing adequate municipal services" is not operational. The goal of "maintaining a low fire loss rate," however, is more or less operational; and a residential inspection program constitutes a more or less independent set of activities directed toward the (operational) subgoal of preventing fires (which is directed, in turn, toward the goal of maintaining a low fire loss rate).

Along with such a specification of a goal structure, an organization has a hierarchy of formal authority relations. We wish to relate this structure of formal authority to the hierarchy of means and ends previously described. For clarity, call the entire system we are considering the "organization"; the largest subparts, the "departments"; the subdivisions of departments, "divisions."

Consider the whole cluster of means and ends relating to the first operational goal, the cluster of means and ends relating to the second operational goal, etc. Now if we compare these clusters with the organizational units, we will discover variations among organizations with respect to the congruence between goal structure and organization structure.

Each of the clusters may represent the domain of a single department, so that each operational subgoal is the goal of a department. In this case we refer to the departments as *unitary* organizations, the organization as a whole as a *federal* organization. The divisions are *component* organizations of the unitary departments (Simon, Smithburg, and Thompson, 1950, pp. 268–72).

Each of the clusters may lie partly within the province of one or more departments, so that the organization as a whole is the smallest unit that contains an entire cluster. In this case, we refer to the organization as a whole as a *composite* organization, and the departments and divisions as *component* organizations.

There are, of course, other possibilities than the two that have been mentioned, but they are the "pure" types at the ends of the spectrum of possibilities.

Let us propose some slightly more formal definitions. An organization is *unitary* to the extent that the scope of its activity coincides with a means-end structure organized around a single operational goal. An organization is *federal* if it is composed of a number of unitary subdivisions. An organization is *composite* if the scope of its activity encompasses more than one means-end structure organized around operational goals, and if it is not composed of unitary subdivisions. Organizational units that are parts of unitary or composite organizations are referred to as *component* units.

In a hierarchy of organizational units, there will be a lowest level at which units encompass entire goal structures. The units at this level may be unitary or composite. We call this level the *level of integration:* it is the lowest level at which all activities relating to a particular operational goal can be coordinated through the formal authority mechanisms.

One particular form of composite organization deserves notice, because it is a highly prevalent form. The major subdivisions (departments) of an organization may be unitary organizations except for certain "housekeeping" activities that are split off and assigned to special departments that perform these activities for the entire organization. This kind of structure is often called line-and-auxiliary (or, less accurately, "line-and-staff") organization. The "nearly unitary" departments are called line departments, and the departments performing the common housekeeping activities are called auxiliary (or staff) departments. Examples of auxiliary departments are personnel departments, legal departments, purchasing departments, and the like.

From the standpoint of nonprogrammed decision-making, line-and-auxiliary organizations more nearly resemble federal organizations (with the departments as unitary subdivisions) than they do composite organizations. However, which they resemble most closely depends upon *how much* of the activity relating to the operational goals of each line department is separated out and assigned to the auxiliary units. The fewer the auxiliary activities (i.e., the more nearly self-contained are the line departments), the more the organization will operate as a federal structure; the more the auxiliary activities, the more the organization will operate as a composite structure.

The several operational subgoals of an organization may be independent of each other—i.e., they may compete only for organizational resources and in no other way—or they may be directly competitive. Thus, if a company has two product divisions in rather distinct lines of business, the goals of these divisions are likely to be independent rather than competitive. On the other hand, the subgoals of sales department and production department in a business are likely to be competitive in some respects (since courses of action that reduce production costs may make the product harder to sell, whereas sales practices that would attract customers may create production difficulties).

One of the central propositions on operational goals is worth mentioning here: Where a choice of a course of action requires comparison of several operational goals, which are not themselves subgoals to a common operational goal, the decision-making process will be characterized by bargaining. Where the alternatives under consideration are all directed to the same operational goals, analytic decision-making processes will predominate. Hence, the prevalance of bargaining is a symptom *either* that goals are not operational or that they are not shared.

Where goals are ostensibly shared (e.g., agreement that profit maximization is the goal of the firm) but not operational, then two subcases need to be distinguished, a distinction that is significant for the character of the decision-making process. The shared goals may be held in common because they have been internalized by the members of the executive group; or they may be common organization goals that the executives accept because of the reward structure. In the former case, we would expect a good deal of ideological conflict in the bargaining process—genuine disagreement as to which means will best implement the goals. In the latter case, we would expect the bargaining to be of a more opportunistic sort, characterized by rationalizations attempting to "clothe private aims with a public interest."

Finally, we postulate that any concrete program of action will acquire a set of operational goals. They may be the goals that originally motivated the initiation of the program (if those goals were operational); or they may be goals evolved after the program was instituted (if the original goals were not operational). Once acquired, the operational goals will provide the basis for evaluation of the action program.

Specialization of Innovative Functions by Level. At any point in the organization we would expect *sensitivity to innovations* to be a function of *relevance of the innovation to the needs of the specific unit involved.* Thus, the top executive levels of an organizational unit will be particularly sensitive to needs for innovation with respect to the goals of that unit —as distinct from either particular subgoals assigned to subunits or general organizational goals. This sensitivity will be exhibited both (*a*) through what matters attract attention and (*b*) through the priority matters obtain after they have been noticed.

When the goal of a proposed innovation is inappropriate in scope (too broad or too narrow) for the particular organization level that is attending to it, it is likely to be filtered in two respects: it is less apt to receive attention or high priority than it would if it were of the "appropriate" scope; if it receives attention, the action is likely to be a referral for consideration and program elaboration to the appropriate organization level.

Suppose that a program change is proposed, or a new action program. The change may refer to one of the existing operational goals of the organization, or it may lie outside these goals and refer to a nonoperational goal of a federal unit. In the latter case, initiation involves the elaboration of a new program that falls outside the province of any of the existing unitary organizations. This is the "appropriate" and hence the characteristic type of innovative activity that will take place at top levels of a federal organization—the initiation of new programs and the definition of new operational goals that fall outside the present scope of the activities of any of the operational units.

In composite organizations, on the other hand, where the whole organization is the smallest unit that encompasses individual operational goals, we expect to find a wider range of innovative activity at the top levels. The line-and-auxiliary structure may be expected to fall between a federal structure and more extreme types of composite structure; a large part of the innovation with respect to existing operating goals can be expected to be performed at the level of the line departments rather than at the top level.

Where innovation in a federal organization (to a lesser extent, in a line-and-auxiliary organization) relates to existing operational goals, most program elaboration will take place within the unitary subdivisions of the organization; the participation of the higher levels in initiation will be confined largely to program approval. We would predict that for the various innovative functions, the relative participation of unitary subdivisions as compared with overhead levels will vary (from greatest to least) as follows: initiation, elaboration of alternatives, elaboration of consequences, evaluation, recommendation, approval.

A major significance, therefore, of the assignment of an activity or of an operational goal to a definite, recognized organizational unit is that this creates a group of employees concerned with the activity on a full-time basis—an important point of initiation for further program elaboration relating to that goal.

At the same time, in a federal or composite organization, the extent to which innovation involves levels above the unitary components depends partly on the *type of coordination* used. Coordination by feedback will increase, and coordination by plan decrease, the *extent of involvement of top levels in innovation.*

In line-and-auxiliary organizations, the locus and rate of innovation will depend on the degree of self-containment of the unitary line departments. In many cases, potential innovations and new programs require changes in organization structure and in existing programs of activity. In general, the proposer of an innovation will regard elements of structure and existing programs that are more than one or two steps removed from him in the formal structure as "given" and unchangeable. Hence, the greater the *interdependence among subunits* and the higher the dependence of line units on auxiliary units, the less vigorous will be the innovative activity of the line units. When self-containment is low and new activities are to be elaborated, innovation will be consummated only when resources are allocated to interdependent departments as well as to the department originating the innovation.

The extent of involvement of top levels in the innovative process depends on a number of factors in addition to those we have already mentioned. In general, vigorous innovative activity will take place only in organizational units that are not assigned substantial responsibilities for programmed activity. Hence, the level at which innovation will take place depends on the levels at which there are individuals or units having planning responsibilities without heavy operating responsibilities.

In general, the pattern of attention will be less stable, the higher the organizational level. Hence the participation of high levels in particular innovative efforts will vary greatly with the number of other high-priority items on the agenda.

The attention of high levels, particularly those above the unitary organizations, will be directed principally to those proposed innovations that have significance for the maintenance of organization structure, for the survival of the organization, or for activities in more than one organization subdivision. Hence, "procedural" aspects of decisions take on increasing importance as we move upwards in the structure.

If the top levels of an organization have a program for the periodic review of the "organization character," this program will become an important stimulus to innovation at that level and lower levels.

The locus of innovation in an organization also has important consequences for the distribution of power and influence. There are two reasons for this: (1) Because of the asymmetries, noted earlier, between persistence and change, and between inaction and action, an organization's pattern of activity is as much influenced by the processes that originate proposals for activity as by the processes that evaluate proposals. (2) Because of the need for uncertainty absorption—the relatively greater ease of communicating conclusions than of communicating the evidence they are drawn from—the evaluation of proposals is much influenced by the location of the inference processes. A great deal of uncertainty absorption normally takes places near the locus where proposals originate.

That the right to initiate is a source of power is common knowledge to executives in most organizations. It probably accounts for an attitude toward delegation that is also widespread; at each administrative level in an organization, there is a favorable attitude toward centralization of decision-making up to that level, but decentralization from above down to that level.

REFERENCES

Bales, R. F., and F. L. Strodtbeck. Phases in group problem-solving. *Journal of Abnormal and Social Psychology*. 1951, Vol. 46, pp. 485–495.

Brown, W. H. Innovation in the machine tool industry. *Quarterly Journal of Economics*. 1957, Vol. 71, pp. 406–425.

Coleman, J., E. Katz, and H. Menzel. Diffusion of an innovation among physicians. *Sociometry*. 1957, Vol. 20, pp. 253–270.

Cyert, R. M., and J. G. March. Organizational structure and pricing behavior in an oligopolistic market. *American Economic Review.* 1955, Vol. 45, pp. 129–139.

Cyert, R. M., and J. G. March. Organizational factors in the theory of oligopoly. *Quarterly Journal of Economics.* 1956, Vol. 70, pp. 44–64.

Cyert, R. M., H. A. Simon, and D. B. Trow. Observation of a business decision. *Journal of Business.* 1956, Vol. 29, pp. 237–248.

Gaus, J. M., and L. O. Wolcott. *Public Administration and the United States Department of Agriculture.* Chicago, 1940.

de Groot, A. D. *Het Denken van Den Schaker.* Amsterdam, 1946.

Haberstroh, C. J. Processes of internal control in firms. Ph.D. thesis, University of Minnesota, 1957.

Hadamard, J. *The Psychology of Invention in the Mathematical Field.* Princeton, 1945.

Katona, G. *Psychological Analysis of Economic Behavior.* New York, 1951.

Lanzetta, J. T., and T. B. Roby. Group performance as a function of work-distribution patterns and task load. *Sociometry.* 1956, Vol. 19, pp. 95–104.

Lindzey, G., ed. *Handbook of Social Psychology.* Cambridge, Mass., 1954.

March, J. G. An introduction to the theory and measurement of influence. *American Political Science Review.* 1955a, Vol. 49, pp. 431–451.

Marschak, J. Rational behavior, uncertain prospects, and measurable utility. *Econometrica.* 1950, Vol 18, pp. 111–141.

Newell, A., J. C. Shaw, and H. A. Simon. Elements of a theory of human problem solving. *Psychological Review.* 1958, Vol. 65, pp. 151–166.

Plato, *meno.*

Selznick, P. *Leadership in Administration.* Evanston, Ill., 1957.

Simon, H. A. *Administrative Behavior.* New York, 1947.

Simon, H. A. A behavioral model of rational choice. *Quarterly Journal of Economics.* 1955, Vol. 69, pp. 99–118.

Simon, H. A., D. W. Smithburg, and V. A. Thompson. *Public Administration.* New York, 1950.

Thorndike, E. L. The effect of discussion upon the correctness of group decisions when the factor of majority influence is allowed for. *Journal of Social Psychology.* 1938, Vol. 9, pp. 343–362.

Mechanistic and Organic Systems

TOM BURNS AND G. M. STALKER

We are now at the point at which we may set down the outline of the two management systems which represent for us (see Chap. 5) the two polar extremities of the forms which such systems can take when they are adapted to a specific rate of technical and commercial change. The case we have tried to establish from the literature, as from our research experience exhibited in the last chapter, is that the different forms assumed by a working organization do exist objectively and are not merely interpretations offered by observers of different schools.

Both types represent a "rational" form of organization, in that they may both, in our experience, be explicitly and deliberately created and maintained to exploit the human resources of a concern in the most efficient manner feasible in the circumstances of the concern. Not surprisingly, however, each exhibits characteristics which have been hitherto associated with different kinds of interpretation. For it is our contention that empirical findings have usually been classified according to sociological ideology rather than according to the functional specificity of the working organization to its task and the conditions confronting it.

We have tried to argue that these are two formally contrasted forms of management system. These we shall call the mechanistic and organic forms.

A *mechanistic* management system is appropriate to stable conditions. It is characterized by:

(*a*) The specialized differentiation of functional tasks into which the problems and tasks facing the concern as a whole are broken down.

(*b*) The abstract nature of each individual task, which is pursued with techniques and purposes more or less distinct from those of the concern as a whole; i.e., the functionaries tend to pursue the technical improvement of means, rather than the accomplishment of the ends of the concern.

(*c*) The reconciliation, for each level in the hierarchy, of these distinct performances by the immediate superiors, who are also, in turn, responsible for seeing that each is relevant in his own special part of the main task.

(*d*) The precise definition of rights and obligations and technical methods attached to each functional role.

(*e*) The translation of rights and obligations and methods into the responsibilities of a functional position.

(*f*) Hierarchic structure of control, authority and communication.

(*g*) A reinforcement of the hierarchic structure by the location of knowledge of actualities exclusively at the top of the hierarchy, where the final reconciliation of distinct tasks and assessment of relevance is made.[1]

(*h*) A tendency for interaction between members of the concern to be vertical, i.e., between superior and subordinate.

(*i*) A tendency for operations and working

From *The Management of Innovation*, London, Tavistock Publications Ltd., 1961, pp. 119–125. Reprinted with permission of the publisher.

[1] This functional attribute of the head of a concern often takes on a clearly expressive aspect. It is common enough for concerns to instruct all people with whom they deal to address correspondence to the firm (i.e., to its formal head) and for all outgoing letters and orders to be signed by the head of the concern. Similarly, the printed letter heading used by Government departments carries instructions for the replies to be addressed to the Secretary, etc. These instructions are not always taken seriously, either by members of the organization or their correspondents, but in one company this practice was insisted upon and was taken to somewhat unusual lengths; *all* correspondence was delivered to the managing director, who would thereafter distribute excerpts to members of the staff, synthesizing their replies into the letter of reply which he eventually sent. Telephone communication was also controlled by limiting the numbers of extensions, and by monitoring incoming and outgoing calls.

behaviour to be governed by the instructions and decisions issued by superiors.

(*j*) Insistence on loyalty to the concern and obedience to superiors as a condition of membership.

(*k*) A greater importance and prestige attaching to internal (local) than to general (cosmopolitan) knowledge, experience, and skill.

The *organic* form is appropriate to changing conditions, which give rise constantly to fresh problems and unforeseen requirements for action which cannot be broken down or distributed automatically arising from the functional roles defined within a hierarchic structure. It is characterized by:

(*a*) The contributive nature of special knowledge and experience to the common task of the concern.

(*b*) The "realistic" nature of the individual task, which is seen as set by the total situation of the concern.

(*c*) The adjustment and continual re-definition of individual tasks through interaction with others.

(*d*) The shedding of "responsibility" as a limited field of rights, obligations and methods (problems may not be posted upwards, downwards or sideways as being someone's else's responsibility).

(*e*) The spread of commitment to the concern beyond any technical definition.

(*f*) A network structure of control, authority, and communication. The sanctions which apply to the individual's conduct in his working role derive more from presumed community of interest with the rest of the working organization in the survival and growth of the firm, and less from a contractual relationship between himself and a non-personal corporation, represented for him by an immediate superior.

(*g*) Omniscience no longer imputed to the head of the concern; knowledge about the technical or commercial nature of the here and now task may be located anywhere in the network; this location becoming the *ad hoc* centre of control authority and communication.

(*h*) A lateral rather than a vertical direction of communication through the organization, communication between people of different rank, also, resembling consultation rather than command.

(*i*) A content of communication which consists of information and advice rather than instructions and decisions.

(*j*) Commitment to the concern's tasks and to the "technological ethos" of material progress and expansion is more highly valued than loyalty and obedience.

(*k*) Importance and prestige attach to affiliations and expertise valid in the industrial and technical and commercial milieux external to the firm.

One important corollary to be attached to this account is that while organic systems are not hierarchic in the same sense as are mechanistic, they remain stratified. Positions are differentiated according to seniority—i.e., greater expertise. The lead in joint decisions is frequently taken by seniors, but it is an essential presumption of the organic system that the lead, i.e., "authority," is taken by whoever shows himself most informed and capable, i.e., the "best authority." The location of authority is settled by consensus.

A second observation is that the area of commitment to the concern—the extent to which the individual yields himself as a resource to be used by the working organization—is far more extensive in organic than in mechanistic systems. Commitment, in fact, is expected to approach that of the professional scientist to his work, and frequently does. One further consequence of this is that it becomes far less feasible to distinguish "informal" from "formal" organization.

Thirdly, the emptying out of significance from the hierarchic command system, by which co-operation is ensured and which serves to monitor the working organization under a mechanistic system, is countered by the development of shared beliefs about the values and goals of the concern. The growth and accretion of institutionalized values, beliefs, and conduct, in the form of commitments, ideology, and manners, around an image of the concern in its industrial and commercial setting make good the loss of formal structure.

Finally, the two forms of system represent a polarity, not a dichotomy; there are, as we have tried to show, intermediate stages between the extremities empirically known to us. Also, the relation of one form to the other is elastic, so that a concern oscillating between relative stability and relative change may also oscillate between the two forms. A concern may (and frequently does) operate with a management system which includes both types.

The organic form, by departing from the familiar clarity and fixity of the hierarchic structure, is often experienced by the individual manager as an uneasy, embarrassed, or chronically anxious quest for knowledge about what he should be doing, or what is expected of him, and similar apprehensiveness about what others are doing. Indeed, as we shall see later, this kind of response is necessary if the organic form of organization is to work effectively. Understandably, such anxiety finds expression in resentment when the apparent confusion besetting him is not explained. In these situations, all managers some of the time, and many managers all the time, yearn for more definition and structure.

On the other hand, some managers recognize a rationale of nondefinition, a reasoned basis for the practice of those successful firms in which designation of status, function, and line of responsibility and authority has been vague or even avoided.

The desire for more definition is often in effect a wish to have the limits of one's task more neatly defined—to know what and when one doesn't have to bother about as much as to know what one does have to. It follows that the more definition is given, the more omniscient the management must be, so that no functions are left wholly or partly undischarged, no person is overburdend with undelegated responsibility, or left without the authority to do his job properly. To do this, to have all the separate functions attached to individual roles fitting together and comprehensively, to have communication between persons constantly maintained on a level adequate to the needs of each functional role, requires rules or traditions of behaviour proved over a long time and an equally fixed, stable task. The omniscience which may then be credited to the head of the concern is expressed throughout its body through the lines of command extending in a clear, explicitly titled hierarchy of officers and subordinates.

The whole mechanistic form is instinct with this twofold principle of definition and dependence which acts as the frame within which action is conceived and carried out. It works, unconsciously, almost in the smallest minutiae of daily activity. "How late is late?" The answer to this question is not to be found in the rule book, but in the superior. Late is when the boss thinks it is late. Is he the kind of man who thinks 8.00 is the time, and 8.01 is late? Does he think that 8.15 is all right occasionally if it is not a regular thing? Does he think that everyone should be allowed a 5-minute grace after 8.00 but after that they are late?

Settling questions about how a person's job is to be done in this way is nevertheless simple, direct, and economical of effort. We shall, in a later chapter, examine more fully the nature of the protection and freedom (in other respects than his job) which this affords the individual.

One other feature of mechanistic organization needs emphasis. It is a necessary condition of its operation that the individual "works on his own," functionally isolated; he "knows his job," he is "responsible for seeing it's done." He works at a job which is in a sense artificially abstracted from the realities of the situation the concern is dealing with, the accountant "dealing with the costs side," the works manager "pushing production," and so on. As this works out in practice, the rest of the organization becomes part of the problem situation the individual has to deal with in order to perform successfully; i.e., difficulties and problems arising from work or information which has been handed over the "responsibility barrier" between two jobs or departments are regarded as "really" the responsibility of the person from whom they were received. As a design engineer put in, "When you get designers handing over designs completely to production, it's their responsibility now. And you get tennis games played with the responsibility for anything that goes wrong. What happens is that you're constantly getting unsuspected faults arising from characteristics which you didn't think important in the design. If you get to hear of these through a sales person, or a production person, or somebody to whom the design was handed over to in the dim past, then, instead of being a design problem, it's an annoyance caused by that particular person, who can't do his own job—because you'd thought you were finished with that one, and you're on to something else now."

When the assumptions of the form of organization make for preoccupation with specialized tasks, the chances of career success, or of greater influence, depend rather on the relative importance which may be attached to each special function by the superior whose task it is to reconcile and control a number of them. And, indeed, to press the claims of one's job or department for a bigger share of the firm's resources is in many cases regarded as a mark of initiative, of effectiveness, and even of "loyalty to the firm's interests." The state of affairs thus engendered squares with the role of the superior, the man who can see the wood instead of just the trees, and gives it the reinforcement of the aloof detachment belonging to a court of appeal. The ordinary relationship prevailing between individual managers "in charge of" different functions is one of rivalry, a rivalry which may be rendered innocuous to the persons involved by personal friendship or the norms of sociability, but which turns discussion about the situations which constitute the real problems of the concern—how to make products more cheaply, how to sell more, how to allocate resources, whether to curtail activity in one sector, whether to risk expansion in another, and so on—into an arena of conflicting interests.

The distinctive feature of the second, organic system is the pervasiveness of the working organization as an institution. In concrete terms, this makes itself felt in a preparedness to combine with others in serving the general aims of the concern. Proportionately to the rate and extent of change, the less can the omniscience appropriate to command organizations be ascribed to the head of the organization; for executives, and even operatives, in a changing firm it is always theirs to reason why. Furthermore, the less definition can be given to status, roles, and modes of communication, the more do the activities of each member of the organization become determined by the real tasks of the firm as he sees them than by instruction and routine. The individual's job ceases to be self-contained; the only way in which "his" job can be done is by his participating continually with others in the solution of problems which are real to the firm, and put in a language of requirements and activities meaningful to them all. Such methods of working put much heavier demands on the individual. The ways in which these demands are met, or countered, will be enumerated and discussed in Part Three.

We have endeavoured to stress the appropriateness of each system to its own specific set of conditions. Equally, we desire to avoid the suggestion that either system is superior under all circumstances to the other. In particular, nothing in our experience justifies the assumption that mechanistic systems should be superseded by organic in conditions of stability.[2] The beginning of administrative wisdom is the awareness that there is no one optimum type of management system.

[2] A recent instance of this assumption is contained in H. A. Shepard's paper addressed to the Symposium on the Direction of Research Establishments, 1956. "There is much evidence to suggest that the optimal use of human resources in industrial organizations requires a different set of conditions, assumptions, and skills from those traditionally present in industry. Over the past twenty-five years, some new orientations have emerged from organizational experiments, observations and inventions. The new orientations depart radically from doctrines associated with 'Scientific Management' and traditional bureaucratic patterns.

"The central emphases in this development are as follows:

1. Wide participation in decision-making, rather than centralized decision-making.
2. The face-to-face group, rather than the individual, as the basic unit of organization.
3. Mutual confidence, rather than authority, as the integrative force in organization.
4. The supervisor as the agent for maintaining intragroup and intergroup communication, rather than as the agent of higher authority.
5. Growth of members of the organization to greater responsibility, rather than external control of the member's performance or their tasks."

A Behavioral Theory of Organizational Objectives [1]

R. M. CYERT AND J. G. MARCH

Organizations make decisions. They make decisions in the same sense in which individuals make decisions: The organization as a whole behaves as though there existed a central coordination and control system capable of directing the behavior of the members of the organization sufficiently to allow the meaningful imputation of purpose to the total system. Because the central nervous system of most organizations appears to be somewhat different from that of the individual system, we are understandably cautious about viewing organization decision-making in quite the same terms as those applied to individual choice. Nevertheless, organizational choice is a legitimate and important focus of research attention.

As in theories of individual choice, theories of organizational decision-making fall into two broad classes. Normative theorists—particularly economic theorists of the firm—have been dedicated to the improvement of the rationality of organizational choice. Recent developments in the application of mathematics to the solution of economic decision-problems are fully and effectively in such a tradition (Cooper, Hitch, Baumol, Shubik, Schelling, Valavanis, and Ellsberg, 1958). The empirical theory of organizational decision-making has a much more checkered tradition and is considerably less well-developed (March and Simon, 1958).

The present efforts to develop a behavioral theory of organizational decision-making represent attempts to overcome the disparity between the importance of decision-making in organizations and our understanding of how, in fact, such decisions are made. The research as a whole, as well as that part of it discussed below, is based on three initial commitments. The first of these is to develop an explicitly empirical theory rather than a normative one. Our interest is in understanding how complex organizations make decisions, not how they ought to do so. Without denying the importance of normative theory, we are convinced that the major current needs are for empirical knowledge.

The second commitment is to focus on the classic problems long explored in economic theory—pricing, resource allocation, and capital investment. This commitment is intended to overcome some difficulties with existing organization theory. By introducing organizational propositions into models of rather complex systems, we are driven to increase the precision of the propositions considerably. At present, anyone taking existing organization theory as a base for predicting behavior within organizations finds that he can make a number of rather important predictions of the general form: If x varies, y will vary. Only rarely will he find either the parameters of the functions or more elaborate predictions for situations in which the *ceteris paribus* assumptions are not met.

The third commitment is to approximate in the theory the process by which decisions are made by organizations. This commitment to a process-oriented theory is not new. It has typified many organization theorists in the past (Marshall, 1919; Weber, 1947). The sentiment that one should substitute observation for assumption whenever possible seems, *a priori*, reasonable. Traditionally, the major dilemma in organization theory has been between putting into the theory all the features of organizations we think are relevant and thereby making the theory unmanageable, or pruning the model down to a simple system, thereby making it unrealistic. So long as we had to deal primarily with classical mathematics, there was, in fact, little we could do. With the ad-

From *Modern Organization Theory*, Haire (ed.), New York, Wiley, 1959, pp. 76–90. Reprinted by permission of the publisher.

[1] The research is supported by grants from the Graduate School of Industrial Administration, Carnegie Institute of Technology, from the school's funds and from Ford Foundation funds, given for the study of organizational behavior.

vent of the computer and the use of simulation, we have a methodology that will permit us to expand considerably the emphasis on actual process without losing the predictive precision essential to testing (Cyert and March, in press, 1959).

In models currently being developed there are four major sub systems. Since they operate more or less independently, it is possible to conceive them as the four basic sub-theories required for a behavioral theory of organizational decision-making: first, the theory of organizational objectives; second, the theory of organizational expectations; third, the theory of organizational choice; fourth, the theory of organizational implementation. In this paper we discuss the first of these only, the theory of organizational objectives.

The Organization as a Coalition

Let us conceive the organization as a coalition. It is a coalition of individuals, some of them organized into sub-coalitions. In the business organization, one immediately thinks of such coalition members as managers, workers, stockholders, suppliers, customers, lawyers, tax collectors, etc. In the governmental organization, one thinks of such members as administrators, workers, appointive officials, elective officials, legislators, judges, clientele, etc. In the voluntary charitable organization, one thinks of paid functionaries, volunteers, donars, donees, etc.

This view of an organization as a coalition suggests, of course, several different recent treatments of organization theory in which a similar basic position is adopted. In particular, inducements-contributions theory (Barnard, 1938; Simon, 1947), theory of games (von Neumann and Morgenstern, 1947), and theory of teams (Marschak, in this volume). Each of these theories is substantially equivalent on this score. Each specifies:

1. That organizations include individual participants with (at least potentially) widely varying preference orderings.
2. That through bargaining and side payments the participants in the organization enter into a coalition agreement for purposes of the game. This agreement specifies a joint preference-ordering (or organizational objective) for the coalition.
3. That thereafter the coalition can be treated as a single strategist, entrepreneur, or what have you.

Such a formulation permits us to move immediately to modern decision theory, which has been an important part of recent developments in normative organization theory. In our view, however, a joint preference ordering is not a particularly good description of actual organization goals. Studies of organizational objectives suggest that to the extent to which there is agreement on objectives, it is agreement on highly ambiguous goals (Truman, 1951; Kaplan, Dirlam, and Lanzillotti, 1958). Such agreement is undoubtedly important to choice within the organization, but it is a far cry from a clear preference ordering. The studies suggest further that behind this agreement on rather vague objectives there is considerable disagreement and uncertainty about sub-goals; that organizations appear to be pursuing one goal at one time and another (partially inconsistent) goal at another; and that different parts of the organization appear to be pursuing different goals at the same time (Kaplan, Dirlam, and Lanzillotti, 1958; Selznick, 1949). Finally, the studies suggest that most organization objectives take the form of an aspiration level rather than an imperative to "maximize" or "minimize," and that the aspiration level changes in response to experience (Blau, 1955; Alt, 1949).

In the theory to be outlined here, we consider three major ways in which the objectives of a coalition are determined. The first of these is the bargaining process by which the composition and general terms of the coalition are fixed. The second is the internal organizational process of control by which objectives are stabilized and elaborated. The third is the process of adjustment to experience, by which coalition agreements are altered in response to environmental changes. Each of these processes is considered, in turn, in the next three sections of the paper.

Formation of Coalition Objectives through Bargaining

A basic problem in developing a theory of coalition formation is the problem of handling side payments. No matter how we try, we simply cannot imagine that the side payments by which organizational coalitions are formed even remotely satisfy the requirements of unrestricted transferability of utility. Side payments are made in many forms: money, personal treatment, authority, organization policy, etc. A winning coalition does not have a fixed booty which it then divides among its members. Quite to the contrary, the total value of side payments available for division among coalition members is a function of the composition of the coalition; and the total utility of the actual side payments depends on the distribution made within the coalition. There is no conservation of utility.

For example, if we can imagine a situation in which any dyad is a viable coalition (e.g., a partnership to exploit the proposition that two can live more cheaply in coalition than separately), we would predict a greater total utility for those dyads in which needs were complementary than for those in which they were competitive. Generally speaking, therefore, the partitioning of the adult population into male-female dyads is probably more efficient from the point of view of total utility accruing to the coalition than is a partition into sexually homogeneous pairs.

Such a situation makes game theory as it currently exists virtually irrelevant for a treatment of organizational side payments (Luce and Raiffa, 1957). But the problem is in part even deeper than that. The second requirement of such theories as game theory, theory of teams, and inducements-contributions theory, is that after the side payments are made, a joint preference ordering is defined. All conflict is settled by the side-payment bargaining. The employment-contract form of these theories, for example, assumes that the entrepreneur has an objective. He then purchases whatever services he needs to achieve the objective. In return for such payments, employees contract to perform whatever is required of them—at least within the range of permissible requirements. For a price, the employee adopts the "organization" goal.

One strange feature of such a conception is that it describes a coalition asymmetrically. To what extent is it arbitrary that we call wage payments "costs" and dividend payments "profits"—rather than the other way around? Why is it that in our quasi-genetic moments we are inclined to say that in the beginning there was a manager and he recruited workers and capital? For the development of our own theory we make two major arguments. First, the emphasis on the asymmetry has seriously confused our understanding of organizational goals. The confusion arises because ultimately it makes only slightly more sense to say that the goal of a business organization is to maximize profit than it does to say that its goal is to maximize the salary of Sam Smith, Assistant to the Janitor.

Second, despite this there are important reasons for viewing some coalition members as quite different from others. For example, it is clear that employees and management make somewhat different demands on the organization. In their bargaining, side payments appear traditionally to have performed the classical function of specifying a joint preference ordering. In addition, some coalition members (e.g., many stockholders) devote substantially less time to the particular coalition under consideration than do others. It is this characteristic that has usually been used to draw organizational boundaries between "external" and "internal" members of the coalition. Thus, there are important classes of coalition members who are passive most of the time. A condition of such passivity must be that the payment demands they make are of such a character that most of the time they can be met rather easily.

Although we thereby reduce substantially the size and complexity of the coalition relevant for most goal-setting, we are still left with something more complicated than an individual entrepreneur. It is primarily through bargaining within this active group that what we call organizational objectives arise. Side payments, far from being incidental distribution of a fixed, transferable booty, represent the central process of goal specification. That is, a significant number of these payments are in the form of policy commitments.

The distinction between demands for monetary side payments and demands for policy commitments seems to underlie management-oriented treatments of organizations. It is clear that in many organizations this distinction has important ideological and therefore affective connotations. Indeed, the breakdown of the distinction in our generation has been quite consistently violent. Political party-machines in this country have changed drastically the ratio of direct monetary side payments (e.g., patronage, charity) to policy commitments (e.g., economic legislation). Labor unions are conspicuously entering into what has been viewed traditionally as the management prerogatives of policy-making, and demanding payments in that area. Military forces have long since given up the substance—if not entirely the pretense—of being simply hired agents of the regime. The phenomenon is especially obvious in public (Dahl and Lindblom, 1953; Simon, Smithburg, and Thompson, 1950) and voluntary (Sills, 1957; Messinger, 1955) organizations; but all organizations use policy side payments. The marginal cost to other coalition members is typically quite small.

This trend toward policy side payments is particularly observable in contemporary organizations, but the important point is that we have never come close to maintenance of a sharp distinction in the kinds of payments made and demanded. Policy commitments have (one is tempted to say always) been an important part of the method by which coalitions are formed. In fact, an organization that does not use such devices can exist in only a rather special environment.

To illustrate coalition formation under conditions where the problem is not scarce resources for side payments, but varying complementarities of policy demands, imagine a nine-man committee appointed to commission a painting for the village hall. The nine members make individually the following demands:

Committeeman A: The painting must be an abstract monotone.
Committeeman B: The painting must be an impressionistic oil.
Committeeman C: The painting must be small and oval in shape.
Committeeman D: The painting must be small and in oil.
Committeeman E: The painting must be square in shape and multicolored:
Committeeman F: The painting must be an impressionistic square.
Committeeman G: The painting must be a monotone and in oil.
Committeeman H: The painting must be multicolored and impressionistic.
Committeeman I: The painting must be small and oval.

In this case, each potential coalition member makes two simple demands. Assuming that five members are all that are required to make the decision, there are three feasible coalitions. A, C, D, G, and I can form a coalition and commission a small, oval, monotone, oil abstract. B, C, D, H, and I can form a coalition and commission a small, oval, multicolored, impressionistic oil. B, D, E, F, and H can form a coalition and commission a small, square, multicolored, impressionistic oil.

Committeeman D, it will be noted, is in the admirable position of being included in every possible coalition. The reason is clear; his demands are completely consistent with the demands of everyone else.

Obviously at some level of generality the distinction between money and policy payments disappears because any side payment can be viewed as a policy constraint. When we agree to pay someone $35,000 a year, we are constrained to that set of policy decisions that will allow such a payment. Any allocation of scarce resources (such as money) limits the alternatives for the organization. But the scarcity of resources is not the only kind of problem. Some policy demands are strictly inconsistent with other demands. Others are completely complementary. If I demand of the organization that John Jones be shot and you demand that he be sainted, it will be difficult for us to stay in the organization. This is not because either bullets or haloes are in short supply or because we don't have enough money for both.

To be sure, the problems of policy consistency are *in principle* amenable to explicit optimizing behavior. But they add to the computational difficulties facing the coalition members and make it even more obvious why the bargaining leading to side payment and policy agreements is only slightly related to the bargaining anticipated in a theory of omniscient rationality. The tests of short-run feasibility that they represent lead to the familiar complications of conflict, disagreement, and rebargaining.

In the process of bargaining over side payments many of the organizational objectives are defined. Because of the form the bargaining takes, the objectives tend to have several important attributes. First, they are imperfectly rationalized. Depending on the skill of the leaders involved, the sequence of demands leading to the new bargaining, the aggressiveness of various parts of the organization, and the scarcity of resources, the new demands will be tested for consistency with existing policy. But this testing is normally far from complete. Second, some objectives are stated in the form of aspiration-level constraints. Objectives arise in this form when demands which are consistent with the coalition are stated in this form. For example, the demand, "We must allocate ten percent of our total budget to research." Third, some objectives are stated in a non-operational form. In our formulation such objectives arise when potential coalition members have demands which are non-operational or demands which can be made non-operational. The prevalence of objectives in this form can be explained by the fact that non-operational objectives are consistent with virtually any set of objectives.

Stabilization and Elaboration of Objectives

The bargaining process goes on more or less continuously, turning out a long series of commitments. But a description of goal formation simply in such terms is not adequate. Organizational objectives are, first of all, much more stable than would be suggested by such a model, and secondly, such a model does not handle very well the elaboration and clarification of goals through day-to-day bargaining.

Central to an understanding of these phenomena is again an appreciation for the limitations of human capacities and time to devote to any particular aspect of the organizational system. Let us return to our conception of a coalition having monetary and policy side payments. These side-payment agreements are incomplete. They do not anticipate effectively all possible future situations, and they do not identify all considerations that might be viewed as important by the coalition members at some future time. Nevertheless, the coalition members are motivated to operate under the agreements and to develop some mutual control-systems for enforcing them.

One such mutual control-system in many organizations is the budget. A budget is a highly explicit elaboration of previous commitments. Although it is usually viewed as an asymmetric control-device (i.e., a means for superiors to control subordinates), it is clear that it represents a form of mutual control. Just as there are usually severe costs to the department in exceeding the budget, so also are there severe costs to other members of the coalition if the budget is not paid in full. As a result, budgets in every organization tend to be self-confirming.

A second major, mutual control-system is the allocation of functions. Division of labor and specialization are commonly treated in management textbooks simply as techniques of rational organization. If, however, we consider the allocation of functions in much the way we would normally view the allocation of resources during budgeting, a somewhat different picture emerges. When we define the limits of discretion, we constrain the individual or sub-group from acting outside those limits. But at the same time, we constrain any other members of the coalition from prohibiting action within those limits. Like the allocation of resources in a budget, the allocaton of discretion in an organization chart is largely self-confirming.

The secondary bargaining involved in such mutual control-systems serves to elaborate and revise the coalition agreements made on entry (Thompson and McEwen, 1958). In the early life of an organization, or after some exceptionally drastic organizational upheaval, this elaboration occurs in a context where very little is taken as given. Relatively deliberate action must be taken on everything from pricing policy to paper-clip policy. Reports from individuals who have lived through such early stages emphasize the lack of structure that typifies settings for day-to-day decisions (Simon, 1953).

In most organizations most of the time, however, the elaboration of objectives occurs within much tighter constraints. Much of the situation is taken as given. This is true primarily because organizations have memories in the form of precedents, and individuals in the coalition are strongly motivated to accept the precedents as binding. Whether precedents are formalized in the shape of an official standard-operating-procedure or are less formally stored, they remove from conscious consideration many agreements, decisions, and commitments that might well be subject to renegotiation in an organization without a memory (Cyert and March, to be published, 1960). Past bargains become precedents for present situations. A budget becomes a precedent for future budgets. An allocation of functions becomes a precedent for future allocations. Through all the well-known mechanisms, the coalition agreements of today are institutionalized into semi-permanent arrangements. A number of administrative aphorisms come to mind: an unfilled position disappears; see an empty office and fill it up; there is nothing temporary under the sun. As a result of organizational precedents, objectives exhibit much greater stability than would typify a pure bargaining situation. The "accidents" of organizational genealogy tend to be perpetuated.

Changes in Objectives through Experience

Although considerably stabilized by memory and institutionalization-phenomena, the demands made on the coalition by individual members do change with experience. Both the nature of the demands and their quantitative level vary over time.

Since many of the requirements specified by individual participants are in the form of attainable goals rather than general maximizing constraints, objectives are subject to the usual phenomena associated with aspiration levels. As an approximation to the aspiration-level model, we can take the following set of propositions:

1. In the steady state, aspiration level exceeds achievement by a small amount.
2. Where achievement increases at an increasing rate, aspiration level will exhibit short-run lags behind achievement.
3. Where achievement decreases, aspiration level will be substantially above achievement.

These propositions derive from simpler assumptions requiring that current aspiration be an optimistic extrapolation of past achievement and past aspiration. Although such assumptions are sometimes inappropriate, the model seems to be consistent with a wide range of human goal-setting behavior (Lewin, Dembo, Festinger, and Sears, 1944). Two kinds of achievement are, of course, important. The first is the achievement of the participant himself. The second is the achievement of others in his reference group (Festinger, 1954).

Because of these phenomena, our theory of organizational objectives must allow for drift in the demands of members of the organization. No one doubts that aspirations with respect to monetary compensation vary substantially as a function of payments received. So also do aspirations regarding advertising budget, quality of product, volume of sales, product mix, and capital investment. Obviously, until we know a great deal more than we do about the parameters of the relation between achievement and aspiration we can make only relatively weak predictions. But some of these predictions are quite useful, particularly in conjunction with search theory (Cyert, Dill, and March, 1958).

For example, two situations are particularly intriguing. What happens when the rate of improvement in the environment is great enough so that it outruns the upward adjustment of aspiration? Second, what happens when the environment becomes less favorable? The general answer to both of these questions involves the concept of organizational slack (Cyert and March, 1956). When the environment outruns aspiration-level adjustment, the organization secures, or at least has the potentiality of securing, resources in excess of its demands. Some of these resources are simply not obtained—although they are available. Others are used to meet the revised demands of those members of the coalition whose demands adjust most rapidly—usually those most deeply involved in the organization. The excess resources would not be subject to very general bargaining because they do not involve allocation in the face of scarcity. Coincidentally perhaps, the absorption of excess resources also serves to delay aspiration-level adjustment by passive members of the coalition.

When the environment becomes less favorable, organizational slack represents a cushion. Resource scarcity brings on renewed bargaining and tends to cut heavily into the excess payments introduced during plusher times. It does not necessarily mean that precisely those demands that grew abnormally during better days are pruned abnormally during poorer ones; but in general we would expect this to be approximately the case.

Some attempts have been made to use these very simple propositions to generate some meaningful empirical predictions. Thus, we predict that, discounting for the economies of scale, relatively successful firms will have higher unit-costs than relatively unsuccessful ones. We predict that advertising expenditures will be a function of sales in the previous time period at least as much as the reverse will be true.

The nature of the demands also changes with experience in another way. We do not conceive that individual members of the coalition will have a simple listing of demands, with only the quantitative values changing over time. Instead we imagine each member as having a rather disorganized file case full of demands. At any point in time, the member attends to only a rather small subset of his demands, the number and variety depending again on the extent of his involvement in the organization and on the demands of his other commitments on his attention.

Since not all demands are attended to at the same time, one important part of the theory of organizational objectives is to predict when particular units in the organization will attend to particular goals. Consider the safety goal in a large corporation. For the safety engineers, this is a very important goal most of the time. Other parts of the organization rarely even consider it. If, however, the organization has some drastic experience (e.g., a multiple fatality), attention to a safety goal is much more widespread and safety action quite probable.

Whatever the experience, it shifts the attention-focus. In some (as in the safety example), adverse experience suggests a problem area to be attacked. In others, solutions to problems stimulate attention to a particular goal. An organization with an active personnel-research department will devote substantial attention to personnel goals not because it is necessarily a particularly pressing problem but because the sub-unit keeps generating solutions that remind other members of the organization of a particular set of objectives they profess.

The notion of attention-focus suggests one reason why organizations are successful in surviving with a large set of unrationalized goals. They rarely see the conflicting objectives simultaneously. For example, let us reconsider the case of the pair of demands that John Jones be either (*a*) shot or (*b*) sainted. Quite naturally, these were described as inconsistent demands. Jones cannot be simultaneously shot and sainted. But the emphasis should be on *simultaneously*. It is quite feasible for him to be first shot and then sainted, or vice versa. It is logically feasible because a halo can be attached as firmly to a dead man as to a live one and a saint is as susceptible to bullets as a sinner. It is organizationally feasible because the probability is low that both of these demands will be attended to simultaneously.

The sequential attention to goals is a simple mechanism. A consequence of the mechanism is that organizations ignore many conditions that outside observers see as direct contradictions. They are contradictions only if we imagine a well-established, joint preference ordering or omniscient bargaining. Neither condition exists in an organization. If we assume that attention to goals is limited, we can explain the absence of any strong pressure to resolve apparent internal inconsistencies. This is not to argue that all conflicts involving objectives can be resolved in this way, but it is one important mechanism that deserves much more intensive study.

Constructing a Predictive Theory

Before the general considerations outlined above can be transformed into a useful predictive theory, a considerable amount of precision must be added. The introduction of precision depends, in turn, on the future success of research into the process of coalition formation. Nevertheless, some steps can be taken now to develop the theory. In particular, we can specify a general framework for a theory and indicate its needs for further development.

We assume a set of coalition members, actual or potential. Whether these members are individuals or groups of individuals is unimportant. Some of the possible subsets drawn from this set are viable coalitions. That is, we will identify a class of combinations of members such that any of these combinations meet the minimal standards imposed by the external environment on the organization. Patently, therefore, the composition of the viable set of coalitions will depend on environmental conditions.

For each of the potential coalition members we require a set of demands. Each such individual set is partitioned into an active part currently attended to and an inactive part currently ignored. Each demand can be characterized by two factors: first, its marginal resource requirements, given the demands of all possible other combinations of demands from potential coalition members; second, its marginal consistency with all possible combinations of demands from potential coalition members.

For each potential coalition member we also require a set of problems, partitioned similarly into an active and an inactive part.

This provides us with the framework of the theory. In addition, we need five basic mechanisms. First, we need a mechanism that changes the quantitative value of the demands over time. In our formulation, this becomes a version of the basic aspiration-level and mutual control theory outlined earlier.

Second, we need an attention-focus mechanism that transfers demands among the three possible states: active set, inactive set, not-considered set. We have said that some organizational participants will attend to more demands than other participants and that for all participants some demands will be considered at one time and others at other times. But we know rather little about the actual mechanisms that control this attention factor.

Third, we need a similar attention-focus mechanism for problems. As we have noted, there is a major interaction between what problems are attended to and what demands are attended to, but research is also badly needed in this area.

Fourth, we need a demand-evaluation procedure that is consistent with the limited capacities of human beings. Such a procedure must specify how demands are checked for consistency and for their resource demands. Presumably, such a mechanism will depend heavily on a rule that much of the problem is taken as given and only incremental changes are considered.

Fifth, we need a mechanism for choosing among the potentially viable coalitions. In our judgment, this mechanism will probably look much like the recent suggestions of game theorists that only small changes are evaluated at a time (Luce and Raiffa, 1957).

Given these five mechanisms and some way of expressing environmental resources, we can describe a process for the determination of objectives in an organization that will exhibit the important attributes of organizational goal-determination. At the moment, we can approximate some of the required functions. For example, it has been possible to introduce into a complete model a substantial part of the first mechanism, and some elements of the second, third, and fourth (Cyert, Feigenbaum, and March, 1959). Before the theory can develop further, however, and particularly before it can focus intensively on the formation of objectives through bargaining and coalition formation (rather than on the revision of such objectives and the selective attention to them), we require greater empirical clarification of the phenomena involved.

REFERENCES

Alt, R. M. 1949. The internal organization of the firm and price formation: an illustrative case. *Quarterly J. of Econ.* **63**, 92–110.

Barnard, C. I. 1938. *The functions of the executive.* Harvard University Press, Cambridge.

Blau, P. M. 1955. *The dynamics of bureaucracy.* University of Chicago Press, Chicago.

Cooper, W. W., C. Hitch, W. J. Baumol, M. Shubik, T. C. Schelling, S. Valavanis, and D. Ellsberg. 1958. Economics and operations research: a symposium. *The Rev. of Econ. and Stat.* **40**, 195–229.

Cyert, R. M., and J. G. March. 1956. Organizational factors in the theory of oligopoly. *Quarterly J. of Econ.* **70**, 44–64.

Cyert, R. M., W. R. Dill, and J. G. March. 1958. The role of expectations in business decision making. *Adm. Sci. Quarterly.* **3**, 307–340.

Cyert, R. M., and J. G. March. To be published, 1959. Research on a behavioral theory of the firm. *Management Rev.*

Cyert, R. M., E. A. Feigenbaum, and J. G. March. 1959. Models in a behavioral theory of the firm. *Behavioral Sci.* **4**, 81–95.

Cyert, R. M., and J. G. March. To be published, 1960. Business operating procedures. In B. von H. Gilmer (ed.), *Industrial psychology.* McGraw-Hill, New York.

Dahl, R. A., and C. E. Lindblom. 1953. *Politics, economics, and welfare.* Harper, New York.

Festinger, L. 1954. A theory of social comparison processes. *Human Relations.* **7**, 117–140.

Kaplan, A. D. H., J. B. Dirlam, and R. F. Lanzillotti. 1958. *Pricing in big business.* Brookings Institution, Washington.

Lewin, L., T. Dembo, L. Festinger, and P. Sears. 1944. Level of aspiration. In J. M. Hunt (ed.), *Personality and the behavior disorders.* Vol. I. Ronald, New York.

Luce, R. D., and H. Raiffa. 1957. *Games and decisions.* Wiley, New York. Chaps. 7 and 10.

March, J. G., and H. A. Simon. 1958. *Organizations.* Wiley, New York.

Marschak, J. Efficient and viable organization forms. In this volume.

Marshall, A. 1919. *Industry and trade.* Macmillan, London.

Messinger, S. L. 1955. Organizational transformation: a case study of a declining social movement. *Amer. sociol. Rev.* **20**, 3–10.

Selznick, P. 1949. *TVA and the grass roots.* University of California Press, Berkeley.

Sills, D. L. 1957. *The volunteers.* Free Press, Glencoe, Ill.

Simon, H. A. 1947. *Administrative behavior.* Macmillan, New York.

Simon, H. A., D. W. Smithburg, and V. A. Thompson. 1950. *Public administration.* Knopf, New York. Chaps. 18 and 19.

Simon, H. A. 1953. Birth of an organization: the economic cooperation administration. *Public Adm. Rev.* **13**, 227–236.

Thompson, J. D., and W. J. McEwen. 1958. Organizational goals and environment; goal setting as an interaction process. *Amer. sociol. Rev.* **23**, 23–31.

Truman, D. B. 1951. *The governmental process.* Knopf, New York. Pages 282–287.

von Neumann, J., and O. Morgenstern. 1947. *Theory of games and economic behavior.* Second edition. Princeton University Press, Princeton.

Weber, M. 1947. *The theory of social and economic organization.* Translated by A. M. Henderson and T. Parsons. Oxford University Press, New York.

Foundations of the Theory of Organization

PHILIP SELZNICK

Trades unions, governments, business corporations, political parties, and the like are formal structures in the sense that they represent rationally ordered instruments for the achievement of stated goals. "Organization," we are told, "is the arrangement of personnel for facilitating the accomplishment of some agreed purpose through the allocation of functions and responsibilities." [1] Or, defined more generally, formal organization is "a system of consciously coordinated activities or forces of two or more persons." [2] Viewed in this light, formal organization is the structural expression of rational action. The mobilization of technical and managerial skills requires a pattern of coordination, a systematic ordering of positions and duties which defines a chain of command and makes possible the administrative integration of specialized functions. In this context *delegation* is the primordial organizational act, a precarious venture which requires the continuous elaboration of formal mechanisms of coordination and control. The security of all participants, and of the system as a whole, generates a persistent pressure for the institutionalization of relationships, which are thus removed from the uncertainties of individual fealty or sentiment. Moreover, it is necessary for the relations within the structure to be determined in such a way that individuals will be interchangeable and the organization will thus be free of dependence upon personal qualities.[3] In this way, the formal structure becomes subject to calculable manipulation, an instrument of rational action.

But as we inspect these formal structures we begin to see that they never succeed in conquering the non-rational dimension of organizational behavior. The latter remain at once indispensable to the continued existence of the system of coordination and at the same time the source of friction, dilemma, doubt, and ruin. This fundamental paradox arises from the fact that rational action systems are inescapably imbedded in an institutional matrix, in two significant senses: (1) the action system—or the formal structure of delegation and control which is its organizational expression—is itself only an aspect of a concrete social structure made up of individuals who may interact as *wholes*, not simply in terms of their formal roles within the system; (2) the formal system, and the social structure within which it finds concrete existence, are alike subject to the pressure of an institutional environment to which some over-all adjustment must be made. The formal administrative design can never adequately or fully reflect the concrete organization to which it refers, for the obvious reason that no abstract plan or pattern can—or may, if it is to be useful—exhaustively describe an empirical totality. At the same time, that which is not included in the abstract design (as reflected, for example, in a staff-and-line organization chart) is vitally relevant to the maintenance and development of the formal system itself.

Organization may be viewed from two standpoints which are analytically distinct but which are empirically united in a context of reciprocal consequences. On the one hand, any concrete organizational system is an *economy;* at the same time, it is an *adaptive social structure*. Considered as an economy, organization is a system of relationships which define the availability of scarce resources and which may be manipulated in terms of efficiency and

From *American Sociological Review*, Vol. 13, Feb. 1948, pp. 25–35. Reprinted with permission of the author and the publisher, American Sociological Association.

[1] John M. Gaus, "A Theory of Organization in Public Administration," in *The Frontiers of Public Administration* (Chicago: University of Chicago Press, 1936), p. 66.

[2] Chester I. Barnard, *The Functions of the Executive* (Cambridge: Harvard University Press, 1938), p. 73.

[3] Cf. Talcott Parsons' generalization (after Max Weber) of the "law of the increasing rationality of action systems," in *The Structure of Social Action* (New York: McGraw-Hill, 1937), p. 752.

effectiveness. It is the economic aspect of organization which commands the attention of management technicians and, for the most part, students of public as well as private administration.[4] Such problems as the span of executive control, the role of staff or auxiliary agencies, the relation of headquarters to field offices, and the relative merits of single or multiple executive boards are typical concerns of the science of administration. The coordinative scalar, and functional principles, as elements of the theory of organization, are products of the attempt to explicate the most general features of organization as a "technical problem" or, in our terms, as an economy.

Organization as an economy is, however, necessarily conditioned by the organic states of the concrete structure, outside of the systematics of delegation and control. This becomes especially evident as the attention of leadership is directed toward such problems as the legitimacy of authority and the dynamics of persuasion. It is recognized implicitly in action and explicitly in the work of a number of students that the possibility of manipulating the system of coordination depends on the extent to which that system is operating within an environment of effective inducement to individual participants and of conditions in which the stability of authority is assured. This is in a sense the fundamental thesis of Barnard's remarkable study, *The Functions of the Executive*. It is also the underlying hypothesis which makes it possible for Urwick to suggest that "proper" or formal channels in fact function to "confirm and record" decisions arrived at by more personal means.[5] We meet it again in the concept of administration as a process of education, in which the winning of consent and support is conceived to be a basic function of leadership.[6] In short, it is recognized that control and consent cannot be divorced even within formally authoritarian structures.

The indivisibility of control and consent makes it necessary to view formal organizations as *cooperative* systems, widening the frame of reference of those concerned with the manipulation of organizational resources. At the point of action, of executive decision, the economic aspect of organization provides inadequate tools for control over the concrete structure. This idea may be readily grasped if attention is directed to the role of the individual within the organizational economy. From the standpoint of organization as a formal system, persons are viewed functionally, in respect to their *roles*, as participants in assigned segments of the cooperative system. But in fact individuals have a propensity to resist depersonalization, to spill over the boundaries of their segmentary roles, to participate as *wholes*. The formal systems (at an extreme, the disposition of "rifles" at a military perimeter) cannot take account of the deviations thus introduced, and consequently break down as instruments of control when relied upon alone. The whole individual raises new problems for the organization, partly because of the needs of his own personality, partly because he brings with him a set of established habits as well, perhaps, as commitments to special groups outside of the organization.

Unfortunately for the adequacy of formal systems of coordination, the needs of individuals do not permit a single-minded attention to the stated goals of the system within which they have been assigned. The hazard inherent in the act of delegation derives essentially from this fact. Delegation is an organizational act, having to do with formal assignments of functions and powers. Theoretically, these assignments are made to roles or official positions, not to individuals as such. In fact, however, delegation necessarily involves concrete individuals who have interests and goals which do not always coincide with the goals of the formal system. As a consequence, individual personalities may offer resistance to the demands made upon them by the official conditions of delegation. These resistances are not accounted

[4] See Luther Gulick and Lydall Urwick (editors), *Papers on the Science of Administration* (New York: Institute of Public Administration, Columbia University, 1937); Lydall Urwick, *The Elements of Administration* (New York, Harper, 1943); James D. Mooney and Alan C. Reiley, *The Principles of Organization* (New York: Harper, 1939); H. S. Dennison, *Organization Engineering* (New York: McGraw-Hill, 1931).

[5] Urwick, *The Elements of Administration, op. cit.*, p. 47.

[6] See Gaus, *op. cit.* Studies of the problem of morale are instances of the same orientation, having received considerable impetus in recent years from the work of the Harvard Business School group.

for within the categories of coordination and delegation, so that when they occur they must be considered as unpredictable and accidental. Observations of this type of situation within formal structures are sufficiently commonplace. A familiar example is that of delegation to a subordinate who is also required to train his own replacement. The subordinate may resist this demand in order to maintain unique access to the "mysteries" of the job, and thus insure his indispensability to the organization.

In large organizations, deviations from the formal system tend to become institutionalized, so that "unwritten laws" and informal associations are established. Institutionalization removes such deviations from the realm of personality differences, transforming them into a persistent structural aspect of formal organizations.[7] These institutionalized rules and modes of informal cooperation are normally attempts by participants in the formal organization to control the group relations which form the environment of organizational decisions. The informal patterns (such as cliques) arise spontaneously, are based on personal relationships, and are usually directed to the control of some specific situation. They may be generated anywhere within a hierarchy, often with deleterious consequences for the formal goals of the organization, but they may also function to widen the available resources of executive control and thus contribute to rather than hinder the achievement of the stated objectives of the organization. The deviations tend to force a shift away from the purely formal system as the effective determinant of behavior to (1) a condition in which informal patterns buttress the formal, as through the manipulation of sentiment within the organization in favor of established authority; or (2) a condition wherein the informal controls effect a consistent modification of formal goals, as in the case of some bureaucratic patterns.[8] This trend will eventually result in the formalization of erstwhile informal activities, with the cycle of deviation and transformation beginning again on a new level.

The relevance of informal structures to organizational analysis underlines the significance of conceiving of formal organizations as cooperative systems. When the totality of interacting groups and individuals becomes the object of inquiry, the latter is not restricted by formal, legal, or procedural dimensions. The *state of the system* emerges as a significant point of analysis, as when an internal situation charged with conflict qualifies and informs actions ostensibly determined by formal relations and objectives. A proper understanding of the organizational process must make it possible to interpret changes in the formal system—new appointments or rules or reorganizations—in their relation to the informal and unavowed ties of friendship, class loyalty, power cliques, or external commitment. This is what it means "to know the score."

The fact that the involvement of individuals as whole personalities tends to limit the adequacy of formal systems of coordination does not mean that organizational characteristics are those of individuals. The organic, emergent character of the formal organization considered as a cooperative system must be recognized. This means that the *organization* reaches decisions, takes action, and makes adjustments. Such a view raises the question of the relation between organizations and persons. The significance of theoretical emphasis upon the cooperative *system* as such is derived from the insight that certain actions and consequences are enjoined independently of the personality of the individuals involved. Thus, if reference is made to the "organization-paradox"—the tension created by the inhibitory consequences of certain types of informal structures within organizations—this does not mean that individuals themselves are in quandaries. It is the nature of the interacting consequences of divergent interests within the organization which creates the condition, a result which may obtain independently of the consciousness or the qualities of the individual participants. Similarly, it seems useful to insist that there are qualities and needs of leader*ship*,

[7] The creation of informal structures within various types of organizations has received explicit recognition in recent years. See F. J. Roethlisberger and W. J. Dickson, *Management and the Worker* (Cambridge: Harvard University Press, 1941), p. 524; also Barnard, *op. cit.*, c. ix; and Wilbert E. Moore, *Industrial Relations and the Social Order* (New York: Macmillan, 1946), chap. xv.

[8] For an analysis of the latter in these terms, see Philip Selznick, "An Approach to a Theory of Bureaucracy," *American Sociological Review*, Vol. VIII, No. 1 (February, 1943).

having to do with position and role, which are persistent despite variations in the character or personality of individual leaders themselves.

Rational action systems are characteristic of both individuals and organizations. The conscious attempt to mobilize available internal resources (e.g., self-discipline) for the achievement of a stated goal—referred to here as an economy or a formal system—is one aspect of individual psychology. But the personality considered as a dynamic system of interacting wishes, compulsions, and restraints defines a system which is at once essential and yet potentially deleterious to what may be thought of as the "economy of learning" or to individual rational action. At the same time, the individual personality is an adaptive structure, and this, too, requires a broader frame of reference for analysis than the categories of rationality. On a different level, although analogously, we have pointed to the need to consider organizations as cooperative systems and adaptive structures in order to explain the context of and deviations from the formal systems of delegation and coordination.

To recognize the sociological relevance of formal structures is not, however, to have constructed a theory of organization. It is important to set the framework of analysis, and much is accomplished along this line when, for example, the nature of authority in formal organizations is reinterpreted to emphasize the factors of cohesion and persuasion as against legal or coercive sources.[9] This redefinition is logically the same as that which introduced the conception of the self as social. The latter helps make possible, but does not of itself fulfill, the requirements for a dynamic theory of personality. In the same way, the definition of authority as conditioned by sociological factors of sentiment and cohesion—or more generally the definition of formal organizations as cooperative systems—only sets the stage, as an initial requirement, for the formulation of a theory of organization.

Structural-Functional Analysis

Cooperative systems are constituted of individuals interacting as wholes in relation to a formal system of coordination. The concrete structure is therefore a resultant of the reciprocal influences of the formal and informal aspects of organization. Furthermore, this structure is itself a totality, an adaptive "organism" reacting to influences upon it from an external environment. These considerations help to define the objects of inquiry; but to progress to a system of predicates *about* these objects it is necessary to set forth an analytical method which seems to be fruitful and significant. The method must have a relevance to empirical materials, which is to say, it must be more specific in its reference than discussions of the logic or methodology of social science.

The organon which may be suggested as peculiarly helpful in the analysis of adaptive structures has been referred to as "structural-functional analysis."[10] This method may be characterized in a sentence: *Structural-functional analysis relates contemporary and variable behavior to a presumptively stable system of needs and mechanisms.* This means that a given empirical system is deemed to have basic needs, essentially related to self-maintenance; the system develops repetitive means of self-defense; and day-to-day activity is interpreted in terms of the function served by that activity for the maintenance and defense of the system. Put this generally, the approach is applicable on any level in which the determinate "states" of empirically isolable systems undergo self-impelled and repetitive transformations when impinged upon by external conditions. This self-impulsion suggests the relevance of the term "dynamic," which is often used in referring to physiological, psychological, or social systems to which this type of analysis has been applied.[11]

[9] Robert Michels, "Authority," *Encyclopedia of the Social Sciences* (New York: Macmillan, 1931), pp. 319ff.; also Barnard, *op. cit.*, c. xii.

[10] For a presentation of this approach having a more general reference than the study of formal organizations, see Talcott Parsons, "The Present Position and Prospects of Systematic Theory in Sociology," in Georges Gurvitch and Wilbert E. Moore (ed.), *Twentieth Century Sociology* (New York: The philosophical Library, 1945).

[11] "Structure" refers to both the relationships within the system (formal plus informal patterns in organization) and the set of needs and modes of satisfaction which characterize the given type of empirical system. As the utilization of this type of analysis proceeds, the concept of "need" will require further clarification. In particular, the imputation of a "stable set of needs" to organizational systems must not function as a new instinct

It is a postulate of the structural-functional approach that the basic need of all empirical systems is the maintenance of the integrity and continuity of the system itself. Of course, such a postulate is primarily useful in directing attention to a set of "derived imperatives" or needs which are sufficiently concrete to characterize the system at hand.[12] It is perhaps rash to attempt a catalogue of these imperatives for formal organizations, but some suggestive formulation is needed in the interests of setting forth the type of analysis under discussion. In formal organizations, the "maintenance of the system" as a generic need may be specified in terms of the following imperatives:

1. *The Security of the Organization as a Whole in relation to Social Forces in its Environment.* This imperative requires continuous attention to the possibilities of encroachment and to the forestalling of threatened aggressions or deleterious (though perhaps unintended) consequences from the actions of others.

2. *The Stability of the Lines of Authority and Communication.* One of the persistent reference-points of administrative decision is the weighing of consequences for the continued capacity of leadership to control and to have access to the personnel or ranks.

3. *The Stability of Informal Relations within the Organization.* Ties of sentiment and self-interest are evolved as unacknowledged but effective mechanisms of adjustment of individuals and sub-groups to the conditions of life within the organization. These ties represent a cementing of relationships which sustains the formal authority in day-to-day operations and widens opportunities for effective communication.[13] Consequently, attempts to "upset" the informal structure, either frontally or as an indirect consequence of formal reorganization, will normally be met with considerable resistance.

4. *The Continuity of Policy and of the Sources of its Determination.* For each level within the organization, and for the organization as a whole, it is necessary that there be a sense that action taken in the light of a given policy will not be placed in continuous jeopardy. Arbitrary or unpredictable changes in policy undermine the significance of (and therefore the attention to) day-to-day action by injecting a note of capriciousness. At the same time, the organization will seek stable roots (or firm statutory authority or popular mandate) so that a sense of the permanency and legitimacy of its acts will be achieved.

5. *A Homogeneity of Outlook with respect to the Meaning and Role of the Organization.* The minimization of disaffection requires a unity derived from a common understanding of what the character of the organization is meant to be. When this homogeneity breaks down, as in situations of internal conflict over basic issues, the continued existence of the organization is endangered. On the other hand, one of the signs of "healthy" organization is the ability to effectively orient new members and readily slough off those who cannot be adapted to the established outlook.

This catalogue of needs cannot be thought of as final, but it approximates the stable system generally characteristic of formal organizations. These imperatives are derived, in the sense that they represent the conditions for survival or self-maintenance of cooperative systems of organized action. An inspection of these needs suggests that organizational survival is intimately connected with the struggle for relative prestige, both for the organization and for elements and individuals within it. It may therefore be useful to refer to a *prestige-survival motif* in organizational behavior as a short-hand way of relating behavior to needs, especially when the exact nature of the needs

theory. At the same time, we cannot avoid using these inductions as to generic needs, for they help us to stake out our area of inquiry. The author is indebted to Robert K. Merton who has, in correspondence, raised some important objections to the use of the term "need" in this context.

[12] For "derived imperative" see Bronislaw Malinowski, *The Dynamics of Culture Change* (New Haven: Yale University Press, 1945), pp. 44ff. For the use of "need" in place of "motive" see the same author's *A Scientific Theory of Culture* (Chapel Hill: University of North Carolina Press, 1944), pp. 89–90.

[13] They may also *destroy* those relationships, as noted above, but the need remains, generating one of the persistent dilemmas of leadership.

remains in doubt. However, it must be emphasized that prestige-survival in organizations does not derive simply from like motives in individuals. Loyalty and self-sacrifice may be individual expressions of organizational or group egotism and self-consciousness.

The concept of organizational need directs analysis to the *internal relevance* of organizational behavior. This is especially pertinent with respect to discretionary action undertaken by agents manifestly in pursuit of formal goals. The question then becomes one of relating the specific act of discretion to some presumptively stable organizational need. In other words, it is not simply action plainly oriented internally (such as in-service training) but also action presumably oriented externally which must be inspected for its relevance to internal conditions. This is of prime importance for the understanding of bureaucratic behavior, for it is of the essence of the latter that action formally undertaken for substantive goals be weighed and transformed in terms of its consequences for the position of the officialdom.

Formal organizations as cooperative systems on the one hand, and individual personalities on the other, involve structural-functional homologies, a point which may help to clarify the nature of this type of analysis. If we say that the individual has a stable set of needs, most generally the need for maintaining and defending the integrity of his personality or ego; that there are recognizable certain repetitive mechanisms which are utilized by the ego in its defense (rationalization, projection, regression, etc.); and that overt and variable behavior may be interpreted in terms of its relation to these needs and mechanisms—on the basis of this logic we may discern the typical pattern of structural-functional analysis as set forth above. In this sense, it is possible to speak of a "Freudian model" for organizational analysis. This does not mean that the substantive insights of individual psychology may be applied to organizations, as in vulgar extrapolations from the individual ego to whole nations or (by a no less vulgar inversion) from strikes to frustrated workers. It is the *logic*, the *type* of analysis which is pertinent.

This homology is also instructive in relation to the applicability of generalizations to concrete cases. The dynamic theory of personality states a set of possible predicates about the ego and its mechanisms of defense, which inform us concerning the propensities of individual personalities under certain general circumstances. But these predicates provide only tools for the analysis of particular individuals, and each concrete case must be examined to tell which operate and in what degree. They are not primarily organs of prediction. In the same way, the predicates within the theory of organization will provide tools for the analysis of particular cases. Each organization, like each personality, represents a resultant of complex forces, an empirical entity which no single relation or no simple formula can explain. The problem of analysis becomes that of selecting among the possible predicates set forth in the theory of organization those which illuminate our understanding of the materials at hand.

The setting of structural-functional analysis as applied to organizations requires some qualification, however. Let us entertain the suggestion that the interesting problem in social science is not so much why men act the way they do as why men in certain circumstances *must* act the way they do. This emphasis upon constraint, if accepted, releases us from an ubiquitous attention to behavior in general, and especially from any undue fixation upon statistics. On the other hand, it has what would seem to be the salutary consequence of focusing inquiry upon certain necessary relationships of the type "if . . . then," for example: if the cultural level of the rank and file members of a formally democratic organization is below that necessary for participation in the formulation of policy, then there will be pressure upon the leaders to use the tools of demagogy.

Is such a statement universal in its applicability? Surely not in the sense that one can predict without remainder the nature of all or even most political groups in a democracy. Concrete behavior is a resultant, a complex vector, shaped by the operation of a number of such general constraints. But there is a test of general applicability: it is that of noting whether the relation made explicit must be *taken into account* in action. This criterion represents an empirical test of the significance of social science generalizations. If a theory is significant it will state a relation which will either (1) be taken into account as an element of achieving control; or (2) be ignored only at the risk of losing control and will evidence itself in a ramification of objective or unintended consequences.[14] It is a corollary of this principle of significance that investigation must search out the underlying factors in organizational action, which requires a kind of intensive analysis of the same order as psychoanalytic probing.

A frame of reference which invites attention to the constraints upon behavior will tend to highlight tensions and dilemmas, the characteristic paradoxes generated in the course of action. The dilemma may be said to be the handmaiden of structural-functional analysis, for it introduces the concept of *commitment* or *involvement* as fundamental to organizational analysis. A dilemma in human behavior is represented by an inescapable commitment which cannot be reconciled with the needs of the organism or the social system. There are many spurious dilemmas which have to do with verbal contradictions, but inherent dilemmas to which we refer are of a more profound sort, for they reflect the basic nature of the empirical system in question. An economic order committed to profit as its sustaining incentive may, in Marxist terms, sow the seed of its own destruction. Again, the anguish of man, torn between finitude and pride, is not a matter of arbitrary and replaceable assumptions but is a reflection of the psychological needs of the human organism, and is concretized in his commitment to the institutions which command his life; he is in the world and of it, inescapably involved in its goals and demands; at the same time, the needs of the spirit are compelling, proposing modes of salvation which have continuously disquieting consequences for worldly involvements. In still another context, the need of the human organism for affection and response necessitates a commitment to elements of the culture which can provide them; but the rule of the superego is uncertain since it cannot be completely reconciled with the need for libidinal satisfactions.

Applying this principle to organizations we may note that there is a general source of tension observable in the split between "the motion and the act." Plans and programs reflect the freedom of technical or ideal choice, but organized action cannot escape involvement, a commitment to personnel or institutions or procedures which effectively qualifies the initial plan. *Der Mensch denkt, Gott lenkt.* In organized action, this ultimate wisdom finds a temporal meaning in the recalcitrance of the tools of action. We are inescapably committed to the mediation of human structures which are at once indispensable to our goals and at the same time stand between them and ourselves. The selection of agents generates immediately a bifurcation of interest, expressed in new centers of need and power, placing effective constraints upon the arena of action, and resulting in tensions which are never completely resolved. This is part of what it means to say that there is a "logic" of action which impels us forward from one undesired position to another. Commitment to dynamic, self-activating tools is of the nature of organized action; at the same time, the need for continuity of authority, policy, and character are pressing, and require an unceasing effort to master the instruments generated in the course of action. This generic tension is specified within the terms of each cooperative system. But for all we find a persistent relationship between *need* and *commitment* in which the latter not only qualifies the former but unites with it to produce a continuous state of tension. In this way, the notion of constraint (as reflected in tension or paradox) at once widens and more closely specifies the frame of reference for organizational analysis.

For Malinowski, the core of functionalism was contained in the view that a cultural fact must be analyzed in its setting. Moreover, he apparently conceived of his method as pertinent to the analysis of all aspects of cultural systems. But there is a more specific problem, one involving a principle of selection which serves to guide inquiry along significant lines. Freud conceived of the human organism as an adaptive structure, but he was not concerned with all human needs, nor with all phases of

[14] See R. M. MacIver's discussion of the "dynamic assessment" which "brings the external world selectively into the subjective realm, conferring on it subjective significance for the ends of action." *Social Causation* (Boston: Ginn, 1942), chaps. 11, 12. The analysis of this assessment within the context of organized action yields the implicit knowledge which guides the choice among alternatives. See also Robert K. Merton, "The Unanticipated Consequences of Purposive Social Action," *American Sociological Review, I*, 6 (December, 1936).

adaptation. For his system, he selected those needs whose expression is blocked in some way, so that such terms as repression, inhibition, and frustration became crucial. All conduct may be thought of as derived from need, and all adjustment represents the reduction of need. But not all needs are relevant to the systematics of dynamic psychology; and it is not adjustment as such but reaction to frustration which generates the characteristic modes of defensive behavior.

Organizational analysis, too, must find its selective principle; otherwise the indiscriminate attempts to relate activity functionally to needs will produce little in the way of significant theory. Such a principle might read as follows: *Our frame of reference is to select out those needs which cannot be fulfilled within approved avenues of expression and thus must have recourse to such adaptive mechanisms as ideology and to the manipulation of formal processes and structures in terms of informal goals.* This formulation has many difficulties, and is not presented as conclusive, but it suggests the kind of principle which is likely to separate the quick and the dead, the meaningful and the trite, in the study of cooperative systems in organized action.[15]

The frame of reference outlined here for the theory of organization may now be identified as involving the following major ideas: (1) the concept of organizations as cooperative systems, adaptive social structures, made up of interacting individuals, sub-groups, and informal plus formal relationships; (2) structural-functional analysis, which relates variable aspects of organization (such as goals) to stable needs and self-defensive mechanisms; (3) the concept of recalcitrance as a quality of the tools of social action, involving a break in the continuum of adjustment and defining an environment of constraint, commitment, and tension. This frame of reference is suggested as providing a specifiable *area of relations* within which predicates in the theory of organization will be sought, and at the same time setting forth principles of selection and relevance in our approach to the data of organization.

[15] This is not meant to deprecate the study of organizations as *economies* or formal systems. The latter represent an independent level, abstracted from organizational structures as cooperative or adaptive systems ("organisms").

It will be noted that we have set forth this frame of reference within the over-all context of social action. The significance of events may be defined by their place and operational role in a means-end scheme. If functional analysis searches out the elements important for the maintenance of a given structure, and that structure is one of the materials to be manipulated in action, then that which is functional in respect to the structure is also functional in respect to the action system. This provides a ground for the significance of functionally derived theories. At the same time, relevance to control in action is the empirical test of their applicability or truth.

Cooptation as a Mechanism of Adjustment

The frame of reference stated above is in fact an amalgam of definition, resolution, and substantive theory. There is an element of *definition* in conceiving of formal organizations as cooperative systems, though of course the interaction of informal and formal patterns is a question of fact; in a sense, we are *resolving* to employ structural-functional analysis on the assumption that it will be fruitful to do so, though here, too, the specification of needs or derived imperatives is a matter for empirical inquiry; and our predication of recalcitrance as a quality of the tools of action is itself a *substantive theory*, perhaps fundamental to a general understanding of the nature of social action.

A theory of organization requires more than a general frame of reference, though the latter is indispensable to inform the approach of inquiry to any given set of materials. What is necessary is the construction of generalizations concerning transformations within and among cooperative systems. These generalizations represent, from the standpoint of particular cases, possible predicates which are relevant to the materials as we know them in general, but which are not necessarily controlling in all circumstances. A theory of transformations in organization would specify those states of the system which resulted typically in predictable, or at least understandable, changes in such aspects of organization as goals, leadership, doctrine, efficiency, effectiveness, and size. These empirical generalizations would be systematized as they were related to the stable needs of the cooperative system.

Changes in the characteristics of organizations may occur as a result of many different conditions, not always or necessarily related to the processes of organization as such. But the theory of organization must be selective, so that explanations of transformations will be sought within its own assumptions or frame of reference. Consider the question of size. Organizations may expand for many reasons—the availability of markets, legislative delegations, the swing of opinion—which may be accidental from the point of view of the organizational process. To explore changes in size (as of, say, a trades union) as related to changes in non-organizational conditions may be necessitated by the historical events to be described, but it will not of itself advance the frontiers of the theory of organization. However, if "the innate propensity of an organization to expand" is asserted as a function of "the inherent instability of incentives"[16] then transformations have been stated within the terms of the theory of organization itself. It is likely that in many cases the generalization in question may represent only a minor aspect of the empirical changes, but these organizational relations must be made explicit if the theory is to receive development.

In a frame of reference which specifies needs and anticipates the formulation of a set of self-defensive responses or mechanisms, the latter appear to constitute one kind of empirical generalization or "possible predicate" within the general theory. The needs of organizations (whatever investigation may determine them to be) are posited as attributes of all organizations, but the responses to disequilibrium will be varied. The mechanisms used by the system in fulfillment of its needs will be repetitive and thus may be described as a specifiable set of assertions within the theory of organization, but any given organization may or may not have recourse to the characteristic modes of response. Certainly no given organization will employ all of the possible mechanisms which are theoretically available. When Barnard speaks of an "innate propensity of organization to expand" he is in fact formulating one of the general mechanisms, namely, expansion, which is a characteristic mode of response available to an organization under pressure from within. These responses necessarily involve a transformation (in this case, size) of some structural aspect of the organization.

Other examples of the self-defensive mechanisms available to organizations may derive primarily from the response of these organizations to the institutional environments in which they live. The tendency to construct ideologies, reflecting the need to come to terms with major social forces, is one such mechanism. Less well understood as a mechanism of organizational adjustment is what we may term *cooptation.* Some statement of the meaning of this concept may aid in clarifying the foregoing analysis.

Cooptation is the process of absorbing new elements into the leadership or policy-determining structure of an organization as a means of averting threats to its stability or existence. This is a defensive mechanism, formulated as one of a number of possible predicates available for the interpretation of organizational behavior. Cooptation tells us something about the process by which an institutional environment impinges itself upon an organization and effects changes in its leadership and policy. Formal authority may resort to cooptation under the following general conditions:

1. When there exists a hiatus between consent and control, so that the legitimacy of the formal authority is called into question. The "indivisibility" of consent and control refers, of course, to an optimum situation. Where control lacks an adequate measure of consent, it may revert to coercive measures or attempt somehow to win the consent of the governed. One means of winning consent is to coopt elements into the leadership or organization, usually elements which in some way reflect the sentiment, or possess the confidence of the relevant public or mass. As a result, it is expected that the new elements will lend respectability or legitimacy to the organs of control and thus reestablish the stability of formal authority. This process is widely used, and in many different contexts. It is met in colonial countries, where the organs of alien control reaffirm their legitimacy by coopting native leaders into the colonial administration. We find it in the phenomenon of "crisis-patriotism" wherein normally disfranchised groups are temporarily given representation in the coun-

[16] Barnard, *op. cit.*, pp. 158–9.

cils of government in order to win their solidarity in a time of national stress. Cooptation is presently being considered by the United States Army in its study of proposals to give enlisted personnel representation in the court-martial machinery—a clearly adaptive response to stresses made explicit during the war, the lack of confidence in the administration of army justice. The "unity" parties of totalitarian states are another form of cooptation; company unions or some employee representation plans in industry are still another. In each of these cases, the response of formal authority (private or public, in a large organization or a small one) is an attempt to correct a state of imbalance by *formal* measures. It will be noted, moreover, that what is shared is the *responsibility* for power rather than power itself. These conditions define what we shall refer to as *formal cooptation.*

2. Cooptation may be a response to the pressure of specific centers of power. This is not necessarily a matter of legitimacy or of a general and diffuse lack of confidence. These may be well established; and yet organized forces which are able to threaten the formal authority may effectively shape its structure and policy. The organization in respect to its institutional environment—or the leadership in respect to its ranks—must take these forces into account. As a consequence, the outside elements may be brought into the leadership or policy-determining structure, may be given a place as a recognition of and concession to the resources they can independently command. The representation of interests through administrative constituencies is a typical example of this process. Or, within an organization, individuals upon whom the group is dependent for funds or other resources may insist upon and receive a share in the determination of policy. This form of cooptation is typically expressed in informal terms, for the problem is not one of responding to a state of imbalance with respect to the "people as a whole" but rather one of meeting the pressure of specific individuals or interest-groups which are in a position to enforce demands. The latter are interested in the substance of power and not its forms. Moreover, an open acknowledgement of capitulation to specific interests may itself undermine the sense of legitimacy of the formal authority within the community. Consequently, there is a positive pressure to refrain from explicit recognition of the relationship established. This form of the cooptative mechanism, having to do with the sharing of power as a response to specific pressures, may be termed *informal cooptation.*

Cooptation reflects a state of tension between formal authority and social power. The former is embodied in a particular structure and leadership, but the latter has to do with subjective and objective factors which control the loyalties and potential manipulability of the community. Where the formal authority is an expression of social power, its stability is assured. On the other hand, when it becomes divorced from the sources of social power its continued existence is threatened. This threat may arise from the sheer alienation of sentiment or from the fact that other leaderships have control over the sources of social power. Where a formal authority has been accustomed to the assumption that its constituents respond to it as individuals, there may be a rude awakening when organization of those constituents on a non-governmental basis creates nuclei of power which are able effectively to demand a sharing of power.[17]

The significance of cooptation for organizational analysis is not simply that there is a change in or a broadening of leadership, and that this is an adaptive response, but also that *this change is consequential for the character and role of the organization.* Cooptation in-

[17] It is perhaps useful to restrict the concept of cooptation to formal organizations, but in fact it probably reflects a process characteristic of all group leaderships. This has received some recognition in the analysis of class structure, wherein the ruling class is interpreted as protecting its own stability by absorbing new elements. Thus Michels made the point that "an aristocracy cannot maintain an enduring stability by sealing itself off hermetically." See Robert Michels, *Umschichtungen in den herrschenden Klassen nach dem Kriege* (Stuttgart: Kohlhammer, 1934), p. 39; also Gaetano Mosca, *The Ruling Class* (New York: McGraw-Hill, 1939), pp. 413ff. The alliance or amalgamation of classes in the face of a common threat may be reflected in formal and informal cooptative responses among formal organizations sensitive to class pressures. In a forthcoming volume, *TVA and the Grass Roots,* the author has made extensive use of the concept of cooptation in analyzing some aspects of the organizational behavior of a government agency.

volves commitment, so that the groups to which adaptation has been made constrain the field of choice available to the organization or leadership in question. The character of the coopted elements will necessarily shape (inhibit or broaden) the modes of action available to the leadership which has won adaptation and security at the price of commitment. The concept of cooptation thus implicitly sets forth the major points of the frame of reference outlined above: it is an adaptive response of a cooperative system to a stable need, generating transformations which reflect constraints enforced by the recalcitrant tools of action.

The Analysis of Goals in Complex Organizations

CHARLES PERROW

Social scientists have produced a rich body of knowledge about many aspects of large-scale organizations, yet there are comparatively few studies of the goals of these organizations. For a full understanding of organizations and the behavior of their personnel, analysis of organizational goals would seem to be critical. Two things have impeded such analysis. Studies of morale, turnover, informal organization, communication, supervisory practices, etc., have been guided by an over-rationalistic point of view wherein goals are taken for granted, and the most effective ordering of resources and personnel is seen as the only problematical issue. Fostering this view is the lack of an adequate distinction between types of goals. Without such clarification it is difficult to determine what the goals are and what would be acceptable evidence for the existence of a particular goal and for a change in goals.

It will be argued here, first, that the type of goals most relevant to understanding organizational behavior are not the official goals, but those that are embedded in major operating policies and the daily decisions of the personnel. Second, these goals will be shaped by the particular problems or tasks an organization must emphasize, since these tasks determine the characteristics of those who will dominate the organization. In illustrating the latter argument, we will not be concerned with the specific goals of organizations, but only with the range within which goals are likely to vary. Though general hospitals will be used as the main illustration, three types of organizations will be discussed: voluntary service organizations, non-voluntary service organizations and profit-making organizations.

The Over-Rationalistic View

Most studies of the internal operation of complex organizations, if they mention goals at all, have taken official statements of goals at face value. This may be justified if only a limited problem is being investigated, but even then it contributes to the view that goals are not problematical. In this view, goals have no effect upon activities other than in the grossest terms; or it can be taken for granted that the only problem is to adjust means to given and stable ends. This reflects a distinctive "model" of organizational behavior, which Gouldner has characterized as the rational model. Its proponents see the managerial elite as using rational and logical means to pursue clear and discrete ends set forth in official statements of goals, while the worker is seen as governed by nonrationalistic, traditionalistic orientations. If goals are unambiguous and achievement evaluated by cost-accounting procedures, the only turmoil of organizational life lies below the surface with workers or, at best, with middle management maneuvering for status and power. Actually, however, nonrational orientations exist at all levels, including the elite who are responsible for setting goals and assessing the degree to which they are achieved.

One reason for treating goals as static fixtures of organizational life is that goals have not been given adequate conceptualization, though the elements of this are in easy reach. If making a profit or serving customers is to be taken as a sufficient statement of goals, then all means to this end might appear to be based on rational decisions because the analyst is not alerted to the countless policy decisions involved. If goals are given a more elaborate conceptualization, we are forced to see many more things as problematic.

Official and Operative Goals

Two major categories of goals will be discussed here, official and "operative" goals. Official goals are the general purposes of the

From *American Sociological Review*, Vol. 26, 1961, pp. 854–865. Reprinted by permission of the author and the publisher, the American Sociological Association.

organization as put forth in the charter, annual reports, public statements by key executives and other authoritative pronouncements. For example, the goal of an employment agency may be to place job seekers in contact with firms seeking workers. The official goal of a hospital may be to promote the health of the community through curing the ill, and sometimes through preventing illness, teaching, and conducting research. Similar organizations may emphasize different publically acceptable goals. A business corporation, for example, may state that its goal is to make a profit or adequate return on investment, or provide a customer service, or produce goods.

This level of analysis is inadequate in itself for a full understanding of organizational behavior. Official goals are purposely vague and general and do not indicate two major factors which influence organizational behavior: the host of decisions that must be made among alternative ways of achieving official goals and the priority of multiple goals, and the many unofficial goals pursued by groups within the organization. The concept of "operative goals" will be used to cover these aspects. Operative goals designate the ends sought through the actual operating policies of the organization; they tell us what the organization actually is trying to do, regardless of what the official goals say are the aims.

Where operative goals provide the specific content of official goals they reflect choices among competing values. They may be justified on the basis of an official goal, even though they may subvert another official goal. In one sense they are means to official goals, but since the latter are vague or of high abstraction, the "means" become ends in themselves when the organization is the object of analysis. For example, where profit-making is the announced goal, operative goals will specify whether quality or quantity is to be emphasized, whether profits are to be short run and risky or long run and stable, and will indicate the relative priority of diverse and somewhat conflicting ends of customer service, employee morale, competitive pricing, diversification, or liquidity. Decisions on all these factors influence the nature of the organization, and distinguish it from another with an identical official goal. An employment agency must decide whom to serve, what characteristics they favor among clients, and whether a high turnover of clients or a long run relationship is desired. In the voluntary general hospital, where the official goals are patient care, teaching, and research, the relative priority of these must be decided, as well as which group in the community is to be given priority in service, and are these services to emphasize, say, technical excellence or warmth and "hand-holding."

Unofficial operative goals, on the other hand, are tied more directly to group interests and while they may support, be irrelevant to, or subvert official goals, they bear no necessary connection with them. An interest in a major supplier may dictate the policies of a corporation executive. The prestige that attaches to utilizing elaborate high speed computers may dictate the reorganization of inventory and accounting departments. Racial prejudice may influence the selection procedures of an employment agency. The personal ambition of a hospital administrator may lead to community alliances and activities which bind the organization without enhancing its goal achievement. On the other hand, while the use of interns and residents as "cheap labor" may subvert the official goal of medical education, it may substantially further the official goal of providing a high quality of patient care.

The discernment of operative goals is, of course, difficult and subject to error. The researcher may have to determine from analysis of a series of apparently minor decisions regarding the lack of competitive bidding and quality control that an unofficial goal of a group of key executives is to maximize their individual investments in a major supplier. This unofficial goal may affect profits, quality, market position, and morale of key skill groups. The executive of a correctional institution may argue that the goal of the organization is treatment, and only the lack of resources creates an apparent emphasis upon custody or deprivation. The researcher may find, however, that decisions in many areas establish the priority of custody or punishment as a goal. For example, few efforts may be made to obtain more treatment personnel; those hired are misused and mistrusted; and clients are viewed as responding only to deprivations. The president of a junior college may deny the function of the institution is to deal with the latent terminal student, but careful analysis such as Clark has made of operating policies, personnel practices, recruitment procedures, organizational alliances and personal characteristics of elites will demonstrate this to be the operative goal.

The Task–Authority–Goal Sequence

While operative goals will only be established through intensive analysis of decisions, personnel practices, alliance and elite characteristics in each organization, it is possible to indicate the range within which they will vary and the occasion for general shifts in goals. We will argue that if we know something about the major tasks of an organization and the characteristics of its controlling elite, we can predict its goals in general terms. The theory presented and illustrated in the rest of this paper is a first approximation and very general, but it may guide and stimulate research on this problem.

Every organization must accomplish four tasks: (1) secure inputs in the form of capital sufficient to establish itself, operate, and expand as the need arises; (2) secure acceptance in the form of basic legitimization of activity; (3) marshal the necessary skills; and (4) coordinate the activities of its members and the relations of the organization with other organizations and with clients or consumers. All four are not likely to be equally important at any point in time. Each of these task areas provides a presumptive basis for control or domination by the group equipped to meet the problems involved. (The use of the terms control or dominance signifies a more pervasive, thorough and all-embracing phenomenon than authority or power.) The operative goals will be shaped by the dominant group, reflecting the imperatives of the particular task area that is most critical, their own background characteristics (distinctive perspectives based upon their training, career lines, and areas of competence) and the unofficial uses to which they put the organization for their own ends.

The relative emphasis upon one or another of the four tasks will vary with the nature of the work the organization does and the technology appropriate to it, and with the stage of development within the organization. An organization engaged in manufacturing in an industry where skills are routinized and the market position secure, may emphasize coordination, giving control to the experienced administrator. An extractive industry, with a low skill level in its basic tasks and a simple product, will probably emphasize the importance of capital tied up in land, specialized and expensive machinery, and transportation facilities. The chairman of the board of directors of a group within the board will probably dominate such an organization. An organization engaged in research and development, or the production of goods or services which cannot be carried out in a routinized fashion, will probably be most concerned with skills. Thus engineers or other relevant professionals will dominate. It is also possible that all three groups—trustees, representatives of critical skills, and administrators—may share power equally. This "multiple leadership" will be discussed in detail later. Of course, trustees are likely to dominate in the early history of any organization, particularly those requiring elaborate capital and facilities, or unusual legitimization. But once these requisites are secured, the nature of the tasks will determine whether trustees or others dominate. The transfer of authority, especially from trustees to another group, may be protracted, constituting a lag in adaptation.

Where major task areas do not change over time, the utility of the scheme presented here is limited to suggesting possible relations between task areas, authority structure, and operative goals. The more interesting problems, which we deal with in our illustrations below, involve organizations which experience changes in major task areas over time. If the technology or type of work changes, or if new requirements for capital or legitimization arise, control will shift from one group to another. One sequence is believed to be typical.

Voluntary General Hospitals

We will discuss four types of hospitals, those dominated by trustees, by the medical staff (an organized group of those doctors who bring in private patients plus the few doctors who receive salaries or commissions from the hospital), by the administration, and by some form of multiple leadership. There has been a general development among hospitals from trustee domination, based on capital and legitimization, to domination by the medical staff, based upon the increasing importance of their technical skills, and, at present, a tendency towards administrative dominance based on internal and external coordination. (The administrator may or may not be a doctor himself.) Not all hospitals go through these stages, or go through them in this sequence. Each type of authority structure shapes, or sets limits to, the type of operative goals that are likely to prevail, though there will be much variation within each type.

Trustee Domination. Voluntary general hospitals depend upon community funds for an important part of their capital and operating budget. Lacking precise indicators of efficiency or goal achievement, yet using donated funds, they must involve community representatives—trustees—in their authority structure. Trustees legitimate the non-profit status of the organization, assure that funds are not misused, and see that community needs are being met. Officially, they are the ultimate authority in voluntary hospitals. They do not necessarily exercise the legal powers they have, but where they do, there is no question that they are in control.

The functional basis for this control is primarily financial. They have access to those who make donations, are expected to contribute heavily themselves, and control the machinery and sanctions for fund raising drives. Financial control allows them to withhold resources from recalcitrant groups in the organization, medical or non-medical. They also, of course, control all appointments and promotions, medical and non-medical.

Where these extensive powers are exercised, operative goals are likely to reflect the role of trustees as community representatives and contributors to community health. Because of their responsibility to the sponsoring community, trustees may favor conservative financial policies, opposing large financial outlays for equipment, research, and education so necessary for high medical standards. High standards also require more delegation of authority to the medical staff than trustee domination can easily allow. As representatives drawn from distinctive social groups in the community, they may be oriented towards service for a religious, ethnic, economic, or age group in the community. Such an orientation may conflict with selection procedures favored by the medical staff or administration. Trustees may also promote policies which demonstrate a contribution to community welfare on the part of an elite group, perhaps seeking to maintain a position of prominence and power within the community. The hospital may be used as a vehicle for furthering a social philosophy of philanthropy and good works; social class values regarding personal worth, economic independence and responsibility; the assimilation of a minority group; or even to further resistance to government control and socialized medicine.

Such orientations will shape operative goals in many respects, affecting standards and techniques of care, priority of services, access to care, relations with other organizations, and directions and rate of development. The administrator in such a hospital—usually called a "superintendent" under the circumstances—will have little power, prestige or responsibility. For example, trustees have been known to question the brand of grape juice the dietician orders, or insist that they approve the color of paint the administrator selects for a room. Physicians may disapprove of patient selection criteria, chafe under financial restrictions which limit the resources they have to work with, and resent active control over appointments and promotions in the medical staff.

Medical Domination. Trustee domination was probably most common in the late nineteenth and early twentieth century. Medical technology made extraordinary advances in the twentieth century, and doctors possessed the skills capable of utilizing the advances. They demanded new resources and were potentially in a position to control their allocation and use. Increasingly, major decisions had to be based upon a technical competence trustees did not possess. Trustees had a continuing basis for control because of the costs of new equipment and personnel, but in many hospitals the skill factor became decisive. Some trustees felt that the technology required increased control by doctors; others lost a struggle for power with the medical staff; in some cases trustees were forced to bring in and give power to an outstanding doctor in order to increase the reputation of the hospital. Under such conditions trustees are likely to find that their legal power becomes nominal and they can only intervene in crisis situations; even financial requirements come to be set by conditions outside their control. They continue to provide the mantle of community representation and non-profit status, and become "staff" members whose major task is to secure funds.

It is sometimes hard to see why all hospitals are not controlled by the medical staff, in view of the increasing complexity and specialization of the doctor's skills, their common professional background, the power of organized medicine, and the prestige accorded the doctor in society. Furthermore, they are organized for dominance, despite their nominal status as "guests" in the house. The medical staff constitutes a "shadow" organization in hospitals, providing a ready potential for control. It is organized on bureaucratic principles with admission requirements, rewards and sanctions, and a committee structure which often duplicates the key committees of the board of directors and administrative staff. Nor are doctors in an advisory position as are "staff" groups in other organizations. Doctors perform both staff and line functions, and their presumptive right to control rests on both. Doctors also have a basic economic interest in the hospital, since it is essential to most private medical practice and career advancement. They seek extensive facilities, low hospital charges, a high quality of coordinated services, and elaborate time and energy-conserving conveniences.

Thus there is sufficient means for control by doctors, elaborated far beyond the mere provision of essential skills, and sufficient interest in control. Where doctors fully exercise their potential power the administrator functions as a superintendent or, as his co-professionals are wont to put it, as a "housekeeper." The importance of administrative skills is likely to be minimized, the administrative viewpoint on operative goals neglected, and the quality of personnel may suffer. A former nurse often serves as superintendent in this type of hospital. Policy matters are defined as medical in nature by the doctors, and neither trustees nor administrators, by definition, are qualified to have an equal voice in policy formation.

The operative goals of such a hospital are likely to be defined in strictly medical terms and the organization may achieve high technical standards of care, promote exemplary research, and provide sound training. However, there is a danger that resources will be used primarily for private (paying) patients with little attention to other community needs such as caring for the medically indigent (unless they happen to be good teaching cases), developing preventive medicine, or pioneering new organizational forms of care. Furthermore, high technical standards increasingly require efficient coordination of services and doctors may be unwilling to delegate authority to qualified administrators.

Various unofficial goals may be achieved at the expense of medical ones, or, in some cases, in conjunction with them. There are many cases of personal aggrandizement on the part of departmental chiefs and the chief of staff. The informal referral and consultation system in conjunction with promotions, bed quotas, and "privileges" to operate or treat certain types of cases, affords many occasions for the misuse of power. Interns and residents are particularly vulnerable to exploitation at the expense of teaching goals. Furthermore, as a professional, the doctor has undergone intensive socialization in his training and is called upon to exercise extraordinary judgment and skill with drastic consequences for good or ill. Thus he demands unusual deference and obedience and is invested with "charismatic" authority. He may extend this authority to the entrepreneurial aspects of his role, with the result that his "service" orientation, so taken for granted in much of the literature, sometimes means service to the doctor at the expense of personnel, other patients, or even his own patient.

Administrative Dominance. Administrative dominance is based first on the need for coordinating the increasingly complex, non-routinizable functions hospitals have undertaken. There is an increasing number of personnel that the doctor can no longer direct. The mounting concern of trustees, doctors themselves, patients and pre-payment groups with more efficient and economical operation also gives the administrator more power. A second, related basis for control stems from the fact that health services in general have become increasingly interdependent and specialized. The hospital must cooperate more with other hospitals and community agencies. It must also take on more services itself, and in doing so its contacts with other agencies and professional groups outside the hospital multiply. The administrator is equipped to handle these matters because of his specialized training, often received in a professional school of hospital administration, accumulated experience and available time. These services impinge upon the doctor at many points, providing a further basis for administrative control over doctors, and they lead to commitments in which trustees find they have to acquiesce.

The administrator is also in a position to control matters which affect the doctor's demands for status, deference, and time-saving conveniences. By maintaining close supervision over employees or promoting their own independent basis for competence, and by supporting them in conflicts with doctors, the administrator can, to some degree, overcome the high functional authority that doctors command. In addition, by carefully controlling communication between trustees and key medical staff officials, he can prevent an alliance of these two groups against him.

If administrative dominance is based primarily on the complexity of basic hospital activities, rather than the organization's medical-social role in the community, the operative orientation may be toward financial solvency, careful budget controls, efficiency, and minimal development of services. For example, preventive medicine, research, and training may be minimized; a cautious approach may prevail towards new forms of care such as intensive therapy units or home care programs. Such orientations could be especially true of hospitals dominated by administrators whose background and training were as bookkeepers, comptrollers, business managers, purchasing agents, and the like. This is probably the most common form of administrative dominance.

However, increasing professionalization of hospital administrators has, on the one hand, equipped them to handle narrower administrative matters easily, and, on the other hand, alerted them to the broader medical-social role of hospitals involving organizational and financial innovations in the forms of care. Even medical standards can come under administrative control. For example, the informal system among doctors of sponsorship, referral, and consultation serves to protect informal work norms, shield members from criticism and exclude non-cooperative members. The administrator is in a position to insist that medical policing be performed by a salaried doctor who stands outside the informal system.

There is, of course, a possibility of less "progressive" consequences. Interference with medical practices in the name of either high standards or treating the "whole" person may be misguided or have latent consequences which impair therapy. Publicity-seeking innovations may be at the expense of more humdrum but crucial services such as the outpatient department, or may alienate doctors or other personnel, or may deflect administrative efforts from essential but unglamorous administrative tasks. Using the organization for career advancement, they may seek to expand and publicize their hospital regardless of community needs and ability to pay. Like trustees they may favor a distinctive and medically irrelevant community relations policy, perhaps with a view towards moving upward in the community power structure. Regardless of these dangers, the number of administration dominated hospitals oriented towards broad medical-social goals will probably grow.

Multiple Leadership. So far we have been considering situations where one group clearly dominates. It is possible, however, for power to be shared by two or three groups to the extent that no one is able to control all or most of the actions of the others. This we call multiple leadership: a division of labor regarding the determination of goals and the power to achieve them. This is not the same as fractionated power where several groups have small amounts of power in an unstable situation. With multiple leadership, there are two or three stable, known centers of power. Nor is it the same as decentralized power, where specialized units of the organization have considerable autonomy. In the latter case, units are free to operate as they choose only up to a point, when it becomes quite clear that there is a centralized authority. In multiple leadership there is no single ultimate power.

Multiple leadership is most likely to appear in organizations where there are multiple goals which lack precise criteria of achievement and admit of considerable tolerance with regard to achievement. Multiple goals focus interests, and achievement tolerance provides the necessary leeway for accommodation of interests and vitiation of responsibility. Many service organizations fit these criteria, but so might large, public relations-conscious business or industrial organizations where a variety of goals can be elevated to such importance that power must be shared by the representatives of each.

In one hospital where this was studied it was found that multiple leadership insured that crucial group interests could be met and protected, and encouraged a high level of creative (though selective) involvement by trustees, doctors, and the administration. However, the problems of goal setting, assessment of achievement, and assignment of responsibility seemed abnormally high. While the three groups pursued separate and unconflicting operative goals in some cases, and were in agreement on still other goals, in areas where interests conflicted the goal conflicts were submerged in the interests of harmony. In the absence of a single authority, repetitive conflicts threatened to erode morale and waste energies. A showdown and clear solution of a conflict, furthermore, might signal defeat for one party, forcing them to abandon their interests. Thus a premium was placed on the ability of some elites to smooth over conflicts and exercise interpersonal skills. Intentions were sometimes masked and ends achieved through covert manipulation. Assessment of achievement in some areas was prevented either by the submergence of conflict or the preoccupation with segmental interests. Opportunism was encouraged: events in the environment or within the hospital were exploited without attention to the interests of the other groups or the long range development of the hospital. This left the organization open to vagrant pressures and to the operation of unintended consequences. Indeed, with conflict submerged and groups pursuing independent goals, long range planning was difficult.

This summary statement exaggerates the impact of multiple leadership in this hospital and neglects the areas of convergence on goals. Actually, the hospital prospered and led its region in progressive innovations and responsible medical-social policies despite some subversion of the official goals of patient care, teaching, research, and preventive medicine. The organization could tolerate considerable ambiguity of goals and achievements as long as standards remained high in most areas, occupancy was sufficient to operate with a minimum deficit, and a favorable public image was maintained. It remains to be seen if the costs and consequences are similar for other organizations where multiple leadership exists.

Application to Other Organizations

Voluntary Service Organizations. Other voluntary service organizations, such as private universities, social service agencies, privately sponsored correctional institutions for juveniles, and fund raising agencies resemble hospitals in many respects. They have trustees representing the community, may have professionals playing prominent roles, and with increasing size and complexity of operation, require skilled coordination of activities. Initially at least, trustees are likely to provide a character defining function which emphasizes community goals and goals filtered through their own social position. Examples are religious schools, or those emphasizing one field of knowledge or training; agencies caring for specialized groups such as ethnic or religious minorities, unwed mothers, and dependent and neglected children; and groups raising money for special causes. Funds of skill and knowledge accumulate around these activities, and the activities increasingly grow in complexity, requiring still more skill on the part of those performing the tasks. As the professional staff expands and professional identification grows, they may challenge the narrower orientations of trustees on the basis of their own special competence and professional ideology and seek to broaden the scope of services and the clientele. They may be supported in this by changing values in the community. Coordination of activities usually rests with professionals promoted from the staff during this second character defining phase, and these administrators retain, for a while at least, their professional identity. Trustees gradually lose the competence to interfere.

However, professionals have interests of their own which shape the organization. They may develop an identity and ethic which cuts them off from the needs of the community and favors specialized, narrow and—to critics—self-serving goals. Current criticisms of the emphasis upon research and over-specialization in graduate training at the expense of the basic task of educating undergraduates is a case in point in the universities. There is also criticism of the tendency of professionals in correctional institutions to focus upon case work techniques applicable to middle-class "neurotic" delinquents at the expense of techniques for resocializing the so-called "socialized" delinquent from culturally deprived areas. The latter account for most of the delinquents, but professional identity and techniques favor methods applicable to the former. Something similar may be found in social agencies. Social workers, especially the "elite" doing therapy in psychiatric and child guidance clinics and private family agencies, may become preoccupied with securing recognition, equitable financial remuneration, and status that would approach that of psychiatrists. Their attitudes may become more conservative; the social order more readily accepted and the deviant adapted to it; "worthy" clients and "interesting cases" receive priority.

It is possible that with increasing complexity and growth in many of these voluntary service organizations, administrators will lose their professional identity or be recruited from outside the organization on the basis of organizational skills. In either case they will be in a position to alter the direction fostered by selective professional interests. Of course, the problem of coordinating both internal and external activities need not generate leadership seeking broadly social rather than narrowly professional goals, any more than it necessarily does in the hospital. Administrative dominance may stunt professional services and neglect social policy in the interest of economy, efficiency, or conservative policies.

Non-Voluntary Service Organizations. A different picture is presented by non-voluntary service organizations—those sponsored by governmental agencies such as county or military hospitals, city or county welfare agencies, juvenile and adult correctional agencies. Authority for goal setting, regulation, and provision of capital and operating expenses does not rest with voluntary trustees, but with governmental officials appointed to commissions. In contrast to volunteers on the board of a private service organization, commissioners are not likely to be highly identified with the organization, nor do they derive much social status from it. The organizations themselves often are tolerated only as holding operations or as "necessary evils." Commission dominance is sporadic and brief, associated with public clamor or political expediency. On the other hand, the large size of these organizations and the complex procedures for reporting to the parent body gives considerable importance to the administrative function from the outset, which is enhanced by the tenuous relationship with the commissioners. Consistent with this and reinforcing it is the low level of professionalization found in many of these agencies. The key skills are often non-professional custodial skills or their equivalent in the case of public welfare agencies (and schools). Administrators are often at the mercy of the custodial staff if, indeed, they have not themselves risen to their administrative position because of their ability to maintain order and custody.

Nevertheless, professional influence is mounting in these organizations, and professional groups outside of them have exercised considerable influence. Professionals may assume control of the organization, or administrators may be brought in whose commitment is to the positive purposes of the organization, such as rehabilitation of the clients, rather than the negative custodial functions. This appears to have happened in the case of a few federal penal institutions, a few state juvenile correctional institutions, and several Veterans Administration mental hospitals. Even where this happens, one must be alert to the influence of unofficial goals. The organizations are particularly vulnerable to exploitation by the political career interests of administrators or to irresponsible fads or cure-alls of marginal professionals. In summary, the sequence of tasks, power structure, and goals may be different in non-voluntary service organizations. The importance of administrative skills with system maintenance as the overriding operative goal does not encourage a shift in power structure; but where new technologies are introduced we are alerted to such shifts along with changes in goals.

Profit-Making Organizations. Our analysis may appear less applicable to profit-making organizations for two reasons. First, it could be argued, they are not characterized by multiple goals, but relate all operations to profit-making. Second, skill groups are not likely to dominate these organizations; owners control the smaller firms, and professional executives the larger ones. Thus power structure and possibly goals may merely be a function of size. We will discuss each of these points in turn.

If profit-making is an overriding goal of an organization, many operative decisions must still be made which will shape its character. Even where technology remains constant, organizations will vary with regard to personnel practices, customer services, growth, liquidity, an emphasis upon quality or quantity, or long or short run gains. An adequate understanding of the organization will require attention to alternatives in these and other areas.

Furthermore, it has often been asserted that the importance of profits, *per se*, has declined with the increased power of professional management, especially in large organizations. The argument runs that since management does not have a personal stake in profits, they consider them less important than stability, growth, solvency, and liquidity. The impressionistic evidence of those who assert this is not supported by a study of James Dent. When asked, "What are the aims of top management in your company?", the response of executives of 145 business firms showed no greater mention of "to make profits, money or a living" among large than small firms, nor among those with professional managers than owner-managers. Because goals stated in this form may not reflect actual policies and because of other limitations, one is somewhat reluctant to take this as a fair test of the hypothesis.

Even though his sample was not representative, and the question asked does not get at what we have called operative goals, his study provides good evidence of variations of stated goals in profitmaking organizations. Responses coded under the category "to make money, profits, or a living" were mentioned as the first aim by 36 per cent of the executives; "to provide a good product; public service" by 21 per cent, and "to grow" was third with 12 per cent. When the first three aims spontaneously mentioned were added together, profits led; employee welfare tied with "good products or public service" for second place. Dent found that the variables most associated with goals were size of company and "proportion of employees who are white-collar, professional or supervisory." While goals no doubt are influenced by size, this accounted for only some of the variance. Holding size constant, one might discover the effects of major task areas. The association of goals with the "proportion of employees who are white-collar . . ." supports this argument.

R. A. Gordon and others have asserted that in large corporations it is the executive group, rather than stockholders or the board of trustees, that generally dominates. A study of the role of trustees, frankly in favor of their exercising leadership and control, actually shows through its many cases studies that trustees exercise leadership mainly in times of crisis. The generalization of Gordon, almost a commonplace today, appears to be sound: he asserts that the common pattern of evolution is for active leadership by owners in the early years of the firm, then it is passed on to new generations of the families concerned, and gradually responsibility for decision-making passes to professional executives who frequently have been trained by the original leaders. Goals likewise shift from rapid development and a concern with profits to more conservative policies emphasizing coordination, stability and security of employment.

But does this mean that for large, old and stable firms that operative goals are substantially similar, reflecting professional administration? Does it also mean that for profit-making organizations in general there are only two alternative sources of domination, trustees (including owners) and professional administrators? Our theoretical scheme suggests that neither may be true, but the evidence is scanty. Certainly within the organizations dominated by professional managers there is ample opportunity for a variety of operational goals less general than, say, stability and security of employment. Even these are likely to vary and to shape the nature of the firm. (We exclude, of course, the failure to achieve these broad goals because of poor management or environmental factors over which the organization has no control; we are dealing with operating policies which may not be achieved.) Gordon notes that the "historical background" of a company (he does not elaborate this phrase) and especially the training received by its leading executives may be a powerful factor in shaping management decisions. "It is the 'Rockefeller tradition' rather than the present Rockefeller holdings which actively conditions the management decisions in the Standard Oil companies. This tradition is largely responsible for present methods of management organization and internal control, use of the committee system, and the domination of boards of directors by (company executives)." Historical factors will certainly shape decisions, but the nature of technology in the oil industry and the trustees' awareness of the prime importance of coordination may have been decisive in that historical experience.

Domination by skill groups is possible in two ways. On the one hand, a department—for example, sales, engineering, research and development, or finance—may, because of the technology and a stage of growth, effectively exercise a veto on the executive's decisions and substantially shape decisions in other departments. Second, lines of promotion may be such that top executives are drawn from one powerful department, and retain their identification with the parochial goals of that department. Gordon asserts that chief executives with a legal background are conservative in making price changes and find "order in the industry" more appealing than aggressive price competition. It is possible that engineers, sales executives, and financial executives all have distinctive views on what the operating policies should be.

Thus, goals may vary widely in profitmaking organizations, and power may rest not only with trustees or professional administrators, but with skill groups or administrators influenced by their skill background. Of course, one task area may so dominate a firm that there will be no shifts in power, and operative goals will remain fairly stable within the limits of the changing values of society. But where basic tasks shift, either because of growth or changing technology, the scheme presented here at least alerts us to potential goal changes and their consequences. An ideal-typical sequence would be as follows: trustee domination in initial stages of financing, setting direction for development and recruitment of technical or professional skills; then dominance by the skill group during product or service development and research, only to have subsequent control pass to coordination of fairly routinized activities. As the market and technology change, this cycle could be repeated. During the course of this sequence, operative goals may shift from quantity production and short-run profits as emphasized by trustees, to the engineer's preoccupation with quality at the expense of quantity or styling, with this succeeded by a priority upon styling and unessential innovations demanded by the sales force, and finally with an emphasis upon the long-run market position, conservative attitude towards innovation, and considerable investment in employee-centered policies and programs by management. It is important to note that the formal authority structure may not vary during this sequence, but recruitment into managerial positions and the actual power of management, trustees or skill groups would shift with each new problem focus. Multiple leadership is also possible, as noted in an earlier section.

There are many critical variables influencing the selection of key problem areas and thus the characteristics of the controlling elite and operative goals. They will be applicable to the analysis of any complex organization, whether business, governmental, or voluntary. Among those that should be considered are capital needs and legitimization, the amount of routinization possible, adaptability of technology to market shifts and consumer behavior, possible or required professionalization, and the nature of the work force. Our analysis of profitmaking organizations suggests that we should be alert to the possibility of a natural history of changes in task areas, authority, and goals which parallels that of hospitals and other voluntary service organizations. Non-voluntary service organizations may systematically deviate from this sequence because of the source of capital (government) which influences the commitments of appointive trustees (commissioners), and the character of the administrative tasks. The scheme presented here, when used in conjunction with the concept of operative goals, may provide a tool for analyzing the dynamics of goal setting and goal changing in all complex organizations.

A Comparative Analysis of Some Conditions and Consequences of Intra-Organizational Conflict

CLAGETT G. SMITH

With the recognition that intergroup conflict is a characteristic phenomenon of organizations and not simply a manifestation of irrationality negating the harmonious functioning of bureaucratic organizations, increasing attention is being devoted to the conditions generating intra-organizational conflict and their management. Despite the growing concern with conflict and its resolution on the international level, little systematic research on this problem has been undertaken in complex organizations. This paper attempts to complement other studies by reporting the results of a comparative analysis of some of the conditions generating intra-organizational conflict in complex organizations and their consequences.

Approach

Three limited aspects of the problem of intra-organizational conflict are considered:

1. What are the interpersonal processes underlying, or resulting in conflict between members occupying different levels in the organizational hierarchy?
2. What are the social-structural determinants of such interpersonal processes?
3. What are some of the organizational mechanisms that influence the consequences of interlevel conflict for the effectiveness of an organization?

Thus conceived, a basic premise of the problem is that intraorganizational conflict has its source in the nature of the organization as a social system, in the way it is structured and in the manner in which the component subsystems are interrelated. It is further proposed that the effects of structural variables in generating interlevel conflict are mediated by interpersonal processes. The final premise is that the effect of intra-organizational conflict on organizational functioning will depend partly upon the mechanisms used by the organization to manage or control the conflict.

For formulating specific hypotheses, some interpersonal processes underlying conflict suggested in the literature are reviewed, together with their accompanying structural determinants; then some of the factors conditioning the effects of intergroup conflict are considered. The specific focus will be limited to interlevel conflict; i.e., conflict involving lower participants (the rank and file) and those higher in the organizational hierarchy.

Determinants of Intra-Organizational Conflict. Intergroup conflict in organizations has been attributed to (*1*) problems of communication between the parties involved, (*2*) differences in basic interests and goals, and (*3*) a lack of shared perceptions and attitudes among members at different echelons.

COMMUNICATION HYPOTHESIS. The first approach concentrates upon the barriers to adequate communication between echelons. If the information given is sufficient quantitatively and qualitatively, effective and acceptable decisions can be made, and the required coordination can be achieved through the development of common programs and feed-back processes. Such decisions and concerted action would mitigate against the development of any high degree of conflict.[1]

From *Administrative Science Quarterly*, Vol. 10, March 1966, pp. 504–529. Reprinted by permission of the author and publisher.

[1] For a review of the communications approach employed in the study of complex organizations, see summaries by Clagett G. Smith and Michael A. Brown, Communication Structure and Control Structure in a Voluntary Association, *Sociometry*, 27 (1964 A), 449–468; and Jay M. Jackson, "The Organization and Its Communication Problems" (Paper presented at the seventh annual meeting of the Society of Public Health Educators, Atlantic City, N. J., Nov., 1956).

According to this familiar hypothesis, achieving adequate interlevel communication is a problem inherent in large complex organizations.[2] Organizational size inevitably gives rise to specialization and a proliferation of organizational roles. Because of this, increasing reliance is placed upon supervisory roles and the supporting staff functions to achieve the necessary coordination.[3] Achieving coordination in this manner has the effect of placing further impediments to the flow of information in the organization.

CONFLICT OF INTEREST HYPOTHESIS. This explanation views conflict as stemming essentially from basic differences of interests between participants occupying different positions in the organizational hierarchy. Katz emphasizes that conflict arises not simply from "misunderstandings," but from differences among subgroups who are in functional competition with one another, rationally pursuing different goals and struggling for limited organizational rewards.[4] Such differences are viewed as inherent in a hierarchical organization. The increase in supervisory or leadership roles, together with the accompanying differentiation of authority, lead to increased centralized control. As a consequence of the disproportionate representation of the interests of the leaders, such centralized control has the effect of displacing organizational goals, so that they are even less of a reflection of the interest of those lower in the hierarchy. Moreover, as Thompson observes,[5] hierarchical organization increases the disparity between authority, technical competence, and share in the rewards of the organization. As a result, most of the participants become less committed to the organization and fail to accept the goals of the organization.

[2] For an examination of the effects of size on communication processes, see Bernard P. Indik, Some Effects of Organizational Size on Member Attitudes and Behavior, *Human Relations,* 16 (1963), 369–384.

[3] See for example Victor A. Thompson, Hierarchy, Specialization, and Organizational Conflict, *Administrative Science Quarterly,* 5 (1961), 485–521.

[4] Daniel Katz, "Approaches to Managing Conflict," in Robert L. Kahn and Elsie Boulding (eds.), *Power and Conflict in Organizations* (New York: Basic Books, 1964), ch. vii, pp. 105–114.

[5] Thompson, *op. cit.*

CONSENSUS HYPOTHESIS. This approach interprets intra-organizational conflict as stemming essentially from a lack of shared perceptions and attitudes among members at different echelons.[6] In this view, member consensus arises primarily through processes of cohesiveness and participation in the group or organization. Participation, particularly when communication channels are adequate, permits members to ascertain the norms of the organization or other echelons, as well as facilitating their enforcement. Under conditions of high cohesiveness, members would be motivated to accept influence attempts and adhere to normative prescriptions. A variant of this view also would highlight the importance of shared perceptions and attitudes in the prevention of conflict, but would stress the importance of "pre-programming" of consensus through selection for organizational roles, career perspectives, or other latent roles.[7]

Although there is some empirical and conceptual support for each of these approaches, no attempt has been made to assess their tenability by comparative analysis of different types of organizations. As Smith and Brown note, different types of organizations face different system problems, whether these involve pursuing objectives efficiently, achieving member involvement in the organization, integrating the organization into the institutions of the larger social system, or achieving coordination with the environment.[8] Consequently, the relationships to be expected in different organizations may not be simple or invariant. Furthermore, identification, consensus, and interlevel communication may not interact in a simple additive fashion in the generation of

[6] For a more complete discussion of this viewpoint with particular reference to organizational control, see Clagett G. Smith and Oguz Ari, Organitional Control Structure and Member Consensus, *American Journal of Sociology,* 69 (1964), 623–638.

[7] James D. Thompson has presented a discussion of some of the mechanisms used in different organizations to build in consensus through selection procedures; cf., Organizational Management of Conflict, *Administrative Science Quarterly,* 4 (1960), 389–409.

[8] Clagett G. Smith and Michael A. Brown, "A Comparative Analysis of Factors in Organizational Control" (Unpublished report, Institute for Social Research, The University of Michigan, 1964 B).

organizational conflict. For example, Thompson and Tuden observe that the type and degree of consensus in organizations will dictate different optimal strategies of decision making, such as a reliance on facts or compromise. In turn such strategies will condition the level of cooperation or conflict.[9] Then whether such decision processes actually occur will depend upon existing practices for communication in the organization. Moreover, in the light of Newcomb's discussion of balance theory,[10] the effect of consensus in the prevention of interlevel conflict may be expected to vary depending upon the nature and level of commitment of organization members.

Consequences of Intra-Organizational Conflict. Two aspects of this phase of the problem are considered: (*1*) the consequences of intra-organizational conflict for achieving organizational objectives; (*2*) the processes alleviating or intensifying such consequences. Intra-organizational conflict is not considered as invariably having dysfunctional consequences for the performance of an organization. Although conflict may in some instances be so intense as to destroy the organization, in other instances, it may stimulate creative problem-solving and innovation.[11] This view is consistent with that of Litwak, who states that the traditional bureaucratic organization can tolerate very little conflict, the human-relations organization somewhat more, whereas the professional organizations are structured to permit a great deal of conflict.[12] The organizations included in the present analysis represent a range along this continuum.

Equally important, it is assumed that the consequences of intra-organizational conflict for the functioning of an organization will depend to a large extent upon the processes employed to control or manage the conflict. As Katz observes,[13] the strategies utilized in organizations for dealing with various types of conflict range from those which simply attempt to make the system work, to those which introduce additional machinery for conflict adjudication, to those involving restructuring the organization to reduce built-in conflict. A few of these strategies are examined in the present analysis: (*1*) the reliance upon general bureaucratic rules, as a means of "making the system work"; (*2*) leadership practices of planning, coordinating, and providing supportive functions as a way of either preventing conflict or adjudicating it once it has arisen; (*3*) the effects of a system of high mutual influence crosscutting specialities and hierarchical levels as a means of restructuring an organization to reduce built-in conflict. The relative efficacy of these three processes is assessed in different types of organizations, which, in view of their different system problems, might be expected to stress different mechanisms of conflict resolution.

Procedure

Sample of Organizations and Source of Data. In a test of the alternative hypotheses of the determinants and consequences of intra-organizational conflict, a comparative analysis was made in approximately 250 separate organizational units from six organizations.[14] The six organizations include the following:

[9] James D. Thompson and Arthur Tuden, "Strategies and Processes in Organizational Decision," in *Comparative Studies of Administration* (Pittsburgh, Pa.: University of Pittsburgh Administrative Science Center, 1959).

[10] Theodore M. Newcomb, "Individual Systems of Orientation," in S. Koch (ed.), *A Study of Systematic Resources* (Washington, D. C.: American Psychological Association and National Science Foundation, 1961).

[11] The findings of Donald Marquis and his associates on the prediction of scientific performance suggest that when conflict consists of differences in ideas and approaches, in contrast to differences in values and basic motivations, it may have a constructive and stimulating effect; cf. W. M. Evan, R. R. Blain, and G. R. Mackethan, "Four Types of Conflict in Research and Development Performance," in Donald G. Marquis, *Organizational Research Program* (Cambridge, Mass.: Massachusetts Institute of Technology, Dec. 9, 1963). L. Richard Hoffman has recently attempted to specify conceptually the conditions under which such differences will lead to problem solving and creative solutions; cf. Conditions for Creative Problem Solving, *Journal of Psychology*, 52 (1961), 429–444.

[12] Eugene Litwak, Models of Bureaucracy Which Permit Conflict, *American Journal of Sociology*, 67 (1961), 177–184.

[13] Katz, *op. cit.*

[14] This comparative analysis complements that of Smith and Brown, *op. cit.*, (1964 B), which is devoted to an assessment of factors underlying or-

1. Four locals of an international trade union.
2. A sample of 112 local leagues of the League of Women Voters.
3. Thirty geographically separate stations within a nationally organized delivery company.
4. Thirty-three geographically separate dealerships of an automotive sales organization.
5. Forty geographically separate agencies of a nationally organized insurance company.
6. Thirty-six branch offices of a national brokerage firm.

Several aspects of these organizations lend themselves to a comparative analysis: (1) Each organization has component units with identical purposes, similar technologies, and comparable formal structures. (2) The component units generally operate within similar environments and are located in or near large metropolitan areas. (3) Each organization exhibits significant variation with respect to the general level of intra-organizational conflict. (4) Comparable measures of social structure, interpersonal processes, and organizational performance are available, particularly with respect to the conceptual definitions of these variables.

Equally important, the six organizations differ greatly in organizational structure, purposes, and the participants who benefit from the output of the organization. This makes it possible to ascertain the general or limited applicability of the explanations being assessed. For example, the unions and the voluntary associations, with their member orientation, contrast sharply with the business organizations, with their emphasis on the efficient pursuit of objectives established by the owners. Consequently, the potential for intra-organizational conflict, as well as the mechanisms employed for managing conflict, can be expected to differ markedly in these two clusters of organizations.

The information about each of these organizations came originally from the organizations and their members as a product of collaborative research with the Survey Research Center of the University of Michigan. The data are taken from the research archives of this research center. The data on organizational performance, as well as on most of the measures of social structure, are based on official organizational records or reports of individual organization members. The data on interpersonal processes are derived from questionnaires administered by Survey Research Center personnel to members of these organizations.

Intra-Organizational Conflict. "Conflict" was defined as a situation in which the conditions, practices, or goals for the different participants are inherently incompatible. Responses of members of each organization to similar questions ascertained on a five-point scale the amount of conflict and tension between all possible combinations of hierarchical groups within the organizational unit. The amount of conflict between two hierarchical levels in an organizational unit was computed by averaging judgments of respondents about the two levels in question. An index of the general level of intra-organizational conflict was derived by computing for each organizational unit, the sum of the averaged judgments of all possible combinations of hierarchical groups. In the interests of comparability and of limiting the index to a measure of *intra*-organizational conflict alone, a measure of direct conflict between the company and the union was excluded from this computation.

Two reservations must be made. Although the questions were similarly phrased in all organizations, one cannot be entirely sure that respondents in different organizational contexts attributed precisely the same meaning to the question. The data obtained, however, indicate that this is not a serious problem. Moreover, the present preliminary investigation is limited to a concern with conflict as a general phenomenon and does not deal with different varieties of conflict in all their complexity.

Social Structure. Five measures of social structure were developed which were thought to bear either on the generation of interlevel conflict or on its resolution. These included organizational size, complexity or specialization, differentiation, and two measures of organizational control structure. Size was operationalized in terms of the total number of

ganizational control and its effects, and which gives a more extensive description of the general approach utilized, the organizations studied, and the specific operationalization of the measures common to both analyses.

members in each organizational unit. For all organizations, complexity was defined simply as the number of formal positions in the organizational unit. It was determined by summing the total number of formal positions specified in the organizational chart at both the rank-and-file and officer level, thus indicating the degree of specialization or complexity of the role system. Differentiation refers to the development of the officer or supervisory level, and was operationalized in terms of the ratio of actual supervisory or officer personnel (including staff or advisory personnel) to the size of the organizational unit.

Control refers to "any process in which a person (or group, or organization) determines or affects what another person (or group, or organization) will do." [15] Measures of control were based on responses of members in each organization to similar questions ascertaining (on a five-point scale) the amount of influence that each of several hierarchical groups or persons had upon activity within the organization. The amount of control exercised by each of the hierarchical levels in a given organizational unit was computed by averaging judgments of respondents about each of the levels. Indices defining the pattern of control included the relative distribution of control among hierarchical levels—whether centralized or decentralized—and the total amount of control exercised by all hierarchical levels. Measures of the relative distribution of control were derived by computing for each organizational unit the average of the algebraic differences between the amount of influence reported to be exercised by successive hierarchical levels. A high score would represent high rank-and-file control relative to upper echelons, a low score the converse. The total amount of control was computed for each organizational unit simply by summing the amount of control reported to be exercised by all the various hierarchical levels. Previous research suggests that these indices provide reasonably valid measures of control structure, even though they are subject to some unreliability.[16]

It was expected that conflict between lower participants and those higher in the organizational hierarchy would be most directly related to how closely the goals or subgoals of the organization were oriented toward the rank-and-file members; i.e., represented their interests. For the six organizations, this was measured as shown in Table I.

Table 1. Measures of Member-Oriented Goals

ORGANIZATION	MEASURE
Brokerage firm	Whether policies were oriented toward the account executives or the firm
Insurance company	Economic gain of the agents relative to the volume of sales
Automotive sales	Personal gain on the part of the salesmen if the dealership was successful
Delivery company	Extent to which the company was interested in its employees
Voluntary association	Extent to which sociability among members was emphasized
Union locals	Degree to which specific utilitarian goals existed

Interpersonal Processes. Member attitudes toward the organization, participation in the organization, consensus of organizational members, and interlevel communication were thought to have a strong effect on interlevel conflict. These measures of members' attitudes toward their organization were taken as repre-

[15] This definition follows that of Arnold S. Tannenbaum, Control in Organizations: Individual Adjustment and Organizational Performance, *Administrative Science Quarterly*, 7 (1962), 236–257. For a further discussion of this concept, see that of Smith and Ari, *op. cit.*

[16] See for example, Arnold S. Tannenbaum and Clagett G. Smith, The Effects of Member Influence in an Organization: Phenomenology versus Organizational Structure, *Journal of Abnormal and Social Psychology* 69 (1964), 401–410; and Jerald Bachman, Clagett G. Smith, and Jonathan A. Slesinger, Control, Performance, and Satisfaction: An Analysis of Structural and Individual Effects, *Journal of Abnormal and Social Psychology* (in press).

Table 2. Measures of Interpersonal Processes

ORGANIZATION	COMMITMENT	PARTICIPATION	INTERLEVEL COMMUNICATION	FORMAL RULES AND PROCEDURES
Brokerage firm	Indices of general satisfaction derived from items which included policies and goals of firm	Members reports on average number of hours per week	Adequacy of knowledge about the office	Two questions about the importance of rules and regulations and willingness of members to set aside rules in interest of production
Insurance company	As in brokerage firm	As in brokerage firm	Ease of obtaining technical information	The degree to which work procedures are programmed
Automotive sales	Preference of salesmen to remain in their particular dealerships given the possibility of moving to another	As in brokerage firm	Adequacy of knowledge about dealerships	Extent to which general rules govern relations among salesmen
Delivery company	Level of morale which members judged to exist in their respective stations	This index not available since length of work week constant	Adequacy of knowledge about the job	Inversely indicated by percent of respondents who answered that there were no work standards
Voluntary association	Index of member loyalty; i.e., the willingness of members to expend additional effort if existence of organization was threatened either by external or by internal circumstances	Number of meetings of various kinds attended and involvement of members in various committees	Total amount of communication between members and board members	Degree of understanding by members of formal procedures and objectives of the League
Union locals	As in voluntary association	As in voluntary association	Measure of communication not available	Degree of observance of formal democratic procedures

senting identification with or commitment to the organization and its goals and are described in Table 2.

The participation of members in the organization was taken as the degree of time and energy they devoted to organizational activities (Table 2). Consensus was defined as agreement in attitude among organizational members toward the job, the policies and goals of the organization, its manner of operation (including its pattern of control), or other organizationally relevant attitudes. In each organization, questionnaire items were selected which pertained to areas in which differences might be expected to generate friction or conflict among members and ultimately impede concerted activity. After items were selected in terms of this criterion, as well as a statistical one which would rule out the possibility of any ceiling effect, inverse of variances were computed from member responses for each organizational unit in each of the six organizations. The data on the separate items were then averaged to provide measures of general consensus for each organizational unit. The specific items utilized in each organization have been previously described by Smith and Brown.[17]

Measures of interlevel communication considered the amount or adequacy of communication between lower participants and those higher in the organizational hierarchy, and are described in Table 2.[18]

Measures of organizational mechanisms which were thought to have implications for the resolution of interlevel conflict, or for preventing it, included the existence of general rules and types of leadership practices. The other hypothesized mechanism of conflict resolution is the total amount of control resulting from the mutual influence occurring across specialities and hierarchical levels.

In each organization, indices were developed to indicate the degree to which formal rules and procedures were available for carrying out the objectives of the organization, and are described in Table 2. For the present analysis two major leadership functions were developed: an "initiation of structure" function and a "supportive" function. The first was defined as the degree to which the leaders in each organizational unit performed a planning, administrative, or coordinative function. This func-

Table 3. Measures of Effectiveness

ORGANIZATION	MEASURE
Brokerage firm	Average standardized performance of office salesmen measured in dollar productivity with the effects of differential individual experience eliminated
Insurance company	Productivity records provided by company officials indicating their annual volume of business
Automotive sales	Extent to which actual sales met assigned sales quotas in each dealership
Delivery company	Objective productivity measures provided by the company
Voluntary association	Ratings of 29 officers of the national headquarters of the League who evaluated the local leagues they were familiar with in terms of formal objectives established for the local leagues by the national organization
Union locals	Judgments by original researchers of the union's power vis-à-vis their respective managements

[17] Smith and Brown, *op. cit.* (1964 B).

[18] The measures of communication thus employed are not strictly comparable in the six organizations, particularly the measure employed in the voluntary association as compared to those used in the business organizations. Such differences should be borne in mind in the ensuing analyses. Under conditions of free and open communication in the voluntary association, however, it was thought that the measure of the amount of communication employed would be highly correlated with its adequacy, if such a measure were available.

tion was thought to be of primary importance in developing a setting that would encourage cooperative, consistent, interrelated activity. The supportive function pertains to the material or social rewards in response to the followers' needs for achievement or affiliative experiences, needs which might be expected to be substantially frustrated by an overbureaucratized or hierarchical form of organization. In each organization, similar indices were derived which reflected the basic aspects of these two functions. The specific operations employed in each organization to define these functions have been described previously.[19]

Analysis and Results

The hypotheses to be tested in this paper involve essentially hypothesizing relationships among an independent variable, one or more intervening or mediating variables or processes, and a dependent variable, the latter in turn serving as an independent variable in another set of processes. In order to test the hypotheses in this manner, a correlational procedure was adopted, which was originally suggested by Simon,[21] and is illustrated in the work of Indik.[22] The procedure is illustrated

Table 4. Determinants of Intra-Organizational Conflict: Comparison of Hypotheses

VARIABLES CORRELATED	HYPOTHESIS	UNION LOCALS	VOLUNTARY ASSOCIATION	DELIVERY COMPANY	AUTOMOTIVE SALES	INSURANCE COMPANY	BROKERAGE FIRM
r_1 Identification; member consensus	+	1.00 †	0.53 †	0.42 †	0.53 †	0.29 †	0.43 †
r_2 Identification; interlevel communication	+	NA	0.38 †	0.63 †	0.38 †	0.29 †	0.36 †
r_3 Identification; organizational conflict	—	0.80 *	0.07	−0.76 †	−0.22	−0.20	−0.29 †
r_4 Member consensus; interlevel communication	+	NA	0.31 †	0.63 †	0.38 †	0.20	0.16
r_5 Member consensus; organizational conflict	—	0.80 *	−0.03	−0.57 †	−0.20	−0.49 †	−0.18
r_6 Interlevel communication; organizational conflict	—	NA	−0.09	−0.72 †	0.09	−0.44 †	−0.10

NA missing data.
* Significant at the 0.10 level of confidence.
† Significant at the 0.05 level of confidence or greater.

Effectiveness. Following Georgopoulos and Tannenbaum,[20] organizational effectiveness was defined as the extent to which an organization, given certain resources and means, achieves its objectives without incapacitating its means and resources, and without placing undue strain on its members. The actual measures of effectiveness employed (see Table 3) while consistent with this definition, varied in the different organizations studied.

in the figures below Tables 4 through 7. The explanation is taken as valid if all the variables are significantly related in the manner specified in the figures. The assumption of mediating variables is particularly critical for the validity of the hypotheses. A variable which is related both to the measures of the independent variable and the dependent variable is taken as representing a mediating or intervening variable. A variable which is related to the independent variable but not to the dependent

[19] Smith and Brown, *op. cit.* (1964 B).
[20] Basil Georgopoulos and Arnold S. Tannenbaum, A Study of Organizational Effectiveness, *American Sociological Review*, 67 (1961), 177–184.
[21] Herbert A. Simon, *Models of Man* (New York: Wiley, 1957).
[22] Indik, *op. cit.*

variable is taken as representing one which conditions the effects of the independent variable. Strictly speaking, this technique does not by itself permit conclusions about causality with respect to the place of a variable in a given chain of events. If the relationship obtained is consistent with the *a priori* conceptual explanation, it affords us partial confidence in the type of relationship obtained, but the conclusion must be buttressed by additional (longitudinal) analyses and strong theory.

Determinants of Intra-Organizational Conflict. Table 4 presents the basic results bearing on the tenability of the relationships expected in terms of the three hypotheses. The relationships obtained in terms of Explanation 1, the communication hypothesis, are presented in Table 5. Table 6 summarizes the relationships obtained in terms of Explanation 2, the conflict of interest hypothesis. Table 7 summarizes the relationships obtained in terms of Explanation 3, the consensus hypothesis. Table 4 summarizes the intercorrelations among identification, consensus, and interlevel communication. This allows us to compare their respective contribution to the level of intra-organizational conflict in the organizations studied.

COMMUNICATION HYPOTHESIS. This hypothesis on the importance of adequate interlevel communication in the prevention of conflict seems more appropriate to the business organizations than to the union or the voluntary association. In Table 4 it can be seen that especially in the delivery organization ($r_6 = -0.72$) and in the insurance company ($r_6 = -0.44$), the predicted correlations between the measures of interlevel communication and intra-organizational conflict are significantly substantiated. The small number of significant relationships, however, temper any general conclusion, and indicate that, for the organizations in general, poor communication and lack of understanding between members oc-

Table 5. Determinants of Intra-Organizational Conflict: Communication Hypothesis

VARIABLES CORRELATED	HYPOTHESIS	UNION LOCALS	VOLUNTARY ASSOCIATION	DELIVERY COMPANY	AUTOMOTIVE SALES	INSURANCE COMPANY	BROKERAGE FIRM
r_1 Size; interlevel communication	—	NA	−0.51 †	−0.26 *	−0.26 *	0.30 †	−0.07
r_2 Size; complexity	+	1.00 †	NA	0.84 †	0.66 †	0.62 †	NA
r_3 Size; differentiation	+	−0.15	0.13	0.39 †	−0.36 †	−0.30 †	0.31 †
r_4 Complexity; differentiation	+	−0.15	NA	0.57 †	0.13	0.39 †	NA
r_5 Complexity; interlevel communication	—	NA	NA	−0.19	−0.05	0.51 †	NA
r_6 Differentiation; interlevel communication	—	NA	0.07	−0.23 †	0.43 †	0.35 †	−0.06

NA missing data.
* Significant at the 0.10 level of confidence.
† Significant at the 0.05 level of confidence or greater.

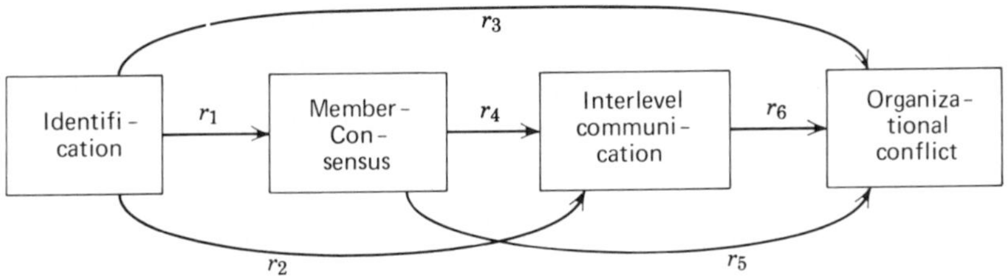

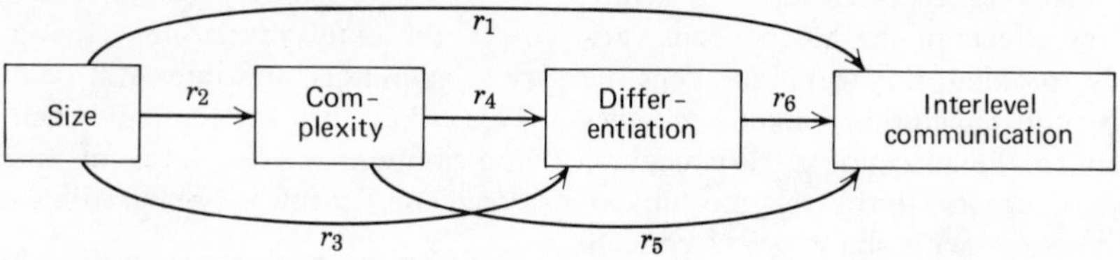

cupying different positions in the hierarchy are are not in themselves inevitably a major source of inter-level conflict.

These results seem partially explainable in terms of the relationships found with respect to the structural factors associated with the adequacy of communications, as summarized in Table 5. Although size is accompanied by an increased complexity of roles, in most cases complexity does not lead to an increased differentiation of the leadership or to poor interlevel communication. Furthermore, a relatively high ratio of leadership roles, as indicated by differentiation, does not generally lower the adequacy of communication between rank-and-file members and officers; in fact in the automotive sales organization and the insurance company it facilitates interlevel communication. Although large size does have some of the effects predicted by this hypothesis, size does not appear to affect communications to the degree that would by itself lead to serious conflict between echelons.

CONFLICT OF INTEREST HYPOTHESIS. This hypothesis also receives partial confirmation, as indicated by the correlations between the measures of identification and intra-organizational conflict (see Table 4). Again, this hypothesis seems more appropriate to the business organizations than to the union or the voluntary association. It is particularly in the brokerage firm ($r_3 = -0.29$) and in the delivery organization ($r_3 = -0.76$) that significant correlations emerge. By contrast, the predicted relationships are not obtained in the voluntary association or in the union; in fact, in the union, high loyalty among the members is accompanied by heightened conflict between members and officers ($r_3 = 0.80$). It is also evident in Table 6 that although differentiated structure does not necessarily lead to hierarchical or centralized control, centralized control is generally accompanied by organizational goals which do not reflect the interests of the rank and file. In all six of the organizations, this is associated with lower identification with the

Table 6. Determinants of Intra-Organizational Conflict: Conflict of Interest Hypothesis

VARIABLES CORRELATED	HYPOTHESIS	UNION LOCALS	VOLUNTARY ASSOCIATION	DELIVERY COMPANY	AUTOMOTIVE SALES	INSURANCE COMPANY	BROKERAGE FIRM
r_1 Differentiation; identification	—	0.15	0.03	—0.42 †	0.14	0.38 †	—0.05
r_2 Differentiation; hierarchical control	+	0.95 †	—0.23 †	—0.11	—0.15	0.45 †	—0.12
r_3 Differentiation; member-oriented goals	—	0.35	0.08	—0.33 *	0.05	—0.05	0.37 †
r_4 Hierarchical control; member-oriented goals	—	0.25	—0.28 †	—0.35 †	—0.31 †	0.06	—0.37 †
r_5 Hierarchical control; identification	—	—0.40	—0.25 †	—0.05	0.25	0.06	0.02
r_6 Member-oriented goals; identification	+	0.65	0.36 †	0.63 †	0.37 †	0.34 †	0.10

NA missing data.
* Significant at the 0.10 level of confidence.
† Significant at the 0.05 level of confidence or greater.

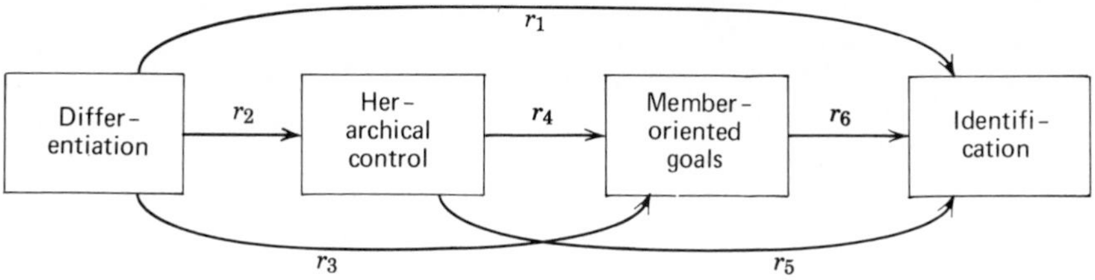

organization, but as the results above indicate, lack of identification is related to organizational conflict only in the business organizations.

CONSENSUS HYPOTHESIS. This hypothesis also seems tenable, as indicated by the correlations between the measures of consensus and interlevel conflict summarized in Table 4. Here too, the hypothesis seems particularly appropriate to the business organizations and receives significant support in the delivery organization ($r_5 = -0.57$) and in the insurance company ($r_5 = -0.49$). From the structural correlations of consensus in Table 7, it is evident that identification with the organization is strongly associated with a high level of member consensus in all six of the organizations. Frequency of participation in the activities of the organization does not, however, appear to be an important condition mediating this relationship. Rather, consensus appears to have a motivational basis as indicated by the significant correlations between the measures of identification and member consensus obtained in all six organizations. Although lack of shared perception and attitudes may have the general effect of impeding coordination, it does not seem sufficient to bring about actual conflict in the union or the voluntary association. In fact, member consensus operates to increase the degree of interlevel conflict in the union ($r_5 = 0.80$).

Table 7. Determinants of Intra-Organizational Conflict: Consensus Hypothesis

VARIABLES CORRELATED	HYPOTHESIS	UNION LOCALS	VOLUNTARY ASSOCIATION	DELIVERY COMPANY	AUTOMOTIVE SALES	INSURANCE COMPANY	BROKERAGE FIRM
r_4 Identification; participation	+	0.80 *	0.56 †	NA	0.27	0.13	0.12
r_5 Identification; member consensus	+	1.00 †	0.53 †	0.42 †	0.53 †	0.29 †	0.43 †
r_6 Participation; member consensus	+	0.80 †	0.35 †	NA	0.23	0.19	0.33 †

NA missing data.
* Significant at the 0.10 level of confidence.
† Significant at the 0.05 level of confidence or greater.

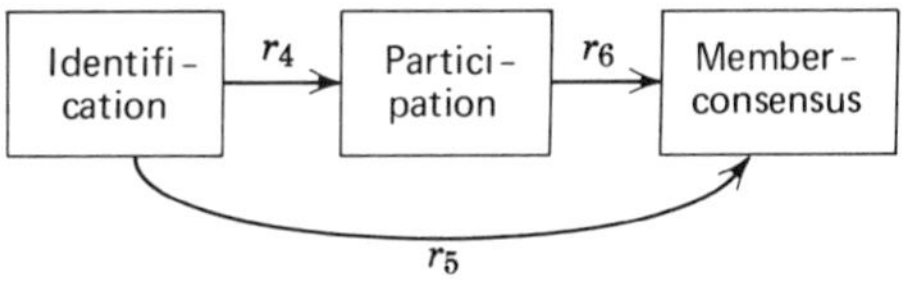

Discussion of Results. Taken together, the general pattern of results indicates that each hypothesis is more appropriate to the business organizations than to the union or the voluntary association. These findings are not unexpected. As Litwak notes,[23] the potential for conflict tends to be greater in centralized, bureaucratic organizations. Furthermore, as a consequence of the limited material or "utilitarian" type of compliance in these organizations,[24] any condition which further decreases

[23] Litwak, *op. cit.*

[24] This follows the postulate presented by Amitai Etzioni, *A Comparative Analysis of Complex Organizations* (Glencoe, Ill.: The Free Press, 1961).

the commitment of members (or increases their alienation), or makes for disagreements in perceptions and attitudes (both reflecting unfavorable rewards or returns) is more likely to result in conflict in these organizations.

It is not entirely clear why the generally positive findings are stronger in the delivery company and insurance company than in the brokerage firm, and are very slight in the automobile dealerships. Perhaps goals are more operational or the tasks are more highly interdependent and require more concerted activity in the delivery and insurance companies; this seems to be particularly the case in the delivery organization. If the hypothesis of March and Simon [25] is valid, there should be a greater need for joint decision making; and organizational strains arising from a complex, differentiated role structure and centralized control are more likely to give rise to problems in interpersonal relations. In short, under conditions of a heavily structured organization where there is need for joint decision making, the possibility of conflict is greater. Another possibility is that competition may be less exclusively regulated by bureaucratic mechanisms in the brokerage firm and even less regulated in the automobile dealerships. In the dealerships, competition may be controlled or regulated by informal means, so that it does not develop into actual conflict. In effect, there may be more flexible means for dealing with problems of communications, and differences in perceptions, attitudes, and interests. But it should be emphasized that in all the business organizations the relationships are generally in the expected direction. The variations in the

Table 8. Consequences of Intra-Organizational Conflict

VARIABLES CORRELATED	HYPOTHESIS	UNION LOCALS	VOLUNTARY ASSOCIATION	DELIVERY COMPANY	AUTOMOTIVE SALES	INSURANCE COMPANY	BROKERAGE FIRM
r_1 Intra-organizational conflict; organizational effectiveness	—	0.80 *	0.22 †	−0.55 †	−0.16	−0.25 †	0.19
r_2 Intra-organizational conflict; general rules	—	0.00	0.15	−0.12	0.06	−0.14	−0.28 †
r_3 Intra-organizational conflict; initiation of structure	—	0.00	−0.09	−0.61 †	0.02	−0.37 †	−0.17
r_4 Intra-organizational conflict; supportiveness	—	0.00	−0.15 †	−0.64 †	0.12	−0.70 †	−0.32 †
r_5 Intra-organizational conflict; total amount of control	—	0.80 *	0.03	−0.68 †	−0.29 †	−0.46 †	−0.22
r_6 General rules; organizational effectiveness	+	0.40	0.10	−0.10	−0.03	0.02	−0.14
r_7 Initiation of structure; organizational effectiveness	+	0.40	0.15 †	0.34 †	−0.29 †	0.59 †	0.34 †
r_8 Supportiveness; organizational effectiveness	+	0.40	0.12	0.44 †	0.10	0.43 †	0.28 †
r_9 Total amount of control; organizational effectiveness	+	1.00 †	0.18 †	0.46 †	0.11	0.49 †	0.30 †

NA missing data.
* Significant at the 0.10 level of confidence.
† Significant at the 0.05 level of confidence or greater.

[25] James G. March and Herbert A. Simon, *Organizations* (New York: Wiley, 1958), ch. v.

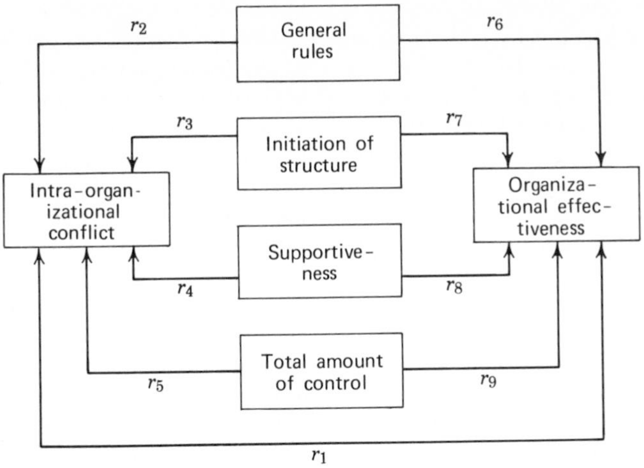

strength of the relationships for the different business organizations may simply reflect statistical "noise" or lack of strict comparability of the measures.

There is a notable lack of support for the three hypotheses in the voluntary association and the union; in fact, the evidence is negative for the union. These findings are also not unexpected. These member-oriented organizations are designed to promote the shared values and goals of the members; consequently there are no basic differences of interests between the rank-and-file members and the officers, even though this condition may develop in other types of trade unions or voluntary associations. Furthermore, the union and voluntary association examined are structured to facilitate majority rule, freedom of discussion and dissent, and joint decision making; consequently, interpersonal problems generated by an over-structured, bureaucratic organization are less apt to arise. If anything, high identification with the organization and consensus among members tends to increase intra-organizational conflict in the union (r_3, $r_5 = 0.80$). In contrast to the voluntary association, these union locals have predominantly bread-and-butter goals and the rank and file have a utilitarian orientation. It is not surprising then that, under conditions of high identification and basic consensus, members' actions should result in conflict that may reflect disagreements as to the *means* of actualizing their interests, or dissension that is encouraged by the officers and the executive committee. Such disagreements and dissension of a self-interested nature are likely to be minimized or more formally regulated in the voluntary association.

Consequences of Intra-Organizational Conflict. Table 8 presents some findings on the consequences and management of intra-organizational conflict. This table summarizes the correlations between general rules, initiation of structure, supportiveness, and the total amount of control and organizational conflict and organizational effectiveness. The relationships between the independent variable of intra-organizational conflict and these four mediating variables are assumed to operate in both directions; that is, these variables are assumed to operate either to prevent conflict or to reduce its consequences for the effectiveness of the organization. The findings are striking in indicating that intra-organizational conflict does not inevitably have negative consequences for the effectiveness of an organization. As expected, the measure of interlevel conflict is negatively related to performance in three of the four business organizations: $r_1 = -0.55$ in the delivery company; $r_1 = -0.16$ in the sales organization; $r_1 = -0.25$ in the insurance company. This finding is again consistent with the contention of Litwak,[26] that if conflict arises in the traditional bureaucratic organization, it is likely to impede the coordinated pursuit of objectives. And it is particularly the organiza-

[26] Litwak, *op. cit.*

tions that have a complex, differentiated structure with control centralized in the upper echelons (the delivery company and the insurance company) that conflict has the most significant consequences. As was also seen in Table 4, conflict in these organizations is accompanied by low identification on the part of members and lack of shared perceptions and attitudes. Under these conditions, conflict between echelons has its most detrimental effects.

By contrast, intra-organizational conflict is positively associated with effectiveness in the union ($r_1 = 0.80$) and in the voluntary association ($r_1 = 0.22$). With the basic agreement in interests and attitudes, and high loyalty in these member-oriented organizations, interlevel conflict has constructive consequences for organizational performance. Instead of a bitter struggle for limited rewards by interest groups pursuing different goals, conflict in these organizations probably reflects discussion, dissent, and a conflict over means rather than ends. This is the type of conflict that the formal machinery of these organizations strives to promote, and that increases the effectiveness of these organizations.

It was further proposed that the consequences of intra-organizational conflict for the functioning of an organization would depend upon the techniques for managing the conflict. As seen from the data in Table 8, general bureaucratic rules alone have little relevance in either preventing or managing intralevel conflict (with the exception of the brokerage firm). This may mean that simply applying general rules to resolve conflict; i.e., attempting to make the system work better, has little effect in solving basic problems of communication, consensus, or conflicting interests, particularly when the rules are imposed by groups at the top of the hierarchy.

On the other hand, effective leadership seems to be an important variable in the prevention or resolution of conflict. Advanced planning and coordination, as indicated by the index of initiation of structure, appear to be important in some of the organizations, specifically, in the delivery organization ($r_3 = -0.61$) and the insurance company ($r_3 = -0.37$), in managing conflict generated by an over-bureaucratized form of organization. In these organizations, this leadership practice probably introduces flexibility and direction, so that interlevel conflict is either controlled in advance or mediated once it has arisen.

More important, supportiveness on the part of the leaders appears to have a more general applicability in managing conflict; significant negative relationships between the measures of this function and intra-organizational conflict occur in four of the six organizations examined. By providing practical or social support, the leadership may operate as a compensatory mechanism to offset problems of communication, organizational commitment, or differences of interests generated by a hierarchical form of organization. In effect, there are actually fewer differences in status, the technical competence of members of lower echelons is utilized more, and the gap between the unequal rewards accruing to the members and the leaders is bridged to some extent. This interpretation is particularly tenable in three of the four hierarchically organized business organizations, where the relationships are most definitive.

If the results suggest factors generating intra-organizational conflict that are ultimately inherent in large, hierarchical organization, they also indicate a way of restructuring the organization to reduce built-in conflicts. A pattern of high mutual influence among organizational members that crosses hierarchical levels and specialities may prevent destructive conflict, or it may help manage it once it has arisen—as indicated in three of the four business organizations—or stimulate constructive conflict—as in the union. This pattern of control may be effective partly because of better communications and interpersonal relationships, allowing a more flexible way of resolving conflicts. From earlier research,[27] this pattern of reciprocal influence is also likely to facilitate the development of a broader range of shared perceptions and attitudes among organizational members. Probably of most significance, the expansion in the control exercised by those lower in the hierarchy tends to counteract the consequences of hierarchical organization and serves to equalize, to some extent, the differences in status, authority, and organizational rewards which appear to be significant in the development of conflict in organizations.

[27] See Arnold S. Tannenbaum, Control Structure and Union Functions, *American Journal of Sociology*, 61 (1956), 536–545; and Smith and Ari, *op. cit.;* and Smith and Brown, *op. cit.* (1964 B).

The efficacy of this pattern of control in the prevention or management of conflict also obtains under conditions where such mutual influence complements the hierarchical form of organization. If carried to the extreme where there is no centralized direction, it might create new problems of communications, decision making, and coordination. As Zald's study suggests,[28] a system of shared influence among the parties can operate to intensify the level of conflict, particularly where there is a lack of agreement over ultimate goals and values to be pursued, or when the "game" is actually "zero-sum" in nature.

Summary and Conclusions

This study has presented a comparative analysis of some determinants and consequences of intra-organizational conflict in complex organizations. A test of three hypotheses about the structural and interpersonal processes generating intra-organizational conflict indicates that each is valid to some extent, but none completely represents the complexities of the relationships. Instead, the factors or combination of factors significant in the development of serious interlevel conflict depends upon the type of organization examined; some organizations, such as the business organizations, are more conflict-prone than others. Furthermore intra-organizational conflict does not inevitably have negative consequences for the performance of an organization. In certain types of organizations, as in the union and voluntary association, intra-organizational conflict may have constructive effects. Also, the consequences of intra-organizational conflict for the functioning of an organization seem to be contingent upon the techniques employed to manage the conflict. The findings suggest that two such techniques may be important: certain techniques of supportive leadership, and a system of high mutual influence crosscutting specialities and organizational echelons. They seem to provide counter-balances to the strains induced by hierarchical organization. Although this study has been limited to certain aspects of the problem of intra-organizational conflict, and consequently has underemphasized other aspects, it is hoped that the findings will provide hypotheses for more extensive comparative analyses.

[28] Mayer N. Zald, Power Balance and Staff Conflict in Correctional Institutions, *Administrative Science Quarterly*, 7 (1962), 22–49.

Selections from The Theory of the Growth of the Firm

EDITH PENROSE

"Inherited" Resources and the Direction of Expansion

The emphasis of our analysis now shifts from the limits on expansion to the direction of expansion. At any time a firm will have a variety of inducements to expand in one or more specific directions; but at the same time there will be a variety of difficulties to be overcome in planning and executing an expansion programme in any given direction. The inducements as well as the difficulties may be outside the firm, in the external world, or within the firm—in the "internal world" so to speak. They create conditions enhancing or restricting the profitability or practicability of expansion in particular directions.

The external inducements to expansion are well known and require little discussion. They include growing demand for particular products, changes in technology which call for production on a larger scale than before, discoveries and inventions the exploitation of which seems particularly promising or which open up promising fields in supplementary directions, special opportunities to obtain a better market position or achieve some monopolistic advantage, and similar conditions and opportunities. They also include changes which might adversely affect a firm's existing operations and against which it could protect itself through expansion in particular directions, for example through backward integration to control sources of supply, diversification of final products to spread risk, or expansion of existing or allied products to preclude the entry of new competitors.

External obstacles to expansion are equally well known. They include keen competition in markets for particular products which makes profitable entry or expansion in those markets difficult or necessitates expensive selling efforts and the acceptance of lower profit margins; the existence of patent rights and other restrictions on the use of knowledge and technology; high costs of entry into new areas; or difficulties of obtaining raw materials, labour, or specialized technical or managerial personnel.

While external inducements and difficulties have been widely discussed, little attention has been paid, in a systematic way at least, to the equally important internal influences on the direction of expansion. Internal obstacles arise when some of the important types of specialized service required for expansion in particular directions are not available in sufficient amounts within the firm—in particular when not enough of the managerial capacity and the technical skills required for the planning, execution, and efficient operation of a new programme can be had from among existing experienced personnel. Internal inducements to expansion arise largely from the existence of a pool of unused productive services, resources, and special knowledge, all of which will always be found within any firm. Most of this chapter will be devoted to the explanation of why there will always be unused productive services within a firm, and to a discussion of the significance of the existence of such services for the "external" opportunities for expansion as perceived by the firm.

We should note in passing that it is important to discuss separately the nature of the inducements and obstacles to expansion instead of simply "net inducements to expand", because different kinds of inducements and difficulties influence differently both the direction and the method of expansion chosen. If, for example, the external inducement to expand is the profitability of a new and growing market, but there is an external obstacle to entry in the form of, say, patent rights, the external inducements and obstacles may both be high and the only feasible method of expansion may be acquisition of another firm. Or, if the incentive to expand is the fear of adverse changes

From *The Theory of the Growth of the Firm*, New York, Wiley, 1959, pp. 65–76, 88–101. Reprinted by permission of the publisher.

in the external world the effects of which might be offset by diversification, the problem will be one of finding suitable fields in which neither the external nor the internal obstacles to expansion are great. On the other hand, a firm may have a strong internal inducement to expand provided by the presence of an energetic and ambitious entrepreneur with many ideas, but if at the same time the firm lacks the managerial abilities or technical skills to carry his ideas into action, a significant internal obstacle to expansion exists which again will influence the direction, and in particular, the method of expansion chosen. This type of problem will be taken up in the chapters on diversification, merger, and the factors affecting the rate of growth of firms.

The Continuing Availability of Unused Productive Services

Resources are defined to include the physical things a firm buys, leases, or produces for its own use, and the people hired on terms that make them effectively part of the firm. Services, on the other hand, are the contributions these resources can make to the productive operations of the firm. A resource, then, can be viewed as a bundle of possible services.

For any given scale of operations a firm must possess resources from which it can obtain the productive services appropriate to the amounts and types of product it intends to produce. Some of the services will be obtained from resources already under the control of the firm in the form of fixed plant and equipment, more or less permanent personnel, and inventories of materials and goods in process; others will be obtained from resources the firm acquires in the market as occasion demands. Although the "inputs" in which the firm is interested are productive services, it is *resources* that, with few exceptions, must be acquired in order to obtain services. For the most part, resources are only obtainable in discrete amounts, that is to say, a "bundle" of services must be acquired even if only a "single" service should be wanted.[1] The amount and kind of productive services obtainable from each *class* of resource are different, and sometimes, particularly with respect to personnel, the amount and kind of service obtainable from each *unit* within a resource-class are different. Having acquired resources for actual and contemplated operations, a firm has an incentive to use as profitably as possible the services obtainable from each unit of each type of resource acquired.

It follows, therefore, that as long as expansion can provide a way of using the services of its resources more profitably than they are being used, a firm has an incentive to expand; or alternatively, so long as any resources are not used fully in current operations, there is an incentive for a firm to find a way of using them more fully. Unused productive services available from existing resources are a "waste," sometimes an unavoidable waste (that is to say, it may not pay to try to use them) but they are "free" services which, if they can be used profitably, may provide a competitive advantage for the firm possessing them.

The next question to explore is whether or not it is likely that a firm will ever reach a position in which it will have no incentive to expand in order to use the productive services available from its existing collection of resources more profitably than they are being used. In the language of traditional theory, can we say that a firm will ever reach an "equilibrium position" in which there is no further internal incentive to expand?

The attainment of such a "state of rest" is precluded by three significant obstacles: those arising from the familiar difficulties posed by the indivisibility of resources; those arising from the fact that the same resources can be used differently under different circumstances, and in particular, in a "specialized" manner; and those arising because in the ordinary processes of operation and expansion new productive services are continually being created.

Indivisibility and the "Balance of Processes." The "balance of processes" or the "principle of multiples" has been explicitly discussed by economists for over 100 years with respect to

[1] Even those raw materials which are in principle finely divisible must usually be acquired in minimum-sized bundles because to acquire less than the "standard unit" is usually disproportionately expensive. However, this type of indivisibility is probably not of much practical importance.

the optimum size of plant.[2] It is an application of the principle of the "least common multiple". If a collection of indivisible productive resources is to be fully used, the minimum level of output at which the firm must produce must correspond to the least common multiple of the various maximum outputs obtainable from the smallest unit in which each type of resource can be acquired. The principle has usually been applied to machines, and even in this case it has been pointed out that it may be necessary to plan production on a very large scale in order to use all machines at their most efficient level of operation.[3]

If we consider the *full* range of resources used in any firm of even moderate size, including its various grades of management personnel, its engineers and other technical specialists, the minimum sales force needed to reach its market and sell its products, its financial specialists, and even its research personnel, it is clear that this "least common multiple" may call for an enormously large and varied output. This is, of course, the result of the indivisibility of the units in which resources can be acquired; even though a firm may not need a full-time salesman, engineer, or "trouble shooter", it is often impossible, or at best difficult and disproportionately expensive, to acquire a part-time one, and for a given scale of operations it may be preferable to acquire a resource and use it only partly than to do without it.

From our point of view, the significance of indivisibility does not lie so much in the fact that large units of equipment or large-scale processes may be most efficient in certain types of production—the traditional examples being railways, public utilities, mass production industries, etc. It lies rather in the fact that a large number and variety of indivisible resources are used. None of these need be very large, but if each is capable of rendering not only different amounts, but also different *kinds* of services, a combination that achieves the full utilization of all of them may perforce call for an output much larger and more *varied* than can be organized by a firm in any given period of time.

We have seen that there is a limit on the amount of expansion a firm can undertake at a given time. Obviously the output that will fully use the productive services available from every one of the firm's resources can be reached only if there is no limit short of this output on the availability of any of the productive services required to produce that output. If we take into account all of the resources used by a firm, the limit on the amount of expansion it can plan may well force it to forgo the use of many of the services available to it. In other words, in putting together the jig-saw puzzle of resources required in an expansion programme, the firm may find that a number of awkward corners persist in sticking out.[4]

On the other hand, we have also seen that the limit on expansion is a receding one; in the next period the firm can undertake still more. But in the process of expansion the firm will acquire still further resources, and the individual units of many of these will vary in the amount and type of service they can provide. Thus the "multiple" will again be changed, and further expansion may be called for; the firm may be aware that this will be the case even before it undertakes the expansion, but be unable to do anything about it; the firm needs the resources it acquires, but at the same time

[2] In 1832 Charles Babbage pointed out: "the extent of a factory . . . ought to consist of such a number of machines as shall occupy the whole time of one workman in keeping them in order, and in making any casual repairs; if it is extended beyond this, the same principle of economy would point out the necessity of doubling or tripling the number of machines, in order to employ the whole time of two or three skilful workmen". Charles Babbage, *On the Economy of Machinery and Manufactures* (London: Charles Knight, 1832), p. 175. So far as I know, E. A. G. Robinson was the first to use the term "balance of processes". *The Structure of Competitive Industry* (New York: Harcourt Brace, 1932), pp. 31–35. P. Sargant Florence uses the term "principle of multiples", *The Logic of British and American Industry* (London: Routledge and Kegan Paul), p. 51.

[3] See, for example, E. A. G. Robinson, op. cit., p. 33.

[4] For example, an industrial engineer in charge of product development in a firm is quoted as having stated: "Every time we make something, we have something left over, and have to find something to do with that. And when we find something to do with it we usually find that leaves us with something else. It is an endless process." A. D. H. Kaplan, *Big Enterprise in a Competitive System* (Washington D.C.: Brookings Institution, 1954), footnote, p. 191.

it cannot plan a programme large enough to use all of them fully.

The jig-saw puzzle becomes more complicated when we consider imperfections of the market, whether they arise from transport costs, monopoly positions, competitive differentiation of products, or the necessity of incurring selling costs. The full use of important resources in the process of production may, under such conditions, require some diversification of output because further expansion of some existing product lines may not be warranted by market conditions at the time, even though further growth in demand for these products may be expected in time.

When, however, a firm embarks on a programme of diversification, new types of resources rendering services quite different from those required to produce its older products will be added to the firm's collection of resources, and the problem of "balancing processes" may carry the firm off in entirely new directions.[5] Examples of this process will be given in Chapter VII, which deals with the economics of diversification.

Since attempts to achieve a "balance" in the utilization of resources can never reach the continually receding goal, some resources will always be only partly used and some will be used less efficiently than they would have been in the absence of the restriction on the firm's expansion. "Idle" services range from those available from resources which could be by-products but which are in fact treated as waste products and thrown away or dumped (because the firm cannot organize the profitable exploitation of them and is unable to sell them) to idle man- or machine-hours at various points in the production process and in the managerial staff.[6] By-products and certain other types of potential joint-products have in fact provided an important basis for expansion for some firms, once the energies of management could be released from the task of expanding the firm's primary lines.

The Specialized Use of Resources. The avoidance of "idleness" in resources is only one aspect of the problem posed by the indivisibility of resources and by the logical implications of the "principle of multiples" for the planning of the most efficient scale of a firm's operations. A firm has an incentive not only to engage in operations large enough to eliminate pools of idle services, but also to use the most valuable specialized services of its resources as fully as possible. A small firm may employ a chemist to test products in the process of production even though his services as a chemist are required only a few hours a day. The rest of his time may be used in checking inventories or in sending out accounts; he is not "idle," but neither are his most valuable services fully used because the firm's output is too small to permit their use. In general, the extent to which a firm can employ the most advantageous division of labour depends on the scale of its operations; the smaller its output the less can resources be used in a specialized manner.

That increasing division of labour is promoted by large markets, and that division of labour makes possible a more efficient use of resources, are among the most firmly accepted of the principles of economics. An increase of efficiency in the use of resources through the specialization of firms on narrowly defined products or processes was early seen to be a characteristic of the "industrial revolution."[7]

[5] For a good discussion see P. Sargant Florence, op. cit., pp. 74 ff. He summarizes his argument as follows: "The economy of integration due to common costs boils down to this, that if a manufacturer has a certain unused capacity in equipment or in research or in finance (or brains of himself and staff), it may pay to 'balance up' by taking on as a side line new processes or products using that idle capacity. As a summary to the American survey puts it under the heading of utilization of resources, 'diversification may result from an attempt to make full use of managerial or manufacturing capacity'". op. cit., p. 76. The "American survey" referred to is that of the Temporary National Economic Committee, *The Structure of Industry*, Monograph 27 (Wash., D.C., 1941).

[6] Not all "idle" or "free" services, however, provide genuinely profitable opportunities. The problems of expanding on such a basis—sometimes called "burden absorption" or "creep" are discussed in Chapter VII.

[7] See, for example, Allyn Young, "Increasing Returns and Economic Progress", *Economic Journal*, Vol. XXXVIII, No. 152 (Dec., 1928), pp. 527-542. The increasing scope for the division of labour led to a disintegration of industry in the sense that different processes became concentrated in separate specialized firms. There is no technological or organizational necessity for division of labour to take this form; it could just as well have

But just as the division of labour in the economy as a whole is limited by the demand for goods and services, so within a firm the division of labour, or the specialization of resources, is limited by the total output of the firm, for the firm's output controls its "demand" for productive services. If the chemist in our example were used only as a chemist, then other workers would have to be employed to check inventories and to send out accounts, but the employment of these new personnel becomes profitable only if the scale of operations is enlarged.[8]

Thus specialization can take place within a firm only to the extent that the output of the firm is large enough to justify it. In other words, increasing advantages from further division of labour within a firm are available to the firm only if it can grow. By the same token, to expand efficiently, a firm must effect a a division of labour appropriate to the size of the expansion it wants to undertake.

An extreme illustration of this was given earlier in another connection where it was pointed out that if the manager of a small firm is unwilling to relinquish any of his functions to others he creates a bottleneck which will effectively restrict further growth. In general, it can be said that when the demand for specialized services is sufficient to justify the specialization of resources, a failure on the part of a firm to effect at least a minimum degree of specialization will lead to such inefficiency that even firms in highly protected positions will run into serious administrative or technical trouble with a consequent severe increase in costs. A firm with only half a dozen administrative personnel would hardly consider a type of organization where there was no division of labour at all between the administrators, each doing a bit of everything in turn.

As a firm grows in size, therefore, it will reorganize its resources to take advantage of the more obvious opportunities for specialization. As a result, a higher level of output will be required if full use is to be made of resources. In consequence, the process of growth which itself necessitates, at least up to a point, increasing specialization, gives rise at the same time to higher and higher "lowest common multiples" with respect to the output which will fully use the specialized services of the resources acquired. This has been called the "virtuous circle" in which "specialization leads to higher common multiples, higher common multiples to greater specialization."[9]

The mere fact, however, that a higher level of output is called for does not mean that a firm can plan the amount of expansion necessary to produce it. To the extent that the problem is primarily one of attaining the lowest-cost scale of production for a given product, it seems probable that a point will be reached where no further gains are to be obtained from specialization. But the process is a good deal more than this, for the advantages of using the specialized services of resources may themselves lead a firm to diversify its final output. It often happens, for example, that there are "stages" in the processes of production in which significant economies can be obtained if sufficient use can be made of specialized resources. This may promote diversification of final output by encouraging a firm to produce a group of products which require the same productive services at some stage, for example, products that use raw materials processed in common, or products that are sold through the same channels of distribution. In other words, if a group of products have costs in common, specialization at the point of com-

taken the form of a division of function between different establishments of the same firm or different parts of the same establishment, and if there were no restrictions on the rate of growth of firms I should expect this to have occurred. One reason for the limit to the rate of expansion of firms was the difficulty of obtaining capital for expansion by the individual firm, particularly in the days before the corporation or joint-stock company was the normal form of industrial enterprise and equity markets little developed. But in addition the fact that the rate of internal expansion of firms is limited under any circumstances encourages specialization of firms in periods of rapidly growing demand. This limit on expansion was even more restrictive in the 19th century than it is to-day, for acquisition and merger were not common means of expansion before the "corporate age".

[8] There are many discussions of the relation between specialization and the scale of operations of firms and there is no need to give an extensive review of the subject here. Among the more comprehensive discussions is that of P. Sargant Florence in the works already cited.

[9] P. Sargant Florence, op. cit., p. 52.

mon cost may reduce the cost of production of any one of them. And once new products are added, new types of specialized resources may be required at other stages of production or distribution, and a new series of advantages from further specialization in still different directions may become obtainable.

The new resources required are, of course, not only managerial, but include other types of personnel, such as engineers and salesmen, as well as physical resources, such as plant and equipment. Moreover, with larger outputs it becomes profitable to use different kinds of resources and processes. In particular, it becomes profitable to employ expensive capital equipment instead of, or in addition to, specialized labour resources, and to undertake activities unprofitable at smaller scales of operation, such as extensive advertising, market analysis or other research. The total of the productive services available to the firm is again enlarged, and the "jig-saw" puzzle changes in size. But there is every reason to assume that the problem of fully using all resources will never be solved, partly for the reasons discussed above, but partly also because *new* services will become available from existing resources—services which were not anticipated when the expansion was originally planned. Why new services from managerial resources will be created has already been demonstrated; but the change in the services of managerial resources also changes the nature of the productive services available from other resources, as well as the significance to the firm's management of existing services. Let us see how.

The Heterogeneity of Resources. Productive services are not "man-hours," or "machine-hours" or "bales of cotton," or "tons of coal," but the actual services rendered by the men, machines, cotton, or coal in the productive process. Although it is manifestly services in this sense that are the actual (physical) "inputs" in production, a less specific or more indirect definition is usually required when services must be expressed as measurable homogeneous *quantities*, for example, if it is desired to measure the *cost* of certain productive services or to construct technological production functions for certain outputs. In the theory of production, therefore, man-hours, machine-hours, acre-years, or the units in which a resource is acquired, are themselves often treated as the productive services of the resource.[10] Such generalized definitions of services are sufficient where it is the *homogeneity* of the services per unit of any given resource that is relevant for the analysis; they are not useful where the *heterogeneity* of the services contained in resources makes a fundamental difference.

For many purposes it is possible to deal with rather broad categories of resources, overlooking the lack of homogeneity in the members of the category. Economists usually recognize this, stating that for convenience alone resources are grouped under a few heads—for example, land, labour and capital—but pointing out that the sub-division of resources may proceed as far as is useful, and according to whatever principles are most applicable for the problem in hand.[11] There are many resources of which each unit is so much like every other unit that a homogeneous category can be established which includes a large number of units. This is true of many materials. With respect to other resources, however, each unit may be so unique that any classification, except one that makes each unit a separate resource, must disregard some heterogeneity; this is the case for human beings, land, and certain other types of resources.

The lack of homogeneity within any classification of resources does not much matter if we are concerned only with the analysis of the supply of particular services (as is true for the most part in the theory of production) and if there is a reasonable relation between the

[10] As a matter of fact, no consistent principle other than practical convenience has been adopted. In some circumstances the service itself can be expressed in homogeneous units (BTU's for coal, haulage-miles for trucks) and these units may be used; in others a unit of the resource itself has to be used (bales of cotton, pounds of sulphuric acid). The chief problem is to obtain a classification related to the nature of the resource within which the required degree of homogeneity exists. When a choice of units is feasible, measures that reflect most directly the actual services rendered tend to be preferred.

[11] The subdivision cannot go so far that each input is defined as a separate resource, however. The only purpose of devising a "unit" of resources or services is to enable us to measure the number of units within a given category. If this number is always one, no purpose is served by the classification.

amount of service supplied and the measure of the service in terms of the resource. For some productive services even this is lacking: entrepreneurial services are the classic example and many economists have refused to include entrepreneurs among the "factors of production" since the heterogeneous nature of entrepreneurial services is such that no "unit" of input can be devised. The number of entrepreneurial man-hours has surely very little relation to the "amount" of service rendered. This is equally true of research personnel, of the higher grades of managerial personnel, and similar types of human services. In all these cases, not only is each resource unique, but many of its services are unique in the sense that the same service is not repeatable. An idea produced, a decision made, an important employee grievance settled, are each a unique operation of value in the organization of production—services performed which cannot be repeated. There is no supply curve or production function into which such services can be fitted, but they are nevertheless inputs in production.

The fact that most resources can provide a variety of different services is of great importance for the productive opportunity of a firm. It is the heterogeneity, and not the homogeneity, of the productive services available or potentially available from its resources that gives each firm its unique character. Not only can the personnel of a firm render a heterogeneous variety of unique services, but also the material resources of the firm can be used in different ways, which means that they can provide different kinds of services. This kind of heterogeneity in the services available from the material resources with which a firm works permits the same resources to be used in different ways and for different purposes if the people who work with them get different ideas about how they can be used. In other words there is an interaction between the two kinds of resources of a firm—its personnel and material resources—which affects the productive services available from each.

The Economies of Size and the Economies of Growth

The proposition that enterprising firms have a continuous incentive to expand and that there is no limit to their absolute size (other than that imposed by our conception of the nature of an industrial firm) stands in sharp contrast to the notion of an "optimum" size of firm. We have argued that the expansion of firms is largely based on opportunities to use their existing productive resources more efficiently than they are being used. In so far as a firm's opportunities are not based on the possession of gross monopoly power to exploit suppliers or consumers, expansion that uses resources more efficiently may be an efficient process from the point of view of society as a whole as well as from the point of view of the firm. As a result of the process, firms become larger and larger, and the question arises whether the large firms, because they are larger, are more efficient than smaller firms would be. The biggest firms in the economy today will continue to grow; does this justify the assumption that they will become more efficient as they grow, that each of their product-lines will tend to become cheaper, of better quality, or more adapted to the wants of consumers because they are produced within the administrative framework of a larger organization? Are there economies still to be obtained which relate directly to the increased size of the firms? Growth is a process; size is a state. Our task now is to examine whether there may be economies from the point of view of the efficient utilization of the resources of society which relate to the process but which do not pertain to the "state," to the size that is the by-product of the process.

I shall first describe very briefly the nature of the economies of size as they are usually presented. I shall not go into detail, or attempt to evaluate the relative significance of the different kinds of economies or the conditions under which they arise. The economies of size have been extensively and competently described by others, and my purpose in the following summary is merely to provide a background for some important distinctions and relationships between the economies of size and those of growth.[12]

[12] Nearly every economist concerned with the operations of industry has at some point discussed this subject from Babbage in 1832, through Marshall both in the *Principles* and in his *Industry and Trade*, up to the modern discussions of E. A. G. Robinson in *The Structure of Competitive Industry* (New York: Harcourt Brace, 1932), and P. Sargant Florence in *The Logic of Industrial*

The Economies of Size

Economies of size are present when a larger firm, because of its size alone, can not only produce and sell goods and services more efficiently than smaller firms but also can introduce larger quantities or new products more efficiently. In discussions of the economies of size, so-called "technological economies", derived from producing large amounts of given products in large plants, are commonly distinguished from "managerial" and "financial" economies, derived from improved managerial division of labour and from reductions in unit costs made possible when purchases, sales, and financial transactions can be made on a large scale. Moreover, one can distinguish the economies of size applying to plants from those applying to firms, but the distinction between plant and firm is not coterminous with the distinction between technological and managerial economies.[13] The size of plant is not independent of managerial and financial economies; nor is the size of firm independent of technological economies, although technological economies relate most directly to the organization of plants.

Technological Economies. A plant, unlike a firm, is necessarily confined to a given geographical location. From the point of view of the present discussion a "plant" or "factory" is characterized chiefly by the fact that the activities contained within it and the products produced by it, are technically related to each other in the process of production.[14] Technological economies arise, when, under given conditions, for given products, changes in the amounts and kinds of resources used in production permit a larger output to be produced at lower average cost. Thus, technological economies arise when costs can be reduced through an increase in the specialization of labour; the introduction of automatic machinery, assembly-line techniques, or mechanized internal transport systems; the installation of large units of equipment capable of producing larger quantities at lower unit cost if used to capacity; and other similar technical alterations in the organization of production.

The effect of any of these technological changes on costs depends not only on the physical productivity of the combination of "inputs," but also on the prices of the factors of production required. Hence the "technically optimum" size of plant is as much a function of prices as of technology, and the concept of technological economies of scale can only mean that with given prices of productive resources a larger scale of output permits changes in the productive techniques or resources used which reduce the average cost of output.[15] If the change in the type of input

---

Organization (London: Kegan Paul, 1933) and *The Logic of British and American Industry* (London: Routledge and Kegan Paul, 1953). Abba Lerner in *Economics of Control* (New York: Macmillan, 1944) and Fritz Machlup in *Economics of Sellers' Competition* (Baltimore: Johns Hopkins Press, 1952) have useful theoretical discussions. A recent review of the empirical work on the subject as well as a penetrating analysis of the theoretical and conceptual problems can be found in Caleb Smith, "Survey of the Empirical Evidence on Economies of Scale", in *Business Concentration and Price Policy* (New York: Princeton Univ. Press for the National Bureau of Economic Research, 1955), pp. 213 ff. Many competent industry studies, too numerous to list, are also available.

[13] P. Sargant Florence, for example, discusses the economies of large-scale operation in a very generalized form, recognizing that the same fundamental principles lie behind all kinds of economies regardless of which type of organization they apply to. He analyzes three basic principles: the "principle of bulk transactions"; the "principle of massed (or pooled) reserves; and the "principle of multiples". *The Logic of British and American Industry*, op. cit., pp. 50–51.

[14] Where this is not true, the mere fact that a variety of productive activities are carried on in close geographical proximity does not provide an economic reason for calling the collection of activities a single plant.

[15] It should also be noted that changes in the price of the final product change the opportunity cost of resources used in its production and therefore their value to the firm. This has relevance not only for the optimum size of plant in an industry, but also for the scale on which each of the particular products of a multi-product firm will be produced. In addition, even if an important resource used is specific to a single product and has no opportunity cost to the firm, its value will change with the price of the product and rent should be imputed to the resource and added to the cost of production. This, too, will change the optimum size of plant. For a full discussion of this point see Fritz Machlup, op. cit., pp. 288–299.

required to produce a larger output of given product in a larger plant calls for an increased use of more expensive resources, costs may not fall as the scale of production is enlarged; while if the same resources were cheaper, the larger size of plant could produce at lower cost. Thus, where capital equipment, or the skilled labour necessary to operate it, is relatively expensive, the introduction of more capital-using mass-production techniques may not reduce costs, and the most efficient size of plant will be smaller than it would have been if capital had been cheap and skilled labour less scarce and expensive. Furthermore, if transportation costs of either the raw materials or product are high, a given plant may be faced with increasing costs on this account as output expands, and the most profitable size will be appropriately limited.

Moreover, management varies in ability, and the size of plant that can be operated most efficiently by one type of management may not be an efficient size for another type. Small plants run by unspecialized and relatively untrained men may compete successfully with larger plants run by highly skilled, specialized, but more expensive managers, if the lower cost of management offsets the technical disadvantages of the smaller plants.[16]

Nevertheless, it often happens that when the scale of output is increased technological considerations are of such overwhelming importance that changes in managerial or transport costs may be of negligible significance. In this case we may neglect them, and plants taking advantage of technological economies will always be able to produce at lower costs than plants that do not, and will therefore tend to dominate the industry. It may be that this is a fairly common situation in some industries, particularly in the large-scale mass-production industries, such as automobile assembly, and in industries in which the most efficient units of productive machinery are very large. Thus, where technological economies of size are very great and can be achieved without the aid of exceptionally scarce managerial or other productive factors, and when they more than offset any increases in transport costs as output increases, the size of plant that can survive in an industry will have to be large enough to take advantage of the production methods which make possible the bulk of the economies. Technological economies will affect the minimum size of plant, and therefore of firm in such industries. Furthermore, where a large plant is necessary to achieve low-cost production, the minimum amount of expansion planned by firms will have to be fairly large.

The size of plant can be measured in different units, with different results. A measure of plant size in terms of employment will understate the effects of increasing mechanization, while a measure in terms of capital equipment will distort comparison of plant sizes between regions where the relative prices of labour and capital are different, or between periods of time in which the "utilization" of plant has changed.[17] Within the same industry, the volume of output is the simplest measure, but between industries "outputs" are difficult to compare and some other measure must be adopted. In considering the effect of the size of plant on the size and growth of firms we must, of course, measure plant size in the same units as we do the size of firms and, as we shall see in Chapter IX, if we measure both by the capital equipment employed, there is reason to believe that the amount of expansion a given firm can plan is greater when the most profitable plant requires a large amount of capital.

Managerial Economies. Large firms are for the most part multi-plant firms, and economies of multi-plant operation must in general be sought in other sources than technology—in

[16] This is not a fanciful illustration. Executives of a large firm will often tell you of smaller firms—sometimes very small firms—that can produce one of the large firm's products at the same, or lower cost merely because the small firm does not have the managerial overhead of the larger.

[17] W. Baldamus, in a very interesting article, has attempted to explain the trend in plant size in a variety of industries in Britain in terms of the relative influence of "mechanization" and "utilization"—the former being an increase in output by expansion of plant, the latter, by more intensive utilization of existing plant. He found that in the "newer" industries, mechanization, i.e., "technical progress", tended to be largely responsible for rapid increases in the size of plants. "Then there comes a point when utilization takes over as the dominant principle controlling expansion, because it is no longer possible or profitable to carry through radical technological innovations." W. Baldamus, "Mechanization, Utilization and Size of Plant", *Economic Journal*, Vol. LXII (March 1953), p. 68.

what are known as "managerial economies" which, in the broadest sense, include marketing, financial, and research economies. Managerial economies are held to result when a larger firm can take advantage of an increased division of managerial labour and of the closely allied mechanization of certain administrative processes; make more intensive use of existing managerial resources by the "spreading" of overheads; obtain economies from buying and selling on a larger scale; use reserves more economically; acquire capital on cheaper terms; and support large-scale research.[18]

When the scale of production is sufficient to justify a specialized production manager, a sales manager, a financial expert, or a specialist in raw-material buying, for example, each function is performed more efficiently than it would be if all of them were performed by one person. An excellent plant manager may make a poor financial manager indeed. For any given degree of specialization, further economies may often be obtained by the spreading of managerial overhead cost, thus reducing average cost as output increases. This may be possible because existing personnel have been used below capacity or because a given function or service required for one scale of operation need not be increased proportionately for larger outputs. For example, if a firm employs a specialized market-analyst, a research staff, specialized salesmen, etc., it may be able to plan an output appreciably larger than the minimum that would justify their original employment, thereby reducing their cost per unit of product. The same market forecast may be as applicable to an output of 500,000 units as for an output of 50,000 units.

When a larger output can be produced more cheaply than a smaller output without any change in the basic techniques of production, simply because at the larger scale of operations it is possible to employ specialized managerial talent and so to improve the efficiency of operations that savings are made in materials cost, labour cost, fuel or any other cost, these savings may properly be classed as a managerial economy.

If some of the reduced cost can be attributed to basic changes in production techniques (e.g., to increased mechanization), managerial economies may in some sense be part of the total economies of the changed scale of operation, but they could never be identified. This is, of course, the more usual case in reality. Managerial and technological reorganization proceed *pari passu* with increasing size of firm, and an increased division of managerial labour is often necessary to keep costs from rising at higher levels of output; it is an adaptive procedure undertaken to permit economies to be achieved elsewhere. Average cost of output may fall, but average managerial cost may remain constant or even rise as additional managerial personnel are acquired to fulfil more and more specialized functions. Even when it is possible to prevent the emergence of managerial diseconomies by appropriate distribution of the various managerial functions among a larger number of people, it does not necessarily follow that any part of the lower cost of the greater output can be traced to managerial economies.

Economies in selling come from the increased efficiency resulting when specialized sales personnel can be employed and from producing on a scale sufficiently extensive to use their full selling capacity. There may also be economies in large transactions and in handling bulk quantities; in maintaining an advertising programme sufficiently extensive to ensure not only that all potential consumers are aware of the kind and quality of product available, but also to persuade them that they need the particular brand of product produced; and in maintaining a sales organization that reaches well forward towards the final consumer.

A great deal of the superior selling strength of large firms as compared with small firms is undoubtedly of a "monopolistic" variety in the economist's sense. This is especially true of advertising and certain types of sales technique. Yet, given the natural imperfections of the market—the difficulties consumers have in knowing what is available at what prices and where, the physical arrangements necessary to bring seller and buyer together, the education and instruction of the consumer in the use and care of products, and similar problems—selling

[18] The reader will notice the similarity between the discussion of the economies of size and our earlier analysis of the significance of unused productive services. Since the two discussions are merely different ways of analyzing the same problem, some repetition is inevitable but will help to bring out the relation between the economies of size and those of growth.

efforts on a sufficient scale to meet the real needs of consumers are surely an economy for the consumer as well as an economy of scale for the firm. There is little doubt that the smallest firms often cannot support sales organizations and programmes that can serve consumers as effectively in such matters as do those of larger firms.

A firm needs a variety of "reserves" for its operations, whether they be financial reserves, inventory reserves, or labour reserves. With large-scale operations, economies may be obtained in the use of reserves because the proportion of total reserves to total operations can be reduced. This is perhaps most clearly seen in the case of inventories. A small repair shop, for example, may have to carry reserves of parts of all kinds but cannot easily adjust the size of the stock of each part to requirements because the small scale of operations makes it difficult for the firm to predict with any accuracy the demand for any particular part. The larger shop, on the other hand, can, because of the "law of large numbers," predict demand for each kind of part more successfully and can more accurately trim its inventories accordingly.[19]

As to financial economies and the ability to support research, the advantages of the large firm are self-evident. The greater security offered to investors, the easier access to capital markets, the greater public knowledge of the firm's existence and operations, the fact that it is often cheaper within limits to borrow large than small amounts of funds, all combine and interact to place the larger firm in a better financial position than the smaller firm. When research personnel and laboratories are expensive, the large firm can support more of them than can the small firm; when research operations require a large organization, the larger firm can administer them with greater ease than can a smaller firm. We shall have more to say in the next section about the question of treating the ability to support research as an "economy of size".

Economies in Operations and Economies in Expansion. Clearly the several economies of size refer to different types of operation: some economies apply to the large-scale production of given products in large plants; some relate to the improved utilization of an administrative organization and have no relevance to any particular products; some are economies in expanding into new fields. But when we speak of "economies" that apply to different sets of existing products, or to new products yet to be created or produced, we have departed a considerable distance from the traditional economies of large-scale production, commonly called "increasing returns."

The theoretical analysis of the economies of large-scale production has been developed most rigorously within the context of the "theory of the firm" or "theory of the industry" and refers, not to the growth of an administrative organization producing many products, but rather to the production of a given product on an increasing scale. In this context, the costs of production as the "firm" grows in size, as well as the costs of production of different "firms" in the same "industry," are always comparable because "firm" and "industry" are defined as producers of a given product. Within a firm the existence of economies of scale can be shown by a "reversible cost curve" that declines as output increases in volume (i.e., the "firm" increases in size) and rises as one traces the curve backwards to smaller outputs.

In the more descriptive analyses, on the other hand, many of the economies of size apply to firms defined differently and presumably influence the cost of any number of products; further, some of them, notably economies in the ability to support research and

[19] This principle has been particularly stressed by P. Sargant Florence under the name of "massed (or pooled) reserves." He points out that it appears in ". . . many apparently unrelated branches of economic life . . . in schemes for the decasualization of labour at the docks and underlies all forms of insurance and banking; the reserves that are economized may in fact be labour, liquid monetary resources, stocks of goods and materials or any other factors in production, when the demands upon these factors are somewhat uncertain in their incidence." It illustrates "the statistical theory of large numbers, based on probable error, that the greater the number of similar items involved the more likely are deviations to cancel out and to leave the actual results nearer to the expected results. The probable deviation in orders for similar items that a reserve guards against is thus proportionately less when orders are many, and the cost of reserves per unit of output falls correspondingly." P. Sargant Florence, op. cit., pp. 50–51.

certain economies of selling, apply primarily to the development or introduction of new products. The word "economies" implies that in some sense output is "cheaper," and this in turn implies a comparison with some other output of the same or very similar products. Here we have two possibilities: first, the average cost of a larger output produced by a firm may be compared with the cost of a smaller output produced by the same firm. If the cost of the larger output is lower, economies of large-scale production are present and we can unequivocably say that the same firm is more efficient when it is larger than when it is smaller. Second, the average cost of additional output may be compared with the cost of the same output in some other firm. Here the "additional output" may consist of products very different from those the firm has been producing and the appropriate comparison is with the cost of producing the additional output in some other firm. If this cost is cheaper in a larger firm than in a smaller one, where size is the only variable, then economies of size are present, though not necessarily economies of large-scale production, for the lower cost of the additional output may be due only to the size of the firm that undertook it and not to the scale on which the new output itself is produced. In this case we can say that a large firm is more efficient than a smaller firm, but we cannot say that the same firm is more efficient when it is larger than it was when it was smaller.

Economies of operation refer to the average cost of production and distribution of additional output *after* an expansion has been completed. Here we can compare the average cost of the new output by one firm either with the cost of the same firm's previous output, or with the cost of similar products in another firm. Economies of expansion do not refer to the costs of production after production has been established, but only to the cost of effecting an expansion. This includes the cost of establishing additional production on a smoothly operating basis and of enlarging or creating the market for the additional output. Here the appropriate comparison is only with the cost that another firm would incur if it undertook to initiate the production and marketing of the same products; though not necessarily on the same scale. Needless to say, if the volume of output of two firms is different, cost per unit of output must be compared. If a large firm, because of its size alone, would be able to take up production at a lower average cost than that of any smaller firm, then economies of size are present; and this would be true even if after the new productive activities were well established by the larger firm they could be separated from it and carried on independently at no increase in cost.

In including among the economies of size such things as the ability to support research, the ability to capture the confidence of consumers through extensive advertising that is made possible only because the firm is large, or merely the financial security which is not easily acquired by smaller firms, I have not departed from the customary treatment.[20] Yet there is a fundamental difference between these and the economies of large-scale production and operation that depend essentially on the efficiency with which resources are used for the production and distribution of existing products.

To illustrate, suppose a firm, large enough to support an extensive research organization, perfects a new product and proceeds to introduce it. Assume that the product could not have been perfected or introduced by a smaller firm, but that it is produced by a separate division in separate plants of the large firm. Once the investment to manufacture and distribute the product is made and the product clearly established in the market, it may well be possible to separate the production of the new product from the firm, thus reducing the size of the firm, without causing any increase in the costs of production in any part of the firm. Or again, suppose expansion of the production of a given product has been made possible because of an advertising programme so extensive that only a large firm could have undertaken it. This is an economy to the firm (and perhaps also to consumers if the product could not have been made so widely known in the absence of the selling effort of the firm); but again, once the product is established, no increase in the cost of producing or distributing it need follow if production is transferred to a separate firm.

Thus, economies attributable to the size of firms may, up to a point, not only be responsi-

[20] See, for example, E. A. G. Robinson, op. cit., pp. 39–40; and P. Sargant Florence, op. cit., p. 52.

ble for lower costs in the production and distribution of the existing products of larger firms, but also for lower costs and competitive advantages enabling larger firms to expand in certain directions. These latter are economies of size whenever their existence is directly correlated with the size of the firm enjoying them. They would not be available if firms were sufficiently reduced in size; but they are economies which are applicable only to the process of growth and, once taken advantage of, their fruits may remain in existence and be enjoyed by society even if separated from the tree that bore them—a subsequent reduction in the size of the firm need not lead to increased costs of production or distribution of any of its existing products.[21]

The distinction between economies in operations and economies in expansion throws light, I think, on some of the difficulties with the notion of an "optimum" size of firm. Economies of large-scale production or operation have traditionally been associated with the concept of an optimum firm—a firm large enough to take full advantage of all economies of size but not so large that it runs into net diseconomies. Diseconomies of size arise from excessively diminishing returns to scale, but diminishing returns depend upon the existence of a "fixed factor" in the operations of the firm. As we have earlier noted, management has often been treated as the "fixed factor" giving rise to increasing costs; while this may be legitimate for many particular firms, it is not appropriate for all firms. Under competition, and in the presence of economies of large-scale production and operation, there may be a *minimum* size of firm, but we have rejected the proposition that there is for every firm some *optimum* size beyond which it will run into diseconomies. Only for firms incapable of adapting their managerial structure to the requirements of larger operations can one postulate *an* optimum size.

For any given product there may be decreasing costs as the scale of production is increased, but after a point costs must increase when all costs, including the opportunity costs of resources, are taken into consideration.[22] In other words, there may be an "optimum" output for each of the firm's product-lines, but not an "optimum" output for the firm as a whole.[23] In general we have found nothing to prevent the indefinite expansion of firms as time passes, and clearly if some of the economies of size are economies of expansion, there is no reason to assume that a firm would ever reach a size in which it has taken full advantage of all these economies. But the notion of "decreasing costs" is inapplicable to economies of expansion unless, after an expansion has been completed, one can compare the new output with the old and find it cheaper.

The Economies of Growth

Economies of growth are the internal economies available to an individual firm which make expansion profitable in particular directions. They are derived from the unique collection of productive services available to it, and create for that firm a differential advantage over other firms in putting on the market new products or increased quantities of old products. At any time the availability of such economies is the result of the process, discussed in the previous chapter, by which unused productive services are continually created within the firm. They may or may not be also economies of size.

Economies of size do not provide economies

[21] I am not suggesting that the persistent removal of the fruit would not reduce the future supply of fruit; I am only concerned to make clear the distinction between the two types of economies of size. Incidentally, that there may be economies in expansion without enduring economies of size often helps to explain the voluntary reduction in the size of a firm when it sells one of its "businesses" to another firm. See the discussion below in Chapter VIII of the "Purchase and Sale of Businesses That are Not Firms."

[22] The significance of this is discussed more fully in the next chapter, which deals with the economics of diversification.

[23] It should be clear, once again, that in rejecting the notion of an optimum size of firm in this context we are not quarrelling with the concept of the optimum size of firm as it appears in the "theory of the firm," since the "optimum firm" in that context is merely the optimum output of a given product. Furthermore, the above discussion refers only to the firm, and not to the plant—there probably is in any particular economy an optimum size of plant for many industries.

of growth for firms that are unable to expand sufficiently to obtain them. If there are substantial economies in the large-scale production of particular products, but if at the same time there are already in existence large firms whose selling prices reflect the low costs of production obtainable only at large outputs, small firms may survive in the interstices of the market, but their expansion in competition with the larger firms may be precluded if the amount of expansion required to obtain the lower costs of large-scale operation is beyond their ability to plan or to execute.

Thus, it is not necessarily capital that prevents the expansion of the small firms often found on the fringes of an industry; it may just as well be that the organization and execution of an expansion on the required scale is only possible for firms already large.[24] The small firms may survive because of some small advantage in some special market, but they will not in such circumstances become large producers in the industry. New entrants to the industry, if any, will consist of large firms, usually from related industries, which are able to undertake the necessary expansion.

All of the economies of size that we have discussed—whether they be economies of larger-scale production or operation, or economies of expansion—also provide economies of growth for any firm that can take advantage of them. On the other hand, economies of growth may exist at all sizes, and some of them may have no relation either to the size of the firm before it undertakes an expansion based on them, or to any increase in efficiency due to a larger scale of production. Economies of size do not exist if smaller firms could produce or introduce the same products at no higher cost than larger firms when size is the only factor considered. Nevertheless, under given circumstances, a particular firm may be able to put additional output on the market at a lower average cost than any other firm, whether larger or smaller. In this case, economies of growth are present, but not economies of size. A firm may find it profitable to expand even though, after its expansion, it may have no advantages other than those that would have accrued to any other larger or smaller firm that had had equivalent productive services available at the time. For one of the significant characteristics of the economies of growth is that they depend on the particular collection of productive resources possessed by the particular firm, and the exploitation of the opportunities provided by these resources may be quite unrelated to the size of the firm.

Obviously expansion always implies an increased size of firm, but even the firm itself may see no particular advantage in being larger, and in fact may deplore the increase in size which necessarily follows the exploitation of a profitable opportunity, because size creates administrative problems the firm would have preferred to avoid.[25] One does often find that a firm expanded because it was aware that a larger size of operation was necessary for the effective exploitation of its opportunities; but in firms already large, the economies perceived relate primarily to the particular opportunity being exploited and not to the increased size of the firm as a whole. It is only in relatively small firms that management itself seems to think that a greater size of the firm as a whole would lead to more efficient production.[26]

[24] Essentially the same point is made by E. A. G. Robinson with respect to the costs of selling: "The cost of selling is only in part, and in certain conditions, a cost of production. At other times and in other conditions, it is a cost not of producing but of growing. For once the market has been won, it can be retained at a lower selling cost than is necessary to secure it initially. We have, then, two quite distinct questions to which we must give an answer. First, is a larger firm more efficient than a smaller firm? Second, will it pay to grow from being smaller to being larger? The high cost of selling may be, paradoxically, at the same time a source of economy, making the already large firm more efficient than the smaller firm, and a cost of growth which makes it unprofitable for the small firm to grow up to its most efficient size." E. A. G. Robinson, op. cit., p. 67.

[25] For example, the executives of one prominent United States firm that I studied felt strongly that increased size brought nothing but administrative headaches; at the same time they knew they could not afford to pass up promising opportunities for expansion.

[26] On the other hand, many large firms insist on the social advantages of their large size, largely, I suspect, because they feel they must justify their existing state. Even if size is no advantage, no firm wants to be broken up by outside action.

Author Index

Subject Index